Neo-African Literature and Culture

Edition Ethnos

Mainzer Afrika-Studien 1

Herausgeber:
Gerhard Grohs, Ernst W. Müller, Leo Stappers
und Erika Sulzmann;
Institut für Ethnologie und Afrika-Studien,
Mainz

Editors
Bernth Lindfors and Ulla Schild

Neo-African
Literature and Culture

Essays in memory of Janheinz Jahn

B. Heymann

Dieser Band gilt zugleich als Band 8 der Schriften der Vereinigung von Afrikanisten in Deutschland (VAD)

Type-setting by H. Unnewehr Maschinensetzerei, Eppstein (Taunus)

Printed by Druckerei Ebenhoch, Niedernhausen

Printed in the Federal Republic of Germany

ISBN 3/88055/500/1

Contents

Geleitwort

Das Institut für Ethnologie und Afrika-Studien eröffnet mit diesem Band eine Reihe, in der es seine auf Afrika bezogenen Arbeiten der Öffentlichkeit vorstellt.

Es erscheint uns ein besonders glücklicher Umstand zu sein, daß wir mit einer Festschrift für Janheinz Jahn beginnen können, da wir mit dem Erwerb seiner Bibliothek die Verpflichtung übernommen haben, die Arbeiten fortzuführen, die mit seinem Tode unterbrochen wurden.

Ein Teil der in dieser Festschrift veröffentlichten Texte sind Vorträge, die auf einem Symposium gehalten wurden, das in Erinnerung an Jahn am 7.—8. April 1975 in der Universität Mainz veranstaltet wurde. Zu dieser Tagung hatten die Vereinigung von Afrikanisten in Deutschland (VAD) und das Institut für Ethnologie und Afrika-Studien der Johannes-Gutenberg-Universität, Mainz, das für die Vorbereitung verantwortlich war, eingeladen.

An dieser Stelle soll allen denen gedankt werden, die zum Gelingen des Symposiums beigetragen haben, sei es durch ihre Mitarbeit oder durch ihre finanzielle Unterstützung, wobei besonders das Auswärtige Amt der Bundesrepublik Deutschland und das Auslandsamt der Universität Mainz erwähnt werden sollen.

A black-bordered card from Germany

(In Memory of Janheinz Jahn)

Just like the other pieces of mail
I'd received throughout the years

(whether they were translation-queries,
requests for biographical details,

news of our Thirties political poets
who had quietly slipped their moorings
and moved country and tone
or written themselves out
with the hopelessness of exile),

this black-bordered card from Germany
was equally short and sharp.

You had left, it said simply.

Andrew Salkey

FOREWORD

Janheinz Jahn may need no memorial. His voluminous writings on neo-African literature and culture will serve as his monument for many years to come, reminding us not only of his extraordinary energy and creative imagination but also of the impressive contribution one man was able to make to the development of a field he himself helped to define. Any effort by friends and colleagues to eulogize his pioneering achievements would therefore seem supererogatory. A more appropriate way of expressing appreciation would be to try out new approaches to subjects that he found interesting, for the sincerest tribute one can pay to an original thinker is not to follow doggedly in his footsteps but to strike out in new directions over the terrain he surveyed. This collection of essays seeks to honor the memory of Jahn not by complimenting the man but by complementing his ideas.

Of course, it would be impossible to treat in one volume all the subjects that absorbed Jahn's attention. He studied black expressive cultures in three parts of the world—Africa, Afro-America and the Caribbean—focussing primarily on Africa in his later years. Represented here are a good many of his African interests but only a few of his West Indian and Afro-American enthusiasms. It is pleasing to note that original literary works have been contributed by three distinguished creative writers—Bernard Dadié of the Ivory Coast, Wilson Harris of Guyana and Andrew Salkey of Jamaica.

Some of these essays were solicited by the editors and some were read as papers at an International Symposium on the Social Significance of Modern African Literature held in memory of Jahn at the University of Mainz in April 1975. The editors would like to express their gratitude to the Institute of Ethnology and African Studies at the University of Mainz and the German Society of Africanists (Vereinigung von Afrikanisten in Deutschland), whose annual meeting was made to coincide with the symposium, for sponsering and organising the symposium and for making the papers available for inclusion here. The editors regret, that the lectures delivered to the symposium by Papa Gueye N'Diaye, Abiola Irele and Gerd Meuer have not arrived by the time this volume went into print. Gerhard Grohs' contribution was published in the meantime in *Modern African Studies*.

Bernth Lindfors
Ulla Schild

The Works of Janheinz Jahn

Bernth Lindfors

In *Through African Doors* Janheinz Jahn told of an amusing experience he once had when crossing the border between Dahomey and Nigeria. A Dahomean customs official, on seeing him describe himself on one of the customs forms as a writer, eagerly engaged him in conversation about Gide, Colette and several French West African poets and novelists he had read. Delighted to meet someone with whom he could discuss literature, the official offered to buy Jahn a beer and invited him to have a look at his library, but because Jahn was travelling in a car with others who were ready to depart, he could not accept these kind offers. A few miles further down the road at the Nigerian border station he had to fill out a similar form in order to reenter Nigeria. According to Jahn:

> The customs official watched intently every movement of the ball-point pen. In the little box for "profession" I put „writer," and in the one for "employed by" I put a stroke. I was going on to the next question when the official suddenly said: "Stop."
> "What is it?"
> "What is that you have written here?" he asked. "There is no such profession. 'Writer' is a man who writes."
> "Exactly," I said, laughing.
> "Are you trying to make fun of me?" said the man, very conscious of the dignity of his office. " That is not a profession. Writing is something we all do. Anybody who can write could write 'writer' there. All Europeans are writers, but you are supposed to write your profession in this place."
> I tried to explain the thing to him. "'Writer' is not simply any man who writes. 'Writer' is a profession, it is the same as 'author.'"
> "Author?" The customs man had evidently not yet come across this word. The policeman, however, who had been casually listening to the conversation as he stamped the passport, now intervened. "'Author,'" he said, "I know that. I once read a book: *The Author of the Crime*. An author ist the man who does it, a criminal." .After this remark, philologically accurate enough, he gave me e piercing look and said: "What do you want in Nigeria, sir?"

Jahn tried to explain that he wrote books, and when this led to further confusion, he put it in the simplest terms he could:

> "I write something on paper, and what I write there is then printed."
> The customs man sighed with relief and gave a laugh of triumph. "Ah, now

we have it, he is a journalist. But then, sir, you must fill in here which paper employs you." . . .

"I am not employed by any paper; I write books."

"Books are not written but printed," said the policeman.

"So you are a printer," said the customs man. "Good, and now just tell us which firm of printers employ you."

"But gentlemen," I protested, "I am not employed by any printers. Please try to understand: a 'writer' is free, as free as a poet."

"I must warn you sir", said the customs man, "you must not keep using words which are not proper words."

I was starting to explain the word "poet" as well, when the policeman cut short the debate. "So you are an unemployed printer. That will do."[1]

And it was with this ignominious title that Jahn was permitted to cross the border.

This bizarre episode in cross-cultural misunderstanding was typical of Jahn's life. In some places in the world he received recognition for the work he did; in others—particularly in centers of learning where diplomas and certificates are regarded as passports to respectability—he was often eyed with suspicion because he earned his living by writing. There are still many customs officials performing duties in academic ivory towers who are unwilling to accept his credentials, who look upon him as no more than a journalist, a fast-talking author who committed his crimes in print. They claim that he misused words, that he frequently misled people by pretending to understand what no European could possibly fathom, that his translations of African culture were incorrect, that though he produced a lot of books he was never gainfully employed. Such policemen of the intellect might even now refuse to allow Jahn to enter another world with the word "scholar" beside his name.

Not that he would have coveted this title. Indeed, he might have considered it a mild insult. There were mindless academic tasks for which he had no appetite and certain kinds of scholarship for which he possessed neither patience nor respect. Jahn was not a pedant who concentrated on writing footnotes to other scholars' opinions. He was an original thinker with an audacious spirit, a pioneer willing to take risks with ideas, to speculate and hypothesize, to stir up controversy, to attack dogma. He believed in basing his theories on facts, but he was not afraid to allow his theoretical constructs to float free on the bouyancy of their own logic when it was impossible to adequately document everything he wanted to put forward. If he were asked to compose his own epitaph, he would probably still list himself simply as a writer rather than attempt to pass himself off as a scholar. Some might prefer that he be called a "creative writer" or "pseudo-scholar" because they find it difficult to persuade themselves to take the work of such a free-spirited individual seriously. But instead of merely calling Jahn names, let us review his career. To measure the achievements of any man, it is necessary to look back at his life and see what he did with it.

I know very little about Jahn's early life except what he told me in the spring of 1972 when he was living in my home while serving as Visiting Professor of English and of General and Comparative Studies at The University of Texas at Austin. After finishing dinner or a game of chess or several bottles of beer, we would sometimes sit and talk for hours, touching upon all kinds of subjects, including many of his past experiences. He was an entertaining conversationalist with a flair for drama and a talent for comic embroidery that often made me wonder how much of what he was telling me was really true. Now, several years later, I cannot vouch for the absolute accuracy of my own recollections either, but will try to reconstruct a few details about Jahn's life as faithfully as I can remember them. It should be understood, of course, that I do not claim to be speaking the whole truth and nothing but the truth about this unusual man.

Jahn was born in Frankfurt in 1918, the eldest of two sons in a wealthy family. When he was a young man, his parents had the means to send him to a different country each summer to learn a new language, and in this way he acquired a knowledge of four or five European tongues before entering the University of Munich where he studied, among other subjects, Classical Arabic. The Second World War interrupted his education, but his language ability earned him a noncombat position as an interpreter in the German Army. When the war ended, he did not go back to his studies but became a full-timer writer. He took odd jobs as a journalist (including writing the horoscope columns for a daily newspaper), and his success in getting a few short stories published in literary magazines encouraged him to attempt writing a novel, which he later admitted was a complete failure. In the early 1950s he fell in love with a woman from a poor, working-class family with whom his bourgeois parents did not wish to be associated, much less related. When he ignored their protests and married her in 1955, his father disinherited him, leaving him penniless and completely on his own. These were lean, postwar years but Jahn's wife knew how to make ends meet on a skimpy budget, and they managed to survive on the little he earned as a free-lance writer.

The turning point in Jahn's life came in 1952 when Léopold Sédar Senghor, then a member of the French Parliament (and since 1960 President of Senegal), visited Frankfurt and gave a public lecture. Jahn was in the audience and, greatly stimulated by the lecture, sought out Senghor afterwards to learn more about African literature and culture. By then Senghor had already published his first three volumes of poetry and only four years earlier had edited the remarkable *Anthologie de la nouvelle poésie nègre et malgache de langue française* with its famous introduction, "Orphée Noir," by Jean-Paul Sartre. Jahn was instantly seized with an ambition to translate these works into German, and he began to do research not only on the literature produced by Africans and West Indians in Paris but also on the cultural background from which it had sprung. He wanted to find out everything he could about African life styles, African social structure, African art,

African symbolism, African thought. He read Lévy-Brühl, Frobenius and other early cultural anthropologists; he devoured a new French translation of Rev. Placide Tempels' *Bantu Philosophy* published in 1952 by Présence Africaine; he studied the works of Césaire, Damas and other originators of the Negritude movement. He also began perusing Afro-American literature, especially the works of poets and novelists associated with the Harlem Renaissance.

Soon he was writing about these authors, their books and their ideas. His first article on modern black poetry appeared in *Die Literatur* on August 15, 1952.[2] Within two years he was publishing essays on such varied topics as Bantu ontology and "The Contribution of the West Indiens to Poetry," essays reflecting the range of his widening interests.

But his primary occupation during this period was translating into German the works of African, Afro-Caribbean and Afra-American writers. His first anthology, *Schwarzer Orpheus,* which borrowed its title from Sartre's influential essay, appeared in 1954 and was an immediate success. A second edition was published the following year and a third in 1959; a new enlarged edition, brought out in 1964, was reissued in 1973 and is still in print today. It was this book that established Jahn's early reputation as a translator of the new black culture—not only the new expressive culture of Africa but also that of the African diaspora in the New World. A German scholar has attributed much of the success of *Schwarzer Orpheus* to its novelty: "Germans were surprised to discover that Africa had a literature apart from folktales, a written literature with new metaphors, rhythms and styles"[3] In his translations Jahn tried to remain faithful to these idioms, rendering Senghor's polyrhythmic lyricism, Cécaire's surrealism, Langston Hughes's verbal jazz and blues into innovative Teutonic equivalents. In all, there were 82 poets represented in *Schwarzer Orpheus* by 161 poems; roughly one-third were African, one-third Caribbean and one-third Afro-American. Jahn's enthusiasm knew no geographical boundaries; he was interested in creative expression in the entire black world.

After the success of *Schwarzer Orpheus* he set to work to make the literatures of the black world better known in Germany. In 1955 he published *Tam-Tam Schwarz,* a booklength translation of Senghor's poetry, and the following year he published four books, including the first German translation of Césaire's poetry, of Césaire's first play, of Barbadian writer George Lamming's autobiographical novel *In the Castle of My Skin,* and of the poetry of Sam Allen, an Afro-American who wrote under the pseudonym "Paul Vesey". During this very fruitful period in the mid-1950s he also gave a number of radio talks on black literature, focussing sometimes on individual writers and sometimes on broader topics such as rumba rhythms in Afro-Cuban poetry, the language of modern African literature, or the black renaissance in Africa and the New World—topics which gave him the latitude to comment on new trends and timely issues in contemporary black culture. It may have been during one of these radio talks broadcast in 1957 that he first coined the term "Neo-African literature"[4] to distinguish the new writing emerging in the black world from the traditional oral literature which many Europeans still presumed to be the only mode of literary expression utilized by black peoples. Jahn was soon the major European publicist of black literary achievements the world over.

In September 1956 Jahn attented the first World Congress of Black Writers and Artists, which was convened in Paris by Présence Africaine. There he met not only such illustrious authors as Richard Wright, George Lamming, Frantz Fanon, Jacques Rabemananjara, Ferdinand Oyono, Bernard Dadié, Davidson Nicol and Mercer Cook but also a German writer named Ulli Beier who had been teaching phonetics in Nigeria for several years and doing research on Yoruba culture. Jahn and Beier agreed that it would be an opportune moment to start a literary journal in Nigeria, one which would carry original works written in English by African and Afro-American authors and also English translations of poetry and prose by prominent writers from French and Portuguese areas of Africa and the New World. They decided to call the journal *Black Orpheus,* giving it the same title as Sartre's essay and Jahn's anthology.[5] The first issue appeared in September 1957 and within a few years *Black Orpheus* had established itself as the most influential literary journal in all of Africa. Beier, who continued to edit the magazine until the eruption of the Nigerian civil war in 1967, must of course be given most of the credit for *Black Orpheus's* remarkable success. Jahn served as co-editor for only two years before being replaced by Ezekiel Mphahlele and Wole Soyinka. But Jahn was instrumental in getting this crucial literary venture started and he supported it with frequent contributions of critical essays even after he was no longer on the editorial board. *Black Orpheus* was another one of his pioneering efforts which led to greater international awareness and appreciation of modern black literatures.

Greater achievements were yet to come. By 1958 Jahn was already fairly well-known in Germany for his translations. In the six years since first meeting Senghor he had published twelve books, seven of them translations of novels, plays or collections of poetry by individual African, Afro-Caribbean and Afro-American authors, five of them anthologies of translated prose and poetry from the same areas as well as from Indonesia and the Hispano-Arabic world. He had also written nearly two dozen essays and given a score of radio talks during these active years. However, the book which was to earn him an international reputation, good and bad, was *Muntu: An Outline of Neo-African Culture,* published in 1958. By 1961 it was available in Swedish, English, American, French and Italian editions, and subsequently was translated into at least three more languages—Spanish, Norwegian and Dutch. *Muntu* was the book which transformed Jahn from a translator to an interpreter of modern black culture.

But Jahn's interpretation was controversial. Few reviewers took a neutral position on *Muntu.* Some praised it, some condemned it, some tempered praise for its analytical clarity with condemnation of its tendency toward sweeping generalizations and overstatements, some were impressed with Jahn's erudition, some were indignant about his lack of knowledge of many areas of Africa. The South African novelist Peter Abrahams, reviewing the book in the *New York Times Book Review*, called it

> a brilliant and painstaking piece of scholarship... I think this is the first time that any Western writer has gone below the surface of what is glibly called "the African personality" and come up with a true picture. This, I think, is as near as anybody who is not himself an African will get to understanding what makes the African tick. This is how the African sees his world; these are his beliefs; and here, too, I think, the thoughtful reader will find an indication of what is likely to happen in tomorrow's continent.[6]

For Abrahams, Jahn was both a scholar and a seer.

But for the anonymous reviewer in the London *Times Literary Supplement* Jahn was merely refurbishing old academic clichés and trying to give them a new respectability by clothing them in African terminology. His work was neither original nor African in its intellectual orientation.

> What Mr. Jahn has to say here about the significance of sacrifice, of ancestors, of spirit-cults and spirit possesion, and of religious syncretism, has been a commonplace of ethnological studies for many years. But then so has almost everything African he refers to.
> If, as is claimed, this book is intended for the general public rather than for anthropologists or art-historians, so much the more important that it should embody a sense of proportion both about Africa and about what its readers might take for granted. The intelligence of the general public is certainly not overestimated here... The use of a few African words does not save this modern view of African from being yet another reflection of European values, and such internal standards of criticism as an African culture might be supposed to have and to develop systematically never appear.[7]

Antoher British reviewer, Neal Acherson, writing in *The Spectator*, was even more scathing in his appraisal of *Muntu:*

> Mr. Jahn's essay on the elements of "the African culture" is strident with jargon and with existentialist arrogance... His book has been cooked out of enormous reading with no discernible care or humility, and the bibliography is as menacing as a machine-gun belt. Essentially, on the other hand, it is not a work of scholarship at all. Assembling a number of classifying words from several African languages, Mr. Jahn then proclaims them master-concepts and selects whatever evidence he can find to fit them.

But the same reviewer then went on to say:

> And yet he scores. His philosophical apparatus of Modalities and Designations and Determinations does help to describe the nature of African creativity and shows it functioning both in Leadbelly in Texas and in the guitarist Jean-Bosco Mwenda in Katanga. No "African philosophy" exists in the usual sense, but the material for one ist ready.[8]

In other words, *Muntu* was full of mystical popularized pseudo-science but somehow it worked. Despite his limitations and quirks, Jahn had managed to perform an impressive feat of intellectual voodoo in outlining neo-African culture.

It is not difficult to see why some Africanists were upset with *Muntu*. The book was ambitious in scope and polemical in tone. Since sub-Saharan Africa is huge and its peoples diverse in language, custom and belief, any attempt to "determine what is 'really African'" and then define "to what extent [African poetry, literature and art] are 'really African' and to what extent they are not"⁹ would seem doomed to failure. It would be too easy for ethnologists, folklorists and literary critics familiar with Africa's complexity to cite counter-examples or to demonstrate where Jahn's theory did not fit the facts in a particular corner of Africa. Professional nit-pickers could have their fun poking holes in such an all-embracing hypotheses. And many did. Several were especially scornful of Jahn's nomenclature, pointing out that it was foolish to apply Bantu and Dogon philosophical terminology borrowed from Abbé Alexis Kagame, Placide Tempels and Marcel Griaule—words such as Muntu, Kintu, Hantu, Kuntu and Nommo—to non-Bontu and non-Dogon conceptual systems. What might be true for the Dogon of Mali or the Bantu peoples of Ruanda might not be equally true for the Tiv of Nigeria, the Luo of Kenya or the Khoisan peoples of Southern Africa. There were too many exceptions to consider for the theory to have uniform applicability to the entire continent, much less to the black diaspora.

Yet, as one disgruntled reviewer admitted, the system Jahn devised —artificial, schematic and simplistic as it was—did seem to work. It was a useful shorthand for expressing essential African ideas, a workable tool for probing certain African realities. Jahn may have ignored or overlooked numerous specific truths about Africa in order to make his total argument more coherent and persuasive, but in so doing he may have arrived at a much larger, more profound truth about at least one aspect of contemporary African experience —the persistence of tradition in modern black expressive culture. His contribution here was unique and unprecedented. He had attempted a synthesis and distillation of notions about the African arts such as no one had dared to attempt before. Whether he actually succeeded may still be open to debate but at least he tried to go beyond the usual boundaries of inquiry by plunging into uncharted territory. He was still functioning as a pioneer.

If *Muntu* had been published in 1975 instead of 1958, it probably would not have commanded so much attention. In the late 1950s and early 1960s the wold was hungry for information about Africa because the colonial era was finally ending and new African nations were gaining their independence at a rate of one or two per month. Sociopolitical changes in Africa dominated the international news. *Muntu,* arriving at this time, provided a reasonably concise explanation of Africa's ability to adapt to cultural change without losing its identity. Such a book helped Europe and America to understand some of the forces at work in modern African society. *Muntu* was the thinking man's Baedeker to metamorphosis in the African continent.

After *Muntu*, Jahn began his bibliographical researches into black literature, publishing in 1959 (with John Ramsaran) a booklet entitled *Approaches to African Literature,* the first attempt at a bibliography of African writings. He also travelled through parts of West Africa in 1958—59, documenting his trip in *Through African Doors,* published in 1960. And of course he continued writing essays on African, Afro-Caribbean and Afro-American literatures.

Through African Doors is an amusing account of Jahn's adventures in Nigeria, Dahomey and Ghana. Eager for an authentic African experience, he eschewed European modes of transportation and travelled about on foot or bicycle or aboard African lorries, taxies, boats and trains, buying a third-class ticket whenever possible. He tried to acquire a taste for African food and a mastery of African table manners and other forms of indigenous etiquette. He fraternized with the high and the low, entering with equal curiosity the pa-laces of kings, the homes of the *nouveaux riche,* the sleazy nightclubs in the city and the rough huts of peasants in the country. Ever the enthusiastic student of African folkways, he sought in his daily experiences evidence to verifv his theories of cultural change.

But he was not obsequious among his hosts. Sometimes he would delibe-rately provoke an argument when he found middle-class Africans attempting to emulate European ways. On other occasions he would put up with personal discomfort rather than allow his host to offer him accomodations superior to those an African visitor would be offered. Jahn did not want to be mistaken for a tender-skinned colonialist. As in his literary research, he jumped into new experience with gusto, seeking to taste the full flavor of everything he came across. His appetite for adventure was insatiable.

Jahn spent the next few years involved in his usual academic activities. He translated more of Césaire and Senghor as well as a lengthy autobiographical novel by Bloke Modisane entitled *Blame Me On History.* He wrote more essays for journals, magazines and newspapers. He gave more talks on the radio, sometimes branching out into subjects such as African art and African medicine in addition to covering literary developments in the black world. In 1964 he made his first lecture tour of the United States. But his two major works during this phase of his career were *A Bibliography of Neo-African Literature from Africa, America and the Caribbean* (1965) and *A History of Neo-African Literature: Writing in Two Continents* (1966—German edition).

The *Bibliography* was another ground-breaking achievement. Although several specialized bibliographies on black literature had already appeared, none was as detailed or as comprehensive as Jahn's, which attempted to list "all the works which might be considered as belonging to neo-African literature."[10] This took in not only writings by Africans but also writings by Afro-Carib-beans and Afro-Americans. Moreover, if Jahn's stilistic criteria for the iden-tification of neo-African literature were followed rigorously, even the works of Euro-African and Euro-American writers could be included if they manifested "the overlapping of two historically different literatures: (1) traditional Negro-African literature, and (2) Western literature."[11] However, Jahn admitted that such stylistic discriminations were difficult to make and subject to dispute, so until his criteria could be further refined and applied with some analytical precision, he was content to list all creative works—essays and unpublished manuscripts as well as novels, plays, volumes of poetry, and autobiographies—produced by black writers in Africa and the New World. In other words, his bibliography included rather than excluded writings that failed to meet his own "neo-African" criteria. This must be stressed because several obtuse reviewers unjustly accused him of deliberately omitting a number of black authors because their writings did not manifest what Jahn was imagined to regard arbitrarily as the hallmarks of "neo-African style." As Jahn said clearly in his introduction,

> Whether the user agrees or disagrees with my definition of neo-African literature, whether he interprets my term 'neo-African literature' as meaning 'modern literature in Negro-Africa', 'literature of Negro-Africans and Afro-Americans' or 'Negro literature', he will find the related works in this volume.[12]

Following this catholic principle, Jahn was able to list 3566 works by more than 1400 authors, recording each volume in the fullest possible bibliographical detail. Literary anthologies and translations in thirty-eight different languages were included, too. Jahn's *Bibliography* immediately became the indispensable reference tool for any scholar working in black literatures. Indeed, it helped to established such literatures as legitimate subjects for academic inquiry. Jahn, more than any other individual researcher, must be given credit for accelerating the pace of scholarly activity in these new literary fields.

But Jahn didn't confine himself to bibliographical endeavors. His book, *A History of Neo-African Literature: Writing in Two Continents*, published a year after the *Bibliography*, was one of the first scholarly works to attempt to cover this history of black writing in two worlds. Other scholars such as Bakary Traoré, Lilyan Lagneau-Kesteloot, Thomas Melone, Ezekiel Mphahlele, Gerald Moore, Judith Gleason and Claude Wauthier had examined more restricted topics in some detail, but no one had tried systematically to relate the literature of Africa to those of Afro-America and the Caribbean.

Any effort to do this was bound to be controversial, and Jahn's *History* got the same mixed reaction from critics and reviewers as *Muntu* had received eight years earlier. Readers were impressed with Jahn's wide-ranging research which took him into such remarkably varied areas as sixteenth century Latin poetry by Alfonso Álvares (the first known Negro writer), African praise-songs, Hausa and Swahili traditions of verse, early Southern Bantu writings, Afro-American slave narratives, New World minstrelsy and voodoo, Negro spirituals, blues and calypso, the Harlem Renaissance, Cuban Negrism and the evolution of Negritude. But while critics were willing to concede that

Jahn has done an enoumous amout of reading and thinking on these hetero-geneous subjects, they were still suspicious of his underlying theory and felt that some of his ideas, though extremely stimulating, were not adequately proven by the few examples he cited or the brief analyses he offered. They were also upset once again by his terminology, especially by the new word he coined for sub-Saharan Africa—Agisymba. The reaction of the reviewer in the *Times Literary Supplement* to the original German edition of Jahn's *History* was typical of the bemused skepticism that greeted this ambitious book:

> His theory seems to be that the black African cultures south of the Sahara form a cultural unit. In spite of local differences they share basic philosophic concepts. Herr Jahn assumes than he has proved this in his earlier book *Muntu*. In this new volume he takes it for granted that readers have accepted his argument that Alexis Kagame's controversial book *Bantu Philosophy* is valid, by and large, for the whole of Negro Africa and he can therefore proceed to give this country a name: Agisymba is what we are expected to call this territory now. Herr Jahn found the word on an old map of Africa drawn by Ptolemy. There it seemed to signify all those countries which Ptolemy knew nothing about. It would be kinder not to draw the com-parison.

But even after his negative opening and a few examples of Jahn's inability to demonstrate some of his theories, the anonymous *Times* reviewer felt com-pelled to add that Jahn's *History* had some redeeming qualities:

> Herr Jahn's new book is full of such bold ideas, most of them unproved, but many worth discussing. Like *Muntu* and other writings by this prolific apostle of negritude, *Geschichte der neoafrikanischen Literatur* leaves the reader entirely unconvinced but greatly stimulated and entertained.[13]

This, it could be argued, was Jahn's primary achievement as a scholar. He was able to provoke, to stimulate and to entertain. He didn't seek definitive proof of many of his ideas because often there was not enough evidence available to examine. His role was that of an instigator, someone who goaded others into activity by suggesting something they could test independently by examining a larger body of evidence. As Jahn himself stated in the first chapter of his *History:*

> When considering a living literature like the neo-African, historians of literature must except to be deepening and widening their observations all the time ... An introduction to the neo-African literature, in fact, is neither a complete history of this literature nor a conclusive study of its styles; a great deal of further research is needed before works of that sort can be carried out. The purpose of the present book is to point out the problems and classify provisionally the material to be analysed.[14]

In other words, Jahn was not attempting to provide unassailable answers to the riddles posed by this new literature; he was merely trying to raise relevant questions which others could investigate in greater depth and detail. He was urging scholars and academicians to thoroughly explore new frontiers. And when he himself sought to make bold leaps forward into these unknown regions, he was still being stopped at the border by literal-minded customs officials who suspected his papers were not in order.

After writing his *History*, Jahn returned to his habitual activities, producing two or three major translations and anthologies each year in addition to publishing essays, broadcasting radio talks and lecturing on African literature at the University of Frankfurt. Between 1966 and 1970 he translated books by Senghor, Césaire, V. S. Naipaul, Roger Mais, Cameron Duodu and Marcel Griaule as well as all the material which went into three anthologies of African, West Indian and Afro-American tales, proverbs, songs and love stories. He wrote and spoke on Negritude, on Senghor, on the cultural festivals he attended in Dakar, Algiers and Ife, on academic conferences and book fairs, on the growth and development of African literatures, on corruption, magic and polygamy in modern Africa—on literally anything that intersted him. He also edited for Kraus-Thomson Reprints a critical selection of the earliest and most important African and West Indian literary works, journals and scholarly monographs. He was now internationally recognized as a leading authority on African and New World black culture, and his talents were in great demand.

His next major opus was the comprehensive *Bibliography of Creative African Writing* which he compiled with the assistance of Claus Peter Dressler, a trained librarian who had worked for him for several years and had helped to collect, transcribe and record data for his earlier *Bibliography of Neo-African Literature*. The new bibliography was even more impressive than the first, though it was far narrower in scope, covering only the creative writing produced in sub-Saharan Africa. Jahn and Dressler managed to list 2130 individual works by 1127 authors writing in 51 African languages as well as in English, French and Portuguese. They also provided full documentation on 202 anthologies, 36 literary magazines, 33 bibliographies and 8 "forgeries" or works published by non-Africans under African pseudonyms. But the greatest improvement in coverage lay in the inclusion of bibliographical data on the hundreds of books and essays that had been written on African literatures; this important body of critical and scholarly commentary had never been adequately recorded in one volume before, and though Jahn and Dressler's coverage was by no means complete, their new *Bibliography* provided the most comprehensive single source of information yet compiled on the vast and widely scattered secondary literature that had grown up so rapidly around several of the new literatures of sub-Saharan Africa. In addition, their coverage of the primary works was remarkably thorough, embracing not only the various editions in which each title had appeared but also all known translations in 45 different languages of the world. This book instantly became the bibliographical Bible for all denominations of scholars working in African literatures. If Jahn had done nothing else in his lifetime, this *Bibliography* alone would have earned him an international reputation as a scholar.

But of course he did much more than this. His next book was another fundamental reference work, *Who's Who in African Literature: Biographies, Works, Commentaries*, which he completed in 1972 in collaboration with two of his closest associates, Ulla Schild and Almut Nordmann. Again, nothing quite like it had ever been done for African literature before. The book contained basic biographical information on nearly 450 African authors as well as a selection of diverse critical opinions on their works taken from standard secondary sources. Whenever possible, Jahn and his co-editors made an effort to contact the authors personally or by mail to check on the biographical data they had collected; they had also scoured maps of Africa trying to verify the existence of all the towns, districts and geographical features mentioned in their research notes on individual writers. The result, they admitted, was "not wholly balanced" since some of the information they sought could not be obtained, but it was nonetheless the fullest biographical handbook that had been produced on the lives of African writers. As such, it was an indispensable companion to Jahn and Dressler's *Bibliography*, to which it had been keyed by numerous cross-references to avoid unnecessary repetition of basis bibliograhical data. Jahn, with the help of his collaborators, had scored another impressive first in African literary studies.

It was to be his last major contribution. Within a year he was dead, having suffered several heart attacks after recovering from a long illness contracted while leading a group of wealthy tourists through West Africa to the land of the Dogon. He died at home on October 20, 1973, just two days after interviewing for German television the African poet who had launched him on his career twenty-one years earlier—Léopold Senghor. It was a fitting conclusion to a life dedicated to disseminating information about literary and cultural achievements in modern Africa.

Throughout his career Jahn remained a tireless worker who never lost his enthusiasm for his chosen vocation. He thrived on accepting challenges which tested his mental and physical resources, making demands on his enormous fund of creative energy. Though he had an eye for detail and meticulous accuracy, he never stooped to trivial or petty pursuits which would not advance understanding and appreciation of black expressive cultures. Through his translations, anthologies, bibliographies, interpretations, lectures, essays and numerous controversies, he contributed more than anyone else to worldwide recognition of Africa's unique contributions to twentieth century civilization. He was Africa's best literary agent and promoter.

How did he succeed in accomplishing all he did? How did he manage to find the time and stamina to write, translate, edit and compile fifty-four books in the last two decades of his life? How did he keep up such a hectic pace year after year and still maintain the ability to travel, lecture and enjoy life as much as he did? His secret, he once told me with a twinkle in his eye, was that he didn't really write his books; he dictated them. A tape recorder was his amanuensis. Even *Muntu*, he insisted, had been put together from the transcripts of a series of lectures he had delivered orally. Translations were even easier. He merely read a work, circling the words he did not know, then asking his friends and assistants to look these up in a dictionary and to write their German equivalents in the margins. After this had been done, he would sit down with the book again and read his translation of it onto cassette tapes, which unemployed housewives in his village would transcribe to earn a little pocket money. In this way he was able to translate lengthy books or the numerous excerpts included in his anthologies very speedily. It took a bit longer to assemble a scholarly book using such methods but he claimed this was how he usually first got his ideas down on paper. Later he would revise and polish up the transcript but his work at that stage would be mainly editorial. When formulating his ideas or translating a text, he always relied more heavily on his tongue than on his pen.

Though Jahn may have been exaggerating slightly for dramatic effect (it is inconceivable, for example, that his newspaper articles could have been composed in this manner), his account of his methods of composition nevertheless sheds interesting light on his working habits and personality. In his own writings he fused oral and written modes of communication, shaping his African material into recognized and accepted forms of European expressions. Thus, in a sense, he himself was operating according to neo-African artistic principles. He had bridged not just two disparate cultures but two disparate techniques of creative expression. He was Germany's most African writer.

In an essay completed a few months before his death, Jahn appraised the career of Germany's most famous Africanist, Leo Frobenius. It was the Frobenius centennial year, and Jahn, with characteristic iconoclasm and calculated mischief, attacked the great man's scholarship and unscientific practices, debunking the theories and intuitions upon which his reputation was based. Instead of humbly placing a wreath on his tomb, Jahn defaced it with bold graffiti, labeling him a "demonic child," "a pacesetter of fascism," "a post-Wilhelminian barroom philosopher," "a retarded petty bourgeouis," "a pseudo-scholar," "a sentimental author of *Kitsch*."[15] Yet Jahn also respected Frobenius for his enormous productivity, his huge collections of well-organized data, his vitality and his love for Africa. And he praised him for having made the world aware of the dignity and beauty of African art, literature and culture. "Africa," he said, "will remember him for that. He helped Africans and Afro-Americans to find a new consciousness of themselves within the African heritage."[16]

The same could be said of Jahn himself. Though his theories remain controversial, though some may still regard him as having been too enthusiastic and unscholarly in his approach to black expressive culture, though some might yet be tempted to call him the same names he called Frobenius, we cannot fail to be impressed with the monumental works he left behind. Nor can we deny him the credit he merits for having helped to make the world conscious of the cultural wealth of modern Africa. Janheinz Jahn deserves to be issued with a new international passport, one in which he is properly identified not as an unemployed printer but as a very important writer, certainly the most important writer on African literatures that Germany has yet produced.

Notes

1 Janheinz Jahn, *Through African Doors* (London, 1962), pp. 141—42.
2 For a complete list of Jahn's writings, see Ulla Schild, "A Bibliography of the Works of Janheinz Jahn," *Research in African Literatures,* 5 (1974), 196—205.
3 Ulla Schild, "Janheinz Jahn, 1918—1973," *Research in African Literatures,* 5 (1974), 194.
4 In 1957 he gave a talk on „Zwischen zwei Zivilisationen: Eine Analyse der neoafrikanischen Literatur" on Hessischer Rundfunk. See Schild, "Bibliography," p. 204.
5 For a history of this journal, see my "A decade of *Black Orpheus,*" Books *Abroad*, 42 (1968), 509—16.
6 Peter Abrahams, "Africa on the Move," *New York Times Book Review,* 14 May 1961, p. 10.
7 *Times Literary Supplement*, 11 August 1961, p. 498.
8 *The Spectator*, 31 March 1961, pp. 451—52.
9 Janheinz Jahn, *Muntu* (New York, 1961), p. 21.
10 Janheinz Jahn, *A Bibliography of Neo-African Literature from Africa, America and the Caribbean* (London, 1965), p. viii.
11 Ibid., p. vii.
12 Ibid, p. viii.
13 *Times Literary Supplement*, 8 September 1966, p. 816.
14 Janheinz Jahn, *A History of Neo-African Literature: Writing in Two Continents* (London, 1966), pp. 23—24.
15 Janheinz Jahn, *Leo Frobenius: The Demonic Child* (Austin, 1974), pp. 17, 20.
16 Ibid., p. 20.

A Bibliography of the Works of Janheinz Jahn

Ulla Schild

BOOKS

1. *Muntu: Umrisse der neoafrikanischen Kultur.* Düsseldorf: Eugen Diederichs, 1958. 262 p. + 8 p. ill.
   Muntu: neoafrikansk kultur i vardande. Tr. Ake Sparring. Stockholm: Rabén & Sjörgen, 1960. 247 p + 8 p. ill.
   Muntu: an outline of neo-African culture. Tr. Marjorie Grene. London: Faber & Faber, 1961. 267 p. + 16 p. ill.
   Muntu: the New African Culture. Tr. Marjorie Grene. New York: Grove Press, 1961. 267 p. + 16 p. ill. In paperback 1969.
   Muntu: l'homme africain et la culture néo-africaine. Tr. Brian de Martinoir. Paris. Edition du Seuil, 1961. 293 p.
   Muntu: la civiltà africana moderna. Tr. Gustavo Glaesser. Introd. Ernesto de Martino. Torino: Einaudi, 1961. xiv + 279 p. + 14 p. ill.
   Muntu: las culturas neoafricanas. Tr. Jasmin Reuter. Mexiko, Buenos Aires: Fondo de Cultura Económica, 1963. 348 p. + 8 p. ill.
   Muntu: mot en ny afrikansk kultur. Tr. Amund Hønningstad. Oslo: Dreyer, 1966. 159 p. (Perspektivbokene 18.)
   Moentoe: Contouren van de neo-Afrikaanse cultuur. Tr. Wouter Gortzak. Amsterdam: Moussault, 1967. 240 p.
   Muntu: las culturas de la negritude. Tr. Daniel Romero. Madrid: Guadarrama, 1970. 299 p. (Punto Omega 98).
2. *Anders gläubige Kunst.* [Essay] Stierstadt im Taunus: Eremiten Presse, 1958. 25 p. + 16 p. ill. by Susanne Wenger.
3. *Approaches to African Literature.* [Essay] Ibadan (Nigeria): Ibadan University Press, 1959. 31 p.
4. *Durch afrikanische Türen: Erlebnisse und Begegnungen in Westafrika.* Düsseldorf: Eugen Diederichs, 1960. 279 p.; Frankfurt am Main: Büchergilde Gutenberg, 1962. 269 p.; Frankfurt am Main: Fischer Bücherei, 1967. 237 p. (Fischer Bücherei 821.)
   Through African Doors: experiences and encounters in West Africa. Tr. Oliver Coburn. London: Faber & Faber, 1962. 232 p. + 8 p. ill.; New York: Grove Press, 1962. 235 p. + 8 p. ill. In paperback 1969.
   Skozi Afriska Vrata: dozivljaji in srecanja v zahodni Afriki. Tr. Peter Kolar. Maribor: Zalozba Obzorja, 1962. 273 p.
   Africa Puertas Adentro: hechos, cosas y gentes de Africa occidental. Tr. Ingeborg S. de Luque. Buenos Aires: Compañia General Fabril Editora, 1963. 251 p. (Los libros del mirasol.)
5. *Geschichte der neoafrikanischen Literatur: Eine Einführung.* Düsseldorf: Eugen Diederichs, 1966. 285 p.
   A History of Neo-African Literature: Writing in two continents. Tr. Oliver Coburn & Ursula Lehrburger. London: Faber & Faber, 1968. 301 p.
   Neo-African Literature: A history of black writing. Tr. Oliver Coburn & Ursula Lehrburger. New York: Grove Press, 1968. 301 p. In paperback 1969.

Manuel de Littérature neo-africaine du XVIe siècle à nos jours, de l'Afrique à l'Amérique. Tr. Gaston Bailly. Paris: RESMA. Distribution Sedim, 1969. 293 p.
Las Literaturas neoafricanas. Tr. Daniel Romero. Madrid: Guadarrama, 1971. 362 p. (Punta Omega 107.)

6. *Leo Frobenius: The Demonic Child.* [Essay] Tr. Reinhard Sander. Pref. Ulla Schild. Austin: African and Afro-American Studies and Research Center, The University of Texas at Austin, 1974. 23 p. (Occasional Publication 8.)

REFERENCE WORKS

7. *Die neoafrikanische Literatur: Gesamtbibliographie von den Anfängen bis zur Gegenwart.* Düsseldorf: Eugen Diederichs, 1965. xxxv + 359 p. *A Bibliography of Neo-African Literature from Africa, America and the Caribbean.* London: André Deutsch, 1965. xxxv + 359 p.; New York: F. A. Praeger, 1965. xxxv + 359 p.

8. Janheinz Jahn and Claus Peter Dressler. *A Bibliography of Creative African Writing.* Nendeln (Liechtenstein): Kraus Reprint, 1971. xl, 446 p. 2nd rev. ed. Milwood, N.Y.: Kraus Thompson, 1972. xl, 446 p.

9. Janheinz Jahn, Ulla Schild, Almut Nordmann. *Who's Who in African Literature: Biographies, Works, Commentaries.* Tübingen: Horst Erdmann, 1972. 406 p.

ANTHOLOGIES

10. *Schwarzer Orpheus: Moderne Dichtung afrikanischer Völker beider Hemisphären.* München: Carl Hanser, 1954; 2nd ed., 1955. 139 p.; 3rd ed., 1959. 149 p.; Frankfurt am Main: Fischer Bücherei, 1960. 181 p. (Fischer Bücherei 350). New edition: München: Carl Hanser, 1964. 323 p.; München: Sonderreihe dtv, 1973. 293 p.

11. *Andalusischer Liebesdiwan: Nachdichtungen hispanorabischer Lyrik.* Freiburg im Breisgau: Klemm, 1955. 138 p.

12. *Schwarze Ballade: Moderne afrikanische Erzähler beider Hemisphären.* Düsseldorf: Eugen Diederichs, 1957. 243 p.; Frankfurt am Main: Fischer Bücherei, 1965. 237 p. (Fischer Bücherei 680.)

13. *Rumba Macumba: Nachdichtungen afrocubanischer Lyrik.* München: Carl Hanser, 1957. 79 p.

14. *Reis und Hahnenschrei: Moderne Lyrik von den Inseln Indonesiens.* With W. A. Braasem. Heidelberg: Wolfgang Rothe, 1957. 59 p.

15. *Sirih und rote Hibiskusblüten: Indonesische Volksdichtung.* With W. A. Braasem. München: Langen-Müller, 1959. 115 p., ill.

16. *Afrikanische Impressionen.* Fotos und Zeichnungen von Helmut Lander, Einleitung und Übersetzungen von Janheinz Jahn. Darmstadt: Peter-Presse, 1962. 99 p., ill.

17. *Negro Spirituals.* Frankfurt am Main: Fischer Bücherei, 1962. 196 p. (Fischer Bücherei 472.)

18. *Das Herz auf dem Opferstein: Selbstzeugnisse der Azteken,* gesammelt von Fray Bernardino de Sahagún, dt. von Edmund Seler, herausgegeben von Janheinz Jahn. Köln, Berlin: Kiepenheuer & Witsch, 1962. 316 p.

19. *Die Welt ist Wind: Afrikanische Pointen.* München: Ehrenwirth, 1962. 96 p., ill.

20. *Dunkle Stimmen (Schwarzer Orpheus + Schwarze Ballade).* Frankfurt am Main: Büchergilde Gutenberg, 1963. 416 p.

21. *Das junge Afrika: Erzählungen junger afrikanischer Autoren.* Wien, München, Basel: Kurt Desch, 1963. 596 p.

22. *Afrika erzählt: Erzähler südlich der Sahara.* Frankfurt am Main: Fischer Bücherei, 1963. 180 p. (Fischer Bücherei 555.)

23. *Blues und Work Songs.* Frankfurt am Main: Fischer Bücherei, 1964. 185 p. (Fischer Bücherei 597.)
24. *Wir nannten sie Wilde: Begegnungen in Übersee einst und jetzt.* Aus alten und neuen Reisebeschreibungen zusammengestellt und kommentiert. München: Ehrenwirth, 1964. 200 p. + 16 p., ill.
25. *Das Schlangenorakel: Erzählungen junger afrikanischer Autoren.* München: Goldmann, 1965. 179 p. (Goldmanns gelbe Taschenbücher 1618.)
26. *Die Zauberkatze: Erzählungen junger afrikanischer Autoren.* München: Goldmann, 1965. 169 p. (Goldmanns gelbe Taschenbücher 1624.) (Selected from No. 20.)
27. *Jubeltag auf Jamaica: Westindien in Erzählungen der besten zeitgenössischen Autoren.* Herrenalb (Schwarzwald): Horst Erdmann, 1965. 447 p. (Geistige Begegnung 13.)
28. *34 × schwarze Liebe: Erotische Erzählungen aus Afrika, Westindien, Nordamerika.* Frankfurt am Main: Bärmeier & Nikel, 1968. 350 p.
29. *Afrika lacht: Sinnliche, freche und witzige Geschichten, Pointen und Songs aus Afrika, Westindien und Nordamerika.* Frankfurt am Main: Bärmeier & Nikel, 1968. 296 p.
30. *Entflammte Rivalen: Afrikanische Liebesgeschichten.* München, Wien, Basel: Kurt Desch, 1969. 137 p. (Bücher der Liebe 53.)
31. *Süß ist das Leben in Kumansenu und andere Erzählungen aus Westafrika.* Tübingen, Basel: Horst Erdmann, 1971. 455 p. (Geistige Begegnung 31.)

TRANSLATIONS

32. Léopold Sédar Senghor. *Tam-Tam Schwarz. Gesänge vom Senegal (Auswahl).* Heidelberg: Wolfgang Rothe, 1955. 63 p.
33. Aimé Césaire. *Sonnendolche — Poignards du Soleil. Lyrik von den Antillen.* (Zweisprachige Auswahl.) Heidelberg: Wolfgang Rothe, 1956. 88 p.
34. Aimé Césaire. *Und die Hunde schwiegen. Drama.* Introd. Arthur Müller. Emsdetten (Westfalen): Lechte, 1956. 95 p.; Bühnenrechte: Kiepenheuer & Witsch, Köln. 1960, Stadttheater Basel.
35. Paul Vesey. *Elfenbeinzähne — Ivory Tusks. Gedichte eines Afro-Amerikaners* (zweisprachige Ausgabe). Heidelberg: Wolfgang Rothe, 1956. 47 p.
36. George Lamming. *Mit dem Golfstrom. Roman.* München: Carl Hanser, 1956. 351 p.
37. Adalberto Ortiz. *Juyungo. Roman.* Tr. with Hans Platschek. Frankfurt am Main: G. B. Fischer, 1957. 312 p.; Berlin: Volk und Welt, 1958. 300 p.; Hamburg: Deutsche Hausbücherei, 1960. 254 p.
38. Alejo Carpentier. *Die Flucht nach Manoa. Roman.* Tr. with Hans Platschek. München: R. Piper & Co., 1958. 369 p.
39. Aimé Césaire. *Zurück ins Land der Geburt — Cahier d'un retour au pays natal* (zweisprachig). Frankfurt am Main: Insel Verlag, 1962. 95 p.
40. Léopold Sédar Senghor. *Botschaft und Anruf. Sämtliche Gedichte, französisch und deutsch.* München: Carl Hanser, 1963. 229 p.; (German text only) München: Deutscher Taschenbuchverlag, 1966. 149 p. (Sonderreihe dtv 54.)
41. Aimé Césaire. *Die Tragödie von König Christoph. Bühnenmanuskript.* 110 p., mimeographed. Bühnenrechte: Kiepenheuer & Witsch, Köln, 1964. Also in *Theater heute,* No. 10 (Okt. 1964), pp. 55—68.
42. Bloke Modisane. *Weiß ist das Gesetz. Autobiographischer Roman.* München: Droemer/Knaur, 1964. 354 p.
43. Nabi Youla. *Moussa, Enfant de Guinée — Mussa, ein Kind aus Guinea* (zweisprachig). Regensburg: Josef Habbel, 1964. 68 p., ill.
44. V. S. Naipaul. *Blaue Karren im Calypsoland. Eine Geschichte aus Trinidad.* Herrenalb (Schwarzwald): Horst Erdmann, 1966. 248 p.

45. Léopold Sédar Senghor. *Négritude und Humanismus.* Düsseldorf: Eugen Diederichs, 1967. 322 p.
46. Roger Mais. *Sie nannten ihn Bruder Mensch. Roman.* Freiburg, Basel, Wien: Herder, 1967. 222 p.; Berlin: Evangelische Verlagsanstalt, 1971. 228 p.
47. Aimé Césaire. *An Afrika. Gedichte (zweisprachige Ausgabe).* Übersetzt unter Mitarbeit von Friedhelm Kemp. München: Carl Hanser, 1968. 198 p.
48. Cameron Duodu. *Flucht nach Akkra. Roman der unruhigen Jugend Afrikas.* Tübingen, Basel: Horst Erdmann, 1970. 268 p.
49. Marcel Griaule. *Schwarze Genesis. Ein afrikanischer Schöpfungsbericht.* Freiburg, Basel, Wien: Herder, 1970. 205 p.

EDITIONS

50. *The Black Experience. Four hundred years of black literature from Africa and the Americas. Series 1.* A critical selection, edited and annotated by Janheinz Jahn. Nendeln (Liechtenstein): Kraus Reprint, 1969.
51. *The Black Experience. Four hundred years of black experience from Africa and the Americas. Series 2. Monographs.* A critical selection, edited and annotated by Janheinz Jahn. Nendeln (Liechtenstein): Kraus Reprint, 1971.
52. *The Black Experience. Four hundred years of black experience from Africa and the Americas. Series 1 and Series 2. Journals.* A critical selection by Janheinz Jahn. Nendeln (Liechtenstein): Kraus Reprint, 1972.

RECORD

53. *Schwarzer Orpheus — Rumba Macumba Neoafrikanische Lyrik,* übersetzt und ausgewählt von Janheinz Jahn. Sprecher: Siegfried Wischnewski, Susanne Eggers und Alwin Michael Rueffer (Kommentar). Ariola — Athena 51188. 30 cm. 33 rpm.

ESSAYS AND ARTICLES

"Moderne Neger-Lyrik," *Die Literatur,* II (15 Aug. 1952).
"Voltaires Frankfurter Abenteuer," *Antares,* 1, 7 (1953), 3—17.
"Fleisch vom Fleisch der Welt. Onthologie der Bantu," *Frankfurter Hefte,* 9, 8 (1954), 604—15.
"The contribution of the West Indies to poetry," *Bim,* 6, 21 (1954), 16—22.
"Eine abenteuerliche Korrespondenz," *Die Gegenwart,* 16 (31 June 1954).
"Die afrikanische Literatur und die Freiheit. Der erste Weltkongreß schwarzer Autoren," *Texte und Zeichen,* 2, 6 (1956), 657—63.
"Die Ägäis der Neuen Welt. Götter und Menschen auf den Antillen," *Agorá,* 6 (1956), 60—74.
"Aimé Césaire und der Surrealismus," *Texte und Zeichen,* 2, 4 (1956), 430—33.
"Zum Übersetzungsproblem: Dante, übersetzt," *Akzente,* 5 (1956), 405—14.
"Die Kunst zwischen den Stühlen. Ein Dialog," *Akzente,* 5 (1956), 426—31.
"Een internationale organisatie van neger-schrijvers. Aan de blanken de vriendenhand toegestoken," *Het Vaderland,* 27 Oct. 1956.
"Aber bewahre mich, Herz, vor allem Hasse. Der erste Weltkongreß schwarzer Autoren," *Frankfurter Allgemeine Zeitung,* 5 Oct. 1956.
"Die Amerikaner hatten einen schweren Stand. Die schwarzen Dichter trafen sich zu einem ersten internationalen Kongreß in Paris," *Handelsblatt,* 19 Oct. 1956.
"Ich komme mir lächerlich vor im Smoking," *Frankfurter Allgemeine Zeitung,* 24 Nov. 1956.
"World congress of black writers," *Black Orpheus,* 1 (Sept. 1957), 39—46.
"Lyrik und Rumba. Moderne kubanische Gedichte," *Deutsche Universitätszeitung,* 3 (1957), 16—19.
"Het eerste congres van neger-schrijvers," *Studium Generale,* 2 (1957), 44—46.
"Aimé Césaire," *Antares,* 2 (1957), 25—28.

"Aus der Werkstatt des Übersetzers. Der Schreibtisch ist meine Hobelbank," *Antares*, 6 (1957), 19—23.
"Die afrikanische Kultur und die Freiheit. Der erste Weltkongreß schwarzer Autoren," *Texte und Zeichen*, 10 (1956), 657—63.
"Die moderne Lyrik der Schwarzen," *Die Horen*, 2, 6 (1957), 1—15.
"Poetry in Rumba rhythms," *Black Orpheus*, 3 (May 1958), 32—36.
"Wodu," *Du*, 18, 9 (1958), 39—40, 55—56.
"Aimé Césaire," *Black Orpheus*, 2 (Jan. 1958), 32—36.
"Discussion on Camara Laye. Camara Laye: an interpretation," *Black Orpheus*, 6 (Nov. 1959), 35—38.
"Über Tchicaya U Tam'si," *Blätter und Bilder*, 11 (Nov./Dec. 1960), 43—44.
"Mittelamerikanischer Aufruhr und französische Klarheit verbinden sich im Werk des Martinikesen Aimé Césaire," *Der Tagesspiegel*, 22 Oct. 1960.
"Richard Wright. Tragiker zwischen Schwarz und Weiß," *Christ und Welt*, 8 Dec. 1960.
"Aspekte afrikanisch-europäischer Kulturbeziehungen," *WUS-Nachrichten*, special issue: Afrika — Essay, Bericht, Information, (1960), 7—18.
"Die neoafrikanische Literatur," *Das Schönste*, 7, 5 (1961), 67—69.
"Dichter und Staatsmann. Léopold Sédar Senghor spricht heute in Frankfurt," *Neue Presse*, 11 Nov. 1961; *Hannoversche Presse*, 14 Nov. 1961.
"Der Dichter als Staatschef. Léopold Sédar Senghor auf Staatsbesuch in Deutschland," *Stuttgarter Zeitung*, 6 Nov. 1961.
"Die Dichtung in der afrikanischen Kultur," *Schauspielheft*, 11 (1962/63). (Landestheater Hannover.)
"Geschichte der neo-afrikanischen Literatur: die frühen Zöglinge," *Katholisches Missionsjahrbuch der Schweiz*, 29 (1962), 22—25.
"Afrikanische Medizin," *Therapie des Monats*, 12, 2 (1962), 53—64; 12, 3 (1962), 100—12.
"An der Tür zum schwarzen Afrika. Amos Tutuola, Nigerias bekanntester Erzähler, verdient sich seinen Lebensunterhalt als Portier," *Der Tagesspiegel*, 12 April 1962.
"Common market of culture," *WAY Forum*, 45 (Nov. 1962), 39—41.
"Stimme des schwarzen Orpheus," *Epoca*, 1, 3 (1963), 64—70.
"Sur la littérature africaine," *Présence africaine*, nouv. série, 48 (1963), 151—62.
"Dichter und Politiker: Césaire. Zur deutschen Erstaufführung der Tragödie 'Und die Hunde schwiegen'," *Hannoversche Presse*, 19 April 1963.
"Die Dichtung des schwarzen Kontinents," *Der Literat*, 7, 11 (1964), 128—29; *Die Welt der Literatur*, 14 (17 Sept. 1964), 417.
"Blues — Dichtung und Gesang. Von Janheinz Jahn und Alfons Michael Dauer," *Der Monat*, 16, 186 (1964), 54—64.
"Afrikanische Literatur in Deutschland. Eine Übersicht," *Frankfurter Allgemeine Zeitung*, 20 Nov. 1964.
"Grundzüge der neoafrikanischen Literatur," *Neusprachliche Mitteilungen aus Wissenschaft und Praxis*, 1 (1965).
"Afrika, der neue Partner der Weltgeschichte," *Propyläen-Weltgeschichte*, II (1965).
"Rhythmes et style dans la poésie africaine," *Actes du colloque sur la littérature africaine d'etpression française*. Dakar: Université, 1965, pp. 227—37.
"Ein Festival afrikanischer Kunst," *Frankfurter Allgemeine Zeitung*, 23 Dec. 1965.
"Senghor without propeller," *Black Orpheus*, 19 (1966), 40—44.
"Der Philosoph der Negritude — Léopold Sédar Senghor," *Der Literat*, 12 (1966), 183.
"Und Afrika tanzt. Die Weltfestspiele der Negerkünste in Dakar," *Der Literat*, 5 (1966), 67—68.

"Négritude — weltoffen. Die Literaturpreise des Festivals von Dakar," *Frankfurter Allgemeine Zeitung*, 18 May 1966.

"Ein dynamisches Museum für die Kunst Afrikas. Die Ausstellung aus Dakar übersiedelt nach Paris," *Frankfurter Allgemeine Zeitung*, 11 June 1966.

"Afrika tanzt in Dakar. Die ersten Weltfestspiele der Negerkünste," *Frankfurter Allgemeine Zeitung*, 27 April 1966.

"Trommel und Telefon," *Darmstädter Echo*, 15 July 1967.

"Von Cologne nach Addis Abeba. Alter Streit und notwendige Ergänzung," *Die Zeit*, 14 April 1967.

"Komfort und Abenteuer," *Darmstädter Echo*, 2 Sept. 1967.

"Die Auseinandersetzung um Biafra. Ihr Ablauf und die Hintergründe," *Frankfurter Hefte*, 23, 11 (1968), 756—66.

"Léopold Sédar Senghor," *Der Literat*, 10, 9 (12 Sept. 1968), 129.

"Der Poet Léopold Sédar Senghor," *Tele Africa: Senghor Senegal*. Stuttgart: Tele Africa Verlagsges., 1968, pp. 27—34.

"Meine erste Begegnung mit Senghor," *Darmstädter Echo*, 20 Sept. 1968.

"Léopold Sédar Senghor, Friedenspreisträger 1968," *Börsenblatt für den Deutschen Buchhandel*, (28 Aug. 1968), pp. 5—18.

"Senghors Dichtung — Kraftquelle der Politik. Der Sänger von Joal als Friedenspreisträger des Buchhandels," *Rheinische Post*, 7 Sept. 1968.

"Legalisierung eines Unrechts. Entwicklungshilfe, die Freiheit der Literatur und die Stockholmer Empfehlungen zum Urheberrecht," *Frankfurter Allgemeine Zeitung*, 29 May 1969.

"Der Akzent liegt in Afrika. Die ersten panafrikanischen Kulturfestspiele (Algier)," *Frankfurter Allgemeine Zeitung*, 26 July 1969.

"Tanzende, dampfende Wirklichkeit. Buntes Kulturprogramm auf dem Panafrikanischen Festival," *Frankfurter Allgemeine Zeitung*, 1 Aug. 1969.

"Nicht nur Sonnenschein und Rosen in Afrika. Olympische Medaillen beim Panafrikanischen Festival in Algier," *Frankfurter Allgemeine Zeitung*, 11 Aug. 1969.

"Der Umfang der modernen afrikanischen Literatur," *Internationales Afrika-Forum*, 5, 9/10 (Sept./Oct. 1969), 596—99.

"Ein Kongreß platzt. Der internationale Kongreß der Afrika-Studien in Montreal," *Frankfurter Allgemeine Zeitung*, 28 Oct. 1969.

"Von europäischen Fesseln befreit. Das Universitätsfestival in Abidjan an der Elfenbeinküste," *Frankfurter Allgemeine Zeitung*, 21 May 1970.

"Haitis Herren und Götter," *Kunst aus Haiti*, Sammlung Kurt Bachmann, Museum am Ostwall, Dortmund, 1969—1970, pp. 5—7.

"Von der Kunst, afrikanische Literatur zu übersetzen (Dankrede zum Übersetzerpreis)," *Internationales Afrika-Forum*, 6, 9/10 (Sept./Oct. 1970), 564—66.

"The Scope of Modern African Literature," *Research in African Literatures*, 1, 2 (1970), 167—75.

"Arts festival tribute to Senghor," *Times* (Lagos), 16 Dec. 1970.

"Triumph afrikanischer Laien in Ife. Kunstfestspiele in Ife," *Frankfurter Allgemeine Zeitung*, 29 Dec. 1970.

"Négritude und Afrikanität," *Theoretische Probleme des Sozialismus in Afrika*. Hamburg: Buske, 1971, pp. 11—20.

"Modern African Literature: Bibliographical Spectrum," *Review of National Literatures*, 2, 2 (1971), 224—42.

"Freiheit im Exil. Zur Mobilität afrikanischer Autoren," *Afrika heute*, 18 (Sept. 1971), 394, 397.

"Freedom in Exile: On the mobility of African Writers," *Pan-African Journal*, 4, 4 (1971), 473—76.

"Von der Négritude zum Volkstheater," *Schweizer Monatshefte*, 51, 7 (1971), 495—505.

"Was haben wir eigentlich von diesen Afrikanern?" *Entwicklung und Zusammenarbeit*, 10 (1971), 7—8.

"Adebisi Fabunmi," Catalogue of the *Agisymba-Galerie*, Berlin, Dec. 1971.

"Ghana's written literature," In *Ghanaian Writing*, ed. by A. W. Kayper-Mensah and Horst Wollf, Tübingen: Erdmann, 1972, pp. 234—39.

"Afrika: nicht mehr 'in'?" *Frankfurter Allgemeine Zeitung*, 2 Oct. 1972.

"Entdecker im Dunst. Kritisches Gedenkblatt für Leo Frobenius," *Stuttgarter Zeitung*, 30 June 1973.

"Nochmals Frobenius: Ein Geist über den Erdteilen," *Internationales Afrika-Forum*, 9, 9/10 (Sept. 1973), 524—36.

"African literature and the process of decolonization," *Ufahamu*, 4, 1 (1973), 34—44.

"Two African Writers: Nathaniel Nakasa and Issa Traoré," *Research in African Literatures*, 5, 1 (1974).

RADIO ESSAYS

Totem und Trommel. Ein Abendstudio über Geisteshaltung und Musik der Tropenvölker. *Hessischer Rundfunk*, 15 May 1951, 60'.

Die Renaissance der Schwarzen. Moderne Negerlyrik. *Hessischer Rundfunk*, 23 April 1953, 30'.

Lyrik im Rumbatakt. Moderne kubanische Lyrik. *Hessischer Rundfunk*, 10 June 1954, 30'.

Die Ägäis der Neuen Welt. Götter und Menschen auf den Antillen. *Hessischer Rundfunk*, 13 July 1954, 60'.

Lyrik von den Antillen. *Hessischer Rundfunk*, 1954, 15'.

Meine schwarzen Puppen. Südamerikanische Negerlyrik. *Hessischer Rundfunk*, 2 Dec. 1954, 30'.

Zum Schauen bestellt. Wandlungen europäischer Weltsicht von Herodot bis Overhoff. *Hessischer Rundfunk*, 24 May 1955, 60'.

Verrat an der Muttersprache? Probleme moderner afrikanischer Lyrik. *Radio Bremen*, Feb. 1956, 30'.

Die schwarzen Prosaisten Adalberto Ortiz und George Lamming. *Hessischer Rundfunk*, 8 April 1956, 30'.

Rumba Macumba. Afrocubanische Lyrik. *Südwestfunk*, 5 Oct. 1956, 30'.

Die Philosophie der Bantus. *Norddeutscher Rundfunk*, Dec. 1956, 60'.

Gedicht und Gedanke: "An Afrika" von Aimé Césaire. *Hessischer Rundfunk*, 1957 (?), 10'.

Zwischen zwei Zivilisationen. Eine Analyse der neoafrikanischen Literatur. *Hessischer Rundfunk*, 1957, 60'.

Der Tod in Afrika. (Diop, Senghor, Tempels, Beier, "Dr. Henshaw".) *Südwestfunk*, 1957, 30'.

Aimé Césaire — Léopold Sédar Senghor. Zwei Möglichkeiten schwarzer Dichtung. *Süddeutscher Rundfunk*, 25 March 1957, 30'.

Ham — Parade der Vorurteile gegenüber Afrikanern. *Hessischer Rundfunk*, 1958 (?), 60'.

Vom Gottsucher zum Geisterbusch. Fünfzig Jahre neoafrikanischer Literatur. *Hessischer Rundfunk*, 15 July 1958, 60'.

Die Zauberkraft des Wortes. Prinzipien afrikanischer Dichtung und Medizin. *Hessischer Rundfunk*, 28 Oct. 1958, 60'.

Wortzauber und Exempel. Neoafrikanische Dichtung und Prosa. *Hessischer Rundfunk*, 4 Nov. 1958, 60'.

Die Stadt von morgen prophezeien. Eine Sendung über Léopold Sédar Senghor. *Rias Berlin*, 3 July 1961, 30'.

Aus der Vormundschaft entlassen. Zur Geschichte der neoafrikanischen Literatur. *Hessischer Rundfunk*, 3 Oct. 1961, 60'.

Heilkunst oder Hokuspokus? Die Heilpraktiken in Afrika. *Norddeutscher Rundfunk,* 20 Aug. 1962, 30'.
Europa und die afrikanische Kunst. Hundert Jahre Kunstbetrachtung in ihrem Ablauf dargestellt. *Hessischer Rundfunk,* 19 Jan. 1964, 60'.
Der kongolesische Lyriker Felix Tchicaya U Tam'si. *Hessischer Rundfunk,* Nov. 1965, 30'.
Kultur und Kritik 1: Sédar Senghor 60 Jahre. *Hessischer Rundfunk,* 9 Oct. 1966, 5'.
Zwischenlandung Dakar. Ein Reisehörbild. *Süddeutscher Rundfunk,* March 1967, 60'.
Zwischen Musterdemokratie und Völkermord. *Hessischer Rundfunk* and *Sender Freies Berlin,* Dec. 1967, 60'. (The same under the title "Zwischen Musterdemokratie und Schlachthaus," *Westdeutscher Rundfunk,* 15 May 1968, and under the title "Zwischen Musterdemokratie und Stammesfehde," *Südwestfunk,* 5 Sept. 1968.)
Die zwei Gesichter der Korruption. Szenen aus dem modernen Afrika. *Hessischer Rundfunk,* 7 June 1968, 60'.
Polygamie — eine afrikanische Lebensform. *Hessischer Rundfunk,* 21 July 1968; *Radio Bremen,* 9 March 1969; *Deutschlandfunk,* 27 Sept. 1971, 60'.
Dichtung der Négritude. *Bayerischer Rundfunk,* 15 Oct. 1968, 30'.
Die Gefangenschaft des Obatalla. (The imprisonment of Obatala, dt.) Nach der englischen Bühnenbearbeitung von Ulli Beier ins Deutsche übertragen und als Hörspiel eingerichtet. *Westdeutscher Rundfunk,* 1968, *Süddeutscher Rundfunk,* 26 May 1971, 90'.
Das Ziegenherz unterm Bett. Magie im modernen Afrika. *Hessischer Rundfunk,* 7 Febr. 1969, 60'.
Tübinger Afrika-Tage. *Sender Freies Berlin,* 9 July 1970, 20'.
Von der Négritude zur Selbstkritik. Moderne afrikanische Prosa. *Sender Freies Berlin,* 6 Oct. 1970, 60'.
Zwischen National- und Volkstheater. Modernes afrikanisches Drama. *Sender Freies Berlin,* 3 Nov. 1970, 65'.
Afrikanische Literatur auf der Frankfurter Buchmesse 1970. *Hessischer Rundfunk,* 25 Nov. 1970, 7'.
Die Abwendung von Europa. Moderne afrikanische Lyrik. *Sender Freies Berlin,* 1 Dec. 1970, 30'.
Von Abidjan bis Ife. Probleme der Sprachbarrieren in Afrika. *Hessischer Rundfunk,* 12 April 1971, 60'.
Neue Tempel für alte Götter. Susanne Wenger und die Heiligtümer von Oshogbo. *Hessischer Rundfunk,* 1971, 60'.
Drei Freier — ein Ehemann. Komödie von Guillaume Oyono-Mbia. Übersetzt und als Hörspiel bearbeitet. *Hessischer Rundfunk,* 5 Oct. 1971, 90'.
Afrikanische Literatur auf der Buchmesse 1971. *Hessischer Rundfunk,* 15 Oct. 1971, 5'.
Magie im modernen Afrika. *Südwestfunk* and *Süddeutscher Rundfunk,* 17 Jan. 1972, 60'.
Afrikanische Literatur auf der Buchmesse 1972. *Hessischer Rundfunk,* Oct. 1972, 5'.
Literatur in der Diktatur. Südafrika. *Hessischer Rundfunk,* 13 May 1973, 30'.
Reiseziel Deutschland. Kulturbetrieb in afrikanischer Sicht. Ein Bericht von Peter Russell, dargestellt von Janheinz Jahn. *Hessischer Rundfunk,* 29 July 1973, 30'.

Concerning African Performance Patterns

Roger D. Abrahams

It is, of course, dangerous to make generalizations about all of sub-Saharan African anything, because of the great institutional and cultural diversity one encounters there. The same might be said for Europe. Yet I am enboldened to do so, for there have been a number of others including some very careful Africanists, who have preceded me in this. For instance, one of these, William Bascom, notes in a recent survey article that one type of traditional story, the *dilemma tale*, is "characteristically African." Judiciously, he points out that they are "not unique to Africa"; however, he notes the high incidence of the form there, and the relative scarcity of it elsewhere. "Dilemma tales" Bascom notes, then, "constitute a large, varied, and widespread class of folktales in Africa." He proceeds to describe them as:

> Narratives that leave listeners with a choice between alternatives, such as which of several characters deserves a reward, or which of them has done the best. Sometimes they have a "correct" answer, but often they do not. Usually the narrator ends his tale with an unresolved question, often explicitly stated, to be debated by his audience. Even when they have standard answers, dilemma tales generally evoke spirited discussions, and they train those who participate in the skills of debate and argumentation.[1]

The importance of skill in such oral disputation, furthermore, is widely attested to in both Africa and Afro-America. But this is not what interests me about the dilemma tale; rather, I am taken with the principle that stories may be told which have no ending, and which are calculated to bring about dispute, characteristics someone from my culture (whatever that may be) finds very difficult to handle. "Stories" we somehow learn, should have a strong sense of ending, and a sense of wholeness that will seldom call for even discussion of motives, much less argument. Yet in both my American and West Indian storytelling experiences I have been struck by the strong tendency to ameliorate any sense of ending—by, say, repeating a punch-line three or four or five times in the case of a joke, or by discussing the dramatic situation and the characters after the story has been, from my cultural perspective, completed.

This open-ended, on-going quality, moreover, is assigned high value by the native aestheticians with whom I've discussed the matter. To one of them, Percy Silva of Richland Park, St. Vincent, the difference between a "wet" (good) and a "dry" (bad) story turned on the opportunities a story provided for repitition, for it is at such places that the audience is called on to demonstrate their involvement in the proceedings, by joining in with the restatement of the memorable line in the "easy" song (in the case of the cantefable.)

Thus, open-endedness and repetition are resolutely connected in the minds of the community with involvement, and thus with noise. It is, in fact, this quality more than any other which most upsets the performance expectations of Europeans, leading to confusion and embarrassment. On one occasion, I attended a *college* for orators in preparation for a *tea meeting* (oratorical contest), and witnessed how much time and effort the young *scholars* (for this is what Vincentians call them) invested in learning their elaborate speeches.[2] Without ever having witnessed a tea meeting in St. Vincent, I was made a judge (they discovered I was a "professor"). Thus, when the speeches began, and the audience enthusiastically heckled the speakers, I was immensely uncomfortable. I asked a friend, "Why they make such noise—so?" to be greeted with howls of laughter and the explanation that a tea meeting would not be a tea meeting without noise. It seems that the crowd was testing the powers of *cool* of the orators.

It is precisely this, "the aesthetic of the cool" (to use Robert Farris Thompson's term), which accounts for the seemingly contradictory characteristics of encouraging argumentation and noise, while placing very high value upon performing with great dignity and self-control. The two become one through active juxtaposition. Or to quote Thompson, commenting on the strength of this performance pattern in the Old and New Worlds:

> The grandeur of the tradition perenially imparted strength. In the midst of the turbulence of the festival was the learning of valor under provocation, balance in competing rhythms, and the sweetness of matched densities of interest and comon purpose.[3]

For some time, I tried to get at some of the aesthetic differences as they manifested themselves in American life by making reference to a judgmental dichotomy much in evidence in both white and black talk in the sixties (but clearly derived from black *hip talk*): the distinction between something being *square* and something being *groovy*. The latter term, it seems clear, comes from the action of a phonograph needle as goes around a record, a circular and vertiginous movement quite in contrast to the figure of the square. Though the distinction designates something which is "good" or "bad," "beautiful" or "ugly," it also provides a useful set of descriptive contrasts that, in fact, tell us a good deal about Euro-American and Afro-American performances (including, of course, in some dimensions, white performances which imitate black performances).

The Euro-American aesthetic does indeed rely upon artistic forms built on the principle of fours. One need only point to the standard folk-dance form of the *square dance*, or to the basic step of American social dancing, the *box-step*, to make the point. But even more noteworthy is the development of popular song out of folk forms. The standard folk meter in English (in both music and lyric) is a line of four stresses or pulses, each of which is divided by a caesura in the middle to achieve a sense ob balance. Further, songs are built in stanzaic form, the most common pattern being the four-line stanza, in which both text and tune come to a pause at the end of the second and fourth lines, with the message being underlined by end-rhyme. Finally, in the sentimental "ballad" tradition characteristic of songs in the first sixty years of this century, the stanzas are grouped together in fours, (*á la* the sonata allegro form of classical music) in which there is an opening statement, a restatement (with approximately the same tune as the first), a "bridge" or "channel," and a final reiteration of the first. Commonly the fourth lines of the first quatrain ist repeated in the same position in the second and the fourth quatrains, thus underlining the squaring of the squares.

With black song, there is not only not such a profound sense of squaring off with a beginning and ending, but the tunes tend toward the circular, as do the dances that accompany them. There is a clear rejection of the square aesthetic with those getting *into it* (or, as it was put in the Thirties and Forties, getting "in the groove"). Whereas Euro-American songs and dances emphasize balance and coordinated order, those of Afro-Americans underline circular movements (especially of the hips), participation and *doing your thing*.

It is precisely this concept of *doing your thing* that provides (for me at least) the connection with the dilemma tale. For what this means in black talk (as opposed to what the same term means when used by whites) is that *within the performance* everyone is free to play off against the others, contributing to the effect of the whole. As in other Afro-American performance genres, this usually means doing some *cutting*—that is, entering into competition or debate, not waged to determine a winner but rather to make the action more interesting. This establishment of opposites for their own sake, seems to me to be the most salient feature of both African and Afro-American performance forms.

But this is dealing with the familiar (perhaps overfamiliar) materials of everyday American life. I am encouraged to see this repeated in much broader and more Old World terms in the careful observations of a number of ethnographers, and other students of culture.

One thing that can be argued with a high degree of certainity is that the African aesthetic, whatever it may be, is very different from the European and Euro-American aesthetic and that this difference is, in great part, due to the relative importance of the devices of self-conscious style or "performance" in the broadest sense, in life. Thus, one often encounters a statement such as "Art permeates African culture, which in turn permeates African art. Art is not set aside from "real life"—it cannot be among a people who do not make such distinctions."[4] But it is not just that the Western analytic distinctions between art and life is not meaningful in dealing with African expressive culture, but that the distinction actively threatens the lifeblood of the

African sense of community. Elimo P. Njau, at the first meeting of the Congress of Africanists, eloquently made just this point:

> Before African art was known in its own right, before African music was known as music in its own right, African art and music were the true cement of the African community.
>
> African art and music were so much part and parcel of the daily life of the community that when you talked about art and music you actually talked about the people themselves, their daily activities, their day-to-day aspirations as a community, their joys together, the enemies they fought together and the tears they shared together.
>
> When you talked of African art and music you talked about a common language that expressed the body and soul of an African community...
>
> African art and music were an inspiring means of education, a means of uplifting man from his self-centered animal state to a spiritual understanding with fellow members of the community.
>
> African art and music expressed their faith in man as a component part of his small community and proved the inadequacy of the individual by himself.[5]

It would be a serious mistake to look at statements such as this and to simply dismiss them as chauvinistic romantic nationalism. Other less involved and more analytic observers have made the same point, using a more objective comparativist schema. For instance, Alan Merriam argues:

> The stress placed upon musical activity as an integral and functioning part of the society is a feature that music shares with other aesthetic aspects of culture in Africa and one which is emphasized in almost all non-literature societies. In Euro-american society, in contrast, there is a tendency to compartmentalize the arts and divorce them from aspects of everday life; thus we have "pure" art as opposed to "applied" art, as well as the "artists" and "commercial artists" or "craftsman," who are also differentiated both in role and in function. A further distinction is made in Western society in terms of "artist" and "audience,", with the first group tending to be limited in number; ... relatively large numbers of people within a non-literate society are competent in the arts, and aesthetic activities are closely related to the whole functioning culture.[6]

But the rejection of Western notions concerning art is not just focussed on the difference in the role of the artist and the art object in everyday life. In fact, some of the most perceptive acts of critical judgement with regard to the patterns of African performance arts have emerged as a result of this rejection of European norms. Often, the arguments waged have been directed at the Western analytic frame of reference. Léopold Sédar Senghor, for instance, seeks to purge from the discussion of African arts the use of European aesthetic concepts. This he pursues as part of his argument for negritude, but he is joined by numerous non-African Africanists who find through their field experiences that in African arts there is a "dynamic sensibility" that fuses "energy and decorum in a manner that confounds the either/or categories of Western thinking."[7]

It is precisely this "dynamic sensibilty" that seems to be the central feature African commentators want to protect, having observed the threat to it by Western technology and its attendant Western analytic modes of thought.

This is not to argue that Africans have no analytic mode and no sense of categories, discretions, and opposites. Rather, it is to assert that they handle these distinctions and oppositions very differently than Westerners, seeing in them both a threat to community order and an opportunity for the demonstration of group vitality. The reason why artistic performance is so focal in African community life resides in its ability to take oppositional forces and to embody them in perpetual balance. These posed oppositions are through performance, made to interpenetrate each other, and therefore the dominant African performance pattern is one in which socio-aesthetic synthesis is achieved. This synthesis, especially in rituals, is brought about in the face of potential social division and is a response to shared anxieties. It is hardly surprising, then, to discover a reaction against modes of analysis which emphasize distinctions and develop forms which distract from this synthetic focus.

Discussions of the symbolic progression of rituals provide us with some of our clearest insights into these principles of complementarity and interpenetration. James Fernandez, for instance, briefly notes of a *Bwiti* (northern Gabon) cult ritual "that we get a constant recasting of experience from one 'vocabulary' [semantic and symbolic domain] to another—whether by congruence of association or by the provocation of opposites. The process is one of constant transformation . . . This looping through various 'vocabularies' produces that 'thick complex condition' the experience of which is potent and meaningful."

Fernandez notes that this "provocation of opposites" is not just characteristic of the Bwiti cult, but is observable on many levels of Fang artistic behavior as well as in social interactions:

> . . .what is aesthetically pleasing to the Fang has . . . a vitality that arises out of a certain relationship of contradictory elements. The Fang not only live easily with contradictions; they cannot live without them.[8]
> . . . when Fang assume a posture of aesthetic scrutiny the presence of skillfully related oppositions constitutes an important part of their delight and appreciation. This is so because vitality arises out of complementary oppositions and for them what is aesthetically satisfying is the same as what is culturally alive.[9]

Aesthetic canons of pleasure among the Fang, then, rely upon the dramatizing of opposition without attempting resolution. Specific oppositions often relate to concepts of maleness and femaleness, especially those visible in interlocking relationships between hot (male) and cold (female), day and sun (male), night and moon (female), earth (female) and sky (male), flesh, bone and bloody organs of the body (female), bones, sinews, and brains (male) and so on. To so relate the oppositions is to create a world of reference in which basic stuff of life is constantly available as a means of demonstrating vitality-in-opposition.

I would not emphasize such a description of one small group in Africa were there not so many other ethnographic descriptions of performance and world order that, though different in particulars, shared this basic ethical, structural, and aesthetic presumption of how the world is put together.

For instance, this richness of texture achieved through the interpenetration of oppositions is brought out most forcefully and poetically in Victor W. Turner's studies of Ndembu rituals. Repeatedly he demonstrates, with regard to one or another potential conflict within the Ndembu conceptual system that "Ndembu, in the symbolic idiom . . . have elected to emphasize the aspect of opposition and complementarity . . . when they exhibit the process of uniting the components of the dyad, they represent this process as a coincidence of opposites . . . social forces approximately equal in strength and opposite in quality are exhibited as working in harmony."[10] The meaning of this movement is both social and aesthetic: "Such symbols . . . unite the organic with the sociomoral order, proclaiming their ultimate religious unity, over and above conflicts between and within these orders."[11] "Every opposition is overcome or transcended in a recovered unity, a unity that, moreover is reinforced by the very potencies that endanger it."[12]

Generalizing this pattern does not detract from the uniqueness of the oppositions and the ultimate orders achieved by specific African groups. One need only read the Turner books or Griaule's *tour de force, Conversations with Ogotommêli,* to recognize that the complexities differ in intensity, texture and color from one group to another. On the other hand, there are those who will argue (with some degree of validity) that these remarks on the synthesizing dimensions of African performances are characteristic of ritual and myth processes among nonliterate peoples in general. Though this may prove true, it is not the direction of the sociomoral or aesthetic process which is most important to the present discussion, but rather the patterns of performance by which these synthetic moves are enacted which seem uniquely African and Afro-American.

In demonstrating the distinctiveness of this pattern one is aided immeasurably by the cantometric analyses of Alan Lomex and his associates, for Lomax's description of African musical style indicates immediately not only that we can generalize in a number of ways about African performance patterns but that the terms of generalization emphasize the principles of complementarity, interlock, and synthetic cohesiveness. What one observes in Africa is an "extraordinary homogeneity" of song style arising from a "highly cohesive, complexly integrated song model. Black Africans synchronize their motor and vocal acts more tightly than the people of other culture regions," a coordination which Lomax correlates with a high degree of social complementarity between males and females, community cohesiveness, and a multi-leveled ability to integrate the potentially disparate.[13]

The image of African performance which emerges here is of the community celebrating its sense of groupness through the coordination of energies in the common creative enterprise, and doing so by taking binary oppositions, embodying them in a complexly integrated traditional form which utilizes these oppositions in the form of complementarities. This group focus is guaranteed through the practice of *interlock,* in which the distinction between performer and audience is made meaningless, for alle perform to some degree. The good performers, then, differ from others in the community only in quality of performance. Channelled energies devoted to the demonstration of community will be valued by any group, but in those (like so many African groups) which conceive of life in terms of a reservoir of vital spirit residing apart from individuals, the elicitation and coordination of energy is regarded as the basis of the continuation of group life.[14]

But one must not emphasize such coordination without recognizing the way in which the individual expresses himself. When an individual sets himself apart from the group, he does so not to demonstrate his individual talents but rather to set up a dialogue between himself and the rest of the group. The individual and the group interact to thicken the texture of the performance, by establishing interlocking voices (whether it be in drumming, singing, dancing, or orating). The more interlock, the greater the complexity, of course, and the more vitality the community feels is being channelled through them. Thus, there is a high value placed on what Thompson has called "apart playing": "each [performer] . . . intent upon the production of his own contribution to the polymetric whole."[15] It is in this metrical dimension of performance, whether in song, ensemble playing, or dancing, that we see the principle of apartness most clearly enunciated. And it is precisely this moral and aesthetic principle that I referred to above as "doing your thing!"

Polymeter, the thick texture of impulses played against each other, is probably most easily recognized in drumming, for here our major focus is on the pulses alone. The characteristic sound of African drumming is the superimposition of a number of different (and often shifting) metrical patterns. But this type of complexity in apart playing is equally characteristic of dancing, certain modes of song, and even heroic singing and formal speechmaking, in which the counterpoint between audience noise and oration has often been noted.[16] Perhaps the ultimate expression of this complexity in apartness is to be seen in the polymetric way by which the individual may organize his physical performance. For instance, in African dance the body divides in two at the hips; the movement of the hips commonly provides the primary meter and the focus of movement, but the hips, legs, torso play against each other metrically. The great dancer will respond with some part of his body to all of the pulse-patterns provided by the drums.

Perhaps this polymetric complexity established through apartness could also be conceived of as an extension of the principle of complementarity. When a chanter-response dialogue is established between a single performer and the rest of the group, there arises a sense of mutual supportiveness, of counterpositioning between the two. This becomes clear in those West African groups (such as the Yoruba) who conceive of performances in terms of the demonstration of the community ideal of the *cool* — "an ancient indigenous ideal: patience and collectedness of mind."[17] As one might suppose, both noise and complexity are conceived of as *hot* in such a perspective, as is any licentious (*i.e.,* apparently uncontrolled) performance. But in line with the pattern of complementarity, cool implies hot and vice-versa. That is, beneath hot is always the cool; the ideals of the community are judged not in terms of the constancy of collectedness of mind but rather in how much heat can be balanced by the performer asserting this collectedness and patience in this midst of expressions of its opposite. Man's spirit, in these terms, is most engaged, most ratified, most celebrated, when both hot and cool are brought into dialogue. Performance then signals action, eliciting energy, fortifying the group through its creative individuals playing together while apart.

The African aesthetic, in this complex way, calls for the dramatization of the wholeness, the integrity of experience, through the yoking together of opposites. The either/or categories of Western analyitc thought, so helpful in learning to control nature through technology, actively threaten this integrative socially-based conceptual system. Sound and silence, or *hot* feeling and *cool* reason and patience, cannot meaningfully be thought of as separates, for each implies the other, not by contrast but by complement. To reduce it to simple form, life is idealized as constantly changing multileveled performance involving the entire group. Each performance is, in part, a realization of this metaphor and a way of demonstrating the wholeness and vitality of the community.

Life is conceived in terms of the expenditure of energy, energy ist most fully realized in action, and a performance is where the action is most fully and self-consciously to be found. Performers are valued because they bring on-going expressions of energy to those valuing and seeking action. This vision of life, in placing performance at its center of focus, differs greatly from the Western (and especially Euro-American) system which tends to project life as an individual journey, and which relegates affective, group-ratifying (irrational) performance to the periphery of cultural concerns. Having travelled this far, then, and while still emboldened by my enthusiasm for the task, let me compare in far too simle a manner, the tendencies of African participative danced arts, "arts in motion," with the most extreme examples of European monumental art.

African and Afro-American	*European and Euro-American*
Emphasis on whole-group involvement in performance; individual plays "apart" to add to the complexity of the ensemble in the total event; interlock of individuals in total event; interlock of individuals in total group performance; performance not separated from everyday reality but seen as its ultimate expression; virtuosity, when it occurs, is defined in terms of the performer representing the group.	Emphasis on individual performer, virtuosity, subtlety; strong performer-audience, performance-reality (subject-object) dichotomies; in situations in which a group performs together, strong emphasis is placed on coordination.

African and Afro-American	*European and Euro-American*
Circular, vertiginous organization of performing group; heavy emphasis on involvement through repetition of sound and movement; retreat from closure in favor of the ongoing and open-ended (*running the changes*); tendency to break up performance into short units or episodes, each of which is a whole, related to the other units because of intensity of contrast.	Linear, progressive organization driving toward climax and catharsis (insight and relief of tension); repetition not valued and when it occurs, employed for intensifying tension, or for comic effect; tendency to operate harmonically, subordinating smaller "passages" to the larger overall statement of unity.
Multiple and shifting dramatic focus; polymetric rhythmic organization; in ensembles, emphasis on individuals asserting contrastive alternatives (*apartness*); emphasis on complexity, density and richness of texture.	Single dramatic focus; unimetric rhythmic organization; in ensembles, synchronized performances; emphasis on subtlety; synchronization achieved through use of highly redundant and predictable pulses, organized on principles of balance and squaring.
Creative vitality comes from source outside the individual, is called into play by performer and performance; individual performer is regarded as the instigator of action only; he brings group into performance, sharing in the energy souce.	Creative vitality comes from within the performer; though he may regard himself as channel of tradition, it is his energies, abilities which are drawn upon and focussed upon by the audience; he leads them by the hand.
Audience is part of the performance through actual physical involvement; approval and involvement are indicated by continuatives (*amen, right on*, etc.).	Audience involvement indicates distancing, sympathetic, vicarious involvement; performance encouraged by silence, continuing eye-contact, laughter when appropriate.
Oppositions, conceived as complementaries (in perpetual contrast and balance), expected and converted into expression of energy; need for continuing interlock, interplay.	Oppositions conceived in agonistic terms; need for victory, defeat, compromise, as means of achieving dramatic closure, sense of relief and repose; continuing sense of opposition feared.
Synthetic frame of reference; distinctions made in order to articulate interplay; demonstration of ultimate and continuing unity of group, life, etc.	Analytic frame of reference; distinctions made in order to demonstrate diversity; unity assumed but not demonstrated.

But now, looking back over these contrasts, I see that they have been made at the expence of the principles of the ethical-aesthetic balance most characteristic of the black performances. In spite of our stereotype notions of the sensuality and emotionalism of blacks on both sides of the Atlantic, the most salient and grand feature of their art is the transcendent balance which is brought about because of involvement, interlock and overlap, because of the superimposition of the many meters and the contrasting ethical and aesthetic ideas. Let me allow my friend Robert Farris Thompson to have the final words here, for he is the poet of this sensibility. Here he comments on sculpture and dance, but broader application is obvious.

> ... West Africans cultivate divinity through richly stabilized traditions of personal balance.... the notion of "streightness," in the sense of the maintaining of the commanding vertical position of the human body, has consistently loomed as an important issue.
> However, the convention would doubtless soon wax boring, were it not honored so magnificently in the breach by kicks, spins, and leaps...
> The African image stands not only fully upright ["straight], but is evocative of balance in another sense—degree of realism. Representational balance is as important as stability *per se*, and can be identified in imagery which is not too real and not too abstract, but somewhere in between...

Mid-point mimesis or balance in the mode of representing visual reality defines the African aesthetic as a mediating force... Humanity generalized by rhythmic impulse, in sculpture and dance, is humanity divested momentarily of the heat of personal ambition and individualism, detached from emotion, and shaped within images of ideal vital character—[all leading to the means] to find identity through merger with a larger social whole.[17]

Notes

1   William Bascom, "African Dilemma Tales: An Introduction," in *African Folklore*, ed. Richard M. Dorson (New York, 1972), pp. 143, 153.
2   For a description of the speeches and the learning process, see my "Training of the Man of Words in Talking Sweet," *Language in Socitey*, 1 (1972), 15—29.
3   Robert Farris Thompson, "An Introduction to Transatlantic Black Art History: Remarks in Anticipation of a Coming Golden Age of Afro-Americana," in *Discovering Afro-America*, ed. Roger G. Abrahams and John F. Szwed (forthcoming).
4   Paul Bohannan, *Africa and Africans* (Garden City, New York, 1964), p. 150.
5   Elimo P. Njau, "African Art," in *Proceedings of the First International Congress of Africanists*, ed. Lalage Bown and Michael Crowder (London, 1964), pp. 237—38.
6   Alan Merriam, "African Music," in *Continuity and Change in African Cultures*, ed. William Bascom and Melville J. Herskovits (Chicago, 1959), pp. 49—50.
7   Robert Farris Thompson, "An Aesthetic of the Cool: West African Dance," *African Forum*, II, 2, (1966), 85.
8   James Fernandez, "Principles of Opposition and Vitality in Fang Aesthetics," in *Art and Aesthetics in Primitive Societies*, ed. Carl F. Jopling (New York, 1971), p. 358. The entire essay deals with this sense of creative opposition in art and in society among the Fang.
9   Ibid., p. 370.
10   Victor W. Turner, *The Ritual Process* (Chicago, 1969), p. 50.
11   Ibid., p. 52.

12   Ibid., p. 93.
13   Alan Lomax, *Folk Song Style and Culture* (Washington, D. C., 1968), pp. 182—92.
14   Cf. Placide Tempels, *Bantu Philosophy* (Paris, 1959), and Janheinz Jahn, *Muntu* (New York, 1961).
15   Thompson, "An Aesthetic of the Cool," p. 93.
16   See, e. g., the African examples in Karl Riesman, "Cultural and Linguistic Ambiguity in a West Indian Village," in *Afro-American Anthropology: Contemporary Perspectives*, ed. Norman E. Whitten, Tr., and John F. Szwed (New York, 1970), pp. 129—44.
17   Thompson, "An Aesthetic of the Cool," p. 87.
18   This comes from Robert Farris Thompson's magnificent exhibit catalog, *African Arts in Motion* (Los Angeles, 1974), pp. 24—27. I am indebted throughout this paper to Thompson for his friendship and constant enthusiastic illumination on all manner of subjects aesthetical. John Szwed also has discussed these matters with me early and often, as have Alan Lomax and Karl Riesman. To them my enduring thanks. Dan Ben-Amos offered extremely useful comments on this paper when I first read it at the Conference on African Folklore at Indiana University, July 16—18, 1970. Richard Dorson kindly made that forum available to me, just one of his many kindnesses over these years. The revisions were, for the most part, completed while I was on a grant from the Center for Urban Ethnography, University of Pennsylvania, PHS Research Grant no 17 216.

Negritude and Structuralism

Sunday O. Anozie

> « Dans les oeuvres poetiques, le lin-
> guiste discerne des structures dont l'ana-
> logie est frappante avec celles que l'ana-
> lyse des mythes révèle à l'ethnologue.
> De son côté, celui-ci ne saurait mécon-
> naître que les mythes ne consistent pas
> seulement en agencements conceptuels :
> ce sont aussi des oeuvres d'art . . . »

With this preface, Lévi-Strauss and Roman Jakobson embarked upon
one of the rare interdisciplinary collaborations in recent memory between
an ethnologist and a linguist—the dissection of Baudelaire's poem, "Les
Chats."[1] Sence this date and as a result of innovative work in generative
grammar[2] and in semiotics[3], critics especially in the United States and France
have begun to show some interest in the structural linguistic analysis of
literary works, particularly poetry[4]. In each case the underlying assumption
is twofold. The first is the realization that a poetic work contains a system
of ordered variants which can be isolated and represented vertically in the
form of superimposed levels such as phonology, phonetic, syntactic, prosodic,
and semantic. The second is that modern structuralism—especially in the
form of its offshoot, generative grammar—provides an adequate theory and
method for accounting for such levels and in dealing with the internal coherence of the given work of art.

Some African critics of African literature have objected to this search
for internal coherence. Abiola Irele, a Nigerian critic well-known for his
several defenses of negritude, for example, has argued strongly in favor of a
"sociological imagination" on the part of a critic of African literature,
without showing in what essential way(s) this differs from a structuralist
imagination.[5] Is it true, for example, that the assertion that man is a structural
animal precludes the African?[6] On the contrary, the present writer has argued
elsewhere that no adequate sociological theory of African literature, the
novel in particular, can be formulated outside a framework of structuralism.[7]
More recently, too, I have insisted on the possibility of defining such a
structuralist framework within the terms, necessarily more narrow, of the
conceptual framework of negritude.[8] Such integration will serve not only to
revitalize but also to provide negritude with the one thing it so far lacks—
scientific method of inquiry.

In the present contribution, I wish to add to this argument by submitting that negritude and structuralism have more in common than at first may strike the eye of a casual observer, and, consequently, that the search for internal coherence in an African or any other work of art does not necessarily detract from its aesthetic or ideological value as such; if anything, it can enhance appreciation and respect for both.

The paper falls into two parts. In the first part, I will sketch a brief structural analysis of one of Senghor's shorter poems, "Le Totem." In the second part, I will examine, also briefly, a few developments within negritude, especially Senghor's, in relation to the concept of structuralism, especially Lévi-Strauss's. This movement from practice to theory will, I hope, underline if not the innate scientific disposition of negritude, at least our belief in its potential to develop into one.

The concept of "problematic" in poetry

Two remarks must be made from the outset. The first is that the composition of Senghors's "Le Totem" contains no diachronic problematic. As an isolated event, it has no special recorded "history" of its own (if it does, this paper is not at any rate interested in that, but in the poem itself as a synchronic event) beyond the fact that it is the fourteenth poem in the author's 1945 collection of poems published under the title of *Chants d'ombre.*[9] I use the term "problematic" in the same way as both Althusser and Lévi-Strauss to define a particular theoretical system or "thought structure."[10] Glucksmann has cogently demonstrated the correlations between the uses of the concept of "problematic" by Althusser to define the specificities of Marx's theory and by Lévi-Strauss to designate systems of totemic classification in "primitive cultures." Thus in refusing to see Senghor's "Le Totem" as a diachronic problematic, I merely deny that it provides any substantive account of history. Instead the poem's, any poem's, problematic should be sought in the fact that it is first and foremost a synchronic event (in it, as in any language system, history is transfixed, so to speak, into an instant of time), and therefore essentially mythical. According to Lévi-Strauss:

> Mythical thought, that bricoleur, builds structures by bitting together events, or rather the remains of events, while science, "in operation" simply by virtue of coming into being, creates its means and results in the form of events, thanks to the structures which it is constantly elaborating and which are its hypotheses and theories... the scientist creating events (changing the world) by means of structures, and the 'bricoleur' creating structures by means of events.[12]

Lévi-Strauss's concept of the problematic is therefore in direct relationship to objective knowledge and cosmology in "primitive" societies where myths are shown to operate from an awareness of oppositions to their satisfactory mediation. Recently too, Senghor has spoken of the problematic of negritude in an attempt to reevaluate this ideology in the context of a global awareness of developments in the social sciences and the humanities.[13] I shall return to this point later.

The second remark I wish to make is that it is especially not difficult to assign a correct reading to the Senghor poem, "Le Totem." A careful attention to the organization of details in the poem coupled with a knowledge of its cultural codes (the African totemic configuration) will certainly enable an alert critic, native or foreign, to read a correct meaning into the poem. Thus, in an explicatory footnote to the poem, Shelton rightly observes:

> This is the actual totem. A totem is the spirit of an animal, usually, considered to have aided a founding ancestor in a critical moment at the beginning or early part of the clan's history, or considered spiritually related to the members of the clan. Among the Wolof (Senghor is Serer, a related group), each clan group has totem animals: Diop, the crown bird; Njai, the lion; Toure, the frog, etc. *The totem in the poem suggests the real self of the poet, as distinct from the artificial, Europeanised surface of the acculturated African.*[14]

I have italicized in the above quotation the senctence that appears to me to contain a crucial interpretation of the Senghor poem. Similarly referring to the frequency in Senghor's peotry of images derived from the vegetable and animal kingdom, Robert Mercier speaks of

> ... une influence de la coutume africaine attribuant à chaque individu, comme « totem », un animal dont il revêt plus ou moins la personnalité. L. S. Senghor fait allusion lui-même à cet usage et à l'interdiction de révelér aux autres ce patronage.

Continuing, he says,

> Mais si le secret doit être gardé par chacun sur son propre totem, les rapprochements métaphoriques, fondés sur la ressemblance de caractères entre un homme et un animal, sont un jeu inoffensif... Ce double sens des échanges entre l'homme et le monde est une constante de l'imagination de L. S. Senghor.[15]

Mercier is not content with merely pointing at "totem" as a cultural code in Africa, but with showing it as performing a significant metonymic function in Senghor's poetry. Finally, Bâ seeks to integrate the Senghorian concept and use of "totem" within the wider philosophical context of African lifeforces —first enunciated by Father Tempels and remarkably evident in Jahn's work as part of the criteria of neo-africanism:

> In a world where significance is attributed to all forces and with such interdependence of action, the wisdom of the ages is implied by the basic principle of life forces and simplified by the concrete nature of its expression. It is these concrete symbols that the initiate learns to understand. We can now better understand why Senghor insists that totemism only seems monstrous.

Some animal or tree is often identified with a clan through the common ancestor whose life is then made known through a totemic or astral myth. This tendency toward identification with inferior, that is, nonrational, forces is described by Senghor as anthropsychism: the tendency to relate to other objects or forces as though they were persons. The purpose of such identification with totem is the appropriation of the psychic force associated with the particular totem. The ancestortotem constitutes a doubly protective force, destined by its very nature and composition to preserve the life principle of those under its tutelage.[16]

Thus from the recognition of "totem" in the Senghor poem as denotative of acculturation (Shelton's distinction between real self/surface "self," Europeanized/African is clear-cut) to that of "totem" as a cultural code with stylistic function (Mercier calls it an imaginative "constant") in Senghor's poem, finally, to Bâ's assimilation of "totem" into an ideology based upon "life—forces," it can be inferred that the semantic component of "Le Totem" is both normatively circumscribed and exhaustive; in other terms, that no meaning can be assigned to this poem, outside the referential framework of "totem" as a "thought structure." This inference is valid—for reasons I prefer not to elaborate here and now. Consequently, further attempts at interpretation in this paper can only serve one useful purpose—to relate the semantic component of the poem to its syntactic structure, that is to say, define the nature of the poem's problematic.

Syntactic structures in "Le totem"

I	Il me faut le cacher/**a** au plus intimes de mes veines/**b**
II	L'Ancêtre/**c** à la peau d'orage sillonnée d'éclairs et de foudre/**d**
III	Mon animal gardien/**e**, il me faut le cacher/**f**
IV	Que je ne rompe le barrage des scandales/**g**.
V	Il est mon sang fidèle/**h** qui requérit la fidélité/**i**
VI	Protégéant mon orgueil nu/**j** contre
VII	Moi-même/**k** et la superbe des races heureuses/**l**.

I must hide him in my innermost veins
The Ancestor with the stormy skin streaked with thunder and lightning
My guardian animal, I must hide him
That I may not burst the dam of scandal.
He is my loyal blood that demands loyalty
Shielding my naked pride against
Myself and the arrogance of the blessed races . . .[17]
Shielding my naked pride against
Myself and the arrogance of the blessed races . . .[17]

The period at the end of the fourth line divides this seven line stanza into two distinct units of thought: a Quatrain and a Tercet. With the exception of the /R/ (in foud*re* and cont*re*) and the /E/ (in fidélit*é* and cach*er*), the poem has no end rhymes. (Senghor's poems do not as a rule depend on end rhymes for effect, but on internal rhythm instead.) Here the rhythm is conveyed through the preponderance of consonantal sounds at the beginning of words: /l/, /p/, /s/, /d/, /f/, /g/, /s/, /m/, /R/, /b/, and of vowel and consonant sounds in the middle.

The quatrain displays on the surface level of propositions, an elegant structural balance. I have denoted with alphabets the different poetic propositions. The term "proposition" as employed here does not necessarily mean a "complete thought" in the sense of a sentence; instead it stands for a phrase structure, the smallest significant unit of meaning, (a *sememe*), as far as this poem is concerned. This said, it is obvious that propositions Ia and IIIf are strictly symmetrical with this significant difference: that the order in which they appear in the lines is reversed. The effect on the two odd lines of the quatrain is identical to the opening and closing of brackets, viz. [ ], implying the exclusion of the even line IV. Given this phenomenon, one could say that the unity of the quatrain has been "broken," the fourth line being abruptly and artificially excluded from the rest. What is more significant, too, the verb (*rompe*) appears precisely in the line where this scandal seemingly occurs, and thereby doubly underlines and reinforces the poet's intention and fear. Mercier (cf. above) has rightly spoken of "l'interdiction de révéler aux autres ce patronage." And I have shown that this semantic interpretation cannot be divorced from the very syntactic structure of line IV which expresses the interdiction, the central theme of the quatrain. On the contrary, the sense absolutely inheres in the form of the expression. The unity in Africa between man and his "totem" which consists in a system of both cognitive and existential relations (if we admit also the Negritude ideology of "life-forces") is thus reflected in the poem structurally as a system of grammatical interrelationships within the quatrain.

Apart from being related as the two external lines of a quatrain, line IV and line I are linked by other ties: semantically, *veines* and *barrage,* for instance, belong to the same category (they are both containers of fluid); morphologically, they are both preceded by identical *des* and are genitive substantives; finally, both lines end with an identical consonantal inflectional suffix "-s" (*veine-s, scandale-s*) indicating plurality,

Similarly, the propositions Ib and IId appear to be parenthetically separate, the one from the verb *cacher,* the other from the noun *l'Ancêtre* to which they respectively act as complements. This time, however, the evidence of the "break" is more phonological than syntactical: the presence of vowels and consonants: /o/, /p/, /l/ (in Ib); /a/, /l/, /p/ (in IId). In fact, not only does this situation now justify our establishing a syntagmatic parallelism between Ib and IId, but the phonemic and morphological index, particularly at the beginning of each proposition, seems to point towards a closer link or identity between, thus the inseparability of, *cacher* and *l'Ancêtre* (Ia, IIc) as a syntagmatic category. Thus the relationship of IIc to Ia, namely, the logical finite predicate, is the same as that of IIIc to IIIf. This further suggests that the initial "break" in the natural order and balance (*Il me faut le cacher* → *l'Ancêtre*) appears now rectified but in a somewhat, odd that is, reversed manner (*Mon animal gardien* ← *il me faut le cacher*). It is also significant that this artificial disjunction is expressed in the odd lines of the quatrain. In line II this disjunction is partly metonymical (*peau d'orage*) and partly a deliberate search for rhythmic balance (*d'orage/d'éclairs/de foudre*). Finally, in line IV, the same phenomenon becomes, on the part of the poet, consciousness of a taboo, expressed in a deprecatory subjunctive mood. (*Que ie ne rompe...*) Also this line contains the only subjunctive verb in the whole poem which links it as an adverb proposition to Ia and IIIf.

Consciousness of an initial separation followed by a search for the restoration of primitive balance and order constitutes not only the global symmetry but also the meaning of "Le Totem." Senghor's stylistic execution of this structural principle in the quatrain is literally scientific.

The structure of propositions in the quatrain is defined by the following logical relations.

Ia	$\equiv$ IIIf	Equivalent propositions
IIb	// IId	Parallel propositions
Ia	$\rightarrow$ IIc	Finite predicate (broken order)
IIIe	$\leftarrow$ IIIf	Finite predicate (reverse order)
IIc	= IIIe	Equal propositions
IV	$\longleftrightarrow$ I + III	Subjunctive/Adverb Proposition

Strictly within the context of these paradigms, is it possible to define other syntagmatic features which will enable us to relate or map the quatrain to the tercet, at the dual levels of the deep and surface structure?

Yes. Such evidence is, to take the most obvious case, provided in the form of a substantive followed by an adjective and a pronoun in the second odd line of the quatrain and the first odd and even lines of the tercet. The result is his symmetrical pattern, with identical morpheme {mɔ̃}:

Pro	$\rightarrow$ N	$\rightarrow$ N
mon	*animal*	*gardien* (IIIe)
Pro	$\rightarrow$ N	$\rightarrow$ Adj
mon	*sang*	*fidèle* (Vh)
mon	*orgueil*	*nu* (VIj)

A disjunctive sequence is found in the second odd line of the tercet:

Pro	V N	$\rightarrow$ N	$\rightarrow$ Adj
Moi-même	*Superbe*	*races*	*heureuses* (VII)

(as if the poet wishes to emphasize the uniqueness of this closing line of the tercet, also of the poem, in relation to the rest of the lines.) Note that the lexical categories contained in III, V, VI are also present in VII but in varying combinations, and with this morphological difference: that the initial pronominal item changes from the possessive form *mon* (mɔ̃) to the direct object form *moi* (mwa). (Other obvious relations of a semantic nature exist between *veines* $\rightarrow$ *sang* (I, V); *gardien* $\rightarrow$ *fidèle*; (*fidélité*) $\rightarrow$ *Protégéant* (III, V, VI.)

A second evidence, this times less obvious because it relates to the deep structure level, yields itself when we seek to interpret the above change with reference to other syntactic features of the tercet. Consider that the only logical, i.e., grammatical, link between VI and VII is the preposition *contre:* it serves to map the only participial proposition in the poem to the two conjoined propositions: *contre moi-même* and *(contre) la superbe des races heureuse.* The effect of this conjunction is accentuated only if we admit a disjunction, a break, between VIIk and VIII similar to that witnessed in IV; that is, if we read VI, taking a breath pause after *moi-même* in VII. However, whereas the evidence in IV is inclusive (it has nothing to do with breath pause), the disjunction that occurs in VII must be seen as functionally exclusive: it opposes VIIk to VIII by juxtaposing them.

What one witnesses here is an intriguing phenomenon of balancing opposites, characteristic of Senghor's art in this poem. Furthermore, this can be illustrated even by isolating from VI and VII lexical entries pertaining to the same category: *moi-même/races, orgueil/superbe, heureuses/nu.* These pairs constitute a system of binary oppositions which can be represented, both horizontally and vertically in the form of two intersecting circles:

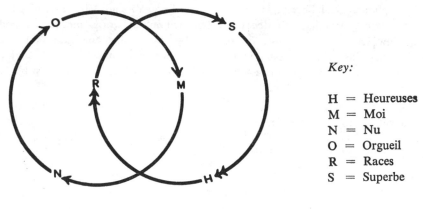

Key:

H = Heureuses
M = Moi
N = Nu
O = Orgueil
R = Races
S = Superbe

Fig I

The geometrical figure has at the least the merit of displaying visually the area in which the poet's meaning may be said to be embedded. An existentialist predicament expressed in terms of racial (cf. the tercet) and religious (cf. the quatrain) consciousness thus constitutes the problematic of the poem. Such interpretation will confirm Senghor's, who, drawing upon the philosophy of vital forces, has described the black man's metaphysics as an existential ontology.[18]

Let me now briefly summarize the data so far presented in this section. Starting with a division of Senghor's poem "Le Totem" into two distinct parts, I have tried to reconstitute the unities of the Quatrain and of the Tercet as well as the relationship between these two parts, by relying almost solely upon the syntactical features, the structure of propositions, in the poem. The poem, as has been seen, contains a striking symmetry of organisation, with the Tercet seemingly responding to and complementing the Quatrain, but clearly exhibiting unique syntagmatic features of its own.

The results can be shown graphically as follows:

Lines	QUATRAIN		Lines	TERCET
I	a	b		
II	c	d	V	h i
III	e	f	VI	j
IV	g		VII	k

Fig II

Even a schema as simple as the above can serve to illustrate the internal mechanism of the poem, the principle of binary oppositions by which it functions, and finally, the attempt at reconciliation, or the restoration of the primary ontological unity. Note that in explaining how this theme is structurally articulated in line VII, I have taken what may appear to be a slight phonological liberty, in insisting that lines VI and VII be read as if there were a breath pause (*caesura*) between initial words *moi-même* and *et*. Now let me correct this impression by saying that the fact that one recognizes this morphophonemic change or not, may not have any major incidence on the analysis since what really counts in the line in question is the syntagm or juxtaposition.

As a final and more technical evidence of the poet's delicate art of balancing, mention should now be made of the fact that the poem contains a total of fourteen nouns (I regard *animal gardien* as a substantive unit) numerically distributed as follows:

Lns M F		NOUNS				
I — 1		Masculine	Feminine		Lns M	1
II 3 2	QUATRAIN	5	4		VI 1	—
III 1 —		2	3	TERCET	VII 1	F
IV 1 1		7	7		V —	2

Fig III

This table permits the identification of a number of relations, either identical, inverse or parallel (e. g., 5:4 : : 3:2 or 5:3 : : 4:2; V:IV, : : VI:III or III:IV : : VI:V, etc.); it may possibly also constitute a system of permutations.

Totemism, Lévi-Strauss and Senghor

The choice of the poem "Le Totem" as the subject of analysis in Section 3 is not fortuitous; in fact, as announced above, the reason can now be explicited. Viewed as an isolated synchronic event, this poem affords as good a starting point as any other for illustrating some of the basic relationships and assumptions of negritude and structuralism. If thus I say that the poem "Le Totem" stands in relation to Senghorian Negritude as "Totemism" does in relation to Lévi-Straussian Structuralism, I have merely posed a hypothesis. Such a statement may or may not invite justification or proof. It is not my intention to offer or even attempt any here. Instead I will confine myself in the remaining pages to indicating a line of inquiry which may prove useful in dealing with such a problem.

Senghor's earlier observations about traditional African metaphysics, his attempts to formulate on the basis of these a theory of African creativity, constitute a major contribution to negritude. Not only do these pronouncements embody important structuralist insights, but, in some respects, they reflect, or at least are reconcilable with, the views expressed by Lévi-Strauss. Take African art, for instance. In Senghor's opinion, all arts in Africa are social, that is, functional in the sense that they are both collective and committed. This view, which is largely shared by several modern scholars,[19] is not much different from that held by Lévi-Strauss. However, when Senghor further asserts that African arts constitute "techniques of essentialisation" for the individual, it is clear that he is endorsing the traditional viewpoint of descriptive anthropologists according to which African art has an exclusive religious determination. Lévi-Strauss differs on this point, since he is more inclined than Senghor to recognize the personality of the artist both as an individual and as a creator. For example, he claims that:

> Des travaux récents sur le sculpture africaine montrent que le sculpteur est un artiste, que cet artiste est connu, quelquefois très loin à la rondc, et que le public indigène sait reconnaître le style propre de chaque auteur de masque ou de statue.[20]

Thus whereas Senghor defends traditional art as an existentialist problematic for the individual, Lévi-Strauss views artistic production as a process of individualization.

Next, Senghor sees African poetry as a form of discourse on the grounds that it rejects the idea of the permanence of art, preferring instead the novelty of what the poet calls "idées-sentiments" and the dramatic progression of rhythm. On this premise Senghor also condemns the classical Greek and Roman theory of archetypes and mimesis as alien and inapplicable to Africa. The same goes for the art of writing with regard to which he claims in his 1958 preface to *L'Anthologie de la vie africaine* as follows:

> ... l'écriture appauvrit le réel. Elle le cristallise en categories rigides ; elle le fixe quand-le propre du réel est d'être vivant, fluide et sans contours.[21]

Now, all structuralists of Lévi-Straussian inspiration will agree that poetry is a form of linguistic discourse. Lévi-Strauss himself does not have anything complimentary to say about the art of writing which he associates with the

origin of social cleavages such as the slave, the class, and the caste systems—
and with the capitalization and totalization of knowledge:

> L'écriture elle-même ne nous parait associée de façon permanente, dans ses
> origines, qu'à des sociétés qui sont fondées sur l'exploitation de l'homme par
> l'homme.[22]

Roland Barthes, in particular, would not hesitate to agree with Senghor that
writing impoverishes reality by crystallizing it so as to clarify further the
perspective of modern semiology.[23] One need, however, not go into the other
negritude view somewhat contradictory to Senghor's, according to which
Africa is not entirely without her share of the blame for the invention of
the art of writing.[24] Instead it is more significant to point out that as early
as 1958 Senghor has been aware of the structuralist movement in France.
The first reference made by him to Lévi-Strauss is contained in the 1958
preface where the French ethnologist's remarks in favor of "primitive"
people are approvingly quoted. I should add at this point also that the
second and apparently the last explicit reference to Lévi-Strauss is contained
in Senghor's 1959 essay, "Eléments Constitutifs . . ." This time the context
is religion—magic and totemism—and the reference is a negative one:

> Prise dans son sens le plus étroit, la magie peut être definie avec Claude
> Lévi-Strauss, ‹ comme un systeme d'opérations et de croyances qui prétend, à
> certains actes humains, la même valeur qu'à des causes naturelles.› Prise dans
> son sens large, la magie est un dogme selon lequel ‹le visible est la mani-
> festation de l'invisible.› On reconnait là definition du mysticisme. C'est le
> sens que je retiendrai.[25]

That Senghor prefers a definition of magic which derives from a marriage
of mysticism and surrealism (in the passage in question, for example, he sees
Elias Lévi through the eyes of André Breton!) to that deriving from
structural anthropology, may by itself be instructive, but not a surprise. In
fact, this may be seen as part of the general theoretic eclecticism which
characterized the development of Senghor's negritude vis-à-vis its treatment
of and relationship to other intellectual movements, marxism, existentialism
or structuralism; they served only as expedient reinforcement to the former.
What is surprising then is the fact that the difference between the two
definitions proposed above is indeed more terminological—"system" and
"dogma," I take it, are inductively synonymous or nearly so—rather than
real. It is thus a matter of the levels of empiricism at which each observer
situates himself in relation to the object. For further evidence of this, one
need only consider the inductive parallelism established by Lévi-Strauss
between science and magic.[26] These are considered as "two parallel modes
of acquiring knowledge," or two systems which require the same sort of
mental operations and which differ not so much in kind as in the different
"types of phenomenon" to which they are applied. Hence what Senghor
views as mystical about magic it seems to me may be nothing but the pure

supernatural state of magic considered as a "life-force," its abstract power of symbolization, not the fact that magic may also constitute an integral science whose operations can be rationally explicated and understood.

A delightful sense of magic in the sense already indicated, which stems partly from his intensely African religious background and partly from the influence of French medieval and modern mystics, poets, and philosophers, also underlines Senghor's views on African poetic rhythm and imagery. Let me note in passing that a similar romantic strain runs through much of the anthropological writings of Lévi-Strauss, who besides has claimed Jean Jacques Rousseau as a major influence. On the subject of poetic image, Senghor argues:

> Il s'agit de la double valeur du mot. Celui-ci peut être perçu comme signe ou comme sens ; très souvent, en poesie, comme signe et sens en même temps. Le mot peut avoir la valeur quasi-abstraite d'un signe algébrique.[27]

Clearly then Senghor recognizes not only the double quality of denotation and connotation in words but also the relationship between the signifier and the signified, a central point in structural linguistics.[28] One would have wished that Senghor had developed further these technical insinuations in a way that would have been both consistent and beneficial in any methodological considerations within negritude.

As for "rhythm", Senghor defines it variously as "the architecture of being," "the internal dynamism," "the system of waves," "the pure expression of the Life-force," and so on. Now, all these are imprecise and, strictly from the point of view of analytic methodology, unreliable definitions. They do not transcend the level of mysticism, nor were they originally intended to, in delineating this particular problematic, Senghor's negritude. But far from dismaying by their so-called impreciseness, such definitions should impress by the structural perspective within which they already appear to be inscribed, namely, that of descriptive exhaustion of the object contemplated —in other terms, the perspective of phenomenology.

Phenomenology, according to Senghor, is nothing but

> la description des faits pour en comprendre les significations. C'est la dialectique vécue de l'objet et du sujet, de l'abstrait et du concret, de la théorie et de la pratique, de l'action et de la mystique.[29]

It is therefore in this dialectical sense that one must interpret Senghor's equation of Life-forces with super- or sur-reality as indeed no more than a mystical affirmation of structural relationships within a given system, whether of cosmology such as the African universe in which man, according to the poet-humanist, holds the central place; or ontology, such as the relationship between an individual and his clan totem in traditional Africa. In any case, this interpretation if upheld should lead us to reconsider the role and meaning of the term "Life-force" in negritude, in such a way

as may enable us to appreciate the close resemblance between the use of
the term "life-force," in Senghor's phenomenology of religious and cultural
perception, and the idea of "structure," particularly in the reductionist
phenomenology of Husserl and Merleau Ponty.* In either case, the concepts
are used in a transcendental and subjective manner to invoke a systemic, in
the sense of a rational and objective view of the world. Hence the poet has
argued, too, that the perception of "life-forces" is possible only through
emotion and *intuition*—two modes upon which he conferred an epistemologi-
cal and cognitive role among the Blacks.

> * Phenomenology developed with Edmund Husserl as a protest against Neo-
> Kantism (strong in German universities at the turn of this century) and
> empiricism. It was presented as a principle or method of description of things
> which would give priority of consideration not to any pre-existing conceptual
> framework but to the intuitive rapport between the subject and the object.
> For things in their raw state (that is, the world) do not possess a meaning;
> they do so, that is become "phenomena" only when they are *lived*, that is,
> illuminated by an act of consciousness of the subject (the "transcendental
> Ego"). Sometimes referred to as "a science of essences" (or "eidetic" science),
> one of phenomenology's many concerns is therefore to discover, using its
> own method of intuitive reasoning, the transcendental structures of the con-
> sciousness which is present in every signifying act. Thus the evolution of
> Husserl's phenomenology can be said to be towards a philosophy of per-
> ception and of history. In this respect, Merleau Ponty was his principal
> continuator and disciple in France. I can understand any critic who prefers
> to link Senghor's negritude, in terms of direct influence, with Bergson's de-
> scriptive psychology rather than with Merleau Ponty.

However, in a recent review of the problematic of negritude, Senghor has
again defended his position against his critics by rightly emphasizing that
"emotion" signifies "intuitive reason." Although this position is by no
means new, Senghor nevertheless ascribes it to what he terms "the triumph
of the new epistemology." Also, without specifically mentioning the name
of Lévi-Strauss as one of the architects of "the new epistemology," it is clear
that Senghor had the ethnologist in mind when he referred to the recent
development of the structuralist and functionalist theories in the human
sciences, and when he argued:

> La connaissance contemporaine est une confrontation du sujet et de l'objet,
> dont l'initiative, au demeurant, n'est pas toujours du sujet. C'est une parti-
> cipation, une communion, où le sujet et l'objet sont, chacun et en même
> temps, regardant et regarde, agent et agi. C'est l'acte d'amour de laison-oeil
> et de la raison-toucher. Or, c'est ainsi, par les mots de ‹participation› et
> ‹communion›, que les ethnologues ont toujours defini la connaissance des
> Nègres.[30]

Senghor's claim, implied above, that the orthodox position of negritude
has been vindicated by developments in contemporary knowledge, is
characteristic but vague. The question is indeed not whether terms like

"participation" and "communion" have been employed by past anthropologists[31] to describe the people whose cultures they studied, but whether the properties of the terms have been correctly described and specified and by what methods. A significant development in Senghor's new thinking, as defined in the above, is therefore the implied critique of "reductionism" which in Husserl's philosophical system argues that all signification attached to the world of phenomena originates from the consciousness, that is, the intentionality, of the contemplating subject, since "all consciousness is of something." Also Senghor correctly states the position of modern structuralism, considered as a system of epistemology, when he acknowledges that the "initiative" (in determining the structure of signification, that is), does not always lie with the subject. In the methodological specification of the laws governing the new "participation" and "communion" between subject and object, which Senghor refers to, however, structuralism has progressed, whereas negritude has remained static.

Lévi-Straussian structuralism is a paradigmatic science. Its method consists essentially in erecting conceptual models which mediate between contradictory, or binary relations.[32] Myths, for example, are considered not only as systems of abstract relations but also as aesthetic objects. The creative act which gives rise to myths, he claims

> ... is in fact exactly the reverse of that which gives rise to works of art. In the case of works of art, the starting point is a set of one or more objects and one or more events which aesthetic creation unifies by revealing a common structure. Myths travel the same road, but start from the other end. They use a structure to produce what is itself an object consisting of a set of events (for all myths tell a story). Art thus proceeds from a set (object + event) to the discovery of its structure. Myth starts from a structure by means of which it constructs a set (object + event).[33]

Senghor's poem "Le Totem" provides an eminent illustration of this statement. As a form of myth, it starts from a given structure, namely, the primitive unity within the dualism which is part of the totemic belief; as an art, that is a conscious exploration in the medium of language, it moves from a series of disjunctions (images, symbols or propositions) towards a search for the principle of their unification. Thus the same system of permutations, which in totemism mediates ideal relations between the two privileged series of Nature and Culture, are also present at a phenomenological level of perception in Senghor's "Le Totem."

Notes
1   Roman Jakobson and Claude Lévi-Strauss, «‹ Les Chats › de Baudelaire,» *L'Homme,* 2, 1 (1962), 5—21.
2   Noam Chomsky, *Syntactic Structures* (The Hague, 1957) and *Aspects of the Theory of Syntax* (Boston, 1965).
3   Roland Barthes, « Elements de semiologie,» *Communication,* 4 (1964), 91—135.
4   See, e. g., S. Levin, *Linguistic Structures in Poetry* (The Hague, 1969).

5   "The Criticism of Modern African Literature," in *Perspectives on African Literature*, ed. Christopher Heywood (New York, 1968), pp. 9—30.
6   Cf. Roland Barthes, *Essais Critiques* (Paris, 1964).
7   In *Sociologie du roman africain* (Paris, 1970) and "Genetic Structuralism as a Critical Technique," *Conch*, 3, 1 (1971), 33—44.
8   "Structuralism in East and West Africa," in *Structuralism around the World*, ed. T. E. Sebeok (forthcoming).
9   Léopold Sédar Senghor, *Chants d'ombre* (Paris, 1945).
10   L. Althusser and Etienne Balibar, *Reading Capital* (New York, 1970); Claude Lévi-Strauss, *The Savage Mind* (Chicago, 1966).
11   M. Glucksmann, *Structuralist Analysis in Contemporary Social Thought* (London, 1974).
12   *The Savage Mind*, p. 22.
13   « Problématique de la Négritude,» *Présence Africaine*, 78 (1971), 3—26.
14   Austin J. Shelton, *The African Assertion* (New York, 1968), p. 73.
15   Robert Mercier, « L'Imagination dans la poésie de Léopold Sédar Senghor,» *Literature East & West*, 12, 1 (1968), 44—45.
16   Sylvia Washington Bâ, *The Concept of Negritude in the Poetry of Léopold Sédar Senghor* (Princeton, 1973), pp. 61—62; Placide B. Tempels, *La Philosophie Bantoue* (Paris, 1949); Janheinz Jahn, *Muntu* (Paris, 1958).
17   Translation by Bâ, p. 197.
18   *Liberté I: Négritude et humanisme* (Paris, 1964), p. 203.
19   W. L. d'Azevedo, ed. *The Traditional Artist in African Societies* (Bloomington, 1973).
20   J. Charbonnier, *Entretiens avec Claude Lévi-Strauss* (Paris, 1961), p. 70.
21   *Liberté I . . .*, p. 240.
22   Charbonnier, pp. 33, 71.
23   Roland Barthes, *Le Degre zero de l'écriture* (Paris, 1964).
24   C. A. Diop, *The African Origin of Civilization* (New York, 1974).
25   *Liberté I . . .*, p. 267.
26   *The Savage Mind*, p. 12.
27   *Liberté I . . .*, p. 161.
28   Cf., e. g., Ferdinand de Saussure, *Cours de linguistique générale* (Paris, 1968).
29   *Liberté I . . .*, p. 386.
30   « Problématique de la Négritude,» pp. 13—26.
31   Cf. Lucien Lévy-Bruhl, *Les Carnets de Lucien Lévy-Bruhl* (Paris, 1949).
32   Sunday O. Anozie, "Structuralism in Poetry and Mythology," *Conch*, 4, 1 (1972), 1—21.
33   *The Savage Mind*, pp. 25—26.

Migration d'un mouvement: Le cas de la négritude

Mineke Schipper-de Leeuw

Au risque d'être classée parmi « ces blancs passionnés qui veulent en toute conscience être justes cette fois-ci et éviter les erreurs de la colonisation », selon l'expression d'Ezekiel Mphahlele dans son *African Image*, nous essaierons de dégager quelques idées au sujet de la négritude en tant que mouvement littéraire[1].

Notons d'abord qu'il est impossible de mettre toute la littérature africaine dans le même sac, comme plusieurs théoriciens et défenseurs ont essayé de le faire dans le passé. Cette tendance a provoqué des protestations de la part d'écrivains et de critiques non seulement dans le camp anglophone, mais encore parmi les francophones : pensons à Mphahlele, Soyinka, Franklin ou Adotevi pour ne citer que ceux-là. Parfois des protagonistes se sont transformés en adversaires de la négritude et vice-versa, mais les textes des auteurs ne changent pas et c'est sur eux que nous nous sommes basée pour voir un peu plus clair dans ce sujet complexe. Des auteurs noirs américains, antillais et africains se sont inspirés de thèmes communs, les thèmes de la négritude. Ce « message de la race noir » comme l'a définie Thomas Melone, l'un des fidèles défenseurs de la négritude, a voyagé de l'Amérique aux Antilles, des Antilles à l'Europe et aux pays de l'Afrique. Les thèmes ont été abordés par des écrivains de l'Afrique occidentale avant d'être utilisés en Afrique centrale : la plupart des Zaïrois ont ignoré jusqu'au concept de la négritude — ils n'avaient d'ailleurs guère écrit — avant l'indépendance de leur pays, grâce à la politique de l'isolement que les Belges ont appliqués dans leur colonie. A partir des années soixante, la négritude connaît une période de floraison au Zaïre[2], tandis que depuis les années soixante-dix elle semble trouver des adeptes en Afrique du Sud, parmi les victimes de l'Apartheid.

Il nous semble inutile de revenir ici aux changements que la négritude a voulu effectuer dans le domaine culturel ou littéraire. L'historique du mouvement a été fait par Lilyan Kesteloot, par Janheinz Jahn et par d'autres[3]. Nous connaissons les origines du mouvement, la *Negro-Renaissance* aux Etats Unis et les activités littéraires aux Antilles, antérieures à la naissance même du terme négritude qui date des années trente à Paris. Dans un article entitulé *Parallelisms and divergencies between "negritude" and "indigenismo"*, le professeur Coulthard estime que le "gradual build-up to negritude and the final elaboration of the concept of negritude took place largely in the West-Indies"[4]. Cependant les Antilles néerlandaises et le Surinam n'y ont pas participé : à en juger d'après leur production littéraire, les auteurs n'en sont pour l'instant qu'aux débuts de leur « négritude ».

Avant d'examiner les textes des plus près, nous croyons devoir poser une autre question, celle de savoir ce que c'est qu'un mouvement littéraire. Dans son livre *The Theory of the Avant-Garde*, Poggioli consacre tout un chapitre à ce problème. Il est d'avis que le terme *d'école* est hors d'usage depuis le Romantisme et que les artistes eux-mêmes préfèrent parler de leur appartenance à un *mouvement*. En général le terme mouvement sert à désigner un groupe d'auteurs qui écrivent plus ou moins dans le même esprit, mais cette « esprit » du mouvement est parfois, dans sa définition même, source de divergences. Dans le cadre de leur mouvement des auteurs publient des périodiques qui ont un caractère de manifestes et qui ont en général la vie brève. Toujours selon Poggioli, le mouvement a des bases idéologiques et psychologiques et il aspire au succès, c'est-à-dire à la confirmation de son esprit dans le domaine culturel. Dans la plupart des cas le mouvement constitue une réaction, il réagit contre la tradition, une autorité, le public ou bien contre tout cela à la fois[5].

Les traits mentionnés ci-dessus se retrouvent aussi dans la négritude, depuis les sens divergents en passant par des manifestes publiés — citons *Légitime Défense* ou *L'Etudiant noir* — jusqu'aux bases idéologiques et aux réactions contre l'ordre culturel occidental établi. Cela nous semble justifier l'emploi du terme mouvement. Et le terme négritude? Dans l'histoire littéraire il arrive qu'un mouvement reçoive son nom longtemps après sa disparition. Pensons aux noms de Renaissance ou de Baroque qui ne furent attribués ces périodes respectives que quelques siècles plus tard. Cependant il arrive aussi que le terme désignant un mouvement lui soit attribué par les artistes mêmes qui y participent. Cela prouve en général que ces artistes travaillent consciemment et il est alors probable que cette conscience influence profondément leurs œuvres. Ceci vaut sans doute pour certains artistes du Romantisme qui se sont servi de ce terme, mais aussi pour des écrivains de la négritude tels que Césaire, Senghor, Damas et d'autres qui ont été influencés par les manifestes et les théories du mouvement. D'autre part, il est certain que pas mal d'écrivains ont écrit dans le même sens sans avoir adhéré consciemment au mouvement, sans se servir du terme négritude et même avant que le terme ne fût né. Les textes littéraires prouvent que, à un moment donné, des auteurs noirs ont créé une littérature nouvelle dans des pays, voire des continents, différents, dans des langues différentes et à des moments différents de l'histoire.

En relisant certains passages sur le Romantisme dans les *Concepts of criticism* de René Wellek, on est frappé par quelques analogies qui s'offrent entre ce mouvement européen et la négritude : tout d'abord l'un et l'autre ont voyagé, se sont déplacés d'un pays à l'autre. Ensuite, les deux mouvements ont été définis de plusieurs manières, recevant tantôt un sens global y compris des aspects culturels et politiques, tantôt un sens strictement littéraire. Il y a un troisiéme point de comparaison : Wellek signale qu'aucun poète anglais ne s'est jamais considéré comme un poète romantique[6]. N'en est-il pas ainsi de bon nombre de poètes africains anglophones qui n'ont jamais reconnu ou voulu reconnaître la négritude ? Dans son article *Thèmes de la poésie africaine d'expression anglaise*, J. P. Clark, découvre chez ses confrères poètes anglophones l'amour des thèmes de la négritude, comme celui de « Afrique perdue et reconquise ». Il note : « Les poètes de langue française, selon la manière méthodique de leur maître, ont créé, pour désigner cette grande passion commune, le mot magnifique de « négritude ». Quant à nos poètes anglophones, si peu assimilés qu'ils soient, la sophistication britannique a dû quelque peu déteindre sur eux, car bien qu'ils ne portent aucune étiquette et n'appartiennent à aucune école, ni à aucun mouvement célèbre, le nom même de l'Afrique est pour eux « comme une cloche qui les rappelle » vers leur passé glorieux de « palmiers élancés », de « brises rafraîchissantes se levant au-dessus de jolis lagons », de « vierges aux seins nus » et « d'hommes simples, ayant perdu, chez eux, toute dignité humaine », ou bien confiants « à la tête et aux muscles solides », « trompés et traîtreusement emmenés en esclavage vers les pays lointains »[7].

Ce que Wellek a dit au sujet du Romantisme nous semble s'appliquer également à la négritude. Apparemment l'histoire d'un terme et son introduction ne peuvent pas dicter son utilisation à l'historien de la littérature, car celui-ci serait alors forcé de respecter des repères qui ne se justifieraient pas lorsque l'on veut tenir compte des courants littéraires mêmes. Aussi Wellek conclut-il : "The great changes happened independently of the introduction of these terms, either before or after them and only rarely approximately at the same time"[8]. Il serait intéressant de comparer les deux mouvements d'une façon détaillée, d'autant plus que plusieurs critiques africains ont déjà fait allusion aux éléments romantiques qui caracteriseraient la négritude. Ici cependant nous devrons nous limiter aux thèmes et textes de la négritude.

Les thèmes communs se trouvent surtout dans la poésie, ce qui, selon Samuel Allen, n'est pas dû au hasard. Si la négritude a donné naissance à des poèmes plutôt qu'à des œuvres romanesques, c'est que le romancier doit tenir compte de la réalité, de l'intrigue, du "setting", de l'évolution de ses caractères : "He is constrained to a certain degree of reasonableness. The poet has probably a greater chance to penetrate at once without apology and without a setting of the worldly stage to the deepest levels of his creative concern"[9].

Dans l'univers poétique, les auteurs vont à la recherche de leurs propres valeurs et de leur propre identité qui seront alors en même temps les valeurs et un l'identité des frères de race, leur histoire commune d'hommes opprimés en route pour la liberté. Les thèmes révèlent que pour les poètes il s'agit de se définir comme des hommes autres que le Blanc, de se définir négativement par rapport au monde blanc, pour ainsi dire. Les thèmes en témoignent nettement : ce sont surtout celui de la souffrance, celui de la révolte, celui du triomphe ou de l'idéalisation de l'Afrique et de l'homme noir, et pour terminer il y a le dialogue interracial qui semble marquer le moment final du mouvement.

Le thème de la souffrance

Sartre analyse le phénomène de la souffrance nègre dans son célèbre essai *Orphée noir* où il parle de la Passion (avec P majuscule) de la race : « Le Noir conscient de soi se représente à ses propres yeux comme l'homme qui a pris sur soi toute la douleur humaine et qui souffre pour tous, même pour le Blanc »[10]. Cette Passion de la race tout entière a inspiré bon nombre de poètes. On évoque le passé, on analyse l'histoire, on diagnostique le mal : les douleurs de l'homme noir résultent fatalement de la sauvagerie du Blanc. Il fallait qu'on le dise ! Voici un bref fragment de *Et les chiens se taisaient* d'Aimé Césaire. L'auteur y semble obsédé par la vision des cruautés commises par le Blanc. Les atrocités prennent des formes concrètes. La mer, le soleil, le ciel, le vent, les nuages, la nature entière, tout constitue un tableau horrifiant où sont incarnés les souffrances des frères, les gémissements des victimes :

« ... Le nuage a la tête du vieux nègre que j'ai vu rouer vif sur une place, le ciel bas est un étouffoir, le vent roule des fardeaux et des sanglots de peau suante, le vent se contamine de fouets et de futailles et les pendus peuplent le ciel d'acéras et il y a des dogues de poil sanglant et des oreilles ... des oreilles ... des barques faites d'oreilles coupées qui glissent sur le couchant (...) Une rumeur de chaînes de carcans monte de la mer ... un gargouillement de noyés, de la pense verte de la mer ... un claquement de feu, un claquement de fouet, des cris d'assassinés ... la mer brûle »[11].

Les souffrances décrites sont d'ordre physique et moral : il n'y a pas que la traite et l'exploitation, il y a aussi l'aliénation causée par la destruction de l'ancienne société et l'imposition de l'économie et de la culture étrangères. Cette situation est présente à la mémoire des fils d'esclaves et des anciens colonisés, mais elle est la réalité quotidienne des victimes du royaume de l'Apartheid, de l'Afrique du Sud de nos jours. C'est cette réalité misérable qui a inspiré James Matthews dans son recueil de poèmes *Cry rage* (paru en 1972), lorsqu'il fait allusion à la politique scandaleuse de délogement que le gouvernement de Prétoria applique impunément. Les gens « inutiles » sont « réinstallés » dans les « aixes de recasement », tels que Limehill et Dimbaza :

> "The people of Limehill and Dimbaza
> like those of Sada and Ilinge
> are harvesting crops of crosses
> the only fruit the land will bear
> with the fields of their villages
> fertilised by the bodies of children
> and bones of the ancient ones
> Cinderella resettlement areas, government gifts,

> are graveyards they stumble through
> as hunger roosts on their shoulder
> waiting for them to fill the earth
> . . . . .
> Mute evidence of white man's morality
> are the legions of walking death
> the people of Limehill and Dimbaza
> and those of Sada and Ilinge"[12].

Peu de temps après la parution de *Cry rage*, le livre tomba sous le *banning-order* du gouvernement : d'après Nadine Gordimer c'est le premier recueil de poèmes publié et « banni » en Afrique du Sud même[13].

Les deux exemples, celui de Césaire et celui de Matthews, ont été choisis parmi des dizaines d'autres poèmes de langue française, anglaise, portugaise ou néerlandaise qui ont pour sujet la souffrance de la race noire exploitée par l'homme blanc. Le poème de Matthews démontre que le thème dont Césaire s'est servi il y a une trentaine d'années est vivant et actuel dans le contexte de l'Afrique du Sud des années soixante-dix.

Le thème de la révolte

Pour le poète qui chante la souffrance, la révolte n'est jamais loin : il proteste contre le tort infligé à ses frères de race. La parole du poète est son arme dans la lutte de libération, une arme forgée du matériau de la langue européenne, car on dirait que cette poésie s'adresse tant aux Blancs qu'aux Noirs. Voici un petit poème de David Diop s'adressant aux Africains qui devront refuser leur situation misérable.

Défi à la force

> « Toi qui plies toi qui pleures
> Toi qui meurs un jour comme ça sans savoir pourquoi
> Toi qui luttes qui veilles pour le repos de l'Autre
> Toi qui ne regardes plus avec le rire dans les yeux
> Toi mon frère au visage de peur et d'angoisse
> Relève-toi et crie : NON ! »[14]

Des poèmes qui respirent le même esprit sont cités par Pol Ndu dans un article intitulé *Negritude and the new breed* qui traite de la poésie noire américaine actuelle : "the poems of the battle-criers are action-charged, ringing with blood, fire and avalanche of some global doomsday (. . .) The poets, as it were, are impatient. For them the offensive is on . . ." Et l'auteur cite le poème *Black art* de Leroi Jones :

"We want 'poems that kill'
we want a black poem. And a
Black World.
Let the world be a Black Poem
And let All Black People Speak This Poem
Silently
or Loud"[15].

Le monde et le poème doivent être noirs parce que la révolte se dirige contre la domination blanche qui la conditionne. Si l'Autre n'existait pas, la révolte serait superflue et ces thèmes de poésie inexistantes. Dans la poésie la civilisation blanche est attaquée dans tous ces aspects : à travers son œuvre poétique, Aimé Césaire, par exemple, condamne successivement la raison, la culture, la technique, les idéologies et le christianisme[16].

Le thème de l'Afrique idéalisée

L'idéalisation de l'Afrique ancestrale, celle qui n'avait pas le malheur de connaître des Blancs est un thème fréquent dans la poésie de la négritude. Nous n'avons qu'à penser aux poèmes relatifs au « Royaume de l'Enfance » de Senghor. Dans le monde anglophone aussi il y a des odes à l'Afrique : Clark, dans son article cité plus haut, est d'avis que ce thème a été utilisé plus tôt en Afrique occidentale qu'en Afrique orientale ou centrale. Des exemples bien connus sont *African heaven* du Ghanéen Kobina Parkes ou *Sounds of a cowhide drum* du Sud-Africain Oswald Mtshali. Le thème est cher aussi aux poètes zaïrois des années soixante tels que Kadima-Nzuji[17].

Ce n'est pas seulement l'Afrique qui est idéalisée, mais aussi l'Africain et l'homme noir en général. Bernard Dadié remercie son Dieu de l'avoir créé noir, puisque « le blanc est une couleur de circonstance ». C'est bien la vue romantique de l'Afrique exclusive, symbole de la pureté, en face de l'Europe corrompue et destructrice. C'est aussi le cri triomphant du *black is beautiful* que Léon Damas pousse dans son poème *Black Label* dont nous ferons suivre quelques vers :

> « Jamais le Blanc ne sera nègre
> car la beauté est nègre
> et nègre la sagesse
> car l'endurance est nègre
> et nègre le courage
> car la patience est nègre
> et nègre l'ironie
> car le charme est nègre
> et nègre la magie
> car l'amour est nègre
> et nègre le déhanchement
> car la danse est nègre

> et nègre le rythme
> car l'art est nègre
> et nègre le mouvement
> car le rire est nègre
> car la joie est nègre
> car la paix est nègre
> car la vie est nègre
> T'EN SOUVIENT-IL »[18].

Le dialogue

Les trois thèmes mentionnés, la souffrance, la révolte et le triomphe, excluent le dialogue ; ce sont trois phases pendant lesquelles le poète se définit en face de l'Autre qui au cours de l'histoire, n'a pas non plus cherché le dialogue. Les poètes de la négritude attestent souvent qu'ils veulent rendre le monde plus humain et Senghor a dit que « le poème nègre n'est pas monologue mais dialogue »[19]. Cependant ce dialogue n'est pas inconditionné, il faut d'abord que les préjugés soient balayés et qu'il existe les même droits chez les deux groupes concernés. Dans la poésie, ces conditions ne sont pas toujours formulées. En Europe Senghor a souvent été considéré comme le réconciliateur des Noirs et des Blancs. Son œuvre littéraire est beaucoup moins agressive que celle d'auteurs tels que Césaire ou David Diop. Senghor explique cela par son « harmonie avec la nature africaine ». Cela explique-t-il que déjà en 1945 il ait pu écrire son poème *Prière de Paix* ?

> « Au pied de mon Afrique crucifiée depuis quatre cents ans et
> pourtant respirante
> Laisse-moi Te dire Seigneur, sa prière de paix et de pardon
> Seigneur Dieu, pardonne à l'Europe blanche ! »[20].

Ce pardon global et généreux de la part du père de la négritude n'a pas enchanté tous les Africains. Le Camerounais Marcien Towa reproche à Senghor d'être si pacifique qu'il se montre prêt à pardonner des crimes à une Europe qui n'aspire pas au pardon africain et qui n'a pas l'air de renoncer à des crimes nouveaux[21].

D'autres poètes font la distinction entre ceux qui sont au pouvoir et qui par conséquent sont responsables des injustices infligées aux peuples de couleur, et ceux qui dans le monde occidental sont eux aussi des victimes, les petits paysans et les ouvriers. Dans son poème *Pour saluer le Tiers Monde,* Césaire imagine comment l'Afrique est la première à tendre la main aux « damnés » des autres continents : l'Afrique

> « C'est une main tuméfiée
> une-blesée-main-ouverte,

tendue,
  brunes, jaunes, blanches,
à toutes mains, à toutes les mains blessées
du monde »[22].

Jacques Roumain ne pardonne pas aux coupables. Dans son *Nouveau ser-mon nègre,* ce poète compare le Noir souffrant au Christ souffrant, mais lors-que Jésus demande au Père de pardonner à ses ennemis qui ne savent pas ce qu'ils font, Roumain s'écrie : « Nous ne leur pardonnerons pas, car ils savent ce qu'ils font »[23]. Cependant sa solidarité ne se limite pas aux frères de race, témoin la fin du poème *Bois d'ébène :*

  « Comme la contradiction des traits
  se résout en l'harmonie du visage
  nous proclamons l'unité de la souffrance
  et de la révolte
  de tous les peuples sur toute la surface de notre terre
  et nous brassons le mortier des temps fraternels
  dans la poussière des idoles »[24].

Avec la conscience des classes, la négritude perd sa raison d'être : une autre solidarité se forge qui n'exige plus que l'homme mette en relief la cou-leur de sa peau ou son appartenance à telle ou telle race. « C'est le Blanc qui a créé le nègre », a dit Fanon, et la négritude a réagi contre cet état des choses, mais elle l'a aussi prolongé dans un certain sens puisque les auteurs se sont définis « en fonction de la couleur des autres », selon l'expression de Sembène Ousmane dans son avant-propos au *Mandat*[25].

      *   *   *

Après cet inventaire sommaire des thèmes et de leur migration, il est peut-être utile de voir où en sont les discussions actuelles autour de la négritude, ses défenseurs et ses adversaires. La négritude telle que nous l'avons reconnue dans les thèmes de la poésie constitue d'après Adotevi, la négritude de la pre-mière heure, « ce coup de pistolet au beau milieu du concert », lorsque « l'Af-rique, l'Amérique et les Antilles, tous les nègres du monde se retrouvent hors de l'humanité connue, hors de l'humanité du Blanc, pour affirmer leur huma-nité ». Cette « fin d'un silence », dit-il, c'est la négritude réelle, celle qui n'est pas encore pervertie, celle qui a permis de faire connaître l'Afrique grâce aux thèmes hurlés de nos poètes ». Ces thèmes marquent pour lui « l'acte de nais-sance d'une nouvelle littérature africaine ». Après ces réflexions positives dans *Négritude et négrologues,* Adotevi met en doute l'existence d'une unité durable parmi les Noirs de pays et de continents différents : Qu'est-ce qui les unit à part la couleur de la peau et « ce fond commun de trois siècles de traite ou d'inconscient collectif ? Même à l'égard de ce « fond commun » Adotevi se montre sceptique, à cause des variations historiques, géographiques et sociologiques qui, dans l'art des peuples de ces deux continents, ont abouti à des expressions différentes. Et il ajoute : « Même en Afrique les problèmes diffèrent pour peu qu'on passe du Dahomey à la Côte d'Ivoire, de la Côte d'Ivoire au Ghana. Et que dire de l'Afrique du Sud, du Kenya, du Rwanda ? . . . »[26].

Les « thèmes hurlés » dont parle Adotevi et qui ont voyagé entre les Etats Unis, les Antilles et l'Afrique font l'unité du mouvement. Rien d'autre que l'expérience commune de l'opression blanche ne permet de généraliser au sujet de l'homme noir, selon cet auteur. A un tel point de vue s'opposent les convictions d'Abiola Irele : dans son article *A defence of negritude,* lui aussi atteste d'abord le caractère révolutionnaire de la littérature du mouvement, mais pour lui, il y a plus que le point de départ de la protestation. Selon Irele, la négation de l'Europe constitue en même temps la recherche de soi et le retour aux sources. Comme Senghor, il estime que "the negro being is rooted in African tradition which is unified by a common philosophical acception (. . .) a common ontological outlook which governs the African psyche and in which the negro in America can rightly be supposed to share." Et plus loin : "there is something in common: I find nothing to contradict the thesis of a unified African universe." Pour Irele il existe ce je-ne-sais-quoi-nègre qu'il appelle "total African cosmology", l'ensemble des valeurs africaines de Senghor, dont il partage le point de vue, du moins le faisait-il en 1964 en écrivant cet article[27]. Adotevi par contre cite Peter Abrahams et Richard Wright pour défendre ses idées. Ces deux écrivains n'ont pas ressenti l'unité fraternelle noire lors de leur séjour en Afrique occidentale. Wright dit ceci : « J'étais noir et ils étaient noirs et cela ne m'a servi à rien ». Et Abrahams : « La conscience de race si aiguë chez le noir américain ou chez celui de l'Afrique du Sud, victime de l'Apartheid, lui (c'est-à-dire à l'Africain de l'Afrique indépendante) est étrangère. La race et la couleur étaient ses dernières préoccupations avant qu'on ne le contraigne à y penser. Et la « Mère Afrique est trop vaste pour lui inspirer un sentiment global »[28].

Or, la conscience raciale ne préoccupe plus tellement les Africains de l'Afrique indépendante, tandis que les auteurs noirs américains s'en servent encore dans leur poésie, car ils représentent toujours une minorité opprimée dans la société où ils vivent. Les « cris de guerre » de ceux que Pol Ndu a appelés "the new breed" retentissent dans cette littérature de nos jours comme par le passé. Il en est de même dans les pays africains d'expression portugaise. Mario de Andrade atteste « l'unité certaine des thèmes » dans la poésie de ces pays : c'est une poésie de combat, c'est le temps de « vaincre ou de mourir », mais lui aussi ajoute que cette poésie est circonstanciée[29].

Les thèmes de la négritude sont vivants pour ceux qui sont encore opprimés et nous avons mentionné le nom de James Matthews pour l'Afrique du Sud, mais il y a beaucoup d'autres poètes qui écrivent dans le même sens[30]. En

dehors de l'Afrique du Sud, on a tendance à citer Mphahlele comme le représentant légal du point de vue sud-africain de la négritude. Bien qu'il ait
revu quelque peu ses idées à ce sujet dans la seconde édition de son *African
Image,* Mphahlele reste d'avis (dans un chapitre intitulé « Négritude re-
visited ») que la négritude en tant que programme artistique est "unwork-
able" pour l'Afrique moderne et que les facteurs historiques ayant engendré
la négritude n'y existent plus[31]. Cependant Mphahlele ne représente pas *le*
point de vue des auteurs sud-africains, et il ne le ne prétend d'ailleurs pas lui-
même. Bien que de ton beaucoup plus modéré que leurs confrères négro-
américains — ce qui s'explique par la censure impassible — les poètes sud-
africains non-exilés manient les thèmes de la négritude. La domination
blanche y anime, dirait-on, la conscience noire des années soixante-dix. Des
termes tels que *blackness, black culture* et *black conscienceness* répondent à
la situation cuisante dans ce pays. Au mois de décembre de 1974, la première
Black Renaissance Convention a eu lieu à Hammanskraal en Afrique du Sud.
Des Noirs y ont affirmé fermement leur solidarité d'hommes de couleur en
face des Blancs de leur pays, maintenant qu'ils se sont rendus à l'évidence
que tout effort de dialogue a échoué sur les écueils de l'Apartheid. Depuis les
annés soixante-dix, les leaders de la SASO, 'organisation des étudiants noirs de
l'Afrique du Sud, organisent des programmes culturels populaires de poésie et
de théâtre qu'ils ont intitulés "into the heart of negritude" et qui contiennent
des poèmes de Senghor, de Dadié, de David Diop à côté des œuvres de Mtshali, Serote, Gwala et d'autres Sud-Africains.

Lors d'un entretien que nous avons eu avec eux à Durban il y a deux ans,
ils nous ont expliqué qu'à l'heure actuelle la négritude est une phase culturelle
indispensable qui ne sera pas dépassée avant que la liberté acquise n'ait ouvert
de nouvelles perspectives. Ces « radicaux », comme on les appelle en Afrique
du Sud, rattachent eux aussi la négritude à leur lutte de libération.

Jusqu'ici nous n'avons guère parlé des théories senghoriennes qui ont peut-
être le plus contribué à fonder et à faire connaître le mouvement. Senghor
donne à la négritude un contenu non pas passager mais durable. Dans une
interview qu'il nous avait accordé lors de sa visite aux Pays Bas en octobre
1974, le père de la négritude a réaffirmé l'unité des valeurs de la civilisation
du monde noir, bien que les circonstances et les thèmes changent aujourd'hui.
Il ne s'agit plus de «polémiquer» contre la civilisation européenne mais la
négritude reste. Dans la « Civilisation de l'Universel », l'Europe et l'Afrique
auront des apports bien définis: «L'Europe nous apportera, essentiellement,
avec son esprit de méthode et d'organisation, ses découvertes scientifiques et
techniques, L'Afrique, je veux dire l'Afrique noire, apportera ses vertus com-
munautaires et artistiques, singulièrement sa philosophie de la vie, fondée sur
la complémentarité, et, dans les arts, son sens de l'image analogique, du
rythme et de la mélodie »[32]. Il reste des particularités conditionnées par l'appartenance à telle ou telle race, car si l'Afrique avait pu coloniser l'Europe,
les Africains auraient mieux traités les Blancs que les Blancs n'ont traités les
Noirs en Afrique ; la preuve est fourni par des cas historiques où des

groupements noirs ont soumis des populations blanches tels que les Almora-
vides qui ont conquis le Maroc: « Jamais les Noirs ayant le pouvoir n'ont fait
de racisme contre les Blancs », dit le Président-Poète. A la question de savoir
s'il existe des analogies entre la situation des femmes et celle des Noirs dans
le monde (« les unes et les autres s'émancipent aujourd'hui d'un même pater-
nalisme », celui de l'homme blanc, lit-on dans *Le deuxième sexe* de Simon de
Beauvoir), Senghor répond: « Il y a, certainement, des similitudes, non seulement entre les conditions de la femme occidentale et du Négro-Africain, mais
encore entre les vertus féminines et les vertus négro-africaines. Que les conditions de la femme en Occident et du Négro-Africain dans le monde soient
semblables, c'est l'évidence même. L'Euramérique, on le sait, a commencé par
nier les vertus du Nègre comme l'homme de l'Occident avait nié celles de la
Femme. Ce qui paraît moins évident, ce sont les similitudes entre les vertus
de la Femme et les vertus du Nègre. Et pourtant il y a, ici et là, le même
besoin d'expression, exprimée par l'image analogique et le rythme. Il y a,
surtout, chez le Nègre, comme chez la Femme, la puissance d'emotion et,
partant, d'identification. D'où la fausse impression chez l'Euraméricain,
comme chez l'homme de l'Occident, que l'on peut assimiler le Nègre, comme
la Femme »[33]. On peut se demander ce que devient la femme noire dans ces
conditions là. Cependant si la négritude est une qualité éternelle unissant
les Noirs du monde entier, comment faut-il alors s'expliquer que Senghor accorde à un tout petit peuple comme celui des Pays Bas une *néerlandité* (basée
sur le *robur Batavorum* dont parla déjà Tacite) et à un autre peuple européen,
le peuple portugais, la *lusitanité* faite de l'énergie lusitanienne de sa sensibilité
profonde, de sa gentillesse, de sa tristesse et de sa nostalgie, comme il nous
explique dans un des derniers numéros de *Jeune Afrique*[34].

« Tant qu'il y aura un Etat néerlandais, il y aura une néerlandité » et « tant
qu'il y aura une ethnie nègre il y aura la négritude », selon Senghor[35]. En
quoi consiste alors l'ethnie nègre et pourquoi ne pas attribuer aux différents
Etats noirs une propre « -ité » ou « -itude », comme il l'a fait pour plusieurs
peuples européens?

« La négritude, connais pas ». dit Sembène Ousmane, « elle est pour moi
comme le sexe des anges. » Cet auteur n'a jamais reconnu la négritude, bien
qu'il ait admis dans un pays comme l'Afrique du Sud elle pourra jouer
un rôle positif, mais rien que temporairement : « Ce n'est que demain que les
Noirs sudafricains comprendront où se trouve le noyau du problème et alors
ils ne continueront certainement pas à courir après la négritude. » C'est la révolution qu'il leur faudra selon lui, et la négritude ne peut pas la réaliser[36].
C'est là le reproche qui est adressé très souvent à la négritude : elle s'oppose-
rait à révolution africaine. Selon Adotevi elle a raté sa vocation politique
et révolutionnaire : « Si la négritude ancienne est un refus de l'humiliation; le
nègre qui aujourd'hui parle au nègre, doit être au centre du drame de son
peuple, conscient de soi, c'est-à-dire aux tâches de l'heure. » Et Mphahlele
conseille à la négritude "to stop telling the masses how beautiful they are
while they are starving, while they swelter under new lords"[37]. Pour Adotevi

la négritude d'aujourd'hui, c'est le discours actuel du néo-colonialisme. La négritude, c'est la manière *noire* d'être *blanc*. » Cet auteur se réclame des idées de Fanon qui lui aussi a refusé d'appartenir à un rameau particulier de la race humaine, d'être fixé par l'histoire, car pour chaque homme il s'agit de dépasser la donnée historique et d'introduire le cycle de sa liberté. Aussi Fanon s'est-il refusé à faire « le bilan des valeurs nègres » en disant en 1952 déjà : « Moi, l'homme de couleur, je ne veux qu'une chose : Que jemais l'instrument ne domine l'homme. Que cesse à jamais l'asservissement de l'homme par l'homme. C'est-à-dire de moi par un autre. Qu'il me soit permis de découvrir et de vouloir l'homme, où qu'il se trouve.

Le nègre n'est pas. Pas plus que le Blanc »[38].

L'écho de propos pareils à travers le monde est à la base du déclin actuel de la négritude. Il va de pair avec le développement du nouveau réalisme qui marque de plus en plus nettement le visage de la littérature dans l'Afrique indépendante de nos jours.

Notes

1   E. MPHAHLELE, *The African Image*, Revised Edition, New York, 1974, p. 79.
2   Voir notre article *Littérature zaïroise et société decolonisée*, dans *Kroniek van Afrika*, Leyden 1972/4, pp. 187—194.
3   L. KESTELOOT, *Les écrivains noirs de langue française: naissance d'une littérature*, Bruxelles, 1963. J. JAHN, *A history of Neo-African literature. Writing in two continents*, New York, 1968.
4   Dans *Caribbean Studies*, vol. 8/1, avril 1968, p. 46.
5   R. POGGIOLI, *The theory of the Avant-Garde*, Cambridge/Mass., 1968, pp. 17—40.
6   R. WELLEK, *Concepts of Criticism*, New Haven, 1963, p. 151.
7   Dans *Présence Africaine*, 54, 2e trim. 1965, pp. 99—100.
8   WELLEK, o. c., p. 151.
9   Cité par MPHAHLELE, o. c. première édition, Londres, 1962, p. 50.
10 Dans *Situations III*, Paris, 1949, p. 270. Ce phénomène n'est d'ailleurs pas inconnu; d'autres peuples aussi ont cru qu'ils avaient à jouer le même rôle, comme par exemple les Juifs, les Polonais, les Russes.
11 *Et les chiens se taisaient*, Paris (1946) 1961, pp. 151, 186.
12 J. MATTHEWS et G. THOMAS, *Cry rage*, Johannesbourg, 1972, p. 8.
13 N. GORDIMER, *The black interpreters*, Johannesbourg, 1972, p. 70.
14 D. DIOP, *Coups de pilon*, Paris, (1961) 1973, p. 48.
15 P. NDU, article dans *Présence Africaine*, 86, 2e trim. 1973, pp. 130 ss.
16 Voir notre article *Noirs et Blancs dans l'oeuvre d'Aimé Césaire*, dans *Présence Africaine*, 72, 4e trim. 1969, pp. 124—147.
17 CLARK, art. cit., p. 102; F. E. K. PARKES, *African heaven*, dans *An African treasury*, selected by L. HUGHES, New York, 1961, pp. 170—172; O. M. MTSHALI, *Sounds of a cowhide drum*, dans le recueil du même nom (1971), Londres, 1974, pp. 71—72; D. KADIMA-NZUJI, *Afrique*, dans *Anthologie des écrivains congolais*, Kinshasa, 1969, p. 235.
18 L. DAMAS, *Black Label*, Paris, 1956 p. 52.
19 L. S. SENGHOR, *La littérature africaine d'expression* française, dans *Liberté I, Négritude et humanisme*, Paris, 1964, p. 401.
20 Idem, *Poemes*, Paris, 1964, pp. 92—93.

21 M. TOWA, *Léopold Sédar Senghor: négritude ou servitude*, Yaoundé, 1971, p. 72.
22 A. CESAIRE, *Ferrements*, Paris, 1960, p. 85.
23 J. ROUMAIN, *La montagne ensorcelée*, Paris, 1972, p. 238.
24 Ibid., pp. 234—235.
25 SEMBENE, *Le Mandat*, Paris, 1965, p. 15.
26 S. S. K. ADOTEVI, *Négritude et négrologues*, Paris, 1972, 306 pp.
27 IRELE, *A defence of negritude*, dans *Transition*, 13, mars—avril 1964, pp. 9—11.
28 ADOTEVI, o. c., pp. 47, 48.
29 M. de ANDRADE, *La poésie négro-africaine d'expression portugaise*, Paris, 1969, pp. 26—28.
30 Voir par exemple le récent recueil *Poets to the poeple. South African Freedom Poems*, B. FEINBERG (ed.), Londres, 1974.
31 MPHAHLELE, o. c., (2e éd.), p. 81.
32 Entretien, octobre 1974.
33 Lettre du 21 novembre 1974.
34 L.-S. SENGHOR, *Lusitanité et Africanité*, dans *Jeune Afrique*, 21 mars 1975, pp. 22—25.
35 Entretien, octobre 1974.
36 Entretien, février 1975.
37 ADOTEVI, o. c., pp. 151, 152, 207.
38 F. Fanon, *Peau noire, masques blancs*, Paris, 1952, pp. 206, 207.

The Natur of Being in Contemporary Francophone African Literature

Gerald Moore

It may seem unreasonable, on the face of it, to expect of modern literary artists in Africa the statement of any coherent view of the nature of the world, or of man's existence within it, which we could place beside the traditional cosmologies offered in a collection like *African Worlds,* or in a recent addition to scholarship like Goody's recording of the Bagre Myths of the Lo Dagaa people of Ghana. If the origins of the Western novel, for example, lie in bourgeois realism, and if Western models have been a decisive influence on the francophone novelists of Africa, we might expect to find a fiction wherein the important variables are status, money education, race and perhaps tribe, but where fundamental questions about man's origin, nature and purpose will be avoided. Likewise, the francophone poet of today does not usually attempt the didacticism or inclusiveness of the great epic or mythic texts which were orally transmitted from the past. No modern poetry festival in Dakar or Lomé seems to offer the same kind of significance as a great annual ritual of recitation like that described by Dr. Goody, or to rival the cosmological myths recorded from the Western Sudan by Hampaté Ba and Marcel Griaule.

Such a conclusion would not do full justice to the present state of either fiction or poetry in francophone Africa. Since the 1920s the French novel itself has moved far away from bourgeois realism, and the works of novelists like Céline, Montherlant, Camus, Sartre or Malraux, not to mention numerous products of the *nouveau roman,* do address themselves precisely to the sort of primal questions about time and perception which the nineteenth century often felt able to ignore. Turning to poetry, it was W. B. Yeats who said that any major modern poet must develop a total view of the world to which all his works can be related, which will both sustain them and draw nourishment from them, if he is to give some unity to his vision and his achievement. Even if we concede, therefore, that the extreme centralism of French colonial and educational policy has made the literature of France a major feature in the experience of many African writers, we can still expect them to display some of the ideological and cosmological ambitions which have become the common stock of literature in France itself. But there is another and more important reason why an African writing today is likely to concern himself with such matters. It is no longer enough to ridicule the religious and administrative certitudes of colonial France, as writers like Ferdinand Oyono, Mongo Beti and David Diop did so brilliantly in the fifties. The very disillusionments of the independence period—the recognition of corruption, political disintegration and arbitrary military rule as evils that will not soon be eradicated— have forced upon many writers an anguished search for some meaning beneath the bewildering flood of experience. New codes of living are sought, to replace those destroyed or mortally injured during the colonial interlude. Codes which are capable of growth, yet discernibly related to the life of the past, and which draw their strength from some consistent view of the nature of external reality.

One of the most eloquent manifestations of this kind of vision is Camara Laye's third book *Dramouss*, published in 1966. Although unsatisfactory as a novel, by reason of its outbursts of authorial confusion and terror at what is passing in Guinea, *Dramouss* contains some of the most intense and searching pages to be found in recent African writing. Having expressed in his first two books a lyrical faith in the continued vitality of African humanism, Laye returns to a Guinea where it seems to be utterly denied; where arrest, imprisonment and execution have become daily events; where arson and terror are regarded as legitimate means of political debate among fellow Africans. It is for the moment irrelevant whether Laye's view of Guinea today is a totally just and balanced one, for he does not write as a political journalist. We can demand that it be a consistent one, and that it be sustained by his own clearly articulated beliefs. By these tests, *Dramouss* emerges as a work of remarkable interest and importance.

Towards the end of the book, when Laye is about to leave Guinea once more, his father gives him a little ball covered in cowries to set under his pillow, so that he may dream the future of the country. Symbolic dream or vision has always played an important part in Laye's fiction (one thinks of Clarence's successive dreams and stupors in *Le Regard du Roi* and of that remarkable story, «The Eyes of the Statue" and the dream here is a slightly altered and elaborated version of one which he recounted to a writers' conference at Freetown in 1963. It begins with a vision of Guinea as a vast circular prison with immensely high walls into which the dreamer is helplessly thrust by an involuntary ascent which drops him at its gate. Starved, bullied, flogged and even eviscerated by their gigantic guard, the prisoners seem completely inured to their fate, but the dreamer insists on conducting a series of conversations with him. A sardonic, argumentative and bloodthirsty lout of a man, this guard is one of Lay's most sinister creations:

> — Tu es comme le *linké*, hurlait-il. Exactement comme cette arbre géant, qui, au lieu de porter son ombre à son pied, la porte bizarrement à des lieus à la ronde, abondannant ainsi ses racines au soleil, bien que celles-ci aient besoin d'humidité pour que l'arbre survive.
> — Mais ! . . . risquais-je
> — Non, disait-il, laisse-moi parler. Je sais que lorsque tu vois le dernier des hommes, tu t'y attaches. Et même tu lui donnes de l'argent, tu lui voues

des sentiments charitables. Bien plus, tu le considères comme un frère . . .
Et tu es tellement naif que tu attends quelque chose de l'homme. Tu at-
tends de lui de la reconnaissance. Seulement, en portant ton ombre ail-
leurs, en te privant pour les autres, tu te condaisnes toi-même. Tu ne dois
donc t'en prendre qu'à toi-même.
— Ce que je fais pour mon prochain, je le fais pour moi-même et pour Dieu,
repliquais-je.
— Pas de tout ! faisait-il. Tu n'es qu'un naif, m'entends-tu ? . . . un crédule !
— C'est ma crédulité et ma naiveté qui me valent la paix de la conscience.
— C'est ce que te condamne ! Hurla-t-il . . .
— Faites ce que vous voulez. Votre prison ne changera nullement le fond de
ma pensée. Je garderai mes convictions.
— La bonté paie-t-elle jamais ? . . . Or, toi, tu as le cœur d'une sensibilité,
d'une sensiblerie à ne pas croire ! . . . Le cœur d'une mère pour ses petits !
. . . C'est une honte, d'avoir si bon cœur. La bonnaisserie ruine l'homme.[1]

Persisting in his questions and in his attempts to soften the guard's ferocity,
the dreamer is condemned to death by public burning. Marched out before
the assembled prisoners and fastened to the pyre, he finds himself ascending,
like the smoke of a burnt-offering, high above the scene of his "death." In
a series of rapid transformations, the dreamer now becomes a sparrowhawk,
but his flight weakening, is in danger of falling back into the prison when
he is rescued by a black serpent which shoots "like a rocket" into the sky.
As in the earliest pages of Laye's first work, *l'Enfant Noir*, this serpent
appears to symbolize the prophetic and protective wisdom of the ancestors;
the dreamer is rescued because of his faith in man, the faith of the traditional
African civilization in which he was reared.

There follows a sequence in which the snake, descending to earth in a
neighboring land, assumes the features of the tall, commanding woman called
Dramouss. After wandering through the familiar but sadly changed streets
of Samakoro, a village of Upper Guinea, the dreamer finds himself at the foot
of a huge *cailcedrat* tree, beneath which hundreds of corpses lie ranged. Dramouss orders him to bring one more body to complete the rows, but he at
first refuses, believing the man she indicates to be merely asleep. He returns
to Dramouss:

— Mais . . . il n'est pas mort ! . . . C'est un dormeur ! balbutiais-je.
— Non, ripostait Dramouss. C'est un des morts de la révolution.
— De quelle révolution ?
— De votre révolution
— Bien ! murmurais-je avec résignation (pp. 224—25)

Returning to gather up the body, he finds it stiff and heavy with death
—but, while he is setting it on his shoulder, the corpse awakes and vanishes
like a lightning-flash. Is this body his own, and its miraculous resurrection
his own also?

Tout s'était passé comme si j'avais été moi-même le mort réveillé, le mort ra-
nimé. (p. 227)

Finally, the vision closes with yet another movement of ascent. A flood of icy water gradually swallows the earth and drives the dreamer into the topmost branches of the tree. There Dramouss reappears and lights for him a vision of judgement in the skies. Between the files of the damned and the blessed appears a huge black tablet on which is inscribed:

SUR LA TERRE, L'HOMME NE FAIT RIEN POUR PERSONNE, NI RIEN CONTRE PERSONNE : IL FAIT TOUT POUR LUI-MÊME ET TOUT CONTRE LUI-MÊME (pp. 224—25, 227)

Dramouss tells him that the revolution has swallowed everything: she has been able to rescue only the gun, the hoe and the assagai, which she has conferred on the Black Lion. For the dreamer she has nothing but a golden staff (this staff proves to be a propelling pencil, the tool of the artist). The moon now descends onto the surface of the immense flood and, balloon-like, opens its doors to offer him rescue. There sits the Black Lion, presiding over the moon's safe ascent towards the sun, to which it proves to be tied by a great cord. Ever more rapidly, lion and dreamer hurtle towards "the source of light." Gradually the moon itself becomes coterminous with the whole redeemed, resurgent world of Africa:

A ce moment, regardant autour de moi, je voyais, je reconnaissais distincte-ment dans la lune, ma Basse-Guinée, ma Moyenne-Guinée, ma Haute-Guinée natale. J'apercevais ma Guinée forestière, jadis traquée, terrorisée par le «gaillard». Je les voyais heureures, profondément et pleinement.
Oui, je reconnaissais ces filles vêtues de *témourés* et de pagnes chatoyants, ces hommes et ces vieux, ces femmes et ces vieilles. Je contemplais ma Gui-née, guidée avec sagesse par le Lion Noir, l'héroique et sage Lion Noir. (p. 231)

This complex and extraordinary vision, with its constant transformations and repeated movements of ascent and descent, may be interpreted on many levels. At the most banal of these, the "source of light" is no more than the burning thatch of Laye's hut which he sees overhead as he awakes from the dream. At a slightly bolder level, the sequence may be seen as analogous with his own escape from Guinea, as the forces making for his arrest closed even upon men like Keita Fodeba, and his decision to seek refuge in neighboring Senegal. But would not anyone familiar with the symbolism of Manding culture recognize here its rearrangement in a way that speaks of Laye's undimmed hope in the eventual resurgence of a humane civilization, founded upon what seem, through every vicissitude, the most enduring things in the life of Africa? Particularly striking is the concept of the moon as a kind of intermediary and vehicle between man and the sun. Is not the moon often regarded, in the Western Sudan, as a repository for the souls of the dead? Does not the sun speak, not merely of light, but also of rebirth? And what of the juxtaposition of the tree, the serpent-woman and seeker after know-ledge? The antiquity and ubiquity of the imagery we associate with Genesis are as evident here as in the Myth of the Black Bagre, recorded far to the southward of Upper Guinea, where the first woman learns the art of sexual intercourse from a serpent encountered under a tree, and then teaches it to her mate.

The imagery of the sacrificial smoke ascending from the prison is particularly interesting, because the imagery of sacrifice is found in several other African writers of the last decade. It is at its clearest and most specific in a work like Cheikh Hamidou Kane's *L'Aventure Ambiguë,* where la Grande Royale unflinchingly presents to her family the real cost, and the real expectation, implied in sending their beloved son **Samba Diallo** to the schools of the white man.

Even Samba Diallo's Koranic education has given him faith only in death and its meaning. As a mere child, he has terrorized the mortal villagers with utterances like this:

> « Gens de Dieu, songez à votre mort prochaine. Éveillez-vous, oh, éveillez-vous ! Azrael, l'ange de la mort, déjà fend la terre vers vous. Il va surgir à vos pieds. Gens de Dieu, la mort n'est pas cette sournoise qu'on croit, qui vient quand on ne l'attend pas, qui se dissimule si bien que lorsqu'elle est venue plus personne n'est là . . . »
>
> « Gens de Dieu, vous êtes avertis . . . On meurt, lucidement, car la mort est violence qui triomphe, négation qui s'impose. Que la mort dès à present soit familière à vos esprits . . . »[2]

In a sense, la Grande Royale is only asking her society to accept its own death, just as it has always accepted the fact of death itself. If the death of each believer is seen by the community as an affirmation of communal life, an earnest of continuity and renewal, then must not the whole society consent to die, in the faith that another will be born from the fallen seed? Looked at in this way, the "death" of Samba Diallo, who is a kind of sacrifice offered up on the altar of the white man's technology and secular power, is merely symbolic of a larger death, undergone in the same spirit of sacrifice. It is the very custodians of the Toucouleur culture, its chiefs, elders and Imans, whom she urges to push their children into the French school:

> — L'école où je pousse nos enfants tuera en eux ce qu'aujourd'hui nous aimons et conservons avec soin, à juste titre. Peut-être notre souvenir lui-même mourra-t-il en eux . . . Ce que je propose c'est que nous acceptions de mourir en nos enfants et que les étrangers qui nous ont défait prennent en eux toute la place que nous aurons laissée libre . . .
>
> — Mais, gens de Diallobé, souvenez-vous de nos champs quand approche la saison des pluies. Nous aimons bien nos champs, mais que faisons-nous alors ? Nous y mettons le fer et le feu, nous les tuons. De même, souvenez-vous : que faisons-nous de nos réserves de graines quand il a plu ? Nous voudrions bien les mangers, mais nous les enfouissons en terre.
> (pp. 62—63)

The ghost-like Samba Diallo who returns, years later, from the Sorbonne, unable to pray, unable to work, unable to rest, compelled at last to run towards the physical death that can alone resolve the spiritual one, has been prefigured in these sombre words. But what is the truth that Samba Diallo discovers in death, which his father has always insisted can be found there and only there? To learn this we must study the difficult dialogue of the last chapter, where a voice (the Master's? God's?) instructs the newly-dead Samba Diallo in the nature of being and the meaning of existence.

In the aftermath of death, Samba Diallo is still close to "la rondeur fermé" of the world, to the bright surface of appearance which throws back to us the glance we turn upon it. As the voice leads him away from illusion, he too, like the dreamer in *Dramouss,* feels the sensation of a mounting stream, but the stream is within him, it is himself, and he cries out:

> — Où es-tu ?. Je ne te vois plus. Il n'y a que cette turgesence qui sourd en moi, comme fait l'eau nouvelle dans le fleuve en crue.

and the voice replies:

> — voici que tu renais à l'être. Il n'y a plus de lumière, il n'y a plus de poids, l'ombre n'est plus. Sens qu'il n'existe pas d'antagonismes. (p. 203)

Now the dead man feels, for the first time, that his baffled thought no longer returns to him "like a wounded bird" but soars on into the infinite. Sight and sound are no longer turned back towards their human source by the hard surface of appearance. The old self is dying and he is gradually filled, drowned by the new awareness:

> — Je suis deux voix simultanées. L'une s'éloigne et l'autre croît. Je suis seul. Le fleuve monte ! Je déborde . . . (p. 204)

The last paragraph of the book carries a complex realization of the relationship between instant and infinity. The thought of man matches itself to the pulse of the instant it inhabits, like the breath in a blowpipe. Within the fortress of the instant, man is king, for the instant is infinite, *as long as it lasts.* "La pureté de l'instant est faite de l'absence du temps." Within the brilliant dome of the instant man flutteres and creates himself, for when he turns his look upon a wave in the ocean of time, it hardens into Being.

The visions of reality which close these two novels of the Western Sudan may be compared with the pagan faith in continuity which sustains the old blind woman, Naana, in Ayi Kwei Armah's *Fragments.* It is convenient at this moment to step out of francophone literature, for the opening and closing pages of Armah's Ghanaian novel provide the completest exposition in recent African fiction of a view of continuity less metaphysical than that found in the Islamic writers. It is true that even la Grande Royale's analogy of the burnt field and the buried seed is pagan in feeling, since it appeals to the manifest circularity of the seasons and the crops to establish faith in the return of life. But this kind of autochthonous faith is more pervasive in *Fragments,* where no appeal is made to a world religion to reinforce its direct reference to human observation of decay and renewal.

Fragments also offers an imagery of sacrifice surrounding the departure of the chosen son overseas; like Samba Diallo, he is as one killed and sent to the spirit-land in order that his ghost may return with good things; but the expectations of this family are poisoned with materialism and Naana is fearful of what the perverted rituals will produce. Baako, her beloved grandson, will return; but for what, and as what?

> Each thing that goes away returns and nothing in the end is lost. The great friend throws all things apart and brings all things together again ... That is how all living things come back after long absences and in the whole great world all things are living things. All that goes will return. He will return.
> How can I not know it when all my years I have watched the sun go down times unending toward the night only to come again from the dawn the opposite way? Too true, it is so long since last I saw the sun going and coming. But my skin continues still to tell the heat from the cold, and I know it is I who have changed, not the changing circle of the world itself.[3]

Her dread is realized in the event, for the Baako who returns is torn between his disgust at the world that awaits him, and his guilt at feeling that disgust. He withdraws into an isolation as complete as Naana's but less tolerable in the young than in the old and blind. The strain of standing alone not only looks like insanity in a self-busy world: perhaps it is insanity. Naana can do nothing to help him, herself an outcast on the threshold of death, but she alone understands his anguish. Finally, she can only cross that threshold towards which her impatient relatives have thrust her. Like the two novels we began with, *Fragments* also ends in a confrontation with the eternal return:

> ... For what purpose do you throw us such blinding sweetness when our end is death?
> I am approaching you. Forgive me. I know of the screens of life you have left us: veils that rise in front of us, cutting into easy pieces eternity and the circle of the world, so that until we have grown tall enough to look behind the next veil we think the whole of life is the little we are allowed to see, and this little we clutch at with such desperation ...
> I am here against the last of my veils. Take me—I am ready. You are the end. The beginning. You who have no end. I am coming. (pp. 286—87)

Naana's final response to death is to recognize at last her involvement with it. By a total participation in the physical world of earth and sea; of animal, plant and tree; man experiences the world existentially and cannot see his death as an isolated fact, or as any significant interruption in the affirmation of life.

This experiencing of the world is particularly evident in the work of another francophone writer, the Congolese poet Tchicaya U Tam'si. His published work is so extensive that it seems best, for purposes of a short paper, to confine our examples to a single volume, *Feu de Brousse,* which was published in 1957. The poem "Presence" is a particularly intense expression of the very process of participation, of that opening of oneself to the world of which the voice spoke to Samba Diallo. And, as so often in poetry, it is where sea and light intermix, in the green half-light of the seaweed and the shrimp, that U Tam'si detects the elements of rebirth:

> n'ayant pas trouvé d'hommes
> sur mon horizon
> j'ai joué avec mon corps
> l'ardent poème de la mort
> j'ai suivi mon fleuve,
> vers des houles froides et courantes
> je me suis ouvert au monde,
> des algues
> ou grouillent des solitudes
> aux solitudes ouvrez les halliers
> au soleil
> ouvrez ma chair
> au sang mûr des revoltes
> le sperme réel par des souffles m'assimile
> aux levures des feuilles et des tornades
> ma chevelure rèche à tous les vents
> s'arc boute
> mes mains humides à tous les germes
> portent mes pieds profonds à toutes latitudes
> a toute les latitudes
> la mort lente avec ses soleils richissimes m'assimile
> présence truquée
> je serai perfide
> puis dieu des armées
> le christ m'a trahi
> en se laissant trouer le peau
> qui voulait qu'on fit le preuve de sa mort
> christ traître
> voici ma chair de bronze
> et mon sang fermé
> par d'innombrables moi cuivre et zinc
> par les deux pierres de mon cerveau
> eternel par ma mort lente
> poisson coelacanthe[4]

Perhaps it would be useful to offer a translation of this fairly complex poem, which borrows from the Surrealists a form without punctuation or syntactical divisions; relying upon a rapid flow of imagery to make its effects:

> Having found no men
> on my horizon
> I played with my body
> the ardent poem of death
> I followed my river
> to the cold and surging billows

I opened myself to the world
of sea weeds
where solitudes crawl
open the thickets to solitude
to the sun
open my flesh
to the ripe blood of riots
the breath of sperm mingles me
into the yeast of leaves and storms
and my hair roughened by all the winds
stands on edge
my hands moist to all seeds
carry my feet deep into space
into all latitudes
and I resemble slow death with its rich suns
faked presence I shall be unfaithful
for christ the god of armies
has betrayed me
when he allowed his skin to be pierced
to offer us the mere proof of his death
treacherous christ
here is my flesh of bronze
and my blood closed
by the numberless I copper and zinc
by the two stones of my brain
eternal by my slow death
a coelacanth

In the opening lines, the interpenetration of the poet with the world is surely analogous with the way death interpenetrates all nature and thereby asserts its continuity, just as the setting sun is a necessary prelude to the risen? So that when the poet reaches his maximum extension of sensibility, he resembles "slow death with its rich suns." Then comes the juxtaposition with Christ who "allowed his skin to be pierced." In other words, the image offered to the world by Christ's death is a false one, which suggests that penetration of the human citadel by external reality constitutes death. On the contrary, it is the mingling of oneself with "the yeast of leaves and storms" which constitutes the process of both death and rebirth, of cyclical change and of the continuity it expresses. Because the poet's attitude towards "mingling," towards "opening himself to the world," is positive and outflowing, it is also invulnerable, like "copper and zinc," compared to the pricked puppet which is the image of Christ in this poem. Finally comes the image of the coelacanth, lurking and reproducing in the depths for millenia after its supposed extinction. For better effect, it is in the deepest seas around Africa that it lives.

Other poems of *Feu de Brousse* offer striking conceptual similarities with the literature looked at earlier. This despite the immense physical and cultural distance separating the Congo from the Senegal and the Upper Niger, and the fact that the external religious influence working upon immemorial African pagan concepts is here Roman Catholicism rather than Islam. The

first poem of the collection offers lines which recapture the imagery of the
ascending smoke of the burnt offering, itself redemptive and transformative,
which we saw in the prison scene of *Dramouss* and to some extent in the fire
imagery used by la Grande Royale:

A Travers Temps et Fleuve

un jour il faudra se prendre
marcher haut les vents
comme les feuilles des arbres
pour un fumier pour un feu
qu'importe
d'autres ages feront de nos âmes
des silex
gare aux pieds nus
nous serons sur tous les chemins (p. 7)

Here U Tam'si, who is often like Aimé Césaire in the rapidity of his transformations, jolts us with the sharp pain of recognition; what a moment before
was whirling above our heads now threatens our naked feet, like a jagged flint
in the pathway of "time," our illusory journey.

The other example comes from the closing lines of the poem "Vertige,"
where U Tam'si, after a long struggle to place in relationship the broken
rhythms of the river's flow, the burnt bush, the torn thighs of human suffering, suddenly recovers his faith in human solidarity and the return of life.
Once again there are men on his horizon: he understands the meaning of fire
and the brief flame of sex, which is nevertheless an ever-flowing source. All
can be knit together by the griot's (poet's) tongue, for he alone has the audacity to become the rainbow, the covenant of renewal, which the snake only
dreams of becoming (the rainbow-snake is another image travelling with us
from the Senegal to the Congo). In the structure of this poem, penis and tongue become alternatives in the search for vital connection, which only the
latter can truly discover:

sous les paupières
le long d'une nuit lourde
le griot revient déjà

cache son sexe
crache sa langue aux savanes claires
le soleil s'étonne
de les voir reverdir sous nos yeux
nous sommes sauvés

rhythmes cassés sauvés
brousses brulées sauvées
reins cassés sauvées
le fleuve s'en va droit à la mer

il est un main ici
il est un cil ici
il est un bras ici
et tous deux revenons solidaires
je vois des hommes
au delà de leur propre horizon
et je comprends le feu comme ma présence
je suis la chair
de ceux qui me portent
j'ai compris ma source comme la flamme d'un sexe
à laver l'approbre

comme va la fleuve
nous sommes sauvés

mes yeux sont des matrices
le serpent revait d'être arc-en-ciel
il lui manquait l'audace
ou la perfidie
mais moi j'ai cette perfidie . . .
ordonnez-moi la chair humaine
je suis le frère d'homme
rejoignez-moi
où va le fleuve (pp. 29—30)

The very river whose broken waves precipitated all the hesitations and doubtful eddies of the poem, asserts with its underlying flow all those perceptions which finally complete its unity. It is when the poet "spits his tongue into the bright savannahs" that he is able to march and mingle with that flow.

Can we attempt to say what unites these four writers, of Guinea, Senegal, Ghana and Congo, in their view of the nature of being? It is surely their common insistence that man realizes his being only in participation with the world, not in withdrawal from it. Denial of death, which reaches its apotheosis in the funeral parlors of California, comes only when man refuses to recognize his identity with the flowing and recurring patterns of nature. On the level of human affairs, this identity asserts itself in love (quite opposite to the cold separation of lust) and in mutual responsibility—"I am the flesh of those who carry me." Everything that makes for individual isolation, accumulation, competition and its inevitable concommitant of subjugation, is here rejected. It is the stuff of death in its most negative sense, and the only thing that makes it absolute[5]. It is a real acceptance of the conquest of Africa to accept uncritically the values which conquered it.

I am aware that there are many features of African life today which run counter to all these assertions. Perhaps I shall be accused of caution in taking my examples from major literary artists rather than from the presidential palace or the military camp. But then, are we to deny altogether to the writer his own witness, or that responsibility for the fate of others which he is ready to accept? Each of these men has had to come to terms in his own way with the world which has also shaped the politician and the soldier. It was Tchicaya U Tam'si who wrote:

I have often seen
carcasses in the air
where my blood burns.

Notes

1 Camara Laye, *Dramouss* (Paris, 1966), pp. 201—04. All quotations are from this edition.
2 Cheikh Hamidou Kane, *L'Aventure ambiguë* (Paris, 1961), pp. 26—27. All quotations are from this edition.
3 Ayi Kwei Armah, *Fragments* (Boston, 1970), p. 1. All quotations are from this edition.
4 Tchicaya U Tam'si, *Feu de Brousse* (Paris, 1957), pp. 35—37. All quotations are from this edition.
5 Cf. Ruskin in *Unto This Last:* "competition is (in all things) the law of death."

L'evasion de Gola

Bernard B. Dadié

On l'appelait l'Empereur! Un homme bien frêle, le pagne toujours autour des reins, calme, souriant, l'allure souple. Tout le monde le respectait. La prison semblait être son domaine. Sur lui, on racontait de merveilleuses histoires, ses exploits colportés de prison en prison avaient tissé sa légende. On le disait capable de passer au travers des murs les plus épais. Ne s'était-il pas évadé des prisons les mieux surveillées ? N'avait-il pas faussé compagnie aux cerbères les plus vigilants ? Homme de parole lorsqu'il avait dit vouloir s'évader, il s'évadait. Cela tout le monde le savait, les policiers, les régisseurs, les porte-clefs, les gendarmes, toute la gent qui rayonne autour des prisons.

Donc depuis deux jours Gola chaintait:

« Je briserai mes chaines
Le ciel bleu me l'ordonne
Je briserai mes chaines
Le vent rageur me l'ordonne ».

La veille il n'avait pris aucun repas. Il disait avoir la nostalgie, la nostalgie du grand air, et lorsque les copains l'appelaient il répondait :

« Quoi qu'on fasse, on ne fera jamais manger de l'herbe à un aigle, il faut que je m'en aille. La prison, c'est bon pour les blancs, ça fait partie de leur système. Il nous faut refuser leur système. » Et Gola chantait d'une voix qui obligeait chacun à l'écouter, chacun à réfléchir sur son sort... Il disait que personne ne doit accepter les chaines de qui que ce soit. Parce que Gola chantait, les autorités avaient doublé la garde, vérifié les portes, les serrures, remplacé toutes les ampoules grillées, éclairé la cour, les alentours de la prison.

Les condamnés vaquaient à leurs occupations habituelles : travailler à l'extérieur, balayer les rues, des bureaux, les marchés, nettoyer les W. C. publics. Les prévenus dont la plupart attendaient depuis des années d'être jugés, se tassaient au long des murs à la recherche d'ombres bien chétives. Un silence pesait sur eux. Non seulement la surveillance venait d'être renforcée, mais ils apprenaient la mort, au lazaret et à l'hôpital, de trois détenus que les gardes avaient battus férocement, pour l'exemple. Une conscience plus aiguë de leur condition d'homme sans défense s'imposait à eux.

Et depuis deux jours Gola chantait, et les autres prisonniers l'écoutaient chanter. Ce qu'il disait remuait des fibres, revigorait des nerfs détendus par l'inaction ; des yeux lançaient des éclairs. On regardait les porte-clefs avec plus de haine, on murmurait des insultes au passage du régisseur, un homme pourtant pas foncièrement mauvais. Oui, au dehors il y a d'autres ignames, de plus belles ignames pour les repas, du riz d'une autre saveur, des fleurs, des papillons, des oiseaux, de l'eau qui coule en jouant avec les roseaux, des brindilles, de l'eau que frôlent des libellules qui se pourchassent, de l'eau libre. Au dehors, il y a des femmes avec leur démarche coquine, leurs rires provocateurs, leurs œillades qui fouettent le sang, des femmes qui laissent sur leur passage un parfum tout différent de l'odeur de moisissure, de sueur rance, de cuir pourri, de linge sale, de crotte, d'urine que distillent les cellules. Une odeur qui vous colle à la peau, vous sort de tous les pores, une odeur qu'aucun parfum n'arrive à vaincre aisément, l'odeur spécifique de la prison coloniale, où les détenus couchaient sur des planches ou à même le sol, entassés, collés les uns aux autres comme du bétail.

Gola chantait. Naguère, il allait par les villages, libre ; libre de marcher, libre de s'arrêter, libre de tous ses gestes, respirant l'air à pleins poumons, un air pur, tonique.

Il avait ses petites amies qui à cause de lui se querellaient. Dans combien de villages, n'avait-il pas provoqué des dissensions dans des ménages ? Plus craint que l'épervier ! Lorsque Gola venait chanter dans un village, les époux n'étaient guère tranquilles ; il faut reconnaître qu'il s'en allait toujours après avoir enlevé soit une jeune fille, soit une épouse. Il chantait sa vie, Gola.

Tout avait débuté simplement, tout bêtement. Boy chez un agent des affaires indigènes, il lui avait un jour pris cinquante centimes. Conduit au commissariat de police, il avait résisté aux policiers qui le battaient. A proprement parler, il n'avait pas résisté. Ils étaient six à lui taper dessus, de toutes leurs forces. L'un d'eux lui ayant saisi la gorge, il lui fallait se défendre. Il ne se souvenait plus de rien, lorsqu'il revint à lui, on lui dit qu'il avait brisé deux dents à l'un des policiers. On l'avait menotté, promené par la ville, au marché avant d'aller l'enfermer. La semaine suivante à l'audience des flagrants délits, il fut condamné à quatre ans de prison ferme pour vol, violence, résistance à agent de la force publique, coups et blessures. Nul n'est censé ignorer la loi, surtout lorsqu'elle est importée. A ce tribunal il y avait des assesseurs indigènes. C'était pour la forme. En flagrant délit point n'est besoin de chercher midi à quatorze heures. Les faits parlent d'eux-mêmes et la sanction tombe, lourde. Quatre ans de prison. Lui qui avait été battu, lui qui s'était évanoui sous les coups des policiers. Fallait-il se laisser battre ? Torturer ? La force publique ! A six pour battre un homme. Dans le code d'honneur de chez lui, les policiers auraient dû être sanctionnés et lui, chanté par les jeunes filles pour avoir tenu tête à six hommes. Un autre monde maintenant et il ne comprenait pas.

Pourquoi voulait-on le battre puisqu'il avait reconnu les faits ? Etait-ce une maladie chez les policiers de toujours battre les gens ? Maintenant, il se couchait et se réveillait au son des sifflets, il mangeait et accourait au son des sifflets. Plus de nom, mais un matricule, le numéro d'écrou. Plus de sortie le jour, la nuit. Il se couchait dès dix sept heures avant même les poulets au village. Des étoiles, il n'en voyait plus, or Dieu sait s'il aime les regarder, s'il aime regarder la lune chevaucher les nuages. Non, il n'était pas fait pour être prisonnier. Qu'avait-il de commun avec les autres qui subissaient leur sort comme une fatalité ? Evidemment, s'il avait comme tous les autres pris une somme énorme, il aurait pu assurer sa défense, mais . . .

Au cours d'une corvée, il prit le large. Rattrapé, il eut quatre ans de plus. Ne supportant pas le climat des prisons, il s'évada encore. Repris, il eut dix autres années. Deux ans après, il reprit sa liberté. Elément extrêmement dangereux, recherché à toutes les frontières, dans les colonies voisines, il fut repris dans son village auprès de ses parents. Nouvelle condamnation qui le conduisit dans les pénétenciers les plus durs d'alors, notamment à Fobato. Trois ans s'écoulèrent, le temps d'étudier les lieux et d'endormir la vigilance des gardiens. Un matin, il faussa compagnie à ses géoliers. Plus de six évasions toutes réussies. Les prisonniers venaient d'avoir leur empereur.

Parce que depuis deux jours il chantait, on l'avait mis aux fers par précaution. Il chantait, Gola, et personne ne dormait. Il chantait sa jeunesse, ses parents, son village, ses femmes, ses enfants . . . Sa voix emplissait la prison, sortait de la prison. Il chantait la pluie, le soleil, le vent, la brise, les fleurs, les parfums des sous-bois, les ébats des jeunes gens. Il chantait tout ce qui hors des murs hérissés de tessons de bouteilles, avait corps, mouvement.

> Je briserai mes chaines
> Le ciel bleu me l'ordonne
> Je briserai mes chaines
> Le vent rageur me l'ordonne

A ses yeux défilaient les rizières, les bananeraies, les palmeraies, à ses narines passait et repassait le fumet si spécial du nouveau riz accompagné de poulet bien gras.

Gola tira sur ses chaines, les chaines résistèrent . . . Il savait qu'il bravait un régime d'oppression, aussi méprisait-il les gardes-cercle vils serviteurs des occupants que ses grands pères avaient combattus glorieusement. Ils étaient tous morts la lance au poing pour ne pas survivre à la mort de leurs droits. Gola tira sur les chaines. Les chaines résistèrent. Dans la cour le vent balayait les feuilles et passait rageur dans les arbres. Le bruit de l'océan s'enflait, tout à coup le tonnerre gronda, au loin ... Dans sa cellule étroite, couché sur le dos, à même le sol, Gola s'était tu. Un silence profond tout d'un coup pesa sur la prison. On entendait des gens tousser, le coassement des crapauds ... Gola tirait sur ses chaines, lentement, longuement, douloureusement. Le porte-clefs par le judas vint observer Gola toujours couché sur le dos, revérifier les serrures et, rassuré, s'en alla la lampe tempête dans la main gauche. Gola tira sur ses chaines patiemment, décidé à les briser, à se libérer. Les pieds et les poignets saignaient. Dans sa jeunesse l'éducation l'avait formé pour se dominer. Ce fut donc les chaines qui crièrent, desserrèrent les dents, vaincues. La lutte dura plus de deux heures. La lutte entre l'homme et les fers.

La chaine de la main droite fut la première à céder puis, la main gauche et ensuite celle des pieds. Gola était libre. Il entendit des clefs tinter. C'était la seconde ronde du porte-clefs. Il resta couché. Le porte-clefs ouvrit le judas, les clefs tintèrent une éternité Gola et le garde se regardèrent dans les yeux comme pour se narguer. Il ne bougeait pas. Le porte-clefs l'appela, il répondit. Les clefs tintèrent, puis s'éloignèrent. Le vent toujours soufflait et le sable et les feuilles tourbillonnaient. Une porte fut rabattue bruyamment. Le porte-clefs était rentré. Un répit d'une demi-heure à mettre à profit. Gola se dressa. Il ne semblait pas sentir les douleurs qu'il avait aux poignets et aux chevilles. Il recula, prit son élan, s'accrocha aux barreaux. Comment s'y prit-il ? Il en brisa trois et par cette ouverture sauta dans la cour. Fit-il du bruit ? Est-ce réflexe de limier ? L'un des porte-clefs jouant aux cartes dans une salle enfumée, leva la tête, tendit l'oreille, hésita, jeta un coup d'œil par la fenêtre ouverte, tira sur sa cigarette et reprit le jeu. Gola n'avait plus peur lorsqu'il s'évadait, étant devenu un spécialiste, un expert dans ce domaine. Là où tous les autres perdraient la tête, il gardait la sienne froide. Maître de la situation.

Le policier qui avait levé la tête, remonta la mèche de la lampe, regarda encore dans la cour, soupçonneux. Gola le vit allumer une autre cigarette et lancer la fumée en l'air. Le tonnerre continuait de gronder, annonçant l'imminence de la pluie. On l'entendait rugir du côté de la forêt, du côté de l'océan. On aurait dit que tous les bruits s'étaient concentrés sur la prison. Un coup sec, la foudre venait de tomber quelque part. Les lampes s'éteignirent brusquement et la pluie se mit à tomber ... Le porte-clefs ferma sa fenêtre ; du seuil de la porte il jeta un coup d'œil dans la cour. Le vent qui soufflait fort éteignit la lampe tempête qu'il avait levée à hauteur de sa tête pour examiner la cour. Il crut avoir entendu un rire, des pas, avoir aperçu une ombre. On racontait aussi que la prison certaincs nuits était visitée par des génies et des revenants. Il rentra et tira la porte. Après tout pour ce qu'il gagnait par mois. La solde du régisseur ne dépassait-elle pas celle des huit porte-clefs indigènes ? Il tira encore la porte, plus fort.

Gola était au dehors. Devant lui la route, la route de la liberté dans le chant des coqs et des muezzins.

Les débuts du roman de moeurs sénégalais

Eberhard Müller-Bochat

La naissance du mouvement de la négritude a été décrite par Lilian Kesteloot et est bien connue depuis.

En 1932 parut à Paris une revue dont les collaborateurs étaient de jeunes étudiants martiniquais ; elle s'intitulait : « Légitime Défense ». D'un manifeste elle avait à la fois le ton et le caractère et revendiquait une littérature authentique et autochtone pour les Antilles. Cette littérature devait avoir pour point de départ la réflexion sur le fait que le monde des Antilles porte davantage l'empreinte de l'Afrique que celle de l'Europe. Les parents spirituels de cette idée étaient en premier lieu les auteurs de la « négro-renaissance » aux Etats-Unis et l'ethnologue haitien Price-Mars.

Un tel programme n'était ni du goût des Français ni de celui des Antillais de la vieille génération. La revue « Légitime Défense » dut cesser de paraître dès le premier numéro. Ses jeunes éditeurs l'avaient plus ou moins prévu. Toujours est-il que, dans ce premier et unique numéro, on peut lire cette phrase : « Cette petite revue, outil provisoire, s'il casse, nous saurons trouver d'autre instrument ».[1]

Et de fait, il se trouva bientôt un autre instrument pour répandre la conscience maintenant éveillée de la culture africaine. En 1934 la revue « L'Etudiant noir » fait son apparition à Paris ; elle continuera de paraître jusqu'en 1940. Cet organe n'était plus seulement le porte-parole des intellectuels des Caraïbes mais établissait le lien avec Africains d'Afrique — de la « mère Afrique — », et devenait la tribune où se célébraient les valeurs spécifiques de la civilisation africaine. Ce pont jeté dans la direction de la vraie Afrique en même temps que la connaissance de ce qui constituait à l'époque l'africanistique moderne (Frobenius, Delafosse, etc.) voilà en quoi consistait l'élément à proprement parler nouveau de la « négritude » francophone, par rapport à la négro-renaissance nord-américaine.

Les jeunes auteurs de la revue, qui dans l'histoire du mouvement de la négritude devaient s'attacher la plus grande célébrité, étaient des lyriques. C'étaient le Guyanais Léon Gontran Damas, le Sénégalais Léopold Sédar Senghor et le Martiniquais Aimé Césaire. C'est dans les années quarante que leur étoile commença de briller.

D'autres Sénégalais que Senghor faisaient partie du groupe de « L'Etudiant noir », notamment Birago Diop et Ousmane Socé Diop. Celui-ci fut le premier à prendre la plume en tant que romancier et à aborder le public avec son livre : *Karim, roman sénégalais* (1935).

Encore avant que ce cercle lyrique ne commençât de rayonner, ce « roman sénégalais » constitue la pierre de base d'un complexe de littérature néo-africaine et plus particulièrement, de littérature sénégalaise. Nous le désignerons avec circonspection comme un « roman de moeurs ». Force nous est d'être circonspect quant à l'emploi de ce terme, dans la mesure où la description des moeurs et du mode de vie a une autre raison d'être ici que dans le groupe de romans européens pour lequel on a, au début, créé ce mot. Il n'est pas jusqu'à la fonction que le roman de moeurs est appelé à remplir auprès de son public qui ne soit spécifique et ne s'applique à la situation particulière dans laquelle le mot d'ordre de la négritude pouvait prendre naissance et produire son effet électrisant.

Ce n'est pas un hasard si les premiers pas sur le terrain littéraire furent faits par des auteurs sénégalais. La place occupée par le Sénégal à l'intérieur de l'ensemble des anciennes colonies françaises sur le sol africain, était, sous bien des rapports, une place particulière. La présence française remontait là à très longue date et la tradition française y était plus profondément enracinée que dans les autres territoires. Dès le XVIIème siècle, il existait là des communes françaises (Saint-Louis, Rufisque, Gorée). En 1857 Dakar était fondée, une ville qui, grâce à la situation remarquable de son port gagnait rapidement en importance et devait devenir plus tard la capitale non seulement du Sénégal, mais de toute l'Afrique occidentale française. Les habitants de ces 4 communes jouissaient de privilèges, dont ce n'est pas la place ici de raconter l'histoire ni les avatars. D'un autre côté, nulle part ailleurs en Afrique, les immigrants français ne furent aussi nombreux de sorte que les contacts entre Français et Africains étaient particulièrement intenses.

Cette étroite interpénétration du Sénégal et de la France n'était pas sans poser de problèmes sur lesquels les esprits devaient se diviser. La possibilité de l'assimilation s'offrait là plus fortement que partout ailleurs en Afrique noire. Mais les opinions des Africains pouvaient fort diverger dans leur appréciation de la situation. Les uns voyaient un idéal dans l'européanisation, les autres se croyaient appelés à découvrir l'authenticité de leur propre physionomie culturelle et à la mettre en valeur. Ce dernier point justement constitue le credo du mouvement de la négritude qui, pour ce qui est de ses tenants africains — fut et est assumée en majeure partie par les auteurs sénégalais. La composition du groupe de « L'Etudiant noir » le montre pour la période qui va jusqu'à débâcle de 1940. Ce jugement est confirmé pour la période qui suivit la deuxième guerre mondiale par la revue « Présence Africaine », qui est restée jusqu'à aujourd'hui, l'organe de l'Afrique francophone.

Mais les Sénégalais avaient encore une raison de plus que les autres Africains de faire de leur relation avec la France un sujet de réflexion et de se sentir mis au défi de se prendre eux-mêmes pour sujet de représentation, car non seulement ils se voyaient confrontés dans leurs pays à un milieu français solidement structuré et établi de longue date, mais encore c'étaient eux aussi qui, en raison de leurs vieux privilèges, venaient nombreux en France, voire, qui prenaient même part en tant que soldats aux deux guerres mondiales. Ceci explique que pour le Français moyen, ils aient été le prototype du noir d'Afrique et de ce fait, la cible de nombreux préjugés.

L'auteur nord-américain Claude McKay — un noir lui aussi, en contact à Paris avec les jeunes protagonistes de la négritude, a décrit dans son roman *Banjo* (1928) ce que signifiait, dans la France d'alors, d'être un Sénégalais. Ci-dessous, brièvement, l'épisode qui s'y rapporte. Le personnage de roman Ray fait connaissance à Marseille d'un étudiant martiniquais noir qui est la personnification même de ce zèle spécifiquement martiniquais fi l'assimilation. Selon lui, la plus grande gloire de sa patrie insulaire consiste à avoir donné à la France, la mère patrie, Joséphine de Beauharnais, une blanche qui, en tant que soi-disant créole, crée le lien entre les Martiniquais de couleur qui, selon la terminologie du pays porte aussi le nom de créoles.

> — Je ne vois pas tes raisons d'être si fier, lui dit Ray. Ce n'était pas une femme de couleur.
> — Non ... Mais elle était créole et, à la Martinique, nous sommes plutôt des créoles que des noirs. Nous sommes fiers de l'impératrice, à la Martinique ; là-bas, la bonne société est très distinguée et elle parle un français très pur qui n'a rien à faire avec ce français vulgaire de Marseille.

Le jeune Noir martiniquais condamne catégoriquement le célèbre roman africain de son compatriote René Maran *Batouala* : « C'était un livre dangereux, très fort, très fort ... ».

Finalement Ray invite le Noir martiniquais au café — lieu de rencontre des Africains —.

> L'autre refusa, disant qu'il ne tenait pas à fréquenter les Sénégalais, et que le bar était d'ailleurs un bar des bas-fonds. Il crut devoir mettre en garde Ray contre les Sénégalais.
> — Ils ne sont pas comme nous, lui dit-il. Les blancs se conduiraient mieux avec les noirs, si les Sénégalais n'étaient pas là. Avant la guerre et le débarquement des Sénégalais en France, c'était parfait pour les noirs. On nous aimait et l'on nous respectait, tandis que maintenant ...[2]

La diversité des points de vue dans cet épisode est extrêmement significative. Le Nord-américain est le plus émancipé. L'Antillais, en proie à tous les complexes de l'assimilé, connaît tous les faux-fuyants intellectuels du Noir qui voudrait passer pour un Français.[3] Les Sénégalais, eux, sont, pour finir, le bouc émissaire, qu'ils rendent responsables de l'aversion qu'éprouvent les Blancs pour les Noirs.

Nous retrouverons le titre *Banjo* quelques années plus tard dans la bibliothèque d'un étudiant de philosophie africain, qui joue un rôle dans le second roman d'Ousmane Socé Diop *Mirage de Paris* (1937).[4] Et là aussi nous verrons confirmé que pour le Français moyen, les Sénégalais personnifient les Africains en-soi : « . . . car tous les Noirs d'Afrique ne sont pas des Sénégalais comme l'usage le veut en France »[5].

Il faut situer *Karim — roman sénégalais* devant la toile de fond de ces problèms. Toutefois, on s'interdira la compréhension de ce livre, qui, en quelque sorte, marque le commencement de la littérature sénégalaise et fait aujourd'hui partie des canons classiques de l'école sénégalaise, si, suivant l'invite du sous-titre « roman », on s'attend à ce que l'accent soit mis sur l'enchevêtrement de destins humains. Nous avons plutôt affaire ici à l'aimable simplicité d'une églogue qui, d'une manière poétique, donne de l'éclat à la vie sénégalaise.

Le fait que l'ébauche d'une action confère au livre un caractère encore plus sensiblement romanesque, montre combien nous sommes proches de l'inspiration bucolique. Il n'est pas jusqu'à la fable elle-même qui, de par sa structure thématique, ne soit comparable aux fables bucoliques. Le jeune Karim tombe amoureux d'une jeune fille qui lui rend son amour. L'apparition d'un rival qui fait un étalage tapageur de sa richesse trouble l'idylle. Karim, blessé dans son honneur et son amour-propre s'en va au loin et auprès d'autres femmes chercher le bonheur, mais à la fin, le cercle se ferme. Karim rentre et épouse la première fiancée.

On ne peut concevoir histoire plus simple, ni, si l'on veut, plus naive, mais l'action n'est qu'un prétexte. Elle est, à l'instar du genre bucolique, le fil sur lequel on enfile, comme des perles, des textes de caractère différent. Des passages de prose narrative ou descriptive alternent avec des dialogues, de petits morceaux en vers et des enclaves qu'on pourrait définir comme des « poèmes en prose ». Pas la moindre trace d'approfondissement psychologique. Karim est — disons-le paradoxalement — l'apothéose d'un jeune et gentil Sénégalais moyen: beau, bien fait, sympathique, fier, loyal et intelligent, mais rien dans son histoire qui fasse s'égarer le lecteur à la recherche de détails qui individualisent sa personne.

Cette technique est familière à qui pratique la littérature pastorale. Le « héros », aussi gentil qu'abstrait, n'est rien qu'une plaisante marionette servant à visualiser une casuistique.

Cette casuistique, à son tour est là, pour dresser le tableau d'une civilisation à l'encontre de tous les préjugés, bien policée, enjouée, tout compte fait exubérante, autonome, sans pour autant éviter les contacts avec l'Europe.

Ecrit à Paris, ce petit roman est un vademecum nostalgique pour Africains en même temps qu'un abécédaire explicite pour Européens, une fable, dans laquelle les notions sénégalaises de bonheur, de civilisation et de sociabilité sonst exemplifiées. C'est un inventaire — dans sa majeure partie apologétique, mais aussi, par endroits, ironique et critique —, un livre d'images poétique, riche en miniatures colorées, lequel pousse à l'absurde la conception d'une Afrique non civilisée.

Karim est conduit de situation en situation mais, ainsi que nous l'avons déjà dit, aucune d'elle n'est humainement parlant extraordinaire ; elles visent toutes au typique. Elles illustrent les moeurs sénégalaises et la civilité sénégalaise. Par « illustrer », nous entendons le mot dans son double sens de: « mettre en lumière » et de « transfigurer ».

Certes, ce roman transfigure. Le repos bien mérité après le travail, les dimanches et les fêtes jouent un rôle prépondérant. Même la description du quotidien à un je ne sais quoi qui rappelle la fête.

Cependant ceci ne veut aucunement dire que Karim fuie le travail ou ne soit pas à la hauteur de sa tâche dans la vie quotidienne. Bien au contraire. Le jeune homme est présenté comme un comptable vraiment capable et estimé. Mais le quotidien est européen, parce que les maisons de commerce sont européennes et seuls, le repos, les dimanches et les jours de fête permettent de peindre ce qui est le thème de ce roman, c'est-à-dire le charme et la courtoisie des moeurs sénégalaises.

Le répertoire des fêtes et des réjouissances est tout à fait éclectique et reflète la symbiose de civilisations différentes, caractéristique du Sénégal. Il y a les cérémonies privées: les visites de courtoisie, fiançailles et mariages. Il y a les fêtes nationales, à commencer par le 14 juillet. Il y a les fêtes musulmanes, mais aussi les chrétiennes (telle la procession à laquelle Karim est convié par une jeune fille chrétienne).

Il faut voir un rapport direct entre l'atmosphère de fête du roman et la profusion de détails avec laquelle le conteur dépeint l'habillement. Karim aime les vêtements majestueux aux couleurs éclatantes, de son pays, mais il se laisse aussi, un temps prendre au charme de la mode européenne. Mais surtout, ce qu'il décrit, ce sont le soin et le goût que les femmes et les jeunes filles mettent à combiner les différentes parties des vêtements. C'est une revue de couleurs et d'étoffes magnifiques. Dans ces descriptions s'exprime toute la fierté éprouvée devant l'originalité de culture sénégalaise qui porte l'empreinte du monde arabe, de l'Afrique noire et récemment aussi, de l'Europe. A la manière critique, mais cependant non polémique dont sont présentées les influences européennes, s'annonce déjà la formule d'un « métissage intellectuel » qui caractérisera Ousmane Socé dans son roman suivant et qui n'est pas éloigné du programme que Senghor préconise depuis longtemps sous la devise « culture de l'universel ».

Les thèmes de la galanterie, de l'amitié et de l'hospitalité constituent d'autres points de cristallisation de l'action. La mentalité sénégalaise est décrite avec une certaine satisfaction, mais non sans autocritique ironique. Karim et ses camarades sont généreux et orgueilleux, et ils le sont jusqu'à l'exagération. (Le conteur se plaît au jeu des exagérations). Leur amitié est désintéressée, fidèle et loyale. Finalement un rôle non négligeable dans l'économie du livre est attribué au personnage du « griot » (musicien et rhapsode), autrement dit à la musique et à la poésie dans la vie du Sénégal traditionnel; cet aspect lui aussi fait partie du caractère de fête qui est celui de tout le livre.

Nous avons, pour prendre le contre-pied de malentendus et de fausses espérances que pourrait éveiller ce « roman », assimilé Karim à la littérature bucolique. Cependant le milieu où se situe l'action n'a absolument rien de champêtre. Bien au contraire, tout se joue dans la vieille ville coloniale, riche de tradition de Saint-Louis, où a vécu Karim et à Dakar, ambitieuse ville commerciale et industrielle, où il essaie d'oublier ses chagrins d'amour et de faire fortune. Et pourtant la vie qu'il dépeint est très éloignée des problèmes qui occupent le roman européen des grandes villes des 19 et 20 e siècles, problèmes qui jouent également un rôle important dans le roman african depuis les années 50 (qu'on pense à Mongo Beti ou à Ousmane Sembène). Ce que Karim dépeint, à côté de quelques soucis journaliers bénins racontés sur le ton badin, ce sont les joies innocentes de la vie citadine. Et si l'histoire littéraire connaît déjà une « ecloga pastoralis » et une « ecloga piscatoria », on serait tenté ici de parler d'une « ecloga urbana ». La spontanéité, la cordialité et la grâce de moeurs, tout empreints de tradition, sont les traits dominants d'une vie dont, apparemment, sont absents les problèmes graves.

On pourrait aussi à l'égard de ce petit roman parler d'un réalisme utopique. Le réalisme existe, car il s'agit là de l'inventaire sociologique et folklorique d'une réalité urbaine. Utopique, cet inventaire l'est parce qu'il fait abstraction des ombres inhérentes à cette réalité, et qu'il fait de la fête quelque chose d'exemplaire. Un voile de mélancolie plane sur cette utopie parce qu'il s'agit d'un inventaire de valeurs morales et esthétiques, qui en raison de progrès de la civilisation moderne pourrait n'appartenir bientôt plus qu'au passé.

Qui aborde ce roman, plein de l'arsenal de nomenclature de l'histoire littéraire européenne, lui associera vite les concepts de « couleur locale » et de « pittoresque ». Ce n'est d'ailleurs pas totalement faux. Cependant il ne faut pas perdre de vue que « couleur locale » et « pittoresque » ont ici une tout autre fonction que dans la littérature européenne correspondante des 19 et 20e siècles. Ce n'est pas un monde étranger qui est décrit ou suggéré ici, mais la personnalité authentique de son propre peuple et de sa propre civilisation. Qu'un Noir africain vivant en Europe, ait pu se pencher avec amour et fierté sur l'image qu'offraient les moeurs de son pays, n'aurait pas été possible sans le programme et l'idéologie de la « négritude ».

Le « roman sénégalais » d'Ousmane Socé a engendré deux sortes de prolongements — ou mieux : de correspondances — ce sont : *Mirages de Paris* (également d'Ousmane Socé) et *Maïmouna* (d'Abdoulaye Sadij).

Deux ans après *Karim*, Socé publiait l'histoire d'un jeune Sénégalais dont le rêve d'aller à Paris pour y vivre, se réalise. Les conditions de vie sont donc ici à l'opposé de celles de Karim, mais l'intention de l'auteur est identiqué. Fara, le protagoniste, fait lui-même l'expérience des préjugés des Français; dans une série de situations, il gagne leur confiance (et, ce faisant, tout naturellement aussi celle de son lecteur européen). Il fait ses preuves en tant que jeune ambassadeur de son pays, voire de son continent, non seulement en incarnant la civilité de son pays dans son comportement, mais aussi en sachant l'expliquer théoriquement. Les causeries avec les Français sur l'Afrique constituent une partie importante du livre et lui confèrent en même temps un caractère à la fois didactique et apologétique.

La véritable action romanesque puise sa substance dans les rapports avec une jeune Française. Mais qui classe ce roman sous la rubrique « love-story », comme l'a fait la critique, commet à coup sûr, une erreur. Il s'agit là beaucoup plus d'un roman-essai sur l'Afrique avec, en supplément, l'amour qu'inspire Paris et la réflexion mélancolique sur la difficulté pour les deux races d'établir entre elles des relations libérées de préjugés. Cette mélancolie a recours à un moyen littéraire et fait mourir les amants de mort romantique afin d'éviter de poser le problème dans toute son âpreté morale et sociale. Si le destin du jeune Africain et de la jeune Française était le thème no 1 du livre, ce serait peut-être une solution facile, mais justement, nous avons affaire là à un exposé sur l'Afrique et l'africanité. En attribuant l'échec de ses protagonistes non pas à leurs problèmes concrets, mais à leur destin romantique, l'auteur a voulu faire preuve de tact humain et politique. Ce roman ne voulait pas être polémique, mais au contraire ébaucher le programme d'une « culture métisse », sans pour autant en escamoter les difficultés humaines.

S'il existe un autre roman complémentaire de *Karim* à bien des égards, c'est *Maïmouna* d'Abdoulaye Sadij.

Sadji est de la même génération qu'Ousmane Socé. Tous deux étaient liés d'amitié. Socé a dédié un de ses livres à Sadji.

Il semble que *Maïmouna*, bien que paru beaucoup plus tard, ait été écrit ou du moins ébauché dès le fin des années 30 — soit peu après *Karim*. Dans l'avant-dernier chapitre, une lettre est datée du 15 septembre 193 . . .; il y est question de la déclaration de la 2ème guerre mondiale. Comme cette déclaration de guerre ne joue pas le moindre rôle dans l'action, ce passage n'est là que pour renseigner sur la date où fut rédigé le roman.

Le roman *Maïmouna* est lui aussi pour une part importante un inventaire des us et coutumes sénégalais reliés avec grâce à l'histoire d'une jeune fille. Le destin personnel du personnage central est ici plus fortement accentué que dans *Karim,* mais les passages où sont décrites les moeurs sont multiples et détaillés. Son intérêt théorique, pour ne pas dire scientifique pour les traditions sénégalaises et leur fonction sociale, Abdoulaye Sadji l'a, du reste, également prouvé dans son dernier livre posthume, paru avec une préface de Senghor: « Education africaine et civilisation ».

Maïmouna complète *Karim* presque point par point en ce qui concerne le thème. L'histoire de Karim se joue entre Saint-Louis et Dakar. Maïmouna, par contre, a grandi dans un petit bourg de l'intérieur ; comme Karim, elle tente sa chance à Dakar pour finir par retourner à son milieu rural, avec cette différence toutefois que le jeune homme rentre vainqueur, alors que la jeune Maïmouna retourne vaincue à ses origines sociales.

Il n'est pas sans intérêt pour comprendre le caractère complémentaire des deux romans de souligner le fait que dans le premier, le protagoniste est un jeune homme alors que dans le second, c'est une jeune fille. Cette différence ouvre des perspectives, elles aussi différentes, sur le panorama des moeurs sénégalaises. Et, compte tenu de leur intérêt théorico-folklorique, les deux oeuvres sont tellement un roman que, dans chaque cas, la perspective considérée est une composante de la forme littéraire.

Cette étude de moeurs dans *Maïmouna* embrasse deux milieux qui forment contraste. La jeune fille grandit à l'intérieur du pays, pauvrement, entourée de la sollicitude maternelle. Nous sont décrits, le milieu défini par les voisins, les formes qui régissent les relations sociales, l'éducation de la jeune fille, le choix des vêtements dans les différentes circonstances, les coiffures appropriées aux différents âges, enfin — et ce n'est pas le moindre — toutes sortes de problèmes psychologiques nés du mélange de religion et de superstition.

Devenue une grande et belle jeune fille, Maïmouna se rend à Dakar, chez sa soeur qui y est mariée. Elle y fait la connaissance d'une vie relativement aisée. La maison de son beau-frère est hospitalière ; les amis y vont et viennent. Qu'il se trouve quelques parasites parmi ces amis, cela est donné à entendre au lecteur avec une fine ironie. Ainsi, comme *Karim*, ce roman critique la prodigalité sénégalaise. Mais surtout la maison du beau-frère est là pour nous faire voir les habitudes d'une famille citadine musulmane d'une grande libéralité.

Maïmouna doit être mariée à Dakar. Les prétendants sont nombreux. Sa beauté lui vaut d'avancer rapidement au rang d' « étoile de Dakar », pour employer la terminologie du cercle qu'elle fréquente, mais son coeur n'appartient à aucun des notables qui lui font la cour. Au contraire, son penchant secret va à un pauvre diable aussi beau et jeune que sympathique. Avec une naïveté totale et sans bien comprendre ce qui lui arrive, elle se laisse séduire. Enceinte et déshonorée, elle retourne au pays, chez sa mère. La petite vérole fait le reste et défigure ce visage naguère si agréable. Maïmouna retourne dans le milcu dont elle voulait se libérer par mariage. Elle devient vendeuse de marché, comme sa mère et accepte son destin.

> « Elle découvrit rapidement un charme profond dans cette perpétuelle exposition des denrées du marché, dans les airs fanfarons de marchandes, dans la succession des foules et jusque dans les odeurs dont l'atmosphère était saturée.
> Avec la fuite des jours son existence passée s'en allait, s'évanouissait, enveloppée dans un nuage aux contours imprécis. Il lui semblait maintenant que ce passé n'avait jamais été qu'un rêve.
> Avec la fuite des jours, la vraie vie, la vie réelle sans tendresse ni leurre, Maïmouna commençait à la découvrir, à l'aimer du même amour que sa brave mère. »

Dans *Karim*, cette ecloga urbana, le destin personnel du protagoniste n'était, ainsi que nous l'avons vu ci-dessus, qu'un canevas. Dans *Maïmouna* le destin personnel de la jeune fille est beaucoup plus accentué sans pour autant que le tableau de moeurs passe à l'arrière-plan. Abdoulaye Sadji, cela est certain, ne voulait écrire ni un roman psychologique ni un roman social, même si les motifs de la séduction et de la maladie constituent le coeur de l'intrigue. Dans l'économie du livre, les pages descriptives l'emportent. Le thème n° 1 est la vie sénégalaise dans son autonomie culturelle, morale et psychologique. Cette description de l'authentique est d'autant plus convaincante qu'elle ne prend jamais la forme d'une glorification fanatique, mais qu'elle se contente d'embrasser les phénomènes avec tendresse et compréhension et que parfois, elle laisse percer un doute ironique sur le bien-fondé de telle ou telle tradition.

Les deux romans traités ici constituent une première phase du roman sénégalais, sinon du roman négro-africain. Ils ne sont certes pas sans scepticisme à l'endroit des influences européennes, toutefois, ils ne polémiquent pas. D'autre part, ils sont de ces premiers témoignages de la prose, où apparaît clairement que les Africains se sont libérés de leurs complexes d'infériorité culturelle, conséquence de l'histoire coloniale, et ont su trouver une manière aussi chaleureuse que naturelle pour peindre leur mode de vie et, plus généralement, l'authenticité de leur civilisation et de leur morale (éthique), authenticité qui n'est pas dénuée d'éclat, que lui confère la transfiguration poétique.

Bientôt d'autres types de roman viendront occuper le champ de la littérature. Leurs thèmes, il les puiseront dans le problème colonial, le problème racial et le problème social. Enfin tout un groupe de romans auront pour thème la confrontation de la culture africaine avec la civilisation scientifique européenne.

Notes

1 Cité d'après L. Kesteloot, *Anthologie négro-africaine* (Verviers, 1967), p. 78.
2 Pour des raisons d' homogénéité linguistique, nous citons ici la traduction française et, plus précisément, d'après Kesteloot, p. 28 f.
3 Le Martiniquais a consacré à ce phénomène une analyse psychiatrique : *Peau noire — masques blancs,* (Paris, 1954).
4 Ousmane Socé, *Mirages de Paris,* (Paris, 1964), p. 145.
5 Ibid., p. 123.

Fonction du heros
dans les oeuvres narratives d'Ousmane Sembene

Roger Mercier

Dans les romans écrits par des auteurs africains d'expressions française, nombreux sont les récits dominés par la figure d'un héros central, qu'une référence explicite soit faite à celui-ci dans le titre (Camara Laye, *L'Enfant noir* ; Bernard Dadié, *Climbié* ; Aké Loba, *Kocoumbo l'étudiant noir*) ou que sa personnalité apparaisse seulement à la lecture du livre (Camara Laye, *Le Regard du roi* ; Cheikh Hamidou Kane, *L'Aventure ambiguë* ; Ahmadou Kourouma, *Les Soleils des indépendances*). La prééminence du personnage ne signifie d'ailleurs pas toujours qu'il ait une dimension héroïque, et il arrive qu'il soit en position de victime humiliée ou ridiculisée (Ferdinand Oyono, *Une Vie de boy, Le Vieux Nègre et la médaille* ; Mongo Beti, *Mission terminée*), sans perdre pour autant ni sa valeur significative, ni le relief que lui confère son choix comme « foyer » du récit, que ce dernier soit au reste écrit à la première ou à la troisième personne.

Un simple coup d'oeil jeté sur la liste, déjà assez longue, des oeuvres narratives d'Ousmane Sembene, le romancier et cinéaste sénégalais, révèle qu'un seul titre, celui de son premier roman, *Le Docker noir*, désigne à l'attention du lecteur le personnage dont les sentiments et l'aventure seront le centre de l'action. Des deux autres titres où l'on croit déceler à première vue le même procédé, l'un, *Voltaïque*, simplement repris de la dernière nouvelle du recueil, renvoie au narrateur de l'anecdote, un mythe avec lequel il n'a d'autre rapport que la nationalité, l'autre, *Vehi Ciosane*, couplé avec celui d'une autre nouvelle, *Le Mandat*, est le nom d'une petite fille de quelques jours, qui symbolise l'Afrique future. Les autres titres témoignent d'une imagination riche et parfois expressive. *Le Mandat*, c'est l'objet qui va causer les malheurs d'Ibrahima Dieng. *Xala*, c'est le sortilège qui empêche El Hadji Abdou Kader Bèye de consommer son mariage avec N'Goné. *O Pays, mon beau peuple* est une sorte d'invocation lyrique. « *Les Bouts de bois de Dieu* » sont une formule usitée dans un dénombrement, à la place du nom des êtres vivants, pour ne pas attirer sur eux le mauvais sort. Enfin *L'Harmattan* est à la fois le titre d'un tableau de Lèye, et le symbole, contenu dans le tableau lui-même, du « sanglot de quatre siècles, soufflé par des millions et des millions de voix ensevelies » et apporté par le vent qui vient du désert. De cette énumération se dégagent deux traits de l'inspiration romanesque de Sembene : l'attention portée à la vie collective, le goût des symboles. C'est à cette lumière que l'on comprendra la fonction qu'il donne aux personnages dans ses romans et ses nouvelles.

Une lecture hâtive des oeuvres de Sembene a parfois conduit les critiques à les classer sous l'étiquette du réalisme (sinon même du réalisme socialiste, puisque le romancier n'a jamais fait mystère de ses convictions marxistes) et à y voir des documents sur la situation matérielle et morale de l'Afrique coloniale et post-coloniale, sur les sentiments des Africains face à leur destinée dans les vingt ou trente dernières années. Avec d'autant plus d'empressement que les indications fournies par Sembene favorisaient la paresse intellectuelle et semblaient dispenser de tout effort de réflexion, on a relevé les coïncidences des intrigues avec la réalité : la vie de docker que Sembene avait menée à Marseille après la fin de la seconde guerre mondiale ; la grève des cheminots du Dakar-Niger, du 10 octobre 1947 au 19 mars 1948, cadre dans lequel se déroulent *Les Bouts de bois de Dieu* ; la campagne pour le référendum de septembre 1958, à laquelle prennent part tous les personnages de *L'Harmattan*.

Outre que ce jugement répond à des conceptions littéraires dont la critique récente a établi le caractère idéaliste insoutenable, reposant sur la division fallacieuse entre le réel et l'écrit, entre le fond et la forme, il méconnaît les déclarations faites par Sembene lui-même, par exemple dans l'Avertissement de *L'Harmattan*. Il commence certes par affirmer son intention de « rester au plus près du réel et du peuple », il se décrit cheminant « sur les sentiers africains, à dos de chameau, en pirogue, en bateau, en auto et à pied pendant six mois » pour rassembler la documentation dont il avait besoin. Mais il précise bien que « *L'Harmattan* ne se passe dans aucun des Etats africains dits d'expression française », qu'il « emprunte à chacun un fait, un événement de la vie de la cité », afin « que chacun y décèle, y voie un peu de lui-même selon la vie qu'il mène ». S'il se défend de faire « la théorie du roman africain », il définit fort bien sa propre pratique:

> J'avertis que je ne tente ni oeuvre d'historien ni oeuvre de chroniqueur. Les hommes, les femmes et les enfants évoqués en ces pages sont nés de ma plume et des faits que j'interprète. « Je n'aime pas les héros, ils meurent jeunes », ceux-ci n'en sont pas. Les personnages sont mes enfants. Pour vous des compagnons, avec nos défauts, nos ambitions, nos désirs et nos rêves pour l'avenir.

Ce sont là précisément les problèmes que nous nous proposons d'examiner : la naissance des personnages, leurs rapports avec l'auteur, les modalités de leur présentation ; la manière dont ils sont implantés dans le monde de la fiction, leur existence en tant qu'individus et en tant que membres d'une collectivité ; enfin la relation que l'auteur cherche à nouer avec son lecteur.

En règle générale, Sembene ne commence pas un roman par la présentation directe du personnage qui y jouera le rôle principal. Il arrive qu'il paraisse dès les premières pages, mais au milieu d'un groupe dont il fait partie et où sa personnalité se dissout en quelque sorte, chacun des autres membres étant au fond semblable à lui, et l'individu choisi étant représentatif de l'ensemble :

tel est le cas d'El Hadji Abdou Kader Bèye parmi les « Hommes d'affaires » de la Chambre de Commerce dans *Xala*. Dans *Le Docker noir*, roman dont la construction est particulièrement soignée, l'entrée en scène de Diaw Falla est préparée par une présentation indirecte, l'image que se font de lui, à la veille de son procès, sa mère, sa compagne Catherine et ses amis les Noirs de Marseille : trois images inspirées par la sympathie et qui nous disposent favorablement malgré l'accusation de meurtre portée contre Diaw. Dans *Les Bouts de bois de Dieu* et dans *L'Harmattan*, l'action est engagée par des personnages secondaires. L'épisode initial de *L'Harmattan*, le meurtre d'Antoine Faure et de Rémy Soglo, aura des répercussions sur la suite de l'intrigue, mais son auteur, Digbé, reparaîtra à peine ultérieurement, et il ne contribuera en rien à la connaissance des principaux personnages. Le cas des *Bouts de bois de Dieu* est le plus digne d'attention. De même que dans *O Pays, mon beau peuple,* nous assistons aux efforts d'un personnage lucide et énergique pour transformer la condition de ses compatriotes et compagnons de travail. Mais alors que, dans *O Pays, mon beau peuple,* Oumar Faye était presque continuellement présent, animait les discussions et l'action par ses interventions personnelles, que même son assassinat n'interrompait pas son oeuvre, puisque l'enfant porté par sa femme Isabelle était garant de la continuité, la présence de Bakayoko dans *Les Bouts de bois de Dieu* est d'un ordre différent. Les membres de sa famille, ses compagnons du syndicat, parlent de son attitude envers les siens, de ses conceptions politiques, de sa tournée de long de la ligne de chemin de fer pour soutenir le moral des grévistes. Nous le connaissons donc bien, à travers les jugements des autres, parmi lesquels quelques discordances nous montrent qu'il n'est pas une personnalité d'une seule pièce, mais il ne paraît lui-même, à l'improviste, qu'aux deux tiers du roman, il ne participe du reste en personne qu'à un petit nombre de scènes. C'est donc un personnage dont nous retenons finalement moins quelques traits de caractère individuels que le rayonnement sur les esprits, le rôle d'animateur de foules.

Le mode de présence des personnages, les techniques de caractérisation et de narration sont par suite, dans l'oeuvre de Sembene, très différents de qu'ils étaient dans le roman balzacien aussi bien que de ce qu'ils sont dans le nouveau roman. Plus exactement des transformations fondamentales se font jour au cours de cette production romanesque échelonnée sur dix-sept ans, de 1956 à 1973. Dans *Le Docker noir* (1956), l'innovation technique, encore timide, consiste seulement dans l'adaptation du procédé cinématographique du retour en arrière : l'action ne se déroule pas selon une ligne chronologique rectiligne, mais commence quelques jours avant le procès de Diaw Falla, puis celui-ci, au cours de l'audience, revit les événements passés, et un bref épilogue se situe trois ans après sa condamnation. Si les quelques premières pages nous montrent Diaw à travers la conscience des autres, et si le recours au dialogue est fréquent tout au long du livre, la partie essentielle est conçue selon la formule de la focalisation interne, et c'est le point de vue de Diaw Falla qui prévaut pour le récit de son aventure et pour la peinture de la situation à laquelle lui-même et le cercle de ses proches ont été réduits par son emprisonnement.

Dans ces deux dernières parties l'analyse reste assez proche des procédés du roman français traditionnel, et si le sort de Diaw Falla est donné comme exemple typique de la condition de l'Africain dans le monde créé par la civilisation occidentale, le personnage a une densité psychologique incontestable, peut-être due au fait que, si les événements sont inventés, le milieu et les sentiments sont peints d'après l'expérience personnelle de l'auteur.

Dans la série des trois romans suivants, *O Pays, mon beau peuple* (1957), *Les Bouts de bois de Dieu* (1960), *L'Harmattan* (1964), Sembene a renoncé à la focalisation interne pour revenir à la focalisation zéro du roman classique. Cette transformation dans la technique correspond à un changement de statut du héros. Dans *O Pays, mon beau peuple*, Oumar Faye domine encore largement l'action, mais alors que Diaw Falla représentait, parmi les travailleurs africains de Marseille, un cas exceptionnel par sa conscience syndicale et par ses dons d'écrivain, Oumar Faye n'est plus que le centre d'un petit groupe de militants, noirs et blancs d'ailleurs, où la réflexion sur la situation de l'Afrique et les remèdes à y apporter est le résultat d'une mise en commun des intelligences et des volontés, bien marquée par l'importance donnée aux scènes de discussion et de dialogue. Comme Manuel dans *Gouverneurs de la rosée* de Jacques Roumain, modèle qu'Ousmane Sembene a suivi d'assez près, Oumar Faye est l'éveilleur, et sa disparition est sans conséquences autres que sentimentales, car le mouvement qu'il a lancé a bien démarré et peut continuer sans lui. Dans *Les Bouts de bois de Dieu*, il subsiste un héros dont l'intelligence et l'autorité transcendent celles des autres personnages, qui est pour eux un modèle admiré ou jalousé, à moins qu'il ne soit un adversaire envers qui les sentiments vont de la haine aveugle à l'estime et au respect. Cependant Bakayoko, avons-nous vu, est absent d'une bonne partie des épisodes du roman, et Sembene lui donne alors divers substituts, qui gardent leur individualité propre, Doudou, le secrétaire syndical maladroit et ambitieux, Penda, la prostituée passionnée et généreuse, mais dont la fonction est la même que la sienne, de faire prendre au peuple conscience de lui-même. Dans *L'Harmattan*, la fonction même de héros est supprimée. Sembene présente un petit groupe de personnages dont chacun est représentatif d'un choix politique devant le référendum de septembre 1958, qui devait décider du sort des anciennes colonies françaises. Deux se détachent parmi eux : Tangara, le médecin, partisan du *non*, mais qui maintient une stricte distinction entre ses idées politiques et l'accomplissement de son devoir professionnel, tout en se demandant si cette attitude ne fait pas de lui un bourgeois ; Tioumbé, l'institutrice, qui organise la propagande pour le *non* et milite en même temps pour l'émancipation des femmes, et qui sacrifiera sa vie sentimentale à son devoir politique, laissant partir son amant Sori seul pour la Guinée. Autour de ces deux personnages principaux gravitent quelques figures secondaires, Lèye le peintre, Sori le réparateur de cycles, Koffi le médecin adjoint de Tangara. Aucun d'entre eux ne répond à la conception du héros romanesque, et celui-ci laisse en fait la place à la cellule politique, où les tensions entre orientations individuelles n'empêchent pas l'unanimité à l'heure de l'action.

Cette disparition du héros est plus accentuée encore dans les oeuvres qui ont suivi *L'Harmattan*. Les personnages cessent d'avoir une volonté propre et de conduire leur destinée, ils sont le jouet des événements et des hommes et sont ballottés de mésaventure en mésaventure. Dans *Le Mandat* (1966), Ibrahima Dieng, à partir du moment où il a reçu le mandat de son neveu Abdou, est victime des exigences administratives, qui l'empêchent de le toucher immédiatement, des sollicitations de ses voisins, empressés à profiter de la bonne aubaine, de la méchanceté des hommes, insolence du commis du photographe, vol au préjudice de son cousin Mbaye, si bien qu'à la fin il se retrouve plus malheureux qu'avant, n'ayant pas touché l'argent du mandat et davantage endetté. Dans *Xala* (1973), El Hadji Abdou Kader Bèye, qui vient d'épouser une troisième femme moins par passion que par ostentation, victime d'un sortilège qui le rend impuissant, mais aussi de l'incurie qu'il déploie dans la gestion de ses affaires, se trouve abandonné par sa nouvelle femme, ruiné, et dans la dernière scène, pour mettre fin au sortilège, il s'expose volontairement aux crachats de tous les mendiants de Dakar et à l'humiliation publique. L'un comme l'autre, Ibrahima Dieng et Bèye, sont dépouillés de toute personnalité. Dieng n'a d'autre réalité que la double image que se font de lui ses femmes et ses voisins : pour ses femmes, chef apparemment respecté de la famille, mais homme faible, qu'il faut protéger contre les autres et contre lui-même ; pour ses voisins, source inépuisable de profits par sa vanité et son impuissance à résister aux quémandeurs. Bèye a dans sa famille même deux faces différentes : pour sa première épouse et pour les enfants de celle-ci, mari aimé et père respecté malgré ses défauts et ses fautes : pour les deux autres femmes, un sexe et un portefeuille, et quand des circonstances malheureuses lui ont fait perdre ces attributs, il est abandonné sans pudeur. Dans le public, auprès de la foule et des « Hommes d'affaires », son prestige repose sur sa réussite et ne résiste pas à sa déconfiture financière. Toute cohérence interne est donc déniée à ces personnages, ils ne sont rien d'autre que leur apparence sociale, la qualification qui leur est donnée par l'opinion. Devant des héros aussi pitoyables on se prend à songer aux pantins que Voltaire présente dans ses contes et qu'il promène de catastrophe en catastrophe, êtres inconsistants que transforment d'instant en instant les rencontres ménagées par la fantaisie de l'auteur.

Mais pas plus que la fantaisie de Voltaire n'est arbitraire, les vicissitudes que traversent les personnages de Sembene ne sont purement capricieuses. Le déroulement de ces existences correspond à une conception sociale et politique de la personnalité humaine, des rapports de l'individu et de la collectivité. Cette philosophie de l'homme, qui doit pour parts égales à la tradition africaine et au marxisme, reste sous-jacente à l'oeuvre. Elle n'occupe pas la place évidente que tiennent les préoccupations politiques, la lutte des ouvriers contre l'exploitation des patrons, la lutte des peuples colonisés contre l'oppression coloniale. Le besoin de donner aux idées politiques une expression claire commande la présence de scènes de discussion, où les opinions adverses sont confrontées, où les tendances divergentes d'une même doctrine se nuancent, mais ces scènes attirent à elles tout ce qui dans l'oeuvre est idéologie et laissent ainsi en dehors d'elles de vastes zones disponibles. La philosophie de l'homme, au contraire, jamais présentée explicitement, imprègne la totalité de l'oeuvre, et ce sont les éléments romanesques eux-mêmes qui ont la charge de l'exprimer. C'est d'ailleurs à cette condition qu'il est possible de parler d'oeuvre littéraire et non d'ouvrage de propagande.

Les passages où cette philosophie se condense, faussant peut-être le ton et faisant glisser le roman au didactisme, sont les réflexions de Diaw Falla dans sa prison, à la fin du *Docker noir*. Du moins ces réflexions nous fournissent-elles des formules bien frappées, qu'il est possible de prendre comme fil directeur. Diaw Falla, condamné à la prison perpétuelle, écrit : « Je ne purge pas ma peine. Je suis rayé de la masse. » A la dernière page, dans une perspective d'ailleurs différente et qui pourrait déboucher sur un mysticisme bien éloigné de la pensée de Sembene, il dit encore : « Tout en moi me paraît néant. » Telle est en effet l'idée qui prévaut dans toute l'oeuvre de Sembene : l'individu n'est rien par lui-même, il n'est rien quand, par sa volonté ou par les circonstances, il est coupé de la collectivité. Cela est vrai naturellement en premier lieu de Diaw Falla, que son emprisonnement retranche matériellement du monde et empêche de jouer son rôle de chef de famille auprès de Catherine et de leur enfant, de défenseur des exploités parmi les dockers noirs de Marseille. Mais pour ne pas être victimes de la même coupure matérielle, maints autres personnages n'en sont pas moins livrés à leurs seules forces et réduits à l'impuissance, souvent par leur propre faute. Ainsi Guibril Guedj Diob est-il, dans *Vehi Ciosane*, retranché de la communauté par l'inceste commis avec sa fille et devient-il la cause des plus grands malheurs pour lui-même et pour son clan, suicide de sa femme Ngoné War Thiandum, parricide de son fils Tanor frappé d'égarement mental, fuite de sa fille Khar, bouleversement des structures sociales et religieuses dans leur village de Santhiu-Niaye : on ne peut limiter les conséquences de l'individualisme passionnel qui prétend s'affranchir des règles ancestrales. C'est le même individualisme, non plus de la sexualité, mais de la cupidité et de l'ambition, qui cause la perte d'El Hadji Abdou Kader Bèye : respectueux de la lettre de la loi coranique, il en a rejeté l'esprit, et le mendiant qui lui jette le sortilège et lui inflige l'humiliation est l'homme qu'il a autrefois dépouillé en vendant comme sien un terrain appartenant au clan, première étape de son ascension financière. Des exemples analogues paraissent dans *Les Bouts de bois de Dieu* : tous ceux qui succombent à la tentation d'assurer leur situation individuelle en méconnaissant la solidarité, Sounkaré, le gardien dévoré par les rats dans son dépôt ; Diara, le contrôleur qui a repris son travail malgré la grève et qui est jugé par les siens ; Doudou, le secrétaire syndical, qui, avide de succès et jaloux de la popularité de Bakayoko, abandonne son métier au moment où les grévistes vont triompher. Bakayoko lui-même n'est pas à l'abri de tout reproche : il n'est sans doute conduit par aucun motif personnel, mais, trop sûr de sa supériorité, il agit en solitaire, éloigné des hommes qui respectent spontanément une distance envers lui, ignorant ou repoussant les femmes qui sont prêtes à l'aider, son épouse Assitan, Penda, N'Deye Touti qui voudrait devenir sa seconde épouse, ne trouvant quelque chaleur humaine que pour la petite Ad'jibid'ji, la fille de sa femme. Il prend du moins conscience de sa solitude à la fin et tente d'y remédier en complétant l'instruction d'Assitan pour lui permettre de le comprendre.

Cette méfiance à l'égard de l'individualisme apparaît plusieurs fois dans la conduite privée des personnages. Il y a deux hommes en Diaw Falla, le militant, tout dévoué aux autres, et l'auteur du roman *Le Dernier Voyage du négrier Sirius,* qui rêve de réussite personnelle, alors que, comme le lui dit le syndicaliste Pipo, on ne peut devenir un bon écrivain qu'à condition de défendre une cause. Son malheur est dans une certaine mésure la conséquence de la coupure qu'il a entretenue entre les moitiés de son être. Dans *L'Harmattan,* les personnages ont compris les leçons de l'expérience. Lèye et Tioumbé se dévouent tout entiers à la cause commune : Lèye cesse d'écrire, moyen d'action trop peu efficace, et se fait peintre pour pouvoir parler à tous, même aux illetrés ; Tioumbé renonce à sa liaison avec Sori, parceque lui est Guinéen, elle Sénégalaise, et que leur place de combat est pour chacun dans son pays. Seul Tangara, le médicin, opte pour la vie privée : arbitrairement congédié de son poste de médecin-chef, il se refuse à rejoindre le Front, dont il vient de démissionner, ne voulant pas paraître agir par un motif personnel, et on le devine trouvant le bonheur dans une liaison avec Charlotte Faure, l'Européenne dont le mari a été assassiné. Mais malgré la supériorité de son intelligence et l'honnêteté, de toute sa conduite, il est visiblement l'object d'une réprobation nuancée d'estime, tant de la part de ses compatriotes que de la part de l'auteur.

L'homme, pense Sembene, ne trouve de force véritable que dans son intégration à un ensemble qui le dépasse. Pour un au moins de ses personnages, il s'agit de la communion avec une puissance transcendante. Dans *Les Bouts de bois de Dieu,* Fa Keïta, l'Ancien, le doyen des poseurs de rails, après le jugement de Diara le briseur de grève, où son intervention a été décisive et a évité au coupable tout autre châtiment que l'humiliation d'être flétri comme un traître, commence une retraite d'une semaine pour s'adresser au Tout-Puissant et réfléchir sur les événements. Sa retraite sera interrompue par la perquisition de la police, il sera conduit au camp, où il subira des sévices et des vexations, mais, relâché, il appellera ses amis à dominer leur haine pour faire triompher la vérité. La figure de Fa Keïta est présentée sous un jour sympathique, mais Ousmane Sembene ne croit guère à la valeur et à l'efficacité de la religion, et c'est dans le sentiment collectif que ses personnages puisent en général leur force. L'action des personnages les plus représentatifs, Diaw Falla, Oumar Faye, Bakayoko, n'est pas l'impulsion donnée d'en haut à une foule passive, mais un échange dynamique où le meneur recueille les sentiments nés en chacun de ses compagnons mais restés dans un état de confusion et d'éparpillement, leur donne la clarté qui leur manquait en les fondant sur une analyse politique et idéologique, les concentre et multiplie leur puissance, pour les projeter de nouveau hors de lui et susciter dans la foule l'élan unanime auquel elle ne pouvait parvenir seule. Aussi faut-il compter parmi les plus belles réussites d'Ousmane Sembene quelques scènes de foules où l'on voit la colère ou les aspirations s'organiser sous l'impulsion d'une personnalité issue du groupe, mais sachant, par une lucidité et une énergie plus grandes, unir en un faisceau les forces qui jusque là se perdaient dans l'inefficacité de récriminations individuelles. De telles scènes sont fréquentes dans *Les Bouts de bois de Dieu* : l'émeute des femmes accueillant la police venue interroger Ramatoulaye au sujet du meurtre du bélier, la procession des mêmes femmes accompagnant Ramatoulaye au commissariat, et surtourt le point culminant de l'action, la marche des femmes de cheminots de Thiès à Dakar, sous la conduite de Penda, pour faire abourtir les revendications de leurs maris, épisode où les jalousies, les mesquineries, les faiblesses physiques aussi sont peu à peu surmontées sous l'effet de l'enthousiasme et font place à une unanimité irrésistible. Dans un ton différent il faut citer aussi la scène finale de *Xala*, où la bande des mendiants, représentant toutes les misères de la société postcoloniale, envahit la maison d'El Hadji Abdou Kader Bèye, le profiteur déchu, véritable déchaînement de Cour des Miracles qui atteint au sublime dans l'horreur, presque insoutenable, et qui, transposée dans le film que Sembene a tiré de son roman, a provoqué les critiques de la censure sénégalaise.

Un double problème se pose donc, à l'individu et à la collectivité. Pour l'individu, il s'agit de savoir prendre ses responsabilités. Les romans et les nouvelles d'Ousmane Sembene nous montrent quelques exemples d'hommes qui, par suite d'une faute ou tout simplement en raison de leur lâcheté, ont perdu leur dignité d'homme, de ceux dont un comparse du *Mandat* déclare : « Quand l'homme se dessaisit de son autorité, il ne devient qu'épouvantail. » Ibrahima Dieng, à propos de qui est dite cette parole, est bien entendu du nombre, lui dont les démarches ridicules et la générosité intempestive ont compromis la sécurité de sa famille, et à la place de qui ses deux femmes doivent prendre les initiatives. Dans la même catégorie se rangent tous ceux qui, pour des raisons diverses, recherchent à se soustraire à la loi de la solidarité et font passer avant tout leur plaisir, leur confort ou leur autorité : Guibril Guedj Diob l'incestueux, El Hadji Mabigué le serigne égoïste, El Hadji Abdou Kader Bèye l'arriviste, Koéboghi le père brutal qui prétend interdire à sa femme et à sa fille Tioumbé toute pensée et toute vie personnelles et les bat quand elles n'obéissent pas. En face d'eux se dressant ceux qui ont pris conscience de la réalité, qui se dévouent à leurs frères, leur donnent l'exemple et les mobilisent pour les causes justes. Hommes tels que Diaw Falla, Bakayoko, ou Malic dans la nouvelle « Prise de conscience » du recueil *Voltaïque*, responsables syndicaux qui luttent pour la justice sociale; tels aussi qu'Oumar Faye, qui cherche à initier ses compatriotes casamançais aux méthodes de culture modernes et au système coopératif, pour qu'ils ne soient plus livrés sans défense aux grandes compagnies capitalistes. Mais particulièrement remarquables sont les personnages de femmes que l'on voit assez souvent, chez Sembene, accéder à cette conscience et à cette responsabilité : Ngoné War Thiandum, l'épouse que la faute et la démission de son mari obligent à prendre seule les graves décision qui concernent sa famille, Penda, l'anima-

trice de la marche des femmes sur Dakar, Ramatoulaye surtout, qui, devant
la disette causé par la grève, se révèle un véritable chef, prend l'initiative de
la revolte contre l'injustice, tue le bélier de son frère Mabigué, réussit à sauver
la vie des siens et à imposer son autorité jusqu'aux représentants de l'administration. Les conditions de cette consécration ne sont ni l'instruction, ni
l'expérimence politique, mais l'enracinement dans la réalité quotidienne. Ramatoulaye n'a connu ni la guerre, ni les « inhumaines cadences du travail
ouvrier », ni « de multiples étreintes d'hommes », elle a puisé sa force, tout
simplement, « dans les cuisines aux foyers éteints ».

Au niveau de la collectivité, le premier pas à faire est la reconnaissance de
l'égalité de nature et de valeur entre tous les hommes. Le mépris pour ceux
que l'on juge inférieurs à soi est un crime contre l'humanité. C'est celui des
Blancs à l'égard des Noirs, celui des juges qui refusent de croire aux ex-
plications de Diaw Falla, celui de la Compagnie qui n'accorde pas même
traitement à ses employés blancs et noirs. Mais c'est aussi, parmi les
Noirs, celui des priviligiés et des parvenus, tel, dans la nouvelle « Prise
de conscience », cet Ibra, ancien militant de l'indépendance, à qui la
tête a tourné depuis qu'il est devenue député, et que ses compagnons
condamnent d'une formule sans appel : « Ces types n'ont rien de commun
avec nous ! Ils sont noirs dessus . . . leur intérieur est comme le colonial-
isme . . . » De la solidarité nécessaire pour rendre la vie supportable à tous,
les humbles donnent au contraire l'exemple vivant : dans la vie quotidienne,
les dockers s'associant pour limiter les effets du chômage, les femmes des
cheminots grévistes mettant leurs ressources en commun ; dans les luttes sociales et politiques, la résolution de tenir ensemble jusqu'au succès des revendications, le partage des responsabilités dans la propaganda pour le *non*
au référendum. Encore faut-il que la solidarité repose sur des sentiments
honnêtes. L'exploitation éhontée d'Ibrahima Dieng par ses voisins et voisines
quand la nouvelle de l'arrivée de son mandat s'est répandue est une autre
forme de l'égoïsme et de l'injustice. Le modèle de la véritable solidarité est
donné par les femmes réunies autour de Ramatoulaye pour survivre dans la
dignité et le respect réciproque, ou par le mouvement de révolte et de sacrifice
qui associe les chômeurs et qui suscite, chez un ancien rendu sceptique par
les nombreux échecs du passé, la surprise « de voir tant de gens s'entendre
ainsi ensemble ».

Dans la restauration des vraies valeurs les femmes jouent un rôle plus important encore que les hommes. Ce sont elles qui sont les principales victimes de la
société De l'oeuvre de Sembène monte une plainte de plus en plus amère contre
les humiliations et les souffrances morales infligées aux femmes. Dans *Les
Bouts de bois de Dieu*, une des causes essentielles de la grève est, à côte de la
revendication d'un salaire égal pour les Noirs et pour les Blancs, l'exigence
de l'attribution des allocations familiales, refusées par l'administration aux
polygames parce que leurs mariages ne sont pas reconnus par la loi française.
Et les cheminots font écho avec colère aux paroles de Bakayoko s'écriant :
« On refuse ce que nous demandons sous prétexte que nos mères et nos fem-

mes sont des concubines, nous-mêmes et nos fils des bâtards ! » Dans plusieurs
nouvelles de *Voltaïque*, dans *Xala*, c'est à la polygamie elle-même que s'en
prend Sembene. Il montre le tourment jaloux de la femme attendant en vain
son marie retenu par une co-épouse plus jeune, le désarroi de la jeune femme
mariée à un vieillard installé en France et laissée seule par la mort de son
mari, il dénonce l'avidité des femmes désirant toujours plus de cadeaux à la
fois pour prouver leur pouvoir sur leur mari et pour s'assurer une existence
confortable et indépendante. A ces calculs sordides il oppose, d'une part la
générosité des femmes restées fidèles à la tradition et à leur devoir, la vieille
Niakoro, mère de Bakayoko, Ramatoulaye, Ngoné War Thiandum, d'autre
part l'ardeur novatrice des jeunes, qu'elles finissent par imiter les anciennes,
comme N'Deye Touti, ou qu'elles luttent pour une émancipation totale, comme
Tioumbé ou Rama, la fille d'El Hadji Abdou Kader Bèye. Ce n'est pas seulement à propos de la grève des cheminots, mais de tous les aspects de l'oeuvre
de Sembene, que l'on peut dire « que ce temps, s'il enfantait d'autres hommes,
enfantait aussi d'autres femmes ».

Romans et nouvelles d'Ousmane Sembene sont d'abord une prise de conscience de l'auteur lui-même. Les découvertes qu'il prête à son héros Diaw
Falla, apprenti romancier, sont manifestament les siennes :

> Il savait maintenant que la vie était une lutte de tous les jours ; il apprit à
> détester les poètes et les peintres qui ne montraient que ce qui est beau, qui
> chantaient la gloire du printemps, oubliant l'aigreur du froid. Les oiseaux ne
> sont pas là seulement pour embellir, les fleurs non plus.

Cette déclaration anti-idéaliste est un véritable art poétique. L'écrivain doit
lutter pour dissiper ses rêves et ses illusions, et sa tâche ne sera accomplie
que s'il dissipe aussi ceux de ses lecteurs. D'où la nécessité pour lui de
pratiquer deux tactiques différentes: l'exaltation de quelques figures idéales,
proposant le but à atteindre, et la dérision jetée sur les hommes de tous les
jours, les coupables, les traîtres, certes, mais aussi les victimes innocentes, qui
contribuent à leur écrasement par leur passivité, et c'est un souci de plus
grande efficacité qui a conduit Sembene à insister de plus en plus sur cet
aspect, semblant ainsi se moquer cyniquement des malheureux, car la
découverte de la corruption du monde, du faux calcul que son la résignation
et la compensation illusoire des souffrances par le sentiment de sa propre
innocence, est le moyen le plus rapide de convaincre les hommes qu'en ne
luttant pas contre le mal de toutes leurs forces, ils s'en font objectivement les
complices.

La relation de l'auteur avec le lecteur est d'ordre pédagogique. C'est celle
qui convient aux besoins de l'Afrique contemporaine, où une foule encore
mal préparée doit accéder aussi rapidement que possible à la conscience de
sa situation et à l'action de l'écrivain est la réalité, car la foule ne réagirait
pas si lui était présenté un monde mythique ou imaginaire, mais la technique
appropriée est celle que Lèye emploie dans ses tableaux. Son *Harmattan*

représente un marché africain, mais il y enferme, par la vertu des symboles, tout le passé et tout l'avenir de l'Afrique. De même le romancier, par le choix de ses personnages et la manière dont il les peint, en fait la figuration des éléments en conflit dans la société africaine, anciens attachés à la tradition, jeunes aspirant à la transformation du monde, et aussi profiteurs qui, feignant de contribuer à promouvoir l'Afrique de demain, ne pensent qu'à leur intérêt personnel. La schématisation d'une classe dans quelques individus, le grossissement des traits communs au détriment des particularités de chacun sont les procédés les plus efficaces pour frapper et toucher le public. On peut même dans cette perspective intégrer pleinement au reste de l'oeuvre le roman de *Xala,* dont le thème, le sortilège qui « noue l'aiguillette », est à première vue surprenant chez un auteur qui proclame ses convictions matérialistes. Ce qui importe, c'est moins la croyance sorcellerie en elle-même que l'accent mis sur le complexe de culpabilité que persuade El Hadji Abdou Kader Bèye de la possibilité de telles pratiques, et la scène finale, l'humiliation par les mendiants, prend une valeur incantatoire, préfigurant la chute des privilèges mal acquis et le triomphe de la justice : le présent fictif est le garant de la réalisation de l'avenir attendu.

Remarques sur la naissance du roman policier en Afrique de l'ouest

Alain Ricard

Que vont lire les nouveaux lecteurs de l'Afrique de l'Ouest? Nous pouvons chercher la réponse dans les enquêtes des sociologues, mais aussi dans les textes des écrivains et l'émergence d'un nouveau genre de roman issu de la rencontre d'une attente et d'un nouvel univers[1]. L'urbanisme massive se traduit par le développement de villes comme Accra, Lagos, mais aussi Lomé, Cotonou qui ont toutes en dix ans doublé leur population. Elle se combine avec une forte hausse de la scorlarisation. Le taux en est aujourd'hui dans ces villes voisin de 100 % : la majorité de ces scolarisés ne continuera pas les études et beaucoup resteront en ville chômeurs partiels. Leur expérience urbaine sera celle de la misère : public jeune, lettré, habitant la ville mais en connaissant la dureté, public prêt à entrer de plein pied dans l'univers du roman policier.

Une enquête réalisée en 1967—68 au Centre Culturel Française de Lomé[2], bibliothèque de la capitale du Togo, confirme le désir de lecture « policière » de ces adolescents ou adultes, élèves, apprentis, ou chômeurs. A tel point que, par souci « éducatif », la bibliothécaire a retiré ces ouvrages du prêt. Il est compréhensible que la bibliothécaire se désole de voir l'intérêt à son sens excessif des lecteurs pour ces ouvrages. On peut en effet regretter que l'univers des romans policiers français appelle trop à l'exotisme. Une production locale de romans policiers semble avoir une clientèle toute prête : il est significatif qu'elle commence à la rechercher. Curieusement l'intérêt pour la littérature policière trouve aujourd'hui un écho chez les écrivains. Il s'agit là d'un phénomène nouveau et qui mérite d'être analysé: nous tenterons ici de tracer quelques pistes.

En 1967 et en 1970 paraissent des romans policiers en langues africaines. En 1969 *Aja l'o leru* en yoruba et en 1971 *Ku le xoma*[3] (la mort à domicile) en ewe. Plusieurs millions de personnes lisent le yoruba et plusieurs centaines de milliers de personnes lisent l'ewe. Dans les deux cas la masse « lisante » est suffisamment urbanisée et a atteint le seul critique qui fait apparaître, le motif nouveau de l'enquête urbaine. Ces deux romans, publiés en volumes par des éditeurs établis marquent bien la naissance du genre.

La parution au Ghana en 1970 d'une série policière introduisant le personnage du détective marque une nouvelle étape dans la diversification de la production littéraire. Les deux premiers titres

Cofie Quaye, *Sammy Slams the Gang*
Cofie Quaye, *Murder in Kumasi*[4]

nous entraînent l'un à Accra, l'autre à Koumasi. Le troisième titre nous
promet des aventures à Takoradi, le grand port de l'ouest Ghanéen. Nous
participons à deux enquêtes du détective, Sammy Hayford. Les cloisons entre
les bas-fonds et la police, la police et les milieux d'affaires sont transpercés
par le détective. Cette série policière est à notre connaissance la première
du genre en Afrique à appliquer les recettes du roman policier américain.
Seulement les recettes sont trop visibles, et l'on ne peut encore se prononcer
sur la fertilité de la greffe.

En 1967 parait en feuilleton dans Togo Presse, un « roman policier »: *Ici
bas tout se paie*. De tous les feuilletons publiés par Félix Couchoro dans ce
journal, il est le seul à porter l'étiquette de policier.

Ici bas tout se paie nous raconte les aventures de Bob, le gangster, et de la
belle Ruth, la contrebandière, opposés au policier Jean[5]. Bob abat un douanier
pour 2000 CFA et il est alors traqué par les policiers. En essayant de forcer
un barrage routier, sa voiture explose et brûle, d'où le titre du roman... Ce
roman mérite l'épithète de « policier » parcequ' il fait intervenir le police. Il
s'agit d'un roman d'aventure sur une « frontière » que ni le rythme ni l'organisation interne ne permettraient de rattacher au genre « policier ».

Mais ce roman est un roman de moeurs. A criminalité différente police et
roman policier différents. Une petite capitale africaine, Lomé, du milieu des
années soixante n'est ni Los Angeles, ni New York ni Paris. Dans un pays où
il n'y a rien que deux routes goudronnées en dehors des villes, et moins de quatre mille abonnés à l'électricité on ne peut attendre le « tempo » d' un roman
où autoroute* et téléphone jouent un rôle. Roman de mœurs et roman d'aventure mettant en scène quelques types de criminels bien dessinés, le roman de
Félix Couchoro est une version petite bourgeoise et africaine du roman policier.

Dans la lignée de F. Couchoro paraît au Dahomey depuis 1970, dans le
seul quotidien du pays, la série des *Aventures du commissaire Mamadou*
inventée par D. Titus[6]. Félix Couchoro n'avait pas eu le temps de créer un
héros, de créer son commissaire Mamadou à lui et le réinjecter dans de
nouvelles aventures. Félix Couchoro était à travers son roman policier un
moraliste : un romancier « populaire ». Dominique Titus évite lui la morale
ou plutôt la morale de son roman est la technique du commissaire Mamadou,
qui, assisté de l'inspecteur LeBras dejoue par ses capacités de déduction, les
ruses de charlatans de Cotonou. Personnage sympathique et efficace, le
commissaire Mamadou donne à ses enquêtes un cadre bien délimité : la ville
de Cotonou et la lutte contre le crime organisé du Dahomey. Les ambitions
éductrices et moralisatrices de F. Couchoro sont abandonnées.

Seulement D. Titus n'a publié aucun de ses romans policiers en volume
séparés. Depuis plusieurs années il produit des feuilletons, lus et appréciés mais
aucun éditeur local ne s'est risqué à investir dans la publication de ses

romans. D. Titus, comme F. Couchoro, a un public qui serait sans doute prêt à payer 200 à 300 CFA pour un roman policier. Mais ce public est étroit et l'investissement sans doute trop important. Aussi D. Titus cherchait-il à se faire éditer en France; dans les collections spécialisées dans le roman policier, « l'exotisme » des situations et la présence d'un commissaire africain n'ont pas retenu l'attention des éditeurs. Le milieu urbanisé et scolarisé du Dahomey (2 villes de plus de 100 000 habitants) est encore trop étroit pour soutenir la production d'un roman policier en volume. Mais le succès du feuilleton indique, au Dahomey comme au Togo, la présence d'un milieu de lecteurs urbanisés prêts à accepter le tempo et la démarche du genre, pouvu qu'elle s'inscrive dans leur cadre de vie.

Si l'on admet une division de la fiction en divers sous-genre (sentimental, policier, espionnage etc.) on conviendra de ce que cette division en multiples sous-genres ne se produit pas au début d'une production imprimée. Les premiers romans qui paraissent utilisent des ingrédients sentimentaux, policiers, moralistes pour faire appel au public le plus large possible. Ce n'est qu'après quelques années que le public demande, ou est prêt à recevoir, un type d'ouvrages plus spécialisé dont la construction et le rythme correspondent au tempo de la vie urbaine propre au roman à fort tirage.

Le premier roman « urbain » du Nigéria, oeuvre de Cyprien Ekwensi *People of the City*[7] est une excellente illustration du mélange de sous-genre propre à la fiction imprimée à ses débuts : le héros en est un journaliste, chef d'orchestre, qui se lance dans une enquête policière à travers la ville. Le thème policier est vite perdu de vue, mais il sert un temps à appâter le lecteur.

De la même manière un des auteurs à succès de la littérature ghanéenne donne à ses ouvrages des titres de roman policiers, c'est-à-dire utilise la notion de suspence : *Who Killed Lucy*[8]. Mais au lieu que l'ouvrage soit bâti suivant la progression du suspense, suivant cette linéarité qui trouve un univers homogène nous avons un récit laborieuse et composite (lettres, dialogues, etc.) sur l'éducation des filles et les malheurs d'un amoureuse éplorée. Confusion des genres : mélo sentimental et titre à la Hitchcock . . .

Au Ghana aussi un auteur d'ouvrage à succès sans doute publié à compte d'auteur utilise le motif de l'enquête policière pour ce qui serait plus justement des « souvenirs du barreau ». *The Kidnapping of the Millionaire's Daughter* d'Isaac Ephsom n'est en rien un roman policier et pourtant nous y avons une enquête, et des policiers[9]. L'ouvrage en effet est un récit historique qui ne fonctionne pas comme un policier.

Plusieurs ouvrages de Félix Couchoro font en effet usage des mêmes ingrédients et ne sont pas des romans policiers. Ainsi il intitule un ouvrage qui précède *Ici bas tout se paie* paru peu avant ses « roman policiers », *Gangsters et policiers* mais il ne s'agit pour autant pas d'un « roman policier », mais plutôt d'un roman populaire avec personnages de policiers et de gangsters[10].

Ces notes nous suggèrent qu'entre le roman dit « populaire » et le roman policier existent certes des affinités mais aussi de nombreuses différences. Le roman populaire s'identifie à ses débuts avec le roman feuilleton : il assume donc les fonctions multiples des massmedia imprimés : distraction, éduction et même information par tous les moyens possibles[11]. Le roman policier est lui un type particulier de fiction qui fonctionne par la cohérence entre un univers urbain, un texte imprimé, et la mise en marche chez le lecteur d'une déduction linéaire. Alors que le roman populaire peut charier dans ses intrigues les heurs et les malheurs de vastes populations diverses *(La Porteuse de pain, Sans familie,* etc.), le roman policier se limite à des groupes bien définis du territoire urbain. Il est donc normal que ce soit dans les régions les plus alphabétisées et les plus urbanisées de l'Afrique de l'Ouest qu'apparaissent les premiers romans policiers en volumes autonomes, dans le sud du Ghana et dans l'Ouest du Nigéria. F. Couchoro lui, feuilletoniste togolais a pressenti la richesse du genre mais il n'a pas eu le temps de le spécialiser. D. Titus, romancier dahoméen, se heurte lui à la faiblesse de l'industrie de l'édition dans son propre pays.

Cette brève analyse montre en tout cas qu'on ne saurait définir le roman policier uniquement par son contenu. Le roman policier ne peut fonctionner que dans certains types de structures sociales. Alors que le feuilleton, c'est-à-dire le roman « populaire » est très souvent un amalgame de diverses « formes simples », le roman policier est à notre sens le développement d'un élément particulier du roman populaire — l'enquête policière — inséré dans une société plus controlable et moins « mystérieuse »[12]. Type particulier de fiction répondant à une situation sociale, le roman policier est sans doute un genre littéraire. L'étude de cas concrets ouest-africain en nous montrant la définition progressive du roman policier nous aide à mieux comprendre les mécanismes fondamentaux qui travaillent le texte et la société dans laquelle il s'insère.

Notes

1   Sur les rapports entre le roman policier et le roman populaire, cf. J. Tortel, « Le roman policier, » *Encyclopédie de la Pléïade,* T. III (Paris, 1960).

2   D. Dardrey, *La lecture à Lomé* (Lomé, 1969), 90 p.

3   *Aja l'o leru,* cité dans *The Constituents of Yoruba Studies,* (Ife, 1969). Seth Akafia, *Ku le xome* (Accra, 1970), cité in S. Amegbleame, *Un corpus imprimé africain, l'exemple ewe* (Bordeaux, 1974).

4   C. Quaye, *Sammy Slams The Gang* (Accra, 1970), 62 p. C. Quaye, *Murder in Kumasi* (Accra, 1970), 103 p.

5   F. Couchoro, « Ici bas tout se paie, » *Togo Presse* (Lomé), Feuilleton du 15—12—67 au 16—1—68.

6   D. Titus, « Une aventure du commissaire Mamadou : la vierge et le charlatan, » *Daho Express* (Cotonou), Novembre 1972. Communication personnelle, Porto Novo, Dec. 1971 ; cf. interview in *Bulletin du Cercle de Littérature Comparée* (Lomé, Université du Bénin), n° 3.

7   C. Ekwensi, *People of the City* (London, 1954).

8   E. Mickson, *Who killed Lucy* (Accra, 1967), 102 p.

9   I. Ephsom, *The Kidnapping of the Millionnaire's Daughter* (Accra, 1972), 132 p.

10   F. Couchoro, « Gangsters et Policiers, » *Togo Presse* (Lomé), paru de 31—8—
      1967 au 28—10—67.
11   Un phénomène nouveau est apparu en Côte d'Ivoire en 1969 : des romans
      policiers multigraphiés publiés sous forme de série. Les aventures du mystérieux
      criminel Dragax tiendront-elles en haleine lycéens et écoliers d'Abidjan ? Cf.
      Bibliographie Nationale de la Côte d'Ivoire, 2 et 3.
12   Cf. A. Warren et R. Wellek, *La Théorie littéraire* (Paris, 1971).

Annexe

On nous permettra ici d'ajouter une remarque personnelle : ce texte a été
rédigé à Bordeaux par un bordelais. Or Bordeaux a longtemps été pour ceux
qui voulaient la coloniser, mais aussi pour ceux qui voulaient la connaître et
l'aimer, la porte de l'Afrique. Aussi il nous est agréable de savoir que c'est
de Bordeaux que J. Jahn s'est pour la première fois embarqué pour l'Afrique.
De tels départs donnent à un port toute sa noblesse de lien d'échange frater-
nel.

* Il y a une autoroute entre Accra et Tema ...

E. K. Ogunmola: A Personal Memoir

Ulli Beier

The first time I came across that delightful art form known as "Yoruba Opera" was in Lagos in 1951. Those were the days before the so-called "slum clearance," when the center of Lagos was not yet the anonymous conglomeration of office blocks that it has become since. The triangle between Martin Street, Broad Street (as it was then called), and Nnamdi Azikiwe Street, for example, consisted of small Brazilian style houses, rather overpopulated, it is true, but teeming with life and vibrant with music. In those days I liked to take walks through the dimly lit streets at night. Architecturally the town was extremely pleasing. It was not just the masterpieces of Brazilian architecture, like No. 10 Elias Street and Olaiya's house in Tinubu Square which have survived until today, but the whole intricate pattern of buildings, the wealth of architectural ideas and the imaginative detail that gave old Lagos its particular flair.

On one such night I noticed a poster advertising a play called *Adam and Eve*. I went to the old Glover Hall, having no idea at all what it might be. What I found was a fundraising function of the Seraphim and Cherubim Church. The Hall was crowded, predominantly with women who had come in their best *aso oke* dresses and big headties and many of whom were surrounded by children. I cannot remember the names of any of the actors. In fact, I do not think that there was a program listing them. They appeared to be members of the congregation who had thought up the play in order to help their Church raise some money.

The experience was totally new to me. I had, in my ignorance, not yet come across Hubert Ogunde and his concert party, even though he had been running a professional troupe for several years.

It was a charming performance. The backdrop representing the Garden of Eden was executed in a schoolboy manner, but nevertheless very attractive. For the first time I experienced the gentle sway and rhythmic shuffle that runs like a nerve through the performance. In the Western tradition of theater, actors who are not engaged in actual dialogue or action have to occupy themselves with stage "business" in order not to look stiff or artificial. In Yoruba Opera the problem has been solved simply and beautifully by making such characters unashamedly "onlookers" but letting them sway gently to the rhythm of highlife-derived music. What I remember most clearly of this performance is that Adam and Eve were both dressed in long, black, oldfashioned swimsuits. Adam was a thin and wiry young man, a vivacious actor and clearly the clown as well as the hero of the play. Eve was luscious; the black swimsuit had difficulty in containing her, and Adam, when he woke up from his sleep to see her for the first time, broke out into a flourish of appropriately ribald jokes.

I left charmed and intrigued and slightly puzzled, but I had no idea that Yoruba Opera was to become one of the greatest pleasures of my life. My *real* discovery of Yoruba Opera came a year later when I came across E. K. Ogunmola in Ikerre Ekiti. I think this was my first visit to Ikerre. I came to stay there quite accidentally. I was in fact merely driving through but found myself intrigued by the splendid entrance gate to the place that was surmounted by two very tall cement soldiers. Walking through the gate I discovered one of the most beautiful palaces of Yorubaland and I met Adegoriola, the Ogoga of Ikerre, who kindly invited me to spend some days with him in the palace.

On my last night in Ikerre, Ogunmola's company appeared from Ado Ekiti to perform *Joseph and his Brethren* in one of the schoolrooms. Stylistically the performance was not too dissimilar from the one I had seen a year earlier in Lagos. The music was derived from highlife, with a certain influence of Church hymns clearly detectable. There was the same swaying movement of the actors throughout and also the use of a special kind of *recitative*, to which Yoruba, being a tonal language, lends itself particularly well. (To European ears even spoken Yoruba sounds like recitative!) Ogunmola's play, however, was preceded by a number called the "Opening Glee," in which the audience is told in advance about the story they are about to see, and in which a suitable moral is drawn. This was a particularly charming number. The "Opening Glee" started with a group of shimmying girls, who formed a kind of chorus. When the pace of their dance had heated up, Ogunmola suddenly burst out from behind the simple backdrop curtain to take the lead in their midst and to sing the moral of the song. He was dressed in a kind of Pierrot's costume, with a wide red floppy collar.

What made this performance an experience of a different kind, however, was the quality of the acting. There was a sensitivity here, an attention to detail that was totally captivating. Even with virtually no knowledge of Yoruba one could follow any tiny shade of meaning and mood. The acting was selectively realistic. Realism on stage can often be a bore, but Ogunmola always understood what was *typical* in human behavior and he knew how to isolate it and at times exaggerate it for greater effect. Ogunmola's plays did not present a mirror image of Yoruba life: they gave a sharpened, heightened, concentrated image. He always succeeded in going right to the essence of character. He achieved this not with a complex or philosophical dialogue that would lay bare the souls of the dramatic personae. On the contrary—his dialogue was lifted straight from everyday conversation, and his moralizing was simple to the extent of being naive. In fact his plays do not read particularly well. Ogunmola put his characters across not through words, but through gesture, movement and expression. Often the most powerful effects in a play lay in brief moments of silence.

I was so intrigued by this performance that for the next few days I followed Ogunmola around on his tour of Ekiti. I saw several more performances and among them was the play that was to remain my favorite: *Love of Money*.

The plot of this play is deceptively simple. The hero, Adeleke, enjoys moderate prosperity and happiness with his wife Morolayo and their two children. But already his friends, who form a kind of chorus, warn him of the instability of fate: "Fear the son of man," they say, "because money does not stay in one place for generations." Confusion is soon brought into his life by the shrewd and alluring Mopelola, who appears one day to say that she has decided to marry him. Adeleke is flattered by the beautiful temptress and he walks into her trap immediately. He persuades his wife that she needs a co-wife to help her. The new wife moves in and does not take long to pick quarrels with the senior wife. Infatuated with Mopelola, Adeleke drives his first wife away, and she leaves with her children. Mopelola now finds it easy to get a stronger and stronger hold on him and she is now ready for the final kill. Her accomplice and boyfriend R.S.K. is a "money-doubler." The gullible Adeleke is persuaded to borrow $ 200, so that in twenty-four hours he will see it transformed magically into $ 600. Like a sleepwalker, Adeleke walks into this final trap. Helplessly he finds himself duped by the crooks, and to make his humilitation complete, he sees Mopelola quietly packing her bags. She has no more use for him. "My father who begot me was a rich man; my mother who brought me up was a rich woman; a goat cannot give birth to a kid that grows up a sheep. I am ready to leave — I am going!" Left without wife, without children and with debts, he has to suffer the final humiliation of being blamed for his misfortune by his friends: "A man gets what he deserves; you have been trying to speed the hand of God."

This sounds like an *obvious* story and one that merely lends itself to very banal moralizing: pride goes before the fall; beware of women ("the girls of nowadays are hard — they shave your head and paint it black"), and the fool gets punished even if he is innocent.

Even in Ogunmola's own translation of the play, we get little sense of the excitement and subtlety of the performance. Here and there the language is colorful or humorous — but the play still sounds much too simple in cold print.

To see a performance of *Love of Money* was quite a different matter. Ogunmola's portrayal of Adeleke was always subtle, moving and humorous. Right from the opening scene, where Adeleke goes through the typical self-congratulatory phrases of the successful rich man, Ogunmola was able to suggest his vulnerability. One did not really need the chorus of friends to know that here was a man too vain and too weak to meet any real challenge. All that is not really contained in the text, but it was suggested by Ogunmola's every gesture and movement. Even in that very first performance I saw in Ekiti in

1952 the part of Mopelola was played by the girl who was later to become his wife and who was to perform the part for many years to come, until eventually she switched over to the part of Morolayo, leaving the part of Mopelola to a younger actress. What I witnessed then was the beginning of that mature and subtle teamwork between Ogunmola and his wife that was to delight and astonish us again and again in later years.

The part of Mopelola was acted with beautiful economy. A sense of intrigue and danger was cunningly suggested under the sparkling surface of charm and laughter. A cruder performance would have provoked antipathy in the audience for Mopelola and contempt for the foolish Adeleke who could be corrupted so easily by her deceitful manner. But in fact one felt completely captivated by her. Most men in the audience would have walked knowingly into the trap, just as Adeleke did.

Ogunmola was not only an actor, but also a producer of no mean talent. One scene that is unforgettable from *Love of Money* is the preparation for the wedding of Adeleke and Mopelola. Ogunmola would play this on a completely empty stage, with only himself and Morolayo present. And yet, between the two of them, they managed to convey a busy, bustling, nervous household. This scene became one of the highlights of the play in later years, when Mrs. Ogunmola had taken over the part of Morolayo.

Audiences loved this play because it portrayed Yoruba society knowingly and because they could recognize themselves. Ogunmola knew about every weakness of the human character and he would expose it, but he would expose human beings without harshness. There was no bitter satire in these plays — only understanding. He made us laugh about his stage characters, but it was his particular genius that forced us to include ourselves in the laughter. The moralizing of Ogunmola's text was always mellowed by the performance. He never made us despise people. On the contrary, one loved both the "good" and the "bad" characters, one loved the wise ones and most of all the foolish ones.

I do not know how often I saw *Love of Money* during the following twenty years. I guess about thirty times. I never grew tired of it. Of course, no two performances were ever alike. This was not because Ogunmola had a quick turnover in actors. His leading lady stayed with him to the end of his life and in the photographs of *Love of Money* that appeared in *Nigeria Magazine* No. 44 of 1954 I recognize at least one actor who was with him to the end. Ogunmola inspired great loyalty in his company and kept his troupe together extremely well.

His performances varied because he left much to improvisation on stage. He never wrote down his plays in any detail until he was finally asked by others to do so and even then he never wrote down a very full version. His performances, however well rehearsed, always left room for the inspiration of the moment. Moreover, his performances became more and more subtle and more and more professional as he grew older. His understanding of human nature increased, and so with every performance one felt that one got to know the familiar figures of *Love of Money* a little better.

My first encounter with Ogunmola excited me a great deal. I felt everybody ought to know about this gifted man. I could not understand why he was not famous already and why he had not been given the support to enable him to create a fully professional company. He seemed to be wasting his time teaching in a primary school.

I recorded some of his songs and gave the tape to the Western Nigeria Broadcasting Station who broadcast it. When Ogunmola performed in Oshogbo, for the first time in 1953, I was able to take D. W. McCrow along, the Editor of *Nigeria Magazine*. McCrow enjoyed the performance and we arranged for the company to perform in the open air in Ede the next morning, to enable McCrow to take the pictures which finally appeared in *Nigeria Magazine* No. 44. I also wrote a piece for the *Journal of the African Music Society* (Vol. 1, No. 1, 1954). But for a long time none of this made the slightest difference to his career. The audience in Oshogbo clearly enjoyed his performance, but their approval was guarded ("he is really trying") and they compared him unfavorably with Ogunde, who had been capturing their imagination for years. Perhaps in those years Ogunmola could not match the sheer professionalism of Ogunde, and his more subtle approach did not at first make the same impact as the jazzy glamour of Ogunde's performances. In fact it took some years before local audiences learned to stop comparing the two, before they learned that they were looking at two entirely different things, and that each could be perfect in his own way. There was, by the way, never any rivalry between the actors. They kept cordial relations throughout, and not merely on the surface.

In 1955 Ogunmola moved to Oshogbo, which enabled him to operate from a bigger center. In the same year we managed for the first time to arrange a performance by Ogunmola at the University of Ibadan—but in those days most of the staff still preferred their annual performance of the *Mikado* to any African drama. The real break came for E. K. Ogunmola when Robert July came to Oshogbo and saw him perform. Robert July was then the representative of the Rockefeller Foundation in Nigeria. He was highly impressed by what he saw and negotiated a grant for Ogunmola that gave him a period of six months with the Drama Department at the University of Ibadan, during which he could work on the production of a new play, get acquainted with more complicated stage techniques, experience other productions and demonstrate his skill to the students. At the same time the grant provided money for a lorry, generator, lights, basic costume and a revolving production fund, that would enable Ogunmola to go fully professional at the end of the period.

The result of his stay at the University was the famous production of the *Palm Wine Drinkard*, which was a tremendous success and which Ogunmola finally took to the Algiers Festival. I still find it regrettable that Ogunmola was not given a chance to create his own play out of Tutuola's book, but that he was given someone else's dramatization, that turned the realities of Tutuola's supernatural world into the feeble device of a dream. Even so, the

Palm Wine Drinkard provided Ogunmola with one of his greatest parts and many people will remember him exactly as Segun Olusola described him in *Nigeria Magazine* No. 77 (1963): "In his 'praise song of the spirit palm-wine' he surpasses anything that has ever come on the local stage. Whether he sings it or leads the chorus to recite it, his pauses, nuances, gestures, word associations or the eloquent mimes when he puts his expressive face to full use ... you are witnessing a great performer in the act with a relish for the liquor that is easily transferable to the audience."

Demas Nwoko's production had added some tightness and speed, without interfering with Ogunmola's basic style of performance. His costume design and sets were brilliant and spectacular, thus giving the play a very wide appeal. There was a great deal of humor in these designs too that blended well with the tone of much of Tutuola's writing.

At the end of his stay with the Drama School, Ogunmola achieved his ambition of founding a fully professional company. From then on his popularity rose fast and his perfection grew steadily. I missed few opportunities to see his performances, even though at this stage I had become much more closely associated with another Yoruba Theater company, that of Duro Ladipo. The *Palm Wine Drinkard* remained on Ogunmola's repertoire for years to come, but gradually the costumes and sets became tattered and lost some of their former glamour. The production too moved away gradually from the Arts Theater discipline to Ogunmola's own more relaxed style of production. In some ways this was a pity, but really it merely proved that Ogunmola was a man with a very strong vision of his own, who would not for long incorporate other people's ideas, however brilliant.

In this respect he differed greatly from Duro Ladipo, who always loved to discuss his productions with others, keenly sought criticism of his performances and was wide open to ideas. His approach was completely different from Ogunmola's and he was interested in different aspects of drama. I never saw his theater as being in direct competition with Ogunmola, for they developed quite different styles and talents. The excitement of living in Nigeria at that time was this very profusion and variety of talent that sprouted everywhere.

The two composer-actor-producers did not see themselves as competitors either, until the government's selection of a Yoruba opera for the 1965 Commonwealth Festival in Britain brought some serious misunderstandings and temporarily caused a great deal of bitterness among the companies. With Ogunmola being at the time based in Lagos and in fact banned by the Western Region Government because of his famous play *Yoruba Ronu*, the selectors literally had to make a choice between Ogunmola and Ladipo. It was an almost impossible task, to choose between plays as different as the *Palm Wine Drinkard* and *Oba Koso*. The humor, the refinement of acting, the brilliant timing, the spectacular costumes and designs of the *Drinkard* formed a complete contrast with the poetry, the complex drumming, the real sense of tragedy and the monumental presence of Ladipo in the *Oba Koso*. Unfortunately many of the arguments raised for and against the one or the other play had little to do with theater and a lot with politics. Some comments by adjudicators were indeed trifling and irrelevant. (For example, it was said against the *Palm Wine Drinkard* that "Yorubas drink palm wine from a calabash, not a horn.") If I remember the unpleasant scene correctly, the Western Region selection committee selected *Oba Koso*. The Federal selection committee ordered a replay and favored the *Palm Wine Drinkard*. In the end the Federal Minister of Information overruled and decided on *Oba Koso*. Both companies became pawns of political party squabbles during the time and it left some bitterness and tension between them, antagonisms that were not resolved until much later.

During the coming years Ogunmola led a more and more active life. He took his plays all over the country and drew huge crowds wherever he went. One thing that became clear to me during this time was that he was not merely "popular"; the audience loved him and developed a personal loyalty to him.

In December 1966 I left Nigeria for Papua New Guinea and for some years I was to live without Yoruba Operas. When I returned on a visit in December 1970 in order to attend the Ife Festival of the Arts, I was told that Ogunmola had fallen seriously ill. Wole Soyinka took me to visit him in the University Hospital at Ibadan. To see him prostrate and partly paralyzed was a tremendous shock. I had never known him to be sick, not even mildly. He had always shown incredible stamina; his energy had seemed boundless. I had no idea how old he was: he was one of those alert, ageless people who did not seem to change over the years. Now he looked ravaged, but his courage had not left him. He was a philosopher, who could accept the hardest fate calmly. But it was also clear that he was quietly determined to do the impossible: to get back onto the stage.

Unfortunately Ogunmola was still too ill in December 1971 to witness the first performance of the film *My Brother's Children* at the Fourth Ife Festival of the Arts. This film was made for the International Family Planning Association, and its real purpose was to tell Yoruba people about family planning. The producers, Tony Isaacs and Segun Olusola, had the brilliant idea of asking Ogunmola to write a play on the theme and then they filmed Ogunmola's play. In spite of its strange subject, the film is a monument to E. K. Ogunmola and his genius as an actor and producer. Tony Isaacs, a well-known BBC film producer, was astonished at the sheer professionalism of the company. There is a brilliant quarrel scene in the film, between husband and wife, which was improvised and filmed without rehersal or retake. Tony Isaacs told me that he finished the shooting in less than half the time allotted. It is a great shame that neither the *Palm Wine Drinkard* nor *Love of Money* have been preserved on film, but in the absence of these, *My Brother's Children* will preserve for posterity the greatness of Ogunmola.

Even during these sad times Ogunmola still had time and thoughts for his friends. When the Mbari Club in Oshogbo gave a party for me to mark my return to Nigeria after several years absence, he sent a friend, who presented me with an album and an illuminated address.

During those hard days his wife kept the company together. They continued to play some of the old favorites. But who could play Adeleke like Ogunmola? Who could play the drinkard? Friends rallied to his help. Ogunmola's fellow playwright Wale Ogunyemi stepped into the role of the drinkard in order to give the company a boost.

When I returned to Nigeria a year later in order to take up a position with the University of Ife, Ogunmola was still ill. He lived quietly in Ibadan. His recovery was very slow, but his determination never left him.

Suddenly in May 1972 we heard the incredible news that Ogunmola had announced his return to the stage. His memorable return to the stage had been sponsored by Hubert Ogunde. Peter Brook happened to be on a visit in Ife then and we took him to see Ogunmola's first reappearance in Oshogbo in the Fakunle Major Hotel. It was an incredible event. The nightclub that sometimes serves as a theater for Yoruba Operas could normally hold perhaps three hundred people, but on this occasion there must have been at least a thousand, tightly packed, standing in the aisles, filling out every square inch of the Fakunle Major Hotel and crowding the street outside. The excitement and the noise were incredible.

An incredible roar of delight went up when Ogunmola at last appeared on the stage. Never before has any actor received such a reception. People were beside themselves with joy. Ogunmola had to wait a long time, before the noise had died sufficiently for him to address the crowd. He said that rumors had gone round saying he had died. But thanks to the grace of God he was back there with them and that his greatest wish, to be back on the stage, had been fulfilled. The people laughed and wept and shouted. The noise never died down again and the play had to be acted under this blanket of noise. The actors passed a microphone from one to the other, but even so, we could not hear what they were saying. Nobody cared: Ogunmola was there, alive and back on stage. He was still moving somewhat stiffly, and with difficulty. He was unable to take the lead part and his company had suffered from his long absence. But who cared? Ogunmola was alive and back on stage. We could not hear his words, and it was sad to see him acting a supporting role. But his presence was felt big and strong and warm by everybody. And that incredible, roaring noise was like a kind of ovation. The intense feeling never left the crowd throughout the long evening.

Peter Brook later said he had never seen such strong communication between an actor and his audience. "That man would have communicated with his audience even if he had been invisible."

Ogunmola's return to the stage did not last very long. He struggled gallantly for a while to lead his company. But then he suddenly died. Some felt that he may have hastened his end by exerting himself too much in his comeback. But then it must have been immensely rewarding to him to experience the love his audience felt for him, to see how much he had been missed. That night at the Fakunle Major Hotel was his greatest triumph.

To anyone who ever saw him on stage he remains unforgettable.

Post-Independence Disillusionment in Three African Novels

Emmanuel Obiechina

From the 1940s, when the nationalist movement got under way in Africa, the people were brought to believe that political independence would usher in the millenium, solve all social problems and create a fuller life for everyone. So much was promised and so little was to be realized, or indeed was realizable, given the shortness of vision and the immensity of the difficulties, that disillusionment was bound to set in. From the late 1950s, formal independence was conceded by some of the imperialist powers. In the wake of the euphoria that came with independence, better and better prospects were held out to the masses, more and more promises were made. Post-independence economic plans were based on broad egalitarian precepts which were often an extension of the nationalist rhetoric of the independence struggle. They included commitment to equal opportunities and greater equality in the standard of living, development of opportunities in education, health and employment.

These promises fired the imagination of the different sections of the African population, especially the urban dwellers who stood directly to gain from the transfer of power to the local people. But when it came to "keeping faith" with the people and fulfilling the promises, it became clear that a gulf separated fulfilment from hope. Within a few years of independence, the hopes had collapsed and disillusionment had set in. Political independence was not a panacea. A new black power elite had stepped into the place vacated by the former imperialists. The lot of the common people did not improve as fast as they were led to expect; in some cases, the burden of life became heavier on the poor. The peasantry was becoming pauperized because the agricultural lands were dying from exhaustion; a rapidly increasing population was working the cultivable lands to death, and without new methods of husbandry there was no hope of soil revival. Young semi-literates were deserting the dying villages and drifting into the towns to swell the thousands of unemployed people in the slums and shantytowns. The new political class proved unequal to the challenge of nation-building and incapable of providing moral and civic leadership. The political machinery set up at independence broke down, and there were instabilities attended by coups and counter-coups, with extensive violence. Between 1960 and 1968 alone there were twenty-five unconstitutional changes of government in Africa, of which eighteen were military coups and others were military inspired.[1]

The result of all this has been the alienation of the intellectuals, especially writers and artists, from the politicians and the bureaucratic class which run the post-independence political and administrative machinery. Faced with the new realities of power and politics in Africa, the writers have had to reappraise their role in society. The preoccupation with the past had to give place to concern with the pressing problems of the present.

The reversal of direction has been accompanied by feelings of guilt and self-reproach. Some writers now think their interest in the past was diversionary and wasted resources that could have been more fruitfully expended on the present. It is even being said that preoccupation with the past provided a cover for the post-independence elites to carry on irresponsibly and corruptly.

This view is strongly held by Wole Soyinka and formed the core of his paper presented at the African-Scandinavian Writer's Conference in Stockhom in 1967 on the theme of "The Writer in Modern Africa." Here is part of the essay:

> In the movement towards chaos in Africa, the writer did not anticipate. The understanding language of the outside world, "birth pains", that near-fatal euphemism for death throes, absolved him from responsibility. He was content to turn his eyes backwards in time and prospect in archaic fields for forgotten gems which would dazzle and distract the present. But never inwards, never truly into the present, never into the obvious symptoms of the niggling, warning, predictable present, from which alone lay the salvation of ideas.[2]

He spoke elsewhere in the same paper of "the lack of vital relevance between the literary concerns of writers and the pattern of reality that has overwhelmed even the writers themselves in the majority of modern African states"[3] and later he accused them of an inability to respond with vision to the disturbing and disastrous events which were taking place before them:

> The stage at which we find ourselves is a stage of disillusionment, and it is this which prompts an honest examination of what has been the failure of the African writer, as a writer. And this is not to say that, if the African writer had truly responded to the political moment of his society, he would not still be faced with disillusionment. For the situation in Africa today is the same as in the rest of the world; it is not one of the tragedies which come out of isolated human failures, but the very collapse of humanity. Nevertheless the African writer had done nothing to vindicate his existence, nothing to indicate that he is even aware that this awful collapse has taken place. For he has been generally without vision.[4]

"The very collapse of humanity" is a grandiose phrase. It sounds more imposing than practically relevant. But the general accusation of lack of vision is well grounded, if it implies that the writer should arm himself with a scepticism which will make him, in the midst of popular enthusiasm, a sobering influence, a spokesman for the more durable values. Soyinka had defined the task of the writer in the modern African setting more perceptively at the Unesco Conference on "Colonialism and the Artist's Milieu" in Daressalaam. He said then that "The writer is the visionary of his people, he recognizes past and present not for the purpose of enshrinement but for the local creative glimpses and statement of the ideal future. He anticipates, he warns. It is not always enough for the writer to be involved in the direct political struggle of today, he often cannot help but envisage and seek to protect the future which is the declared aim of the contemporary struggle."[5]

Given the seriousness of events in Africa since independence, the collapse of optimism is understandable, as well as the feeling of guilt and self-reproach among writers that more was not done to warn and admonish. But one must allow for the historical and personal pressures operating on the writers and influencing them to articulate current aspirations. Their perception of the problems of their societies during the struggle for political independence was dominated by nationalist assertiveness. At a time when the nationalist movement called on the corporate energies of the colonized people, the writer had to throw in his lot with the people; he had, as Soyinka has expressed it, to submit "his integrity to the monolithic stresses of the time."[6] As a creative member of his community, his function was to use his art to advance the "cause," and this took the form of a cultural nationalism in which he tried to help his people regain their lost dignity by recreating and interpreting for them their cultural heritage.

The breakdown of this solidarity has been vitalizing to African creative writing. It has, for instance, infused in the writers a certain radicalism as well as sharpened their social instinct. This is evident in the three novels which form the basis of this essay: Soyinka's *The Interpreters* (1965), Achebe's *A Man of the People* (1966) and Ayi Kwei Armah's *The Beautyful Ones Are Not Yet Born* (1968).[7]

The most outstanding feature of these novels is the uncompromising way in which their authors attack the post-independence elite of Africa. Their members are accused of expropriating the masses of the fruits of independence, and, more specifically, of being venal, corrupt, irresponsible, hypocritical and without vision and commonsense. The failure of independence is regarded as evidence of the failure of the elites to justify themselves to the masses and validate their claim to the leadership. The novelists see the post-independence leaders as betraying the pledges they made in the nationalist days to create just, egalitarian and contented new states out of the colonial societies. The writers attack the elite most sharply for creating a standard of living for themselves out of proportion with the national level of economic production, and scandalously higher than that of the rest of society. Most of the social criticism can be traced to this major accusation, that the elite have used their privileged political and administrative position to appropriate the meagre national resources to the near-exclusion of everyone else. David B. Abernathy has tried to find an explanation for this situation: "The government had committed itself to bring about greater equality, yet it was the government officials themselves who were far above the masses in education, income, social status and political power; hence the officials would be the first to suffer losses from any levelling reforms they might institute. This conflict of interest proved difficult, if not impossible, to resolve."[8]

Armah, Soyinka and Achebe adopt an identical narrative approach in their novels. Each sees his subject from behind the mask of a persona or personae. Armah's main persona is the Man, but the Naked Man also conveys some of his other views, the extreme pessimistic ones, which may not synchronize with the consistent image of the Man. Soyinka operates behind his young "interpreters," artists and intellectuals—Sagoe, Sekoni, Kola, Bandele and Egbo— while Achebe uses Odili as mouthpiece. The use of personae allows the writers to explore the questions in all their complexity and to pronounce on them with detachment. The persona is a much more "mobile" personality than the one-dimensional, first-person narrator. Because the persona can represent the author as well as have an independent existence, it is easier for his viewpoint to shift at different stages of the narrative. Moreover, and this is one of the advantages of this narrative approach, the author can, when he so desires, dissociate himself entirely from his persona. He can look critically at the persona while the persona is himself looking critically at specific personal or social evidence. The result is a multiplicity of attitudes, which provides a more complex account than the simple, uncomplicated author-narration. Psychological truth is advanced and the social picture is given more dimensions. The novelists can employ satirical techniques by contrasting viewpoints in this way. Invective, expression of moral outrage or indignation are given "distance," can be played off against each other; when they come directly from the writer they tend to seem simple in their directness. The process itself, of seeing things through other eyes, has a sobering effect.

Soyinka's "interpreters" are very diverse. They are active physically and intellectually and they explore their subjects through action and experience; they are fully participant and comment on social life by their actions as well as by their words. Achebe's Odili is a radical idealist who, like the "interpreters," clarifies the issues through his action and comment, while Armah's the Man ist a contemplative idealist who thinks much and acts little. He keeps the even tenor of his surface life while inwardly, imaginatively and intellectually, he is immensely alive, almost catlike, in his grasp of the nuances of corruption and decay.

The first target of the novels is the tendency for the post-independence elite to "eat up" the meagre national resources of the new states. They are portrayed as having used their position of dominance not to husband national resources, not for stepping up production and disbursing it equitably, but for developing "great appetites" and devouring this wealth almost exclusively. For the members of the elite, the new state is a large and dainty cake to be shared and eaten. The novels borrow these images of "eating" and "sharing" from the politicians who talk of the "sharing of the national cake." The crises in the political and social life of the new states are reducible to the struggles by the elite to decide who should have what portion of the "national cake." The masses are often left out of the calculation, though when the crises hot up for the elite, they often mobilize the support of the masses and sometimes use them as a shield or reduce them to "cannon fodder."

Achebe's *A Man of the People* which deals mainly with the power struggle among the elite is thematically structured around images of "eating" and "sharing." The politics of Chief Nanga and Chief Koko is "eating" politics. Everywhere in the novel, in the parliament, among the people, during political campaigns, the theme is the same: national politics is a frantic struggle for a share of the "national cake." If the nation is not being "eaten," it is being fought over. "Eating-and-sharing" has become an all-pervasive symbol for expressing the absence of health and constructiveness in the body politic; it yields an appropriate metaphor for exploring the corruption and gives a frame to the avariciousness and hedonism of the political class.

A few examples will illustrate the point. In the thick of the conflict between the intellectuals in the parliament and the corrupt philistines, the latter accuse the former of being "snobbish intellectuals . . . (who) sell their mothers for a mess of pottage." (p. 6) When Nanga appeals to Odili to leave his school-mastering in the hinterland and come down to the capital city and join a government department as a civil servant, his reason is expressed in the language of "national cake" politics; he must come and help to secure his people's share of the national cake: "Our people," says Nanga, "must press for their fair share of the national cake." (p. 13) Odili cannot avoid the eating image. He cannot see why "some people's belly is like the earth. It is never so full that it will not take another corpse." (p. 97) Even the names of the two old parties typify the eating tendencies among the politicians. One of them is People's Organization Party (P.O.P.) and the other Progressive Alliance Party (P.A.P.), the one reminds us of "pop-corn" and the other of a popular gruel eaten for breakfast in West African cities. One of the most sustained metaphors of eating is to be found in the section of the novel dealing with the launching of Odili's party, the Common People's Convention, formed by the young radicals to wrest power from the corrupt older parties. In one short passage alone (on pp. 139—40), there are six different references to eating but the crowning image of "eating" politics is in the memorable valediction spoken by Odili about the fall of the politicians and the general state of affairs they have created:

> For I do honestly believe that in the fat-dripping, gummy, eat-and-let-eat regime just ended—a regime which inspired the common saying that a man could only be sure of what he had put away safely in his gut or, in language ever more suited to the times: 'you chop, me self I chop, palaver finish', a regime in which you saw a fellow cursed in the morning for stealing a blind man's stick and later in the evening saw him again mounting the altar of the new shrine in the presence of all the people to whisper into the ear of the chief celebrant—in such a regime, I say, you died a good death if your life had inspired someone to come forward and shoot your murderer in the chest—without asking to be paid. (p. 167)

In *A Man of the People* the politicians are the most inveterate "eaters," but the habit has permeated the rest of the population. For example, Nanga's father-in-law is an avaricious "eater" for whom a prospective son-in-law is an object of exploitation. He explains that the time before one's daughter's marriage is the time to enjoy an in-law, not when he has claimed his wife and gone away. "Our people say: if you fail to take away a strong man's sword when he is on the ground, will you do it when he gets up . . .? No, my daughter. Leave me and my in-law. He will bring and bring and bring and I will eat until I am tired. And thanks to the Man Above he does not lack what to bring. (p. 103) The philosophy of "eating while you may" spreads like a dangerous fungus across the face of national life, destroying and disfiguring it and even threatening to kill the host altogether. Temporary reprieve only comes with a military take-over.

"Eating" and "sharing" images also feature prominently in *The Beautyful Ones Are Not Yet Born* and *The Interpreters*. The hectic scramble for national resources goes on in these two novels too. The politicians as well as lesser citizens are staunch believers in taking what one can out of the general coffers. *The Beautyful Ones Are Not Yet Born* opens with a bus-conductor trying to steal money from passengers' fares. Confronted with an apparently open-eyed watcher (who turns out to be a sleeping passenger), he offers, "You see, we can share." (p. 6) It is all sharing and eating. When the Man attempts to dissociate himself from the shoddy boat deal between Koomson and his mother-in-law, his wife remonstrates with him: "Why are you trying to cut yourself apart from what goes for all of us? . . . you will be eating it with us when it is ripe." (p. 50) Armah sees the fatal social disease in his country as this "eating" propensity. Nothing sums it up better than the crude semi-literate daubing on the wall of a latrine: "SOCIALISM—CHOP MAKE I CHOP, CONTREY BROKE." (p. 124) In *The Interpreters,* Soyinka's eyes see the many ways in which the elite invent occasions to indulge their appetites. One of his "interpreters" seizes on the funeral of Sir Derinola to comment wryly on the interminable orgies and parties of the elite: "The hearse . . . was smothered in wreaths and the mourners carried the extras on their arms. Thank God, said Sagoe, for our orgiastic funerals. If he ever freelanced he knew where to go on lean days. Wedding also, yes, and child-naming, and engagements, and cocktail parties, but a funeral with its night-long waking, its outing, its forty days turning over of the body, its memorial service only a few weeks later, its second turning over of the body, its sudden irrational remembrance feasts—a man could spend his entire life just feasting on a dead man. And many did." (p. 112) The elite go to great lengths to invent excuses for celebrations and indulge their love of ostentation.

But Soyinka and Armah do not stop at describing the eating propensities of the elite; they dwell on the physical corruption that comes with overeating. The elite, glutted with the spoils of their society and given to hedonistic overindulgence, are made to pay a high price in physical and physiological decay and corruption. Soyinka and Armah have given a new dimension to West African fiction by creating in it what may be aptly called the literature of disgust. For example, the Partyman Koomson's moral and political corruption becomes a terrible physical reality when on the day of the military coup he is trapped and cowed in a darkened room. As his confidence deserts him and his fear of being seized by the new regime paralyzes him, he begins to disintegrate and decay physically:

> His mouth had the stench of rotten menstrual blood. The man held his breath until the new smell had gone down in the mixture with the liquid atmosphere of the Party man's farts filling the room. At the same time Koomson's insides gave a growl longer than usual, an inner fart of personal, corrupt thunder which in its fullness sounded as if it had rolled down all the way from the eating throat thundering through the belly and the guts, to end in further silent pollution of the air already thick with flatulent fear. (pp. 191—92)

Already the decadence that comes from overindulgence had been indignantly observed by the Man when he shook hands with the corrupt party-man:

> Koomson . . . looked obviously larger than the chair he was occupying. The man, when he shook hands, was again amazed at the flabby softness of the hand. Ideological hands, the hands of revolutionaries leading their people into bold sacrifices, should these hands not have become even tougher than they were when their owner was hauling loads along the wharf? And yet these were the socialists of Africa, fat, perfumed, soft with the ancestral softness of chiefs who have sold their people and are celestially happy with the fruits of the trade. (pp. 153—54)

Soyinka's Managing Director in *The Interpreters* is part of the same picture of corrupted and decaying human mass created from years of intemperate eating up of the country's limited resources: "The carcass of the Managing Director swelled, spurted greasy globules of the skin in extreme stages of putrefaction and burst in an unintelligible stream through the ruptured throat." (p. 79) Both novels are full of images of throat and belly and of filth and decay arising from intemperate eating. References to bodily secretions, excretions and defecation abound in these novels too, with words like mucus, shit, sweat, urine, lavatory, smears, phlegm, grime and saliva. Indeed, one of Soyinka's "interpreters" invents a "lavatorial" philosophy he calls "voidancy." According to him, "Next to death . . . shit is the most vernacular atmosphere of our beloved country." (p. 108) Blunt speaking, calling things by their proper names, is these writers' device for dealing with the wholesale corruption that has overwhelmed their societies. The tradition goes deep both in writing literature and in the oral cultures of West Africa. It traces its line in Western literature back to the classical satirists through the medieval scatological preachers, Chaucer, Swift and the British "kitchen-sink" dramatists of our own time. Plain speaking is also an element of traditional language, especially in satirical songs and personal altercations. Achebe's rural novels contain very impressive examples of robust rustic bluntness, especially in moments of heated exchange as when the priest of Idemili sends an insulting message to Ezeulu and when the police officer sent to arrest Ezeulu encounters the active challenge of Ezeulu's son. As for satirical bluntness, anyone reading *Igbo Traditional Verse* by Romanus Egudu and Donatus Nwoga, *Orin Ibeji (Songs in Praise of Twins)* by Val

Olayemi, *The Song of Lawino* by Okot p'Bitek and other African work in the vernaculars cannot but be impressed by the absence of bourgeois squeamishness. Chaucer's bluntness is, in this respect, the nearest thing to rustic bluntness in Africa.

The African writers' verbal bluntness can be seen to derive from oral and literary traditions. Or to put it differently, the African writer out to attack social abuse finds ready to hand in the African oral tradition a method which he can pick up, polish and elaborate through his literary medium to produce a powerful neo-African literary mode. And this is what many of them do. In *The Beautyful Ones Are Not Yet Born, The Interpreters* and to some extent *A Man of the People* this bluntness powerfully focusses attention on the social vices being attacked. It is therefore a very effective method of satire.

Scatology has other uses in these works. It is adopted by the writers in order to prick the vast bubble of false respectability blown up by the African elite. Dirt and filth become dialectal instruments for attacking false gentility, philistinism masquerading as civilization, and hedonism and voluptuousness disguised as good living. The elite have set up a front which obscures their own pretentiousness, hollowness and lack of vision, as well as the abject poverty and the indescribable squalor of the lives of the common people and the peasantry. Scatology is a way of answering the elite's claim to have brought progress to the masses and justified the fight for national independence. The writers attempt, through the scatological technique, to prove that the elite have succeeded in inflicting on the masses more disabling disasters than the departed imperialists, that they have strengthened and refined old methods of oppression, forged new chains to hold the masses down and infused their souls with spiritual diseases more damaging than the physical manacles of imperialism. In the midst of so much dirt, filth, squalor, want and disease, the elite attempt desperately to carve out a snug little pocket of cleanness, health, selfsufficiency and prosperity for their members but the filth and squalor find them out and everything is drowned in what Armah calls "victorious filth". (p. 15)

The novelists' most developed satirical instrument is contrast. Each of them contrasts the state of magnificence in which the elite live and the desperate poverty of the rest of the people. In these three novels, the contrast is, in addition, between the spick-and-span plushness of the elite's world and the squalid, filthy world of the poor. Very often, these worlds exist in uneasy juxtaposition. Soyinka makes the office of the *Independent Viewpoint* an illustration of these contrasts. Sagoe's visit to the two toilets—one for the junior staff and the other for the senior staff—is an epitome of contrasting worlds of the elite and the common people. In the one, "(The) cistern was caked and unflushed, and its walls matched the radio station's in suspicious smears," (p. 76) while in the other, after Sagoe has pushed in the Engaged bolt, "Immediately, a light wraith of scented breeze fanned him about the neck and filled the luxurious furnishing of the ante-room. It was an automatic purifier device imported by the Managing Director on his seventh Economic

Mission to Sweden." (p. 82) The board-room bears testimony to the spirit in which the nation is run, almost exclusively in the interest of the elite. (p. 75) The filth that covers the rest of the society now and again spills over and spoils this comfort, as when a nightcart and trailer carrying human waste collide in the middle of a highway and render the road unusable for everyone. The moral is explicit. Selfseeking and concupiscence render the elite insensitive to the plight of the rest of the society, but this insensitivity and neglect of the common people generate their own dynamic which in the end engulfs everyone in a national catastrophe.

Images of filth, squalor and decay are also used to describe the literal physical reality. The persistent hacking at the fact of physical ugliness and filth is of a piece with the novelists' indictment of the society as a whole and the elite who lead it in particular. The inference is often obvious: you cannot produce good men out of squalor and physical dirt. The evocation of dirt and decay is thus a double-edged metaphor. On the one side, it symbolizes the spiritual filth and decay which results from moral corruption; on the other, it symptomizes the general social blindness and ineptitude which prevent the proper organization, development and progress of the society. The inability to maintain physical cleanliness through a proper disposal of refuse indicates the failure of the elite to operate the modern state effeciently.

A very good example is the attempt by the Accra urban council to maintain urban cleanliness. A campaign has been mounted with some success and "big shots" have been pressed into radio appeals, but what follows is an anti-climax. Only a few boxes are supplied "though there was a lot said about the large amount of money paid for them." (p. 9) In other words, someone has used the opportunity for personal gain and sabotaged a worthwhile public project. Next, the few boxes supplied are not emptied periodically as they ought to be. The small boxes are soon filled and people continue to throw their waste not inside but about them. "People still used them, and they overflowed with banana peels and mango seeds and thoroughly sucked-out oranges and the chaff of sugarcane and most of all the thick brown wrapping from a hundred balls of *kenkey*. People did not have to go up to the boxes any more. From a distance they aimed their rubbish at the growing heap, and a good amount of juicy offal hit the face and sides of the box before finding a final resting place upon the heap. As yet the box was still visible above it all, though the writing upon it could no longer be read." (p. 9)

The writing that could no longer be read is "K. C. C. RECEPTACLE FOR DISPOSAL OF WASTE" printed in blue, and "KEEP YOUR COUNTRY CLEAN BY KEEPING YOUR CITY CLEAN," executed in lucent red. At the time of the campaign "the letters had (had) . . . their brief brightness" but now they have irrecoverably faded away. Corruption and official irresponsibility combine to destroy a praiseworthy social project. The failure is an acid comment on the way the post-independence elite are attempting to run the independent states. The effect on the masses is equally profound, for the elite infect the common people with their failings.

It is not hard to see why corruption should have assumed such serious proportions in the post-independence period. Educated West Africans felt frustrated during the colonial period because the colonial regime offered them restricted opportunities to get into lucrative public service or enter commercial or industrial competition against the ruling interests. For them therefore the struggle was essentially to oust the colonial ruling class in order to replace it with an indigenous ruling class drawn from the educated middle class. Independence is seen first and foremost as a transfer of economic control and patronage from a foreign power elite to an indigenous one. The creation of mass parties gave a superficial impression of a populist-based political philosophy and organization; in reality, the dominant ideological orientation remained elitist. If one needed any evidence for this, it is clearly available in the fact that the new independence regimes carried over the colonial structure of administration, privileges and perquisites with as little modification as possible.

The result is far-reaching. The educated middle class which has inherited the privileges of the colonialists is promoting inequality in the new states; its living standards are inflated relative to those of the workers and peasants; this generates resentment among the less privileged and this in turn gives rise to instability. A number of corollaries follow. The elite's high standard of living has a damaging effect on national life by destroying the morale of the masses, and it puts the elite themselves on the defensive, in that they are constantly having to defend their privileges against the pressure of the under-privileged, especially as social alignments are beginning to be defined in terms of "the haves" and "the have-nots." This exacerbates existing conflicts and contradictions. Again, because the middle classes have accepted the principle of unequal distribution of wealth implicit in the colonial structure, they have tended to take up also the capitalist idealogy which supports inequality; their members are instinctively averse to egalitarian social systems. The dilemma of the elite is easy to see. The urge towards the development of a capitalist class is strong, yet the absence of an indigenous source of capital is a constant worry. The meagreness of resources means that it is not easy to take substantial slices away from public resources without being noticed. The absence of a strong indigenous bourgeois class with a capitalist tradition and capital of its own is also a major factor, since anyone aspiring to capitalist accumulation will sooner or later run up against the general anticapitalist tendencies of the population. Given this contradictory situation, the elite's behavior is understandably inconsistent. Sometimes, in their attempt to have the best of all possible worlds, they preach socialism and practice capitalist tenets, and sometimes they evade any ideological or intellectual position at all, hoping that the situation will resolve itself.

The writers recognize both the dilemmas and the ways adopted by the elite to get round them. But they do not approve. Ayi Kwei Armah, for example, indicts the Ghanaian elite for preaching socialism and living capitalism. The Nigerians, Soyinka and Achebe, in whose country the ruling elite have not taken up a public position one way or another, attack the unbridled acquisitiveness of the elite which has brought the new state to grief. Behind these criticisms is the writers' conviction that only a populist, socialist organization of the new states will put them on a proper road to progress. They are therefore uncompromising in their attack on privilege and the tendencies towards property accumulation by those in leadership of the new states.

The writers satirize the corrupt methods used by many people to amass wealth. It is a doleful tale of embezzlement of public funds, appropriation of public resources, diversion of public facilities to private use and the use of bribery and corruption for personal enrichment. A corrupt society is full of thieves, big and small, professional and amateur. In the three novels, embezzlement of public resources by the post-independence rulers of the African states is the central focus of the writers' attack; the biggest public officials, according to them, are the biggest thieves.

In *The Beautyful Ones Are Not Yet Born,* Armah's the Man, watching with dismay the audacity with which public officials appropriate public resources for their personal ends declares that "stealing is a national game" and dismisses the change of government as a result of the February 1966 military coup in Ghana as just "a change of embezzlers", no more. (p. 191)

Leading the line of embezzlers is the corrupt politician, His Excellency Joseph Koomsoon, Minister Plenipotentiary, Member of the Presidential Commission, Hero of Socialist Labour. With a cluster of titles that would do honor to a Gilbertian comic emperor, Koomson is a master of the art of corruption who exploits his public office to enrich himself, destroy the promise of independence and trample down socialism. The most glaring example of Koomson's dishonesty is when, in spite of his ministerial appointment, he borrows state credit under cover names to invest in fishing boats.

> "I had asked Oyo's mother who would pay for the boats, and with a great deal of pride she said the Minister would. Which minister? Koomson, of course. Only she called him Brother Joe. Brother! Aach, so. I said I didn't know Koomson had enough money to buy even one boat. Those things cost thousands and thousands of cedis. My mother-in-law asked me very patiently whether I did not know also that Brother Joe had influence. She called it infruence. I had taken a piece of paper to calculate Koomson's total salary since he joined the Party. Now I dropped the paper and said, 'Oh, I see.' And again with this patience of hers my mother-in-law asked me what I had seen at last. So I got angry enough to tell her I had seen corruption. Public theft." (p. 29)

Koomson of course soon proves the old lady right; he is a staunch believer in the omnipotence of power, in the everlasting possibilities of "influence." His motto is: "Everything is possible, it depends on the person," (p. 175) that is, on who you are and where you stand in the structure of influence and power. Compare the statement in *A Man of the People* that "A common saying in the country after Independence was that it didn't matter *what* you knew but *who* you knew." (p. 19) Finding money for the boats is no insurmountable problem. In fact he says boastfully, "The money ist not the diffi-cult thing. After all, the Commercial Bank is ours, and we can do anything." (p. 160) The Commercial Bank, formed originally to liberalize credit for the people, has become the property of the politicians and a means of serving their greed. Koomson gets the State Furniture Corporation to furnish his house free because, as his shallow wife reminds us, "Joe is like this with the Manager." (p. 174) Koomson uses his "influence" to make a scholarship available to his empty-headed sister-in-law to study dress-making in England and is even expected to make hard-to-come-by foreign exchange available to her to buy a Jaguar car because "She says she has fallen in love with a Jaguar, and she's going to kill herself if she can't have it." (p. 175) Koomson cannot quite reconcile himself to the view that cabinet ministers should not involve themselves in business. This he regards as a "nuisance" and one of the effects of "this foolish socialism that will spoil everybody's peace," (p. 159) as if ministers in capitalist states are not bound by the same rule. Of course, he gets round the problem by finding "somebody to . . . er, lend us the name" and cooperate with him in "a kind of partnership." (p. 161)

In the midst of all the corruption, self-seeking and public embezzlement going on in *The Beautyful Ones Are Not Yet Born,* the ghost of socialism, like the ghost of Banquo at Macbeth's dinner, glides in and out of the con-science of the elite, disturbing its inner peace, jolting its serenity and ruffling its moral assurance. Even the insensitivity of Koomson is threatened by the formal, socialist expectations which represent a certain constraint on evil-doers. Koomson finds these expectations inconvenient: "Now take this boat business, for instance," he cries at one stage, "there is a lot of money to be made in it, but start something, and fools will start shouting slogans at you." And elsewhere "they say we are socialists ministers, so we shouldn't do these things." (p. 160) Armah's disillusionment is not with socialism as such but with the travesty of it, the negation of its promises, and, more specifically, with political leaders and bureaucratic bourgeois who pretend to be socialists while their actions belie their pretences. Armah's disappointment is with the elite who have betrayed independence and infused the masses with cynicism:

> How long will Africa be cursed with its leaders? There were men dying from loss of hope, and other were finding gaudy ways to enjoy power they did not have. We were ready here for big and beautiful things, but what we had was our own black men hugging new paunches scrambling to ask the white man to welcome them onto our backs. These men who were to lead us out of our despair, they came like men already grown fat and cynical with the eating of centuries of power they had never struggled for, old before they had even been born into power, and ready only for the grave. (p. 94)

Perhaps Armah shows naiveté by putting so much trust in the heady natio-nalistic rhetoric and the orchestrated shouts of "Freedom." But he is right to deplore the opportunistic part the elite have played in the post-indepen-dence disaster. Like the school drop-out and ex-docker Koomson, these people passed through the ideological school without letting the ideology pass through them:

> Everybody says with the wave of the hand, "Oh, you know, the ideological thing. Winneba." True. That is where the shit of the country is going nowadays, believing nothing, but saying they believe everything that needs to be believed, so lang as the big jobs and the big money follows. Men who know nothing about politics have grown hot with ideology, thinking of the money that will come. The civil servant who hates socialism is there, singing hosanna. The poet is there, serving power and waiting to fill his coming paunch with crumbs. He will no doubt jump to go and fit his tongue into new arses when new men spring up to shit on us. Everybody who wants speed goes there, and the only thing demanded of them is that they be good at fawning. (p. 104)

Armah hints that there is something wrong with a regime that is so easily exploitable through opportunism. The dissembling game succeeds so well because an adequate structural framework, self-correcting and principle-oriented, is yet to be evolved. Huge ideological gaps exist through which the anti-socialist elite twist, turn and manoeuvre, until they are ready to smash up the machinery. Armah's bitterness is hardly concealed in his scathing criticism of the political and bureaucratic class in Ghana. No one escapes his indignation, from the President to the lowest fawning and scraping little man. But it is obvious that he pities the common people who are the victims.

Soyinka's satire against corruption has no overt indignation but it is barbed with wit and irony. His main targets include the public thieves, hypocrites, apostates, snobs, cunning leaders and overcredulous followers.

Like Armah, he shows up the public men who use their position and political patronage to enrich themselves and further their interests. His strategy is developed around the Board of the *Independent Viewpoint* which is taken as the nation in miniature. The Board members are selected by dubious criteria, chief of which is compensation for political loyalty. They are referred to as "Compensation Members" and Sagoe tries to match them with each "compensation" aspect: "Lost elections, missed nominations, thug recruitment, financial backing, Ministerial in-lawfulness, Ministerial poncing, general arse-licking, Ministerial concubinage . . ." (p. 11) But this general berating of public men is less effective than the satire of specific individuals. The unnamed Managing Director, for example, represents official pomposity and irresponsibility. He floats around the world on interminable economic missions accumulating rubbish instead of promoting the progress of the press over which he presides. His ineffectuality is symbolized by the crude and useless radiogram which takes so much space in the boardroom:

> Like two halves of a broad bean, the pachydermous radiogram and the Managing Director. And his attempt to disown his twin brother proved futile, in spite of the delicate china set from which they all, except Chief Winsala, sipped tea. The Director had picked up the set in the tenth economic mission to American China; he donated it to the Board remarking, "You know, Shanghai Chek has exactly this kind of cup and saucer." (p. 78)

As bad, if not worse, are the Chairman of the Board, Sir Derinola, a retired judge permanently identified by his *abetiaja* clothcap, and Chief Winsala, a gross, spirit-swilling buffoon. Soyinka makes a deft scene of the attempt by Chief Winsala to extract a bribe from Sagoe at the Hotel Excelsior, while Sir Derinola hides in his car outside waiting for his own share of the "kola." Chief Winsala tries by a mixture of half-veiled threats and bonhomie to get Sagoe to pay him fifty pounds for the job for which he has been interviewed by a board. Winsala's first, and quite unexpected, problem is establishing his identity, to a Sagoe deliberately and mischievously pretending ignorance of him. But Winsala rides the difficulty by assumed heartiness: "Let me refresh your memory. You were our interviewee the day before yesterday morning . . . I am a member of the Board to which you came to answer our advertisement . . . By the way, I take schnapps." (p. 83) Winsala goes on to make a number of weighty observations including: "Degree is two for penny . . . No more degree passport", "The job is there, but you have to secure it", "When the Sanitary Inspector looks under the bed he's looking for kola, not tanwiji (mosquito larva)." Of course, he gets no bribe and goes through a mortifiying experience in the hands of the bartenders when he cannot pay for his drinks, Sagoe having meanwhile slipped away under pretence of going to find the bribe. Sagoe in the end saves him by paying for the drinks but the discovery of the meanness and corruption of the Chief and the black knight who is reputed to be a pillar of integrity, proves an embarrassment to him. "He (Sagoe) was the guilty one who had trespassed on secrets that should never be exposed." (p. 86) He has seen these great men in their moral nakedness and the impression is so strong that later, in a state of feverish reverie, he actually imagines Sir Derin emerging naked and maudlin out of Dehinwa's cupboard.

But more sinister than the corruption itself are the hypocrisy and cynicism which refuse to recognise its reality and which continue to whitewash it. So Sir Derin goes to his grave in a blase of glory, with the orator lavishing much flatulent, rhetorical panegyric on him at his graveside, crowned with such lofty sentiments as "his life (is) our inspiration, his idealism our hopes, the survival of his spirit in our midst the hope for a future Nigeria, for moral irridentism and national rejuvenescence . . ." (p. 113) The last bit sounds like a malediction of Nigeria. Corruption has eaten so far into the fabric that the power of moral dicrimination seems also to have died. How can it be otherwise when the organs of mass communication are under the control of corrupt officialdom? Nwabuzor, the hypercynical editor of the *Independent Viewpoint* brings the matter home to Sagoe after his article exposing official scandal has been censored by the hierarchy of his newspaper: "Shut your mouth, I shut mine." (p. 95) The morally sensitive organs of public decency have been blunted by official corruption helped by middle class cupidity and opportunism. Nwabuzor's "But look man, journalism here is just a business like any other. You do what your employer tells you," (p. 95) may sound like a piece of realistic commonsense, but not in a situation of appalling immorality and social disintegration. If the press cannot be a force for moral guidance and for exposing immorality and if the journalist cannot do more than please his employer, the situation is hopeless.

The novelists criticize the elite for complacently creating a different life-style for themselves from the rest of the people. They are shown scrambling to take over the roles, posts and privileges of the former white colonial administrators and to absorb the white man's manners and habits. These "black-white" men (also referred to by Armah as "Golf-course" Blacks) are the pet abomination of the novelist because their uncritical imitation of the white man is symptomatic of the loss of the idealism which, in popular imagination at any rate, animated the struggle for independence. They are easy targets for these catlike satirists who keep their eyes skinned for the absurd and the incongruous in contemporary life. But the "black oyibos" (Soyinka's term for them) are attacked for more substantial reasons. Ridiculous they are, but the novelists also see them as dangerous. Their hankering after European bourgeois elegance is regarded as a deep-seated craving by the class to remove itself from the rest of the people and perpetuate its status as a permanent ruling class, showing its European bourgeois symbols as aspects of its equipment for leadership. The symbols are to mystify the masses, overawe them and compel them to look up to the black bourgeoisie. More important, the situation is regarded by the writers as a reflection of the overall lack of sensitivity, which asserts itself most strongly in the elite's inability to understand or identify with the yearnings of the masses, to evolve original and constructive ideas for the building of the new states, and to give direction and meaning to independence. The more the elite cut themselves off from the rank and file the less they are able to provide adequate leadership. The most serious criticism of the black bourgeoisie is that they absorb the externals of the bourgeois culture while missing its inner qualities: to absorb bourgeois "form" without bourgeois "content," as someone aptly put it. Western bourgeois culture evolved organically out of the historical development of Western society. In Africa, the bourgeois class is largely an adventitious growth. Its impact is therefore largely gestural and diversionary, since it diverts effort away from the development and strengthening of a mass culture that will be more organically based in the African people and society.

That the bitterest attacker of the "black imitators" is Ayi Kwei Armah is not surprising since coastal Ghana (as well as coastal Sierra Leone, Liberia and Gambia) has for a long time had a highly Westernized black bourgeoisie who take their cultural model and attitudes from the Europeans. The coming of independence would not immediately change these people. Indeed, independence makes available to this class the means of expressing its new status through easier espousal of Western status-symbols. Here, for example, Armah catches a group of "Golf Course" blacks in one of their ridiculous postures:

> Five white men and three women came down the road. Hidden in the group, in stiff white uniform, were two Ghanaian men with prosperous-looking bellies. Four little boys struggled behind them all, carrying their bags and

> sticks. As they went past, one of the black men laughed in a forced Senior
> Service way and, smiling into the face of one of the white men, kept saying,
> "Jolly good shot, Jimmy. Jolly good."
> He was trying to speak like a white man, and the sound that came out of
> his mouth reminded the listener of a constipated man, straining in his first
> minute on top of the lavatory seat. The white man grimaced and made a
> reply in steward boy English: "Ha, too good eh?" The black men both
> laughed out loud, and the one who had spoken put both hands to his paunch.
> (pp. 146—47)

Other symbols remind us that nothing has changed with independence.
There are the usual prams pushed by little black baby-minders. The difference
is that the babies are not white but "black as coal." The black bourgeoisie
have found homes in the former all-white surburban reservation, but even
here the desire to be "white" is unmistakeable, the evidence is provided by
"names of black men with white souls and names trying mightily to be white."
"In the forest of white men's names, there were the signs that said almost
aloud: here lives a black imitator. Mills-Hayford . . . Plange-Bannermann . . .
Attoh-White . . . Kuntu-Blankson. Others that must have been keeping the
white neighbours laughing even harder in their homes. Acromond . . . what
Ghanaian name could that have been in the beginning, before its Civil Servant
owner rushed to civilize it, giving it something like the sound of a master
name? Grantson . . . more and more incredible they were getting. There was
someone calling himself Fentengson in this wide world, and also a man called
Binful." (p. 147)

Soyinka also satirizes the "black oyibos" for aspiring to the manners and
cultural habits of white men. But they invariably emerge as caricatures. Professor Oguazor is a regular comic butt, with his affected manner and English
gentleman's accent. He is almost grotesque in his odious preoccupation with
"merals", especially in his fiery denunciation of "meral terpitude" in the
university after a young student has become pregnant. "The college cannot
afford to herve its name dragged down by the meral terpitude of irresponsible
young men. The younger generation is too merally corrupt," (p. 250) he
cries. The morally conscious professor has not been a model of discretion
all his life; indeed, he had had a daughter by his housemaid and had her
"tucked away in private school in Islongton." (p. 149) Faseyi, another of the
phoney "black-white" academics, is a snob and social-climber, obsessed with
etiquette, and riduculously insisting on formality of dress, including "white
gloves for the lady." The lady is his English wife, luckily a sensible girl who
has no time for such silliness.

More crippling to the black bourgeoisie is the demand which the bourgeois life makes on its adherents. To keep up the appearances costs money,
and in desperately underdeveloped states the cost cannot easily be met without
some kind of injustice to someone or some group of people in the society.
The economic equation must be such that those who maintain bourgeois standards do so at the expense of those whose fortunes must be depressed. Since

this class has no independent wealth of its own, it can only sustain its high standard of living by taking more from the common pool than is justly due to it and this gives rise to an endemic state of crises and instabilities in the new states. Because most of the available resources are government controlled, the distribution of these resources is vested in politicians or those who have replaced them as government, and that explains why most members of the elite in the new states are attracted to politics and why the political struggle is so murderous, why anyone in power never wants to let go of the reins. The line that separates a man from great wealth and power and great poverty and obscurity can be very thin indeed, and can be crossed amazingly easily by the loss of an election. A politician is tempted to cling to power at all costs. Also the temptation to "make it" while you may is overwhelming. The prospect of a sudden reversal must be one of the nigthmares haunting public men in Africa.

A vicious circle exists here. Everyone is eager to receive his "fair share" of the national cake. Those in power are aware that to make more than others they must continue as the sharers, that is, they must retain political control. But they are also aware that there are many outside sharpening their knives and eager to get in and cut their own slice. So, while he is at it, the politician tries to cut as much as he can, for the rainy day. Those outside become more and more frantic as those within batten on the national cake. They may try to stop them through constitutional means, but this may not always be possible when those in power neutralize this machinery or those outside are too impatient to go through its processes. The situation generates instability, plots and counterplots, coups and countercoups, most of which may not bring fundamental differences except to replace one set of the "eating bourgeoisie" with another set. There is considerable bitterness and some truth in the words of one of Armah's characters after the first Ghanaian coup that it was only a matter of "new people, new style, old dance . . ." and that soon "another group of bellies will be bursting with the country's riches." (p. 185) Achebe's Odili sums the matter up admirably in *A Man of the People:*

> The first thing critics tell you about our ministers' official residences is that each has seven bedrooms, and seven bathrooms, one for every day of the week. All I can say is that on that first night there was no room in my mind for criticism. I was simply hypnotized by the luxury of the great suite assigned to me. When I lay down in the double bed that seemed to ride on a cushion of air, and switched on that reading lamp and saw all the beautiful furniture anew from the lying down position and looked beyond the door to the gleaming bathroom and the towels as large as a *lappa* I had to confess that if I were at that moment made a minister I would be most anxious to remain one for ever... We ignore man's basic nature if we say, as some critics do, that because a man like Nanga had risen overnight from poverty and insignificance to his present opulence he could be persuaded without much trouble to give it up again and return to his original state.
> A man who has just come in from the rain and dried his body and put on dry clothes is more reluctant to go out again than another who has been

> indoors all the time. The trouble with our new nation—as I saw it then
> lying on that bed—was that none of us had been indoors long enough to be
> able to say "To hell with it". We had all been in the rain together until
> yesterday. Then a handful of us—the smart and the lucky and hardly ever
> the best—had scrambled for the one shelter our former rulers left, and had
> taken it over and barricaded themselves in. (pp. 41—42)

When they create a different world for themselves, the elite lose sight of
the problems of the ordinary people. How could the Koomsons, the Nangas
and the Oguazors really understand the crushing poverty of the masses?
Ensconced in ministerial mansions and surburban villas or in the artificial
cosiness of a professorial mansion in the sedate little world of the academics,
how could these people really understand the plight of Armah's the Man and
the Naked Man and the other unfortunate people trapped in the permanent
maze of poverty and insecurity, those "living dead" about whom Armah writes
so harrowingly and sadly,

> the increasing numbers who had decided they were so deep in despair that
> there was nothing worse to fear in life. These were the men who had finally,
> and so early, so surprisingly early, seen enough of something in their own
> lives and in the lives around them to convince them of the final futility of
> efforts to break the mean monthly cycle of debt and borrowing, borrowing
> and debt ... But perhaps the living dead could take some solace in the half-
> thought that there were so many others dead in life with them. So many, so
> frighteningly many, that maybe in the end even the efforts one made not to
> join them resulted only in another, more frustrating kind of living death.
> (p. 25)

One bourgeois tendency which the writers criticize is the desire of the black
elite to perpetuate themselves by giving their children superior educational
opportunities. There are quality schools, the so-called "Corona" and "Santa
Maria" schools for the children of the black bourgeoisie who can pay the high
fees demanded and bad and indifferent school for the children of the poor.
Armah sees the practice as an indication of an inferiority complex and another
symptom of the desire of the elite to become like the white man. Koomson's
daughter, absurdly named "Princess," is a product of such a school and so
are Nanga's children, though Nanga sensibly insists on taking the children to
the village so that they do not lose the traditional culture altogether and, more
importantly, so that the village influence will cancel out the more objection-
able gloss of the elite school. Mrs. Nanga does not want her children to "become English people.» (p. 43) Children trained in these special schools have
advantages. According to Dr. Barbara B. Llyod, "Children of the educated
elite are taller, heavier, healthier, and begin schooling earlier and with more
skills than the products of illiterate or traditional Yoruba homes. These are
the most obvious results of superior housing, diet, medical care—in fact, of
privilege."[9]

The novelists also accuse the elite, especially the political elite, of being
anti-intellectual. Towards the end of the passage in *A Man of the People* in

which Achebe attempts to diagnose the main cause of the political malaise in
Africa, he speaks of the post-independence politician's tendency, after barricad-
ing himself in the ministerial mansion, to persuade everyone else through
loudspeakers that "all argument should cease and the whole people (should)
speak with one voice and that any more dissent and argument outside the door
of the shelter would subvert and bring down the whole house." (p. 42) There
is one section of the population that by training and historial orientation is
not content to stop all argument and speak "with one voice," a group which
by tradition is more likely to speak in a babel of tongues than "with one
voice." This is the intellectual class. Even if it is only for speaking with a different voice from that of the post-independence politicians, this class would
have rendered itself abhorrent to the politicians. But there are more substantial
reasons why intellectuals are not beloved of the politicians, especially when
things are not going as well as they should. The intellectual class in Africa is
rooted in a world culture and feels most poignantly the possibilities and promises of a new society; it is also acutely aware of lost opportunities and the
dimming of visions. Moreover, the intellectual class has developed a way of
looking at the world which includes constant striving towards the ideal and
the elevated. The spiritual dimension is antithetical to the materialistic obsession of the politicians. Intellectuals are bound, in their quest for the ideal,
to come into conflict with politicians whose actions are governed largely by
expediency. Laurens van der Post sums up the intellectual position of the
African writers as the projectors of ideal values in this way:

> In view of the ominous breakdown in the religious machinery in Africa,
> writers, both in Africa and of Africa, have a tremendous responsibility laid
> upon them. Art to me is the technique of presenting unrealized and hidden
> values to people potentially capable of appreciating and understanding those
> values. It is a means by which men can penetrate places in their minds and
> souls they had never reached before. Writing especially can be a kind of
> magic mirror which holds up to man and society the neglected and unrealized
> aspects of himself and his age.[10]

Because writers and other intellectuals represent a force hostile to the aspirations of the peddlers of corrupt conformism, they are often attacked by corrupt regimes. Achebe speaks in *A Man of the People* of "the . . . general
anti-intellectual feeling in the country." (p. 29) As corruption swamped the
post-independence states and intellectuals of all types became increasingly stri-
dent in their criticisms, the political class became more and more bitterly opposed to intellectualism. All over West Africa, there developed a distinctive
opposition to intellectuals by politicians and to a lesser extent, the bureaucratic
and commercial elite. Political parties used a few intellectuals, of course, but
these were mere hostages of the political machine and constantly at war with
the party bureaucracy which was more often than not manifestly anti-intellectual.

In the novels, anti-intellectualism, philistinism and corruption go together. The characters most thoroughly corrupt tend also to be the most anti-intellectual. Chief Nanga who is supposed to be a minister of culture does not even know the few writers of his country. At a Writer's Society book exhibition which he is to open as the minister in charge of cultural affairs, he is more concerned with the proprieties of dress and address than with culture and literature. He shamelessly acknowledges that he has never heard of his country's most famous novel, yet he is anxious to announce his impending honorary doctorate from an American university for his services to culture. Not surprisingly, when Odili surveys the cultural minister's library, all that it contains are a decorative set of an American encyclopaedia, cheap pulp romances, *She* and *The Return of She* by Rider Haggard, a few books by Marie Corelli and Bertha Clay, and the all-purpose *Speeches: How to Make Them.* (p. 45)

Anti-intellectualism takes different forms in the novels, from Koomson's cavilling at the intellectuals, through Nanga's vulgar jokes at the expense of good education to deliberate obstruction of competently qualified professionals. In *A Man of the People,* anti-intellectualism assumes frighteningly dangerous proportions during the political crisis at the beginning of the novel. The Minister of Finance, "a first-rate economist with a Ph. D. in public finance," has advised cutting the price of coffee in answer to a prevailing slump in the coffee market. The Prime Minister, who is facing an election, will not hear of this; instead, he causes the National Bank to print fifteen million pounds more money. Then he dismisses the Minister of Finance and two-thirds of the cabinet which supports him. He then mounts his anti-intellectual campaign because "the Miscreant Gang" (the name invented for the dismissed men) "were all university people and highly educated professional men." The ground is prepared for Nanga and people like him who shout their way to prominence on the high tide of demagogic anti-intellectualism. The editor of the party newpaper sets the tone of the campaign:

> Let uns now and for all time extract from our body-politic as a dentist extracts a stinking tooth all those decadent stooges versed in text-book economics and aping the white man's mannerisms and way of speaking. We are proud to be Africans. Our true leaders are not those intoxicated with their Oxford, Cambridge or Harvard degrees but those who inspeak the language of the people. Away with the damnable and expensive university education which only alienates an African from his rich and ancient culture and puts him above his people . . . (p. 4)

Though the attack is couched in pseudo-nationalistic terms, the intention is to silence the voice of englightened dissent and of sanity. The Prime Minister caps this incitement with a "solemn" declaration in parliament: "From today we must watch and guard our hard-won freedom jealously. Never again must we entrust our destiny and the destiny of Africa to the hybrid class of Western-educated and snobbish intellectuals who will not hesitate to sell their mothers for a mess of pottage." (p. 6) In other words, the intellectuals have become traitors because they would rather the country experienced economic austerity than senseless inflation. Nanga later speaks disparagingly against African specialists because he is not allowed to build a road to his constituency for his buses because the technical problems need first to be studied. He denounces this as "dillying and dallying" and abuses the specialists, referring to him as "one small boy . . . we all helped to promote last year." (p. 48) He expresses his preference for a white "expert" who is likely to prove more obliging and less obstructive.

In *The Interpreters,* the corrupt speak disparagingly of university education, but the most striking feature is the deliberate frustration of intellectuals. Sekoni, the engineer, comes home from overseas studies well qualified, enthusiastic and patriotic, only to find official prejudice in the way of his using his knowledge unsefully. He is initially reduced to signing bicycle vouchers, approving leave applications and duty rosters and interviewing third class clerks. When Sekoni protests that his professional knowledge is being wasted, he is stigmatized as "one of the keen ones" and sent to work on the "Ijioha Project" for producing cheap electrical power. Now in his proper element, Sekoni builds an experimental power station. The Chairman suborns an expatriate "expert" and has the project discredited:

> To Ijioha Sekoni went, "where you may work with your hands until your back blisters" and Sekoni built a small experimental power station. And the chairman chuckled and said, "I knew he was our man. Get me the expat. expert." Hot from his last lucrative "evaluation", came the expatriate expert. Expatriate, therefore impartial.
> "'Constitute yourself into a one-man commission of enquiry and probe the construction of our power station at Ijioha which was built without estimates approved expenditure."
> "Is it unsafe for operation?" and he winked, a truly expert expat. expert's wink.
> "That's the safest idea. You put it in technical language." And the expatriate expert came to Ijioha, saw and condemned. And the chairman read the report and said, "that expert never fails one", salivating on the epithets, a wasteful expenditure, highly dangerous conditions, unsuitable materials, unsafe for operation.
> "Bring me the Write-off file," chortled the chairman. (p. 27—28)

Sekoni is broken and hounded into a mental hospital while the expatriate expert collects his reward of then thousand pounds, eight for "injuries sustained in the course of duty" and two as "lump sum compensation for the termination of his contract." (p. 94) As in *A Man of the People,* the expatriate becomes a collaborator of the corrupt African leadership to frustrate the course of African progress.

In *The Beautyful Ones Are Not Yet Born,* anti-intellectualism takes the form of active resistance to the theoreticians of socialist ideology. A school of political orientation set up by the political party to wean the political and bureaucratic elite from their old ways fails because of the built-in resistance of the elite. The change requires intellectual commitment to a body of ideas that would constitute the framework of political action. But the elite refuse to make this commitment because such a commitment calls for drastic changes in attitudes to property, status and civil responsibility. There is a wide gap between crypto-capitalism and socialism; the elite refuse to make the leap and reduce the whole program to a joke. The bourgeois intellectual, the bureaucratic elite and the philistine politican make common cause to defeat the social experiment. Armah recaptures this brand of anti-intellectualism in the cleavage between the party theoreticians and the political and bureaucratic elite whom they set out to convert. The scene in which an "ideological" professor attempts without succes to convert an audience to socialism is hilariously described. The story is aptly put in the mouth of Koomson, the corrupt partyman:

> Some people think being a Minister is all good-time. Heh, heh, sometimes I wish I had been a businessman instead. One day they brought a man to give the Ministers and the Parliamentarians and the Party activists a lecture. That was during the Winneba days. The man had many degrees, and he was very boring. In the first place he was dressed like a poor man . . . And for a long time he spoke to us about economics. They say he was telling us how to make poor countries rich. Something called stages of growth. I have tried to find out what he really said, but it seemed I wasn't the only one who slept that day. I woke up when I heard some clapping. The others also woke up, and we clapped and said "yeaah yeah". (pp. 155—56)

The Attorney General, "drunk as usual", treats the audience to what he calls "a vote of thanks" but what turns out to be a mug's lecture on "the stages of booze." These, according to him, were:

> Stage One   — The Mood Jocose
> Stage Two   — The Mood Morose
> Stage Three   — The Mood Bellicose
> Stage Four   — The Mood Lachrymose
> Stage Five   — The Mood Comatose

Quite predictably, the Attorney General falls down after the last stage, to everyone's amusement except the Professor who packs has bags and leaves the country to its jokers.

The attack on anti-intellectualism is aimed at something which is symptomatic. But intellectual commitment is an essential part of charting the course of action and giving a sense of purpose to national life. Ideas rule the world, for they serve as a focus for human energies and a guide to human actions. To run a state without commitment to any body of ideas and principles would be as ineffectual as trying to navigate without a chart. But commitment to ideas and principles is inconvenient to the indolent and the corrupt. The corrupt find that ideas and principles are a measure by which the actions of public officers are judged. The indolent would do without them because ideas and principles make demands on the will, intelligence and judgement.

Those who, in the cultural evolution of the continent, are most capable of calling its leaders to account are the intellectuals, the writers, the artists, professionals and executives of the mass media. Political leaders attempt to buy them over and steamroller them to toe "the party line" or failing that, attempt to silence and constrain them by imprisonment, detention and terror.

In *A Man of the People,* Dr. Makinde and the intellectuals of the People's Organization Party are thrown out of the party and denounced to the people as traiters, decadent stooges, ingrates and enemies of the people. The Professor in *The Beautyful Ones Are Not Yet Born* is driven out by the ridicule of the comedians and the corrupt, while Sekoni and the other "interpreters" in *The Interpreters* are reduced to outsiders in a state to which they have so much to contribute. The effect is to enthrone mediocrity, opportunism and ineffectuality in states needing to use the best in human resources and requiring efficiency and speed in the implementation of national goals.

What is the position of the broad masses in the post-independence drama as reflected in these novels? In the first place, the novelists see the masses without sentimentality. In the corruption created by the elite, the masses are both victims and cynical collaborators. Their initial innocence and naiveté is always assumed and so is the cynicism which results from their lack of trust in new bringers of ideals and hopes. Their naiveté show most starkly in their belief in politicians' promises and their cynicism in their repudiation of all idealism altogether, a feeling that all public promises are mere verbiage, and that one set of politicians is as bad as another. And it would seem that the writers are most angry with the political and bureaucratic elite for so destroying the optimism of the masses and innoculating them with the virus of cynicism.

In *The Interpreters,* Soyinka sees the masses as a victim of the inequalities entrenched in the social structure. The elite are in control of the political and administrative machinery. And they manipulate this machinery to their own advantage and often to the detriment of the common people. In this novel there is a practical illustration when Barabbas the small thief is chased and beaten by a mob while big thieves like the Managing Director, the Manager of *Independent Viewpoint* and other public functionaries despoil the country with impunity. Soyinka gives poignancy to this social inequity in his exhortation to the fleeing thief:

> "Run, Barabbas, run, all underdog sympathetic. Run, you little thief or the bigger thieves will pass a law against your existence as a menace to society."
> (p. 114)

But in the same breath, Soyinka remarks the brutality, gullibility and irrationality of the mob that throws stones and sticks at the little thief and then hails the big public thief grown rich on the spoils of the country's economic resources:

"... Run, Barabbas from the same crowd which will reform tomorrow and cheer the larger thief returning from his twentieth Economic Mission and pluck his train from the mud, dog-wise, in their teeth." (p. 114)

The mob can become brutal and heavy-handed when dealing with its victims. Its ruthlessness is often reserved for its own class: "Like the casual barbarism of such a crowd, their treachery against those who were momentarily below them in daily debasement ... Like sand-elves in *Ogboju Ode,* the mob materialised with every step and every sting of a stone or the passing breath of a near miss made him begin to wish for a merciful release." (p. 115)

This view of the mob has nothing in common with the Coriolanus-like, aristocratic contempt for the common people, the "hydra-headed mob," but is rooted in precise observation of human nature. The poor can be violent and oppressive just like everyone else, but because of their own lack of power, can become tyrannical when they sense they have some advantage over others. The "daily debasement" of the poor drives their violence and oppressiveness inwards, against their own kind, especially those at temporary disadvantage, like Barabbas.

In *A Man of the People,* Achebe underlines this brutality and cynicism. Once they form into a mob the people become willing tools in the hands of demagogues. Their amenability to manipulation is not always a result of ignorance and innocence but often a cynical determination to play their part in compounding the national confusion. They act according to the pressure of the moment. They have come to believe that corruption has become the normal mode of national life, that there is no altruism in social life but calculated self-interest and all public officers are thieves and villains. Odili's father's view of public life, we are told, is that "the mainspring of political action was personal gain," and Odili hastens to add that this view "was much more in line with the general feeling in the country than the high-minded thinking of fellows like Max and I." (p. 128) They see their main interest as trying to find and sustain positions of vantage in the corrupt structure. Their reactions are determined by opportunism.

We first see the mob howling its execrations at the disgraced "intellectual" ministers from the parliamentary gallery. In the conflict between his party, the Common People's Convention and Chief Nanga's party, Odili is chagrined to find the common people he is trying to save siding with Nanga and his corrupt crew. He is even beaten senseless by Nanga's mob. The fact is that the common people are sceptical of all politicians because they have been deceived for so long that they have come to distrust the good intentions of all would-be messiahs. In the crude logic of the benighted time through which they are living, the people would rather trust Nanga and the devils they know than the angels that they do not know.

The common people's scepticism comes out forcefully after Max, the theoretician of Odili's radical party, has tried to project the two older parties as vultures "fighting over what remained of the carcass" of the depreciating national resources. The people should take their gun (the opportunity offered by the impending election) to shoot down the predators. To which a member of the audience answers that "There were three vultures . . . The third and youngest was called C. P. C." (Max's party). (p. 140) When the politicians overreach themselves and plunge the country into chaos, it is not the people who step in to save the situation but the military.

One must suspect that Achebe is overdoing the cynicism. And certainly, he does attribute more political awareness to the common people than they can be expected to possess. The people are no fools but are not in full possession of the facts, have no conception of national goals (the elite do not themselves seem to have clear-cut ideas of these goals) and their response cannot therefore be grounded on rationally considered judgements. Their response cannot be more than a conditioned response. The elite control the machinery of national life, manipulate and juggle it, make available as much information as they consider expedient and withhold what they want, and, in the end, get whatever response they want from the people.

After the launching of the Common People's Convention by Max and Odili in his village, an old man makes reply on behalf of the community. (p. 141) It soon becomes clear that the old man is regurgitating much that was fed into the village. He speaks in the familiar rhythms of traditional rhetoric and makes recognizable references to a sense of community solidarity, yet he is reacting in the terms of modern politicis fed to the villages by the new political elite. The language of "eating" is alien to traditional politics and would hardly have been understood by people in Okonkwo's Umuofia or even those of Ezeulu's Umuaro. They would have had a better criterion of civil leadership than that a candidate could simply increase the communal share of a national good. And even if one accepted to present national politics as a process of sharing between different communities, it must be clear that the substantial truths of modern politics have not been communicated. In view of the total dependence of the common people on the leadership of the educated elite, it is hard to admit the accusation of complicity and cynicism against them. They have been allowed so little participation in the working of the modern institutions and so little inside knowledge that justice demands that they be given the benefit of the doubt. The only image that appears to fit them is that of victim. The educated elite seem to have run away with things, only resorting to the people when they need a validation of their authority. They operate a system little understood by the people, often in a language alien to a vast majority of them. They mystify the people with the new concepts and ideas of government, keep them ignorant as long as it suits them and then rush back to them with passionate harangues when they need the support of the people in their competition with the other members of their class for power. The elite have not succeeded in making the idea of the new nationhood a reality to the masses.

Frantz Fanon in *The Wretched of the Earth* emphasized the collaborative relationship that should exist between leaders and followers in the new nations. His thesis ist that

> The duty of those at the head of the movement is to have the masses behind them. Allegiance presupposes awareness and understanding of the mission which has to be fulfilled; in short, an intellectual position, however embryonic. We must not voodoo the people, nor dissolve them in emotion and confusion. Only those underdeveloped countries led by revolutionary *élites* who have come up from the people can today allow the entry of the masses upon the scene of history.

Fanon warns against the formation of a bourgeois privileged class which he sees as more inhibiting than foreign domination, because, once privileges are created and people have tasted them, it will be difficult to persuade them to let them go for the sake of higher national goals. Fanon's warning is unequivocal:

> We must repeat, it is absolutely necessary to oppose vigorously and definitely the birth of national bourgeoisie and a privileged caste. To educate the masses politically is to make the nation a reality to each citizen. It is to make the history of the nation part of the personal experience of each of its citizens.[11]

Obviously, this ideal has eluded most of the newly independent states. The politics of the "national cake" is no way of making the nation "a reality" to its citizens.

In their attack on the new elite, the writers show attitudes shared with Fanon. Even before they became active Fanonists, their observation of the social and political scene of post-independence Africa led them to the conclusion that the greatest threat to orderly development was the nature of the modern African elite and the style of post-independence political leadership. Fanon confirmed views formed from observation, and gave ideological support to fears and anxieties already felt.

It is clear from Achebe's writing since the end of Nigeria's civil war that he is beginning to see the common people in a new light. He shows in a collection of poems, *Beware, Soul Brother,* many of which deal with wartime experiences, and in a collection of short stories called *Girls at War,* that the common people can show heroism, and that their power of endurance and ability to revive after a major disaster are among their most admirable qualities. In poem after poem and story after story he conveys that his impression of the common people is not that of cynical collaborators in evil and corruption but of a hard-pressed and vulnerable people finding their way out of terrifying group and individual disasters through patience, resignation, and above all, compassion.

Armah sees the common people as first duped by their would-be redeemers and then betrayed through the cupidity and selfishness of the political and bureaucrativ elite. But with time they too become part of the national image of wholesale and unmitigated corruption. They accept with cynical abandon the fact of corruption as the crucial reality of existence and they strive to outdo one another in leaping over the moral barriers to reach the gleam of success. But there is always an implied or overt criticism of the elite who have brouhgt the nation to such a sordid state and blighted the hopes of earlier promise. Certainly the dice are loaded against the common people when their interests and those of the elite clash, because the elite are in control. An example is the commission of enquiry to rid Ghana of corruption. The affair is manipulated in such a way that the big culprits escape and the little "dispensable" fry are sacrificed. We are told that "the net had been made in the special Ghanaian way that allowed the really big corrupt people to pass through it. A net to catch only the small, dispensable fellows, trying in their anguished blindness to leap and to attain the gleam and the comfort the only way these things could be done. And the big ones floated free, like all the slogans." (p. 180)

Like Soyinka, Armah sees the common people in the dual image of victim and evil-doer. But their evil-doing is attenuated by their being vulnerable and lacking in social power. They are reproached for lacking the moral will to resist corruption, but it is also constantly pointed out that they are exposed unceasingly to the seductions of corruption. They observe those who adopt short cuts to fame, wealth and power, and the hardship which is the lot of the honest and the morally fastidious. Nothing is done to give respectability to morality. The few who hold on to their moral integrity, like the Man and his friend the Naked Man, become outsiders and are only saved from destruction by an indomitable pessimism and a tough-minded reliance on their individual integrity. They turn their back on society and seek for strength within themselves, in the knowledge that everything else may collapse except the truth of individual conviction.

It is hard to agree that the answer to social corruption lies in the withdrawal from active participation by good people. The Man does not actually withdraw, as the Naked Man does, but his resistance is too passive to provide an effective answer to social corruption. Soyinka's young activists and Achebe's Odili and Max present a more positive challenge to sozial corruption. Their response, like Dr. Stockman's in Ibsen's *An Enemy of the People,* is to fight back, not to turn the face to the wall. And here is the difference, in the long run, between these writers. Achebe and Soyinka believe in vigorous social action to change the corrupt social order, while Armah thinks the situation is too far gone to be redeemed, at least in the near future. Achebe's young radicals believe in challenging the older corrupt politicians for power; Soyinka's "interpreters" attack and expose the hypocrisy and corruption of the ruling class. Armah on the other hand sees some hope in some distant future, but how this hope will be made to come about is not even remotely hinted at. "Someday in the long future," he writes, "a new life would maybe flower in the country, but when it came, it would not choose as its instruments the same people who had made a habit of killing new flowers." (p. 188) The crucial point is that that "new life" can never come without preparation, a preparation which in its most positive form must involve the deliberate subversion of the old corrupt life. Passivity and inaction are ways of postponing indefinitely this arrival of a desirable new order. The ultimate test of a writer's belief in man and in the power of the people to make destiny is to be found in the vision which animates the writer's work. All the writers discussed have some belief in the people, at least in the idea that they deserve to be and can be saved. Only *The Beautyful Ones Are Not Yet Born,* oddly enough, underplays this positive affirmation that richly distinguishes African literature.

Notes

1 See "The Coups in Upper Volta, Dahomey, and the Central African Republic," in *Protest and Power in Black Africa,* ed. Robert I. Rotberg and Ali A. Mazrui (New York, 1970), p. 1043.
2 "The Writer in a Modern African State," in *The Writer in Modern Africa,* ed. Per Wästberg (New York, 1969), p. 17.
3 Ibid., p. 14.
4 Ibid., p. 16.
5 Wole Soyinka, "The Choice and Use of Language," *Cultural Events in Africa,* 75 (1971), 5. Also quoted in James M. Gibbs, "Wole Soyinka: Bio-Bibliography," *Africana Library Journal,* 3, 1 (1972), 17.
6 Ibid.
7 All quotations are taken from these editions: *The Interpreters* (London, 1965); *A Man of the People* (London, 1966); *The Beautyful Ones Are Not Yet Born* (Boston, 1968). Page numbers are given after each quotation.
8 David Abernethy, *The Political Dilemma of a Popular Education: An African Case* (Stanford, 1969), p. 250.
9 "Education and Family Life in the Development of Class Identification among the Yoruba," in *The New Elites of Tropical Africa,* ed. P. C. Lloyd (London, 1966), p. 164.
10 Laurens van der Post, *The Dark Eye in Africa* (New York, 1955), p. 16.
11 Frantz Fanon, *The Wretched of the Earth* (New York, 1966), p. 159.

Soyinga's Black Orpheus

Dan Izevbaye

> Olóhùn-iyò tuned up and began
> to sing and as he sang flames burst
> out and smoke engulfed us where
> we stood; as it was for us, so also
> for the king of birds and even the
> sand elves, everyone forgot about
> the fight and began to dance.

Forest of a Thousand Daemons

The term "Black Orpheus" was Sartre's description of the *négritude* poets in Senghor's anthology, who had attempted to shake off their alienation from spiritual roots by returning to their native land.[1] This was some time after Fagunwa the Yoruba novelist had adapted the idea in his novel about a quest by a group of Yoruba hunters.[2] Sartre saw a resemblance to the Orpheus myth in the lyrical "descent of the Negro into himself" (p. 21) and interpreted it as a quest for inner harmony by an exiled black soul fleeing through the death corridors of a white culture in order to recover his vital self. Harmony and unity play an important part in Sartre's definition of Black Orpheus. The progress of the black poet begins as a flight from European mineralization of his humanity towards a recovery of his animal or vegetal nature. (p. 48)

But *négritude* poetry which Sartre described in 1948 as "the sole great revolutionary poetry" in our times (p. 11) is described by Soyinka writing twenty years later as the "literature of self-worship." Unlike Sartre who saw a union of two selves as the goal of the Black Orpheus, Soyinka saw a turning into one self and the danger that Black Orpheus might turn narcissist.[3] As many writers have pointed out, Soyinka was rejecting not the main argument of *négritude* but the display.[4] It is easy to find support for the *négritude* quality described by Sartre as the "profound unity of vegetal and sexual symbols in original Negro poetry" by pointing to the primacy of vegetal and sexual imagery in Soyinka's work. Even his famous quip, with its witty "tiger/tigritude," "duiker/duikeritude" pun, refers us to an African vernacular style which depends largely on puns and on references to animal life. The witticism can be used as a gloss on a Fagunwa tale in which the leopard displays his beauty and announces that "if we exempt worthies like the antelope and the duiker, few animals surpass me in beauty."[5]

Sartre and Soyinka also differ in their views of the social status of the black poet. For Sartre the racial issue is at the fore, rather than the place of the poet within his black community. So he uses the idea of an African collective mind to argue that when the black poet expresses himself most lyrically he "attains most surely to great group poetry" and "speaks for all Negroes." (p. 21) Soyinka's interpretation of the Orpheus myth begins from a more dynamic Yoruba conception of the status of the individual in his community. The story of the separation of the gods which we find in Yoruba creation myths appears to be the exemplar for the Yoruba conception of individualism. The myth suggests that separation is an evolutionary stage after original unity and is a necessary stage before meaningful community. The theme of separation or fragmentation appears to be such a fundamental one that the myth contains at least two or three such motifs as variations or as complementary versions.[6] It is from this myth that Soyinka derives the principle of separation in that part of "Idanre" in which he calls for a refusal to become a mere "spoonful of protoplasmic broth" in "one Omni-sentient cauldron" and recommends instead that we "celebrate the stray electron."

Some forms of Yoruba literature celebrate both individualism and the value of the individualist to his society. Folktales with human heroes often celebrate the hunter as an outstanding individual. He can be a benefactor of his community only after fulfilling himself as an individual. It is this two-part principle—the need for individual fulfillment as a condition for community service—which provides the form that is adapted by writers like Fagunwa, Tutuola and Soyinka. In the first part of the story the hero, usually a hunter, wanders into an uncharted forest in quest of fulfillment. The hazards become the test of his manhood, and his achievements in the forest become the criterion for letting him lead a mission on behalf of his community.[7]

The second part of the story is more serious in intent, and deals more or less with the social mission undertaken by the hero. This is the two-part form of *The Forest of a Thousand Daemons* as well as Soyinka's *The Interpreters*. Different as the two works are in other respects, we can relate them by reference to the principle of the two-part "form of criticism" which a discerning critic has introduced into the criticism of *The Interpreters*.[8] In the two novels the first part gives the hero the opportunity to fulfill himself, while in the second part there is an evaluation of the use that has been made of this opportunity. Terror and fear provide both the literary thrill and the spiritual measure in these *rites de passage*. Multiple beads of fearful incidents are strung around the hero's courage in *The Forest of a Thousand Daemons* as a test of his manhood.

In *The Interpreters* fear also becomes a spiritual gateway. Its importance is brought out by the frequency with which it is used to mark the moments of achievement or failure in the characters' opportunity for fulfillment. Chapter nine is full of such moments of fear—Egbo's meeting with Simi and with the girl undergraduate and under Olokemeji bridge; it also occurs elsewhere—Noah at the fire passage, Lazarus's vision of death, and Kola's recognition of his failure as an artist because "he dared not, truly, be fulfilled." (p. 218) The meaning of fear comes through in one of those rare moments when Egbo perceives the meaning of fulfillment. He wakes under the bridge "feeling night a womb of the gods and a passage for travellers" and "left with a gift"—"for which traveller beards the gods in their den and departs without a divine boon." (p. 127) The hunter who ventures into the Forest of a Thousand Daemons also acknowledges the occupational hazards which accompany heroic fulfillment: "The aggressive man dies the death of war, the swimmer dies the death of water, the vainglorious dies the death of women." (p. 36) It is after the hero has fulfilled himself and found fame in the first part of the work that he is chosen in the second part to lead other hunters on a mission for his community in the manner of the Argonauts.

The Forest of a Thousand Daemons relates to the Black Orpheus tradition in two respects. First, there is an occasional revaluation of black cultures and a direct appeal for unity among black communities. Then Orpheus's contest with the sirens is reinterpreted as an allegory of the poet's role in leading the resistance against European cultural assimilation. On their way to their national missions Fagunwa's hunters are lured by a "singing in heaven" so melodious they have never heard the like: "The voices were many and they sang as one." (p. 95) They lose a companion who "plunged into the dome of heaven." Some said that "he was transformed into a ghommid" while others "claimed that the gatekeepers of heaven took pity on him, cloaked him in the garb of immortality and admitted him into heaven." (pp. 95—96) As for the others, it was only the singing of Olóhùn-iyò that saved them by recalling them to their mission. Soyinka's artistes can match this social function. The *àpàlà* drummers in *The Interpreter* "taught style to the new *oyinbos*" (p. 21), working within the same artistic form as the hunter in *The Forest of a Thousand Daemons* who won royal favors by tempting the king to dance:

> When I had truly excelled myself, the king
> himself rose from the throne and plunged into
> the dance. I was now thoroughly aroused and I
> dug the crook into the drum skin, darted into
> the fray and crowded the king with music. (p. 44) [9]

If these artistes win patronage from the great by offering them cultured entertainment, they can retain their professional independence. Soyinka's *àpàlà* drummers "gauged the mood, like true professionals, speaking to each other, not to their audience, who would, if they chose, not *know* this language." (p. 21)

The service of the poet is not to the great alone. It is useful to recall at this stage that in nearly all versions of the Orpheus myth the most important social function performed by the poet comes from his power to tame wild beasts— that is, the power of his music to soothe the savage breast. The universality of this motif clearly testifies to traditional medical faith in the beneficent effect of the poet's art. Yoruba incantations by which men gain control over the forces of evil are not merely magical charms but a distinct poetic genre. Similarly there is a close link between the poetic names of herbs and their healing properties. This has often been used to support the theory that the poetic phrases in incantations are not merely puns but were originally verbal definitions of the curative properties in the herbs used.[10] If tranquilizers used in the treatment of madmen are associated with images and puns in poetry, it is not difficult to see how the practice of healing makes possible the myth about the power of poetry to humanize the man of violence.

This function of poetry explains how the subject of madness and violence relates to the imagery of healing in *Madmen and Specialists,* and it explains the revelation in *Season of Anomy*[11] where a doctor tells the poet-hero how he "gave up this whole business of words" and suddenly "switched over to medicine." (p. 228) Soyinka's interest in the social role of the poet as healer dates from *Idanre and other poems* (1967),[12] a collection which marks the eruption of violence in Nigeria. In "Civilian and Soldier," one of the poems in this collection, a civilian promises to tempt a soldier away from the "lead festival" of the soldier's friends and initiate him into the "trade of living" by shooting him "clean and fair/With meat and bread." (p. 53) The 1966 poems in *Idanre* thus mark the beginning of the poet-as-Orpheus theme. However, this theme is developed mainly in his prose works rather than the poems.

In *The Interpreters*, the work which immediately precedes *Idanre*, Soyinka develops his main characters as Prometheans, and not, as he was later to do, as types of Orpheus. The difference between *The Interpreters* came out when Nigeria was not yet the area of violence presented in *Idanre*. In contrast to *The Man Died* where Soyinka shifts emphasis from social to individual responsibility by arguing that "Violence and death are personal things" (p. 161),[13] *The Interpreters* presents us with Sagoe's vision of a society in which, "next to death . . . shit is the most vernacular atmosphere of our beloved country." (p. 108) The problem in the later works is seen as one of violence, and Soyinka brings an Orpheus to the scene. In *The Interpreters* the problem is that of social development. Sagoe presents that unflattering definition of a developing capital: "Every loud city has its slums, and Isàlè-Èkó symbolised the victory of the modern African capital over European nations in this one aspect of civilisation." (p. 72) To this society Soyinka brings two potential Prometheans. Egbo, invited by his people to be an "enlightened ruler" (p. 12), is fashioned after Ogún, the god of iron and war. Sékoní the electrical engineer is modelled after Sàngó, the god who in tradition possesses the Promethean gift of fire but uses it only as the sign of his wrath. Sékoní starts off with a more earthbound purpose. On his voyage home he has a Promethean dream of using his power over electricity for industrial development on earth:

> He sat on a tall water spout high above
> the tallest trees and beyound low clouds . . .
> he opened his palm to the gurgle of
> power from the charging prisoner,
> shafts of power nudged the monolith
> along the fissures, little gasps of organic
> ecstasy and paths were opened . . . (p. 26)

The god Ogún, after whom Egbo is fashioned, is similarly a pathfinder and human benefactor. He taught men the creative art of metallurgy. But he is also a god of violence and destruction. Egbo is as closely indentified with Ogún as Sékoní is with Sàngó, but only the negative side of Ogún is developed in him, especially the thirst for blood. Apart from his love for sacrificing others to himself, even his pronouncements and deeds are direct allusions to Ogún: the dye drops dripping at the dye pits which he frequented in his youth become Ogún's praise name: the onomatopoetic sound of blood drops becomes a pun on the usual Yoruba salute to royalty: "the indigo streams from *àdìré* hung up to dry, dripping like blood in the *oriki* of Ogun, *tó tó tó tó tó*."[14] (p. 126) At the display of "The Pantheon" the blood link between Ogún and Egbo is again established through Egbo's words: "The moment that you say *tó*, my knife will go in the neck of this ram. *Tó*, and a fountain of blood will strike the ceiling of this studio." (p. 225) The reference here is to bloodshed only; there is nothing of the awesome majesty of blood sacrifice associated with Ogún.

A similar ambivalence exists in Egbo's relation to water. Òshún the sacred river which he frequented in his youth was the legendary secondary wife of Sàngó. Egbo is discovered at her side at midnight. His later failure as an adult is persistently described as "a choice of drowning" (pp. 120, 251), and when he gazes into the water now, what he sees is "a sleepy coil of python . . . voluptuous mermaid arms . . . infinitely coy and maternal." (p. 14) Egbo is unable to leave his adolescence behind, and a regression even occurs during a sexual encounter when he asks to be allowed to lie in darkness and cry. (p. 60) Just as Sagoe, with his "traumatic centre of castor oil" (p. 84), thinks only of voidance, so Egbo relates his life to the drowning of his mother by picking maternal lovers and showing a self-destructive love for water. Egbo's problem is commented on through the fire-eater in the night-club who falls into a small puddle. Egbo's comment, "The night-club salesman of Sango has defected to more watery deities" (p. 158), is an ironical comment on Egbo himself, since he has been described earlier as one unable to avoid "the fate of a burnt-out fire-eater." (p. 12)

If Egbo's failure is wholly a personal one, Sékoní's defeat has a mainly social cause. This Promethean figure "sought the hand of kindred spirits for the flare of static electricity, but it slipped with grease and pointed to his desk . . ." (p. 27) The greased palm is the social corruption that defeated the idealist engineer. These two different kinds of hero may be described as "failed Prometheans," a term borrowed from *The Man Died* (p. 88), Soyinka's personal account of his detention and the main source of material for the second novel. The social cause of Sékoní's frustration provides one explanation why a Promethean should fail. But the story of Sékoní is not merely a story of social frustrations; the portrait of Sékoní betrays a rejection of the Promethean motive because of its implicit questioning of Promethean ambition. Soyinka is only partially sympathetic to Sékoní whom he presents as "short-sighted" (p. 155), presumably for thinking that "the logic of nature's growth" can be "bettered by the cabalistic equations of the sprouting derrick." (p. 27) He nevertheless insists on the social flaw, especially in the tribute to Okigbo in *A Shuttle in the Crypt* where he expresses doubt about the value of Promethean sacrifice.[15] This doubt prepares the way for the final, violent suppression of the Promethean idea whenever it suggests itself in *The Man Died*. It does suggest itself at least once: "My liver is mended. I await the vultures for there are no eagles here." (p. 187) But although the writer's egotism is never conquered in the work, the idea of a Promethean is resolutely suppressed: "History is too full of failed Prometheans bathing their wounded spirits in the tragic stream./ Destoy the tragic lure!" (p. 88)

The egotism which comes through so strongly in *The Man Died* is offered as the precondition for survival. It becomes clear that theories of the African artist as a group representative never included the possibility of a state of anomie in Africa. The egotism emerges from the writer's presentation of himself as a model for lesser beings: "If *he* could break and break so abjectly then anyone can break." (p. 79) The mind that recognizes a threat to its humanity must become a nay-sayer: "The man dies in all who keep silent in the face of tyranny." (p. 13) Inevitably, attention is turned to the prisoners' need to preserve "a spark of human essence" and on "the animality of the gaolers." (p. 98) Humanity can be preserved or recovered through the art of song, as when "the brutalized humanity beneath us" sang, and "involved us all, strangers to their homes, in one common humanity." (p. 110)

The gaolers on the other hand are presented, rather uncharitably, through animal imagery. In accordance with the aesthetic scheme they are depicted as creatures of brute flesh and warm blood lacking in song. First, Polyphemus, "eight feet tall, a thickly cicatriced tower of menace . . . I know Polyphemus will be the priest of the rites of submission." (pp. 125—26) Then comes Hogroth "in the midst of his marshland wanderings . . . *Hraagrh hraagrh hraagrh . . . ptuh—splat! / Pig! . . .* Do you belong to the same species as lay claims to souls, to sensing and thinking?" (p. 133) But the encounter between brute and poet is easy for the poet who, like Adam, conjures by the magic word: "His naming was easy—Hogroth. Slowly the stomach settles back and ceases to heave." (p. 132) In the imagined encounter Wole Beowulf triumphs, as a matter of course: "Hogroth dead. New glow in the universe. I hear the prison celebrating." (p. 133) Inevitably too, we encounter Caliban (not the colonial creature), but his musical ear is not even accepted as an index of his humanity because his creator's malice is far too strong. Caliban sings a "mystery dirge first into himself and then in a reckless challenge to the heavens . . . Caliban never sleeps. Nor do I when Caliban patrols the night." (pp. 134—35 *passim*)

After peopling his world with such creatures Soyinka is now fully prepared to assume the role of Orpheus, the figure who has now displaced Prometheus as his idea of a culture hero. Soyinka shows this new direction to the reader during the account of his nostalgic memory of Cocteau's *Orphée Negre* [sic] which precedes the birth of a child in the prison. The prison becomes "their nether world," and the crying baby is therefore a "full-throated freak." (p. 198) He names her Persephone. But the child has been incorrectly identified. If the child is a freak born in the wrong season, she cannot be Persephone (who, in the winter months, is Queen of the Underworld) unless there is a conflation of the two figures here. She can only be Eurydice. The renaming is done in *Season of Anomy* where the heroine, Ìrìyísé (literally "dew on the feet") is abducted and kept in a prison (described in *The Man Died* as "their nether world"). The hero, Ofeyi (literally either "he loves this one" or more probably "this love") searches for his lost Ìrìyísé, passing through a wasteland, a territory governed by Anubis, the jackal-headed one who brings "the plague of rabid dogs" (p. 159), then through "the formal doorway to the territory of hell." (p. 192) Ofeyi's descent into the mortuary begins on a hopeful note because Soyinka conflates the myths of the Nativity and the *Katabasis* (a technique he attempted with less success in *The Man Died*, p. 198): "There is no more room in the mortuary." (p. 220) It is certain that Ìrìyísè would not be found in this mortuary, but "the ritual had to be undergone." (p. 226) So Ofeyi moves with his companions through the hall of death while their "living bodies felt clammy hands about them sucking their vitality into a universal deathness." (p. 222)

It will be seen from this summary of plot that the outlines of the Orpheus myth are strongly pronounced in *Season of Anomy*, and that Soyinka abandons the veiled allusiveness of *The Interpreters* for an explicitness which ensures that no reader will miss the deliberate focus on the social significance of the myth. There is not much use in retelling a well-known story that is readily available elsewhere if the teller cannot add some new meaning or introduce a new manner in the telling of it. Soyinka offers us both in *Season of Anomy*.

The most important deviation from the usual versions of the myth is the vindication of Ofeyi's conviction that Ìrìyísè could not be in the morgue. Soyinka's interpretation does not differ much from the others. Ìrìyísè, like the dying goddesses before her, and especially like Persephone, is the spirit of spring whose departure marks the descent of winter on the landscape. The induction ceremony of the first chapter marks her out as the goddess of earth, therefore she cannot now be among the dead: "her living essence could not be summed up in one of these wax parodies of the human condition." (p. 226) At this stage Soyinka has stepped beyond the usual meaning of the myth to place his antiscientific definition of man before us. The passage in which he achieves this comes just before Ofeyi's "eternal alarm at human recognition." As poet, Ofeyi is only a popularizer and merely witty. But he is intense enough to elicit some of the book's finest writing from Soyinka as he stands in the mortuary scene before essential organs of human life laid out in a glass chamber. The effectiveness of the passage comes from the functioning of the images. Factual description, compassion, the tragedy of thwarted human aspiration and the futility of monuments are caught in a single set of images:

> The brain was a fallen meteor:
> craters, ridges, a network of

> irrigation channels formed a
> microcosm of the world from
> which it had fallen. A heart sat
> in glazed aloneness on the top
> of a glass case, a funerary
> ornament above a body lying
> piecemeal, not in state. (p. 223)

To match such writing in *The Man Died* we have to turn to the imaginatively evoked primeval world of reptiles in the counterpointed twin chapters, XXXVI and XXXVII, in which the comic world of lizards is placed against the heroic world of geckos. The physical beauty of the reptile's world is a thin veil drawn across the essential violence of the landscape, and the comedy of the lizard chapter is a very thin mask over Soyinka's disapproval of lizards. Lizards "copulate incessantly," cannot keep their minds on the immediate business at hand, are "undignified in hunt, lacking even the failed majesty of the pirate." On the other hand, the more aggressive gecko is presented as a more fascinating creature. Its eyes are "massive Ancient Mariner eyes. One by one the flies come to him unresisting." Since the lizards and the gecko are half-brothers, what is there about the lizard, one may ask, that Soyinka finds so contemptible? What is that "ancestral trauma" needing to be "exorcised some day at some great lizard meet"? The only answer offered is that the lizard "constantly nods his head" in that harsh landscape. To Soyinka the nay-sayer, this is the antithesis of manhood—the man has died in the lizard world, and this robs the male lizard of "a place among the higher predators." (pp. 265—57 *passim*) In other word's, Soyinka constantly emphasizes the importance of the aggressive instinct in the everyday world. This theme has a long history in Soyinka and is not reducible to a clear-cut conflict between violent methods and peaceful ones. It began when Soyinka first became the protégé of Ogún, who is both warrior and artist. Since then the pen and the swords have often been placed in trembling balance rather than in direct opposition—the warrior in Soyinka is not always a villain, but shares honors with the artist: Mulieru with Demoke in *A Dance of the Forests,* Fajuyi with Okigbo in the poems. What is stressed, therefore, is not violence *per se*, but the toughness required to cope with an uncongenial environment. In *Kongi's Harvest* Segi, who dissuades her lover from his vengeful path by urging him to preach life ("only life is worth preaching, my prince"), is contradicted by the realism of a situaion in which the political conflict outlasts the formal limits of the play.

Soyinka revives the tension between the claims of counter-violence and peaceful resistance in the prison diary and the second novel. *The Man Died* reveals how Soyinka personally experienced the dilemma: the suffering spirit who claims he has learnt to starve his violence into calm too quickly turns into a malevolent *anjonnu* straining at the leash of patience as he emerged from the man-made "pit of anguish." Soyinka seeks a less ambiguous resolution in *Season of Anomy* by presenting the problem in the more clearly polarized form of two angels fighting for Ofeyi's soul. Ofeyi's relative quiescence in the midst of all the violence in this work is apparently influenced by a dream which brings him the realization that to meet violence with violence is to trade one's humanity for the bestiality of the aggressor. Attacked by jackals in the dream, Ofeyi involuntarily turns jackal to save himself. This nightmare makes him learn the secret of mob violence: "even innocents donned a mask of the jackal to ensure safety from the hunting pack." (p. 160) Throughout the novel the dentist treats Ofeyi as a naive person for putting off the mask of the jackal. But even the man of violence admits at one point that the naive and simple man may be ennobled by a single heroic effort, like the arduous trek which Ofeyi undertakes for the love of Ìrìyìsè. The actual historical parallels of the trek are inferior to its archetypal significance as an elixir which writers like Faulkner have found useful for injecting into the rustic veins of their simple characters.

It should be conceded that Ofeyi gets caught up in the general preparation for confrontation at the end of the novel—he goes with the Dentist, the man of violence, and parts with that woman of peace, Taiila. But it is also important to remember that he does not sell out to the dentist. He remains "naive" and even takes his role as Orpheus so seriously that he attempts to charm the warder Suberu—who is the watchdog Cerberus—by mere incantation. But although Suberu's face "retained the same mask of blankness" after the verbal persuasion, the attempt actually succeeds. It is made to work because it is partly flattery and partly the self-mockery of an artist reciting his credo before a potential convert. Ofeyi tries to show Suberu, that "dark horse of images," that the artist is more than equal to the warrior: "You grasp a situation of chaos and—bang bang—you impose your order on it. Rather like those men of uniforms who thereby claim to control other lives in perpetuity." (p. 315) In spite of the Dentist's cynicism, therefore, Ofeyi's magic words penetrate the mind of Suberu, so that the two men do not need the strength of a Heracles to drag Suberu with them out of Temoko.

At various points in *Season of Anomy* social problems blend with spiritual meanings, and allegory with symbolism. Ìrìyìsè is made to represent the claims of life. She is the silent arbiter in the struggle for Ofeyi's allegiance carried on by his two "angels," the Dentist, an extractor and agent of violence, and Taiila, an exotic character with other-worldly ideals whose name, I am told, is Sanskrit for oil. Just as the Dentist is concerned with healing by extraction to prevent the spread of infection, so Tailla stands for the soothing power of restorative oil. What she suggests is much more than I can hope to discuss here, but it is not all spiritual. A touch of the mundane occurs in the scene where Ofeyi, exactly like Egbo before him, launches out in a boat to make his choice. Like Osa in *The Interpreters*, this pool "stank of history. Slaves, gold, oil." In one historical vision that reaches back to the slave past, oil is endowed with ambivalent associations: Ofeyi remembers that "the oil trade flowed into a smell of death, disruption and desolation, flowed in turn into tankers for the new oil." But he can also think of "rotted earth-flesh reborn into life-giving oil." (pp. 90—91)

The "rotted earth-flesh" here is the industrial equivalent of the buried corn of mythology which provides the titles of the five sections of the novel; Soyinka is working his country's economic history into this story through the motif of rebirth. It is the importance of this motif as a structuring device which causes Soyinka to make another adaptation of the Orpheus myth by extending Ofeyi's quest beyond the halls of death and into the prison yard. Irìyísè is now discovered in the yard of lunatics beyond the cell of lepers. This extension adds social allegory to the symbolism already implicit in the myth. An allegorical intention has earlier been hinted at in the punning first sentence which suggests contradictory ideas of social order and good government: "A quaint anomaly, had long governed and policed itself, was so singly-knit that it obtained a tax assessment for the whole populace . . ." (p. 2) The social paradox suggested by the opposition between "anomaly" and "governed and policed itself," locates the areas of order and of anomie for the reader. Throughout the book the novelist suggests, through his manipulation of language, that words can give an accurate indication of social health. The Custodian of the Grain insists that his pastoral community Aiyéró (which stands in opposition to the wise, fallen world of Aiyetomo),[16] should be pronounced as Aiyéró, not Aiyéro (i. e. "the world is upright" not "the world is bitter"): "If you find the world bitter don't foist your despair on us. *Aiye ti wa ró*. It works, it is upright and balanced because we have made it so." The old man rejects Ofeyi's quarrel with the fuss about "a little tonal deflection":

> it tells a lot you see. It isn't only that you
> change the meaning to what it isn't, to the
> opposite of what it is, but it tells a lot of
> your state of mind. You've been defeated by life
> and it shows in your tone. (p. 8)

The figures of lepers and lunatics in the last chapter perform a similar function as a language in the first sentence. They are created as the symptoms of the state of social health. The prison yard lepers, "viperous and chastened, predatory and hunted" (p. 295) and fighting over pieces of meat, alienate Ofeyi on his way to recovering Irìyísè. Next come the lunatics, parodying justice. One sat "with a blanket round his shoulders and a headgear, clearly improvised to resemble a turban or wig." Another "held his audience in rapt attention, full of urbane gestures and flourishes." (p. 311) The allegorical hints thrown out by these human figures can be approached only obliquely, not pinned to specific issues.

Referring to the more explicit references and allusions in *The Man Died*, a reviewer criticized Soyinka for his heavy reliance on non-African thinkers.[17] With reference to *Season of Anomy*, may our writers borrow myths from "white" cultures? It is true that the use to which Soyinka puts the Orpheus myth shows his alienation. But the problem takes us back to early attempts to reduce all world cultures to mere variations of Greek and Roman culture. And

Frobenius found Prester John at Ife; Nadel discovered another Byzantium in Bida; Frazier's dying god also died in Benin; and Robert Graves can locate Yoruba evidence that the lost Atlantis is no myth. Africans too have collaborated by tracing cultural sources to Egypt and the Middle East, using similarities of names and structural features as proofs of cultural diffusion and even racial descent.[18]

Perhaps *Season of Anomy* provides one answer to the problem. Soyinka's method distinguishes the vital revival of Orpheus and Eurydice from the merely inert transplant of St. George who "sat symbolical on his leaden steed." (p. 45) It is a moral distinction too, exposing the merely pretentious, the "Florentine moment in the heart of a festering continent." (p. 44) And he shows through word play that a myth can be made indigenous by the right manipulation of language, form and social experience. Ofeyi and Ìrìyísè are meaningful names in Yoruba. They may be unusual, but they are not improbable names. And yet they sound like Yoruba descendants of Greek Orpheus and Eurydice.

Notes

1 Sartre's introduction to Senghor's *Anthologie de la nouvelle poésie nègre et malgache de langue française* (Paris, 1948), is available in an English translation by S. W. Allen, entitled *Black Orpheus* (Paris, 1963). Quotations and page numbers refer to the translation.
2 The novel, *Ogboju Ode Ninu Igbo Irunmale*, was first published in 1938.
3 Wole Soyinka, "And After the Narcissist?" *African Forum*, 1, 4, (1966), 56.
4 See, for example, Janheinz Jahn, *A History of Neo-African Literature*, (London, 1968), pp. 265—66.
5 Wole Soyinka and D. O Fagunwa, *Forest of a Thousand Daemons*, (London, 1968), p. 119.
6 The myth sometimes includes the following incidents: Ògún quarrels with his peers and goes into seclusion; Atowódá the slave rolls a stone on his master, shattering the original godhead into 1001 deities; the aetiological motif of the tortoise shell pieced around divine breath and used as the vessel for creating matter out of the void.
7 In the Tutuola chapter of *Seven African Writers* (London, 1962), Gerald Moore describes the first part of Tutuola's tales as dealing with Initiation.
8 Mark Kinkead-Weekes, *"The Interpreters* — a Form of Criticism," forthcoming in *A Soyinka Symposium*, ed. Abiola Irele. All quotations from *The Interpreters* are taken from the 1965 edition published in London.
9 Hunters have their own poetic genre in *Ijálá* and are expected to know a lot of incantations (òfò). The hunter is thus not only explorer, provider of meat and defender of the town, he is often also drummer, poet and teller of fantastic adventure tales.
10 For example, Pierre Verger, "Tranquillizers and Stimulants in Yoruba Herbal Treatment," in *The Traditional Background to Medical Practice in Nigeria* (Ibadan, 1971), pp. 50—55.
11 *Season of Anomy* (London, 1973). All quotations are from this edition.
12 *Idanre and Other Poems* (London, 1967). All quotations are from this edition.
13 *The Man Died* (London, 1972). All quotations are from this edition.

14 "Tó tó" means "Hail!"
15 *Shuttle in the Crypt* (London, 1972), p. 59.
16 Aiyero is also the fictitious setting of a Yoruba novel *Kékeré Ekùn, by*
   A. Olabimtan (Lagos, 1967). Compare Soyinka's opening sentence in
   Season of Anomy with a Nigerian journalist's description of the Yoruba
   commune of Áiyétòrò (the word means "our world is as peaceful and
   undisturbed as springwater"), the real town from which the fictional town
   derived its name:
   > There is a community town in the Western State [of Nigeria] that
   > goes by the name Aiyetoro which has a [long] tradition of isolation...
   > Apart from the tax which the community pays to the Western State
   > Government they have nothing to do with the outside world. For
   > example, every financial year the community counts all the adults
   > whore are eligible to pay tax and the bulk sum is paid to tax
   > authorities at the other end, no policeman, no law enforcing agencies
   > at Aiyetoro.
   > (Candido, "Nigeria's Weird and Mythical 'Republics'," *New Nigerian,*
   > 4 December 1974, p. 5).
17 Adamu Ciroma in the *New Nigerian*, 5 April 1973, p. 2.
18 For example, J. Olumide Lucas, *The Religion of the Yorubas* (Lagos,
   1948) and, more recently, Modupe Oduyoye, *The Vocabulary of Yoruba
   Religious Discourse* (Ibadan, 1971), and Kemi Morgan, *The Myth of
   Yoruba Ancestry,* (Ibadan, 1974?).

Fate and Divine Justice in THINGS FALL APART

Richard Priebe

Perhaps the least controversial statement one could make in the field of African literature is that Chinua Achebe is a didactic writer. By his own statements and through his work, Achebe clearly shows his belief in the role of the artist as teacher. The pejoration of the word "didactic" in Western criticism, however, makes this statement rather misleading for many readers. Achebe's artistic concerns are with presenting a holistic view of the ethos of his people in an entirely vital, dynamic mode that is expressive of his culture in terms of form no less than content. His works progress in a linear manner and are set in an historical framework that reveals the persistence of cultural continuity despite internal and external threats to the society. Yet there is never a mere photographic rendering of the world he gives us. We confront what I call an ethical consciousness, an authorial presence that leads us into the societal structures of Ibo life and proceeds in a realistic, linear and historical manner, while revealing the depth and breadth of strategies open to the individual and society for coping with reality. Achebe's works are didactic, but not in the manner of a facile, two-dimensional realism where all ethical choices are clear-cut.

Kenneth Burke has suggested that complex literary works can be considered "proverbs writ large."[1] On more than one level Achebe is clearly engaged in writing proverbs. As Burke has explained, the proverb is a very primary unit through which we can see art as equipment for living. Proverbs name and encompass ranges of strategies or attitudes for handling recurrent situations. A strategy, if it is worth anything, must be functional and realistic—in other words it must size things up rather accurately. Above all, the proverb must have vitality:

> The point of issue is not to find categories that "place" the proverbs once and for all. What I want is categories that suggest their active nature. Here is no "realism for its own sake." Here is realism for promise, admonition, solace, foretelling, instruction, charting, all for the direct bearing that such acts have upon matters of welfare.[2]

Few who have seriously looked at Achebe's work would argue with the aptness of Burke's comment on the proverb as a description of the activity Achebe has been engaged in. That Achebe artistically employs proverbs in his writing is not even the central question; it merely underscores the point that is being made here about the complexity of the ethical consciousness reflected in his work.

For the non-African reader the subtleties and complexities of Achebe may indeed be rather difficult to perceive at first. The clues are there, however, and careful reading can lead to an understanding of a great deal that is distinctly African, though comprehensible within Western terms.

In a monograph entitled *Oedipus and Job in West African Religion,* Meyer Fortes explores the way fate and divine justice operate in West African religion.[3] The title sounds arrogantly ethnocentric, but Fortes is careful to avoid any superficially descriptive comparisons of the kind Sir James Frazer made. Instead, he considers the stories of Oedipus and Job from an analytical perspective and shows how they together form a useful paradigm for understanding the paradoxically contradictory and complementary concepts of prenatal fate or destiny and supernatural justice in West Africa. We shall see that this paradigm is one we can also extract from Achebe's *Things Fall Apart.* The point is not to reduce an aspect of Achebe's work to a Eurocentric archetype for we are actually pulling two rather disparate ideas together to create a metaphor that will facilitate an understanding of a religious strategy artistically rendered by an African writer. A tighter argument might be made by taking an emic approach and first going into Ibo religious thought, but the justification for our etic approach lies in what such exegesis will reveal about the accessible pattern in this novel.

A common observation by Western critics has been that *Things Fall Apart* is very much like a Greek tragedy. Okonkwo, like his Greek counterpart, appears to be brought down by a fatal flaw that is beyond his control. Without any doubt Oedipus is the victim of Destiny; personal responsibility or guilt has nothing to do with what happens to him. We also find that Okonkwo's *chi,* his personal god, has quite a lot to do with his destiny, but we are stopped at the very beginning of the novel from pursuing a descriptive comparison for we are told that a man can, in part, shape his own destiny: "If ever a man deserved his success, that man was Okonkwo. At an early age he had achieved fame as the greatest wrestler in all the land. That was not luck. At the most one could say that his *chi* or personal god was good. But the Ibo people have a proverb that when a man says yes his *chi* says yes also. Okonkwo said yes very strongly; so his *chi* agreed. And not only his *chi* but his clan too, because it judged a man by the work of his hands."[4]

Having learned that a man can assert control over his *chi,* we learn a few pages later that the *chi* controls the man. Okonkwo is compared to "the little bird *nza* who so far forgot himself after a heavy meal that he challenged his *chi.*" (p. 28) As there are limitations on how strong the "yes" can be, we are left with an apparent contradiction, a contradiction that seems to raise questions about the nature of Okonkwo's tragedy. How much can he be held responsible for his end and how much can be attributed to an overpowering Destiny?

Keeping in mind these problems let us return for a closer comparison of the structural parallels in the lives of Oedipus and Okonkwo. The summary Meyer Fortes gives of Oedipus's life clearly shows where these parallels lie. Oedipus enters life with an ominous foreboding of an evil Destiny as he is rejected by his parents who physically cast him away. Only for brief moments in his life does he ever escape being an outcast; ultimately his fate overwhelms him. "His tragedy can be described as that of a man blindly seeking to achieve his legitimate place in society, first as son, then as husband, father and citizen against the unconscious opposition of an inborn urge to avenge himself by repudiating his parents, his spouse, and his children. When in the end, he succumbs to this fate he shows his revulsion against himself by mutilating his own eyes and so blotting out his relationship with his kind and his society. He dies in exile, almost like a ghost departing from this world rather than like an ordinary man."[5]

With a few changes of detail, Meyer Fortes could have been talking about Okonkwo. By material standards Okonkwo's father, Unoka, is an outcast in Umuofian society, and by any spiritual measure, he dies one: "He had a bad *chi* . . . and evil fortune followed him to the grave, or rather to his death, for he had no grave." (p. 16) Okonkwo spends his life trying to avoid his father's fate only to succumb to a death that also severs him spiritually from his society. In the course of his life, while attempting to repudiate the "feminine" characteristics of his father, he is respectively alienated from his father, one of his wives, his son, Nwoye, and finally his clan. He treats the memory of his father with contempt; he beats Ojiugo during the Week of Peace; he is horrified by Nwoye's attraction to Christianity; and he is physically exiled when he accidentally kills a young man. His suicide, moreover, is a clear correlative to Oedipus's self-mutilation.

Granted, we are still operating on a rather tenuous descriptive level, but behind both men there is definitely a strong force of Destiny controlling their lives, their parents and their children.[6] With Oedipus this control is complete and with Okonkwo it is partial, though in both cases "it serves to exonerate both society and the sufferer by fixing ultimate responsibility on the ancestors and on a pre-natal, that is pre-social, event."[7] No careful reader of *Things Fall Apart*, any more than a character within Umuofian society, could hold Okonkwo to blame for his fate despite the fact that a good argument can be made for the idea that there are implicit authorial criticisms of both Okonkwo and his society. Within that society we are shown that a man can have either a good or a bad *chi*—Okonkwo's life is simply controlled by an evil Destiny.

Yet such knowledge about a man's fate can only be known for certain after the fact. Moreover, neither the novel, the society, nor Okonkwo's life is all that simple. As Bernth Lindfors has very cogently shown, a very large proportion of the proverbs used by Achebe in *Things Fall Apart* have to do with achievement.[8] Many of these proverbs confirm the idea that in Ibo society a man is not necessarily foredoomed by an evil *chi*. Providing he acts in the appropriate manner, he can say "yes" to a *chi* that says "no": "the sun will shine on those who stand before it shines on those who kneel under them;" (p. 7) "if a child washed his hands he could eat with kings;" (p. 8) "a man who pays respect to the great paves the way for his own greatness;" (p. 16) "as a man danced so the drums were beaten for him." (p. 167)

These proverbs encompass strategies for individual equity that are antithetical to the closed system of prenatal destiny we find in the story of Oedipus. They are, however, rather incisive leads into another dimension of the religious framework of Okonkwo's society—a dimension that can be understood in terms of the patterns of divine justice we find in Job.

Nothing has been pre-established for the course of Job's life. He is free to choose between good and evil, and whatever consequences result from his choices are the rewards and punishments of an omnipotent God. Though personified, and ultimately just and merciful, this God cannot always be comprehended in terms of what the individual perceives as just. Job never admits, nor does he need to admit, any "guilt in the sense of responsibilty for actions that are wicked by ordinary human standards. What he admits is having placed himself on a footing of equality with God, judging for himself what conduct is righteous and what whicked. This wrong relationship was his sin ... Job's sufferings are like severe measures of discipline that a father might use to correct a son who, while exemplary in his conduct, was getting too big for boots and arrogating to himself a status equal to his father's; and Job's salvation might be compared to the son's realizing and accepting his filial dependence."[9]

As we are dealing with a paradigmatic and not a simple descriptive comparison, it might help to momentarily reverse perspectives. Job, in other words, can be seen as one who wrestled with his *chi*, realized his mistake before it was too late, and took the necessary steps to rectify his relationship with his God. Again, the idea here is not in some missionary-like manner to find one-sided "universal" correspondences, but to show that the Western reader should be able to get into the aesthetic complexity of Achebe's work. No injustice to the integrity of the work need be committed by this artifical atomizing so long as we see the process only as a key to a holistic understanding of a work that in its totality is very unlike either the work about Oedipus or Job.

The parallel between Job and Okonkwo that is significant to us is the idea that the ancestors, like Job's God, can be angered or pleased in such a way that they either confirm or override an individual's Destiny, bringing him disaster or good fortune. In discussing this in relation to the religious thought of the Tale, Meyer Fortes makes three generalizations about Tale ancestral belief that we can also draw out of *Things Fall Apart*.[10] These generalizations concern "axiomatic values from which all ideal conduct is deemed to flow. The first is the rule that kinship is binding in an absolute sense. From this follows the second rule, that kinship implies amity in an absolute sense. The third rule is the fundamental one. It postulates that the essential relationship of parent and child, expressed in the parent's devoted care and the child's affectionate dependence, may never be violated and is, in that sense, sacred. It is indeed the source of the other rules.[11] Thus, when Okonkwo is exiled from Umuofia he must flee to the village of his mother. He must accept his relatives there, and they are bound to accept him in complete friendship. Moreover, they are seen almost literally as living extensions of his mother.

Beyond any strict legalistic adherence to these values it is imperative that one have a proper attitude towards the moral relationships that follow from them. Like Job, Okonkwo is an upright and honest man guilty not of any willfully unjust actions, but of an unbending self-righteousness in his relations with his gods, his ancestors and his kin. Moreover, he cannot accept the suffering he is forced to bear. While in exile he is angrily castigated by his kinsman, Uchendu:

> You think you are the greatest sufferer in the world. Do you know that men are sometimes banished for life? Do you know that men sometimes lose all their yams and even their children? I had six wives once. I have none now except that young girl who knows not her right from her left. Do you know how many children I have buried—children I begot in my youth and strength? Twenty-two. I did not hang myself, and I am still alive. If you think you are the greatest sufferer in the world ask my daughter, Akueni, how many twins she has borne and thrown away. Have you not heard the song they sing when a woman dies?
> "For whom is it well, for whom is it well?
> There is no one for whom it is well (p. 122)."

Though Job's relation to his god is unilaterally contractual and Okonkwo's relation is a bilateral one of mutual dependence, the attitudes of both men pose a threat to the religious fabric of their society. God had a bet with Satan that had to be won; Umuofia had its very survival at stake in its confrontation with the white man. This survival of gods, ancestors and kin was more important than the inflexible will of one man: "What the ancestors demand and enforce on pain of death is conformity with the basic moral axiom in fulfilling the requirements of all social relationships; and these are the counterpart, in the domain of kinship, of the obligations posited between persons and their ancestors in the religious domain."[12]

The first thing we learn about Okonkwo is that "his fame rested on solid personal achievements." (p. 3) It is noteworthy that this is followed by our seeing that "he had no patience with his father." (p. 4) Considering the value placed on personal achievement in his society, Okonkwo certainly had no obligation to have patience with his father, who had no rank at all in the society. But there is a more fundamental kinship value that Okonkwo ignores. In a very subtle manner Achebe introduces this tension between individual and communal values and carefully orchestrates its buildup. The proverb that "age was respected . . . achievement . . . revered" (p. 5) lays emphasis on achievement, but indicates a balance between respect and reverence that Okonkwo ignores. His father praises him for his proud heart, but warns him of the difficulty in failing alone (p. 23), advice that Okonkwo is unable to accept. When a joke is made about a man who refused to sacrifice a goat to his father, Okonkwo is uncomfortable, ironically because it reminds him of his father's poverty and not of his own neglect of his father's memory. An old man com-

menting on Okonkwo's success quotes the proverb "Looking at a king's mouth
. . . one would think he never sucked at his mother's breast." (p. 24) The proverb is not used here in any derogatory manner, but is one more sign to the
reader that Okonkwo lives much of his life as if he had no kin.

All this is revealed within the first few chapters. The subsequent action
sharpens our insight into the tragic ordering of values that should be complementary, but in Okonkwo becomes completely oppositional. Communal and
individual values must be in carefully ordered balance. In his extremist actions
Okonkwo shows "no respect for the gods of the clan." (p. 28) Though he may
feel contrite, as he did after beating his wife during the Week of Peace, he
never shows it. The group itself must adjust and change when it is threatened
by its customs; it expects no less of the individual. This point is indirectly, but
firmly underlined by Ezeudu's recounting of the heavy punishments that were
once exacted whenever the Week of Peace was broken. After a while the
custom had to be altered as it destroyed what it was intended to protect.

Without going very far into a Lévi-Straussian type of structural analysis, it
is very obvious that we have here yet another aspect of Okonkwo than can be
understood in terms of the Oedipal paradigm, namely the underrating of blood
relations.[13] Unlike Oedipus in his incestuous relationship with his mother,
Okonkwo never overrates blood relations. Yet comparable to Oedipus's parricide is Okonkwo's rejection of his father and all things feminine. Okonkwo
continually acts in a manner that leads to an absolute rejection of his autochthonous origin. In his participation in the killing of Ikemefuna and in his
reluctant acceptance of his exile in his mother's land, he shows a willful refusal
to submit to the Earth Goddess; in his beating of his wife during the Week of
Peace and in his accidental killing of the boy during Ezeudu's funeral, he com-
mits overt offenses against the goddess.

During a feast at the end of Okonkwo's exile, an old kinsman rises to give
a speech to thank Okonkwo for the great banquet. Very discreetly, however,
he gives a talk on the strength of kinship bonds, while a general warning to
the clan must also be construed as a specific warning to Okonkwo: "A man
who calls his kinsman to a feast does not do so to save them from starving.
They all have food in their own homes. When we gather together in the moon-
lit village ground it is not because of the moon . . . We come together because
it is good for kinsmen to do so." (p. 152) The words, in effect, are beyond
Okonkwo's comprehension. When he returns to Umofia, he is entirely out of
step with his clan. A clear, inexorable logic thus leads him to ultimate offense
against the Earth Goddess, his own suicide.

The logic, however, was inexorable only because of Okonkwo's unbending
will. Had he submitted to the will of the clan, a will dictated by survival, he
too might have avoided a tragic end. Okonkwo's daughter, Ezinma is born
with an evil Destiny. A diviner is consulted and he informs the family that the
child is an *ogbanje*, a spirit that continually returns to the mother's womb in
a cycle of birth and death. Once the proper ritual measures are taken, the

evil *chi* is propitiated and survival from its threat is insured. The implication is clear—Okonkwo never fully propitiates his *chi*.

What Meyer Fortes had noted in a general way we can see very specifically, namely an Oedipal predisposition figuratively transformed into a Jobian fulfillment.[14] Okonkwo is a strong man, but he has limited vision and is caught in the singleminded pursuit of his ambitions and escape from his fears. Only in the end, after he has killed the messenger, does he achieve some tragic recognition: "Okonkwo stood looking at the dead man. He knew that Umuofia would not go to war. He knew because they had let the other messengers escape . . . He wiped his matchet on the sand and went away." (p. 184) But even then, Okonkwo sees only the futility of his own course of action. Complete understanding would entail the perception that "The system as a whole is impregnable, particularly since the criterion invoked is ritual service, not conduct that can be judged by men themselves. Whatever the ancestors do must therefore be, and is, accepted as just, and men have no choice but to submit."[15]

Two scenes that the Western reader is likely to find annoyingly inexplicable can be easily understood in relation to the function they serve in underscoring the need to submit to ancestral control. No reason is given for the Oracle's decision that Ikemefuna must be sacrificed—nor is any reason given for the Oracle's decision to take Ezinma to Agbala's cave for an evening and then bring her home. A boy appears to be senselessly killed and a young girl taken on a seemingly meaningless journey. The point is, however, that man's understanding cannot encompass the ancestor's justice. When Okonkwo attempts to interfere with the Oracle's decision and prevent her from taking his daughter, the priestess warns: "Beware, Okonkwo! . . . Beware of exchanging words with Agbala. Does a man speak when a god speaks? Beware!" (p. 91)

We can see, then, that while prenatal destiny and divine justice appear to be completely oppositional, even antithetical concepts, they are in fact complementary aspects of a logical, well-balanced system in which masculine and feminine values as well as individual and communal values are incorporated without any sense of contradiction. Okonkwo's tragedy is that he fails to recognize this. Like the tortoise in the folktale narrated by Ezinma's mother, Okonkwo tried to have everything his own way. His greed may not be as devious as that of the tortoise who calls himself "All of you," but in the same fundamental sense of selfish desire he sets himself against the group. Likewise, he rejects everything that is feminine in his own nature and others; the group is left with no recourse but to reject him. On the other hand, the imposition of Christianity and the incursion of the European colonial administration afford a great shock to the system, but they do not shatter it.

To return to Burke's idea of novels as proverbs writ large, we can see that *Things Fall Apart* names a strategy for dealing with change. Divine justice and prenatal destiny, the basic components of this strategy, are also the woof and warp of an extremely flexible social fabric. Okonkwo in his political conservatism and obsession with status, poses a threat to the fabric. Existing almost entirely on a physical, material plane and concerned solely with maintaining the status quo, Okonkwo gets into a death lock with his *chi*. The strategy, and mainly the component of prenatal destiny, insures for society that survival is accepted over stasis. It is worth taking note that the last proverb in *Things Fall Apart* is about the bird who is always on the wing: "Men have learnt to shoot without missing their mark and I have learnt to fly without perching on a twig." (p. 183)

Notes

1 Kenneth Burke, *The Philosophy of Literary Form* (New York, 1961), p. 256.
2 Ibid., p. 255. Proverbs are often structured around a metaphor, but if the proverb is to function when used in a social context, the analogue to the real situation must be readily apprehended by those to whom the proverb is directed. Obviously, not all complex literary works are written in a realistic mode. While it takes us beyound the range of this paper, we might note that Burke's idea could be further refined by our thinking not only of "proverbs writ large," but also of riddles writ large. In contrast to the proverb, the riddle is problematic rather than normative, confusing rather than clear. It creates artificial conflict and opens speculation whereas the proverb smoothes over conflict and closes further thought. Thus, Amos Tutuola, Wole Soyinka and other writers who employ a very expressionistic mode in their work might be considered riddlers rather than proverb users.
3 (London, 1959).
4 (London, 1962), p. 25. Subsequent references are to this edition.
5 Meyer Fortes, pp. 70—71.
6 This is borne out in the other two Theban plays of Sophocles and also in Achebe's *No Longer at Ease.*
7 Meyer Fortes, p. 71.
8 "The Palm Oil with Which Achebe's Words are Eaten," *African Literature Today*, 1 (1968), 8.
9 Meyer Fortes, pp. 17—18.
10 The level of generalization is high enough that it should be apparent we are not getting into any of the dangers of cross-cultural camparisons.
11 Meyer Fortes, p. 53.
12 Ibid., p. 54.
13 See Claude Lévi-Strauss, *Structural Anthropology,* trans. Claire Jacobson and Brooke Grundfest Schoepf, 2nd ed. (New York, 1967), p. 211.
14 Meyer Fortes, p. 74.
15 Ibid., p. 59.

Le théâtre africain et son audience européenne et africaine

Robert Cornevin

Le théâtre africain est un monde complexe, divers et qui a pris depuis les indépendances des années 60 une importance nouvelle en raison d'une part des festivals internationaux qui exigent des spectacles susceptibles de plaire aux critiques de théâtre (ce qui n'est pas une garantie de qualité ni d'africanité), d'autre part des restrictions apportées en de nombreux pays d'Afrique à la liberté de l'information qui font que les seuls secteurs laissés libres dans la presse, la radio et la télévision sont précisément ceux de la littérature et plus encore du théâtre.

Par ailleurs si le thème politique est admis lorsqu'il s'agit de l'évocation du gouvernement d'un pays voisin ou du gouvernement précédent la critique n'est admise autrement qu'à travers un thème historique ou étranger.

Ainsi tel tyran du XVIIe ou XVIIIe qui montre avec éclat les mêmes tares que le président en exercice n'appelle de la part de ce président bien installé au premier rang des spectateurs que des applaudissements enthousiastes ... on comprend dès lors l'exceptionnelle faveur du thème historique.

En ce qui concerne le patrimoine étranger il est inutile de rappeler le succès du *Revizor* de Gogol au Mali et au Zaïre en particulier qui pose si bien le problème de la concussion ou celui de *Montserrat* d'Emmanuel Roblès qui pose pour l'Amérique latine du XIXème siècle le problème des otages.

Les festivals internationaux, ceux de Dakar (1966) ou d'Alger (1969) comme ceux, annuels, de Nancy ou Avignon ont valeur d'incitation et de promotion. Certes ils aboutissent à des spectacles de haut niveau. Mais la qualité des critiques européens habitués à des schémas européens à des discussions d'écoles européennes ... aboutissent à des spectacles susceptibles de rentrer en des catégories déjà connues. Les principaux animateurs africains de spectacles formés en Europe souvent conseillés par des Européens, consciemment ou non suivent les mêmes schémas. D'où trop souvent, même en Afrique, un certain eurocentrisme.

Il n'y a donc pas toujours ou pas suffisamment stimulation pour l'auteur dramatique africain malgré la réelle valeur du concours théâtral organisé par les services de la radio française (OCORA puis O.R.T.F./D.A.E.C.).

En ce qui concerne les acteurs noirs, il en existe d'excellents à Paris, Dakar, Abidjan. Ceux de Paris ont les plus grandes difficultés à vivre de leur art en raison du petit nombre de rôles qui leur sont offerts. Ceux de Dakar, Abidjan,

Bamako sont fonctionnaires avec les garanties de carrière qui sont offertes ...
et parfois une certaine tendance à la somnolence chez des artistes qui n'y
croient plus tellement.

En Afrique toutefois il y a lieu de souligner la valeur des troupes d'amateurs
(ce sont des jeunes gens motivés, ils y croient) jouant sur un double registre en
langue africaine et en français.

Ces troupes, dans la brousse, portent un message d'autant plus intéressant
que le cinéma atteint parfois difficilement les régions éloignées.

Les télévisions africaines peuvent elle assurer la rentabilisation des compagnies théâtrales et relancer dans une certaine mesure la création ? C'est la
question que je poserai en terminant.

Je ferai d'abord un bref rappel historique de l'évolution du théâtre dans les
pays d'Afrique Noire ou le français est langue officielle, langue nationale ou
langue de culture puis j'évoquerai les divers problèmes qui se posent au théâtre
africain contemporain.

I. Le théâtre africain autochtone

Ce théâtre autochtone est signalé très tôt par les explorateurs européens
qui ont noté son importance depuis le Chevalier de Boufflers au Sénégal en
1786, jusqu'à l'explorateur Mage qui le décrit en 1868 dans son *voyage dans le
Soudan Occidental* en passant par le Kong Korong du Major Gray (voyage en
Afrique Occidentale, 1826).

Il est indispensable de rappeler que ce théâtre, comme le théâtre européen
du Moyen Age, est très proche des manifestations religieuses. On peut dire
qu'il y a spectacle lorsqu'une manifestation religieuse est vue par quelqu'un
d'un autre culte : la messe apparaît en spectacle pour un Musulman, telle cérémonie juive ou musulmane, constitue de même un spectacle pour le chrétien.
Tous ceux qui ont vécu en Afrique dans la brousse ont été, une fois ou l'autre,
témoins d'une cérémonie coutumière particulièrement remarquable : danse
d'initiation ou célébration des ancêtres. (Les chasseurs de Bassari par example.)

Très proches du théâtre sont les manifestations des Griots correspondant
toute proportion gardée aux monologues dits dans les campagnes européennes,
après les repas de noce ou à l'occasion des veillées de vendange ou des fêtes
de moisson. Le théâtre autochtone est important. Il correspond à la vie culturelle profonde du peuple et après une longue éclipse, on constate à l'heure
actuelle notamment dans le cadre de l'authenticité au Zaïre, au Tchad et au
Togo un retour assez remarquable aux traditions ancestrales.

Toutefois les facilités de communications de la période coloniale ont entraîné
des influences culturelles réciproques que signalait déjà F. V. Equilbecq en
1913.

Pour présenter un spectacle, on est amené à choisir ce qu'il y a de plus
harmonieux, de plus spectaculaire dans l'une ou l'autre ethnie. Sur le plan
musical, le poste à transistor répandu jusqu'au plus lointain village a rompu
complètement l'isolement mais aussi la pureté du patrimoine musical.

Les rythmes afro-cubains ou afro-brésiliens pénétrant jusqu'au village le plus reculé entraine des mélanges au point que pour les régions non encore inventoriées, la collecte risque de devenir bientôt impossible.

La chantefable africaine

Dans la littérature française, la *chantefable* était illustrée par un seul titre *la Chantefable d'Aucassin et Nicolette* (première moitié du XIIIe siècle) qui présente en strophes de vers assonancés entremêlés de prose destinée à être dite, l'idylle d'Aucassin, fils du comte de Beaucaire et de Nicolette une esclave Sarrazine donc africaine.

Le Camerounais Eno Belinga dans *Littérature et Musique populaire en Afrique noire* définit la chantefable comme

« un récit oral de conte ou de fable mêlé de strophes chantées. Le récit et la mélodie se recoupent mutuellement avec harmonie. Il précise que le chant n'est pas un élément accessoire du récit. Plus qu'une simple parure du verbe, il est en fait un élément constitutif et particulièrement important de la narration. Il peut servir de complainte à un thème tragique ou pieux, de dialogue entre les principaux personnages. »[1]

Je pense pour ma part que cette forme (alternance de récit et de chant) correspond aux éléments *variables* (le récit qui dépend de l'humeur de l'auditoire et de l'inspiration de l'aède) et aux éléments *fixes* dont la mémorisation est facilitée par la musique.

Toutes proportions gardées, les chanteurs européens ou américains (je pense aux Québécois Gilles Vigneault ou Pauline Julien par exemple) modifient les propos de leur tour de chant suivant un auditoire qui n'est pas le même à Chicoutimi, à Montréal ou à Paris.

L'épopée vivante et le théâtre épique africain

C'est — je crois — le professeur René Louis qui dans un numéro spécial de *La revue de la table ronde* a imposé le nom d'épopée vivante. Ce médiéviste éminent est l'auteur d'une thèse monumentale sur la geste de Girart de Roussillon, inventeur des thermes gallo-romains de Fontaines salées au pied de Vézelay où Romain Rolland par son centre Jean-Christophe a mis en place un foyer permanent d'amitié franco-allemande.

La définition de René Louis est la suivante :

« L'épopée vivante est la poésie héroïque traditionnelle qui chez les peuples jeunes où l'état de guerre est presque permanent célèbre les hauts faits des guerriers et les transmet de génération en génération par la tradition orale. Loin de commencer et de finir à son auteur » comme les créations de l'activité purement ilittéraire — créations individuelles et fixées dès le principe sous une forme écrite — l'épopée vivante prend sa source dans l'émotion collective d'un groupe humain dont son créateur n'est que l'interprète et elle continue de vivre plus ou moins longtemps après que son créateur l'a mise en circulation dans le public, entraînée dans le cycle de perpétuels renouvellements qu'est la tradition orale . . . »[2]

Cette épopée vivante s'est arrêtée de vivre au moyen âge européen lorsque des clercs ont fixé par écrit ces morceaux de littérature. Au contraire en Afrique nous disposons de griots qui détiennent encore ces épopées et l'Afrique, dans cette perspective a un avantage énorme sur l'Europe puisque le magnétophone permet de noter ces éléments et que nous disposons notamment au Rwanda et au Zaïre de publications avec traductions juxtalinéaires.

Le mythodrame de Samba Guéladio Diégui

L'intérêt des Africains pour le théâtre épique avait été ressenti dès avant la première guerre mondiale par l'administrateur F. V. Equilbecq. Ce dernier a rédigé « à l'africaine » une étonnante pièce de théâtre et avant que n'existe le mot de *psychodrame*, il créait le néologisme de *mythodrame* comme équivalent français du *Märchendrama* allemand. Il me semble que le mythodrame devrait pouvoir être défini comme une pièce de théâtre basée sur des traditions légendaires, ce qui donnerait une appellation commode à toutes les pièces issues du fond historico-légendaire.[3]

Conception africaine et conception européenne du théâtre

Ces conceptions sont fondamentalement différentes d'abord quant à la notion de temps. Sans doute les montres ethorloges ont elles mis longtemps à atteindre les villages de la brousse africaine. Des peuples de paysans vivaient — cela va sans dire — au rythme du soleil et lorsque — la nuit tombée — le moment de la danse était venu il n'était pas question de l'arrêter.

Bernard Dadié nous le rappelait

« Quand quelque chose nous plait, sa répétition nous plait davantage, nous ne nous lassons de chanter que lorsque notre voix s'éraille, de danser quand nos jambes ne nous portent plus . . . »[4] et Bernard Dadié marquait par ailleurs la distinction entre théâtre africain et théâtre européen.

« Si par théâtre on entend un spectacle dans un lieu approprié avec des spectateurs payants et des acteurs payés, avec des décors, des accoutrements, des maquillages, avec des répétitions, des réclames tapageuses, évidemment rien de tel en pays agni, encore qu'il y ait des lieux préférés à d'autres pour le théâtre et qu'il y ait des masques et que les bons conteurs et les musiciens, s'ils ne reçoivent pas d'argent, ne soient pas insensibles aux cadeaux en nature ou même à la bouteille de gin, encore qu'ils sachent soigner leur popularité, se faire attendre et désirer. »

Les concepts varient suivant les régions d'Afrique et les ethnies. On peut en gros distinguer trois phénomènes dans le théâtre autochtone : Cérémonies coutumières, réjouissances coutumières, représentations.

Les cérémonies coutumières ont un caractère religieux et Nicole Labonne dans ses *Recherches sur le théâtre d'expression française au Congo Brazza-*

ville[5] note l'aspect théâtral de cérémonies coutumières de funérailles chez les Batéké, Bakongo, Babembé, mais souligne les réticences des Congolais à prononcer le mot *théâtre* pour ces cérémonies et l'absence de rapport entre cérémonies coutumières et théâtre moderne en République Populaire du Congo.

Les réjouissances coutumières sont ce qui correspond aux fêtes traditionnelles correspondant aux danses, chants, etc. . . .

Enfin il y a *représentation* lorsqu'il y a spectacle, quelles que soient les places réservées aux spectateurs et aux acteurs. En ce domaine le contact public-acteur si passionément recherché à l'heure actuelle est parfaitement naturel en Afrique.

Qu'apportent les manifestations autochtones théâtrales ou parathéâtrales africaines à la civilisation universelle : une illustration éclatante de la chantefable, la valorisation d'une *épopée vivante* que les médiévistes doivent apprécier et ce contact direct entre spectateur et comédien si difficile à obtenir aujourd' hui.

Le théâtre néo-africain : bref rappel historique

C'est à Janheinz Jahn que l'on doit le terme littérature néo-africaine pour la littérature écrite en langue européenne. De même le théâtre néo-africain correspond au théâtre en langue européenne ou en langue africaine dans un cadre non-coutumier.

J'ai rappelé, dans les documents préparatoires au festival d'Alger, dans quelles conditions le théâtre de Bingerville était né en 1932 grâce à Charles Béart[6] alors qu'à l'Ecole Normale William Ponty de Gorée, une tradition existait depuis Georges Hardy, lui-même auteur dramatique.

J'ai personnellement connu Charles Béart et j'ai vu travailler les élèves de l'Ecole Normale William Ponty et je peux témoigner de la qualité technique du travail fourni, mais aussi de la totale liberté dans laquelle était laissée les étudiants, de représenter ce qu'ils voulaient, de choisir eux-mêmes leurs spectacles, leurs thèmes, de construire eux-mêmes leurs dialogues. Il n'y eut jamais, affirmait Charles Béart, aucune contrainte quant à la présentation des spectacles.

« Les étudiants, sur leur théâtre à Sébikotane jouaient tout ce qu'ils voulaient. Ils ont choisi eux-même leur programme quand ils donnaient des représentations ailleurs. Je n'ai opposé mon veto qu'une fois. A propos de la reconstitution d'une *Circoncision chez les Sérères* dont le réalisme était tel que nous eussions certainement eu à Dakar où ils voulaient la jouer des histoires avec la police . . . »

A l'époque de Gorée ou de Sébikotane les représentations données à Dakar dans la grande salle de la chambre de commerce ou à l'occasion de feux de camp en plein air offraient au public colonial et évolué une image de l'Afrique assez exaltante.

Premier contact avec Paris

Grâce à l'inspecteur général Albert Charton, qui devint auprès de Georges Mandel (ministre de la F.O.M.) directeur général de l'enseignement outre-mer, on fit venir les « Pontins » à Paris lors de l'exposition internationale de 1937. Les 12 et 17 août 1937 deux représentations furent données au théâtre des Champs Elysées. On avait eu l'intelligence de demander au gouverneur Henri Labouret de présenter le théâtre africain.

« . . . une compagnie d'élèves-instituteurs qui nous font sentir le charme authentique et la directe vérité de leur monde africain. Il ne s'agit pas d'exotisme pour vous ; ni d'initiation européenne pour eux. Dans une synthèse de danses et de chants, de musique et de littérature, un art dramatique s'éveille qui procède de leur pays et du nôtre, de notre langue et de la leur ».[7]

Deux pièces étaient au programme. L'une, dahoméenne, *Sokamé,* évoque le problème de la sécheresse, le sacrifice de la jeune vierge au serpent maitre des eaux, l'intervention du fiancé, Egblamako, qui tue le monstre, sa condamnation à mort, le tonnerre et la pluie salvatrice au moment où il va être exécuté.

La deuxième pièce, ivoirienne, *Les prétendants rivaux,* correspondait à une farce.

Sokamé fut immédiatement comparée à Iphigénie (non à celle de Racine, mais à celle d'Euripide mais en beaucoup plus vivant et émouvant).

Les prétendants rivaux étaient comparés à Molière,

Bernard Maupoil, l'un des meilleurs administrateurs chercheurs de l'immédiate avant-guerre, au nom de l'authenticité, de la vérité ethnographique partait en guerre contre cette forme de théâtre et « le lourd pavé des réminiscences soigneusement taillé à Paris ».

A ces critiques un africain, Alexandre Adandé répondait dans la revue *Outre-mer :*

« Réunissant dans leur ordre chronologique les pièces théâtrales du Dahomey parues dans le Bulletin de l'Enseignement de l'A.O.F. de 1933 à 1937, M. Maupoil en a fait l'analyse et la critique ; nous lui en sommes reconnaissants. »

« Jusqu'ici, nous avons volé de nos propres ailes, nous avons travaillé sans aucune notion bien précise de l'art nouveau dans lequel nous sommes lancés. Les succès sans cesse croissants que nous remportons sont seuls juges de nos talents. Et nous nous en sommes tenus là, satisfaits des résultats qui suffisent amplement à notre distraction et à la récréation des spectateurs. Somme toute, nous voyons le théâtre selon les critères du dilettantisme. »

« Il apparaît, d'après la critique de M. Maupoil, que notre théâtre, du moins tel qu'il l'entend, est loin de la perfection. La construction d'une pièce théâtrale indigène, en particulier celle qui reconstitue un passé historique, ne doit pas s'effectuer à la légère ; elle doit reposer au contraire sur des bases sérieuses, être entreprise avec le maximum de précautions. »

« Ce qu'il importe de reconnaître, c'est l'esprit impartial et objectif de la critique. Elle dégage des principes, révise des jugements, éclaire notamment notre création d'un jour nouveau. »

« Il ne paraît pas douteux, en tout cas, qu'un tel travail — qui vient à son heure — produise des réactions. Il permettra, à l'avenir, de combler les lacunes et d'éviter les écueils. »

« Toutefois, la critique, en certains points, se révèle quelque peu sévère. »

« Il semble, du reste, que cela provienne de la méconnaissance de notre intention. »

« La conception de nos pièces correspond-elle au but que nous nous proposons d'atteindre ? La réalisation est-elle satisfaisante ? Sur ce dernier point, les succès éclatants que nous avons toujours remportés sont éloquents. Quant au premier point, il y a divergence d'opinions si l'on s'en réfère à la critique et au motif qui l'inspire. Elle semble, en effet, axée sur ce pivot : reconstitution du passé historique ou interprétation de faits strictement localisés. Telle n'est point notre intention. »

« C'est une entreprise incertaine et même hasardeuse, du moins pour nous, que celle d'offrir à la curiosité d'un public étranger, en une représentation théâtrale, les témoignages intégraux du passé historique ou des rites religieux si complexes de notre pays. »

« En abordant nos sujets, nous avons le souci des spectateurs. Aussi nous préoccupons-nous des effets de la réalisation scénique. »

« Est-ce à dire que nos pièces n'ont aucun fond de vérité ? Non. A côté de nombreuses intrigues sérieusement étudiées, nous empruntons parfois, à une région de notre pays, autre que celle où se situe la scène, des éléments dont le pittoresque, pour une même circonstance, présente un puissant intérêt. »

« C'est ainsi que, dans l'Election d'un roi au Dahomey, bien que la cérémonie se déroule à Porto-Novo, nous faisons intervenir les Amazones de l'ancienne capitale du pays des Fon, Abomey, pendant la scène de guerre. Ces personnages jouissent d'une réputation non négligeable et satisfont intensément la curiosité par l'originalité de leur danse guerrière. Ce caractère vraiment typique nous paraissant bien à propos en l'occurence et digne d'intérêt sur une scène, nous l'avons exploité. »

« Disons tout de suite, au sujet de la même pièce, que le défaut dû à la concision qu'on lui reproche ne saurait être retenu. Etant donné le temps et le matériel dont nous disposons, il est absolument impossible d'interpréter, dans leurs moindres détails et avec intégrité, les nombreuses cérémonies fécondes en événements plus ou moins réalisables, qui accompagnent la mort, l'intronisation, le couronnement, voire même les principales fonctions d'un monarque dahoméen. Les grandes lignes des faits que nous évoquons dans cette pièce sont mises en relief en un raccourci qui n'exclut ni l'intérêt ni la compréhension. »

« Dans Sokamé, le personnage du Roi peut être arbitraire, d'après le thème de la pièce : Adaption d'un conte indigène. L'origine du Roi, pas plus que celle des acteurs, n'ont ici, ou ailleurs, aucune espèce d'importance : les personnages des pièces de Molière ou de Corneille en font foi. Ce que nous déplorons, c'est le fait d'avoir choisi un roi exceptionnel en son genre. Il manque de noblesse dans ses paroles et de majesté dans ses faits et gestes. »

« Le serpent des eaux, dont il est question, est universellement connu au Dahomey, à Abomey notamment. Témoin, la statue en bois représentant un reptile légendaire à deux cornes que j'ai achetée dans cette région et qui décore ma chambre. ‹ Ayidohouédo › — tel est son nom — bien que certains chasseurs aient essayé de prouver son existence, ne cesse pas d'être un serpent imaginaire : c'est l'arc-en-ciel ! »

« La superstition lui accorde d'énormes puissances bienfaisantes, entre autres celle de donner le ‹ Dan-mi › (l'excrément du serpent), l'or, autrement dit. »

« Les suggestions que nous notons avec plaisir, malgré l'âcreté de certaines conclusions, sont d'une forte sagacité. Cela tient, disons-le, à la connaissance, par l'auteur, de la mentalité de notre pays ; ses points de vue sur les rythmes sont étayés par des observations contre lesquelles les opinions ne sauraient s'opposer. C'est une conséquence de l'évolution culturelle. »

« M. Maupoil est sensible aux fausses notes, aux ‹ porte-à-faux ›, et son indignation devient manifeste quand ils semblent, au contraire, une concession au goût d'un certain public mal intentionné et ont une tendance à discréditer notre pays et ses traditions. »

« Cet état d'esprit évident prouve bien que cette critique est loin d'être une attaque contre nos ‹ œuvres ›. »

« Dans le numéro de Paris—Dakar du 9 août 1935, un article de fond signé R. Delavignette a parlé de notre pièce : Le Mariage de Sika. Aujourd'hui, c'est une critique qui sanctionne notre production théâtrale. Les pièces dahoméennes intéressent donc le monde ... Souhaitons qu'elles en tirent profit pour une heureuse réforme. »

«Mais, que la critique du théâtre dahoméen soit prise ou non en mauvaise part chez quelques esprits mal intentionnés, une chose est sûre, qu'il importe de retenir : il est l'origine des fêtes scolaires qui honorent l'Ecole W. Ponty. Eloge banal, dira-t-on, mais combien de fois vraiment mérité. »[8]

Le théâtre de Ponty continua durant la guerre sous l'impulsion de Ch. Béart à Sébikotane.

Le théâtre de Côte d'Ivoire

Cependant plusieurs anciens élèves ivoirien de Ponty sous l'impulsion de François Joseph Amon d'Aby créent *Le théâtre indigène de Côte d'Ivoire*, troupe qui devait réussir la performance de jouer en brousse en français et en des conditions tout à fait exceptionnelles, un répertoire qu'il fallait bien entendu améliorer. Ce répertoire correspondait aux idées catholiques de F. J. Amon d'Aby, appartenant à la Jeunesse Ouvrière Chrétienne, d'où les spectacles comme *Noël ! Noël ! Jésus est né, Joseph vendu par ses frères, Le supplice de Jeanne d'Arc*, alors que *L'entrevue de Bondoukou, La mort de la princesse Alloua*, correspondaient à des thèmes historiques locaux, sans manifestations chrétiennes. Amon d'Aby devait donner les objectifs d'un théâtre s'inspirant de l'histoire des coutumes et des légendes, il fallait présenter un théâtre enseignant l'intérêt général *(La mort de la princesse Alloua* et *Le Supplice de Jeanne d'Arc)*, le respect de la parole donnée *(Le drame de Bondoukou)*, la critique d'une civilisation mal comprise qui constitue le défaut général des jeunes gens et l'avarice qui est celui des vieux *(Le mariage difficile* et *Passion)*, lutter contre le charlatanisme qui retarde la civilisation *(La conversion des gens de Yabi, Boussatié, ou le secret du sorcier noir, Wodjé le Karamoko, Le Culte du Mando à Bounoua en 1895)*. Les thèmes du mariage et de la fidélité avec *nos femmes* et *nos maris* étaient abordés comme aussi les thèmes politiques, puisque *Le chant du retour* correspondait à la première pièce de contestation, ce Chant du Retour s'appelait en effet *les Recrutés de M. Maurice*, d'abord interdite par le Gouverneur. Cette pièce fut autorisée en 1943.

Déclin en Afrique. Vitalité en France

On assiste au déclin du théâtre africain de 1946 à 1953. Durant cette période les éléments africains les plus doués vont poursuivre leurs études en Europe, il n'y a plus d'acteurs en Afrique et on assiste à une véritable stagnation. Par contre en Europe, les jeunes étudiants africains qui avaient fait du théâtre en Afrique sont accueillis en France par une personnalité exceptionnelle Habib Benglia qui a toute une carrière dramatique derrière lui des personnalités qui vont y faire carrière comme Keita Fodeba, Douta Seck, etc. . . . Keita Fodeba présente une série d'interprétations les troupes d'acteurs noirs présentent *Negro spiritual* d'Yves Jamiaque, *Homme pour homme* de Bertold Brecht (1955).

Renouveau en Afrique 1953—1957

En 1953 on assiste à un véritable renouveau du théâtre grâce au Haut Commissaire Bernard Cornut-Gentile qui avait créé des centres culturels dans les cercles et lancé une revue *Traits d'Union*. Après des journées d'études des 3—7 novembre 1953, où furent rassemblés les dirigeants des centres culturels fut décidé la création d'un concours des troupes de théâtre et un concours entre auteurs africains. L'animateur de *Traits d'Union* Lompolo Koné décédé voici quelques mois à Banfora anima cette revue jusqu'en 1957 en d'excellentes conditions. Les compétitions théâtrales permirent de redonner vie à des troupes relativement nombreuses dans divers territoires avec des pièces nouvelles, à partir de faits historiques connus. Mais à partir de 1957 l'importance des activités politiques avec la loi-cadre, la communauté, les indépendances devaient mettre en veilleuse les activités théâtrales.

Le théâtre après les indépendances

Les indépendances africaines ne modifient pas du jour au lendemain les perspectives théâtrales, toutefois pour des raisons de prestige sont constitués des ensembles nationaux qui ne sont pas exactement du théâtre mais qui correspondent plutôt à des spectacles de music-hall, destinés à présenter sous leurs meilleurs jours, les diverses cultures des pays africains. Ces ensembles rassemblés à grands frais, furent présentés en Europe et en particulier au Théâtre des Nations (théâtre Sarah-Bernhardt) à Paris avec un certain succès mais dans le cadre de présentations officielles spectacles de gala où les spectateurs invités étaient d'avance gagnés. Ces spectacles de prestige sont montés au détriment des véritables pièces de théâtre, en dehors de l'Oratorioballet de L. S. Senghor sur Chaka il faut mentionner *Une saison au Congo* d'Aimé Césaire, *La Tribu* du Dr Sibney et *l'Oracle* du Congolais Guy Menga. Cette dernière pièce est donc la seule vraie pièce de théâtre d'un auteur africain. Les autres spectacles sont des pièces négro-américaines : *La case de l'oncle Tom* et *Les verts pâturages* réalisés par Jean-Christophe Averty pour les télévisions française et belge, *La fête à Harlem* de Merlin Van Peebles et le *Métro fantôme* et *L'esclave* de Leroi Jones. A signaler aussi le Togolais Alfred Panou et son *Black Power* au théâtre du Lucernaire et le « Mariage » traduction de *Home Free* de l'auteur américain Lanford Wilson au théâtre du Kaléidoscope traduit et monté par l'excellent acteur-cinéaste camerounais Daniel Kamwa avec pour partenaire Marpessa Dawn.

Les comédiens noirs de Paris et leurs problèmes

Les compagnies ont subi des avatars variés. Le problème est qu'il s'agit d'amateurs qui ont un métier. Le guadeloupéen Liensol travaille au Musée de l'Homme, les autres en général font du secrétariat ou de la présentation de mode. Ces acteurs manquent souvent d'occasion pour répéter. Pourtant l'effort est remarquable et beaucoup d'acteurs noirs francophones ont réussi à se dégager complètement des problèmes de la diction française.

Pour les emissions théâtrales vers l'Afrique, les services français de radio font toujours appel à des acteurs noirs pour des rôles africains.

Pour les rôles qui correspondent à des acteurs noirs dans les pièces jouées à Paris il n'existe malheureusement bien souvent que des rôles de serviteurs ou de cuisiniers. Seules des personnalités comme les Sénégalais Douta Seck ou Bachir Touré ou le Camerounais Ambroise M'Bia ont une dimension internationale.

Je passerai rapidement sur le regretté Daniel Sorano, mulâtre de Dakar très clair de peau, qui dirigea le théâtre de Toulouse, mais pour jouer essentiellement des rôles de blancs.

Parmi les initiatives pour essayer de donner au monde du théâtre africain la place qu'il mérite signalons celle de Gisèle Baka de son vrai nom Gisèle Bauche, actrice martiniquaise qui avait voulu organiser les acteurs parisiens, mais les divisions personnelles, les initiatives de Med Hondo et son T.E.F. (théâtre d'expression française) ne devaient pas permettre de donner une suite à ces projets.

Le spectateur européen devant les Africains

Il est navrant de penser que quinze années après l'indépendance le téléspectateur européen ne connaît de l'Afrique que certaines danses coutumières et n'a eu que très rarement l'occasion d'apprécier le théâtre africain. On en est à l'Afrique Safari, la pire du point de vue culturel, celle de bourgeois nantis d'Europe ou d'Amérique qui viennent, caméra en bandoulière, prélevés des images qui leur permettront de jouer à l'explorateur devant des assistances étonnées et ravies. Pourtant les thèmes du théâtre africain sont d'une facile compréhension et au besoin quelques lignes d'introduction suffiraient pour mettre le spectateur dans le bain.

En octobre 1964 était inauguré par un écrivain marocain Driss Chraïbi la série du *théâtre noir* qui avait lieu sur France Culture le premier samedi de chaque mois. Ce théâtre noir comporta surtout des adaptations : *Le chant du lac* d'Olympe Bhély Quenum, *Cette Afrique-là* de Jean Ikelle Matiba, *Le mandat* et *Blanche-Genèse* de Sembene Ousmane, *Mission terminée* de Mongo Beti, *Sur la terre en passant* de François-Borgia Evembe. Les seules pièces jouées dans cette série furent à ma connaissance *Agapes des Dieux* de Jacques Rabemananjara, *L'os* de Birago Diop et *Fo Yovo* du Togolais Joseph Amegboh. Driss Chraïbi fit aussi des adaptations de Wole Soyinka *(Frère Jèro, Les habitants du marécage)*, Chinua Achebe *(Le monde s'effondre)* Ezekiel Mphalele *(Au bas de la seconde avenue)*, Alex La Guma *(Promenade dans la nuit)* et *Camaxillo* de Castro Soromenho.

Depuis cette époque, depuis 10 ans, on peut dire que l'audience européenne du théâtre africain est très médiocre si on excepte le talent de quelques metteurs en scène progressistes comme Jean-Marie Serreau, qui fut rappelons-le en France l'introducteur de Brecht, de Blin et de quelques autres à noter au festival d'Avignon *la Béatrice du Congo* de Bernard Dadié. Mais en fait on pourrait dire que les spectacles africains sont actuellement moins bien connus qu'il a 10 ou 12 ans.

Le concours interafricain de l'O.R.T.F.

Pourtant sur le plan des auteurs, la situation est plutôt meilleure grâce en particulier au concours organisé à partir de 1967 chaque année par la D.A.E.C. (Direction des Affaires extérieures et de la coopération) de la ci-devant O.R.T.F.

Les responsables en effet avaient noté le cercle vicieux du théâtre africain.

« Par son insuffisance d'un répertoire correspondant aux aspirations de leur public, les troupes africaines ne peuvent fonctionner régulièrement ; d'où l'absence de comédiens et ce manque d'interprètes conduit les écrivains à abandonner le théâtre pour la nouvelle ou le roman. »

C'est pourquoi ce concours fut organisé qui voit chaque année depuis 1967 de 4 à 600 pièces de théâtre présentées au concours. Certes beaucoup de ces pièces sont médiocres ou nulles. Malgré les propos pessimistes de notre collègue Albert Gérard de Liège* je pense que les résultats sont dans l'ensemble honorables comme en témoigne le répertoire publié l'an dernier par l'O.R.T.F.

Mais ces pièces sont jouées à la radio pour les auditeurs africains des radiodiffusions nationales d'Afrique Noire.

Publications

Au point de vue des publications, Présence Africaine d'une part, P. J. Oswald d'autre part et la radio diffusion nationale française, publient des séries de pièces qui dans le domaine littéraire ont un certain succès et témoignent du talent littéraire des auteurs.

Théâtre en Afrique

En Afrique le Festival des Arts Nègres (1966) de Dakar devait permettre l'inauguration du théâtre Daniel Sorano qui vit d'importants spectacles et en particulier un Macbeth d'Hermantier et de Maurice Sonar Senghor. Mais je trouve dommage que l'on ait monté un Macbeth, c'est-à-dire qu'on ait emprunté au patrimoine culturel européen, toute chose égale d'ailleurs, ce qui existe dans le fond historique africain. A signaler parmi les créations du théâtre Daniel Sorano : *La fille des dieux* d'Abdou Anta Ka, *Delo*, de Tierno Ba, *L'os de Mor Lam* de Birago Diop. Le Festival mondial des arts nègres de Dakar, fut en avril 1966, un sommet et une occasion de montrer à la critique européenne ce qu'il fallait signaler à la fois du théâtre africain et des acteurs africains. Ce fut *La tragédie du Roi Christophe* qui remporta tous les suffrages, tant par la qualité des acteurs que par les thèmes, mettant en question les problèmes de coopération.

Les troupes nationales appointées (Sénégal, Mali, Côte d'Ivoire, Zaïre) assurent permanence et formation des acteurs. Leur vitalité dépend du directeur, de son talent, de son esprit d'entreprise, de son autorité. Elle dépend aussi de l'appui gouvernemental.

Les autres compagnies formées presque exclusivement d'amateurs ont une vitalité proportionnelle à l'esprit d'entreprises de leurs animateurs.

La critique théâtrale

Dans la presse quotidienne en Afrique des articles de plus en plus nombreux apparaissent sur la philosophie du théâtre africain ou sur les pièces.

Ainsi en septembre 1971 paraissait dans *l'Essor* de Bamako une série d'articles sur *La nécessité d'un théâtre national et populaire au Mali* par Amadou Gagny Kanté qui déplorait le rythme de création (une pièce par an) du théâtre national.

Antoine Chonang, dans *Cameroon Tribune* n° 159 du 6 janvier 1975 consacre un article au théâtre de Guillaume Oyono Mbia sous-titré « par delà le rire l'autopsie d'une société. »

Mais c'est peut-être dans la presse du Zaïre, dans *Salongo* (quotidien du matin) ou *Elima* (quotidien du soir) que les chroniques théâtrales sont les plus vigoureuses.

Perspectives nouvelles du théâtre négro-africain

Quinze ans après les indépendances africaines, quelques mois avant le festival de Lagos, le bilan du théâtre négro-africain de langue française présente des séries alternées d'ombres et de lumières.

Un grand nombre de pièces d'inégale valeur dont une faible proportion seulement a été « rédigée, rabotée, rafistolée, construite » au magnétophone ce qui semble la formule la mieux adaptée en tout cas pour la comédie, la satire sociale ou politique.

La diffusion de ces pièces est assurée par la collection de l'ex O.R.T.F./ D.A.E.C., P. J. Oswald, Présence Africaine, le C.L.E. de Yaoundé, les éditions populaires du Mali. Cette diffusion est encore insuffisante et il faudrait généraliser la pratique mise en place par Jean Vilar au T.N.P. de vendre les textes des pièces à l'entrée du théâtre.

Tout en admirant la performance de ceux qui ont sénégalisé Macbeth j'estime que l'Histoire précoloniale et coloniale est suffisamment riche pour fournir les thèmes nécessaire aux auteurs.

La télévision doit pouvoir fournir une solution aux problèmes de la rentabilisation des spectacles et des compagnies des spectacles africains peuvent pour la plupart être traduits en anglais, en portugais, dans les grandes langues véhiculaires africaines. Pour les spectacles susceptibles d'intéresser l'Europe, des traductions sont également envisageables en allemand, russe, etc. . . .

Ce serait une excellente application de la coopération : rendez vous du donner et du recevoir. Dans les problèmes de droits d'auteur ce serait aussi une bonne formule.

Pour la rentabilisation des acteurs, le cinéma doit être exploité au maximum. Le personnage à peau noire passe beaucoup mieux à la télévision en couleur que le blanc.

Pour ma part je crois préférable de fournir au téléspectateur européen des films africains plongeant dans la réalité du monde noir contemporain plutôt que les sempiternels *Westerns*.

L'U.N.E.S.C.O., me semble-t-il, aurait dans cette perspective un certain rôle à jouer. Ces propos, me semble-t-il sont dans le droit fil de l'idéal de vie de connaissance mutuelle et d'amour de l'Afrique qui fut celui de Janheinz Jahn.

Notes

1 Eno Belinga, *Littérature et musique populaire en Afrique noire* (Cujas 1966), p. 55—56.
2 *Revue de la table ronde*, déc. 1958, p. 9 cité dans mon *Histoire des peuples de l'Afrique noire* (Paris 1960), p. 53—54.
3 cf mon *Le théâtre en Afrique noire et à Madagascar* (Paris 1970), p. 38.

4 Bernard B. Dadié, *Mon pays et son théâtre* (Education africaine 1937), p. 61.
5 Diplôme présenté sous la direction du professeur Scherer à Paris en décembre 1968.
6 *Le théâtre en Afrique noire et à Madagascar*, op. cit., p. 52—54.
7 Robert Delavignette, *Bulletin du Comité Historique et Scientifique de l'A.O.F.*, (sept. 1937), p. 471.
8 Alexandre Adandé, « Réponse à Bernard Maupoil », *Outre-mer*, sept. 1937, no. 3, p. 318—320.
9 Albert Gérard, « La francophonie dans les lettres africaines », *Revue de Littérature comparée*, XLVIII (1974), III—IV, 371—386.

* « Les initiatives étatiques, inévitablement entachées de propagande, sont rarement efficaces : la publication de la collection ‹ Théâtre africain › par l'O.R.T.F. a surtout permis l'impression d'un nombre affligeant de ‹ navets ›. »[9]

Pour une histoire litteraire de l'Afrique orientale

Albert Gérard

L'Afrique Orientale comprend trois états qui n'ont guère qu'une chose en commun : ils ont été tous trois soumis pendant un certain temps à l'autorité du Royaume-Uni. C'est à ce titre qu'ils nous intéressent, car c'est pour cette raison qu'ils ont pu apporter une contribution à la littérature africaine d'expression anglaise. A part cela, il n'y a guère de similitudes, et même les différences, non seulement littéraires, mais culturelles et politiques, semblent destinées, après quelques vains efforts d'entente et d'unification, à croître rapidement, entre le Kenya, la Tanzanie et l'Ouganda. Il s'agit au surplus d'états multinationaux, dont chacun est peuplé de tribus très diverses, dotées souvent d'une longue tradition d'hostilité mutuelle. A l'intérieur d'un même état subsistent donc côté à côté des peuples qui parlent des langues très différentes, chacune ayant produit sa propre littérature.

Une fois reconnu ce fait élémentaire mais trop souvent oublié, il convient d'établir une première distinction. C'est que la plus grande partie de la production littéraire de l'Afrique orientale en est encore au stade oral ; faute de documents écrits et datables, elle n'est donc pas susceptible d'investigation historique : au point de vue littéraire, de nombreuses tribus (ou nations), de nombreuses langues, ne sont pas encore sorties de la préhistoire. Ceci n'empêche pas qu'une partie de l'Afrique orientale a aussi une tradition écrite, plus ancienne qu'en aucune autre région de l'Afrique au sud du Sahara, l'Ethiopie mise à part. C'est l'histoire de cet ensemble d'œuvres écrites qui nous intéresse aujourd'hui, car la littérature de langue anglaise, si elle est la seule qui nous soit accessible, est venue s'insérer tardivement dans un contexte au sein duquel il est nécessaire de définir sa situation si on veut en comprendre la portée.

Au milieu du siècle dernier, un missionnaire allemand, Ludwig Krapf, qui était au service de la London Missionary Society, ramena en Allemagne des manuscrits écrits en alphabet arabe et en langue swahilie. Ces curieux documents restèrent longtemps ignorés, enfouis dans les oubliettes des musées. C'est seulement en 1887, donc après que le Congrès de Berlin eut suscité pour l'Afrique un intérêt qui n'avait pas de rapport immédiat avec la littérature, que les manuscrits récoltés par Krapf furent enfin publiés et étudiés. Et à partir de 1890, nombre de missionnaires, de linguistes et autres savants, surtout allemands et anglais, aidés par des érudits locaux, ont découvert et publié, traduit et étudié une quantité stupéfiante d'œuvres poétiques de type *ajami*, c'est-à-dire écrites en langue vernaculaire au moyen de l'alphabet arabe. Le plus ancien de ces manuscrits date de 1728 et est connu sous deux titres : *L'Epopée d'Heraklios* ou *Le Livre de la bataille de Tambuka*. C'est le premier exemple connu du genre qui domine l'ancienne littérature swahilie : l'*utendi* ou *utenzi*, long poème narratif de forme strophique très stricte ; il raconte un épisode apparemment légendaire du conflit qui opposa Mahomet à l'empereur de Byzance au début du septième siècle.

Cependant l'*Utendi wa Herekali* n'est pas la première œuvre qui ait été écrite en Swahili. D'autres manuscrits du dix-huitième siècle se révèlent, à l'analyse linguistique, être des copies d'œuvres plus anciennes dont il est évidemment impossible de dater la composition. Il est probable que la plupart des écrits antérieurs au dix-huitième siècle ont disparu au cours de la période de déclin économique et culturel qui fut marquée par la prédominance portugaise dans l'Océan Indien, depuis l'arrivée de Vasco de Gama à Mombasa en 1499 jusqu'en 1752 lorsque les Portugais furent définitivement éliminés, par les troupes du sultan d'Oman, des territoires situés au nord du Mozambique. Il n'est nullement invraisemblable que la littérature écrite soit née à Zanzibar, dans les îles voisines et dans les villes côtières à la suite de la pénétration graduelle, commerciale d'abord, puis culturelle et religieuse, des Arabes et de l'Islam. Aainsi se forma sans doute une culture hybride, arabo-bantoue, la culture swahilie. Celle-ci s'incarna, du onzième au quinzième siècles, dans ce mystérieux empire « Zenj » qui semble avoir consisté en une sorte de confédération très lâche de villes musulmanes s'étendant de Mogadiscio au Nord à Sofala au Sud. Il faut espérer que les recherches actuellement en cours permettront de jeter quelque lumière sur les origines historiques de la littérature swahilie.

Dans l'état actuel de nos connaissances, nous pouvons seulement constater que la littérature swahilie du dix-huitième siècle s'est principalement développée dans les îles de Pate et de Lamu, au large de l'actuel Kenya. Elle est essentiellement d'inspiration musulmane, et nombre d'œuvres épiques remontent à des originaux arabes relatifs à la vie du Prophète et à ses guerres contre les infidèles. Mais à côté de ces poèmes narratifs qui célèbrent la croissance de l'Islam, il en est d'autres, plus directement didactiques, qui traitent d'une manière édifiante et conventionnelle le thème de la vanité des choses humaines, avec des motifs analoques à ceux qui imprègnent une bonne partie de la poésie de notre moyen âge occidental : le *contemptus mundi*, l'*ubi sunt*, le *memento mori*.

Une nouvelle phase s'inaugure lorsque le sultan d'Oman, Sayyid Saïd, obtient des Anglais la reconnaissance de son hégémonie sur Zanzibar et la côte africaine en échange de certaines restrictions au commerce de esclaves. Ce fut le traité Moresby de 1822. Afind'asseoir effectivement son autorité, le sultan entra en conflit avec certaines villes de la côte, et notamment Mombasa, gouvernée depuis près d'un siècle par la famille arabe des Mazrui. A en juger par les documents découverts jusqu'à présent, c'est alors qu'apparaît, à côté de l'inspiration religieuse qui avait été, et qui devait d'ailleurs rester, le courant central de la poésie swahilie, une nouvelle orientation qui est, cette fois, sécu-

lière et même engagée. Il semble que cette innovation ait été œuvre de Muyyaka bin Hadji al-Gassaniy (*ca* 1776-*ca* 1840), dont on dit souvent qu'il « sor-
tit la poésie de la mosquée pour l'amener sur la place du marché ». Le fait est
qu'une bonne partie, la plus originale, de la poésie de Muyyaka chante la résistance des dirigeants et de la population de Mombasa à l'impérialisme du
sultan d'Oman.

Résistance vaine, d'ailleurs, et au surplus malavisée, car la victoire et la domination de Saïd, qui transféra sa capitale à Zanzibar en 1840, devaient apporter à toute la région swahilie une stabilité et une prospérité sans précédent
jusqu'à la fin du dix-neuvième siècle. Le temps des Sayyids marque aussi l'apogée de la littérature swahilie classique. Sans doute celle-ci continue-t-elle à
dériver en partie de la littérature arabe : c'est ainsi que le Cheik Muhyi 'l-Din
(1789—1869) donne une des prémières versions vernaculaires du genre narratif arabe appelé *mi'raj*, c'est-à-dire « échelle », qui relate le rêve au cours
duquel le Prophète fut transporté de la Ka'aba au temple de Jérusalem, et de
là au septième siel, où Allah lui confia sa grande mission. Bien entendu les
poèmes didactiques et moralisateurs se multiplient. Mais le genre dominant,
l'*utendi*, reçoit une forme de plus en plus élaborée et véritablement classique
notamment avec l'histoire Job, *Utendi wa Ayubu*, qu'un contemporain de
Muhyi 'l-Din, Umar bin Amin al-Ahdal (1796—1870) acheva en 1835 : le récit
est construit selon une structure ternaire admirablement concertée, qui organise le schéma général et se retrouve dans les moindres épisodes. C'est également au cours du dix-neuvième siècle que se répand un genre plus séculier et
moins conventionnel : l'épître en vers ; elle traite généralement de problèmes
familiers, de questions de morale, de points de droit, mais il arrive aussi qu'elle
se rattache à la satire politique. Chose plus importante, la sécularisation de l'art
littéraire commencée par Muyyaka se poursuit et s'accomplit dans l'utilisation
de l'*utendi* pour la relation poétique d'événements contemporains. C'est ainsi
qu'un autre auteur de la même génération, Abdallah bin Masud al-Mazrui
(1797—1894), dans son *Utendi wa al-Akida* raconte sur le mode épique une
révolte du commandant (*akida*) de Mombasa contre le Sultan de Zanzibar
Sayyid Bargash, en 1875.

On retiendra donc, qu'au moment de la Conférence de Berlin (1884—1885),
il existait une abondante littérature en Swahili, issue principalement d'une
double inspiration, l'une religieuse, l'autre séculière. Les œuvres majeures appartiennent au genre épique, narratif, appelé *utendi*. Outre des récits traditionnels consacrés surtout aux épisodes militaires des débuts de l'Islam, ce genre
comprenait des chroniques en vers rapportant les conflits politiques locaux.
Cette littérature, il s'en fallut de peu qu'elle ne dépassât le stade manuscrit
lorsqu'un de ses représentants les plus prolifiques, connu sous le nom de Sayyid Mansab (*ca* 1828—1922), envoya un recueil de ses poèmes à Bombay pour
y être imprimé. Mais il semble que le navire fit naufrage et que les manuscrits
furent perdus. En tout état de cause, cette littérature écrite n'émanait que d'une
partie très limitée de l'Afrique orientale : les populations de l'immense hinterland qui s'étend jusqu'aux Grands Lacs enétaient restées au stade oral.

L'impact de la conquête européenne devait évidemment modifier profondément cette situation. Mais pour comprendre la suite de l'histoire littéraire de l'Afrique orientale, il est nécessaire de rappeler quelques faits relatifs à l'histoire de la colonisation elle-même.

Au milieu du siècle, missionnaires allemands et britanniques avaient joué un rôle capital dans l'exploration de ces vastes régions. Lorsque la conférence de Berlin eut donné le feu vert aux appétits coloniaux des grandes puissances, ces territoires firent l'objet de marchandages qui aboutirent au traité de Héligoland en 1870. Par ce traité, Zanzibar était placé sous la protection de la couronne d'Angleterre ; sur le continent, la région appelée depuis Kenya était accordée à la Grande-Bretagne, tandis que le Tanganyika allait à l'Allemagne. En 1894, les Anglais octroyaient le statut de protectorat au royaume du Buganda sur la rive occidentale du lac Victoria. En 1920, la Société des Nations faisait du Tanganyika un territoire sous mandat confié à la Grande-Bretagne.

Il faut maintenant examiner les conséquences littéraires de ces événements dans trois domaines : d'abord, l'évolution ultérieure de la littérature swahilie ; ensuite l'apparition de littératures écrites en d'autres langues vernaculaires ; et enfin la naissance d'une littérature (ou peut-être vaudrait-il mieux dire de plusieurs littératures) en langue anglaise.

C'est évidemment par la littérature swahilie qu'il faut commencer, puisqu'elle est, à ce moment, la seule écrite, donc la seule connaissable.

Dès les débuts de la période coloniale, Anglais et Allemands témoignèrent d'un intérêt très vif pour la langue swahilie — non plus seulment au titre d'une érudition presque pure comme cela avait été le cas depuis le milieu du siècle, mais aussi en tant que langue d'administration. Après tout, les nombreuses et diverses tribus de l'intérieur comprenaient et parlaient plus ou moins le Swahili grâce au privilège, par ailleurs douteux, qu'ils avaient eu d'être fréquemment en contact avec les trafiquants arabes. Le Swahili devint donc, au Kenya et en Ouganda comme au Tanganyika, le langage commun de l'administration et de l'instruction scolaire.

La première constatation qui s'impose, c'est l'extrême résilience de la littérature aux impulsions novatrices venues d'Europe. Plus encore qu'en Afrique occidentale, la littérature *ajami* conserve son identité islamique et son orientation dévote, qui se marque, par exemple dans l'*utendi* de *Seyyid Hussein bin Ali*, récit de type *maghazi* qui relate les guerres du petit-fils du Prophète, Hussein, contre le caliphe omayyade de Damas à la fin du septième siècle. C'est l'œuvre de Hemedi bin Abdallah al-Buhriy, poète de grande classe qui était déjà très actif en 1890. Il était originaire du Tanganyika et il est intéressant de noter qu'une distinction se marque très tôt entre les deux territoires. La politique peu systématique des Anglais ne semble pas avoir favorisé un renouveau significatif de la littérature swahilie : à Zanzibar et sur la côte du Kenya, on se préoccupa surtout de recueillir les textes classiques, sans trop chercher à faire œuvre originale. Il n'en alla pas de même au Tanganyika, où une politique assez brutale, appliquée par les Allemands aux tribus de l'intérieur, fournit aux écrivains swahilis des thèmes nouveaux, liés à l'actualité historique, dans la veine inaugurée par Abdallah bin Masud. C'est ainsi que le même Hemedi compose, à la fin du siècle, un *utendi* sur la conquête allemande des régions côtières où certains groupes résistèrent vainement aux Allemands dans l'espoir de maintenir la suprématie du sultan de Zanzibar sur cette partie du continent. Et au début de notre siècle, Abdul Karim bin Jamaliddini écrit un *utendi* sur la rébellion des Maji-Maji, populations animistes de l'intérieur qui s'étaient révoltées vers 1905 à la fois contre la domination allemande et contre les administrateurs musulmans que les nouveaux maîtres avaient hérités du sultan. Tout en reconnaissant les griefs légitimes des insurgés, Abdul Karim ne manque pas d'insister sur leur maladresse guerrière et sur leurs croyances sur-perstitieuses. Jusqu'à la fin de la domination allemande, d'ailleurs, d'autres chroniques en vers devaient être composées par des lettrés qui se montraient d'autant plus loyaux vis-à-vis des conquérants européens qu'ils avaient con-servé, sous le régime allemand, le pouvoir bureaucratique dont ils avaient joui sous les sultans, et qu'ils traitaient d'une répression dirigée contre des infidèles païens.

Cependant, le phénomène le plus décisif pour l'évolution de la littérature swahilie fut évidemment l'introduction de l'alphabet latin et de la presse par les écoles missionnaires. Dès 1867, l'évêque Steere avait adapté certains contes de Charles Lamb ; ceci fut suivi en 1888 d'une version swahilie du *Pilgrim's Progress* et, en 1890, d'une sélection des fables d'Esope — pour ne pas parler des traductions de l'Ecriture Sainte. Bientôt des indigènes instruits virent l'a-vantage de recourir à ce nouveau medium. Tandis que les poètes restaient fidèles à la tradition *ajami*, l'alphabet latin fut surtout utilisé pour écrire des récits historiques ou semi-historiques dont les premiers furent imprimés à Tanga sur la presse de la Universities Mission to Central Africa pendant les années 1890. Après la défaite de l'Allemagne, le Tanganyika, sous le mandat britannique, resta le centre de ce type de production littéraire. Le journal *Mambo Leo* fut lancé à Dar es Salaam en 1923. En 1925, une conférence réunie par le gouverneur du Tanganyika émit l'idée qu'il serait utile et com-mode de faire du Swahili la *lingua franca* des trois territoires. En 1930, après plusieurs années de négociations, fut fondé l'Inter-Territorial Language Com-mittee, dont le but était de promouvoir la standardisation et le développement du Swahili de Zanzibar, notamment en encourageant les auteurs dont la langue maternelle était le Swahili. C'est à la suite des efforts de cette organisation, qui prit bientôt le nom de East African Swahili Committee, qu'apparut une généra-tion nouvelle d'écrivains. Formés dans les écoles missionnaires, en-dehors donc de la tradition des lettrés islamiques, c'étaient principalement des prosateurs ; à côte de leurs écrits historiques, ils publièrent des contes traditionnels oraux, mais aussi des nouvelles et même de courts romans.

Ces œuvres sont en général d'une grande médiocrité. Les auteurs se servaient d'une forme d'expression, la prose, qui ne jouit pas, dans la société tradition-nelle, d'un statut comparable à celui de la poésie. Leur but n'était d'ailleurs pas essentiellement de faire œuvre d'artistes mais d'éducateurs : ces récits en prose étaient destinés à fournir de la lecture agréable et édifiante aux enfants des écoles, à améliorer leur connaissance du Swahili, et ainsi à faire de cette langue un instrument d'unification culturelle à travers toute l'Afrique orientale. Cette entreprise fut un échec. C'est seulement au Tanganyika, devenu Tanzanie, que le Swahili devait se répandre suffisamment — principalement à cause de la faiblesse des autres ethnies et de leurs langues — pour acquérir, après l'indépendance, le statut de langue nationale officielle.

Mais peu après la deuxième guerre mondiale, un effort délibéré fut fait par un autre écrivain du Tanganyika, Shaaban Robert (1909—1962) pour rapprocher les deux courants, le moderne et le traditionnel. Shaaban, dit Lyndon Harries, fut « le premier en Afrique orientale, à pratiquer des genres différents : la nouvelle et l'allégorie politique, l'*utendi* traditionnel et la simple autobiographie, l'essai et la traduction ». A cette diversité inaccoutumée, il faut ajouter deux autres traits caractéristiques de Shaaban, de son œuvre et de sa personnalité. D'une part, il reste très imprégné par le moralisme traditionnel, l'esprit didactique et le sérieux austère de la tradition swahilie. Mais par ailleurs, il est significatif que Shaaban proclamait ostensiblement son identité africaine, déclinant toute ascendance arabe ; ceci était un signe des temps, car les auteurs swahilis traditionnels se réclamaient volontiers de leur origine arabe.

Le premier effet de la colonisation européenne a donc été l'étude de la littérature swahilie classique et la formation d'une littérature swahilie moderne. Il faut noter que cette nouvelle tendance s'est particulièrement développée au Tanganyika, alors que la littérature classique avait connu son apogée à Zanzibar et sur la côte du Kenya. En tout état de cause, cette littérature n'affectait guère que les régions côtières et les îles, même si le East African Swahili Committee eut, à certains moments, une branche à Nairobi (Kenya) et une à Makarere (Uganda) en plus de son centre à Dar es Salaam.

Un deuxième effet de la colonisation britannique fut la réduction d'autres langues vernaculaires à l'écriture et leur utilisation à des fins littéraires — mais seulement en Ouganda et pendant la dernière décennie de la période coloniale. Pour comprendre ce phénomène, il faut se rappeler que l'Ouganda avait un statut politique et linguistique assez particulier. D'une part, en effet, le Swahili n'y était guère connu, sinon comme moyen de communication rudimentaire avec les chasseurs d'esclaves et autres trafiquants arabes ; il n'était la langue maternelle de personne, et il n'éveillait guère, dans l'esprit de la population, que des connotations peu agréables. D'autre part, l'Ouganda n'était pas une colonie comme le Kenya, mais un protectorat. Le statut accordé (ou imposé) dès 1884 au royaume du Buganda, avait été étendu, en 1900, aux petits royaumes voisins du Bunyoro, du Toro et de l'Ankole. La partie dominante restait toutefois le Buganda, où se trouvaient la capitale, Entebbe, ainsi que le centre économique, Kampala, et où devait être fondé, en 1939, le collège universitaire de Makarere. Dès le premier quart de notre siècle, certains indigènes du Buganda, instruits dans les missions, écrivirent en anglais, non dans un but littéraire, mais pour consigner les coutumes et l'histoire de leur peuple. Parmi eux figure notamment Sir Apolo Kagwa, premier ministre du Buganda en 1890, et, par la suite, dirigeant effectif du royaume. Une activité authentiquement littéraire en anglais n'apparut que beaucoup plus tard, comme nous le verrons.

Mais ce qui est plus intéressant pour notre propos, c'est que, au cours des années 1950, le Ganda devint la deuxième langue vernaculaire d'Afrique orientale à pouvoir se targuer d'une production littéraire imprimée. Ce fut là en grande partie le résultat d'une initiative officielle, la fondation de l'East Africa Literature Bureau en 1948. Le Bureau lança un magazine bilingue Swahili-Ganda et publiait quelque 60 à 80 livres par an, en anglais, en swahili et dans plus de vingt autres langues locales ; mais il s'agissait là surtout d'ouvrages didactiques destinés à lutter contre l'analphabétisme et à disséminer des connaissances pratiques sur la vie moderne. C'est seulement en Ganda que parurent à partir de 1953 quelques œuvres de littérature imaginative : poèmes et récits en prose destinés à peu près uniquement à fournir une lecture adéquate aux enfants des écoles.

On peut noter ici, en anticipant quelque peu, qu'après l'indépendance, acquise en 1962, quelques œuvres du même genre furent publiées dans d'autres langues du pays, notamment en Nyoro, en Soga et en Runyankore. Il faut probablement voir là un effet mineur de la politique générale du premier ministre Milton Obote, qui s'efforçait de saper l'hégémonie du Buganda pour mieux assurer l'unité et l'harmonie de l'Ouganda.

Cette littérature vernaculaire est encore très mal connue. Elle n'a guère été étudiée. Sans doute son intérêt proprement esthétique est-il passablement limité. Mais elle témoigne de l'accession de nouveaux groupes humains à la culture de l'écrit et à la production littéraire moderne. Ne fût-ce qu'à ce titre, elle mériterait de faire l'objet de recherches approfondies sur sa genèse, ses thèmes dominants et la manière dont elle a réussi ou échoué à adapter au nouveau medium le style et les techniques de la tradition orale.

Mais le troisième résultat de la colonisation, et bien entendu le plus connu (ou le moins ignoré), c'est l'apparition, en Afrique orientale, d'une littérature en langue anglaise, qui ne devait d'ailleurs se développer vraiment qu'après l'abolition du régime colonial.

Comme je l'ai déjà dit, c'est en Ouganda que voient le jour les premiers écrits indigènes en langue anglaise. Mais il ne s'agissait pas d'œuvres littéraires à proprement parler, et cette initiative resta sans lendemain.

En fait, la littérature est-africaine d'expression anglaise surgit en 1958 sous l'effet de deux facteurs totalement indépendants l'un de l'autre.

Le premier est la révolte Mau Mau de 1952, qui marque le point culminant d'une résistance déjà longue du peuple kikuyu contre les abus les plus criants du système colonial. Les Kikuyus qui occupaient, avant la colonisation, les régions les plus fertiles du Kenya, détenaient une position tout à fait particulière parmi les diverses ethnies du pays. Comme le note John Hatch dans sa *History of Post-War Africa,*

> It was the Kikuyu who felt the racial, economic, and political tensions in
> their severest forms. They lived alongside the White Highlands and around
> the outskirts of Nairobi (...) It was the Kikuyu who were generally the

most advanced tribe, with more educated members and a higher degree of political consciousness. Inevitably, it was those who had approached to the frontiers of western society and then found themselves rejected, who felt discrimination most sharply. It was the Kikuyu also, who formed the largest contingent of the unemployed, homeless and starving in the African locations of Nairobi.

Ces facteurs n'expliquent pas seulement que l'insurrection se soit déclenchée parmi les Kikuyus. Ils expliquent aussi que les Kikuyus aient été les premiers à créer une littérature écrite et qu'ils l'aient créée en langue anglaise. En 1958 paraissait un récit autobiographique au sous-titre révélateur : *Land of Sunshine : Scenes of Life in Kenya before Mau Mau*, par Muga Gicaru (né en 1920). Ce livre manifeste une des grandes tendances de l'ensemble de la littérature africaine moderne : la volonté de tirer parti de l'écriture pour fixer le souvenir des modes de vie traditionnels. Après l'indépendance, obtenue par le Kenya en 1963, il fut suivi de quelques autres récits autobiographiques comme *Mau Mau Detainee* (1963), de Josiah Mwangi Kariuki, qui fut le premier à retracer, de l'intérieur, l'expérience Mau Mau, ou encore comme *Child of Two Worlds* (1964), où Mugo Gatheru relate sa vie d'Africain hautement instruit, qui est parvenu à établir un équilibre entre les croyances et coutumes ancestrales et ses idées d'intellectuel formé à la mentalité de l'Occident.

Mais 1958 fut aussi l'année où parut, à Makarere College, le premier numéro de *Penpoint*, prèmière revue littéraire anglophone, publiée en Afrique orientale. Fondé en 1939, le Collège était une institution inter-territoriale et multiraciale qui allait jouer, pour la littérature de ces pays, un rôle fécondant assez analogue à celui que Fort Hare avait joué en Afrique du Sud dès le dix-neuvième siècle, et à celui d'Ibadan au Nigeria. L'établissement d'une « relation spéciale » entre le Collège et l'Université de Londres en 1953 amena une amélioration spectaculaire de l'enseignement. Dès 1958 le Département d'Anglais devenait le foyer de l'activité littéraire en Afrique orientale, et fournissait les premiers modèles pour des initiatives qui devaient bientôt se multiplier et se répandre à l'extérieur de l'Ouganda. C'est ainsi, par exemple, que la qualité très honorable des œuvres publiées dans *Penpoint* reçut sa consécration en 1965 lorsque l'éditeur anglais Heinemann publia *Origin East Africa*, une anthologie, préparée par David Cook, de récits et de poèmes qui avaient paru dans les seize premiers numéros de *Penpoint*. C'est ainsi encore qu'en 1962 fut jouée, à Makarere, la première pièce anglaise écrite en Afrique orientale, *The Black Hermit*, dont l'auteur, étudiant au Département d'Anglais, était le jeune Kenyan James Ngugi. C'est ainsi toujours que le même département organisa, en 1962 également, une importante conférence des écrivains africains d'expression anglaise. A ce congrès participèrent des auteurs déjà connus comme Chinua Achebe, John Pepper Clark et Wole Soyinka du Nigeria, Ezekiel Mphahlele et Bloke Modisane d'Afrique du Sud, Kofi Awoonor du Ghana, Sarif Easmon du Sierra Leone. Ils prodiguèrent féconds encouragements et conseils judicieux aux écrivains en herbe qui peuplaient, semble-t-il, le département.

On constate aussi que *Penpoint* joue un rôle de précurseur dans le domaine des périodiques littéraires. En 1961 paraît, toujours en Ouganda, une revue de haute tenue, *Transition*, qui l'intéresse aux problèmes politiques, sociaux et culturels aussi bien qu'à la littérature. A partir de 1965, le mouvement se met à essaimer, et d'autres revues littéraires apparaissent dans les nouvelles institutions universitaires créées en Tanzanie et au Kenya. En 1966, *Darlite* est lancé à Dar es Salaam. En 1967, à Nairobi, paraît *Nexus*, remplacé, l'année suivante, par *Busara*. A leur tour, ces revues universitaires suscitèrent des initiatives moins directement reliées au monde académique, principalement à Nairobi. En 1967, la succursale kenyane de l'Oxford University Press lance *Zuka*, présenté comme « a journal of East African creative writing », et en 1958, l'*East Africa Journal* inaugure, sous le titre *Ghala*, un numéro spécial annuel consacré à la littérature.

Comme vous le voyez, ces considérations nous ont amenés au-delà de la période coloniale, qui se clôtura en 1961 pour le Tanganyika, en 1962 pour l'Ouganda, et en 1963 pour Zanzibar et le Kenya. En 1964, Zanzibar et le Tanganyika devaient s'unir pour former la Tanzanie. Il est clair que Makarere College fut le berceau de la littérature de langue anglaise en Afrique orientale. Depuis l'indépendance, comme je l'ai déjà signalé, quelques efforts ont été faits pour promouvoir les littératures vernaculaires écrites en Uganda, et le Swahili est devenu langue officielle en Tanzanie. Mais le phénomène le plus curieux est la croissance extraordinairement rapide de la littérature d'expression anglaise, à vrai dire sous des formes, avec une intensité et selon une chronologie, différentes dans les trois pays.

Très tôt, certains signes avant-coureurs donnèrent à penser que le centre de gravité de cette littérature allait passer de l'Ouganda au Kenya. Tout d'abord, il faut rappeler que dès avant 1965, trois ouvrages autobiographiques écrits par des Kikuyus avaient été publiés en Grande-Bretagne. Par ailleurs, on notera que, parmi les 25 collaborateurs de *Origin East Africa*, huit étaient kényans, alors que cinq seulement étaient originaires du Tanganyika, quatre de l'Ouganda et un de Zanzibar ; les autres venaient pour la plupart d'autres pays d'Afrique, et l'équipe comprenait également un Américain, un Anglais et un Indien. En troisième lieu, il est significatif que quand Ezekiel Mphahlele — dont on sait avec quel inlassable dévouement et quel dynamisme inépuisable il s'est consacré au développement d'une littérature moderne valable dans les régions les plus diverses de l'Afrique — quitta le Nigeria pour lancer, en Afrique Orientale, un mouvement d'animation culturelle analogue au Mbari Club d'Ibadan, c'est à Nairobi qu'en 1963 il fonda son Chemchemi Cultural Centre. Son but était d'atteindre un public plus étendu que les intellectuels formés à Makarere College. Dans l'ensemble, Chemchemi fut un échec ; Mphahlele le reconnut lorsqu'en 1966 il dut quitter le Kenya, où il enseignait au University College de Nairobi, en conséquence, comme il l'écrit avec um humour dépourvu d'amertume, de la politique d'« africanisation » instaurée par les autorités kenyanes.

L'importance rapidement croissante de Kenya dans l'élaboration d'une littérature anglophone en Afrique orientale est en quelque sorte symbolisée par la publication, en 1964, de *Weep not, Child*, roman de James Ngugi, qui a repris aujourd'hui son nom africain, Ngugi wa Thiongo. En effet, Ngugi est le premier écrivain est-africain d'envergure réellement internationale, et dont le talent puisse être comparé, par exemple à celui de Chinua Achebe. A la vérité, il avait déjà écrit une pièce qui avait été représentée en Ouganda en 1962, et qui ne devait être imprimée qu'en 1968, ainsi qu'un premier roman, qui parut en 1965.

Si on examine les œuvres de Ngugi dans l'ordre chronologique de leur composition, on constate un progrès constant dans sa maîtrise de l'art litté-raire, ainsi qu'une évolution thématique qui reflète fidèlement les transfor-mations de la société africaine. La pièce, *The Black Hermet,* était centrée sur un personnage et un thème qui étaient déjà devenus des poncifs de la nouvelle littérature africaine : la situation du jeune homme instruit qui a quitté son village pour vivre à la villa. Mais Ngugi a vu cette situation sous un angle qui lui est personnel : si son protagoniste, Remi, s'attache à la ville, ce n'est pas à cause des plaisirs sophistiqués et passablement vénéneux qu'elle peut lui offrir ; c'est parce que le tribalisme chauvin des villageois le rebute et qu'il veut aider le gouvernement à forger une véritable conscience nationale.

Le premier roman écrit par Ngugi, *The River Between,* est centré sur les problèmes de l'acculturation — le conflit des générations, l'antagonisme entre chrétiens et animistes, entre ceux qui restent fidèles aux coutumes ancestrales et ceux que la fréquentation des écoles a convertis aux idées modernes. Rien de tout cela, n'était bien neuf non plus, même si ces problèmes n'avaient jamais encore été traités dans le contexte est-africain. Mais ici ausssi, James Ngugi introduisait dans le roman anglophone des éléments neufs : d'abord, la capacité de créer et de manipuler des protagonistes à la fois très différents et très convaincants, dans le cadre d'une intrigue complexe et savamment organisée ; ensuite, la faculté poétique d'établir des correspondances symboli-ques entre les personnages et les attitudes qu'ils représentent d'une part, et d'autre part, le paysage africain.

Avec *Weep not, Child* (qui fut son premier livre publié), Ngugi traite de l'époque du mouvement Mau Mau, mais avec une technique narrative à la fois moins systématique et plus raffinée. Se plaçant au point de vue d'un jeune garçon — Ngugi avait 14 ans quand l'insurrection éclata — l'auteur se sert de la succession des générations pour retracer les étapes de la destruction de l'ordre colonial et pour formuler sa haine de la violence et son espoir d'une grande réconciliation des races.

Jusqu'alors, la conscience centrale dans chaque œuvre de Ngugi avait été le représentant d'une jeunesse sensible et idéaliste. Mais avec *A Grain of Wheat* (1967), il abandonne ces personnages non encore mûrs et leur attente utopique pour se tourner vers un monde d'adultes dans le contexte du Kenya indépendant. Et ce qui caractérise cette fascinante évolution du romancier, c'est que cette nouvelle œuvre est marquée par une double désillusion. Dans la mesure où les personnages principaux sont d'anciens membres du mouve-ment Mau Mau qui, traités en héros, prennent néanmoins conscience de l'impureté de leurs mobiles et de l'ambiguïté de leurs actions, cette désillusion est tournée vers le passé. Et dans la mesure où la peinture du Kenya indépendant met en relief l'appétit égoïste de puissance, de richesse et de jouissance qui anime les nouveaux dirigeants, cette désillusion est tournée vers le présent. C'est seulement dans des épisodes symboliques, qu'apparaît le « grain de blé » du titre, le germe d'une nouvelle espérance, qui n'est plus dirigée vers la réalisation d'une société idyllique, mais vers un idéal beaucoup plus individualiste et personnel d'intégrité morale, de compréhension, d'amour et de fécondité.

L'expérience de l'indépendance a détruit beaucoup de mirages parmi les intellectuels d'Afrique noire. Le dernier ouvrage de Ngugi, publié sur place vers 1970, est un recueil de petites pièces assez médiocres, dont l'une montre qu'il se joint au courant grandissant de critique politique et sociale qui envahit aujourd'hui la littérature africaine : elle met en scène la situation des taudisards de Nairobi, dont les autorités font détruire les misérables masures pour ne pas offenser le regard des touristes européens et américains — mais sans faire le moindre effort pour leur procurer des logements plus décents.

Après l'apparition de James Ngugi, le phénomène le plus important pour le développement des littératures est-africaines anglophones, sur le plan quantitatif plutôt que qualitatif, fut la fondation de l'East African Publishing House en 1965. C'est le plus importante maison d'édition de l'ancienne Afrique britannique dont le seul équivalent en Afrique francophone est le Centre de Littérature Evangélique de Yaoundé. Au cours des sept dernières années, la production de l'EAPH a été considérable, particulièrement dans le domaine du roman. Si on essaie de découvrir une sorte de canevas, une structure de tendances dans l'ensemble de cette production, on est amené quelques observations qui ne manquent pas d'intérêt.

En premier lieu, bien que l'entreprise soit internationale, tous les écrivains publiés, nés, en général, vers 1940, proviennent du Kenya, et, dans une moindre mesure, de l'Ouganda. L'absence de la Tanzanie témoigne du fait de plus évident que ce pays suit une voie particulière dans le domaine littéraire aussi bien que dans les autres.

Si on prend comme critère l'appartenance ethnique des écrivains, on observe une nette prédominance des auteurs kikuyus, dont la plupart (je pense par exemple à John Karobi ou à Godwin Wachira) restent obsédés par le traumatisme de l'insurrection Mau Mau et de la répression sanglante qui la suivit. Cela donne à leurs romans une tonalité tragique qui imprègne souvent toute leur conception de la vie. On le voit dans *A Curse from God* (1970) de Stephen Ngubiah : la « malédiction de Dieu » dont parle le titre est la polygamie, mais celle-ci n'est qu'un élément dans une configuration hautement négative, qui comprend non seulement la révolte Mau Mau, mais encore des facteurs comme la division introduite par le christianisme dans la société Kikuyu, la corruption morale et les inégalités socio-économiques provoquées par l'irruption d'une économie monétaire dans une culture dont l'éthique reposait sur une économie de subsistance, et même les famines provoquées périodiquement par la sécheresse : tous ces éléments hétérogènes apparaissent comme autant de signes du destin tragique auquel serait voué le peuple kikuyu. Dans la plupart de ces œuvres, l'insuffisance du style n'a d'égale que la maladresse de la technique. Le seul talent prometteur qui soit apparu depuis James Ngugi est celui de Leonard Kibera, dont le premier roman, *Voices in the Dark* (1970), comme la pièce de Ngugi dont il vient d'être question, confirma l'apparition en Afrique orientale d'une tendance qui existe au Nigeria depuis longtemps : le besoin d'utiliser les ressources du roman pour donner une peinture réaliste, et généralement impitoyablement sarcastique de la nouvelle société africaine où, la domination coloniale étant abolie, « la populace a le privilège de se faire matraquer par son propre gouvernement pour changer »! Le roman de Kibera est une œuvre plus lyrique que narrative, avec une intrigue dérisoire, mais une structure d'ensemble fondée sur le contraste entre la masse réduite à la mendicité et au crime, et la nouvelle classe privilégiée : les capitalistes noirs qui se prélassent dans leurs grosses Mercédès, les politiciens qui agitent fièrement leur chasse-mouche, emblème risible de leur pouvoir, et les soi-disant experts blancs, cyniques et inefficaces, et préoccupés seulement de s'enrichir rapidement.

A côté de cette littérature kikuyu, EAPH a aussi publié quelques œuvres d'auteurs Luos du Kenya comme Grace Ogot, la première romancière d'Afrique orientale. Mais il s'agit surtout de romans ethnographiques rapportant les événements du passé précolonial et décrivant les coutumes traditionnelles.

Chose curieuse, c'est en Ouganda que la littérature Luo d'expression anglaise a produit ses auteurs les plus originaux. En 1966 paraissait *Song of Lawino : A Lament,* version anglaise donnée par Okot p'Bitek d'une œuvre préalablement composée dans le dialecte Acoli du Luo. Ce chant est un long poème en vers libres placé dans la bouche d'une femme qui déplore, mais sur un mode qui est souvent d'une causticité efficacement sarcastique, le mépris de son mari pour les mœurs traditionelles et son admiration éperdue pour la civilisation occidentale, ses gadgets et bidules divers, et l'agréable dérèglement des mœurs qui règne dans les villes. Bientôt d'autres auteurs ougandais, de moindre talent et dont l'origine ethnique ne m'est pas connue, imitèrent la manière dont Okot avait su adapter à la langue occidentale un genre poétique typiquement africain. Tels sont Okullo Oculi dans *Orphan* (1968) et Joseph Buruga dans *The Abandoned Hut.* En 1970, Okot p'Bitek donnait *Song of Ocol,* deuxième panneau de ce qui devenait maintenant un diptyque, puisque c'était le chant du mari de Lawino. Ici la satire prend la forme d'une ironie swiftienne, puisque le héros célèbre l'Afrique moderne en des termes si hyperboliques et malavisés qu'il en paraît parfaitement ridicule.

Toutes ces œuvres ougandaises utilisent le vers blanc et l'élégie orale traditionnelle pour exprimer, avec esprit et humour chez Okot, avec un pathos assez gauche chez les autres, une nostalgie certaine à l'égard d'un monde en voie de disparition et des doutes sérieux sur la qualité intrinsèque d'une nouvelle culture en voie de développement.

Mais dès 1968, Okello Oculi avàit introduit dans la littérature ougandaise le roman à l'occidentale avec *Prostitute,* qui est toutefois entrelardé de passages en vers libres. Du reste, la technique en est essentiellement lyrique, puisqu'il s'agit d'un long monologue intérieur. Ici encore, la modernisation de l'Afrique est présentée sous un jour peu enthousiaste, mais, comme dans les romans kikuyus de la fin des années 1960, la critique s'en prend d'une manière plus directe et plus concrète aux nouvelles classes privilégiées qui se sont constituées après l'indépendance. L'exemple d'Oculi, comme celui de Kibera au Kenya, montre que cette période est celle où les intellectuels d'Afrique orientale prennent ouvertement conscience du fait que si les Noirs ne sont pas des bêtes, ils ne sont pas davantage des anges. Enfin libres de disposer d'eux-mêmes, ils se rendent compte clairement des problèmes existentiels avec lesquels ils sont confrontés, et qui sont très différents de ceux de l'ère coloniale. Ceci se marque encore mieux dans deux romans ultérieurs qui sont aussi les premiers en Ouganda à utiliser les techniques habituelles du roman occidental : *Return to the Shadows* (1969) de Robert Serumaga et *The Experience* (1970) d'Eneriko Seruma. Le premier se situe dans un pays imaginaire à l'époque d'un coup d'état militaire ; Serumaga s'est sans doute inspiré des expériences tumultueuses vécues dans d'autres pays africains, mais il annonce aussi les troubles qui devaient mener, en 1971, à l'éviction du premier ministre Milton Obote. Quant au roman de Seruma, il reprend le thème familier de l'intellectuel idéaliste éduqué en Occident et qui, malgré sa bonne volonté, se trouve aliéné vis-à-vis de son propre peuple ; la fin, symbolique, suggère l'aveuglement de la vieille Afrique, qui détruit ceux qui seraient capables de l'aider à mener à bien son intégration nécessaire au monde moderne.

Cependant, la personnalité la plus remarquable qui soit apparue récemment en Ouganda est celle de Taban lo Liyong (né en 1939), Luo lui aussi, comme p'Bitek, pour la personnalité et l'œuvre de qui il semble nourrir une sérieuse hostilité. Formé aux Etats-Unis, dans le fameux Writers' Workshop de l'Université de l'Iowa, Taban est un écrivain très divers, auteur de nouvelles, adaptateur de récits traditionnels, mais surtout essayiste polémique et critique littéraire. Sa pensée n'est pêut-être pas toujours cohérente : on peut trouver une certaine contradiction entre le mépris qu'il affecte pour la négritude et le conseil qu'il donne aux auteurs africains de s'inspirer de la tradition orale. Il n'en reste pas moins que sa maîtrise de l'anglais est aussi grande que celle de Ngugi ou d'Achebe, et que son style est presque aussi alerte et original que celui de Soyinka. Né en 1939, Taban est sans aucun doute un des grands espoirs de la littérature ougandaise et plus généralement de la littérature est-africaine de langue anglaise.

Si donc l'Ouganda et le Kenya ont d'ores et déjà apporté une contribution significative, tant sur le plan de la qualité que sur celui de la quantité, à la littérature anglophone, il n'en va pas de même au Tanganyika, qui n'a encore donné que deux romans anglais, assez médiocres d'ailleurs : *Dying in the Sun* (1968) de Peter Palangyo et *Village in Uhuru* (1969) de Gabriel Ruhumbika. Une des causes de ce retard est sans aucun doute le nationalisme qui régit la politique culturelle de la Tanzanie et qui se manifeste notamment dans le statut officiel accordé au Swahili et dans les encouragements prodigués à la littérature écrite dans cette langue. Il faut donc s'attendre à ce que le Swahili, et non l'anglais, devienne le medium littéraire propre de la Tanzanie. On sait que le président Julius Nyerere a traduit le *Jules César* de Shakespeare, et j'ai déjà mentionné le nom de Robert Shaaban, qui doit être considéré comme le fondateur de la littérature swahilie moderne. Le successeur le plus important de Shaaban fut Mathias Mnyampala (1919—1969) ; il vaut la peine de signaler que Mnyampala était originaire de l'intérieur et n'avait donc vraisemblablement pas le Swahili comme langue maternelle ; en outre, il était chrétien et est le prémier auteur swahili à avoir utulisé le style et la technique narrative de l'*utendi* pour adapter les récits de l'Evangile. Quant aux œuvres de type moderne, romans et même pièces de théâtre, elles sont relativement nombreuses mais, au contraire de la littérature classique, elles ne sont guère plus étudiées que les œuvres vernaculaires écrites de l'Ouganda. Il serait pourtant bien intéressant de pouvoir se faire une idée de leur valeur esthétique, de leurs dominantes thématiques, et des grandes tendances que peut-être elles illustrent.

Au terme de cet exposé, forcément schématique, de l'histoire littéraire de l'Afrique orientale, on ne peut que se limiter, en guise de conclusion, à quelques constatations et à quelques vœux.

En premier lieu, on rappellera que l'activité littéraire écrite existe depuis plusieurs siècles, du moins dans la région relativement restreinte qui constitue l'aire de culture swahilie. De nombreux textes sont déjà accessibles. D'autres, sans aucun doute, restent à découvrir. Jusqu'à présent, cette littérature n'a été analysée que sous deux angles principaux : celui du message, qui est essentiellement dévotionnel et édifiant ; et celui de la versification. Le moment semble venu de procéder à une étude historique détaillée et à appliquer aux œuvres des critères d'évaluation autres que la simple habilité à manier certaines règles de prosodie.

En second lieu, la colonisation a amené au niveau de l'écrit plusieurs sociétés de l'hinterland. Ainsi ont surgi des littératures « modernes » dans diverses langues. Bien qu'elles n'en soient qu'à leurs premiers débuts — ou plutôt, pour cette raison même — il est urgent de recueillir et de préserver les données documentaires qui sont susceptibles d'éclairer leur genèse et d'expliquer leurs orientations.

En troisième lieu, au cours des années 1960, c'est-à-dire depuis l'indépendance, l'Afrique orientale a commencé à fournir un apport qui n'est nullement négligeable au vaste corpus des littératures de langue anglaise, suivant ainsi, avec deux ou trois décennies de retard, l'exemple donné par l'Afrique australe et l'Afrique occidentale. C'est évidemment celle-là qui intéresse au premier chef les anglicistes que nous sommes. Bien qu'elle n'existe que depuis une douzanie d'années, elle a déjà produit quelques œuvres d'une réele qualité, qui ont fait l'objet d'articles critiques dans les revues spécialisées. Néanmoins, elle suscite nombre de problèmes dignes de retenir notre attention.

J'ai essayé de montrer que la littérature anglophone de ces territoires étendus est loin d'être aussi homogène qu'on ne se l'imagine sans doute généralement. Il conviendrait d'étudier de plus près comment un même idiome, et par surcroît étranger, permet l'expression d'identités collectives distinctes, et cela à deux niveaux : au niveau des entités purement politiques que sont les états, et au niveau des entités ethniques, bien plus organiques, qu'on appelle « tribus ». Il conviendrait d'analyser plus profondément la diversité et la succession des tendances qui parcourent cette littérature en pleine croissance, et de mettre le résultat de cette enquête en corrélation d'une part avec l'évolution historique de la région, et d'autre part avec le substrat autochtone, qu'il s'agisse des cultures variées auxquelles les écrivains anglophones appartiennent, ou, plus particulièrement, de l'influence de la littérature vernaculaire orale sur la littérature écrite en anglais. Enfin, il est indispensable de suivre avec attention l'évolution future de cette littérature engagée dans un processus de croissance rapide. Certes, cela implique la nécessité de lire et d'analyser nombre d'œuvres dont la valeur intrinsèque est pour le moins douteuse. C'est toujours par là que les littératures africaines rédigées en langues européennes ont commencé : dans la maladresse et la gaucherie qu'entraîne inévitablement le recours à une langue étrangère et à des techniques inconnues des littératures orales. Mais, comme le dit un des membres les plus éminents de la nouvelle intelligentsia est-africaine, Ali Mazrui, « All national literatures have grown up within a vigorous relationship of co-existence between the bad and the good. Indeed, that is how aesthetic discrimination becomes meaningful and standards of selectivity in taste attain sophistication ».

The Changing Image of the African
in Portuguese-African Writing

Gerald M. Moser

1. Introduction

a) Premises

One may assume that Portuguese-African writing reflects the conditions under which Europeans and Africans have related to one another. When portraying Africans, it expresses opinions or feelings possible under those conditions. It follows that in the course of over five hundred years, which is the span of history covered by the direct contacts between the Portuguese and the Africans, the image of the latter must have changed with changing conditions. At first glance, this may seem incredible to some, who imagine Portuguese life to be so conservative that attitudes have remained the same even, since the inhabitants of a small fief to the north of the river Douro expanded their kingdom, founded in the XIIth century, farther and farther south, eventually fastening a lengthening chain of trading posts, plantations, ranches, ports, missions, fortresses and naval stations upon the coasts of Africa, beginning in the middle of the XVth century.

This paper attempts to demonstrate, however, that the image of the African has changed—and still is changing—even within Portuguese writing. For the purpose, *Portuguese-African writing* is defined as writing inspired by Africa and composed in the Portuguese language or one of its dialects. It thus falls into both of the categories of literature written in European languages for which Janheinz Jahn used the term "colonialist literature", if written by Europeans from a preponderantly European viewpoint, or "neo-African literature" if written by Africans from a more or less African viewpoint, consciously or unconsciously incorporating African traditions.

"Neo-African literature" will have to include, necessarily in the Portuguese case, a majority of works by authors of racially mixed origins, as well as a very small but significant number of writers of purely European origins who successfully absorbed African elements. All of the "neo-African" writings in Portuguese still belong to what Jahn has aptly named "apprentice literature"; for nowhere in the formerly Portuguese territories has any original writing as yet been attempted in the African languages. The apparent exceptions belong into the realm of Christian mission literature and its derivatives.

By *African* is meant exclusively what belongs to part of the continent lying south and southeast of the Sahara. Another, largely historical study could be made, to be sure, of the image of the North African in Portuguese writing, which would take us back several centuries further, to the early contacts between the Moorish "colonialists" and the Christian Portuguese "resistance fighters" of the Middle Ages.

Image refers to the literary portrayal of the exterior features, but more especially the behavior, feelings and thoughts of Africans, necessarily presented not for their own sake but always brought into a European perspective, if only through the use of a European language.

The procedure that has been followed has been to look at samples of the written evidence. The first work to be chosen is a very recent one written on an Angolan theme by a man of European background who grew up in Angola. The examples it furnishes will then be contrasted with some of the very earliest testimonies dating from the fifteenth century, followed by samples of what can be found in successive periods until we again arrive at our own time. In this way, it should become quite clear what changes have occurred.

There are a few peculiar traits that seem to have characterized the Portuguese in the past, as they traveled, traded, mingled or settled in Africa. Like premises, they should be kept in mind, so as to correct prejudices of long standing that obfuscate to this day the notions most people have about the Portuguese.

The first premise is important for understanding anything relating to Portuguese colonisation and its effects. It is the conviction they held of having a religious mission to help bring about the conversion of the entire world to Christianity. It dates from the very creation of a Portuguese state during the era of Reconquest from Islam. It has survived into this century, in the guise of a civilizing mission with continuing religious undertones. This sense of mission, fostered by the religious orders of the Catholic Church to begin with, led to a constant, though not always consciously experienced conflict with practice, in such old insitutionalized forms of coercion as slavery, piracy, and exploitation of labor.

The second premise is related to the first. The Portuguese remained open-minded, one might even say ingenuous, in their everyday dealings with other peoples, such as the darker Africans and Asians. In this they were not unique, since they merely continued the attitudes of classic Egyptian, Greek and Roman antiquity that did not know race prejudice.[1] However, color blindness ended where clannishness began, especially among the nobility or all those who looked upon themselves as an elite among the Portuguese. Ancestry was important. "Purity of blood" used to be highly valued in the times of the Inquisition, meaning that at least in theory any admixture of Jews, Moors or Blacks excluded a person from many offices. As a result, legally recognized alliances with African women were rare until at least the beginning of this century while concubinage was accepted without leading to inclusion into the family.[2]

On the other hand, anyone who has lived among Portuguese people knows their warmly possessive feelings towards those they consider friends. This, I believe, has led them in their colonial past not merely to gregariousness but to assume that those who consort with them will gladly assimilate Portuguese ways, so as to become *civilisados* and abandon the barbarous customs of the wretched *gentio*. And the truth is that they often succeeded in their endeavor. But N. Sithole, the black nationalist leader in Rhodesia, painted out their cultural one-way street mentality many years ago when he wrote that "the Portuguese are making it appear as though they are accepting the African, when all along they are staunchly refusing to accept the African. (. . .) In accepting the assimilated African, the Portuguese are merely receiving back their own Portuguese they pumped into him. In other words, they are really accepting themselves and not the African."[3]

Still another persistent trait has been observed, for example by the Brazilian social historian Ségio Buarque de Holanda. He was struck by the fact that in the Americas, the early Portuguese were rarely prone to accept fantastic visions of fabulous human or animal monstrosities or boundless riches, while the Spaniards were looking for them everywhere. Something of the sort can be said of the early Portuguese arrivals in Africa. Perhaps the scant credence given to reports of rich silver deposits in central Angola or to the gold of Ophir that was said to exist in central Mozambique are examples of a practical mind concentrating on immediate goals. A further example is the lack of idealization of the African as an unspoilt "child of nature" before the XXth century, whereas the American Indian was idealized as soon as Brazil had become independent. Perhaps the Portuguese in Africa were too close to the realities, especially of the slave trade, to let themselves be persuaded by romantic writers who raved about noble savages.

This does not mean that they lacked sentimentality. But they did not seem to wax sentimental over the alien, the exotic or the faraway. They reserved their sentimental effusions for nostalgia about their home. For a long time one socially useful kind of punishment for criminals was to be cast off—*lançado*—on an African coast in the XVth or XVIth century, and later on, to be transported to such unhealthy places as Luanda, Benguela or the Island of Mozambique, as were the first permanent Portuguese settlers in Angola and Mozambique. Military conquest and penetration of the interior did not form part of traditional Portuguese policy in Africa.

To recapitulate: when looking at the ideas held by Portugues writers in regard to the African, one must not lose sight of old notions, such as a sense of mission, often entering into conflict with brutal practice, an easygoing color blindness, up to a degree, clannishness, and a practical spirit allied to a lack of disinterested scientific curiosity.

b) The Image of the African in a Recent Work of Fiction

At the very end of last year—1974—a remarkable book was published by an Angolan author. It throws such a penetrating light on relations between

Africans and Europeans in the 1950s and 60s. The work in question bears the title *Nós, os do Makulusu,* which might be translated freely as "We, the Gang from the Makulusu", Makulusu being the name of one of the many shanty-town districts surrounding the European core of Luanda, the capital city and principal port of Angola. This particular district no longer exists, having been swallowed up by the *bairros,* or residential European quarters. Its evocation has a nostalgic flavor, as has that of the gang of four boys, one of whom is the now grown-up man, sharing some traits and experiences with the author himself, who reminisces while living through a particular day in his life, the day of his younger brother's funeral.[4]

The author, José Luandino Vieira, enjoys a deserved reputation as an original teller of realistic Angolan stories. He has been experimenting with new styles in Portuguese prose, by africanizing it through the introduction of Angolan speech patterns and a number of Kimbundisms, words and expressions adapted to Portuguese from Kimbundu, the Bantu language spoken in the region of Luanda. Like the unnamed speaker in *Nós, os do Makulusu,* his latest narrative, he was a small boy when his family of Portuguese country folk came to live in one of Luanda's shantytowns, where he grew up among black and mulatto neighbors. Their situation was by no means unique among the poor Europeans or Cape Verdeans. It was remarkable that the young man should have received a good schooling in spite of his slum upbringing and that his talent as a writer and draftsman should have been recognized as early as 1960 at the age of twenty-five, when his first book, *A cidade e a infância* (City and Childhood) was published in Lisbon.[5] His technique in *Nós, os do Makulusu* combines the continuous flow of thought associations in the "stream of consciousness" with narration from a single, autobiographical point of view. It requires alert readers to sense the un-announced shifts in time and to distinguish between the different persons being evoked. As a result, the author creates a dense network of people and events which leave the outsider, that is to say the reader, with the sensation of entering a bewildering, crowded maze, such as a slum would present to him.

The action plunges into the heart of the matter, the future of an Angola of many and discordant populations. It is limited to the day when one young soldier, killed in an ambush while serving in the North of the country, is to be buried in Luanda with military honors. The narrative begins and basically remains a lament for the dead youth, repeatedly referred to as "the best of us all." Towards the end, we become aware of two possible coincidences which would make of the narrator a lone survivor. The first is that the guerilla who shot his brother, and was gunned down in turn, could well have been their childhood buddy. The second is that another young man, who had been arrested and beaten up must have died in jail on the very day of the funeral. These are the four who in their boyhood had formed the Makulusu gang. Their close relationship contains a lesson.

Early in the story, we learn that the narrator's father, Senhor Paulo, the Portuguese immigrant, despises the blacks among whom he has to live because of his poverty. His insults, such as calling his neighbors "mangy dogs" *(cães sarnentos),* are considered commonplace. The daughter, Zabel, whom the older brother teases by calling her with a Kimbundu nickname, takes after her father by looking down on the blacks as "tailless monkeys" *(macacos sem rabo),* and she is even ashamed of telling people that she comes from Luanda, while her brother finds it hard to shed such unconsciously learned prejudices, which "stick to the withe skin from within." (p. 90) The son remembers Senhor Paulo berating the black washerwoman who had at one time accepted him as a lover and belittling the black schoolmaster of his children although he does mind inviting him to a meal. Significantly Senhor Paulo also lards his Portuguese with Kimbundu expressions: his prejudice is inconsistent and incomplete. At least among the poor such as he, prejudice seems bound up with the ideas of an older generation. A shockingly violent instance of it is recalled with shame, of a howling mob, hysteric with fear and hate, giving chase in the city streets to a peaceful black citizen on his way home and lynching him with cries of *Mata o negro* ("Kill the nigger"), in spite of his protestations of innocence. What upset Senhor Paulo's son especially was the fact that the black man was killed by no other than a locksmith who once upon a time had talked to him of class consciousness and of race prejudice being due to nothing but economic inequality. (pp. 55—58)

The narrator's own sense of solitarity with Angolans of all races stemmed from his childhood when he had been one of the four members of the gang: they had called him simply "the Elder" *(o Mais-Velho);* his brother was known as "the Younger" *(o Mais-Novo)* or as "the Kid Brother" *(o Maninho);* the third, the washerwoman's son, who was their blue-eyed half-brother, was called "Daddy" *(Paizinho);* and finally there was a black youngster, proud and hardworking, Kibiaka, the only one to be known to them and to us, the readers, by a personal name, which was an African name as well. The anonymity of three of them could mean that they should be considered as typical of their generation. Being children, their essential quality was their color-blind friendship for one another, which included standing together when there was a fight with another neighborhood gang. Such fights were not too serious; they would symbolically come to an end when all the children would be magnetically attracted by "His Honor Mister Sambo" (Sô Muadiaquimi Sambo) and his marching band. (p. 87) Their feeling of brotherhood developed later on into proletarian class consciousness and this in turn became militancy in an unnamed political organization, where Paizinho, the Mulatto, displayed the same intelligence, bravery, and reliability that already had made him the leader in their childish games. Mais-Velho, the elder of the two brothers, followed Paizinho's lead, whereas Maninho challenged their ideas, seeing no other way than to kill or to be killed in a war that all of them wanted to end speedily. Maninho and Kibiaka, ending up on opposite sides in the war, shared the same idea of masculine dignity: one had to fight back. And yet both were affectionate by nature, the author is at pains to tell us through his narrator. However, none of the other three achieves as great a sense of dignity as Kibiaka, the one who is most vulnerable because he is the poorest of them and has a sister who has fallen prey to prostitution. Kibiaka, fond of birds and children, will not be able to forgive any slight. We see him strangle his white employer who has made an indecent proposition and go off the bush to join the guerrillas with the pistol that is Mais-Velho's farewell gift to him. "He is dignity personified," Mais-Velho says of him with admiration (p. 87), as he says in praise of Paizinho that he will never turn traitor. (p. 138 et al.) Nevertheless, and despite their disagreements, MaisVelho remebers his brother Maninho most fondly of all; the lament that pervades the narrative from beginning to end is therefore mainly reserved for this younger brother who died a heroic but useless death. Why was it that Mais-Velho considered him the "best of us all"? The reason given is remarkable: Maninho was the best and most generous lover. He did not limit himself to one race like Mais-Velho, who never touched mulatto girls out of what in Maninho's opinion was a false respect or reverse prejudice. Maninho maintained that love was "the only way in which one can communicate, find out, learn what it is to be human." (p. 19) He acted on this conviction; he made Rute (Ruth), a perfect mulatto girl, his fiancée, who was to mourn him more than even his own mother and would remain faithful to his memory even though it drove her mad. Mais-Velho, the narrator, puts into Maninho's mouth a tirade in praise of mulatto girls, such as no Brazilian author could improve upon: "You see her firm, scented body and you don't know how soft her skin is with its shades and perfumes, its shiny gloss that surfaces under the perspiration of her love. I'm telling you, they are better women, far more feminine, than those washed-out, so-called intellectual girls of yours. When women are truly in love they are the purest, most revolutionary bcings, Mais-Velho!" (pp. 21—22)

Rute, the mulatto girl, is given the part of the greatest lover among the women, as Maninho is given the same part among the male characters of the narrative. At the earliest moment that is told of her life she is shown practicing the beautiful gesture of ransoming and releasing the caged birds that black Kibiaka used to sell for a living—a gentle gesture that causes both Kibiaka and Maninho to fall head over heel in love with her.

Another great woman, greater in the eyes of the narrator than his own patient mother, is the black washerwoman, who serves Senhor Paulo and his family submissively, without bitterness nor complaint (p. 120), whose eyes are serene (p. 122) and whose voice remains calm, Paizinho's mother, a pillar of strength and goodness, unrecognized by her master. We are not told her given name. Instead, Mais-Velho calls her by the most honored generic name, "Black Mammy" or "Black Mother", *Mãe-Negra*.

The portrayal of these Africans, who are individuals and representative types at one and the same time, would have been incomplete, if the author had not added the inner tension that was caused by what seemed to be irreconcilable attitudes. On one hand, the past is perceived as heroic in the Portuguese tradition, Maninho being identified by Mais-Velho, half in joke, with the tough captains-general of the earliest period, about whom they have read in Cadornega's history of the Angolan wars. Their virility is contrasted with the puny monuments erected in their memory, as if later generations had been ashamed of what once had been the vigorous manhood of the conquest. (p. 46)

On the other hand, the past also appears in its hideous aspects of slavery and exploitation. Mais-Velho romantically associates his own childhood and the «good old days» with the few remaining old streets in the center of the city, "our old Luanda", as he strolls through them, or when he dreams himself back into the miserable shantytown where he and his friends had grown up. Maninho's attitude was different. He wanted to see all those dead vestiges of suffering and poverty razed to the ground so that everything could be made new, *tudo de novo* (pp. 18, 27)

Another contradiction appears in the immediate present. Mais-Velho fondly evokes the brotherly bonds of childhood, symbolized in the unselfconscious manner in which they mixed Portuguese and Kimbundu in their talk. "All of us were practically bilingual." (p. 38) The author raised their talk to a literary level by writing the entire narrative in a language that suggests the same mixture. He gave it a motto in unadulterated Kimbundu, whose meaning is only revealed in a statement on the book's cover, which could easily be overlooked. It reads in translation: "Because nothing can be seen any longer of the place whence we came we are looking for the place toward which we are headed."

But brotherly feeling clashed with distrust: Mais-Velho had been hurt when he had been ignored by the crowd of blacks that had just witnessed with him the arrest of his friend Paizinho, the Mulatto. Instead of sensing his solidarity, they showed him neither "friendship nor hate, neither sadness nor joy." (p. 134) Even worse, all brotherly feeling seemed to vanish in the colonial war, a war of vengeance. (p. 113) Mais-Velho is incapable of overcoming a helpless feeling of catastrophe and in his own mind, of vacillation, *incerteza*, faced with the passions that have been unleashed. Proceeding dialectically, he nevertheless tries to reconcile the logic (*razão*) of Maninho's participation in the war with Paizinho's logic of changing everyone's mentality. His brother's death teaches him that the "old roads" lead nowhere. (p. 15) He can only think of a return to true humanity: "to being just human beings, neither cowards nor heroes." (p. 131)

2. A Glance at the Beginnings: The Earliest Image of the African in Portuguese Writings

"'Here is Africa,' the siren sang—, 'grasping after the good things of this world, uncivilized, full of savagery ... Look out over this whole vast continent, the home of almost countless pagan peoples.'"[6] That was how Camões, the national poet, described the African in his epic of 1572 while glorifying the Portuguese navigators. Was it the image generally shared by the Portuguese, an Africa "full of savagery from end to end", *África inculta, toda cheia de bruteza*? Certain historians have claimed it, among them Randles, and after him the Brazilian Honório Rodrigues.[7] But early accounts dating from the XVth and XVIth centuries tell of a more complex and, on the whole, more sympathetic reaction to reality. Highly educated Europeans, such as the poet Camões or the Christian missionaries, who went from Lisbon and Goa into the recesses of Africa, were fired by an intolerant, crusading spirit, being fully convinced of their religion's superiority. The earlier sailors, explorers, and traders sailed southwards with cooler minds.

In his *History of the Exploits of Guinea (Crónica dos feitos de Guiné)*, composed about 1450, Gomes Eanes de Zurara has preserved for us the reports which the first Portuguese captains gave to Prince Henry the Navigator of their explorations of the African West Coast. Among them are the observations of Álvaro Fernandes, made upon reaching the "Land of the Negroes" *(Terra dos Negros)*—so called to distinguish it from the lands inhabited by the brown Arabs and Berbers. Fernandes met his first Guineans *(guinéus)* in 1445 near Cape Verde at the Senegal River. He described them as "men who came in peace" *(como homens que vinham de paz)*[8], while he and the other early Portuguese raiders had in mind capturing and enslaving these Africans, reserving a few of them for the role of future interpreters. Fernandes' report then characterizes the "Guineans" as brave, strong men *(valentes e fortes,* II, p. 217) who defended themselves in spite of being outnumbered and of having less effective weapons. The Portuguese ought to have been good judges in the matter, filled as they were at that time with notions of chivalric honor, valor, and daring feats.

Zurara notes the intelligence of a black boy who was seized naked in his hut by another commander, Gomes Pires, in 1445, with his little sister, near the Senegal River. Taken to Portugal, he was, the historian says, given a Christian education on Prince Henry's orders, so that "he came to know the precepts of our religion better than many Christians." (II, p. 228) After other such high-handed actions, the same Pires aroused the anger of the blacks, who showed their pride by scorning the three gifts he had left for them on the shore: ". . . and they smashed up the cake and threw it away, and with their darts they shot at the mirror until they had broken it to pieces, and they tore up the piece of paper (on which a cross had been traced), indicating by their actions that they did not care about any of those things." "Since that's the way it is," said Gomes Pires to his crossbowmen, "shoot off your bows at them so that they may at least know us as people who could do them harm if they won't meet us." (II, p. 233) In another report, Captain Álvaro Fernandes told of coming upon a black woman south of the Gambia River in 1446, as she was gathering shellfish in an inlet, having a two-year old boy with her. Of her looks he merely said that they were "reasonable" for a Guinean but what struck him and the historian after him was that having shaken off the Portuguese raiders, she showed a mother's love when she turned back to follow them meekly after they had grabbed her little boy. (II, p. 247) A modern Portuguese historian reproduced the account with indignation: "I confess," he writes, "that I don't understand how some scholars can construe a crusade from feats of that sort." (II, p. 249, n. 6)

Instead of the "brutishness" that the poet stressed, texts about the earliest contacts demonstrate rather a recognition of common human nature, perhaps with some surprise, considering the ancient myths about the monstrous beings inhabiting the equatorial regions which were then current. A rhetorical piece of prose has become a minor classic in Portuguese literature because it presents the same human image. In it Zurara expressed compassion with the Africans of several hues whom he saw being sold off in 1444 in the southern Portuguese harbor of Lagos. (Cf. III, pp. 18—23) He tells how he was moved to tears by the spectacle, because he could not help thinking that these were human beings, also "descended from Adam." (III, p. 20) However, he consoled himself with the further thought that they were probably better off in the long run, since their conversion to Christianity would make their eternal salvation possible. He also was impressed by their readiness to embrace the true faith, in contrast to the Moors the Portuguese knew so well, and he assures the reader that, although they had lived like animals *(bestas)* before, they adopted civilised ways and became loyal servants of their new masters. As Christians, they were not branded but treated like free laborers; some were freed and intermarried or were adopted. The modern reader must conclude that no racial prejudice existed then and that this particular shipment at least was treated better, or at least no worse, than other slaves already living in Portugal, such as Moroccans or Canary Islanders.

The image is reinforced when reading the account of the Venetian merchant Alvise de Cadamosto, who accompanied the Portuguese in 1455 to the Senegal coast. He, and no doubt his Portuguese shipmates, were impressed by the frank sensuality of the Africans, but also by their jealousy (III, p. 148) Moreover, he assures us that the girl he received as a gift from a chief was "very beautiful because she was black." (III, p. 145) Although their religion was already then Islam, the Senegalese did not seem to be fanatic; Cadamosto reports a conversation about religion with the same chief, whom he calls Budumel, which was his title ("Chief of Dumel"). After listening to the Venetian's arguments to prove the superiority and truth of Christianity, Budumel gave him an answer full of humor and cleverness: if God has given you Christians all the good things on earth it goes to show that He who is just will give us Heaven. Then, why should we become Christians?[9] The anecdote was to be the first in a series told through the ages which reflected the European's surprise of seeing their assumptions challenged from a different viewpoint as well as of finding that the so-called savage was also an intelligent human being.

From his encounter with the chief and his subjects, Cadamosto drew the conclusion that Africans were as clever as any of us—*são expertos como qualquer de nós* (III, p. 142) although they might appear backward, for example when, never having beheld sails, they took the Portuguese ships to be big birds with white wings, manned by messengers from the spirit world. Concerning the chiefs, he like later visitors to other parts of Black Africa, was struck by the absolute submission and awe which chiefs, even elected ones, could command. "Even God himself, if he came down to earth, could not be honored and revered more," he remarked. (III, p. 149—150) Clearly, he could distinguish facts from preconceived ideas; for while he noted the African's savagery, nudity, exceeding poverty and unhygienic way of eating, compared to European standards (III, pp. 138, 140, 142), he also appreciated their sense of beauty manifested in the hair styles of the women, their bodily cleanliness, their love of talk, and their great hospitality. (III, pp. 141—142)

Only for special reasons would he say of the tribesmen living near Cape Verde that "they must be very cruel" (III, p. 168), or of others in Gambia that they were "stubborn and obstinate." (III, p. 174) He called them first cruel because the ones killed a black convert whom the Portuguese sent among them shortly after the same coast had been raided by them. The others he called stubborn when they refused to engage in trade with people who reportedly were cannibals!

It is likely that other early visitors brought similar reports back from West Africa. The known ones add up to an image which is a far cry from Camões' "brute Africa." But we shall see that even he, the author of the *Lusiads,* did not always generalize.

The verification that human nature was the same in Africa as in Europe could be expected from people living in the age of humanism, since they prided themselves on relying more on their own eyes than on what the authorities said in their books. The sense of a common human nature, first expressed by Zurara, underlies the comparison of a bushman with a Portuguese in the diary of Vasco da Gama's pilot. The bushman had been caught on Thursday, November 9, 1497, when the pilot jotted down that "he was small of body and looked like Sancho Mexia."[10] Duarte Lopes provided perhaps the best illustration. He was a Portuguese who had lived in Angola at the court of the Christian King of the Congo in the second half of the XVIth century. In Rome he afterwards dictated an account of the Kingdom of the Congo to a priest, Filippo Pigafetta, in whose Italian version it was published.[11] Concerning the physical features of the people inhabiting what is now northern Angola, Lopes had this to say: "The men are black and so are the women, and the color of some even tends more towards olive, and they have curly black hair, and there are also some who have red hair; the men are of medium height, and *except for their black color, they resemble us Portuguese* (italics added): the pupils of their eyes are of various shades of black and of the color of the sea, and their lips are not thick like those of the Nubians and other Blacks, and their features likewise are of various kinds, coarse and fine, as in our countries, and not as among the Blacks of Nubia and Guinea, which are misshapen." (Book I, chapter 2, pp. 6—7)

Turning to works of a more literary nature, we find the black Africans pictured very humanly in the comedies of the Portuguese playwright Gil Vicente, written and staged about 1525. In one of them, the "Ship of Love" *(Nau de*

Amores), he jokes about a black man who has fallen as madly in love as all the other characters. In another, "The Forge of Love" *(Frágua de Amor),* the courtiers are invited to embark for Guinea and trade there to obtain the favors that love can give. This may be the earliest allusion in a Portuguese text to the image of the lovable black woman. A more direct example appeared half a century later when the author of the *Lusiads* addressed a poem to a dark beauty—who could have been African or East Indian *(Pretidão de amor).* Still another fifty years later, numerous verses in praise of mulatto girls were to be written by a Brazilian, Gregório de Matos, who had spent half of his life in Portugal and was exiled to Angola for two years.

In his "Forge of Love", Vicente had perhaps been the first also to create the image of a black man in Europe (in Castile, to be exact), who makes a fool of himself by trying too strenuously to be like a white. He implores Mercury, the God of Trade, guardian of the Forge, to give him a white skin, a thin nose, and thin lips. His wishes are granted, but even the god cannot change one thing, his Guinean way of treating the Portuguese language. Unhappier than before, because everyone pokes fun at him, he asks to be returned to his original state.[12]

The Portuguese tended to divide Africans according to whether they could trade with them or not. Thus we find from the outset some populations being labeled friendly and others hostile or downright barbarian. The sharp distinction between the two opposites was made by Vasco da Gama's pilot in his diary, from where it eventually reached the poet Camões. In his *Lusiads,* Camões differentiated between the hostile bushmen hunters and the friendly Zulu herdsmen (of whom he paints a charming, bucolic picture), or between the treacherous townspeople of Mozambique and Mombasa on one hand and the hospitable citizens of Malindi on the other.

The Portuguese learnt to respect the warlike qualities of many Africans. Already in the middle of the sixteenth century, the most accomplished of the Portuguese historians, João de Barros, who apparently had traveled to West Africa himself, recognized the value that African soldiers might have in the wars in Africa as well as in Europe: "West Africa," he wrote, "yields a numerous and a good people, faithful Catholics, willing workers, and who help us in our needs. And they are so courageous that with them we have conquered the other regions which we hold and which do not produce the like. If I had been trained in the military art, I would rather go to West Africa and enlist soldiers than to the land of the Swiss."[13] Not long thereafter, another classic historian, the humanist Damião de Góis, related how King Manuel of Portugal, hoping to use the forces of the recently converted Afonso, King of the Congo, made him his ally and bestowed on him the Portuguese coat of arms in 1512, an honor never before offered to anyone else.

The bellicose behavior of some peoples quickly became a trait entering the image conceived by the Portuguese. It reminds one of similarly stark impressions left on the white man's imagination in the XIXth century by the ferocious armies of Dahomey with their women's bataillons or by Chaka and other ruthless Zulu conquerors. Thus Diogo Lopes mentioned already the mysterious armed bands marching from the north or center of the continent to devastate southern Africa in his time, the XVIth century, as he also mentioned the legendary women warriors whom the Emperor of Monomotapa employed in the gold-bearing region bordering on what is now the South African Union. The first whom he called *Jacas* (adding that they called themselves *Agagi)* he characterized as "roving nomads, a cruel and murderous people of tall stature and horrible appearance, living on human flesh, ferocious in combat, brave of spirit, (. . .) going naked, and savage in their habits and daily living." *(Relatione . . .,* Book II, chap. 5, p. 59) The Dominican missionary João dos Santos, who knew Mozambique well at firsthand, dismissed Lopes' tale of African Amazons but described the cannibalistic Zimbas about the year 1600 in much the same terms as those used by Lopes to tell about the Jacas. These Jacas were to reappear in every history of Angola, beginning with the earliest, from the pen of the colorful veteran Oliveira de Cardonega, who lived out his life in Luanda during the latter half of the seventeenth century. He told of the *Jagas* (as he spelled their name) with a purpose: to show how their ferocity and efficient organization for warfare made one African ruler redoubtable enough to resist the Portuguese successfully for some thirty years. This ruler was the most remarkable ever encountered by Europeans. To top it off, she was a woman, in whom we behold the combined image of the fear-inspiring, absolute ruler, of the ferocious warrior, of the clever intelligence that matched the European's, and of the perilously attractive black woman. Her personal African name seems not to have come down to us; instead, she is still remembered by her royal title, Nzinga-Mbandi-Ngola, or Queen Ginga, as pronounced by the Portuguese, who also bestowed on her the noble name of Dona Ana de Sousa. Her conversion in 1622 and, following a relapse, her edifying Christian death explain in part why modern Portuguese and Brazilian authors continue to pay their respects to her.[15]

Cadornega, her contemporary, who had taken part in a campaign against her, called her "that Queen Ginga who was as shrewd as she was brave"[16] or "that brave Amazon" (I, p. 150) in his admiring moods, or "that poisonous vermint" *(aquela bicha peçonhenta,* I, p. 402) when he was angry with her for inflicting losses on the Portuguese troops. Ending the account of her death with a eulogy, he concluded: "And what makes her even more outstanding is that she was from this western part of Africa and that her color was black." *(e o que a realça mais é o ser desta Ethyopia occidental e de côr preta."* II, p. 221)

Cadornega provides many insights in the thought of the leading Portuguese residents of seventeenth century Angola. For example, he readily conceded that African girls could be beautiful (e. g. I, p. 409), that the Bantus showed wit in the nicknames they gave to Portuguese officers as well as to their own chiefs (II, pp. 368—369), or that the black auxiliaries, the *guerra negra,* were fine soldiers (I, p. 179 ff.), especially the mixed-breeds.[16]

A very ancient trait in the composite image has barely been mentioned yet, the African as a devout believer in supernatural powers. The early visitors to West Africa had already noticed the hold that snake magic had over the blacks there. Cadornega, like Camões and others before him, had found such faith distasteful from an orthodox Christian standpoint. But on the whole, the Portuguese soldiers and traders seem to have been less upset by magical practices than the fathers belonging to the various missionary orders. In despair over ever achieving conversions peacefully, many a missionary had advocated baptism by force in barbarous Africa, as others had recommended the sword and the iron rod for the Brazilian Indians.[17]

In another part of Africa, Abyssinia, some of the Portuguese missionaries could not help admire the piety of the dark Christians, although at the same time trying so hard to stamp out what they deemed heresy that their intolerance led to the expulsion of all Europeans from the country of the Negus.[18] Their admiration confirms the belief of the ancients that the gods of Olympus loved to visit the Africans and partake of their offerings because they were the most pious of men.[19] A Portuguese layman, the historian Góis, made himself very suspect in the eyes of the Inquisitors by printing his opinion that the Abyssinians' Christian beliefs and practices, while differing from the Roman Catholic variety, were in fact purer.[20]

After a long interval spanning the last part of the XVIIth, all of the XVIIIth, and the first half of the XIXth century, the image of the African reappears only from about 1850 on. The prolonged silence must have been due to the abnormal surge of the tropical plantation economy and the slave trade, leading to merciless competition and a constant state of war inside Africa. Under these circumstances the Muses fell silent. Culture, and literature with it, could not flourish. Neither could human interest in the enslaved races. One has to turn to Brazil to find at least some Portuguese writings mentioning the black people that had been carried off from Africa against their will. In a few cases, authors, all of them priests, kept alive the tradition of charity towards their black brethren, those forced converts to Christianity. One or two dared suggest better treatment, but for the rest of the population, the slave seemed to constitute an indispensible part of the economy. The blacks themselves were not heard from. No one cared about their animal fables, in which the weak got the better of the mighty, the ballads about bandits who took revenge against an unjust society, or the stories about *quilombos*, the armed communities of the runaway slaves, until the study of folklore came into its own and such folk literature was collected and printed. That did not happen in the Portuguese-speaking world, including Africa, until after 1870, however.

In short, the image of the African underwent a radical change from the earliest time to the beginning of the XIXth century, becoming more and more complex and negative, until it almost vanished from literature.

3. From Romanticism to Realism

a) The Image of the African in the XIXth century

It took a long time until the African's ways of living in town and country were considered worth writing poems or stories about. Especially was that the case in the small European settlements, including the few remaining Portuguese trading centers. The slow abolition of slavery, the printing of the first journals, the granting of freedom of the press in 1856, the opening of more schools created indispensible conditions for small groups of Europeans and Mulattos to engage in intellectual activities. Such groups made their appearance in Luanda (Angola) and the Island City of Mozambique in particular. But it was a period of apprenticeship, to use Jahn's term once more, merely a beginning, when European Portuguese standards in language, style and themes were so closely adhered to that it is now almost impossible to tell from a piece of writing, such as a poem, whether the author had grown up in Africa. Some Romantics with a social conscience pictured the African as the victim of greed and sadism during the last stage of the struggle for abolition. As late as the mid-1870s, he thus appeared in stories by Camilo Castelo Branco, the most important Portuguese novelist of the Romantic movement. Even Camilo did not focus so much on the black slaves themselves as on their harsh Portuguese owners and in one case at least, on their common offspring, a lovely, hot-blooded and of course very unhappy Mulatta.[21] Other Portuguese Romanticists, who like Camilo hated their own "commercial century", were ardent humanitarians, yet they barely mentioned the Africans in their works, even after spending years among them. Such is the case with Francisco Maria Bordalo (1821—1861), a naval officer, in whose "Scenes of Slavery" *(Escenas da escravatura,* 1854) we encounter only one black, the noble Jaca, a chief's son from Cabinda at the mouth of the Congo, telling how he was lured aboard a slave ship and sold in Brazil, never to return to his homeland. Others combined folklore motifs with sketches of manners, drawing only hazy portraits. Thus, the misfortunes of Kiangi and Ondetó, a pair of true, black lovers, furnished the story "Guinea Ways" *(Costumes da Guiné,* 1855/56) to Sousa Monteiro, an author from the Cape Verdean Islands. Much closer observation of local creole life animates a mildly satirical tale, "Widow Lady" *(Nga Mutúri,* 1882), which the Portuguese lawyer-journalist Alfredo Troni wrote in Luanda about a black woman who had climbed the social ladder from a Portuguese trader's domestic slave to becoming his recognized free companion in the city. She represents the type of strong woman that dominated creole society.[22]

These stories do not amount to a literature, even if one adds the poems that were for the most part destined for ladies' albums or for popular almanacs. Typical of the poets were two natives of Angola belonging to different generations, Maia Ferreira, who in 1850 published the first book of verse known to have appeared in Portuguese Africa, and Cordeiro da Mata, the author of verses published as a book in 1887. Maia Ferreira wrote many poems inspired by the fair sex and love of country, but he found less to say about his Angolan compatriots than about the early Portuguese discoverers and conquerors. He spoke of both in a long, nostalgic poem on Angola, written in distant Brazil for a friend's album. He confessed that he dared not compare Angola with beautiful Portugal, pregnant with history. Angola could offer no more than the palmtrees among which the *soba* (chief) of a savage tribe drowsily yearned for the cool night breeze, mountains where the renowned African warriors hunted panthers, or lovely damsels in the town, with tiny feet, lacking a snow white skin or social refinements, but who knew how to love faithfully, capable of being as gentle as doves and as fierce as lionesses.[23]

The African chieftain, the African warriors and hunters, the beautiful dark girls, and also his soft-spoken, pious, and loving mother—they form the image of African humanity to which Maia Ferreira, himself born in Africa, hoped to return. The evocation, idyllic rather than exotic, foreshadowed future praises of strong men and loving women. In the latter part of the XIXth century, the African woman was to be exalted in particular, but sometimes with apologies for her color, "black as a dreadful, stormy night" (Cordeiro da Mata). A large number of poems inspired by her appeared in the almanacs, coming from blacks, such as the Angolan Cordeiro da Mata or the young student Costa Alegre, of the Island of São Tomé, as well as from Portuguese residents in Angola, for example Eduardo Neves, who felt moved to address her in her own Kimbundu speech.[24]

This stage of the image survived in the poetry of Tomás Vieira da Cruz, a Portuguese settled in Angola. He married a Mulatto girl and, became very popular about 1930, thanks to his sentimental verses about irresistible black beauty. Characteristically, he felt incapable of taking the decisive step beyond the exoticism to which the colonial writers confined themselves, that "vagrant exoticism" *(exotismo vagabundo),* as he called it.[25] Born in Portugal and remaining loyal to his native country, he visualized Africa as a place of exile, "that Empire made of dream and marvel which was the adorable exile of my soul," to quote his flowery expression.[26]

In his images, he rarely went beyond what was most accessible to him, erotically appealing women of various tribes. Only in contact with them did he dimly perceive the shadows of others moving in the background—dancers of *batuques,* slaves among the ancestors, Bailundo laborers on the road, black fishermen in their boats. It is as if family, children, friends or enemies did not enter his poetic world.

When the image of the African reappeared in Portuguese writing it had at first a pathetic character, then a picturesque or erotic one. In rare cases, certain poems by Cordeiro da Mata and Costa Alegre, both of them blacks, the beauty of blackness was apologetically defended.

b) The Image of the African in the XXth Century

The XXth century was the first in which some writers within the Portuguese sphere, in Brazil as well as in Africa, realized the importance of understanding and interpreting the *alma negra*, the "African soul", i. e. the world of feelings and thoughts within the African as something precious. For the first time also, a large number of writers from Africa proper, especially men and women of partly African partly Portuguese ancestry, had received sufficient schooling to participate prominently in the new enterprise. Thus the image of the African was reoriented. It seemed to be difficult for the Portuguese to abandon their cherished protective, paternalistic view, no doubt because their long acquaintance and intimacy with non-European peoples had made them very confident of knowing exactly how to attract and hold them forever.

The humbler attitude towards black people on a basis of mutual acceptance or cooperation was adumbrated in the earliest times, but it could not prevail over paternalism with its implied coercion until the Portuguese, with the rest of Europe, reached the point of recognizing the existence and, as a next step, the value of the indigenous civilisations in "Black Africa". Some rare precursors appeared in the second half of the past century, whose ideas did not gain acceptance during their lifetime. Those precursors are almost forgotten now. One of them was A. F. Nogueira, a businessman who lived in Africa for twenty-five years, spending those between 1851 and 1862 in southern Angola. He observed Africans with an open heart and mind, coming to the conclusion —so obvious to us at present—that "the Negro is not the absolutely inferior being whom we suppose him to be, and if he needs our help, his help is no less useful to us for the development of our African colonies." These words were published in Lisbon in 1880, when the Portuguese worried about losing their hold on Africa to more powerful European rivals. Because Nogueira, like a few other far-sighted old Africa hands—*africanistas*—such as the botanist Barbosa du Bocage, recognized the existence of African culture, he urged the study of African languages in Portugal, as well as general public education for the black man.[27]

Having much less direct experience, but with a renewed awareness of imminent dangers, the last prime minister of the conservative dictatorial regime, Marcelo Caetano, at least paid lip service to the ideas Nogueira had defended a century earlier, in contrast to his predecessor Oliveira Salazar, who had clung to the notion of Portugal's mission to civilize the "inferior races." Caetano said in one of his broadcasts to the nation, on July 3, 1972: . . ."It is a mistake to think that the only acceptable way of life is the European one. There are values in the traditional African societies that it is important to respect. (. . .) But the African societies have to be constructed in a fraternal spirit by whites and blacks together, with the former contributing their experience and technology, and the latter valid elements of their cultures."[28]

Simplifying matters, one can distinguish between three stages in the evolution of the image since about 1918, or the end of the first World War, when the pioneer work of artists such as Picasso and of anthropologists such as Frobenius could be further developed.

In the first stage, writers attempted to comprehend the African better but retained their sense of a civilising mission. In the second stage, comprehension led to protest against the colonial exploitation. Where this protest remained unheeded, withdrawal into a mythical world of childhood or into past times in general could serve as a prefiguration of the future. In the third stage, writers appeared who felt the need to be "authentic": they turned to a viewpoint, themes, a style, and a language that expressed the experience of their own people in their native environment. This logically led to a rejection of traditional Portuguese models, even among the Portuguese in Portugal itself. The new pride in indigenous development could take the form of Africanization or re-Africanization of the intellectual minority of all shades, impelled by the ideologies of continental solidarity, of negritude, and of nationhood. Africanization actually involved a synthesis that has not yet been completed, between the thought of an African society and its expression in written, literary forms of Portuguese, i. e. European, origins.

The great travelers among the writers belonging to the first stage might still see the blacks as savages, but like Henrique Galvão, for instance, they no longer distinguished between friendly and hostile tribes but between deteriorating societies and others which remained true to their African heritage. Galvão waxed enthusiastic over such peoples as the Cuanhamas, "magnificent, tall, slender, lithe, of proud and attractive bearing, much more intelligent and civilized than their neighbors."[29] In a travel book, he pities the weak chiefs who were the descendants of Queen Nzinga and makes fun of the semi-literate, formally attired notables of Ambaca, an old town east of Luanda, who in the XIXth century had become notorious for their aping of Portuguese ways.[30]

The devoted black woman continued to appear in literature, for example in several novels by Rodrigues Júnior describing the lives of Portuguese bush traders in Mozambique. In spite of his original intentions, the author showed that the traders would not have survived without the moral and material support of the African woman.[31] It was perhaps Galvão who paid the highest tribute to her in his novel "The Golden Fleece" (*O velo d'oiro*, 1930) where he pictured one of her kind uncomplainingly taking care of a white man, a brutal convict who had escaped from prison: "She was so devoted to that hideous gangster, who had reverted to a primitive existence that I remained speechless. The black woman, who could not be older than thirty, showed no bodily deterioration other than missing teeth and repulsively flaccid breasts due to barbarous habits. And yet she would be likely to die of love like the *ingénues* of the Romantics, if she were to lose her man."[32]

The man who went native belongs to the type of the *cafrealizado* ("one who adopts the life of a caffir"), which the Portuguese authors usually treated with the utmost scorn. But Hipólito Raposo had second thoughts about him, as he presents a certain Manuel in his story "White Nigger Boy" (*Branco moleque*, 1926), which concludes as follows: "So ends the true story of Manuel da Silva, a Portuguese from the Azores, who became a respected chief deep in the heart of Angola. He found happiness by voluntarily turning his back on the illusions (of what is called civilisation), which all the rest of us blindly pursue, while deceiving ourselves."[33]

The second stage began gradually with protests that were raised in the name of the white victims, as well as the black ones, due to the plantation system on the tropical cocoa islands of São Tomé and Príncipe. Immorality, corruption and the survival of serfdom are denounced in a documentary novel by Manuel Récio and D. S. de Freitas, "African Fortunes" (*Fortunas de Africa*), as early as 1933. The two authors picture the black man as gentle, hardworking, submissive, childlike and loyal, unless provoked. "*Fortunas de África* is a cry of revolt," they wrote. "Focusing on aspects of life in Africa, we merely wanted to show a small fraction of the embittered existence led by the indigenous workers as well as the white ones . . ."[34]

The contract laborer who was shipped to São Tomé from the Cape Verde Islands and from as far as Angola and Mozambique, did not go there voluntarily. Their miserable silhouettes, appearing in stories and especially in poems by Cape Verdeans, Santomensians and Angolans, became the most haunting figures that contributed to the composite image of the African at this second stage. The *contratado* was joined by the evocations of the *magaíça* or East African laborer who went to the mines of Johannesburg by the thousands, or the laborer recruited from Angolan villages for diamond mines and coffee plantations. One poet saw him being shipped off like dumb cattle[35]; another beheld him returning with flashy clothes that made him look like a clown, but deprived of the bundle of dreams he had carried when he left[36]; a third observed the disconsolate girl he left behind, as she watched the sun and the boat on which he was traveling disappear below the horizon, never to return.[37]

His own early experience as a labor recruiter changed the novelist Castro Soromenho from a sympathetic colonial to a militant opponent of colonialism. In the novel "Dead Land" (*Terra morta*, 1949), he narrated in all its painful details the scene of how a levy of men was assembled to be marched off to work in the distant mines, where they would be as unfree as the slaves had been while their twelve-month contract lasted. Their future resentment is foretold: "Many things did the men learn who went to work in the Northeast. Many things. A great experience. But it would serve them only to spend the rest of their lives lamenting themselves and telling stories. The songs for the dances were replete with tales of what had happened in the mines. And some men mimicked in their dances the chores of opening up the diamond beds and screamed their songs with such utter fury that even the old veterans of the wars against the whites were terrified. It was a sight to behold how their eyes, bleary from marihuana smoke, would light up in anger and their mouths would foam at the corners!"[38]

The resentment of the chiefs, used as tools by the colonial administration, is told in chapter four of the same novel by Castro Soromenho. Similarly, the defeated African warrior, who nurtures a powerless, unspoken hate deep inside, appears in Alexandre Cabral's story of the night watchman Daba-Goma[39]. This figure gains pathetic dimensions when he is seen as an old *cipaio* (or African mercenary in the Portuguese army), who is publicly humiliated after years of faithful service,[40] or as a veteran African official who feels betrayed because his services are no longer sought by a new administration.[41] In a milder, but no less revealing form, the deterioration of the social position and self-image of a mixed minority in the principal towns of Angola has been sketched in the socio-historical writings, the stories and the early poetry of a member of this minority, Mário António Fernandes de Oliveira. He expressed their nostalgia for the past and their sense of "broken roots" when writing verses such as these: "The drama is much greater than he thought: / It is the drama of the pulled-out roots / And of the dreams that were rubbed out / By force, but not by force of time."[42]

Beto, the protagonist o fthe same author's "Chronicle of the Strange City" (*Crónica da cidade estranha*, 1964), retreated into his childhood, "a world that belonged to the past. Or perhaps only for the little group that set its limits at a certain moment in time (. . .) irremediably remote from adults, (. . .) sustained by friendly hearts beating in unison."[43] Many of the poets in particular dreamed of such a time when no barriers seemed to exist, when the family was united, and when they used to ask the traditional puzzles, followed by the traditional stories.

Óscar Ribas, the mestize ethnologist in Luanda, has gathered traditional lore, much of which evokes a recent past that already is gone forever, with its Mardi Gras masquerades, dances and songs, or the story-telling *sunguila* sessions.[44] In modern stories, such sessions are evoked with nostalgia, for example in "The Last Werewolf of the Mukulusu District" (*O último quinzar do Mukulusu*), one of Luandino Vieira's "Old Stories" (*Velhas histórias*, 1974).

A few of the anecdotes collected by Ribas subtly convey an African protest that could not be openly expressed. Here is an example: "A European was hurrying down a sidewalk. His heels hit the pavement hard and loud. Sitting at the curb, a market woman was resting, letting her eyes wander, with her basket next to her. 'Gee! You're fighting with the stones?' she mused to herself. 'Hit them hard, baby, go ahead! They'll have their turn.'"[45]

The third and last stage was already prepared by authors such as Óscar Ribas, who began his writing career in the 1920s, never pretending to be anything but an African, though he was of mixed blood, and although he felt flattered by the attention and the honors the Portuguese intellectuals in high positions showered upon him. Suffice it to mention that the pride in being African was furthered by the international movement of negritude, taken up by an eloquent mestize scholar from São Tomé, Francisco José Tenreiro. He wrote poems and essays inspired by negritude from 1953 on, such as his verses of "With My Heart in Africa" (*Coração em África*). He had had a predecessor of sorts, Pedro Monteiro, in the Cape Verdean Islands, where any affirmation of the African heritage was strenuously resisted by the assimilated elite. But even there, a recent generation has proclaimed its solidarity with the peoples of the African continent, as Mário Alberto da Fonseca did in his poem "Here I am, Africa" (*Eis-me aqui África*): ". . . Oh joy / I find my smile again / And confirmation / That nothing divides us / Neither the sea / Nor the Lusiads / (. . .) / Here I am Guinea-Bissau / With your sons / On your-my borders / Here I am one of your sons / A prodigal son by force / Returning / To my former first forbidden home."[46]

Another Cape Verdean of the same generation, Gabriel Moreno, voiced the hope for a renaissance of "the most despised blood" in "Song of my Island" (*Cantiga da minha ilha*).[47] This hope led a third, Luís Romano, an exile in Brazil, to write not only serious verse, as many had done before him in this century, but serious prose stories as well about the common island folk in their own Creole Portuguese, publishing them under the title "At Dusk" (*Negrume*) in 1973. Cape Verdean Creole suggests a possible development, not without danger for the unity of the Portuguese language. Other writers, such as the poet José Craveirinha in Mozambique or the story writer Luandino Vieira in Angola have initiated adaptations of the literary language by using regional African expressions. They were guided by the mixed language of the unschooled people who have flocked into the cities.

The new African, who asserts his independence, has hardly had time yet to appear in Portuguese African writing, as the furious struggle between "colonialists" and "terrorists", the labels each side used for the other, has barely subsided. The poets have voiced their hopes for unity, for rebirth, for reconciliation. Perhaps the most moving appeal was made by Alda Lara, a white Angolan poetess and doctor, whose life was cut short by illness (1930—1962). Having evoked the powerfully symbolical image of the "Black Mammy" (*Mãe-Preta*) in her poem "Night" (*Noite*, 1948), abstracted as "Mother Africa" (*Mãe África*), the African Mother Earth; in "African Presence" (*Presença africana*) a poem of 1953, she associated herself as a sister and a woman "with all that grows in you / Pure and uncertain." She stretched out her hand— too late!—to João Dias, a black poet from Mozambique, who had just died at an even earlier age than she (1926—1949), telling him in the poem "Direction" (*Rumo*, 1949):

"Brother: / Let me extend my white hands / To clutch with love / your long black hands . . ."[48]

Mother and child, brother and sister—the images of the black African, in relation to the European settler and his descendants, has undergone many changes to arrive once more at the humanism, expressed in the metaphors of family bonds, which had been the ideal and the practice of the ancient cultures of Egypt, Greece and Rome, still faintly remembered in the Age of Discoveries when Portuguese sailors, greedy and crude as many of them were, first looked through unprejudiced eyes at the black peoples of Guinea. Today the image is more fragmented and more complex, carrying with it the thoughts and deeds of five intervening centuries. Returning to the images in Luandino Vieira's recent narrative *Nós, os do Makulusu*, we can appreciate how hard it must be to overcome the humiliation of many an encounter. The images born from superiority complexes, dreams of mission and policies of assimilation are dying. But the essence of certain positive images remains. Such is the image of the strong black fighter, born of admiration, and the image of the beautiful black woman, born of affection.

A great deal of material remains to be collected and analysed before the image of the African in the XIXth and XXth centuries can be traced with complete assurance. All that could be done in this paper has been to outline the image, on the tentative basis of a few samples.

Notes

1 For ample documentation of the lack of bias in Antiquity see Frank M. Snowdon, Jr., *Blacks in Antiquity*, Cambridge, Mass., 1970.
2 The rejection of the halfcaste by the non-African member of the family is the point of a story with the ironic title "Blue-Blooded Mulatto" *(Mulato de sangue azul)* in *Regresso adiado,* by Manuel Rui, Lisbon, 1974.
3 Ndabaningi Sithole, *African Nationalism,* Capetown, 1959, p. 31.
4 José Luandino Vieiro, *Nós, os do Makulusu,* Lisbon, 1974.
5 Vieira had previously published a much smaller book of the same title, a collection of only four stories, which appeared in his hometown Luanda in 1957. Its circulation had been prohibited. Only one of the original four stories was preserved in the 1960 edition. Vieira's reputation soared when he received several literary prizes, among them in 1965 the most important prize that the Society of Portuguese Writers could attribute. It happened at a time when he was in jail as a political prisoner. The attribution of the prize so infuriated the Portuguese Government that it dissolved the Society. Vieira became widely known abroad when one of his tales, "Domingos Xavier's True Life" *(A vida verdadeira de Domingos Xavier)* was published in Paris in a French translation (1971) and shortly thereafter used as the script of the militant motion picture *Sambizanga* which, following the story, told of the activities, jailing, torture and ensuing death of a black Angolan nationalist.
6 Luís de Camões, *Os Lusíadas,* canto X, st. 92, vv. 3—4, 7—8, in W. Atkinson's prose translation, Harmondsworth, 1952, p. 236. The original verses are:
   Vês África, dos bens do mundo avara,
   Inculta et toda cheia de bruteza,
   . . .
   Olha essa terra toda, que se habita
   Dessa gente sem Lei, quase infinita.
7 "Deformed, horrible, cruel, bestial, ferocious, these are the characteristics attributed to the Negroes by Barros, Castanheda, Góis, and Osório. The importance of their descriptions lies in the fact, which Randles has noted, that they served as the basis for the travel narratives and compendia so avidly read by the European public. Thus they set the tone for later judgments upon the Negroes." J. H. Rodrigues, *Brazil and Africa,* Berkeley, California, 1965, p. 6.
8 V. Magalhães Godinho, ed., *Documentos sobre a expansão portuguesa,* vol. II, p. 216. The following quotations are from the same work, which was published in three volumes in Lisbon, 1945 and 1956. The responsibilty for all of the English versions is mine in this paper, except where another translator is mentioned.

9 The passage is reprinted by Godinho, III, p. 151. Other witty remarks were attributed by Damião de Góis to one of the early kings of the Congo, and a hundred years later, by Cadornega and others to the redoubtable Queen Nzinga of Angola.

10 "... era pequeno de corpo e se parecia com samcho mixiaa." Facsimile ed., by A. Baião and A. de Magalhães Basto, Porto, 1945, p. 4.

11 *Relatione del reame di Congo ...,* Rome, 1591.

12 Gil Vicente's two plays are accessible in vol. IV of his *Obras completas,* ed. Marques Braga, Lisbon, 1943.

13 In the first of Barros' *Décadas,* published in 1552. Quoted in the English translation by C. R. Boxer, in *Four Centuries of Portugese Expansion, 1415—1825,* Johannesburg, 1961, pp. 26—27.

14 Damião de Góis, *Crónica de Felicíssimo Rei D. Manuel* of 1566.

15 Henrique Galvão wrote of Queen Nzinga in the early 1940s. The Angolan novelist Castro Soromenho published her eulogy in *Présence Africaine,* Paris, in 1962. She was praised by the Brazilian writers Mário de Andrade, Gilberto Freyre, and Luís da Câmara Cascudo.

16 António de Oliveira de Cadornega, *História geral das guerras angolanas (1680),* ed. Lisbon, 1940, vol. I, p. 293. In the same work, Cadornega wrote: ... "há muitos multatos e pardos (...) que são grandes soldados, principalmente em as gueras do sertão contra o gentio delle: soffredores dos trabalhos, e passão com qualquer couza de sustento, e pouco calçado; delles se fazem grandes homens". (III, p. 30: "In Luanda there are many mulattos and quarteroons [...], who make fine soldiers, principally for the inland campaigns against the natives: supporting every hardship, they sustain themselves on just about anything and need little footwear; some become oustanding".)

17 C. R. Boxer refers to the opinions of Fathers Francisco de Gouveia and Joseph de Anchieta on Angolans and Brazilian Indians respectively in *Four Centuries of Portuguese Expansion, 1415—1825,* Johannesburg, 1961, p. 30.

18 Father Pero Pais, a Castilian who joined the Portuguese Jesuits in their endeavors to make Roman Catholics out of the Abyssinians, had to admit that they were deeply religious, practicing Christians while their social manners gave proof of a higher morality than was usual in Europe. "What quite amazes me," he wrote, is how they control their tempers, or rather, how they hide them. No matter how far away they may be from each other, they rarely give vent to them. On the contrary, they then become even more courteous in their speech, and under no circumstances are there such insults uttered as among other nations". Quoted in Portuguese in H. Cidade, *A literatura portuguesa e a expansão ultramarina,* Coimbra, 1964, vol. II, p. 155.

19 Frank M. Snowden, Jr., *Blacks in Antiquity,* Cambridge, Mass., 1970, p. 146, where Diodorus is quoted.

20 Damião de Góis, *Crónica de Felicíssimo Rei D. Manuel,* Part III, Lisbon, 1567, chapters 60—62.

21 *The beautiful Mulata,* daughter of a slave trader or *negreiro* in West Africa, is the heroine of Camilo Castelo Branco's tale *Aquela casa triste* ("That Sad House", 1874.) Among the same author's other tales, *O degredado* ("The Banished Convict", 1877) revolves around the career of a sadistic slave driver in Eeast Africa.

22 See M. António's sociological essay which serves as the preface of the modern reedition of A. Troni's *Nga Muturi,* Lisbon, 1973.

23 José da Silva Maia Ferreira in his poem *A minha terra* ("My Country"), found in his book of poems *Espontaneidades da minha alma,* Luanda, 1849 (in reality 1850), pp. 13, 14 and 17.

24 For example in Eduardo Neves' poem *A uma africana* ("To an African Girl"), published in the *Novo Almanach de Lembranças Luso-Brazileiro* for 1892, Lisbon, 1891:

> Será feliz queme tu queiras,
> o que teu amor inflame,
> gentil filha das palmeiras,
> *ngu xála, ngâna, ngui 'âme.*

("To whom you give your heart, he will be happy, / Set aflame by your love, / Gentle daughter of the palms, / *I leave you, lady, I depart.*")

25 First line of the poem *Febre lenta* ("Slow Fever") in Tomás Vieira da Cruz, *Tatuagem* ("Tattoo"), Lisbon, 1941.

26 In the dedication of his volume *Saudade negra* ("Black Yearning"), Lisbon, 1932. As the symbol of his understanding and defense of the African in poetry, he chose the popular Angolan *quissange* or "finger piano", to replace at least now and then the classic European symbols of various kinds of poetry—flute, lyre, or trumpet. The complete text of the dedication is as follwos:

> *Ao povo africano:*
> *Ao mundo africano:*
> *A esse Império de sonho e de maravilha que foi, na verde mocidade*
> *e ao acender de gratas ilusões, o adorável exílio da minha alma . . .*
> *Ofereço e dedico as notas mais dolentes do meu saudoso quissange,*
> *as canções mais rítmicas da minha saudade negra.*

("To the African people, to the African world, to that Empire of Dream and Wonder which was the exile of my soul during my tender youth, when I was fired with pleasant illusions . . . I offer and dedicate the most redolent notes of my nostalgic quissange, the most rhythmic songs of my black yearning.")

27 A. F. Nogueira, *A raça negra sob o ponto de vista da civilização da Africa . . .,* Lisbon, 1880, Introduction, p. 7.
On the following page, he refers to conclusions drawn by him and published in articles already in 1871 and 1877 about the Nhaneca and Kumbi tribes of southern Angola: "The Negroes are not (as stupid) as we generally think; they progress and reveal aptitudes that assure them of an important place in the future destinies of mankind."

28 Quoted from "Unidos como um só" (Like One Man), text of a "family chat" by Prime Minister Marcelo Caetano, in *Notícias de Portugal,* Supplement to no. 1314, July 8, 1972, p. 3.

29 Henrique Galvão, *O velo d'oiro,* Lisbon, 1930.

30 In Henrique Galvãos book about a trip across Angola, *Outras terras, outras gentes* ("Other Lands, Other Peoples"), 2 vols., Lisbon, n. d. (c. 1942).

31 Black girls are the heroines of Rodrigues Júnior's novels *Sehura* (1944), *O branco da Motase* (1952), and *Muende* (1960).

32 Henrique Galvão, *O velo d'oiro,* Lisbon, 1933, p. 244.

33 Hipólito Rapose, *Ana a calunga* ("The Sons of the Sea"), Lisbon, 1926, p. 223: *Aqui acaba a história verdadeira de Manuel da Silva, português dos Açores, soba respeitado no interior de Angola, que encontrou a felicidade no desprêzo voluntário daquelas ilusões em que todos nós, por cego engano, a vamos procurando . . .*

34 *"Fortunas de Africa" é um grito de revolta. Focando, como atrás di-*
zemos, aspectos da vida africana, apenas desejamos vir mostrar, um
pouco, a existência amargurada dos trabalhadores indígenas e brancos," . . .
M. Récio and D. S. de Freitas, *Fortunas d'Africa*, Lisbon, 1933, pp. 11—12.

35 The Mozambican José Craveirinha, in *Mamparra m'gaíza*, in Mário de
Andrade, ed., *Poesia*, Algiers, 1967, pp. 224—225.

36 The Mozambican Noémia de Sousa in *Magaíça*, ib., pp. 222—223.

32 The Angolan Agostinho Neto, in "Partida para o contrato" (Departure
for Contract Labor), ib., pp. 216—217.

38 F. Castro Soromenho, *Terra morta*, Rio de Janeiro, 1949, pp. 76—77:
Muitas coisas aprenderam os homens que foram trabalhar ao Nordeste.
Muitas coisas e uma grande experiéncia, mas que só lhes servia para passar
a vida a lamentarem-se e a contar histórias. As canções dos seus batuques
estavam cheias de histórias passadas nas minas. E alguns homens dan-
çavam reproduzindo as fainas da abertura dos jazigos diamantíferos e
cantavam cantigas gritadas com tamanha violência e raiva que até os
velhos guerreiros de tôdas as guerras com os brancos se enchiam de
espanto. E era ver como os seus olhos cansados do fumo da liamba se
acendiam de cólera e os cantos da boca se enchiam de espuma!

39 Alexandre Cabral, "Daba-Goma", *Histórias de Zaire*, 2d ed., Lisbon, 1965.

40 The *cipaio* Caluis in F. Castro Soromenho's novel *Viragem* (The Turn in
the Road), Lisbon, 1957.

41 In the posthumously published novel *Funantes*, by António de Aguiar,
Lisbon, 1969.

42 Mário António, "Drama", *Cem poemas*, Luanda, 1963, p. 32.

43 Mário António, *Crónica de cidade estranha*, Lisbon, 1964, p. 34.

44 In Missosso III, *Izomba* and *Sunguilando,* three of Oscar Ribas' more
recent collections.

45 Oscar Ribas, *Missosso III*, Luanda, 1964, p. 243.

46 M. A. da Fonseca, in M. de Andrade, ed., *Poesia*, Algiers, 1967, p. 176
and 177.

47 Gabriel Mariano, ib., pp. 37—38.

48 Alda Lara, "Rumo", "Noite", and "Presença", to be found in her *Poemas,*
Sá da Bandeira, 1966.

Queen Nzinga in Fact and Fiction
Abstract

Gerald M. Moser

One of the most extraordinary figures in African history was Queen Nzinga, alias Dona Ana de Sousa, who lived in Angola about 1600. She fascinated many poets and novelists who wrote in Portuguese in the XXth century, among them Hipólito Raposo, Aquilino Ribeiro, Castro Soromenho, Geraldo Bessa Victor, Agostinho Neto, and Manuel Pedro Pacavira. They, in addition to Angolan folklore, have portrayed her as an insatiable lover, a ruthless amazon, a restless wanderer, and a fighter for African independence.

I. Introduction

In the opening lines of *Poema del otoño* by the ageing Nicaraguan poet Rubén Darío, there appears the evocation of a historical personage that must have startled his readers, since few of them could have recognized the name. Relating the pleasures of love to the horrors of death, the poet wrote:

> El alma ahita cruel inmola
> lo que la alegra,
> como Zingua, reina de Angola,
> lúbrica negra.[1]

(Surfeited, the soul cruelly immolates what gives it joy, as Zingua had done, the Queen of Angola, that lewd negress.)

The Nicaraguan Modernist poet was dropping a mere hint at an extraordinary African queen, singling out one trait, her cruelty in killing those who had given her sensual pleasure and dismissing her cavalierly as the "lewd negress."

A cruel and lewd queen is impressive enough, but Queen Nzinga had other attributes for which she is remembered to this day, especially in Angola, her own country. During her lifetime, she struck the missionary who definitely converted her to Christianity as a woman "given wholly to the delights of the senses", but also "of intrepid heart," unwilling to submit to foreign invaders. She appeared to a Portuguese *conquistador* as a "fiend in human shape" or "a second Good Thief Dimas, changed into a woman." The same veteran of the campaigns against her was so impressed by her military skill and political acumen that he also referred to her as "aquela ardilosa como valerosa rainha

Ginga," that Queen Ginga who was as crafty as she was valiant. A later Portuguese author, whose *Memórias* were published in 1825, plainly admired her to the point of exclaiming: "If this woman had been born in Europe and had inherited the throne of a great country, she would perhaps have been a second Christina of Sweden or Elizabeth of England." Modern historians of Portuguese Angola echoed these sentiments, calling her "the ancient virago," or more subtly, with a trace of classic learning, "the redoubtable Amazon." A British admirer of Portuguese colonization found her to be "in a sense, one of the most romantic figures in the history of Africa," while a British partisan of the African independence movements hailed her as "that famous Queen Zhinga of Matamba who held the [Portuguese] invaders at bay for year after year"—in fact, she fought them during more than thirty years of her long, adventurous life. An exiled Portuguese, all too familiar with the dangerous game of power politics, considered her "the greatest political genius among Angolan princes of whom history tells," ranking her, aside from social circumstances, with Catherine of Russia and the subtle Maria Theresia of Austria. To a member of her sex, she was a paragon of love, "a female sultan, [. . .] prodigal in giving her caresses to the brave warriors that were winning her battles."[2]

In Angola itself, proof of her enduring fame was found every-where by a Brazilian expert in folklore studies, Luís da Câmara Cascudo, when he visited Africa on a field trip. Cascudo was so impressed by her effective resistance to the Portuguese that he termed her the "ebony Boadicea, who had appeared in a melancholy finale to the autonomous era of Africa."[3]

Cascudo was probably the first scholar to point out that this Queen endures in the printed literature as well as in the oral traditions on both sides of the Atlantic, in Brazil and in Angola: "the only sovereign queen in all Africa who ... continues to live on unmitigatedly ferocious in the Brazilian mind, authentic, because of her strong-willed, decisive, legitimate queenship."[4] Her name is heard in the songs that accompany the dramatic *Congo* or *Congada* dances throughout Northeastern Brazil, Cascudo informs us. One of the principal dancers is her ambassador, whom she has sent across the sea to demand that the King of the Congo be killed. He delivers her message:

> Mandou matar Rei meu senhor!
> E quem mandou foi Rainha Jinga![5]

(Your death has been ordered, my Lord King! Ordered by Jinga the Queen!)

Too little is known directly of the epic and historical traditions that survive among the Bantu peoples of Angola. The task of collecting them, yet to be carried out, will not be an easy one, since the history of each tribe constitutes secret lore that is jealously guarded. But there can be no doubt as to the existence of the traditions, for almost every traveller has reported small bits of them that are tantalizingly vague. Thus we have the testimony of Henrique Galvão, who passed through the lands of the warlike Ginga tribe about 1941 and was profoundly affected by the contrast between the might of their ancient monarchs and the impotence of their modern chief: "The difference," he reported, "must seem even crueler when they are retelling the feats of his forebears with bursts of enthusiasm during the endless nights in his village."[6] In 1957, a Catholic missionary, Father Leguzzano, visited the same village, near which Queen Nzinga is supposed to have been buried. He stated, all too briefly: "No other monarch has remained so alive in the memory of the native population."[7] Cascudo, who went there in 1963 or 64, confirmed this impression, but did not add further details. What is more remarkable is that songs about her are mentioned already by the Italian Capuchins who were her first European biographers. Thus, Father Antonio Laudate da Gaëta, who performed her marriage in 1657, tells of songs recited during her royal wedding celebration, in which the court musicians "sang her praises, her great style of living (*grandezzas*) and the victories she had won over her enemies."[8] And Father Cavazzi, who succeeded Laudate as the Queen's confessor, refers at least twice to songs that had been composed during her lifetime, or shortly afterwards. "Among the various folk songs that were composed about this woman," he writes at one point, "there is a song that tells of the prophecy [made by the soothsayers at the time of her birth]. It says that the soothsayers dared not disclose what they had divined. Surreptitiously eyeing one another, they muttered *Máma ô auê! Máma ô auê!* which means: "Alas, my mother! alas! alas!"[9] Elsewhere Cavazzi mentions songs that narrated the sinister episode of how the Queen had given orders to behead in public a courtier of the newly conquered Matamba Kingdom when he had dared call her cruel to her face, but not until after making him witness the death of his own son.[10]

Cavazzi's testimony is so precious because he knew Queen Nzinga during the last years of her long life, had many conversations with her, and attended her while she was in the throes of death. His account encompasses much more than the Queen's life and reign, however. This is suggested by the title which can be translated as "A Historical Description of the Three Kingdoms of Congo, Matamba and Angola." It was published posthumously in Bologna, Italy, in 1687, slightly retouched by another priest so as to remove certain supernatural elements from the ingenuous missionary's narrative of happenings in Africa. Cavazzi's book remains the chief source of our information on Queen Zinga's career and character.

Other Capuchins have left contemporary accounts. As early as 1669, a Father Francesco Maria Gioia had published an edifying work about the astonishing conversion of the Queen and her Kingdom to the Holy Faith, the diary of the by then deceased Father Antonio [Laudate] da Gaëta, the very priest who had worked the miracle of bringing her back into the fold. A French Dominican, Father J. B. Labat, revived and enlarged Cavazzi's work in the eighteenth century, thus giving it new currency. Important for its own sake but also for checking the accuracy of Cavazzi's history is a work of the same period written by a Portuguese layman with some education, who settled in Luanda, the capital of Angola, after having taken part in the wars of conquest against the Queen. This man, António de Oliveira de Cadornega by name, completed his lively "General History of the Angolan Wars" in 1681, fifteen years after Cavazzi had written his account. But Cadornega's manuscript gathered dust until it was finally printed in our century.

Modern historians have retold the story. They were able to draw on the official documents that have survived from the seventeenth century, such as reports and inquiries by the governors of Angola, particularly Fernão de Sousa, and several letters written by Queen Nzinga herself. One of the historians is a Portuguese, Paiva Manso. An English historian, Charles R. Boxer, speaks of her in his biography of Salvador de Sá, the Brazilian governor who reconquered Angola from its Dutch invaders (1952). A Belgian prelate, J. Cuvelier, made of her life a colorful and dramatic story of a wicked black sinner who repented at last (1957). Minor writings periodically refreshed people's memories of the Queen in Europe, for example a chapbook that was printed in Lisbon during the eighteenth century and magazine articles that appeared in the nineteenth and twentieth centuries, one of which could have been the source of the poet Rubén Darío's cryptic allusion.

II. The Known Facts about Queen Nzinga's Life and Character

Queen Nzinga impressed the Europeans who met her so vividly that several of them have left posterity an account of the chief events in her life, at least after a certain point in time, besides descriptions of her intriguing character. The following emerge as probable facts, based, like the summary of her life that Leguzzano provides,[11] upon a comparison of Cavazzi's and Cadornega's works with the published official records of the seventeenth century.

In order to keep the events in proper perspective, one has to remind oneself that two factors might have muddied those sources. In the case of the missionaries, such as Gaeta and Cavazzi, the Queen might have been painted in the lurid colors of a devilish fiend so as to make her final conversion seem more extraordinary. In the case of Cadornega and the official documents emanating from the Portuguese authorities in Angola, economic and military ambitions probably biased the reporting, especially in view of the stake all of them had in the slave trade, as a modern British historian, David Birmingham, has clearly demonstrated.[12]

(A) Her Life

1. The first fact that can be established concerns Nzinga's birth as one of the children of the ruler of Ndongo, the name of Angola proper, whose title was Nzinga-Mbandi-a-Ngola-Kiluanji. Her mother was one of his several wives, a certain Guenguela-Cacombe. Her own African name is not known, for the name Nzinga was that of her clan and had been given to her as it was to her brother, her father, and her grandfather. The only individual name we have for her is the one the Portuguese bestowed on her when she was baptized a Christian in Luanda: *Ana de Sousa.*

The date of her birth is in doubt. Leguzzano, following Ravenstein,[13] decided on 1582 as most likely. Other conjectures vary between 1580 and 1600.

2. Observing a practice of autocrats, Nzinga's elder brother disposed of possible contenders in the matrilinear family after his father's death in 1617, by killing a younger brother and also his nephew, who was Nzinga's only child. He took further precautions by sterilizing his three sisters, Nzinga among them.

3. A sort of reconciliation must have taken place between Nzinga and her brother, probably as the result of a twofold threat to the independence of the kingdom. On one side, the Portuguese invaded the Ndongo country and build a garrisoned fort (*presídio*) in the heart of it, at Ambaca. On the other side, there was a simultaneous invasion by African warriors led by a commander whom the Portuguese called the Jaga Cassanje. At any rate, we find Nzinga heading an embassy to the Portuguese governor.[14] The embassy arrived in 1622 in the capital of Portuguese Angola, then called São Paulo da Assunção de Luanda. There she concluded a treaty of peace and alliance between Ndongo and Portugal as between equals, impressing the Portuguese with her royal bearing and her diplomatic skill. She won their hearts when she asked to become a Christian. The Governor in person, João Correia de Sousa, served as her godfather and gave her his own family name, one of the oldest and noblest in Portugal.

4. After hostilities had again broken out between the Portuguese and the Angolans of Ndongo, culminating in a decisive defeat of the Ngola-Mbandi, Nzinga's brother, the latter was killed by his own entourage in 1623 on one of the islands in the Kwanza river, where he had taken refuge. According to Cavazzi, he was poisoned at the instigation of his own sister, Nzinga.

5. After her brother had died, Nzinga succeeded him to the throne as Queen of Ndongo and proceeded to kill her brother's only son as treacherously as hers had been done away with. She also joined the mysterious Imbangala brotherhood of warriors known to the Portuguese as the *Jagas*, whom Leguzzano, Cavazzi's modern commentator, has characterized as roving bands of mercenaries. She began her rule by reinstituting the draconic laws of a ferocious African queen, Temba-Ndumba, whom she apparently wanted to emulate. From then on, she and her people led a nomadic life of perpetual warfare on the Portuguese. Her goal was to expel them once and for all from Angola, and with them a half-brother of hers, whom they had set up as a puppet king of Ndongo in 1626, baptizing him one year later and giving him the high-sounding name of Dom Felipe ("Sir Philip"). In the course of these wars, Nzinga moved farther inland, away from the Europeans, and conquered the neighboring kingdom of Matamba in 1623/24 from the widow of its ruler. Matamba became the base of her operations. Hence she was to be known as Queen Nzinga of Matamba.

6. When Dutch invaders occupied Luanda in 1641, in order to take the slave trade away from the Portuguese, she, like the King of the Congo to the north, allied herself with them against the common Portuguese enemy.

7. However, wearying of the long war three years after the Portuguese had expelled the Dutch in 1651, Queen Nzinga asked italian missionaries to come and bring Christianity and peace to Matamba. She had become acquainted with them through her sister Barbara, held captive by the Portuguese, who had one of the Italians as her confessor. Later on several of these missionaries had fallen into her hands as prisoners of war. She calculated correctly that they could bring about the liberation of her sister. They prevailed upon the then governor, Luís Martins de Sousa Chichorro, to return her sister to her in May 1656, and in June she decided to reconvert to Christianity. The Italian fathers were permitted to build a church in her fortified camp town in Matamba.

8. To set a good example, Nzinga married her latest lover in the new church in 1657, at the urging of Father Antonio da Gaëta, who also acted as her emissary to establish peace with the Portuguese at long last.

9. In 1660, she moved her headquarters to a new location on the Uamba river where a new city, Santa Maria de Matamba, was laid out, with a church dedicated to her patron-saint Anne, a house (*hospício*) for the missionaries, and a palace for herself and her courtiers.

10. On December 17, 1663, Queen Nzinga died, assisted by Father Cavazzi. Shortly thereafter her new city was abandoned. "The triumph of the Faith in Matamba unfortunately came to an end with Queen Zinga's death." Thus Father Leguzzano concludes the summary of her life.[15]

(B) Her Character

Considering as fairly certain the facts about Queen Nzinga's life that have just been recapitulated, one is able to accompany the unfolding of her character. But one finds himself limited to the second half of her life, her mature age, since practically nothing is known of what she did before 1617, when she was already about thirty-five years old.

Her confessor, Father Cavazzi, observed in her an indomitable will, above everything else. She did not brook any opposition. He also informs us that her upbringing had made her wanton, because her governess had been "a black woman who was a regular firebrand straight out of Hell" (*um verdadeiro tição do Inferno.*) This woman encouraged her royal pupil to have an abundance of pre-marital sex experiences, "yielding her up to diverse lovers" (*que ... a entregou a diversos amantes.*)[16] Throughout life, Nzinga was to maintain a reputation of unbridled sensuality, and the missionaries reported that she kept a regular harem of lovers far into her old age, treating them as her inferiors, even as slaves, or, to use a modern term, as mere sex objects. On the other hand, she is reported to have been a fond mother until the murder of her only son changed her so radically that she was reputed to hate other women for having children. Considering her efforts to obtain the freedom of her sister Cambo (or Barbara), to find a husband for her and leave her the throne, she must have been very fond of her sisters as well.

The missionary tells us moreover that Nzinga ruled like a spiteful tyrant, striking terror in the hearts of her subjects "because of the frightful manner in which she punished the slightest transgression."[17] Cavazzi paints her in colors more dreadful than the Bible lent to King Herod when he tells us how she carried out the code that Queen Temba-Ndumba had imposed on the Jaga warriors: "Whenever Nzinga would discover a babe of the male sex through her numerous spies, she personally tore out his heart and ate it. There had been instances when she did not wait for the mother to give birth, but opened the womb, tore out the foetus, drank its blood, and cast its flesh to the dogs or had it roasted to be distributed among her vassals."[18] She told Cavazzi often after her reconversion how she had meant to outdo the ferocious Queen Temba-Ndumba.[19]

Queen Nzinga tried to explain her cruelty as a ruler in a letter which she wrote to Governor Chichorro in 1655. A pertinent passage reads as follows: "I complain so much about the past [Portuguese] Governors because they always promised to return my sister in exchange for the countless slaves and thousands of other gifts (*banzos*) that I sent them. Yet they never returned her to me but proceeded to make war on me, not giving me any rest, which caused me to lead the roving life of a *Jaga*, committing tyrannical acts, such as preventing children from being raised since it was contrary to the discipline of a military camp (*quilombo* . . .)"[20]

Another trait of hers which all the Europeans who met her found remarkable was her intelligence, which was aided by an excellent memory. They noticed how well she applied it to shrewd strategy and political maneuvering. Cavazzi wrote that she let it be known among the people that she possessed supernatural powers enabling her to predict future events unfailingly and to change herself into the shapes of "various monsters."[21]

Finally, her wit had a bite to it. Several stories highlight the mocking humor that she displayed now and then in what she said.

Cavazzi relates several anecdotes that reveal those traits—wilfulness, sensuality, cruelty, a sharp mind, and a quick, satirical humor. Since the anecdotes form the basis of later literary treatment of her unique personality, it becomes indispensable to reproduce some of the more telling ones.

(1) It was said that she kept a male harem. But none of her many lovers could ever be sure of her affection. Hiding her innermost feelings, she would show great love at one moment and spite at the next. She made her men dress like women. All of a sudden she would get rid of them so that none might boast that he had conquered her heart.[22] The anecdote seems like a combination of the story of Salome and other female vampires with that of lovelorn Hercules wearing women's gowns.

(2) Nzinga's self-assurance, quick wit, and royal manners are illustrated in the best known anecdote about her, of how she used a human being as a chair. Father Cavazzi told the story as part of the account of her embassy to the Portuguese Governor[23]:

"From Cabaço, the capital of Ndongo [and not Matamba, as Cavazzi wrote], she was carried piggyback, as is the custom of the land, over a distance of a hundred leagues to Luanda. . . . The first time when she went to the

Governor's palace to be received in audience, she showed up laden with precious gems and handsomely adorned with a feather headdress of many hues. She bore herself majestically and was surrounded by a host of ladies, slave girls and male officials of her court.

She entered the hall and, seeing that the place of honor was a velvet-covered, gold-embroidered chair for the Governor, faced by two cushions of gold and velvet on the carpet, after the manner of black princes, she stopped short. Without betraying any embarrassment or uttering a word, she gave a mere wink to one of her ladies. The latter immediately crouched on all fours behind her mistress to serve her as a chair for the duration of the audience. ... At the conclusion of their conversation, the Governor, who was accompanying Nzinga to the door as befitted a princess, politely pointed out to her that the aforementioned lady was still in the same position and that she ought to give her leave to rise. But Nzinga replied that this was no oversight on her part, to leave the woman crouching there on the carpet. It just did not seem right for an envoy of her kingdom to sit twice in the same seat. Since she did not lack chairs of the kind, she cared not what happened to this one and had no more use for it."[24]

The story has European antecedents, as Luís da Câmara Cascudo has conclusively shown. A similar story was told earlier in Spain about an ambassador of the proud Republic of Venice.[25]

(3) How the African Queen preserved her traditional beliefs under a Christian veneer, as long as possible, is illustrated in a third anecdote told by Cavazzi:

"Above all, it seemed extremely difficult to make her relinquish the box in which she continued to keep the remains of her brother, the Ngola-Mbandi. [...] One day, no less than four years after her abjuration of idolatry, she complained to Father Antonio da Gaëta about not yet being admitted to holy communion whereas many of her subjects were. He then talked plainly about the matter of the box. Heaving a sigh, she replied that she no longer felt any reverence for those bones and that she would be willing to cast them into the fire at once. [...] The priest took advantage of the opportunity to extirpate another apparently insignificant practice, which was actually very important. So he said to her: "Milady, as long as I see you wear and keep those superstitious bracelets made for you by your witchdoctor (*xinguila*) to serve as charms against misfortune, I shall not cease to doubt that you are in the proper frame of mind! [...]" The Queen promised that she would not only deliver to him her own bracelets the following morning, but also those of the noblest ladies in the town. She really kept her promise, delivering into the Father's hands about two thousand bracelets. He burned them publicly, together with the bones mentioned above. Many rejoiced and many others were annoyed at this decision, and the Devil himself seemed to show his anger when claps of thunder could be heard coming out of the blue."[26]

Thus it happened that Queen Nzinga gave up her cherished sliver box containing the bones of her royal predecessor, which she used to consult whenever affairs of state had to be decided. And she took leave of the bracelets that were the insignia of her rank and authority. One may wonder, however, if she was capable of abandoning altogether the beliefs connected with those objects.

(4) Her tyrannical cruelty is underlined by the story of how she treated the ruling class of conquered Matamba. Not only did she brand the Queen of Matamba a slave but she terrorized the enemy chiefs, as Cavazzi tells us in the following story:

"One of the chiefs of Matamba, who was more courageous than the rest, told her [to her face] that the way in which she was mistreating her [new] subjects would merely alienate them. . . . In her wrath, the Queen motioned to her guards to cut off his head and that of a young son of his. The wretched father threw himself at her feet and with great presence of mind praised her sentence. He only begged one favor of her: to let him be the first to be executed since he had been born first. But Nzinga laughed at his request and insisted that the boy had to die first. Thereupon an executioner stepped forward, beheaded the son and then cut the father's throat, too, over the dead boy's corpse." Cavazzi adds: "This execrable episode is still recalled in the people's song, and two large boulders on the banks of a creek mark the place where the tragic event occurred."[27]

(5) Finally, there is a story that shows the Queen in a lighter vein. It reports that she played on words when she used to say: "The noble name of Sousa has given me life, death, and ressurrection." She meant by this that Governor João Correia de Sousa had been good to her when he persuaded her to become a Christian, thus giving her life; that Governor Fernão de Sousa had sought her death and caused her to become an apostate, since he took away her kingdom and chased her out of her lands; but that Governor Luís Martins de Sousa Chichorro had ressurrected her to a new life when he restored her sister Barbara to her and made peace with her at long last.[28]

On the whole, Cavazzi's description of Queen Nzinga's character agrees with that of his predecessor, although Antonio da Gaëta's strikes this reader as less colorful but more objective. Gaëta found lasciviousness her outstanding trait, followed by fondness of drinking, music, dancing, smoking, gambling, her liberality in bestowing gifts, which made her popular with vassals and courtiers, a passion for hunting, an unbridled temper, vindictiveness, and a criminal disregard of the rights of her neighbors, whom she plundered and raided to sustain her high living. In short he pictured her not unlike the Renaissance princes of Europe! But one trait struck him most forcefully: her love of independence. "She has always said and keeps on saying that she would rather kill herself than submit to the Portuguese." For that, the Missionary compared her to the dauntless inhabitants of Numantia who resisted the Roman legions to the last man, woman and child.[29]

III. In Literature

The anecdotes told by her European contemporaries already surrounded Queen Nzinga's name with a legendary aura, although she undoubtedly possessed the unusually strong, almost masculine character which those episodes highlighted.

In general, the Franciscan order, of which the Italian Capuchins, to which Fathers Gaëta and Cavazzi belonged, were a branch, could be expected to encourage the change of fact into fiction, because of their propensity to see miracles in daily life and thus to tell wondrous tales in an ingenuous spirit that appealed to many people. The stories about St. Francis and St. Antony, about sermons preached to birds and fishes or about how the wolf of Gubbio was tamed, they all spoke to the imagination, while conveying a simple morality. Cavazzi's account of Queen Nzinga's career similarly was a moral tale, albeit a sensational one, powerfully stirring the minds of its readers with its unfamiliar setting and blood-curdling details. The moral which they could draw for themselves was that no matter how fiendish a life a human being may have led, he or she could be redeemed through a Christian death. The story was the more impressive as it was told of a powerful ruler in the exotically Dark Continent. It shocked because it showed the supposedly gentler sex in a different light. It was novel because the lady in question was a contemporary of the writer and his public. All of these components, with the exception of modernity, have retained their appeal. To be sure, apart from ecclesiastic historians, the black Queen apparently did not catch the attention of writers until the early years of the twentieth century when Black Africa became the last continent to be discovered artistically and literarily speaking, in the wake of its partition among the new industrial empires of Europe. However, at least one case of earlier literary treatment exists, a tragedy about "Nzinga, Queen of Angola," written by J. Nomsz, an obscure author, who published it in Amsterdam in 1791. Nomsz's spelling of the Queen's name betrays French or Italian sources. Perhaps a second exception must be made for a work of the nineteenth century, if it is true that a Christian African in Angola, Cordeiro da Matta, wrote of her in or about 1880, an assertion made by his biographer Mário António Fernandes de Oliveira.[30] At any rate, Matta's papers have been lost, and all that remains is an article of his about "The Real Queen Ginga," which he published in 1883 in order to correct the misrepresentations of a Portuguese writer. Matta's source were "memoirs which," he tells us, "are before our eyes."[31]

The fact that Queen Nzinga's reputation had remained firmly established since the seventeenth century can be inferred from proverbial allusions to her in Portuguese literature, such as the sneering remark made in sonnets of the poet Bocage when he dismissed a rival, the Brazilian Mulatto poet Caldas Barbosa, as an ape and a "grandson of Queen Nzinga," *neto da rainha Ginga*.[32] Caldas Barbosa (1738—1800) was the son of a female slave from Angola.

In Portuguese writings of a literary nature, Queen Nzinga reappeared about 1930, when interest in Africa rose sharply and intellectuals, particularly in Angola, began to pay closer attention to the traditional lore of the African peoples. Thus, an Angolan author of short stories and folklore studies, Óscar Ribas, announced in 1932 that he was working on a historical novel with the title "Rainha Jinga" (insisting on the "J"), "in which this potentate was to be presented with the aureole surrounding her in the minds of some Angolan peoples."[33] Ribas abandoned his project, however, for various practical reasons. A reference to her enduring prestige is found in the novel *O segredo da morta* (1934) by António Assis Júnior, one of whose main characters, Elmira, passes herself off as a descendant of the Queen in order to gain the confidence of a tribe in the interior, her white skin notwithstanding.

The first and so far the best literary treatment of the Queen appeared in the form of a short tale written by a talented Portuguese lawyer of monarchist convictions, Hipólito Raposo. Raposo composed several stories on African themes while spending the year 1922/23 in Luanda. The only one to deal with a historical figure was the story "A Rainha Ginga", which appeared in the volume *Ana a Kalunga [Os filhos do mar]* (Lisbon, 1926). Raposo achieved a marvel of condensation. He began his story by telling how the ambitious dream of Nzinga's brother, to extend the Ngola kingdom to the sea, was quashed by force of arms when the "Sons of the Sea", i. e. the Portuguese, defeated his army. "And then," Raposo wrote, "Gola Ginga Bandi's horn vibrated once again in the air, like a banner of surrender. The black soldiers are running through the *chana*, losing their weapons and howling, howling like driven-off dogs, they are vanishing into the shadowy woods." (p. 69) Raposo then retold Nzinga's embassy to Luanda, enriching it with two episodes, the killing of a monstrous snake by the fearless Princess and her dialogue with a favorite slave companion, who calmed her mistress when the latter perceived mysterious ancestral voices rising from the unfamiliar ocean, tinged blood-red by the setting sun. Her baptism as "Ana de Sousa" follows, being contrasted with atrocities in the train of renewed warfare on the Portuguese and their black allies. The tale ends abruptly with a rapid evocation of "the sad decline of her glory and grandeur." (p. 91) In a last scene, we behold her lying on her deathbed, while a personal letter from His Holiness the Pope is being read to her. "Now, for the last time, she opens her eyes to look at the pain-wracked Savior on the Cross, held up in the friar's hand. Tongue-tied, her mouth utters a murmur of recognition, coming deep from within her hollowed cheeks: 'Praise be to God.'" (p. 97)

That final *tableau* appears also in a book of J. M. Cerqueira d'Azevedo (1949), who fails to give it the solemn air of a historical painting or the musical quality that Raposo achieved by adding an accompaniment of African horns and Portuguese bugles, meant to symbolize the constant warfare. Azevedo's well-documented novel gave a much more gripping account of Queen Nzinga's dying hours, however. She, whose every gesture had been heeded as an absolute command by her subjects, is seen completely alone, abandoned in death by her entire court. Her ladies in waiting have fled, for fear they might be killed in order to serve the Queen as retinue on her journey to the spirit world; none believed that the orders she had given would be obeyed, namely that she should be given a plain burial, clad in the coarse brown cloth of the Capuchin Sisters of Carmel, without any of the bloody funeral rites of a pagan *tambi.*

Once she is dead, Azevedo has everyone reappear for the public farewell parade and the acclamation of her successor, her sister Barbara, to the beat of the big war drums. Once more, the novelist relates, the European missionaries were left alone with the corpse. "Observing from a distance the care with which the Capuchins wrapped Nzinga's remains in the shroud, the women who had been her court ladies approached with some trepidation; for when the body was to be lowered into the grave, a duty that they should have performed, they again took to their heels. Again Brother Gabriel and Brother Ignatius had to take over. They received the coffin at the bottom of the pit when the other friars released the ropes.

Consumed with curiosity, the ladies of the royal household again drew nearer to watch the burial. But as soon as the two friars climbed out a general panic broke out. The men also rushed out of the church, for fear that the cannibalistic rites might be reenacted, as tradition required. And thus, the monks ended up by shoveling the earth into the pit themselves.

Only then, when all these tasks had been completed, did the fear abate."[34] (p. 317)

Azevedo was a Portuguese official who had served in the customs administration. He had written books on economic subjects relating to Angola. His novel was published as a contribution to the celebrations of the tercentenary of the reconquest of Angola from the Dutch, a celebration, by the same token, of Queen Nzinga's defeat. Unlike most writers of historical fiction, Azevedo does not introduce invented characters or romantic subplots. Using his imagination merely to fill in details and giving vent to his own emotions now and then, he produced a straightforward biography that drew on many sources, but mainly on Cavazzi and Cadornega. As a result, his work frequently becomes monotonous and in its initial pages even repulsive, as it retails again and again the atrocities of war. Throughout, Azevedo made an effort to understand the Black Queen's mentality. But whereas he admired her spirit of adventure, as he perceived it, and the courage that were to make her immortal (p. 288), he admitted defeat when trying to fathom her "incomprehensible personality." (p. 261) Nor could he quite accept as genuine her two conversions to Christianity. (Cf. p. 250 f. and 309)

It is a pity that Queen Nzinga's character and career did not yet tempt the pen of a great Portuguese writer, one who would be more knowledgeable than Raposo or Azevedo concerning the customs, beliefs, history and organization of Bantu peoples. At least two fine story writers were attracted by her, but neither gave her the full treatment she deserves: Fernando de Castro Soromenho and Aquilino Ribeiro.

Castro Soromenho was well equipped to understand her, having studied another Angolan tribe, the Lundas, in the northeastern backlands and having shown that he could present black folk credibly in his Angolan tales and novels. Yet he produced merely a brief sketch of her life, and that only towards the end of his career when life in exile and a liver ailment had broken his health. Aquilino Ribeiro, on the other hand, was not personally acquainted with any part of Africa. But he had a flair for unusual character, especially among people who, like those of his native mountains, live close to the soil. He wrote about the Queen incidentally at least. She appears in his story about a Portuguese who served as a simple private in an expeditionary force that had been sent to Angola. Its title is "Jeremelo, expedicionário daquém e dalém-África," and it dates from 1950.[35] This Jeremelo is presented as a village character who had returned destitute from Africa after serving there, as destitute as he had been before his departure for the great adventure. However, he brought back a wealth of extraordinary stories of his own feats, in which he fancied himself a contemporary of Dom Afonso, King of the Congo, and of Queen Nzinga, in whose bed he claimed to have slept.

Aquilino Ribeiro described "Ana Zinga" as an Amazon. "Her agility," according to him, "was such that she ran and leaped, as fast as an arrow or a greyhound jumping over hurdles or a swimmer cutting through the waves." (p. 34) He also saw her as the epitome of ferocity and lust, precisely like the man-hating Berber Queen, ruling a mysterious region in the heart of the Sahara desert, whom the French novelist Pierre Bénoit had made the heroine of his popular L'Atlantide. Aquilino felt that Queen Nzinga must have been the model of Bénoit's white Queen, rather than the Empress Catherine of Russia. Oddly enough, the Portuguese writer did not draw his information about Queen Nzinga from an Italian or a Portuguese source but from the French journal Annales Africaines. He added a personal twist to her story which showed how much he modeled himself on the mocker Anatole France. Having told the anecdote of the straw that persuaded her to return to the Christian faith, according to the missionaries, he claimed that a devilish succubus abandoned her body moments before her pious death, "to roam through all of Africa, raving and famished (as a good father whispered into my ear). Sometimes this demon has the crazy notion to enter the body of a white man [such as Jeremelo] during the sultry hours when the palmtrees waft voluptuousness over the land and malignant, spiteful genie rise from the shaded, cool mire of lagoons and rivers, floating towards the sleepy native villages." (p. 352) Being a realist after all, Aquilino finally feels compelled to explain his man Jeremelo's fancies: Jeremelo, it turns out, had learned about Dom Afonso and Queen Nzinga from one of the cheap little paperbacks he used to peddle in the Angolan countryside for a distributor in Luanda. (p. 361)

One should think that the fierce Queen's love of her only son, her conversion, her long struggles and wanderings, or her lonely death had inspired poetry, perhaps even an epic. In reality, not much Portuguese verse has been composed in her honor. A minor writer, Eduardo Leiria Dias, wrote a short poem with the title *Fala da Rainha Ginga*, "Queen Ginga's Speech," which won him a prize in 1960. In a patronizing manner, he lauds her for becoming a Christian.[36] Little more than a gesture was the feeble attempt made by Eduardo Moreira in his *Bantuânia* (Lisbon, 1939), to sing her in epic verse with other great Bantu leaders, such as Shaka, Kama, and Apollo. But Moreira was the first to recognize that his bits and pieces did not add up to the epic of the Bantu nation he dreamed of. His merit lies in having conceived the idea so early, although he felt certain that Portuguese readers would not care to read the praises of a black Bantu queen:

> uma Mulher de génio alto,
> de nobre porte e de feroz feitio,
> que não deixou as pistas no basalto
> mas deixou-as na mente do gentio.

(a Woman of great genius, of noble bearing and ferocious temper, who left no imprint in basalt but in the native mind.)[37]

More important is the reference made to her by Geraldo Bessa Victor, a black Angolan writer, some years later (1957) in a poem with the title *Momento místico* ("Mystical Moment")[38]:

Ando a conversar com os ventos	(I walk conversing with the winds
para que os ventos me contem, noite	that they might tell me, night and
e dia,	day,
histórias de Quinjango e da Rainha	tales of Quinjango, of Queen Zinga.
Ginga.	
. . .	
E converso com montes e nuvens —	And I converse with peaks and clouds
vultos vivos	—the living figures
de grandes Negros mortos, tão livres,	of our great black dead who never
não cativos.	would be slaves.
(Aiué, Quinjango, aiué!)	(Alas, alas, Quinjango!)
E na forma das nuvens e montes o	And in the shape of clouds and peaks,
meu verso	my verse
tocado pela lenda e pela fé,	is thrilled by legend and by faith
encontra a sua imagem e seu berço.	and finds its image and its root.)

(pp. 77—78)

The identification of the land with its dead warrior heroes arose from the poet's search for roots. The Queen is put in the company of his own ancestor, a *Mestiço* general, son of an expatriate Italian officer and an Angolan woman, who became a legendary figure during the colonial campaigns against the tribes, because of his bravery and his skill as a swordsman, earning for him the nickname Quinjango, "the Sword."

Queen Nzinga's shadow hovers over another of Víctor's poems, *Pedras Negras de Pungo Andongo*, inspired by the famous Black Rocks in the Ndongo mountains:

Conta-me o teu romance, ó tu que
          tens gravados
no corpo, como estranha tatuagem,
os pés da Rainha Ginga!
Que ser tu eras dantes? Que ser vinga
ou se apaga na tua condição?

(Tell me your romance, you that
          guard incised
the imprints of Queen Ginga's feet
like awesome scars on your dark body.
What living soul had you once been?
Thriving or fading in your stony
          state?) (p. 46)

Manuel Bandeira, the Brazilian poet, observed in the preface to Victor's volume that the Angolan had "gathered the best inspiration from the most authentic voices of Africa," the ones that spoke of Queen Nzinga at the Black Rocks. The Queen lives on in the legend of her huge footprints in the Rocks of Pungo Andongo, as she does at the site of her grave on the Kwango River, or in place names, such as Kifuangondo, on the Bengo River, north of Luanda, where she is said to have dropped a copper coin[39], or Mulemba ua-xa-Ngola, six km northeast of Luanda, named after the *mulemba* tree she is reported to have planted there in memory of her passage to Luanda when she went to visit the Portuguese Governor in 1622.[40]

Likewise, her name is preserved, if ever so vaguely, among the descendants of her people that now live in Brazil, whenever they perform the mock fights between Angolans and Congolese that are part of the *congada* dance.

During the years of the guerilla wars, Portuguese poets and novelists in Africa seemed reluctant to mention her name. For in her latest reincarnation, she embodies the spirit of independence among the African nationalists in Angola. Her significance as a defender of Angolan liberty was perceived years ago by the Brazilian folklorist Câmara Cascudo.[41] A modern American historian, John Marcum, pointed it out anew: "And though she and Matamba eventually came to terms with and traded with the Portuguese, she is eulogized by contemporary Angolan nationalists as a legendary heroine, who led her people in thirty years of warfare against 'Portuguese aggressors'."[42] In the same vein, the Portuguese-Angolan novelist Castro Soromenho called her a symbol: "For her own people and today, three hundred years later, for all the peoples of Angola, she is still alive, because she has become a symbol."[43]

Soromenho's prose merely echoed the verses of one of the Angolan nationalist leaders as he envisioned his return to his homeland after final victory would have been won:

Quando eu voltei
qualquer coisa gigantesca se movia
         na terra

. . .

Os braços dos homens
a coragem dos soldados
os suspiros dos poetas
tudo todos tentavam erguer bem alto

acima da lembrança dos Heróis
Ngola Kiluanji

(When I returned
something gigantic stirred in the land

. . .

The people's brawn
the soldiers' courage
the poets' sighs
all of it all of them tried to raise as
         high as they could
above the memory of the Heroes
Ngola-Kiluanji

Rainha Jinga
todos tentavam erguer bem alto
a bandeira da independência.[44]

Queen Nzinga
all tried to raise as high as they could
the banner of independence.)

The name "Ginga" carries nationalist meaning when it is borne by the protagonist's wife in M. Santos Lima's novel *As sementes da liberdade [Seeds of Liberty]* (Rio de Janeiro, 1965). For her sake he returns to till the soil. Their son is to carry on the struggle for the liberty of Angola which he, the father, was unable to undertake.

Another Angolan nationalist, Manuel Pedro Pacavira, wrote an evocative, patriotic novel with the Queen's name as its title: *Nzinga Mbandi*. It was published about the time when Angola won its independence in 1975, but it had been in the making during the war of liberation, while the author was still confined to the Portuguese concentration camp for political prisoners at Tarrafal in the Cape Verde Islands. He weaves an idealized tapestry of Nzinga's life and personality from the threads of her appearances in various of the scenes that make up the novel. The framework is vast and historical, spanning the long conflict between the Portuguese intruders and *os da Pátria*, the native patriots, from the Portuguese captain Diogo Cão's friendly reception by the Congolese in the XVth century on down to the resistance of the Ovimbundu people of Nano, which was not broken until the 1920s. Nzinga Mbandi emerges as the great, shadowy leader of national resistance in a war like the one just concluded. But Pacavira was unprepared or unwilling to narrate her military campaigns or her reign with all the turns they took. Instead of conveying her historically documented complex character, he portrays her most winningly as a representative of her tribe, in sketches of African manners that show her at various stages of life: as a small child with her grandfather the old King, as a little girl listening to traditional stories being told of an evening, as an adolescent visiting the great fair at Luango, as a young woman taking part in a dance at a neighboring court, as her brother's envoy in Luanda, as a queen in her own right, visiting another queen in the Lunda country to the east . . . They, too, are like stories that might be told by the old men who keep the traditions alive. Indeed, the style of the novel is that of a man talking in the present about the history of his country, Angola, before an audience, adding comments and exclamations of his own as he proceeds. "Factos há," he begins, "que nos levam a pensar que ela cresceu bela, carinha bonita, alegre, simpática, sendo o seu defeito: virar bicha-fera-ferida, caso que lhe violassem um direito. Tanto é que uma formidável história ela nos deixou, uma história que mete respeito, o motivo que me traz a conversar aqui com vocês. Mas comecemos pelos tempos dos seus passados." (Certain facts lead us to believe that she grew up to be beautiful, with a cute little face, a cheerful disposition, a popular girl, her one fault being that she would become as ferocious as a wounded wild animal if someone denied her a right. And so she has left us a terrific story, a story that inspires awe and is the reason that has brought me here to converse with you. But let's begin with her grandparents' times.) And then the story starts, like an idyll, to be suddenly troubled: One fine April day, at the mouth of the Zaire . . .

Pacavira's book is like a collection of notes and sketches that may well become the great novel about the Queen in some future version. The setting is there, ready for a royal drama to unfold. He does his theme justice in one important respect: for the first time in a prose work, Nzinga is seen through African eyes, from within the Angolan society to which she belonged.[45]

IV. Conclusion: From Fact to Fiction

Ana de Sousa or Queen Nzinga of Matamba has become a legendary figure as one of the great military leaders, now pressed into the service of the cause of national unity and socialistic organization that bears little resemblance to the autocratic, tribal society for whose survival she fought. The process of making a legend out of this historical personage began more than three hundred years ago, as an homage to her long resistance and her Christian death. Those writers who have had access to the half-forgotten historical literature about her continue to endow her with the baffling, many-sided personality that history records: a woman who was wilful, majestic, vain, strong, nimble, sensual, tyrannical, cruel, bloodthirsty, loving as a sister and a mother, unforgiving, witty, given to pomp, persistent, healty—in short, a very complex human being that is worth remembering. Others, poets especially, and the descendants of her own people in Angola, the Jingas of today, exalt her purely as the strong-willed leader of the nation, perhaps identifying her with other chieftains of past ages, as she herself had done when she took Queen Temba-Ndumba as her model.

To the historian, the folklorist or the literary scholar, she joins a gallery of historic figures that have been sung and told about in the epics of many African countries: the gluttonous, "stiff-legged" Sundiata, who overcame his defects to build the empire of Mali in the thirteenth century; freeborn and frugal Silâmaka ("The Saber") and his companion in arms the brave serf Poullôri, a pair as inseparable as Roland and Oliver, who led a finally victorious, thirty-year-long rebellion of the Peul people against their Bambara overlords in the same country of Mali during the latter half of the eighteenth century; Matope, the "Monomotapa" (Mwana-Mutapa), who in the fifteenth century built an empire in the uplands of the Zambezi valley, whose gold mines fatally attracted the Portuguese; the ruthless Shaka, who united the Zulus of southern Africa in the beginning of the nineteenth century; and the tragic Patrice Lumumba, who in our own times led the Bantu peoples of the Congo to independence.

None of these leaders was quite like Queen Nzinga. None was a woman. Only Cleopatra, the Queen of Egypt, faintly resembles her because of her power over men and her fruitless attempt to save her country and her family from a foreign invader.

Doubtless, more poems, prose fiction or biography will be written about the Black Amazon of Angola, especially if, as is likely, further lore about her will come to light in what was once her kingdom of Matamba.

Among the proverbial riddles that have been collected by Óscar Ribas among the Kimbundu-speaking population of present-day Luanda, one finds a saying which recalls Queen Nzinga and the human chair she refused to take back. Nzinga could have quoted it to the Portuguese Governor whom she confronted. Or did it originate with her? It runs thus:

Question. The bird is a bird of the forest;
The thicket is a thicked of the forest?
Answer. Have you ever seen a bird that carried the thicket away?
Explanatory footnote (by Ribas): After paying a visit, no visitor carries his seat away with him.[46]

Notes

1 Rubén Darío, "Poema del otoño", probably written in 1909, published in 1910. Text reproduced from *Poesías completas*, ed. A. Méndez Plancarte. 9th ed., Madrid, Aguilar, 1961, p. 875.
2 The missionary was Antonio [Laudate] da Gaëta, on whose diary Francesco Maria Gioia da Napoli based his book *La meravigliosa conversione... della regina Singa...*, Naples, 1669; the Portuguese *conquistador* António de Oliveira de Cadornega *(História geral das guerras angolanas*, ms. of 1684); the later Portuguesa memorialist J. C. Feo Cardoso de Castello-Branco e Torres *(Memórias...*, Paris, 1825); the modern historians J. Duffy *Portugal in Africa*, Baltimore, 1963) and Charles R. Boxer *(Salvador de Sá...*, London, 1952); the British admirer of Portuguese colonization F. C. Egerton *(Angola in Perspective*, London, 1957) and the British partisan of the African independence movements Basil Davidson *(The African Slave Trade...*, Boston, 1961); the exiled Portuguese politician Henrique Galvão *(Outras terras, outras gentes*, vol. I, Lisbon, n. d. [1941 or 42]); and Maria Archer, a Portuguese writer who had lived in Angola *(Brasil, fronteira da Africa*, São Paulo, 1963).
3 Luís da Câmara Cascudo, *Made in Africa*, Rio de Janeiro, 1965, p. 30. The legitimacy of her queenship has been seriously questioned by historian Joseph C. Miller. Cf. Note 14.
4 Ibidem, p. 31.
5 Ibidem, p. 32.
6 H. Galvão, *Outras terras, outras gentes*, vol. I, Lisbon, n. d., p. 259.
7 Graciano Maria de Leguzzano, in his Portuguese translation and edition of Cavazzi de Montecuccolo's history. *Descrição histórica dos três reinos do Congo, Matamba e Angola*, Lisbon, 1965, vol. II, p. 171, n. 75.
8 Antonio de Gaëta, *La meravigliosa conversione...*, Naples, 1669, p. 274.
9 Cavazzi de Montecuccolo, op. cit., vol. II, p. 64.
10 Ibidem, vol. II, p. 71.
11 Ibidem, vol. II, pp. 424—28, in an excellent summary of the Queen's life.
12 David Birmingham, *The Portuguese Conquest of Angola*, London, 1965.
13 E. G. Ravenstein, in his notes to *The Strange Adventures of Andrew Battell of Leigh in Angola and the Adjoining Regions*, London, 1901.

14 Joseph C. Miller, an American specialist in Angolan history, casts doubt on Nzinga's having represented her half-brother, the ruler of Ndongo, as she claimed in Luanda. He sees her rise to power as the result of a palace guard coup, for which she cleverly secured Portuguese support. See his "Nzinga of Matamba in a New Perspective", *Journal of African History*, London & New York, vol. XVI, no. 2 (1975), pp. 206—08.

15 "O triunfo da Fé em Matamba, infelizmente, acabava com a morte de Jinga." Note by Leguzzano in Cavazzi de Montecuccolo, op. cit., Lisbon, 1965, vol. II, p. 428. Leguzzano adds that her burial site is well known: "O seu sepulcro está ainda conservado e guardado, perto de aldeia Ngulu-a'Ngola, do posto administrativo de Marimba, numa clareira rectangular, no seio da mata. Clareira e sepulcro são ainda chamados com a palavra portuguesa "igreja", talvez por indicarem o sítio da Igreja de Santa Ana, em que Jinga foi sepultada." ("Her grave is still maintained and guarded near the village of Ngulu-a'Ngola in the Marimba district. It is found in a rectangular clearing in the midst of the woods. Clearing and grave are still called *igreja,* the Portuguese word for church, perhaps because they indicate the location of St. Anne where Jinga had been buried.")

16 Ibidem, vol. II, p. 65.

17 Ibidem, vol. II, p. 75.

18 Ibidem, vol. II, p. 75.

19 Ibidem, vol. II, p. 72.

20 Ibidem, vol. II, p. 351: "Estou tão queixosa dos governadores passados, que sempre me prometérão entregarem minha Irmãa, pela qual tenho dado enfinitas peças e feito milhares de banzos e nunca ma entregaram mas antes movíão logo guerras, com que me inquietárão e fizérão sempre andar feita jaga, usando tiranias, como he não deixar criar creanças, por ser estilo de quilombo, e outras cerimonias e todas deixarei e dou a V. Sa. minha real palavra, tanto que tiver religiosos, que me deem bom exemplo a meus grandes, pera que os ensinem a viver na Santa Fé Catholica, [...] tratarei logo de deixar parir e criar as mulheres seus filhos, cousa que até agora não consenty por ser estilo de quilombo, que anda em campo, o que não haverá, havendo paz firme e perpetua, e em poucos anos se tornarão minhas terras a povoar como dantes, por que até agora me não sirvo senão com gente de outras provincias e nações que tenho conquistado, e me obedecem como sua senhora natural com muito amor e outros por temor."

21 Ibidem, vol. II, p. 74.

22 Ibidem, vol. II, p. 72.

23 Cavazzi de Montecuccolo was the first to tell about the human chair episode. Neither Father Antonio de Gaëta nor Cadornega mentioned it.

24 Ibidem, vol. I, pp. 67 and 68.

25 Luís da Câmara Cascudo, *Made in Africa,* pp. 27 and 28.

26 Cavazzi de Montecuccolo, op. cit., vol. II, pp. 121—22.

27 Ibidem, vol. II, p. 71.

28 Ibidem, vol. II, p. 100.

29 The quotation is taken from Antonio de Gaëta, op. cit., p. 212.

30 Mário António Fernandes de Oliveira, *A sociedade angolana do século XIX e um seu escritor,* Luanda, 1961, p. 120, n. 21.

31 The "memoirs" alluded to by Matta were probably those of Castello-Branco e Torres.

32 One of Bocage's sonnets describes a session of the *Nova Arcádia* group in Lisbon and begins as follows: Preside o neto da rainha Ginga / Á corja vil, aduladora, insana. ("Queen Ginga's grandson presides / Over the vile, fawning, raving pack"). Another sonnet describes the poetaster Caldas: Eis entre os Lusos o animal sem rabo / Prole se aclama da rainha Ginga; (Behold the tail—less beast among the Sons of Lusus / Who claims descent from Queen Ginga") Quoted from *Sonetos*, ed. Hernâni Cidade, Lisbon, [1960], pp. 134 and 139.

33 Oscar Ribas, *Ecos da minha terra*, Luanda, 1932, p. 174. In reply to my inquiry, Sr. Ribas wrote as follows in a letter dated Luanda, September 10, 1973: "Quando tencionava escrever o romance *Rainha Jinga*, projectava deslocar—me ao interior, a fim de recolher os elementos orais que ainda perduram. Para o efeito, comprei um gravador com todos os acessórios para uma segura pesquisa de campo. Cheguei até a ter alojamentos oferecidos. Por razões várias, não me foi possível concretizar tal ideia." ("When I intended to write the novel *Queen Jinga*, I got ready to journey into the interior, in order to collect the oral lore that still remains. For this purpose I bought a tape recorder with all the accessories for reliable fieldwork. I even had gotten to the point where lodgings had been offered to me. Various reasons prevented me from carrying out my idea.")

34 The quotations are from J. M. Cerqueira d'Azevedo, *Jinga, Rainha de Matamba*, Braga, 1949.

35 The story is to be found in Aquilino Ribeiro, *Portugueses das sete partidas*, Lisbon, [1951].

36 Eduardo Leiria Dias' poem was published in *Antologia poética IV*, Benguela, 1971, p. 38.

37 Eduardo Moreira, *Bantuânia. Fragmentos da epopeia de Africa*, Lisbon, 1939, p. 17. "Traces in basalt" alludes to the legend of the Queen's footprints in the Black Rocks of Pungo Andongo.

38 In Geraldo Bessa Victor, *Cubata abandonada*, Lisbon, 1958.

39 The reference to Kifuangondo occurs in H. Chatelain, *Contos populares de Angola*, new ed., Lisbon, 1964, p. 525.

40 Mentioned by Mário de Andrade in his *Antologia temática de poesia africana*, vol. I, Lisbon, 1975, p. 262.

41 See Luís da Câmara Cascudo, *Dicionário de folclore brasileiro*, 2d ed., vol. I, Rio de Janeiro, 1962, p. 230.

42 John Marcum, *The Angolan Revolution*, vol. I, Cambridge, Mass., 1969, pp. 14—15.

43 Castro Soromenho in *Présence Africaine*, Paris, English ed., no. 42/43 (1964), p. 49.

44 Agostinho Neto, "O içar da bandeira", in Mário de Andrade, *Antologia temática de poesia africana*, vol. I, Lisbon, 1975, pp. 254 and 255.

45 Manuel Pedro Pacavira, *Nzinga Mbandi*, n. p., Actualidade Editora, n. d. (Luanda, 1975?). 208 pp. The passage occurs on p. 11, almost at the very beginning of the novel.

46 Oscar Ribas, *Missosso: Literatura tradicional angolana*, vol. III, Luanda, 1964, p. 167, riddle 58.

Appendix

A Short Bibliography on Queen Nzinga of Matamba (Angola) in Chronological Order
1660 Gaëta, Antonio da.

La meravigliosa conversione alla santa fede di Cristo della regina Singa e del suo regno di Matamba ... descritta con istorico stile dal P. F. Francesco Maria Gioia da Napoli ..., Napoli: G. Passaro, 1669. 465 p.
(Father Gaëta, born Emilio Laudate, seems to have written three accounts of how he converted Queen Nzinga. The third, probably written in 1660, was brought to Europe by Father Crisostomo de Genova and edited by Gioia as *La meravigliosa conversione* ...).

1667   or earlier Cavazzi da Montecuccolo, Giovanni Antonio.
Istorica descrizione de tre' regni Congo, Matamba, et Angola situati nell' Etiopia inferiore occidentale e delle missioni apostoliche esercitatevi da religiosi capuccini. Ed. Fortunato Alamandini. Bologna: G. Monti, 1687, xiv, 933 p.
Another ed., Milano, 1690. xvi, 786 p.
Portuguese translation and ed.: *Descrição histórica dos três reinos do Congo, Matamba e Angola*, trans., notes and indices by Father Graciano Maria de Leguzzano. Lisboa: Junta de Investigação do Ultramar, 1965. 2 vols.
(Galotto Cavazzi who adopted the name G. A. da Montecuccolo as a friar was born in Montecuccolo in 1621 and served as a missionary in Angola from 1654 to 1667. Like Father Gaëta, he knew Queen Nzinga personally, assisting her when she died.)
French adaptation: *Relation historique de l'Ethiopie occidentale*, trans. with additions and revisions by Jean Baptiste Labat. Paris, 1732. 5 vols.

1684   Cadornega, António de Oliveira de.
História geral das guerras angolanas, 1680. Ed. José Matias Delgado and M. Alves da Cunha. Lisboa: Agência-Geral das Colónias, 1940—42. 3 vols.
New ed.: Lisboa: Agência Geral do Ultramar, 1972. 3 vols.
(Cadornega wrote his work in Luanda between 1681 and 1684. After many years of army service in Angola he became a judge. The work contains the text of a letter Queen Nzinga wrote to him.)

1732   Labat.
See Cavazzi.

1749   Anon.
Noticia memoravel da vida, e acçoens da Rainha Ginga Amena Natural do Reyno de Angola. Lisboa: D. Gonsalves, 1749. 8 p.

1769   Castilhon, Jean Louis.
Zingha, Reine d'Angola. Histoire africaine ... Paris, 1769. 2 vols.
2d ed.: Paris, 1770.

1791   Nomsz, J.
"Zingha, Koningin van Angola, Treurspel", in *De Nederlandsche dichtkundige schouwburg*, part III. Amsterdam, 1791.

1840   Anon.
"Ana Ginga, rainha de Matamba", in *O Panorama* (Lisboa), first series, vol. IV (1840), pp. 278—80, 298—300.

1882   Matta, Joaquim Dias Cordeiro da.
"A verdadeira Rainha Ginga (Ginga N'Bandi ou Ginga Amena, D. Anna de Souza)", in *Novo Almanach de Lembranças Luso—Brazileiro para 1883.* Lisboa, 1882, pp. 229—32. (The Angolan philologist rectifies in his article a story by A. X. da Silva Pereira. M. A. Fernandes de Oliveira believes that Matta wrote the life of Queen Nzinga about 1880 but that his manuscript was lost (*A sociedade angolana* ..., Luanda, 1961, p. 120, n. 21).

1922/23 Raposo, Hipólito.
"A Rainha Ginga", in *Ana a Kalunga (Os filhos do mar)*. Lisboa: Ottosgráfica, 1926. Pp. 59—97. (Raposo wrote the story probably while in Luanda in 1922/23.)

1924 Cultrera, Samuele.
La conversione della regina Singa. Parma, 1924.

1932 Ribas, Oscar.
"Rainha Jinga." (Abandoned project of a historical novel.)

1949 Azevedo, J. M. Cerqueira d'.
Jinga, rainha de Matamba. Braga: Oficinas Gráficas Augusto Costa & Companhia, 1949. 324 p. (Historical novel.)
Dias, Gastão de Sousa.
A Rainha Jinga. Lisboa: Agência Geral do Ultramar, 1949.

1950 Ribeiro, Aquilino.

1955 Videira, A. G.
"Jeremelo, expedicionário daquém e dalém-África," in *Portugueses das sete partidas*. Lisboa: Bertrand, n. d. [1951], pp. 335—62. (The story is dated Lisbon, 1950.)
"Pedras Negras", in *10 bilhetes postais*, [Lisbon], 1955, pp. 71—84. (Poetic prose evocation of Queen Nzinga's presence at Pungo Andongo.)

1957 Cuvelier, J.
Koningin Nzinga von Matamba. Met medewerking van Jozef Boon. Brugge-Bussum: Desclée, DeBrouwer, 1957. (Dramatic biography written by the former Apostolic Vicar of Matadi.)
Víctor, Geraldo Bessa.
"Momento místico" and "Pedras Negras de Pungo Andongo", two poems in *Cubata abandonada*. Braga: Editora Pax, 1958. 94 p. 2d ed.: Braga: Editora Pax, 1966. Pp. 77—78 and 46 respectively. (The ms. received a prize in 1957.)

1960 Dias, Eduardo Leiria.
"Fala da Reinha Ginga", in *Antologia Poética,* vol. IV. Benguela: Edições Convivium, 1971. p. 38.
(The poem received a prize in 1960.)

1961 Neto, António Agostinho.
"O içar da bandeira", in *Poemas*. Lisboa: Casa dos Estudantes do Império, 1961.
Also in Mário de Andrade, ed., *Literatura africana de expressão portuguesa,* vol. I. *Poesia*. Antologia temática. 2d ed. Algiers: December 1967. Pp. 272—274.

1962 Soromenho, Fernando de Castro.
"Portrait of Queen Jinga", in *Présence Africaine* (Paris), English ed., vol. XIV/XV, no. 42/43 (1962), pp. 44—50.
(Biographical sketch.)

1964 Soromenho, Fernando de Castro.
"Ginga, Reine des N'Golas", in *Révolution* (Paris), no. 12, October—November 1964.
(Biographical sketch.)

1965 Cascudo, Luís da Câmara.
"A rainha Jinga no Brasil", in *Made in Africa*. Pesquisas e notas. Rio de Janeiro: Editôra Civilização Brasileira, 1965. Pp. 25—32.
(Notes on folklore based partly on a field trip to Angola. See also the article on "Congadas, congados, congos" in Cascudo's *Dicionário do folclore brasileiro,* vol. I., 2d ed., Rio de Janeiro: Instituto Nacional do Livro, 1962, with its reference to a festival of the *Rei Congo* and

the *Rainha Xinga* witnessed by Von Martius in June 1818 at Tijuco, now known as Diamantina, in Minas Gerais. The identification of the Queen of the Brazilian pageants with Queen Nzinga of Matamba was first made by Mário de Andrade, the Brazilian musicologist and poet, in his article "Danças dramáticas" of 1934. In a note destined for a revised version, he questioned the identification since he had relied on only one version of the *Congo* found in Paraíba and possibly due to a literate adapter. Cf. his *Danças dramáticas do Brasil*, ed. O. Alvarenga. 3 vols. São Paulo: Martins, 1959, especially vol. I, p. 71, and vol. II, pp. 45—48.)

1975 (?) Pacavira, Manuel Pedro.
Nzinga Mbandi. [Luanda?], Editora Actualidade, n. d. 208 pp. (Novel written during the author's stay in the Tarrafal concentration camp on the Cape Verde Islands, before his release in 1974. Dedicated by him to the soldiers of the *Movimento para a Libertação de Angola* [MPLA].)

Writer, Reader and Character
in
African Language Literature
– Towards a new Definition –

Daniel P. Kunene

In order to understand fully the problem discussed in this paper, we must constantly bear in mind the relationships that are found in oral narrative performance as well as in heroic poetic declamations. For it seems to me that some of the characteristic features of written African literature have a diachronic relationship to characteristic features of oral narrative and heroic poetry.

As far as written literature is concerned, we shall attempt to make our discussion more meaningful and concrete by illustrating our arguments exclusively from the works of one author. For several reasons the choice falls on Thomas Mofolo, the Mosotho author best known for his historical novel *Chaka*. Firstly Mofolo, the first Mosotho novelist, was for a long time the best exponent of the Sesotho language, and as such he eterted a strong and lasting influence on some of his contemporaries, and on many of the following generations of Sesotho writers. Therefore, and secondly, a detailed study of his works lays a good foundation for the evaluation of Sesotho literature as a whole if not, indeed, all of southern Bantu language literature. Thirdly, I have made an in-depth study of Mofolo's works over the years, and can therefore best illustrate my arguments from them.

Thomas Mofolo was born in 1876, forty-three years after the first missionaries came to Lesotho, Mofolo's country of birth, in 1833. In these forty-three years, the missionaries had achieved quite a degree of success in converting the Basotho to Christianity. Mofolo's parents were themselves Christian converts. The schools through which Mofolo learned to read and write and to define his relationship with his fellowmen and with the cosmos, were established and controlled by the missionaries with the specific aim that they be used as aids to facilitate and accelerate the process of Christianization. Christianity, therefore, became a powerful factor in Mofolo's life, in his view of the world, and in his judgement of his fellowmen. And a severe judge he was.

At the same time, the Basotho continued to live according to their traditions which stood strong against the vicious onslaughts of the new religion and its new set of values. Mofolo was thus simultaneously immersed in a virile Sesotho culture marked by an uninhibited relationship of people, both to themselves as physical and spiritual beings with bodies and souls that needed to be revealed and admired and given expression, rather than hidden in some dark recesses of a guilty consciousness, and with those around them who constituted their social environment and provided them not only with companionship, but also with solace and comfort when the need arose.

Mofolo's admonitions to his characters are therefore seen to be often moti-vated by a combination of the traditional and the new, the Sesotho and the Christian, sometimes even while he himself consciously thinks that he is com-mitting himself to a definite choice.

In our illustrations the following abbreviated notations are used: M. for Mofolo's original work which is then designated by its own abbreviation: *Mo.* for *Moeti oa Bochabela,* Pi. for *Pitseng,* and *Ch.* for *Chaka.* M./D. stands for Dutton's translation of *Chaka,* and M./A. for Ashton's translation of *Moeti oa Bochabela.* In all the illustrations the translations are my own, and the page numbers refer to the editions or reprints which I have used, namely: *Moeti oa Bochabela,* Morija, repr. 1957, ed. 1951; *Pitseng,* Morija, ed. 1951; and *Chaka,* Morija, ed. 1957.

As a participant in the oral literature of the Basotho, Mofolo carried on a tradition that, in its folk narratives, sought to maintain harmony in society. This harmony could only be achieved and sustained through the observance of the social mores that then applied. In that all the Basotho of premissionary times subscribed to these ideals, the social function of art was that of integra-tion. The people's behaviour in all its varied aspects, was seen by the artist as being polarized around the social ideal. On the one hand there was the ma-jority of the people who not only subscribed to this ideal, but also strove to keep it alive and meaningful. These were the heroes of the narratives. There were, on the other hand, also the few who, while subscribing to the ideal, none-the-less fell victim to various temptations that brought them into direct con-frontation with their society. These were the villains of the narratives, social misfits who were either rehabilitated or banished or destroyed. The oral artist synthesized all these elements insociety and told a narrative in which they all contributed to the total didactic purpose of the story. Being himself a member of the society, the artist took sides. He liked those characters who were con-stant and steadfast in maintaining the integrity of the social ideal, and disliked those whose antisocial actions placed this ideal in jeopardy.

Christianity introduced a new and very powerful elements into the moral fabric of Basotho society. It created new loyalties, destroying some of the old ones in the process. It brought into being new factions. The verbal artist of this time had a much more difficult task trying to sort out things so that his message could make some sense to his audience. We are talking, in specific terms, about the writer who, in the process of acquiring literacy, was placed, willy-nilly, in the forefront of the movement for change. Circumstances turned him into the most vocal and vehement advocate of the new order. Basically he still considered himself the keeper of the conscience of society, of the people who constituted his audience. This time, however, heroes and villains found new definitions, and many who were the heroes of the old Basotho society became villains solely for their refusal to accept the new dispensation. In the eyes of the writer, much of the old beliefs and customs that the old narratives had sought to hold together were now to be dismantled. Therefore there was need to destroy the old edifice before building the new one. Indeed the new one could only be built on the ground left vacant by the old one. The writer's loyalty was therefore largely alienated from his traditional society and allied to the forces of change, specifically to the missionaries. Again we see how the verbal artist takes sides. He likes those of his characters who accept the new ethical code that he now advocates, and dislikes those who don't.

We can therefore identify the didacticism of the traditional artist as being integrative, and that of the writer of Christian times as being disintegrative.

For our purpose at this point the important consequence of all this is that the writer is involved with his characters as well as the events and conflicts in his story. We see certain very important features of his style arising directly from this involvement.

Now, to come specifically to Mofolo, we have first of all to see how he fits into into the picture described above. Basing our judgement solely on his three published novels, we can say that in *Moeti oa Bochabela* he displays the greatest degree of conscious rejection of Sesotho traditional values. The missionaries of the Paris Evangelical Missionary Society welcomed his manuscript with overflowing enthusiasm not, as it turned out four or five years later when they evaluated *Chaka*, primarily because of its literary merit—indeed they referred to it condescendingly as "a kind of little masterpiece"—but because of its Bunyanesque message of escape from a corrupt society and the search for perfection, a message calculated to advance the cause of Christianity.

In *Pitseng* Mofolo's earlier enthusiasm for the ways of the Whites begins to be tempered by an advocacy of caution. The mystique of the white man's superiority in all things has begun to be replaced by the discovery that he (the white man) is not so perfect or infallible after all, but is sometimes wrong, at times indeed alarmingly so, as in the case of his attitude to love, courtship and marriage.

Mofolo shows much empathy with the Zulu diviner, the Isanusi who, next to Chaka, is the most central figure in *Chaka*, Mofolo's third published novel. This despite the fact that the Isanusi is a traditional Zulu medical doctor-cum-spiritualist. Mofolo is neither apologetic nor condescending as he demonstrates the powers of the Isanusi.

Despite surface indications of alienation in his first two novels, there is no doubt that Mofolo retains a strong, if unconscious, loyalty to Sesotho culture and traditions as well as its definitions of heroism. There is an irrepressible enthusiasm about things Sesotho or, indeed, things African, which surfaces at moments of emotional excitement. Thus we see how, even after declaring over and over that Chaka has lost his claim to humanity and has become totally a beast, especially after his murder of Noliwe, Mofolo still admires certan qualities in him which appeal to his (Mofolo's) sense of manhood, of virility and masculinity. So, towards the end when Chaka is weakened by his evil dreams and frightening nightmares, Mofolo still bubbles over with pure admiration as he says:

> Ya ema tau ya hlakax la ha Zulu, sebata see se nang tshabo, empa ya ema e feletswe ke matla, e sitwa le ho tsosa mohlahla. Ya ema tlou e kgolo, empa

ya ema e theka, e feletswe ke matla, e fehelwa jwale ka kgomo ya lefu la mmamotohwane, le hona e bile e dihile ditsebe. (M. *Ch.* 153, M./D. 195)

He stood up, the lion of Zulu descent, fearless beast of the wilds, but he stood up sapped of his strength, unable even to raise his mane. He stood up, the great elephant, but he stood up unsteady on his feet, sapped of his strength, breathing hard like a bovine suffering from the mmamotohwane disease, with its ears dropping, besides.

Again, Mofolo's reference to Chaka at the very end of the book is in eulogistic terms when he says:

Ho bile jwalo ho fela ha Chaka, mora wa Senzangakhona

(M. *Ch.* 156, M./D. 198)

So it was, the end of Chaka, son of Senzangakhona

The associative reference son-of-Senzangakhona is a powerful affirmation of Chaka as a person of worth. Also, there is an unmistakable tone of nostalgia on Mofolo's part strongly suggested by the inversion of the syntax, which brings about subtle shifts of emphase, in *So it was, the end of Chaka*. This nostalgia comes out a great deal more strongly as a national sentiment of the contemporary Zulu people when Mofolo concludes his powerful narrative with the words:

MaZulu le kajeno a bokajeno ha a hopola kamoo e kileng ya eba batho kateng, mehleng ya Chaka, kamoo ditjhaba di neng di jela kgwebeleng ke ho ba tshoha, le ha ba hopola borena ba bona boo weleng, eba ba sekisa mahlong, ba re: "Di a bela di a hlweba! Madiba ho pjha a maholo!"

(M. *Ch.* 156, M./D. 198)

To this very day the Zulus, when they remember how they were once a great people, in the days of Chaka, and how the nations lived in mortal fear of them, and also when they remember their kingdom that fell, then tears well in their eyes, and they say, "They ferment, they curdle! Even mighty pools do dry away!"

Mofolo's sentiments of admiration and nostalgia are doubly significant in that they come from a severe judge who has previously expressed such negative feelings about Chaka as the following:

Mme jwale ditaba di kgaohile, Chaka o ikgethetse lefu bakeng sa bophelo ka boomo. (M. *Ch.* 40, M./D. 51)

and now the matter has been decided, Chaka has deliberately chosen death for himself instead of life.

a comment made by Mofolo after Chaka decides that he wants the medicine descrubed by Isanusi as being "extremely evil, but also extremely good". (M. *Ch.* 39—40, M./D. 51)

After Chaka chooses *Zulu*, the Heavens, as the new national name for his people, Mofolo remarks:

mme le rona re a makala hore naa ditakatso le boikakaso ba pelo ya Mokone yeo bo ne bo le bokaakang, ha a tla ipapisa le boholo ba mahodimo.

(M. *Ch.* 97, M./D. 125)

and we too wonder how great were the ambition and the impudence of this *Mokone* that he should compare himself with the greatness of the heavens.

And finally, after Chaka kills Noliwe, Mofolo considers him to have lost all claim to humanity:

tlhasenyana ya botho e neng e sa saletse ya tima, ya re lore mafifing aa tsha-
behang a pelo ya hae. ... boyena ba eshwa, ba shwella ruri, ha kena bop-
hoofolo ka ho tlala. (M. *Ch.* 119, M./D. 151)
the little spark of humanity that still remained was extinguished, it became
ashes in the terrible darkness of his heart. ... his self died, it died forever,
and there entered into him the nature fully of a beast.

There is thus an intense relationship between Mofolo the author and Chaka
the character, a relationship whose vicissitudes between love and hate are
paralleled by the author's changing attitudes towards his character. These attitudes in turn are motivated by a variety of stimuli including Mofolo's new
Christian ethic, the old Sesotho ethic, and the traditional admiration for the
qualities of manhood.

There are syncretist tendencies in *Moeti oa Bochabela,* in which Mofolo is
most severe in his criticism of Basotho society, and in *Pitseng.* For example,
the symbolism of light and darkness in Moeti, where Fekisi goes from a morass
of darkness in search of light, the light that he first espies in a dream, which
is to be his guiding light throughout his journey, comes out of Ntswanatsatsi,
the place from which, according to Basotho myths of origins, all the people
and living things originated, a place of birth and renewal. Thus in Fekisi's
search for the Christian God, tradition intervenes, to point the way he is to go.
In *Pitseng* Christian and traditional values are jointly responsible for the upright and virtuous lives of Aria Sebaka and Alfred Phakoe, which is important
since these two characters are the models against whom the intemperate, reckless love lives of the other characters are seen and judged.

It is therefore not a simple context within which Mofolo defines his ethical
standards and on which his judgement of his characters is based. Yet, despite
its complexity, this context still yields but two basic types of character, namely
ones that the author likes, and ones he does not like. There are, of course,
other relationships the author may have with his characters. For example, he
sometimes shows pity for a character who is overwhelmed by events; he may
also display a paternalistic amusement at the foibles of a character; he may
reflect the humility of a character. But all these are manifested within the
broad framework of his affection or disaffection for the character in question.

This relationship of the writer to his characters is at the very center of the
total experience that begins with him and ends with the reader, with the characters and their words and thoughts and deeds serving to bind them all together
in what the author perceives as the pursuit of a common ideal. Like the oral
narrator, the writer not only narrates, but he also reacts to the story, cuing the
audience in the process. Indeed he sometimes becomes part of the audience
and exclaims at the events in the story. This is what happens in *Moeti* where
Mofolo writes that Fekisi has to find shelter in a hole to escape from a lion
and a lioness that are attacking him. The lion pushes its head into the hole in
an attempt to reach him, and he stabs it in the ear with his spear. Mofolo immediately switches roles and sees the whole scene from the point of view of
the audience. He exclaims:

> Joo! Joo! Joo! Ruri jwale ya batla ho hlanya ke kgalefo.
>
> (M. *Mo.* 58, M./A. 100)
>
> Joo! Joo! Joo! Truly now it nearly went mad with anger.

One page later he repeats a closely parallel scene in which Fekisi stabs the lioness in the eye. Again Mofolo reacts in the same manner as he says:

> Ao! Ao! Ao! Ke re ruri ya etsa ntho tsee tshabehang.
>
> (M. *Mo.* 59, M./A. 100)
>
> Ao! Ao! Ao! I say truly it did fearful things.

Before going into a detailed examination of the relationships described above, it is relevant to ask, Why does the author not simply narrate his story and let the characters and their actions speak for themselves? Why does he not detach himself from the action and give the reader an objective, non-partisan view of the story? At the very base of it all lies the fact that the author subscribes to a certain set of moral values which he regards as the *sine qua non* of his society. Like his oral narrative performer counterpart, he believes that justice must always prevail in the end, murder must out, evil must be punished and virtue rewarded. He believes that it is the business of all those who are involved in this human drama—the narrator, the actors and the audience—to ensure that these ends are achieved. The people must sit in judgement over the actions of the characters, with the narrator presiding over this court, so to speak. All through the story they observe the actions and sayings of the characters, they approve or condemn as the case may be. And throughout the story it is the narrator who, by description and impersonation, and by various kinds of reactions, brings together all the participants in the drama, and guides the people towards a fair and just assessment of the situation.

This is communalism at work, operating within the broad framework of humanism. For the writer does not approach his story with the cold detachment of a journalist. On the contrary, he never sees himself as anything but a human being who cannot help reacting, indeed must react, with sympathy to a human situation. Therefore throughout his story he closely watches every move and every syllable of his characters, and he comments on them. He manifests a relationship of Affection/Disaffection with them, loving those who do what he considers to be right, and hating those who do not conform to his patterns of behaviour.

The first indication of Mofolo as a severe judge of human character comes in the very opening sentence of his first book, *Moeti,* and is repeated several times within the first chapter of that book. In *Moeti* as well as in *Chaka,* Mofolo establishes a standard by which he rigorously distinguishes man from beast. Here are the first two sentences of *Moeti:*

> Lefifing le letsho lee reng tsho, mehleng ya ha ditjhaba di sa ntsane di jana jwale ka dibatana tsa naha, motho o ne a le teng yaa bitswang Fekisi.
>
> (M. *Mo.* 1, M./A. 7)
>
> In the black darkness that was pitch black, the days when the nations still ate each other like the wild beasts of the veld, there was a human being called Fekisi.

Using the rhetorical "yes" for emphasis, Mofolo goes on:

> Ee, ke re motho, e seng motho sebopeho le ho tseba ho bua feela, empa motho dipuong, motho diketsong, motho mekgweng yohle; motho sephiring le pontsheng, motho bohlokong le thabong, boiketlong le bothateng, tlaleng le naleng. (M. *Mo.* 1, M./A. 7)
>
> Yes, I say a human being, not a human being in appearance only, and through knowing how to talk, but a human being in his words, a human being in his deeds, a human being in all his ways; a human being in secret and in public, a human being in pain and in joy, in easy times and hard times, in hunger and in plenty.

Having told us that this human being was a "child-who-is-getter-up-with-the-heart-of-yesterday," that is, one who has a consistently good disposition towards other people, Mofolo reinforces his definition even further as he states that

> E ne e le motho ka botlalo bohle ba lentswe lena lee reng *motho*; motho kamoo Mmopi a neng a rere hore motho a be jwalo, setshwantsho sa sebele sa Yaa entseng tsohle, tsee bonwang le tsee sa bonweng, yeo ho neng ho lekanngwa yena yaa jwalo ha ho thwe tsohle dibopuwa tse ding di tla mo tshaba, di tla mo utlwa, di mo hlonephe, ka hobane o na le kganya e nngwe esele, yeo dibopuwa tse ding di se nang yona. (M. *Mo.* 1, M./A. 7)
>
> He was a human being in the fullness of this word that says *human being*; a human being as the Creator had planned that a human being should be, a true image of Him who made all things, both the visible and the invisible, the very human being described when it was said that all other creatures shall fear him, shall obey him, and shall honour him, because he has a glory that is different, which the other creatures do not possess.

This "human being" is Fekisi, the hero of the story, the righteous young man who, having struggled in vain to correct what he perceives as the evils of his society, goes in search of a Utopia and of God. He finds both—and dies.

At the same time as he introduces his ideal human being, Mofolo tells us of "the nations" that "ate each other like the beasts of the wilds". A little later he singles out a neighbour of Fekisi's parents, one Phakoane who "was a human being when he had not taken any drink. But when he was drunk, he was wild beast". Phakoane is a regular drinker and a wife beater who ends up killing his wife in a drunken rage.

The world Mofolo creates for us in his books, then, is a world of human beings and beasts. But since, in fact, Mofolo gives us ample evidence of his admiration for the real beasts, namely the quadrupeds that roam the wilds in pristine innocence, the term *man-beast* more accurately describes the depraved people of his stories. Indeed, as becomes apparent later in this paper, animals which play a significant role in a story often arouse feelings of great admiration in the author, who then conveys his affection for them in the same way he does for a character he loves. Mofolo's message is, consistently, that to be a human being is all right; to be a beast is all right; but to be a man-beast is not all right, in fact, it is abominable.

One of the ways that are open to an involved author like Mofolo to express his involvement, is digression. When a writer uses this method, he has, of necessity, to interrupt his story, to temporarily suspend all action. In this interval he comes out from behind the scenes and speaks direct to his readers.

We have a good example of this in *Chaka*. The fighting that follows Chaka's killing of a hyena to rescue the girl the hyena is carrying away, results in serious injuries for Mfokazana and Dingana, Chaka's half-brothers. Senzangak-hona's senior wives are so furious that they demand that Chaka be killed. Senzangakhona gives the order: "Kill him!" This is a critical moment in Cha-ka's life, a moment of separation. The umbilical cord is snapped, and he is truly on his own. Mofolo concludes this chapter in true Aesopian style when he says:

12. Kgaohanyong ena re fumana hore efela ruri tholwana ya sebe e le boh-loko ka mokgwa oo makatsang, hobane ha re bone tshito ya Chaka ta-beng tsena, empa le ha ho le jwalo ntat'ae o laela hore a bolawe. Mola-tolato, sesosa, ke hobane Nandi hammoho le Senzangakhona ba ne ba na le modimo; mme Senzangakhona, moo a tshabang ha ditaba tsa hae di tsejwa, a ba a rera ho bolaya mora wa hae. Athe hoja Senzangakhona a se etse ditaba tsena tsee dihlong botjheng ba hae, Chaka a ka be a le hae ha habo, Nobamba, e le ngwana wa mpowane, ngwana yaa hlokolotsi haholo ho ntat'ae. (M. *Ch*. 31, M./D. 40)

In this chapter we find that it is indeed true that the fruit of sin is bitter to an amazing degree, because we do not see any transgression on Cha-ka's part in these matters, yet, even though this is so, his father com-mands that he be killed. The real issue, the cause of it all, is that Nandi and Senzangakhona suffer from guilt, and sengangakhona, fearing lest these secret matters should become known, went so far as to kill his own son. Yet, if Senzangakhona had not committed this shameful deed in his youth, Chaka would have been at his home at Nobamba, a precious child, truly beloved of his father.

The detrimental effect of this digression as an interruption of the narrative is mitigated by the fact that it occurs at the end of a chapter, where there is a natural division. The only other such Aesopian conclusion in this book comes at the end of chapter 9 where Mofolo expresses surprise that Chaka fails to tell his mother the whole story about Malunga and Ndlebe, making no mention at all of Malunga and only a casual reference to Ndlebe by saying simply that he had "found himself a fool who will carry his blankets". (M. *Ch*. 56, M./D. 72).

13. Re sa botsa hape hore naa Isanusi o na le eng, le mahlahana a hae a na le eng, ha tsohle tsee bapileng le bona Chaka a di patela mmae? Athe mokgwa wa hae ke ho mmolella ditaba tsohle-tsohle, tse mpe le tse ntle.
(M. *Ch*. 56, M./D. 72)

We ask once more what is it about Isanusi, and what is it about his aids, that makes Chaka hide from his mother everything pertaining to them? Yet his habit has been to tell her his affairs in their entirety, the bad as well as the good.

Most of the digressions in *Chaka* occur in the bodies of the chapters where they are more likely to jolt the reader as intrusive elements. Yet, so much is Mofolo in control of his narrative that the reader tends to be oblivious of these interferences.

Whether, or to what extent, digression can be considered as having a poten-tial for enhancing a writer's style, is a moot point. One incontrovertible fact is that a digression is a very convenient potential vehicle for moral lessons.

Indeed, all the digressions we have quoted or referred to so far have no other purpose but to carry a homily. Therefore while it would, perhaps, be rash to consider them totally without any aesthetic potential in fiction, one must nevertheless point out the unlikelihood of this being the case, and simultaneously the danger that they could be used as propaganda vehicles. There is abundant evidence of this where African language writers plead the cause of the Christian missions and of the westernization process to their readers, while condemning their own.

Further, it should be pointed out that to separate narrative from digression is not always as easy as it might seem. For example, at the end of the first war Chaka fights for Dingiswayo, namely the war against Zwide, Mofolo refers to the songs composed for him by the women, and then goes on to say:

> 14. Hape mohlolo ke hobane ha ho ntse ho bolelwa Chaka, ho binwa Chaka, mabotho a mang ha a ka a kenwa ke mona; ya hla ya eba bona baa rokang Chaka, ba ba ba re morena a mo fetisetse mabothong a hae a maholo, a bahale; mme a fela a etsa jwalo, a ba a mo rwesa mokadi ka ho mo etsa molaodi wa lebotho le leng la a maholo.
>
> (M. *Ch.* 50—51, M./D. —)
>
> Besides, it is strange that as Chaka was being spoken and sung, the other warriors did not become envious; in fact they were the very ones who praised Chaka, and even suggested that the king should advance him into his senior regiments, ones consisting of true braves; and indeed he did so, and honoured him besides by making him a general of one of these senior regiments.

There is here a mixture of Mofolo's parenthetical reaction to a situation in the story, combined with a narrative of that very situation.

But, even with all things considered, it remains nevertheless true that a digression creates a dangerous vacuum in the story, one that is liable to suck in the nearest thing to it. And that, usually, is the message that the writer is either incapable of building into his narrative, or considers to be so important that it needs to be singled out and "told like it is".

A resourceful Sesotho prose writer, however, does not have to rely solely, or even mainly on digression and other interruptions of narrative to convey his reactions to the events and characters in his story. The Sesotho language—its idiom, its syntax, its store of emotive words; the Sesotho tradition that lays so much store on the relationship of a person to other people, and to places of abode or of origin as contextualizing factors that give him strong affirmation as a social being, one who belongs, who has antecedents; the Sesotho traditional communalism that makes every man his brother's keeper—all these factors, as well as others that will emerge in the discussion that follows, are often used by the writer within the stream of his narrative. They then serve the triple purpose of defining the writer's relationship to his characters, advancing the narrative, and enhancing its aesthetic appeal.

Maybe the best way to enter this part of the discussion is via the names of Mofolo's main characters, namely Fekisi in *Moeti oa Bochabela,* Chaka in *Chaka,* and Alfred Phakoe and Aria Sebaka in *Pitseng.* Our first task then will be to determine the alternative names Mofolo uses for each of these characters. *Fekisi* is also referred to as

15. Ngwana-wa-Setsoha-le-pelo-ya-maobane (M. 1, M./A. 7)
    Child-who-is-Getter-up-with-the-heart-of-yesterday
16. moeka (M. 28, M./A. 53 and *passim*)
    big fellow (mock heroic)
17. moshemane-wa-pholo (M. 37, M./A. 67)
    boy-child-who-is-an-ox
18. morena (M. 37, M./A. 67)
    the chief (mock heroic)
19. mohlankana-wa-pholo (M. 38, M./A. 68)
    young-man-who-is-an-ox
20. mothusi-wa-baa-tujwang-le-baa-tlatlapuwang (M. 46, M./A. 81)
    helper of those who are oppressed and those who are robbed of their
    possession

Chaka is also referred to as

21. moshemane-wa-pholo (M. 26, M./D. 34)
    boy-child-who-is-an-ox
22. motho wa ho rata borena (M. 32, M./D. 41)
    person who is noted for his love of kingship
23. motho wa mawala (M. 33, M./D. 43)
    person of quick mind
24. mora wa Senzangakhona (M. 48, M./D. 62 and *passim*)
    son of Senzangakhona
25. mohlankana wa Senzangakhona (M. 88, M./D. 113)
    young man of Senzangakhona
26. moqapa-di-mpe-kaofela (M. 128, M./D. 162)
    originator-of-all-things-evil
27. motho wa ho rata madi (M. 139, M./D. 177)
    person known for his love of the sight of blood
28. tau ya hlaka la ha Zulu (M. 153, M./D. 195)
    lion of Zulu descent
29. sebata see se nang tshabo (M. 153, M./D. 195)
    wild predator that has no fear
30. tlou e kgolo (M. 153, M./D. 195)
    great elephant

Alfred Phakoe ist also referred to as

31. mora wa Phakoe (M. 109 and *passim*)
    son of Phakoe

Aria Sebaka is also referred to as

32. mofumahadi (M. 25)
    the queen (mock heroic)
33. moradi wa Sebaka (M. 90 and *passim*)
    daughter of Sebaka
34. nonyana-ya-seqhala-maraba (M. 90)
    bird that is dismantler of snares
35. tlhapi-ya-sehana-ho-tshwaswa (M. 90)
    fish-that-is-refuser-to-be-caught
36. sekwenya-dilope (M. 90)
    swallower-of-the-bait
37. ngwana enwa wa Sebaka (M. 168)
    this child of Sebaka

From the above we can see how the author reflects his attitude to his characters at any given moment by the identifying label that he chooses for that

character—from the given name, to the eulogue, to words and phrases of mock praise, to terms of filial relationship with the father, etc. Syntactical slots that would ordinarily be filled by the given name can, depending entirely on the author's mood as determined by the events in the story and the behaviour of his characters, be filled by anyone of the various possible aliases for the characters.

Most of these are eulogistic and therefore indicate an affectionate relationship of Mofolo to his characters. The description *son of . . .* or *daughter of . . .*, which we call *filial relationship,* always reflects the author's affection and admiration for the character so identified. Alfred Phakoe is refferred to numerous times as "the son of Phakoe"; similarly Aria Sebaka is referred to numerous times as "the daughter of Sebaka". Many times Chaka is referred to as "the son of Senzangakhona". The filial relationship nomenclature is never used for Fekisi for the simple reason that his father is never mentioned by name.

Some of the surrogate names used are naming eulogues, i. e. names that are praise epithets. Examples of these are *Child-who-is-Getter-up-with-the-heart-of-yesterday* (ill. 15 above), *Boy-child who is an ox* (ills. 17 & 21), *Young man who is an ox* (ill. 19), *Helper of those who are harassed and those who are robbed of their belongings* (ill. 20), *the Son of Senzangakhona* (ill. 24), *Lion of Zulu Descent* (ill. 28), *Wild-Predator-that-has-no-fear* (ill. 29), *Great-Elephant* (ill. 30), *Bird-that-is-Dismantler-of-Snares* (ill. 34), *Fish-that-is-Refuser-to-be-caught* (ill. 35), *Swallower-of-the-bait* (ill. 35).

Some indicate a paternalistic attitude of the author to his characters. He is both superior to them and tolerant and amused by their antics and/or their inflated sense of self-importance. Examples of these are the mock heroic use of some words such as *king, queen, fellow, chief,* and so on.

Some of the above eulogues are fascinating metaphors. For example in illustration 34, Aria Sebaka is a bird, her suitors are hunters, their sweet words of wooing, by which Mofolo suggests they are trying to lure her to some hidden danger, are snares laid out to catch the bird. But Aria is a clever bird that outsmarts its hunters, and, to their eternal chagrin, dismantles their snares. The second last and the last illustrations can be taken together as they both share one and the same basic metaphor. Here Aria is a fish, the coveted prize of the fishermen, namely her young suitors. This time the suitor's eloquence is metaphorically the bait that will attract her and divert her attention from the hook. But this sophisticated fish frustrates the fishermen's plans by either deftly avoiding the hook, or by swallowing everything and remaining defiantly healthy.

There are also deverbative eulogues which arise directly from the action for which the character is praised. *Helper-of-those-who-are-harassed-and-those-who-are-robbed-of-their-belongings* is such a one. Fekisi *helps those who are harassed* etc., and thus earns himself the eulogue *Helper.*

The character has to work his way into the author's heart by doing "good" things. He has to earn the author's affection. Once he has done so, he is worthy of any eulogue or other technique of praise the author may decide to use to describe him, as, for example, the filial relationship technique or the syntax inversion technique. Thus Chaka can only be the *Son-of-Senzangakhona* or the *Great-Elephant* in a rhetorically significant way after he has earned himself a place in Mofolo's heart through his unparalleled prowess even as a youth. Alfred Phakoe and Aria Sebaka similarly deserve the high praise conveyed by the filial relationship phrases the *Son-of-Phakoe* and the *Daughter-of-Sebaka* because they have earned it by being constant and uncompromising in their refusal to be involved in meaningless flirtation under the guise of love, and thus eventually being the ones to demonstrate the value of true, deep, purposeful and lasting love. Their relationship with their parents, full of love, mutual respect, obedience, and openness, is also highly exemplary.

It is intriguing to see how close the story-teller, alias the author, gets to being simultaneously a heroic poet. His relationship to the persons in his story is similar to the heroic poet's relationship to the people around whose lives his poem devolves. People are there to be liked or not to be liked. If you neither like nor dislike them, they don't exist. If you like them you show it; if you don't like them you show it. There are no inhibitions, no punches pulled.

For as long as Chaka is harassed and persecuted by his society, he is pitied by Mofolo. For as long as he shows qualities of bravery, courage, and strength at the time before he is corrupted by ambition, and he is still a potential asset to his community, Mofolo loves him and calls him the *Son-of-Senzangakhona*, the *Boy-Child-who-is-an-Ox*, and so on. However, after he succumbs to his lust for power and uses his endowments to oppress, to lay waste, to murder and in general to systematically destroy love and life and social order, and after he demonstrates the death of his own humanity by treacherously murdering his beloved Noliwe, which is equivalent to murdering love itself, Mofolo, who has been cooling off towards Chaka from the time that he is seduced by the Isanusi, turns around and calls him *Originator-of-all-things-evil*, which helps to underscore Mofolo's ambivalent relationship to Chaka.

From the eulogue to full blown verse is but a short step. The hyena, in *Chaka*, that carries away Mfokazana's girl friend at night, has its praises worked into the grammatical syntax in which Mofolo describes its actions, its physical attributes, as well as its predatory habits:

> E ne e tshajwa thamahane, batho ba thothomela ha ba utlwa tsa yona
>> Thamahane, phiri, sephaka-thamaha,
>> Rangwan'a tau le letlonkana,
>> Ngwana wa merara ee matswedintsweke.
>> Thamahane, ngwana wa madika-tsholo-la-ka-phirimana,
>> Ana motsheare o tshaba'ng ho le dika?
>> Ke tshaba molato nthong tsa batho. (M. *Ch.* 26, M./D. 34)

It was feared very much, the brown hyena, and the people trembled when they heard of its deeds
>> The brown hyena, wolf with a brown coloured forearm,
>> Little father of the lion and the spotted hyena,
>> Child with zig-zag tattoo, mark of brave warriors.
>> Brown hyena, child who is warrior-who-hunts-by-night,
>> What makes you fear to hunt by day?
>> I fear accusations of stealing people's things.

This whole verse occurs in a syntactical slot where it replaces, and can be replaced by, either *thamahane* (hyena) or any of its grammatical substitutes (e. g. pronouns, pronominal phrases, etc.). Thus, in the above usage, it repeats, in a much more forceful way, what has already been conveyed by the pronoun *yona* (it), which it can replace. This little poem is quite complex, including, as it does, a dramatic presentation of the poet challenging the hyena to explain its nocturnal habits, and the hyena replying with the simple logic that he would be caught if he came raiding by day.

In similar fashion the lion's praise verse is used as a delayed subject in

> Ya re feela ham-m-m, ya be e se e le ka hare
> Tshehla ya boMothebele, kokomoha,
> Tshehla, thokwa-lekakuba,
> Ekare o sa je tsa batho,
> O itjella dirobala-naheng!
> Motjhana a se na babo-moholo
> O a n'a bolaya a be a ratha. (M. *Ch.* 15, M./D. 19)

> It just went *ham-m-m,* and was immediately in their midst
> Tawny one, brother of Mothebele, rise up,
> Tawny one, fawn-coloured king of the wilds,
> Why, you eat not what belongs to men,
> But eat, for your part, the sleepers-in-the-veld!
> A nephew bereft of uncles
> Kills and lays claim to all the booty.

The hyena and the lion, which are actors in the story of Chaka, are admired for their qualities of bravery, fearless courage and sheer brutal strength, qualities desired, in those days, for the warrior. And every man was a warrior. Predators like the lion and the hyena thus provided the perfect metaphor for the heroic poet who saw the perfection of the qualities of his hero in the animals, the birds, the insects and the reptiles; in the forces of nature—the angry or smiling skies, storms and hurricanes; in landscape features such as mountains, rivers, gorges, deep pools, and the like.

There are other stylistic techniques which the author uses to define his relationship of affection to his charachters. While we cannot mention them all in this essay, one of them is used sufficiently regularly to warrant at least a passing mention. This is syntax inversion or anastrophe which occurs largely, though by no means exclusively, in the relationship of subject to predicate.

In a simple, matter-of-fact, straight-to-the-point, narrative statement, the subject comes before the predicate, as in

> Fekisi a di hana

> Fekisi rejected them

When, however, the predicate precedes the subject, the latter is rendered unessential for the basic meaning to be communicated. This gives the subject much prominence for the very reason that it is unexpected, and stands in disjunctive relationship to the preceding syntax and in stark aloofness from it. It is in excess of the basic communication needs of the situation. And it is precisely that seeming, contrived, superfluousness that lends it its rhetorical power. The above sentence then becomes

A di hana Fekisi (M. *Mo.* 8, M./A. 19)

He rejected them, Fekisi

But syntax inversion frequently accompanies, or is accompanied by, the naming devices such as filial relationship and so on, as in the following:

A sa qala, a sa qala ho fihla mora wa Senzangakhona (M. *Ch.* 48, M./D. 62)

Even as he initiated, even as he iniated his arriving,
the son of Senzangakhona

This is said in regard to Chaka's killing of a madman who lived in the forest nearby and killed whomsoever he could lay his hands on, which was his (i. e. Chaka's) first deed of bravery shortly after his arrival at Dingiswayo's. Without syntax inversion the above statement would be

Mora wa Senzangakhona a sa qala, a sa qala ho fihla

As a matter of interest we might, in addition to turning around the syntax as above, reduce this phrase to its basic semantic components, including an omission of the rhetorical repetition of *a sa qala.* We then get

Chaka a sa qala ho fihla

Chaka, as he initiated the arriving (i. e. Chaka, as soon as he arrived, . . .)

To convey his dislike for a character, the writer mostly relies on emotive words. So for example Mofolo leaves us in no doubt as to his lack of love for Ndlebe, one of the Isanusi's assistants in *Chaka,* as he, Mofolo, describes him, Ndlebe, through Chaka's point of view as Chaka sees Ndlebe and Malunga for the first time:

Mohlankana wa bobedi yena e le nyafu-nyafu, obu-obuhadi ee dihileng ditsebe, ee rephisitseng melomo, ditsebe di le kgolohadi ho feta tekanyo, di le mahaha, di kgakeleditse moya, re ka re ditaba; mahlo a le mokedi-kedi, a tletse bolotsana le bohlaba-phiyo ka mokgwa oo makatsang . . .
(M. *Ch.* 53, M./D. 68)

The second young man was a formless mass, a big stupid looking thing with drooping ears, and dangling lips. His ears were much larger than they should be, and they were like caves intercepting the wind, or rather we should say the news. His eyes were liquid, they were full of deceit and treachery to an amazing degree . . .

It is extremely difficult to translate such words adequately because of their high emotive content which gives them an extra lexical connotative value.

Conclusion

I have attempted in this paper to establish that Mofolo's style, which is representative of many Basotho writers, and some of whose features probably go beyond Sesotho fiction to embrace the prose fiction of other Bantu languages, is characterized by a breaking down of the barriers that separate the writer from the people of the story world that he creates. Once he has done this, the writer is free to participate, if only as a critical observer, in the events of that world. He emotes, he chides, he commends, he is amused, he exclaims, he advises, and so on as the spirit moves him, or, more to the point, as the events in the story dictate. For he is a human being among other human beings, and he cannot stand aside, cannot maintain that journalistic detachment, from the human drama that is unfolding before him. If he cannot prevent things from going wrong, he can at least make his audience, his readers that is, benefit from the experiences of his characters. His audience is therefore drawn in, both for the reason just stated, but also in order, hopefully, to concur with the moral judgements that he passes from time to time.

Basically the author can make these comments, including his demonstration of his affection or disaffection for any of his characters, in one of two ways. He can either use digressions, stopping the movement of his narrative in order to inject his comments, or he can use anyone of a whole variety of techniques that make his involvement apparent without interrupting the flow of his story. If he handles these techniques with skill, he makes a unique contribution to the general body of critical tools for literary analysis.

There is a wealth of these hitherto undetected stylistic features in the literature written in the African languages of South Africa, and maybe beyond. And it is our duty as critical readers to uncover them and formulate their underlying principles. It appears that by involving ourselves in this investigation, we should, in the process, also uncover some interesting areas where written prose fiction, oral narrative, and heroic poetry, share common sources of inspiration and methods of execution.

An Analysis of Stephen A. Mpashi's
UWAUMA NAFYALA

Daniel P. Kunene

It was somewhere between 1949 and 1953. The British colonial expatriates in Northern Rhodesia, Southern Rhodesia and Nyasaland were planning a federation of the three territories, a move strongly resisted by the Africans. After all, South Africa had formed a Union in 1910 from its erstwhile independent governments of the Transvaal, the Orange Free State, Natal and the Cape Province, and this had not augured well for the Africans there who had from then on been more systematically oppressed since these governments could now have a uniform "native policy."

"Federation" was a hot issue among the Blacks, and there was strong and determined resistance against it.[1] Then there arose that creature called the "informer". The informer was defined, in the popular mind, as the Black who reported the politically active Blacks to the white authorities. He was a spy and a traitor who was, presumably, rewarded monetarily for his treachery. This resulted in mutual suspicion, and no one was able to trust his neighbor. Blacks who showed any sign of increased material comfort or more ready cash than before were immediate targets for gossip and suspicion. Suspicion soon took the semblance of fact, and was acted upon as if it were fact. Indeed the label of "informer" was soon stuck on any Black who perpetrated acts of violence against his fellow Blacks, especially assault, robbery and murder. Such a person was, by implication, being accused of weakening Black solidarity.

Suspicion led to rumor, and rumor attacked insidiously as only rumor can. It was hard to deny because there was no direct accusation and no visible accuser, and the vicious circle simply continued unchecked with the poor victim, who was often innocent, powerless to do anything about it.

In his novel *Uwauma Nafyala*[2], Stephen A. Mpashi makes "federation" a constant topic of conversation at the beer hall, in the shebeens, among the spectators at football games, at the hospital where Joji and Kabanki, the two protagonists, work as medical aids, indeed at just about every conceivable social occasion. Indirect, sarcastic remarks are made in the presence of the "accused", and innuendo usurps the place of direct confrontation. Thus it is fitting that in the very first chapter of *Uwauma Nafyala* the import of the conversation between Joji and Kabanki is the rumor concerning someone who is reported to have turned into an informer.

The tragedy of Joji and Kabanki begins to unfold in the midst of the hum-drum of their daily lives. The main centers of action are the hospital and the beerhall. Some of the action takes place during movement from one place to another, while at other times it is centered around the protagonists' homes.

Mpashi is not slow in introducing the major problem of the story and at once involving the two protagonists in it. At the opening of the story Joji is late in coming to relieve Kabanki at the hospital. He explains that he was delayed by the gossip he heard about Donad[3] and Mwenya having turned infor-mers. Kabanki's first reaction is that of incredulity: "You lie," he tells Joji. "Do you really think that Donad and Mwenya would become informers? No, it does not look like them." But it is all a rhetorical question, and the answer is more a declaration of surprise than an exoneration of Donad and Mwenya. Indeed Kabanki does say, a little later: "This is why we Africans are so poor. We lack unity. Whenever we try to unite, there are some who go to report to the white man." In this little homily, Kabanki reveals to us what he is really thinking concerning Donad and Mwenya.

Joji expresses his bitterness about informers generally and threatens to beat them up. Federation is bad for the African, he declares, and only the stupid can be taken in by the deception. "You will see," says Joji, "when the white people come with this federation, they will take all our land and we shall not even have a place to spit our saliva. They will take even the wild fruits."

Thus we see how right from the beginning Joji and Kabanki are involved with the problem of federation. The question is, What is it going to do to their lives? The answer depends largely on their personalities.

Mpashi maintains an awareness of the problem of federation and the resul-tant informer system by making it the topic of heated discussions, of open or veiled threats. It is constantly on the lips of clusters of people at the beerhall, and of the medical aids and orderlies at the hospital. This way the author successfully creates an all-pervading sense of tension. When he plunges Joji and Kabanki headlong into the controversy by making *them* the suspects, the reader is fully aware of the seriousness of the situation they are in. Also, this provides the opportunity for their personalities to be revealed and to flower. Unfortunately, Mpashi does not exploit this to the fullest advantage.

The plunging takes place in a re-enactment of the opening scene: Joji comes on duty and, when Kabanki is about to leave, tells him, "They are saying that Joji and Kabanki are also informers." This time Kabanki's incredulity is ge-nuine. "There is nothing they have proved," he declares. Later he says, "Just forget it, for it will soon pass."

Joji thinks otherwise: "However much you may deny it, makes no differen-ce with the people once they have put your name in their mouths." Joji's reaction to the accusations is violent: "I will kill one of them, and that's when they will know better. I am mad! Imagine them speaking falsely against me! You will see," he threatens.

Without any effort at all the author has succeeded in revealing the fick-leness of human nature through his two main characters. When other people are accused of being informers, Joji threatens to kill them. When *he* is accused of being an informer, he threatens to kill his accusers. It is the same with Kabanki, except that his is a much milder reaction; he is ready to believe the accusations levelled at other people. Yet when *he* is accused, he expects his innocence to shine through him and become apparent to all who see him.

From this moment on, the author makes every event reinforce the plot and move it towards the crisis point. One example is the scene where Magdalena pleads with Kabanki to give her an injection secretly for a disease she does not want revealed (presumably veneral) and Kabanki persistently refuses. This scene reaches its climax as Kabanki rides off on his bicycle and Magdalena hurls insults at him, crowning it all with the threat. "That's why you people have become informers, selling your own people." Shortly after this he hears a muttered threat at the beerhall uttered by someone in a group looking in his direction.

It is one of the unfortunate consequences of a situation of mutual suspicion and distrust that events that would otherwise have been accepted as the daily irritations of social living—the problems and accidents that are a necessary price for the rewards of communal living—are distorted into monsters that threaten to destroy that very community. Kabanki invites Ollandi Mukwasa to a movie. Shortly after the movie begins he decides he does not like it, leaves Ollandi there and goes home. Unknown to Kabanki, Ollandi is assaulted on his way home. Rumor picks this up: "Informers will kill us all this year," Kabanki overhears some people say in whose company he is cycling to work next morning. "Ollandi Mukwasa had his forehead broken with a chain by informers. They say a friend he went with to the cinema did it. He just took him away from his house pretending to go to the cinema when he had already alerted his fellow informers to go and kill him." The message is beginning to get through to Kabanki, and he is getting alarmed. Joji maintains a constant attitude to the whole thing. He is mad. He will teach them a lesson by killing the originator of the lies once he finds out who he is. Kabanki still maintains a sense of tolerance, even forces himself to see the whole thing as funny, but he does begin to see the serious side of it too: "When I think about it I first laugh because it is untrue. On the other hand it is very bad because people can kill us for no wrong."

Then there is the Kwandangala episode. Kabanki invites Kwandangala to go with him to the Lazymen's Club one Saturday evening to participate in a humorous sketch the management is putting up for the customers. On the way there Kwandangala lags behind and Kabanki assumes he is relieving himself and will soon catch up with him. By the time he realizes that Kwandangala is not coming, he is getting late for the show and decides Kwandangala has probably gone back home. But Kwandangala never reaches home that night, and the next morning Kabanki is confronted by a sorrowful Mrs. Kwandangala together with a group of irate relatives who threaten to kill him if he does not produce Kwandangala. The events involving Kabanki have begun to assume the nature of a vicious circle: The fact that he has been declared not guilty by a white court in the case of Ollandi, instead of making him appear clean in the eyes of the people, does the very opposite because he is now considered to be under the white man's protection as long as he "victimizes" his own people.

The night of the Lazymen's Club and Kwandangala's disappearance follows a day in which, among other things, Kabanki, at the beerhall, overhears two husky strange men in a neighboring shelter asking as they point at him and Joji: "Is it these men?" For better or for worse, Joji does not hear them. Hired assassins? Well, that same night on their return from the Lazymen's Club, Kabanki and Joji are set upon by two men with the words "You are dying today, you informers. You are the ones who kidnap and sell the people." This is the supreme test for the personalities of Joji and Kabanki, and for their relationship. Kabanki acts with discretion and only to the extent demanded by the immediate circumstances. Therefore when Joji has killed one of the men and the other lies disabled in a ditch in which he fell as he pursued Kabanki, Kabanki would leave him there and run away. But Joji reasons otherwise. Invoking the proverb *Uwauma nafyala amumina limo* (He who beats his mother-in-law beats her thoroughly), he argues that "the law says a life for a life." Sparing the second man will make no difference in the severity of their punishment, and will increase the chances of their being caught.

Again Mpashi reinforces Joji's vicious nature and thoroughness by describing in detail the way he kills the second man. "Joji jumped on the man and stabbed him in the ear and then stabbed him again in the throat. Then he grabbed his head and hit it against a rock. Kabanki wanted to run away because Joji was snarling as he did these things. Joji pushed his fingers into the wound in the throat and started to pull in an attempt to break the man's neck. When the man started to struggle between life and death, Joji started hurling stones at his head as if he were killing a snake."

Joji manages to stay calm after this, in complete contrast to the now totally unnerved Kabanki. He warns Kabanki against betraying them. He makes him repeat the formula "*I, Kabanki, have no case,*" and tells him to always counter the feeling of guilt with that formula.

The story has been building towards this point with the characters of Joji and Kabanki being shown to contrast in various ways: Kabanki believes that his innocence is self-evident and, at least at the beginning, he will not go out of his way to prove it to the people. Joji, on the other hand, knows "people psychology": Once your peers have judged you guilty, you have to fight your way out of the situation. Kabanki has an implicit faith in his fellow human being. He is horrified at the accusations leveled at some people he knows. He is totally outraged when the popular finger points at him. Joji considers it much safer to be suspicious and distrustful of other people. They're always wrong whether *they* are accused, or they accuse *him*. Kabanki is patient and accommodating almost to a fault. He assumes other people's good faith unless and until the contrary is proved. Hence his reaction to the accusation of informership, and later to Joji's attempts on his life. Joji on the other hand is impatient, impulsive and easily convinces himself of other people's malicious intentions against him. In fact, towards the end, he is clearly paranoid. His reaction to the accusation of informership is a case in point. But this characteristic is seen at its worst in his conviction that Kabanki has turned against him and must be destroyed. Kabanki is tolerant and slow to anger while Joji's temper rises mercurially at the slightest provocation. The encounter with Maikolo at the beerhall underscores these traits. Maikolo refuses Kabanki's invitation to join him and Joji over a drink of *chibuku* (local Zambian beer) on the pretext that "When I drink kaffir beer I feel something something in my stomach and I also vomit." Kabanki remarks sarcastically: "Yah, you're frightening us. You've turned into a European in such a short time!" Maikolo walks away angrily, threatening to beat up Kabanki. Kabanki lets it pass, but Joji is incensed on his behalf, and later has a scuffle with Maikolo.

It is these personalities that have to react to the violence of a double killing which they are suddenly forced to do in self-defence. Their relationship henceforth has to change: They are either going to be drawn closer together or split apart once and for all. Given Joji's character, we can understand his tragic blind spot. When Kabanki is picked up by the police in connection with Kwandangala's disappearance, rumor simply says "the police have arrested Kabanki and have taken him away." On hearing this, Joji reaches a snap conclusion, namely that the "arrest" is connected with the two men he killed, and he decides to flee to the Congo on his bicycle. When, returning from his abortive escape bid, he sees Kabanki outside his (Kabanki's) house, he concludes that Kabanki has bought his own freedom by incriminating him, Joji. Without taking the trouble to ascertain the facts, he decides on a bloody plan: He is going to blow up Kabanki's house with explosives. Is it right to kill Kabanki's wife and child also? he wonders. Of course, he decides, after all *Uwauma nafyala* . . . When Kabanki and his family escape unhurt from their demolished house, ironically they find shelter in Joji's house. Next he tries to poison Kabanki with strychnine which he puts in Kabanki's tea. Again Kabanki escapes miraculously. This time, however, the veil of naiveté has lifted from his eyes and he knows that Joji is after his life. So he moves himself and his family from Joji's and finds shelter at Luka's house. Finally Joji tries to blow up Luka's house. Unfortunately for him, Kabanki has gone to the cinema and Luka has taken the two women to some drinking place. Luka comes back to check if everything is still in order and sees someone strike a match near his house, and then another. He runs and grapples with the man and during their scuffle two explosives go off one after the other. Joji is fatally injured. Luka is treated and he recovers.

Mpashi's setting is such that most of the locales where he takes his characters are places where people congregate. For he loves observing crowds, and he either does it directly himself, incorporating it into his objective narrative, or through one of his main characters. He describes the individuals in a crowd by some concrete detail that he chooses at random. Individual characteristics stand out precisely because they contrast with those of the other members of the crowd. The very opening scene in the present book gives the visual image of two types of crowd: first, the immobile crowd of patients in a ward in two rows of neatly made beds. "Some (of the patients) were groaning, others were enduring their pain in silence." The other crowd is descending upon the hospital: "Some came on bicycles with plates of food wrapped in cloths and tied to the bicycles; others came on foot carrying umbrellas and wearing boots . . ." These are visitors coming to see their sick friends and relatives. Here at the hospital is where the medical aids, as a social clique, often exchange gossip over a cup of tea or during a few quiet moments from their duties. Here's where Joji twice brings the fateful news of people being accused of being informers. And here's where a crowd of women come wailing over an unconscious man who has been struck by lightning.

Another favorite locale of Mpashi's is the beerhall. People sit in clusters under shelters and chat or discuss serious matters over their beer. The first crowd we see as we follow Kabanki there comprises Nsengas, Lozis, Kaondes and a Bemba. They are talking about federation and the problem of informers. The beerhall is where Kabanki first becomes aware of the two strange men who mutter threats at him and Joji for "being informers." On another occasion Kabanki gets to the beerhall. "He started watching the people. The women were dressed in different kinds of dresses. Some wore short dresses, others long dresses. Some were dressed so well that it made them look more attractive. Some were well suited by their clothes, others were not. . . . Some were going out while others were coming in. Some stood in threes and fours chatting. . . . Some hugged each other over the neck as they walked, others were playfully pretending to quarrel. There were Bembas, Lenjes, Solis, Lozis, Ngonis and Tongas and other groups. Some were short and others were tall." The observation goes on as Kabanki contemplates members of various nationalities and cultural communities, comparing them in respect of their beauty.

Life in its totality still goes on. Thus there are chunks of interludes that add a "whole life" quality to the drama of Joji and Kabanki and thus contextualize it as part of the humdrum of their ordinary existence. Most outstanding of these interludes are the hospital scenes where Mpashi goes into minute details of hospital procedures, medications for patients, bed-to-bed inspection by the doctor and the sister, what the doctor says to each patient, the treatment of specific cases, operation procedures, etc. It is as if one of Mpashi's aims is to show the reader the African adjusting to Western medicine and to hospitalization. Kabanki is a patient and painstaking teacher who advises and cautions with almost missionary dedication: That's why you may go, that's why you must stay a little longer, that's why you have to be operated on, that's why you can't have the same medicine as he, that's why we don't give injections without first diagnosing the disease, and so on.

Mpashi's handling of some of the aspects of his story is unsatisfactory. For example, one does not see enough (if anything) of the development of the characters of Joji and Kabanki. Thus, even though the story does have elements of tragedy, this remains an unrealized potential. At best the author stimulates the reader's expectation that something is going to happen. Major turning points are too abrupt. Thus, even allowing for Joji's temperament, his quick temper and tendency toward snap decisions, his decision, carried out forthwith, to flee to the Congo, jolts the reader. Similarly, when he resolves that Kabanki must die, the reader is shocked because Mpashi has not prepared him for it.

Tle *deus ex machina* stratagem in the poisoned tea episode is perhaps the least convincing. Joji has asked for tea from the kitchen, and this is given him in a teapot. He secretly puts strychnine poison in the tea, puts the teapot on the table outside where the staff always have their tea together. He then invites Kabanki to come and share the tea with him, but then suddenly suggests that Kabanki should go ahead and have his tea while he, Joji, goes to some other part of the hospital for a moment. He goes and invites Webi to join them, his real intention being, however, that Webi should be with him when he "discovers" Kabinki's corpse by the tea table. Meanwhile Kabanki ,pours tea in his cup and begins to raise it to his mouth to drink when a sudden angry call from the sister in charge of the ward summons him to "come and show me where you put the bottle of quinine. Quick! . . ." Kabanki puts down the tea and goes muttering angrily to himself about "these women of federation . . ." But, that he should put down the cup so readily and re-frain from taking even one sip of the tea before obeying the sister's call com-mands little credibility, especially since that reaction is not consistent with Ka-banki's character when confronted with what he whould interpret as white ar-rogance. If he was calm and confident enough to risk being lighthearted and facetious with the white magistrate during the Ollandi Mukwasa hearing, he suddenly seems to lose this self-confidence, this quiet arrogance, in the pre-sence of the irate sister. And therefoe he is saved!

There are other contrived situations. For example, the fact that Kabanki invites Ollandi to see a movie, that he, Kabanki, dislikes the movie so much that he leaves shortly after it starts, and that Ollandi is beaten as he returns home alone, constiututes a series of contrived situations intended to reinforce the people's suspicion that Kabanki is an "informer." Parenthetically, it is noteworthy that "informership" has become a blanket term applied to almost any act committed by one black person against another. In other words, any-thing that seems to weaken the solidarity of the Blacks in their struggle against white oppression is now defined in terms of the "federation." Thus, the con-notative value of this word has grown tremendously, almost completely over-shadowing its denotative significance.

Dialogue is one of the major problems in this book. Mostly Mpashi uses the theatrical format, stating the name of the speaker and then quoting his words. This does not allow for variation, if only to relieve the visual impact. But perhaps more serious is the effect of this on character development. One does not see any development, partly because one does not see or hear the reactions of the characters to the situations in which they are involved. The reader is outside of the characters all the time and relies on the words they speak to know something of what they are thinking. This lack of character perspective or point of view weakens the plot.

In spite of its weaknesses, however, *Uwauma Nafyala* has a wellconceived plot that moves in convincing cause-effect relationships from one stage to the next. The story simply thrives on irony seen, *inter alia,* in the following situations: The friendhip that is secretly undermined by murderous intentions; the Nemesis that overtakes Joji as he is destroyed by the trap he has set for Kabanki; the fact that it is Kabanki who covers the mutilated body of his one-time friend ; and that up till the moment of Joji's death, Kabanki does not know, even though he no doubt has some guesses, why Joji seeks to destroy him. The irony is intensified by the fact that this ending takes place where Joji and Kabanki are first seen as close friends and colleagues, where they have shared so much together. This is the place where they have together engaged in the ritual of signing on and off duty and reporting to each other on the conditions of the patients. This is the place where they have maintained a playful rivalry as they flirted with Florence. This is where they have together witnessed the beginnings of the crises in their lives as the news from the black ghetto and from the streets filtered through to them drawing them willy-nilly into the maelstrom of the black man's unequal yet heroic struggle for liberation.

The movement has therefore been cyclical, and the story ends where it began. The difference is that so many things have been revealed in the intervening period, particularly the reactions of Joji and Kabanki to the vicissitudes of their existence.

Notes

I wish to express my thanks to the Department of Health, Education and Welfare for the Fulbright Hays Fellowship awarded me in 1968—69, which made my research into Zambian literature possible. A major publication from this research is in preparation.

  1 The federation was eventually established in 1953 against strong opposition from all Africans. The Blacks feared for their freedom and their rights, such as they were under the Colonial Government of Northern Rhodesia. But Northern Rhodesia was still accountable to the British Colonial Office for its actions, and this acted as a restraining influence. They feared that the real aim in federating the three territories was to consolidate the Whites' oppressive policies and exploitation of the Blacks. Speeches by Africans of various shades of political opinion showed a remarkable unanimity in their rejection of the idea of federation. Even those who collaborated with the system to the extent that they served on such dummy institutions as the African Representative Council, opposed it. So did the rank-and-file, some of whom, not being literate, received news via radio. They too reacted strongly and with much conviction.

  2 Lusaka: Zambia Publications Bureau, 1955. I have used the 1963 edition. The title is part of the proverb *Uwauma nafyala amumina limo,* "He who beats his mother-in-law beats her thoroughly". The reasoning is that, since the mere fact of raising your hand in anger against your mother-

in-law, even if you may touch her ever so lightly, is punished by depriving you of your wife, if you are going to raise your hand at all, you might as well give her a thorough beating.

3 Donald is sometimes heard as Donad in Bemba pronunciation.

Time, Space and Identity in Athol Fugard's
THE BLOOD KNOT

Anna Rutherford

> And he said, What hast thou done? The
> voice of thy brother's blood crieth unto
> me from the ground.
> > Genesis V. 10.
>
> No smell doth stink as sweet as labour.
> 'Tis joyous times when man and man
> Do work and sweat in common toil,
> When all the world's my neighbour.

The Blood Knot explores what in the world of today can only be termed a myth, namely that all men are brothers, we are all descendants, of Adam and share a universal mother: "There was only one mother, and she's what counts." [1] The theme of universal brotherhood is a seemingly ironic choice of subject for a South African setting, but it is typical of Fugard that he does not use his South African background simply to explore racial problems, but in this play, as in most of his others, takes a particular South African issue and uses it to explore a larger and more universal one.

Subsidiary themes in *The Blood Knot* and ones which are intimately connected with the major theme are those of inhumanity, exploitation, racism (Apartheid, Pass Laws, Immorality Act), the crippling nature of the Boer morality, the repressive nature of the South African regime and the question of identity. These are all themes which Fugard takes up again and again in his later plays: *Statements After An Arrest Under the Immorality Act* (the Immorality Act), *The Island* (the repressive nature of the South African regime), *Hello and Goodbye* (the Boer morality and its effect on people), *Sizwe Bansi is Dead* (the Pass laws), *People Are Living There* (loneliness and the problems of communication), and *Boesman and Lena* (the question of identity). All of Fugard's plays are concerned in varying degrees of intensity with this last theme. [2] What is important to note is that no one play is confined to a single issue; there is a constant interweaving of themes and interchange of symbolic levels not only in each individual play but in his work as a whole. This gives a contrapuntal effect and reminds us of Fugard's statement, "I have learnt more about writing plays from Bach ... than from anything I've ever read by a writer outside of Samuel Beckett." [3] His debt to Beckett is most obvious in *Boesman and Lena* which has strong overtones of *Waiting For*

Godot. The play is a condemnation of racist policies but over and above that it is a Beckett-like study of the misery of human existence. The anxiety, resentment and humiliation of the coloured protagonists is certainly Apartheid-derived but the real concern of the play is with their resilience and will to survive.

> "There will always be thousands of Bantu on the white farms, in the mines, in industry and also as servants in the white homes ... the natives will be there, not as a right but at the bidding and by the grace of the whites."
>
> Minister of Bantu Affairs, 1955.

The title of the play, *The Blood Knot,* indicates the relationship that exists between the two characters, Morris and Zachariah. On the realistic level, as much as there is a realistic level in the play, these two are brothers, born of the same black mother but of different fathers. The result of the different fathers is that Zachariah is black, Morris, white. (on the symbolic level they represent the black and white races.) It is their color that has established their identities in the South African society, not an innate identity, but one created and imposed by outside forces. From the moment of birth skin color has established their fates: fulfilling it would seem Noah's prophecy:

> And he said, Cursed be Canaan; a servant of servants shall he be unto his brethern.
> And he said, Blessed be the Lord God of Shem; and Canaan shall be his servant.
> God shall enlarge Japheth, and he shall dwell in the tents of Shem; and Canaan shall be his servant.
>
> Genesis. X. 25—27.

The story from Genesis finds a direct parallel in a Kono story from Guinea.

> *Death and the Creator*
> At the beginning there was nothing. In the darkness of the world lived Sa, Death, with his wife and only daughter.
> In order to be able to live somewhere, Sa created an immense sea of mud, by means of magic. One day Alatangana, the God, appeared, and visited Sa in his dirty abode. Shocked by this state of affairs, Alatangana reproached Sa fiercely, saying that he had created an uninhabitable place, without plants, without living beings, without light.
> To remedy these faults, Alatangana set out first of all to solidify the dirt. He thus created the earth, but this earth still seemed to him too sterile and too sad, and so he created vegetation and animals of all kinds.
> Sa, who was satisfied with these improvements of his dwelling place, entertained great friendship for Alatangana and offered him much hospitality. After some time Alatangana, who was a bachelor, asked his host for the hand of his only daughter. But the father found many excuses and in the end flatly refused to satisfy his demand. However, Alatangana came to a secret agreement with the young girl. He married her, and in order to escape the wrath of Sa they fled to a remote corner of the earth. There they lived happily and bore many children: seven boys and seven girls—four white boys and girls and three black boys and girls. To the great surprise of their parents, these children spoke strange languages among themselves which their parents did

not understand. Alatangana was annoyed and finally decided to go and consult Sa, and without delay he set out on his way.

His father-in-law addressed him coldly and said: "yes, it was I who punished you, because you have offended me. You shall never understand what your children say. *But I shall give your white children intelligence and paper and ink so that they may write down their thoughts. To your black children, so that they may feed themselves and procure everything they need, I shall give the hoe, the matchet, and the axe.*" (my italics)

Sa, also recommended to Alatangana that the white children should marry among themselves and the black children should do the same. Eager to be reconciled to his father-in-law, Alatangana accepted all his conditions. When he returned he had the marriages of all his children celebrated. They dispersed to all parts of the world and engendered the white and black races. From these ancestors were born innumerable children whom we know today under the names of French, English, Italians, Germans, etc., on the one hand, and Kono, Guuerze, Manon Malinke, and Toma Yacouba on the other.

But the world that had thus been peopled was still living in darkness. Once more Alatangana was forced to ask the advice of Sa. He commanded the "tou-tou" (an early-rising little red bird) and the cock to go and ask Sa's advice.

When he had heard the two messengers, Sa told them: "Enter the house. I shall give you the song by which you shall call the light of day so that men can go about their work."

When the messengers returned, Alatangana became angry and scolded them: "I gave you money and I gave you food for your journey, and you neglected your duty. You deserve death."

But in the end Alatangana mercifully forgave the two unhappy messengers. A little later the tou-tou gave its first cry and the cock too uttered his first song.

And behold, a miracle: hardly had the two birds finished their song when the first day dawned. The sun appeared on the horizon and according to the directions of Sa started on its celestial course. When his journey was completed the sun went to sleep somewhere on the other side of the earth. At this moment there appeared the stars in order to give to mankind some of their light during the night. And since that day the two birds must sing in order to call the light. First the tou-tou and then the cock.

Having thus given the sun, the moon and the stars to mankind, Sa called Alatangana. He said to him: "You took my only child away and in return I have done good to you. It is your turn now to render me a service: as I have been deprived of my child, you must give me one of yours, any time that I choose to call for one. He shall hear a calabash rattle in his dreams when I choose him. This shall be my call which must always be obeyed."

Conscious of his guilt, Alatangana could not but consent. Thus it is because Alatangana disobeyed the custom requiring the payment of the bride-price that human beings must die.[4]

It is a depressing thought that the insidious nature of white propaganda has seeped so far into the black consciousness that a black man would create a tale like the one above. The fate predicted by Noah and Sa alike is the one that has befallen Zachariah. This is revealed when the two brothers start to reminisce about their childhood. Zachariah tells Morris that he never had much to play with. The conversation continues:

> ZACHARIAH: Don't you remember? You got the toys.
> MORRIS: Did I?
> ZACHARIAH: Ja. Like that top, Morrie. Don't you? I have always specially
> remembered that top. That brown stinkwood top. She gave me her old cotton
> reels to play with, but it wasn't the same. I wanted a top.
> MORRIS: Who? Who gave me the top?
> ZACHARIAH: Mother!
> MORRIS: Mother!
> ZACHARIAH: Ja. She said she only had one. There was always only one.
> MORRIS: Zach, you're telling me a thing now! (p. 130)

Zachariah continues to describe the mother he knew (supposedly their
mutual mother) until Morris cries out "Zach, are you sure that wasn't somebody else?"

> ZACHARIAH: It was Mother's feet. She let me feel the hardnesses and then
> pruned them down with a razor blade.
> MORRIS: No, Zach. You got me worried now! A grey dress?
> ZACHARIAH: Maybe.
> MORRIS (persistent): Going to church. She wore it going to . . .
> ZACHARIAH: The butcher shop! That's it! That's where she went.
> MORRIS: What for?
> ZACHARIAH: Offal.
> MORRIS: Offal! Stop, Zach. Stop! We must sort this out, man. I mean . . . it
> sounds like some other mother.
> ZACHARIAH (gently): How can that be?
> MORRIS: Listen, Zach. Do you remember the songs she sang?
> ZACHARIAH: Do I! (He laughs and then sings.)
>
> > My skin is black,
> > The soap is blue,
> > But the washing comes out white.
> > I took a man
> > On a Friday night;
> > Now I'm washing a baby too.
> > Just a little bit black,
> > And a little bit white,
> > He's a Capie through and through.
>
> (MORRIS is staring at him in horror.)
> What's the matter?
> MORRIS: That wasn't what she sang to me.
> ZACHARIAH: No?
> MORRIS: Lullaby-baby it was ". . . You'll get to the top."
> ZACHARIAH: I don't remember that at all.
> MORRIS (anguish): This is some sort of terrible error. (pp. 131—32)

Their almost complete inability to recognize the same woman as their
mother emphasizes the great gap that exists today, a gap that almost makes *us*
forget our common humanity. Morrie persists in his quest for a childhood that
both can recognize and eventually finds a point of common ground in a game
they played when children when they took imaginary rides in an old wreck of
a car. One such ride culminated in their driving into a flock of butterflies:

MORRIS: Look! There's a butterfly.
ZACHARIAH: On your side?
MORRIS: Yours as well. Just look.
ZACHARIAH: All round us, hey!
MORRIS: This is rare, Zach! We've driven into a flock of butterflies.
(ZACHARIAH smiles and then laughs)
You remember, hey! We've found it Zach.
We've found it! This is our youth! (pp. 133—34)

But all that is past; it was in their youth (the beginning of time). The present situation is as Noah predicted it would be. Zach is exploited and insulted by the white man, a victim of prejudice and inhumanity, words which Fugard shows us are empty terms, abstracts, to Morrie, but living realities to Zach.

ZACHARIAH: Ja. They call a man a boy. You got a word for that, Morrie?
MORRIS: Long or short?
ZACHARIAH: Squashed, like it didn't fit the mouth.
MORRIS: I know the one you mean.
ZACHARIAH: Then say it.
MORRIS: Prejudice.
ZACHARIAH: Pre-ja-dis.
MORRIS: Injustice!
ZACHARIAH: That's all out of shape as well.
MORRIS: Inhumanity!
ZACHARIAH: No. That's when he makes me stand at the gate.
MORRIS: Am I right in thinking you were there again today?
ZACHARIAH: All day long.
MORRIS: You tried to go back to pots?
ZACHARIAH: I tried to go back to pots. My feet, I said, are killing me.
MORRIS: And then?
ZACHARIAH: Go to the gate or go to hell ... Boy!
MORRIS: He said boy as well?
ZACHARIAH: He did.
MORRIS: In one sentence?
ZACHARIAH: Prejudice and inhumanity in one sentence! (pp. 119—20)

The white man's prejudiced, archetypal image of the black man is reflected in Zach. He is illiterate, no doubt because he is stupid, he smells and his chief interests are drink and sex. It's perfectly obvious that he is fit for little more than to be a labor machine to make profits for the white man: "I do the work ... But he goes and makes my profit" (p. 91). Zach is no more than a labor unit, one of the group of people described by the South African Deputy Minister of Justice in 1969 as "surplus appendages."

So efficient and ruthless has the white man's propaganda been that Zach begins to doubt his own dignity and beauty. This is revealed in the scene where, in his dream, he confronts his mother. Before doing this he dons Morrie's suit in the hope that he may, through it, assume the white man's identity and then receive the treatment accorded to the white man. The putting on of the clothes is an objective correlative of his own state of mind, an admission of the doubts which assail him. At another stage Morrie also tries to come to an understanding of Zach and of what it means to be Zach by putting on Zach's old coat.

Clothes play a role in the establishment of identity and indicate one's place and position within a society. This is particularly marked, of course, in a divided and highly stratified society. Think for a moment of the beginning of Michael Anthony's *The Year in San Fernando* and the description of Mr. Chandles:

> We had heard only very little about Mr. Chandles. The little we had heard were whispers and we didn't gather much, but we saw him sometimes leaning over the banister of the Forestry Office, and indeed he was as aristocratic as they said he was. He looked tidy and elegant and he always wore jacket and tie, unusual under the blazing sun. These things confirmed that he was well off, and his manner and bearing, and the condescending look he gave everything about him, made us feel that he had gained high honours in life.[5]

The question we ask is, is Mr. Chandles black or white? Dressed as he is, in that society he can be nothing else but white. It is not until chapter four that Mr. Chandles gives himself away; he had mastered the clothes of the white man but had failed to master the language. This shows that clothes are not sufficient in themselves to establish an identity. This is an argument that Morrie uses. He tries to persuade Zach that there's more to the white man's identity than the clothes he wears. Zach goes along with him until Morrie suggests a barefoot white man. "No," says Zach. "Never a barefoot white man" (p. 154). "The settler's feet are never visible." [6] Clothes may not be all but in a society like South Africa they do play a major role. Zach knows this and in desperation enlists Morrie's clothes to come to his aid. Looking ludicrous in the white man's clothes just as Morrie did in Zach's, and proving incidentally, as with Mr. Chandles (1) that clothes are in themselves insufficient to establish identity and (2) that neither can assume the other's identity because "the fit is wrong" Zach appeals to his mother:

> Whose mother were you really? At the bottom of your heart, where your blood is red with pain, tell me, whom did you really love? No evil feelings, Ma, but, I mean, a man's got to know. You see, he's been such a burden as a brother. (Agitation.) Don't be dumb! Don't cry! It was just a question! Look! I brought you a present, old soul. (Holds out a hand with the fingers lightly closed.)
> It's a butterfly. A real beauty butterfly. We were travelling fast, Ma. We hit them at ninety . . . a whole flock. But one was still alive, and made me think of . . . Mother. . . . So I caught it, myself, for you, remembering what I caught from you. This, old Ma of mine, is gratitude for you, and it proves it, doesn't it? Some things are only skin deep, because I got it, here in my hand, I got beauty . . . too . . . haven't I? (pp. 161—62)
>
> > Take up the White Man's burden —
> > Send forth the best ye breed —
> > Go bind your sons to exile
> > To serve your captives' need;
> > To wait in heavy harness
> > On fluttered folk and wild —

> Your new-caught, sullen peoples,
> Half devil and half child.
>   Rudyard Kipling

ZACHARIAH: You see, he's been such a burden as a brother.

Morrie's coming to live with Zach is symbolic on one level of the coming of the white man to South Africa. His dream in the first place, as Zach's brother and as a white man, can be presented thus:

worm   →   butterfly
light half-caste →   white man
white man   →   Lords of Human Kind

But Morrie is a certain king of a white man; he is a liberal, a man with a conscience who has acknowledged his guilt and recognized his tie to the black man (his brother). And so he gives up his original dream and for this he substitutes another, that of the white liberal who believes that the two races can live in harmony togehter. Its "our meaning", he tells Zach, "Me and you . . . in here" (p. 111). This explains his presence in the room, Zach's home. Yet in spite of aligning himself with the black man, "I'm on your side, they're on theirs" (p. 92), he is still destructive of Zach's happiness.

> ZACHARIAH: We . . . had a good time, for a long time. And then you came . . . and . . .
> MORRIS: Say it.
> ZACHARIAH: . . . then you came. That's all. (p. 97)

In giving up his former dream Morrie's ego has managed to triumph over his id. That this has not been an easy task is revealed troughout the play where Morrie's id is constantly trying to assert itself. And what remains quite clear is that Morrie retains a suffficient belief in the superiority of white values to try to impose them on Zach. He displays all the traits of the Boer morality, for example in his frugality and attitude to drink and sex. When Zach dreams of a girl with "tits like fruits" (p. 100), what does Morrie offer as a substitute? "A corresponding pen-pal of the opposite sex" (p. 101). His plans for the future exclude all pleasures.

The absence of women in Zach's life since Morrie entered it can be explained in terms of certain laws have been introduced by the South African government. Zach's relationship with Ethel Lange is out of the question because of the Immorality Act which forbids carnal intercourse between white and coloured persons. Under the act "coloured person" is defined as "any person other than a white person" and "white person" as "any person who *in appearance* (my emphasis) obviously is or who by general acceptance and repute is a white person." But there is another reason which accounts for Zach's lack of women. This is the establishment of the Bantu homelands and the laws that control the entry of coloured people into the White Area, namely the Pass Laws. This has meant the separation of husband from wife, for if a man marries a woman who comes from a rural area, she may not come to live with him in the town, even if he qualifies to life there, unless she can prove that she entered the area lawfully and ordinarily resides with her husband. But there is a total embargo on the entry of black women into the metropolitan area so this is not possible.

As a white person or one who "in appearance" is white, Morrie is obviously able to read and write, and he knows all the social graces (he teaches Zach to use toilet paper!). Because of all of this he at times adopts a patronizing attitude towards his brother, and when challenged, he is ready to assert his superiority: "I win" (p. 138). It is Zach who goes out to work and it is his money that Morrie saves, reminding us that the wealth of South Africa is built on the labor of the black man. It is also the money from Zach's labor that is used to buy the suit that enables Morrie to assume the archetypal role of the white man. Morrie may look upon Zach as his brother but his attitude reflects Albert Schweitzer's statement, "the black man is my brother but my junior brother." I will return to the question of the ambiguity of Morrie's role at a later point in this essay.

The entire action of the play take place in a one-room shack in the Non-White location of Korsten, near Port Elizabeth, South Africa. On the realistic level it is Zach's home which is now being shared by Morrie, whilst on the symbolic level it is a microcosm of South Africa. There is yet another level in which the room is a world within a world in which time and space are sespended to enable Morrie and Zach to assume other identities and to act out their dreams and nightmares. The room, like Style's studio in *Sizwe Bansi* becomes "a strong room of dreams." It would also be possible to postulate that the entire action takes place in the mind of one man, as it does in *Sizwe Bansi is Dead.*

The question of time and space plays an important role in many of Fugard's plays for it is intimately connected to his concern with the question of identity. The two categories are to a certain extent interchangeable dimensions. The Open Space Theatre is particularly suitable to show this, and Fugard uses the technique to advantage in a later play, *Sizwe Bansi*. When we consider time and space as interchangeable dimensions it is interesting to look at Hantu which is the category of time and space in one of the Bantu languages, (Kinyaruanda).

> Space and time fall together into the category *Hantu*. Hantu is the force which localizes spatially and temporally every event and every "motion", for since all things are force, everything is constantly in motion. To the question, "*Where* did you see it?" the answer may be, "Where did I see it? Why, in the reign of King X." That is, a question of place can be answered in terms of time. To the question, "*When* did you see it?" the answer may be: "In the boat, under the liana bridge after Y." Here the question of time is answered by an allocation of place. This is by no means unusual; everyone who looks at a clock reads time by the position of the hands—a determination of place; and the mathematician who wants to represent motion indicates the distance on one axis of his co-ordinates and the time on the other.[7]

To illustrate the interchangeability between time and space and to show the connection between both to identity we can look at a scene from *Boesman and Lena*. Here Fugard uses space to establish identity. This means that when one is disorientated in space, one may establish whatever identity one wants for oneself. Boesman realizes this and so when his pondok is destroyed he cries out in triumph:

> BOESMAN (violently). Yes! *Dankie, baas.*
> You should have said it too, sitting there with your sad story. Whiteman was doing us a favour. You should have helped him. He wasn't just burning *pondoks*. They alone can't stink like that. Or burn like that.
> There was something else in that fire, something rotten. Us! Our sad stories, our smells, our world! And it burnt, *boeta.* It burnt. I watched that too.
> The end was a pile of ashes. And quiet.
> Then ... 'Here!' ... then I went back to the place where our *pondok* had been. It was gone! You understand that? Gone! I wanted to call you and show you. There where we crawled in and out like baboons, where we used to sit like them and eat, our head between our knees, our fingers in the pot, hiding away so that the others wouldn't see our food ... I could stand there! There was room for me to stand straight.
> You know what that is? Listen now. I'm going to use a word. Freedom! *Ja,* I've heard them talk it. Freedom! That's what the whiteman gave us. I've got my feelings too, sister. It was a big one I had when I stood there. That's why I laughed, why I was happy. When we picked up our things and started to walk I wanted to sing. It was Freedom![8]

As long as Boesman wanders aimlessly, tied to no place, he is able to maintain whatever identity he desires. But the moment he picks up the piece of *sinkplaat* his freedom is destroyed, and his old identity, the one imposed by the white man, is once more restored.

> BOESMAN: I saw that piece of *sinkplaat* on the side of the road, I should have passed it. Gone on! Freedom's a long walk. But the sun was low. Our days are too short.
> (Pause)
> Too late, Boesman. Too late for it today.
> So I picked it up. Finish and *klaar*. Another *pondok*. (p. 31)

To turn now to the question of time and identity. One's identity is established partly through memory and this in turn means that it is established in, and must exist in time. One can see this in Beckett for whom, according to Kirsten Petersen,

> a coherent memory is a clue to identity since this allows for changeability of time. Otherwise it would be impossible at any given moment to state one's own identity since it will have changed the next moment. Vladimir and Estragon in *Waiting for Godot* have no consistent memory just as they have no idea of time.[9]

Many of Fugard's characters are endeavoring to establish a consistent identity through memory; Milly in *People Are Living There* and Johnnie in

Hello and Goodbye are obvious examples. *Hello and Goodbye* commences with Johnnie tapping a spoon against the side of a glass and counting:

> JOHNNIE (counting as he taps) . . . fifty-five, fifty-six, fifty-seven, fifty-eight, fifty-nine, sixty!
> (stops tapping.)
> Three hundred and . . .
> (Pause.)
> Five minutes—become hours, become days . . . today! . . . Friday somethingth, nineteen . . . what? . . . sixty-three. One thousand nine hundred and sixty-three! Multiplied by twelve, by thirty, by twenty-four, by sixty . . .
> (Pause.)
> by sixty again! . . . gives you every second. Gee-sis! Millions.
> (Pause.)
> Yes, since Geesis.
> (He starts tapping again but stops after only a few.)
> No! I'm wrong. It's six. Sixty goes six times into three hundred and sixty. It's six minutes!
> (Looks around.)
> Walls. The table. Chairs—three empty, one . . . occupied. Here and now. Mine. No change. Yes there is! Me. I'm a fraction older. More memories. All the others! Same heres mostly. Here. Other nows. Then, and then when this happened and that happened. My milestones, in here mostly. 'And then one day, after a long illness, his . . .'[10]

Johnnie's solution to his problem is to take over his father's identity, (ironically his father is a cripple), and this then provides him with a past: "I'm a man with a story" (p. 51).

The third means of establishing your identity is through your image in the minds of other people, the recognition of yourself through others. In *People are Living There* Don tells Milly:

> You lose your place in the mind of man. With a bit of luck once or twice in your life you have it. That warm nest in another mind where "You" is all wrapped up in their thinking and feeling and worrying about "You". But even if you are one of the lucky ones, sooner or later you end up in the cold again. Nothing is forever.[11]

Or consider Hestor in *Hello and Goodbye*. "Then I started waking in the middle of the night wondering which one it was, which room . . . And later still, who it was . . . Me . . . but what's that mean?" (p. 23). Hestor's tragedy lies in the fact that as a prostitute moving from room to room and man to man she is not able to establish herself either in space, or in someone else's mind, "You're not in his dream" (p. 23). All she can do is wait, "let it happen and wait. For a memory" (p. 23). What we all need is "Eyes. . . . Another pair of eyes. Something to see us" *(Boesman and Lena,* p. 20).

The converse of all of this is that to change one's identity, time and space must be suspended, and this is the situation we have in *The Blood Knot.* The world within the world, the world in which Morrie and Zach play out their dreams/games is one which is controlled by Morrie's alarm clock. Each time the alarm clock rings we are brought back to historical time, to reality, and along with this the two men are brought back to their established identities within South African society. All of this is controlled by the white man and this in turn explains why it is Morrie who sets the alarm. Fugard's choice of the alarm clock is particularly appropriate for his purpose for it is that instrument that constantly wakes us from our dream or nightmare world and plunges us back into the world of reality. Compare Don's experience in *People Are Living There:*

> I have a dream. Music is playing, and I'm in a corner and so far no one has seen me. I think it's a party because there's a lot of people, and ... well, all I know about them really is the noise, because I'm not watching. I'm holding my breath. But the noise is a hubbub—talking and jokes and one very loud voice laughing heartily. Then the music stops. I can't tell you how terrible that is. Just stops. Silence. And sweat. Because I know, I just know that that means *it's my turn.* Don't ask me what. That's the thought. *It's your turn now!* I feel their eyes. Without looking up I know they are staring and waiting and that it is my turn and I must do something. So I move. I walk. One foot up, a second on one leg, then down. Two or three steps, in this silence, safely. Then things start to go wrong. I begin to wobble during that second on one leg. My arms start swinging wildly. There's a feeling that I've got five elbows and they're all sticking out. I'm knocking glasses into people's laps, falling over their legs ...
> MILLY: Wake up!
> DON: I always do. The trouble is I wake up too soon. I never reach the end. The terror, you see. My mind protecting itself. (p. 32)

The Blood Knot is punctuated by the ringing of the alarm. In between the rings the two men play their games in which they switch and change identities and dream their dreams. The novement into this dreamtime is not a clearly defined event. Our only indication that it has taken place is when either man, or both, assumes another identity and it becomes obvious that they are playing a certain role in a game. The games are equated with with their dreams and they may in turn be equated with wish-fulfillment.

The first instance of this taking place in the play is when Zach thinks about his former companion, Minnie, who doesn't come anymore. He goes back into his past and remembers the good times, the fun and happiness he's had with Minnie:

> ZACHARIAH: Standing just right on that spot out there in the street with his bottle and his music and laughing with me. Zach, he says, Ou Pellie, tonight is the night ...
> (The alarm clock goes off.)
> ... is the night ... tonight
> (Zachariah loses the thread of his story. By the time the alarm stops he has forgotten what he was saying.) (p. 94)

Zach's dream of the past has been shattered by the alarm clock which has returned him to the reality of the present in which the past is not even a faint memory.

Morrie too goes back into his past where he dreams first of all the dream of white superiority and then his dream that all men are brothers and can live in harmony together.

> ... Why did I do it? ... Why try to deny it? Because ... because ... I'll tell you the whole truth now ... Because I did try it! It didn't seem a sin. If a man was born with a chance at a change, why not take it, I thought ... thinking of worms lying warm in their silk, to come out one day with wings and things! Why not a man? If his dreams are soft and keep him warm at night, why not stand up the next morning, different ... Beautiful! It's the natural law! The long arm of the real law frightened me—but I might have been lucky. We all know that some are not caught, so ... so ... so what was worrying me? You. Yes, in my dreams at night, there was you, as well. What about you? My own brother. What sort of a thing was that to do to an ou's own flesh and blood brother? Because he is, you know. There was only one mother, and she's what counts. And watch out! She will, too, up in heaven, her two little chickens down here and find one missing. She'll know what you've done! If you don't mind about hell, all right, go ahead ... but even so there was still you, because it wasn't that next life but this old, worn out and wicked one, and I was tired because there was still you. Anywhere, any place or road, there was still you. So I came back. (Pause.) It's not been too hard. A little uneasy at times, but not too hard. And I've proved I'm no Judas. Gentle Jesus meek mild, I'm no Judas! (pp. 159—60)

On this occasion the alarm shatters two dreams. Morrie has, as a white liberal, acknowledged that the dream of God-given white superiority is a false dream, that it is necessary to "get by without the old dreams" (p. 104). "Maybe," he says, "a few new ones will come with time... *and in time please!*" (p. 104) (my emphasis). The play goes on to show that the urgency in Morrie's words, "and in time, please!" is well warranted.

The alarm has also brought them back to a situation where Morrie's idea of universal brotherhood, where black and white can live in harmony, together, is also a dream, an impossibility, given the present South African situation. We are forced at this point to ask ourselves if their childhood in which they played together and were happy is also an illusion, nothing more than a dream. Morrie's statement, "We played our games, Zach" (p. 134), seems ominous.

At this point I would like to take up once more the ambiguity of Morrie's role, and Fugard's attitude towards him. Morrie cries out, "I'm no Judas!" (p. 160). Can the white South African liberal be called a Judas? Has he betrayed his black brother? What has he done to improve the lot of the black South African? Isn't Morrie still imposing the white man's values on Zach? Morrie's terminology can be questioned on several occasions. Consider his analogies from darkness to light, or worm to butterfly. When Zach asks him, "What is there as black as me?", Morrie replies, "To equal you? To match you? How about a dangerous night? Try that for size and colour of its darkness. You go with it, Zach, as with certain smells and simple sorrows too" (p. 145). Even when he puts on Zach's coat to try to get to know him, the first thing he betrays is his Boer mentality. "It was a big help. You get right inside the man when you can wrap up in the smell of him, and imagine the *sins of idle hands in empty pockets* and see the sadness of snot smears on the sleeve" (p. 105) (my emphasis). On both occasions Morrie qualifies his negative statement but it *was* the negative that was apparently uppermost in his mind. When Morrie says to Zach, "I wish that old washerwoman had bruised me at birth" (p. 145), his use of the word "bruised" surely betrays him. The bruise is Zach's blackness, and as a bruise it must be regarded as a flaw which Morrie insinuates was congenital, thus supporting the argument of those who would maintain that the black man is born inferior. The stage direction for this speech of Morrie's is "(quietly and with absolute sincerity)". We are asked to believe that Morrie is truly concerned about Zach and wishes to share his condition. Yet his use of the word "bruised" expresses his subconscious belief in the idea of white superiority which contradicts his avowed liberal sentiments. It is little wonder that Zach "stares strangely at him" (p. 146). What Fugard is perharps suggesting is that just as the propaganda of the South African government has seeped into Zach's subconscious so that at one point he questions his own beauty and dignity, so too has it crept into the white, even of those who would consciously, and in all sincerity, reject it.

Morrie's interpretation of the Blood Knot is a naive, sentimental one of which Zach is justifiably and obviously sceptical. Whilst Morrie raves on about "Brotherhood. Brother-in-arms, each other's arms. Brotherly love. Ah, it breeds, man! It's warm and feathery, like eggs in a nest" (pp. 103—04), Zach sleeps. With seeming awareness of the true situation again and again Zach prods Morrie into betraying himself. One example will suffice. Morrie surreptitiously smells Zach's coat (his concern with the black man's smell should be obvious by now) and says:

> Zach, I think we must borrow Minnie's bath again.
> ZACHARIAH: Okay.
> MORRIS: What about me? Do I smell?
> ZACHARIAH: No. (Pause.) Have I started again?
> (MORRIS doesn't answer. ZACHARIAH laughs.)
> MORRIS: Sweat . . .
> ZACHARIAH: Go on.
> MORRIS: You're still using paper the way I showed you, hey?
> ZACHARIAH: Ja. What's that thing you say, Morrie? The one about smelling?
> MORRIS (quoting): "The rude odours of manhood."
> ZACHARIAH: "The rude odours of manhood." And the other one? The long one?
> MORRIS: No smell?
> (ZACHARIAH nods.)
> > "No smell doth stink as sweet as labour.
> > 'Tis joyous times when man and man

Do work and sweat in common toil,
When all the world's my neighbour."

ZACHARIAH: "When all the world's my neighbour"
(ZACHARIAH starts drying his feet with the towel. MORRIS empties the basin and puts it away.)
Minnie.
MORRIS: What about Minnie?
ZACHARIAH: Our neighbour. Strange thing about Minnie. He doesn't come any more.
MORRIS: I don't miss him.
ZACHARIAH: You don't remember. I'm talking about before you.

(pp. 92—93)

We can see a growing awareness on Zach's part of the ambivalence in Morrie. Consider Morrie's attitude to the discovery that Zach's penpal was a white woman. The historical reality means of course that such a relationship is out of the question. But we would expect Morrie in his role of South African liberal to express opposition to the official attitude. This is not the case. On the contrary, when he says to Zach "I'm telling you it's a dream and the most dangerous one" (p. 129), we have the feeling that he is expressing more then the official attitude. So too does Zach and he chides Morrie for his unwillingness to share "that sweet, white smell" (p. 128) with his brother. "It hurts to think you didn't share a good one like that with your brother. Giving me all that shit about future and plans, and then keeping the real goosie for yourself" (p. 128). Morrie then takes it upon himself to expose Zach, to Zach, in all his blackness and all that goes with it so as to show Zach the complete horror and impossibility of the situation, "of a dark-born boy playing with a white idea" (p. 141). He forces Zach to see himself through the eyes of a white man and presents him with the white man's archetypal image of the black man. Zach thanks Morrie for the exposure: "after a whole life I only seen me properly tonight. You helped me. I'm grateful" (p. 146). Pushed by the white man into the extreme position he decides to accept the consequences of his blackness and act accordingly. He issues due warning of his intentions to the white man:

ZACHARIAH: I take it. I take them all. Black days, black ways, black things. They're me. I'm happy. Ha ha ha! Do you hear my black happiness?
MORRIS: Oh yes, Zach, I hear it, I promise you.
ZACHARIAH: Can you feel it?
MORRIS: I do. I do.
ZACHARIAH: And see it?
MORRIS: Midnight, man! Like the twelve strokes of midnight you stand before my wondering eyes.
ZACHARIAH: And my thoughts! What about my thoughts?
MORRIS: Let's hear it.
ZACHARIAH: I'm on my side, they're on theirs.
MORRIS: That's what they want.
ZACHARIAH: They'll get it.
MORRIS: You heard him.

ZACHARIAH: This time it's serious.
MORRIS: We warn you.
ZACHARIAH: Because from now on, I'll be what I am. They can be what they like. I don't care. I don't want to mix. It's bad for the blood and the poor babies. So I'll keep mine clean, and theirs I'll scrub off, afterwards, off my hands, my unskilled, my stained hands and say I'm not sorry! The trembles you felt was something else. You see you were too white, so blindingly white that I couldn't see what I was doing. (p. 145)

Zach then takes it upon himself to perform the same "favour" for Morrie and give Morrie the benefit of "another pair of eyes." Morrie declines Zach's offer, but Zach insists:

ZACHARIAH: No! I'm not a man who forgets a favour. I want to help you now.
MORRIS: I don't need any assistance, thank you.
ZACHARIAH: But you do. A man can't really see himself. Look at me. I had an odd look at me in the mirror—but so what? Did it make things clearer? No. Why? Because it's the others what does. They got sharper eyes. I want to give you the benefit of mine.
Sit down.
(Morris sits)
You're on the lighter side of life all right, You like that . . . all over? Your legs and things?
MORRIS: It's evenly spread.
ZACHARIAH: Not even a foot in the darker side, hey! I'd say you must be quite a bright boy with nothing on. (pp. 146—47)

From this moment on we have the feeling that Zach is playing with Morrie as a cat with a mouse. He is aware of Morrie's secret longings, how Morrie's id struggles for dominance and with what difficulty his ego subdues it. He in turn forces Morrie into his archetypal role of white man.

It could be argued that the games they play perform a psychological function. Insofar as they force each other into their stereotyped roles and compel each other to see themselves as black or white society sees them, they are in effect acting as Freudian analysts on each other, exposing their neuroses and hopefully, through exposure, curing them. Fugard no doubt is hoping that his play will have a similar effect on the audience.

In the interview entitled "Challenging the Silence," Fugard was asked if he had developed any great optimism for his country. Part of his answer to the question reads as follows:

There is a widening gap of misunderstanding between people, evident in the extent to which whites progressively think of the black stereotype and equivalently, the extent to which blacks now think of the white stereotype; evident in the extent to which people have lost their faces and have become just literally the colour of their skins. The situation is hardening and getting more dangerous. It's going to get worse and, in this respect, I suppose I'm a pessimist. (p. 36)

The final scene of *The Blood Knot* reflects Fugard's pessimism and shows us what can happen if things continue as they are. This game shows us how rapidly dreams can become nigthmares which are also a form of wish-fulfillment. It also shows us the reason behind Morrie's words to Zach on a previous occasion: "All they need for evidence is a man's dreams. Not so much his hate. They say they can live with that. It's his dreams they drag off to judgement, shouting: 'Silence! He's been caught! With convictions? He's pleading! He's guilty! Take him away" (pp. 141—142).

Twice before, in moments of suspended time, Zach had asserted himself, changed identity and assumed control:

> ZACHARIAH: You just keep quiet, Morris, and let me finish this time, and don't think I'm going to get lost in my words again. That bloody clock of yours doesn't go off till bed-time, so I got plenty of time to talk. So just you shut up, please! (p. 110)

A similar situation arises in Scene Three.

The final scene shows us that Zach has learnt his lesson well, the psychotherapy in his case has been extremely successful. Once more he jumps out of his traditional and accepted (in white terms) role and starts to fulfill the promises/threats made in Scene Four. Morrie cannot comprehend the situation:

> MORRIS: But . . . but I thought you were the good sort of boy?
> ZACHARIAH: Me?
> MORRIS: The simple, trustworthy type of Johnboy. Weren't you that?
> ZACHARIAH: I've changed.
> MORRIS: Who gave you the right?
> ZACHARIAH: I took it!
> MORRIS: That's illegal! They weren't yours! That's theft. 'Thou shalt not steal.' I arrest you in the name of God. That's it! God! (Looking around wildly.) My prayers . . . please! My last wish . . . is to say my prayers, please. You see . . . you might hear them.
> (MORRIS: goes down on his knees. ZACHARIAH begins to move to him.)
> Our Father, which art our Father in heaven, because we never knew the other one; Forgive us this day our trespassing; I couldn't help it; The gate was open, God, your sun was too bright and blinded my eyes, so I didn't see the notice prohibiting! And "beware of the dog" was in Bantu, so how was I to know, Oh Lord! My sins are not that black. Furthermore, just some bread for the poor, daily, and let Your Kingdom come as quick as it can, for Yours is the power and the glory, but ours is the fear and the judgement of eyes behind our back for the sins of our birth and the man behind the tree in the darkness while I wait . . . Eina! (pp. 174—75)
> (ZACHARIAH stands above MORRIS on the point of violence. The alarm clock rings. MORRIS crawls frantically away.)

Morrie/Fugard draws back in horror from the consequences of such an Armageddon. His alarm clock, like Don's mind, is a protective device, so that at the very point of violence it rings and we are jerked back into historical time—Morrie still controls historical reality in South Africa. But Zach's victory in suspended time is enough to show Morrie and the audience that the white man is not going to control time forever.

> MORRIS: We were carried away, as they would say, by the game ... quite far in fact. Mustn't get worried, though ... I don't think. I mean, it was only a game ... as long as we play in the right spirit ... we'll be all right. I'll keep the clock winded, don't worry. One thing I'm certain is sure, it's a good thing we got the game. It will pass the time. Because we got a lot left, you know! (Little laugh.) Almost a whole life ... stretching ahead ... in here ... (Pause.) Yes. (Pause.) As I said ... I'm not too worried at all. Not at all ... too worried. I mean, other men get by without a future. In fact, I think there's quite a lot of people getting by without futures these days. (Silence. MORRIS makes the last preparations for bed.)
> ZACHARIAH: Morris?
> MORRIS: Yes?
> ZACHARIAH: What is it, Morrie? The two of us ... you know ... in here?
> MORRIS: Home.
> ZACHARIAH: Is there no other way?
> MORRIS: No. You see, we're tied together, Zach. It's what they call the blood knot ... the bond between brothers. (p. 176)

Here we have the true meaning of the blood knot. The reality lies not in Morrie's sentimental idea but in the mutual dependence of one on the other. In the final scene they both resent and endeavor to chase away the mother; polarized as they are now into black and white roles, they would both deny the connection. But this is not possible; they are bound to one another and they are forced to work out their future, if there is to be a future, within the spatial confines of South Africa.

> Each living man is a fossil in so far as each man carries with himself remnants of his ancestors.
>
>   Jacques Monod

In the terminology of the West Indian author and critic, Wilson Harris, the white South Africans have locked themselves in their own fortresses of culture, their own horizons, so that no dialogue with the past is possible, and if they continue, their future is doomed to destruction, for they have excluded any possibility of revision and renewal.[12] They have polarized their society to such an extent that there is no fertile interaction between the two races. What they have failed to realize is that identity is part of an infinite movement, that one can only come into a dialogue with the past and future, a dialogue which is necessary, if one ceases to invest in a single identity and instead is prepared to participate in a wider community. The promise of fulfillment, Wilson Harris says, lies in a profound and difficult vision of essential unity within the most bitter forms of latent and historical diversity.

It is such a vision that Athol Fugard has presented us with in *The Blood Knot*. He has shown the dynamite-like situation that exists in South Africa today and has made a plea for the circulation of light, the interaction of the races, for it is only in such interaction, in the conjuction of opposites, that regeneration and life consists.

Notes

1 Athol Fugard, *The Blood Knot* (Harmondsworth, 1968), p. 160. All further references are to this edition and will be included in the text.
2 For a discussion of this particular theme see Kirsten Holst Petersen, "The Question of Identity in a South African Context," paper read at Commonwealth Conference, Kampala, 1974. This paper is to be published by *The Literar Criterion,* Mysore.
3 Athol Fugard in an interview with Michael Coveney, "Challenging the Silence," *Plays and Players,* 21, 2 (1973), 37.
4 "Death and the Creator," in *The Origin of Life and Death,* ed. Ulli Beier (London, 1966), pp. 3—6.
5 Michael Anthony, *The Year in San Fernando* (London, 1970), p. 1.
6 Frantz Fanon, *The Wretched of the Earth* (Harmondsworth, 1969), p. 30.
7 Janheinz Jahn, *Muntu: An Outline of Neo-African Culture* (London, 1961), p. 102.
8 Athol Fugard, *Boesman and Lena* (London, 1973), pp. 30—31.
9 Petersen, ms.
10 Athol Fugard, *Hello and Goodbye* (London, 1973), p. 1.
11 Athol Fugard, *People Are Living There* (London, 1970), p. 33.
12 For an introduction to Wilson Harris's critical theories, see the Introduction to *Enigma of Values,* ed. Anna Rutherford (Aarhus, 1975).

Africa, Their Africa

O. R. Dathorne

In isolating David Walker, Henry Highland Garnet, Martin R. Delany and Frederick Douglass for consideration, one is dealing with people who were extremely different in personality but had a single unifying bond. Though born black, they were not subject to the degradation and suffering of their fellow Blacks. The irony of their peculiar situation was as obvious then as it is now, for by averting their eyes they could have afforded themselves some tolerable amount of basic freedom, if not dignity. But they chose, despite their dispensation, to identify themselves with the black slave and to fight for his emancipation.

David Walker is best known for his *Appeal to the Colored Citizens of the World*,[1] constituting one of the first expressions of black assertiveness. Basically the fiery account claimed that the White "God of armies" would side with the Blacks in their need to revolt. If the Whites did not give in, the Blacks would topple them with the help of this Christian god. God, for David Walker, is not to be found in the meek and pious mouthings of the "nigger" minstrel tradition of the slave song. Indeed, Walker goes on to state that Blacks who side with Whites and help to perpetuate the state of ignorance and slavery, should also suffer. Education, Walker argues, would free the black man in that he would not be prepared to subject his family and himself to the adversities of slavery.

Walker's firm statement was the verbalizing of years of discontent. Slaves had always been plotting and seeking ways out of their predicament—escape, suicide, revolution. In 1822 an abortive uprising had taken place led by Denmark Vesey and nine years after (or two years after Walker came out with his activist statement), Nat Turner's rebellion took place. This is the best known of the slave revolts and approximately sixty Whites were killed and a hundred Blacks died before its eventual suppression. Nat Turner himself managed to remain in hiding for over two months before he was captured and hanged. Walker's *Appeal* had contributed in no small way to the rightness of Nat Turner's cause. For by 1830 Walker's little booklet had gone into its third edition and was known in the slave South.

Walker himself had expected no less. He had said that he had assumed he would be labelled "an ignorant impudent and restless disturber of the public peace" and "a mover of insubordination." Indeed his odd disappearance from Boston in 1830, when he was only about forty-five, was most likely an indi-

cation that he had been murdered. Although he was born of a so-called
"free" mother in the south, he himself must have felt the pressures of living in
a racially maladjusted society so acutely that he left for the North when he
was in his thirties. But his links with the South helped to make his *Appeal*
circulate.

Yet the *Appeal* demonstrates certain attitudes worth pointing out. Although
the overall message, poignantly stated time and time again, is that the slaves
should seize their freedom, there are certain give-away parts. For instance
Walker quite obviously sees a distinction in kind between the "free" Blacks
and what he terms "their more ignorant brethren." That is why he wants
"colored people to acquire learning in this country." In turn this attitude
makes him take a firm stance against colonizing. He writes:

> Let no man of us budge one step, and let slaveholders come to beat us
> from our country. America is more our country, than it is the whites—we
> have enriched it with our blood and tears. The greatest riches in all America
> have arisen from our blood and tears—and will they drive us from our
> property and homes, which we have earned with our blood? They must look
> sharp or this very thing will bring swift destruction upon them.

He is a firm integrationist and sees the attempts at founding colonies
overseas and shipping Blacks as a devious way of getting over the consequences of black freedom.

Like Henry Garnet who in 1843 was to deliver a similar attack, he was
suspicious of his fellow Blacks. He can find no accurate comparision between
them and the children of Israel and Moses, for he finds that they are "cour-
ting favor with, and telling news and lies to our *natural enemies.*" Indeed for
people who would seek to perpetuate slavery by not taking a firm stand he
recommends that for them, slavery should continue to exist.

For him God is a rebel. He advises his fellow Blacks that if they revolted
"the God of justice and of armies will surely go before you." There is something distinctly ironical in the invocation of the very god who was to temper
the revolutionary fervor of the slaves. Walker borrows the equipment of the
white slave masters and then turns it against them.

Caution is one of the main themes in the *Appeal*:

> Never make an attempt to gain our freedom or *natural* right, from under
> our cruel oppressors and murderers, until you see your way clear.

But caution does not mean, for Walker, indefinite procrastination. A footnote in the original makes this much clear:

> It is not to be understood here, that I mean for us to wait until God shall
> take us by the hair of our heads and drag us out of abject wretchedness
> and slavery, nor do I mean to convey the idea for us to wait until our
> enemies shall make preparations, and call us to seize those preparations,
> take it away from them and put every thing before us to death, in order

to gain our freedom which God has given us. For you must remember that we are men as well as they. God had pleased to give us two eyes, two hands, two feet, and some sense in our heads as well as they. They have no more right to hold us in slavery than we have to hold them, we have just as much right, in the sight of God, to hold them and their children in slavery and wretchedness, as they have to hold us and no more.

Therefore, Walker goes on in his main text, "if you commence, make sure work."

Slavery is then not only a sin, it emasculates the character of black man; Walker uses the analogy of the black family broken up by slavery to argue that a man who does not actively resist such harm is not even deserving of pity. At one stage Walker explodes "Treat us like men," and in return he advocates that the past should be forgotten. In other words, (and this fits in with his anti-colonization argument) once Whites faced up to the wickedness and evil of slavery, once slaves were free to live normal lives, education (Westernization) would be a means towards integration and "we yet, under God, will become a united and happy people."

He obviously was quite serious in seeing integration as the reward the Black would give the White for emancipation. For in his argument, Walker has made a distinction between "the Americans" (meaning Whites) and Blacks, usually alluded to in the first person plural. When he speaks of integration after freedom the first person plural is *not* restricted to Blacks; Walker is talking about black and white Americans.

On reading Walker a century and a half after his *Appeal* was published, one may be accused quite rightly of ignoring the real issue in any coldhearted examination of what was an emotional piece of writing, intended for a specific people at a specific time. However, it would amount to injustice if some of the discrepancies were not pointed out, since they are indicative of a much larger gap in American life—the polarity, now so painfully apparent, between Black and White and the lack of definite indentity which has plagued black life and culture in America. Walker is extremely contemporary in this way, since one detects between the lines an impassioned groping for a solution.

Hence the painful paradoxes of self-recognition; Walker advocates America as a black homeland and yet describes himself as one of the "wretched sons of Africa." He advocates violence but what little is known of his own life indicates that his *Appeal* was more a war of the pen. He categorically states that only black men deserving the status of slave should cooperate with the white overlord and yet cries out "Treat us like men." In these lapses, or perhaps indications of middle manship, Walker was very much someone of his own time and indeed ours. For Henry Highland Garnet, a minister of a Presbyterian Church in Troy, New York, spoke out even more forcibly in 1843 and still left the same culture chasm unfilled.

Garnet's contribution was a speech delivered at a convention.[2] He begins with an admission that so far the conventions had only concerned themselves with the "free" Blacks. He is logical—coldly and precisely so—in contrast to

David Walker. He is for violence in order to bring about the overthrow of the white slavemaster, and to do this he examines the institutions of America and Africa, debunking the one and advocating the other since, he argues, these very myths have been responsible for the prolongation of slavery.

There is the unintentional giveaway as with Walker. For instance, despite the precise and calculating nature of the argument, he can allude to the non-slave world as "civilized," he can regard the slave-masters as "englightened." Although at one stage he can speak of "our ancestors from the coast of Africa," at another he can allude to the descendant of these very ancestors as "the untutored African who roams the wilds of the Congo." And what Garnet seems to be saying is not so much that slavery in itself was bad but that slavery applied to *evolué* Blacks in America was bad since in fact they were like Whites. The distortion forces him at one stage of the argument to admit as much:

> If a band of heathen men should attempt to enslave a race of Christians, and to place their children under the influence of some false religion, surely Heaven would frown upon the men who would not resist such aggression, even to death. If, on the other hand, a band of Christians should attempt to enslave a race of heathen men, and to entail slavery upon them, and to keep them in heathenism in the midst of Christianity, the God of heaven would smile upon every effort which the injured might make to disenthral themselves.

And yet not much further on, Garnet states that "liberty is a spirit sent out from God, and like its great Author, is no respecter of persons." And even in stronger terms later on—the complete association with Africa—Garnet writes of the "undying glory that hangs round the ancient name of Africa," adding "forget not that you are native born Americans citizens." The culture of the pendulum again.

Despite these lapses the argument is a closely reasoned one. First Garnet identifies the "free" Blacks with the slaves and deplores the fact that little had been done to help. He carries the stage of association one stage further when a cunning pun sums up the relationship—"We therefore write to you as being bound with you." Then, like Walker, the African past is invoked not so much in terms of direct references, but by stressing the exended family links of the black diaspora. This logically leads Garnet to a further stage in the exposition for he can now write to the black slaves that "as such we most affectionately addres you"—i. e. as members of the same black family.

Garnet's imagery is relevant and poignant. Slavery has fixed a "deep gulf" between black people which "shuts out" any friendly help, but God provides a "glimmering ray of hope" which shines out like a "lone star in a cloudy sky." This is powerful and Garnet keeps this up for a paragraph that leads one to the logical conclusion of thought and image—the point at which life and art synthesize—when he says that the "oppressor's power is fading." Darkness, strong light, fading light sum up the predicament and hope of the slaves as well as the ultimate destruction of the slave-master. Yet Garnet's imagery can at times be irritating to the twentieth century reader. He can be as excitingly exotic about Africa as any black writer of the early twentieth century:

> He was a native African, and by the help of God he emancipated a whole ship—load of his fellow men on the high seas. And he now sings of liberty on the sunny hills of Africa and beneath his native palm—trees, where he hears the lion roar and feels himself as free as that king of the forest.

This is a description of Joseph Cinque who led a mutiny and freed the slaves at sea. Equally annoying is his use of "dark"; in one place he alludes to the "dark catalogue of this nation's sins," in another to slavery with its "dark wings of death," although one may concede that he is punning.

The tone of his delivery is at times morbid, as he relates the horrors of the slave system, at times ironical as he describes the hypocrisy of Whites and at other times fierce as he switches from complaint to exhortation—"You can plead your own cause and do the work of emancipation better than any others" or "Tell them in language which they cannot understand, of the exceeding sinfulness of slavery . . ."

His logic develops in sequence like a narrative. First he lists the grievances of Blacks who had been enslaved. Next he plays on the inconsistency of a pepole who had come to America seeking "freedom: and who themselves could enslave others." Then he charts the manner in which slavery was set up to breed a caste of lesser man and within this he attacks cherished white Americans institutions. The war of independence, the declaration (ironically described as a "glorious document") all come in for full-scale attack. Basically, he argues that there was a betrayal of God since the perpetrators of the very evils of slavery were fully aware of the principles of liberty. Therefore slavery was an intentional attempt by Whites to emasculate Blacks. This will be mentioned again and again in Afro-American Literature; it gives added poignancy to David Walker's "Treat us like men"—a plea (and it is a plea) for the reinstatement of manhood. And Garnet means as much when later on he says "they buy and sell you as though you were brute beasts," or even more pertinently *"rather die freemen, than live to be slaves"* (the italics are his).

He debunks the myth of the so-called heroes of the American revolution:

> From the first moment that you breathed the air of heaven, you have been accustomed to nothing else but hardships. The heroes of the American Revolution were never put upon harder fare than a peck of corn and a few herrings per week. You have not become enervated by the luxuries of life. Your sternest energies have been beaten out upon the anvil of severe trial. Slavery has done this to make you subservient, to its own purposes; but it has done more than this, it has prepared you for any emergency. If you receive good treatment, it is what you could hardly expect; if you meet with pain, sorrow, and even death, these are the common lot of slaves.

The suggestion is that the slaves were even more ready for the proclamation of their own freedom since their own courage had been hammered out on the anvil of their bitter life-experience. But the question, implicit but not explicit, "where are the 'slave heroes'"? has to remain unanswered until almost the end of Garnet's search.

No wonder Garnet could switch from the formal opening of "Bretheren and Fellow Citizens" to "Fellow men." The tough texture of oratory has prepared the way for the latter salutation and it is as men that he is addressing his audience, it is as men that they should be prepared to fight.

There are asides that bolster the argument, such as when Garnet cites "the increase of happiness and prosperity in the British West Indies" since emancipation. The economic line was bound to appeal to the white farmers interested in profit—which of course introduces an interesting aspect of the audience-appeal that was less present in Walker, entirely absent in the oral matter, but which comes to be more and more of increasing concern amongst black writers and speakers. This is the frequently unacknowledged presence of the third ear. It makes for a whole new style of writing. The writer/speaker pretends that he is addressing black people, that his only concern is the elevation of Blacks but he assumes that the Whites are also heeding his words. Malcolm X was particularly skillful in this respect.

The argument closes with a factual survey of men who had risked their lives in order to protect freedom—Moses, Toussaint L'Ouverture and Washington appear side by side with the "Patriotic" Turner. Basically they are all fighting for the elevation of the human spirit, Garnet seems to argue, and so the debate is no mere vulgarian's matching of black with white; rather it is the confrontation between captor and captive.

The main points of the argument have been made and now it is only left for Garnet to repeat his call to rebellion, with the fact thrown in (which he is to repeat) that four million Blacks exist. It is only left for him too to chide and mock the "patient people" who surrender their daughters and wives to their overlords. And in conclusion it is only left for him to urge them in the language of the immediate tribal past—"your dead fathers speak to you from their graves"—suggesting that the African presences of their ancestral past also urged them to resist. The tone is high pitched towards the end when he says "Bretheren adieu!" for he has returned to the apparent formality of his opening salutation but not to its docility. The African family ties, the dead presences of Africa, the true African heroes who stood up for liberty, are the actualities of black life. Garnet seeks to replace the myth of the white hero with the substantial one of the black.

At this point one is entitled to ask—Walker had spoken, Garnet had spoken—two men amongst four million? There were only two major slave revolts so what were Blacks doing? The question is a fair one. The answer is not difficult since one must recognize that Walker and Garnet were not just two men who decided to speak up. Walker had an excellent printing and a distribution network behind him; Garnet's speech was given at a National

Negro Convention in Buffalo and was almost adopted. But neither of these men were revolutionaries in the sense that they sought a violent overthrow and would themselves have participated. Their importance lies in the fact that they acted as *disseminators* of thought, of the collective will of large segments of their people. Without them it would not have been possible for Douglass and Delany to have functioned. They set important patterns for others to follow; Douglass and Delany certainly did. Walker and Garnet had ploughed terrain that had hitherto been thought infertile. The harvest was and is still not yet. But the seed had been planted.

National awareness was therefore what Martin R. Delany stressed in his book, *The Condition, Elevation, Emigration and Destiny of the Colored People of the United States, Politically Considered.*[3] Delany was assistant editor and co-founder with Douglass of the *North Star,* but according to him the appendix of the book was written when he was only twenty-four. Apart from the commendable practicality of Delany's plan, what surprises the reader coming to him after Walker and Garnet, is that he should have thought of emigration at all as the only sensible plan for Blacks in America. He did not stick to this and felt that since "one part of the American people" as he puts it "are quite unacquainted with the other" and that "one of the great objects of the author is to make each acquainted."

Within this specific context, Delany's terminology is interesting; Blacks are not singled out as a separate people but a part of the American people. Delany has moved away from supporting the colonization plan for a "far more glorious one," i. e., of educating Whites and Blacks to understand the nature of their proximity. Therefore, like Garnet, Delany has to debunk certain myths of white Americans about themselves and about Blacks. This really is the purpose and body of his book.

However the "Appendix," about which by the time of publication he had only half-hearted feelings, is important since it provided very practical ideas on the return to the motherland. When one considers that Delany was writing this at a time when it was almost anathema to think in this way, he is to be praised for having had the foresight to anticipate the development of the thought of his people. The "Appendix" reveals or rather predates the point at which Blacks would question the legitimacy of white Anglo-Saxon middle class values.

From the first the cultural dichotomy is present—"we are a nation within a nation ... having merged in the habits and customs of our oppressor." At the same time he alludes with relish to the "pristine purity" of Blacks who have been "despoiled of [their] purity." The latter of course harks back to echoes of the noble savage, the Black living at peace with nature, uncorrupted by the advent of the White.

Delany's solution is not in any way a "democratic" one. There is a certain Socratic aloofness about the "true representation of the intelligence and wisdom of the colored freemen" who are to assemble and make specific confidential recommendations" to project any scheme they may think proper for the general good of the whole people." The figures Delany gives are interesting; there are, he says, "six-hundred thousand free and three and a half million bond." So his statistics are used differently from Garnet's who had reminded his audience that they were large enough in numbers to overthrow the Whites. Delany is merely concerned with selecting the best of the best, with convening a Council and a Board of Commissioners "to go on an expedition to the Eastern Coast of Africa" and other places.

But he is like Garnet in that he is aware of his audience. His third ear—and he mentions specifically England and France—is listening. These two countries are to help finance the first expedition and the resettlement since they could hope for "the opening of an immense trade." One is reminded of Garnet's little aside regarding the improvement in the economy of the West Indies since emancipation. The two countries would help without a doubt, Delany believes, since they were willing to do that much "for a little nation—mere nominal nation of five thousand *civilized* Liberians" (the italics are mine), they would do as much for black Americans. This is Delany's quandary and indeed this is the problem of black people in the New World—paying allegiance to alien gods and yet timidly clutching hold of the shadows of their own.

His better-known colleague Frederick Douglass, born a slave arround 1817, was to write "My father is a white man" and in that short terse sentence to have laid bare the entirety of the situation being described here. These black men, Walker, Garnet, Delany and Douglass, to whom one must now come, suffered from the ills of their age—a lack of cultural ethnic direction. True, Delany had suspected the other half of the argument and stated it, but built in the utterances of all these spokesmen was this directionlessness. This is not a sorry reflection on them but on their times since being so close to the slave age, it was extremely difficult for them to think in terms of a slave culture. In this examination some attention has been paid to the backward glance, half-voluntary it would seem at times, when there is evidence of that belonging to the tribal past of Africa.

Therefore, although Douglass is writing in *Narrative of the Life of Frederick Douglass, an American Slave*[4] specifically to condemn slavery, there are, for instance, allusions to family life and its importance. In this connection he writes about separation from his mother:

> For what this separation had done, I do not know unless it be to hinder the development of the child's affection towards its mother, and to blunt and destroy the natural affection of the mother for the child. This is the inevitable result.

He mentions this in decrying this practice of the slave-masters in the part of Maryland where Douglass was brought up. The fact that he saw his mother very few times during his adult life and that she died and was buried unknown to him when he was only seven, shows the high priority he set on this type of relationship. And his priority could not have been derived from personal experience (since he and those near him had no mothers) but from the strong matriachal society to which his ancestors had once belonged.

The Afro-American scene is however Douglass's main concern. He tells of the horrors of miscegenation within the slave society, of mulatto children being constantly whipped to satisfy the wife of the slave-master, of the unnatural cruelty (one is tempted to say un-African) that one member of the family has to practice against the other; as the slave-master stands by and in his role of father would "see one white son tie up his brother, of but a few shades darker complexion than himself."

Like the African art which Douglass would have heard about, his own is linked to the people—in this case their need to survive. Therefore Douglass does not spare detail as he tells about what the slaves received:

> Monthly allowance of food, and their yearly clothing. The men and women slaves received, as their monthly allowance of food, eight pounds of pork, or its equivalent in fish, and one bushel of corn meal. Their yearly clothing consisted of two coarse linen shirts, one pair of linen trousers for winter, one pair of stockings, and one pair of shoes, the whole of which could not have cost more than seven dollars.

Douglass's authority is his own life—he had been a slave and had only managed to free himself after his second attempt at escaping. His statement is therefore not a "bourgeois" empathetic one of atrocities but the mundane recital of the horrors he had personally known.

He provides an answer to a question previously posed. Why did Blacks not revolt more frequently? They faced the threat of imminent death if they were caught but more important, and more subtle, was the "psychological" jurisdiction that was practiced on them. Their owners would ensure that they became inebriated over the few holidays they had that they would rejoice when it was time to commence work. An intentional effort was made to ensure that they were not educated because, as his master said, "learning would spoil the best nigger in the world."

Above all, this is Douglass's own story and it does not suffer half as much from heavyhandedness in style and biblical rhetoric as, say, Ottobah Cugoano's whose account had appeared in England in 1787, or Olaudah Equiano's of 1789. Their purposes were basically the same: to recount a story and at the same time to expose the evils of slave-trafficking and slave-labor. Douglass makes the reader feel that this is very much his story, that he is not going to be led away by alien notions of whom he ought to be. His colleague Delany had complained that:

> politicians, religionists, colonizationists and Abolitionists have each and all, at different times, presumed to think for, to *dictate* to, and *know* better what suited colored people, than they knew for themselves...

and though Douglass joined William Lloyd Garrison, the famous abolitionist, he spoke his language but did not echo his thoughts.

Not surprisingly, his account describes how he began to subscribe to Garrison's paper, *The Liberator*, and how while attending an Anti-Slavery Convention at Nantucket on August 11, 1841, he was encouraged to speak by William C. Coffin. His story is really about how an intelligent black man used his talents for oratory. The speech at Nantucket was the starting point, but there had been a lifetime of preparation, beginning with his learning to read. As Douglass comments:

> In learning to read, I owe almost as much to the bitter opposition of my master, as to the kindly wish of my mistress.

Literacy freed him, taught him about abolition, made him understand his plight. Walker and Garnet had said as much. Literacy made him realize, again much as Walker and Garnet had hinted at, the treachery that lay within, amongst his own people. And he gives an incident in which, despite the close-knit brotherhood amongst "fugitives" in the North, an informer threatened one of them. A meeting was summoned and this was the result:

> A very religious old gentleman was appointed as president, who, I believe, made a prayer, after which he addressed the meeting as follows: "Friends, we have got him here, and I would recommend that you young men just take him outside the door, and kill him."

The nation was coming closer together in having to face common tribulations. And after Douglass's own anxieties of having to face a white audience at Nantucket, Douglass could affirm that "from that time until now, I have been engaged in pleading the cause of my brethren." He did this long after the abolition of slavery, establishing himself as an authentic voice for Blacks.

His resolute intellectual independence was confirmed by his break with Garrison. He came to believe that the dissolution of the union was not necessary to end slavery; instead the ballot would be an effective way of eradicating slavery. It was then that he started his paper, *North Star*, which lasted from 1847 until 1860. He followed a middle-of-the-road line in policy:

> I think the course to be pursued by the Colored Press is to say less about race and claims of justice, liberty and patriotism.

Given the nature of his time and the period of retrogressive measures that were to follow soon, one can see caution and good sense in what he attempted.

Douglass stands out because he was an articulator and activist at an important period in the history of Black America. The end of slavery was the beginning of self-dependence when the cultural dichotomy assumed political overtones—in which direction should the black man go? Toward Africa and the consciousness of kin in the black diaspora? Or towards absorption within the white majority culture? Douglass did not answer the question; he developed countless possibilities for response, for alternative bases of living. Not until the post-Booker T. Washington era when the young DuBois attacked the concept of compromise with a restatement of the urgent presence of Africa was the dormant but never extinct debate to explode with all the fury of a volcano. Its literary splendor was the so-called "Harlem Renaissance."

Notes

1 David Walker, *Walkers Appeal in Four Articles Together with a Preamble to the Colored Citizens of the World, but in Particular and Very Expressly for Those of the United States* (Boston 1930). For a recent reprint of the *Appeal*, see Charles M. Witse, ed. *David Walkers Appeal* (New York, 1965).

2 Henry Highland Garnet, "An Address to the Slaves of the United States", delivered at the National Negro Convention, Buffalo, New York, August 15—19, 1843. A recent reprint can be found in *Early Black American Prose,* ed. William H. Robinson (Dubuque, Iowa, 1971), pp. 84—92. Also see some personal comments by his friend and admirer, Alex Crummel, in *Africa and America* (Miami, 1969), pp. 301—05.

3 (Philadelphia, 1852). Reprinted in *Great Documents in Black American History,* ed. George Ducas and Charles Van Doren (New York, 1970).

4 (Boston, 1845). Three versions exist and one was reissued edited by Benjamin Quarles (Cambridge, Mass., 1960).

Contexts of African Criticism

G. D. Killam

I have called this piece Contexts of Criticism. I mean two things here: first, "contexts" because the essay is selective in its choice of references since one cannot allude to all of the criticism which has been devoted to explaining Africain writing; secondly, and as is obvious, I mean literary criticism. Since the criticisms offered by writers of African literature and its commentators are so varied and sometimes embrace subjects and concerns outside the purely literary, as literary is apprehended in the Western World, I thought I would use the general phrase to describe my purposes and let the qualifications come out as I go along. I was also tempted to turn the title around and call the paper African Contexts of Literary Criticism, the specific purpose of a paper with the title being to answer the claim made by Achebe (at Kampala) and others (elsewhere) that the criticism of African literature has got too much in the hands of expatriates. But I decided that I could not sustain an irony that heavy and so want to look at what recent developments there have been in the sort of criticism that concerns me. But I would like to insist on the word "expatriate" rather than "colonialist.". Part of the purpose of the paper, but not a major purpose, is to show that expatriates have made and will continue to make useful contributions to the interpretation and understanding of African writing. The point needs to be insisted on only because so many seem bent on saying the opposite.

I am concerned here as well with the role the university has played in the context. For when we speak of criticism of the literature of English speaking Africa, or African literature in English, we are speaking for the most part of what the universities, which have been central in the creation and criticism of literature, have done. D. I. Izevbaye, a critic who has been prominent in African literary criticism for six or seven years now, says in a recent issue of *African Literature Today* (which is sub-titled "Focus on Criticism"), that "the responsibility for shaping an African tradition of criticism has passed from its Negritude home to the academy."[1] The Negritude attitude toward criticism is identified as an affective approach which rejects objectivity in criticism, seeks to awaken emotional responses in readers and makes the demand that literature "should be committed to the task of restoring the educated African to a more wholesome mental task."[2] Affective criticism is not concerned with the objective evaluation of art, it is not disinterested;

rather it is interested, it prompts to action. So the theory and the literature are at one, and both are devoted to commitment.

It seems to me that the academies have from the outset been central to the development of literature in African countries, that there has been with few exceptions, an intimate relationship between the writer, the critic (who were and are often the same persons) and the universities. And it seems to me equally that an affective school of criticism (even if divorced from some of the tenets of Negritudism) or at least an affective view of literature still operates in Africa and forcefully too. It is this attitude towards literature studies and criticism (and in Africa the role of the writer as teacher is well known and declaimed or made implicit in the comments of more writers than not), this disposition to see literature not only as a criticism of life, and society, but to be a force in shaping the new society, which is at the heart of the reform which took place in the Literature Department at Nairobi. Ngugi and his colleagues decided that

> ... it is wrong to think of culture as prior to politics. Political and economic liberation are the essential condition for cultural liberation, for the true release of a people's creative spirit and imagination. It is when people are involved in the active work of destroying an inhibitive social structure and building a new one that they begin to see themselves. They are born again.[3]

And this conviction provides the justification for the assertion of Ngugi and his colleagues at Nairobi who said about their proposal to change the nature of the English Department:

> This is not a change in names only. We want to establish the centrality of Africa in the department. This, we have argued, is justifiable on various grounds, the most important one being that education is a means of knowledge about ourselves. Therefore, after we have examined ourselves, we radiate outwards and discover peoples and worlds around us. With Africa at the centre of things, not existing as an appendix or a satellite of other countries and literature, things must be seen from the African perspective. The dominant object in that perspective is African literature, the major branch of African culture. Its roots go back to past African literatures, European literatures, and Asian literatures. These can only be studied meaningfully in a Department of African Literature and Languages in an African University.[4]

And it seems to me that a similar force is in operation in the views about literature expressed by Grant Kamenju when he comments on the achievement of Okot p'Bitek. The article is entitled "Black Aesthetics and pan-African Emancipation" and was published in *Umma*. It gives a vivid idea of the appeal which p'Bitek's writing has for many African intellectuals :

> In his two memorable poems, the *Song of Lawino* and the *Song of Ocol* Okot p'Bitek presents the colonial and neo-colonial Manicheanism that Fanon speaks of in dramatic and vivid poetic form. These two songs demonstrate how out of the Manicheanism of imperialism in Africa flow two rival and conflicting aesthetics: on the one hand, the neo-colonial aesthetics of capitulation and subjugation whose representation and spokesman is the tragi-

comic figure of Ocol, the white-washed, mission-educated graduate of the
colonial university; and on the other, the aesthetics of black pride, black
affirmation, resistance and ultimate liberation confidently articulated by
Ocol's defiant and proud wife, Lawino, the representative of the patriot peasant masses.

The Zombie of a black man that is Ocol is the very triumph of the colonizer's mission in Africa in that not only has he avidly embraced the racist
culture and bourgeoise civilisation of imperialism of which he has become
the faithful sentinel and custodian; he even bitterly laments that he was born
black

> Mother, Mother,
> Why
> Why was I born
> Black?

for the sad fact is that since Ocol believes himself to be "modern", "progressive", and "civilised" he has been educated into the total acceptance of, and
the abject submission to the white coloniser's racist and arrogant doctrine that
black people are evil and savage.

> Ocol pours scorn
> On Black People
> He says we are all Kaffirs
> We do not know the ways of God
> We sit deep in darkness
> And do not know the Gospels . . .
> He says Black people are primitive,
> And their ways are utterly harmful
> Their dances are mortal sins
> They are ignorant, poor and diseased.[5]

The article goes on for a dozen pages in its analysis of the subject, a careful comparison of p'Bitek's poems with Fanon's analysis of the Manicheanism
in the colonial world. Kamenju concludes thus : "On the level of aesthetics,
Lawino's song is, therefore, a clarion call for the defence and support of an
aesthetics among black people from the bondage to the racism, the arrogance
and the barbarism of white cultural imperialism and enhanceful of pan-
African emancipation."[6] Taken to its logical end this would prompt to action
and would use literature to effect that action. And it emanates from the
academies.

The academies and the uses of literacy in Africa have been associated for a
long time. There are exceptions among writers who are not the product of the
universities—Okara, Tutuola, are names which come to mind. Doubtless there
are others. But they are far outnumbered by the university graduates. And
similarly with the critics. It was at Fourah Bay College in 1963, at a conference
on African Writing, attended mostly by university people, that T. R. M. Creighton attempted to define African Literature in this way as "any work in which
an African setting is authentically handled, or to which experiences which originate in Africa are integral."[7] The same definition had been presented to the
Congress of Africanists in Accra in December of 1962, had been accepted by
that meeting, Professor Creighton tells us. But it did not meet with such ready
acceptance by the delegates at Fourah Bay and its reverberations went well

beyond Fourah Bay and well beyond Tom Creighton's expectations. The record of the controversy it occasioned is summarized in Izevbaye's "African Literature Defined" in the first number of *Ibadan Studies in English*.[8] He recalls the reaction of Obi Wali to the Creighton definition which provoked a controversy that flared in the pages of *Transition* throughout 1964. The discussion falls into several parts—an attempt to define a literature concerns its subject matter (as is the case with the Creighton definition and its reference to the authenticity of the theme *vis-a-vis* Africa), and it involves the question of language—which language can carry authentic experience. Izevbaye notes that the major area in which the attempt to solve the problem of the definition was in the universities where experiments with African literary materials in African literature courses responded to the obvious needs and desires of the indigenes (as was the case in the countries where English was or was becoming the *linqua franca*) to contemplate aspects of their nationhood. The major assertion of the central importance and growing worth of African literature so far as the universities is concerned is found in Nairobi where, as we have seen from Ngugi's words, African literature (and therefore culture) is not treated merely as an appendage of the "parent tradition" in English. And this is literature in English with even the local literary material offered in English renderings, and where examples of world literatures, often from languages other than English, are offered in English translations. So Obi Wali's enjoinder in 1968 to fan the flame of the 1964 controversy—"that is impossible to mix African and European writings and label the mixture African literature. It just must have to be one or the other"— did not provoke the response it had four years earlier. But the flame has not entirely guttered out. The issue is raised in a tart contretemps between Achebe and Tai Solarin in the columns of the *Lagos Times*. Achebe rebuts Solarin's suggestion that he, Achebe, writes in English because it is necessary for commercial reasons. Achebe points out what he has said in various places: that English has established itself in Nigeria and that it needs no one to defend it. These succeeding paragraphs are worth recording. Referring to the article, Achebe says:

> The second and third sentences of Solarin's article go on to suggest that since my books are written in English I have a financial interest in defending its use in Nigeria. Very clever, but I'm afraid not clever enough. Have you not heard of translations? My novels are not only in English but in sixteen major languages around the world. And the number is increasing. I am quite confident that if Nigeria decided tomorrow to install Hausa as the national language my books would immediately be translated into it. So, you see, I need not fear such an event. Financially I might even be better-off for it![9]

The fact that Achebe chose to reproduce this letter-to-the-editor in a volume of his collected essays indicates the importance he attaches to the issues that the exchange raised.

Another dimension of this question is seen in an article by C. Jenewari, writing in *Oduma Magazine* (Volume 2, No. 1), who argues the case for the deliberate cultivation of literatures in indigenous Nigerian languages and expresses the hope that the generalized nature of the points he makes will be taken up. Jenewari says that

> One question which has often bothered the minds of people more or less connected with African literature is the relationship between literary content and medium of literary expression. To the world outside Africa, the term African literature is generally associated with the kind of writing done by our elitist artists, expressing an African content through the medium of an European language. But this kind of writing merely constitutes one out of four possible categories of African literature. We have in addition to elitist or modern African literature three other categories, namely (1) oral traditional, (2) written traditional whose medium of expression is the native language and (3) popular African literature—the kind of literature one would characterise as "Onitsha Market Literature". What is common to all four classes of writing is the African content; what distinguishes them is the medium of expression. And it is this medium of expression that makes all the difference in the readership strength and prestige of the different categories of the literature. Of the four categories outlined above, the most widely read (and of course the most prestigious) is certainly the elitist writing. But this kind of writing has two disadvantages... The first, is that it does not quite succeed in integrating content and medium... The second involves the language of expression: since the language of expression is foreign, a considerable portion of the ingroup from which the writer and/or the content derives cannot read and appreciate the literature.

The case that Jenewari makes for the cultivation of the indigenous literatures in indigenous languages is summed up thus:

> ... literature written in the native language ... gives satisfactory and adequate expression to the poignancy and richness of the traditional themes, the subtleties of the language and the thought process. It is also general enough for every literate person within the in-group to read and to enjoy. It must be realised that it is only when we attempt putting the native language to all types of uses—poetry, drama, etcetera that we can properly assess its artistic potential and expressive power.
>
> Indeed there is much the native speaker can benefit from native literature and there is much he can do to develop such a literature. Apparently every people have a culture of which they are proud. But it is not enough to say you possess a proud culture. If indeed you do you would like the world to know that you possess a distinct culture worthy of preserving, then you should be ready to express it in the concrete and permanent form of writing.[10]

These sorts of concerns about language usage will doubtless continue to be expressed. But the debate over languages seems to have subsided. Writing in indigenous, native languages seems to be growing alongside that in world languages. Writing in the vernacular languages will have as many readers of the particular languages as can or as choose to use them. But if one assumes only a percentage of literacy in the users or speakers of any language and only a percentage of these interested in literature, both these percentages being small (the latter even smaller than the former), then we may safely assume that these literatures will have very few readers indeed and that these readers will increase only proportionally with population growth and that an industry devoted to the publication of works in these languages will be on perilous ground from the outset, that in fact such industries dependent on economic and not aesthetic factors in the first and in the final instance, stand little chance of success.

Abiola Irele notes in his introduction to the catalog prepared for the Contemporary African Literature Exhibition mounted at the Ibadan Campus of Ife University, that in fact African writers have forged an independent literary tradition, one related by language to the literatures of the erstwhile colonial masters, but forming not regional schools of the metropolitan tradition, but independent literary areas. No one I think would quarrel with this view now, no more than they would quarrel with Izevbaye's definition of African literature at the close of his assessment of the debate over that definition.

But the question about critical theory and critical systems has not settled down to the same extent. Rand Bishop, Jr., in a doctoral thesis presented to the University of Michigan in 1970, surveys the state of the criticism of African literature between 1947 and 1966. Bishop takes into account what both African and non-African critics have had to say about the subject under these headings —the language question, the audience to which this literature is directed, the relationship of modern African writing to the Western literary tradition and to the African tradition itself; a discussion on realism, surrealism and the African reality; African Literature as a *Literature Engagee*; and a discussion of Negritude. Bishop's survey, which is important reading to anyone interested in the subject, identifies at least six general critical standards which run through the body of African literary criticism of the period he surveys and these may be summarized as follows:

> 1. If critics cannot employ African languages they can "do violence" to the standard forms of the European language and not "ape standards."
> 2. African literature projects an African presence heretofore lacking in the world, it must nevertheless be written primarily for an African audience and not appear to be written primarily for a non-African audience.
> 3. That African writers should show discretion in their borrowings from Western literary traditions, while reflecting, where possible, the forms and content of the—primarily oral—African traditions.
> 4. That African literature must not falsify African realia, whether the writers choose realism or surrealism or some other technique to portray these realia; but that the "information" provided by these realia must be transformed into art, and not presented entirely for their own sake.
> 5. That African literature must somehow be *engagée,* meaning that it address itself to the various problems currently facing Africa, and that it must eschew the principle of "art for art's sake."
> 6. That African *literature* be, somehow, *African,* whether one labels this Africanness as "Negritude" or in some other way, and without becoming *African* at the expense of being at the same time *literature.*[11]

Bishop's conclusions would not distress anyone today except, I think obviously, the final phrase of his sixth point. For the argument about what purposes literature should serve devolves around what literature *is*. And there is no real agreement here as we shall see. It is worth noting how Bishop went about making his determinations since his method originates in the academy and arises out of the systematic contemplation of literature. He adopted from M. H. Abrams in his *The Mirror and the Lamp* four major critical approaches to literature which he defines as follows:

> ... first, Objective Criticism, exemplified by the New and the Neo-Aristo-telian criticism, which concerns itself primarily with the formal characteristics of a literary work, from within the work itself. Secondly, there is a Mimetic Criticism, based on the relationship between the literary work and "the universe" or the real world around it. Thirdly, there is Expressive Criticism, concerned mainly with the work and the author. Finally, there is Pragmatic or Rhetorical Criticism which examines with close attention the relationship between the work and the audience, one which looks at the work of art "chiefly as a means to an end, an instrument for getting something done, and to judge its values according to its success in achieveing that aim."[12]

One might quarrel with the terms, the designations, and prefer other ways of identifying the same tenets. But they do describe literary-critical activity which is familiar and they can be used as guidelines to trace other sorts of literary enquiries.

Bishop's conclusions are valid until 1966. And they suggest the way the discussion and debate have continued to develop since that time, a period which has seen the production of a large number of critical works and commentaries. One need only look at the *Africana Journal* and at *Research in African Literatures* and note the variety of literary critical magazines and journals which have sprung up in North America and which stand alongside their African counterparts to see the extent of this growth. The production of books and collections of critical essays, the development of the monograph as a distinct critical assessment of African authors are noted by Izevbaye in the 7th Number of *African Literature Today,* a number given over to Criticism. Izevbaye's checklist at the close of his article lists 32 book-length studies, collections or anthologies of critical opinion, all but two of which (Jahn's *Muntu* and *History of Neo-African Literature)* have been published since 1966.

And the universities continue to be central in the evolving notions of the criticism best suited to the evaluation of literature from Africa. Irele specified the importance of Western education to this process when he wrote that

> the importance of Western education in this development can hardly be ex-aggerated. In this respect the role of educational institutions in Africa ... have been determinant in producing writers as well as in creating a public for them. More lately, educational centers, by putting African literature courses on their curricula, are also training critics. The special contribution of the institutions of higher learning, both in Europe and abroad, has been to present models in European literature and to create an intellectual disposition towards written expression. The local universities have also served specifically as centers of cultural awareness and it is significant that many African writers began their careers by contributing to student journals such as *The Horn* at Ibadan.[13]

(And to this list one might add the names of *Ghala, Busara, Penpoint, Darlite/ Umma.*) Irele notes that outside of the universities contemporary African literature has developed largely through the efforts of individuals—like Ulli Beier —who were instrumental in creating such centers as Mbari and Chem-Chemi. But it is in the universities that the major contribution has been made.

What are the major points of view which obtain? We have noted Ngugi's expression of what literature studies ought to do and how they ought to be organized to do this. And the next step is to look for literature which will do the job one wants done and this of course implies the operation of a set of critical judgements. For Ngugi, the study of literature is interpreted largely in educational and social terms as assisting the creation of general literacy in a country. As well, it is in the vanguard in creating

> ... a revolutionary culture which is not narrowly confined by the limitations of tribal traditions or national boundaries but is outward looking to Pan-Africa and the Third World and the needs of man. The national, the Pan-African, and the Third World awareness must be transformed into a socialist programme, or be doomed to sterility and death. Any true national culture ... that nurtures a society based on co-operation and not ruthless exploitation, ruthless grab-and-take, a culture that is born of a people's collective labour, such a culture will be best placed to contribute something truly positive and original to the modern world.[14]

Irele is somewhere near this approach, though he deals with the philosophical abstractions of criticism whilst at the same time noting its pragmatic functions in society. He poses a system which depends upon what he calls the "sociological imagination" and which can be summarized in this way:

> Literature takes place within a cultural setting, and no meaningful criticism is possible without the existence of a community of values shared by the writer and the critic which the latter can, in turn, make meaningful to the writer's larger audience. Furthermore, the stream of communication which is established across this line of common relationships in which the critic is a kind of middleman, constitutes an important current in the cultural life of the community.[15]

Irele defines a critical system by which African literature can be judged in terms of the literary and extra-literary factors it must contain. Irele makes a case for a sociological approach, a sociological criticism which he describes in this way:

> The meaning I attach to the application of a "sociological imagination" in the criticism of modern African literature may perhaps now begin to emerge in something of its full light and import. The double relationship of this literature to two cultures and to two imaginative traditions, with the particular forms of human universe which lie behind each of them, calls for a special orientation which is sociological by implication. It involves a process whereby the very differentiation that makes the two frames of reference of this literature imposes upon the critical function important adjustments of

> those principles worked out in the Western tradition, to the peculiar modes
> of sensibility which feature in the African works, and which derive from the
> African background, of which the uses of language, both conditioned by and
> conditioning the traditional modes of feeling and apprehension, constitute a
> distinct social reality.[16]

The criticism exists in and for the society which produces it, just as the work
of the imagination does, whatever wider references and influences they may
have. Irele says:

> The critic of African literature thus has a double responsibility: to show the
> literary work as a significant statement with a direct relevance to the African
> experience; and related to this is what I call the educative role of criticism
> in the present context of the literary situation in Africa. We have a duty not
> only to make our modern African literature accessible to our people in terms
> which they can understand, but also in the process, to promote an understand-
> ing of literature, to widen the creative (as well as the responsive) capabilities
> of our people—the two essential elements in a fruitful literary life."[17]

Irele has attracted his exponents and an interesting manifestation of the application of his theory can be found in the number of *African Literature Today*
mentioned above where, in a review of Eustace Palmer's *Introduction to the
African Novel*, a critic reacts most unfavorably to Palmer's interpretations because he has not based them on Irele's proscriptions. The gist of her argument
is that Palmer fails to recognize and pay tribute to the matter of the commitment of the novelists who have written with the aim of retrieving the Africans'
sense of his own worth, his commitment to the burning social issues of his day.
As well, the reviewer claims that "when it comes to the discrimination of values
and the sharing of insights, we must be cautious in accepting Dr. Palmer's
views which originate entirely from his Western education rather than from
his being conversant with the needs of the majority of the African public." (It
is interesting to note that Irele himself is not much bothered by the fact of
Western education.) Palmer answers by saying that according to this reviewer

> ...the African critic, like the African writer, must be committed and sub-
> jective. This is the enunciation of a critical doctrine which I find both dan-
> gerous and irresponsible, and which totally disregards the needs of readers.
> I will never accept that the critic should allow his commitment to influence
> his criticism. On the contrary, I will maintain that the African critic, like
> other critics, has to strive to be as objective as possible, or his criticism will
> be valueless ... I certainly feel that the novelist must deal with the burning
> issues of his society, and the critic should concern himself with the novelist's
> treatment of these issues ... and should show how relevant these issues are
> to the contemporary situation; but he should also evaluate the novelist's art.
> I certainly do not feel we must commend writers merely for their presenta-
> tion of the oppression and dehumanisation of the African people, if their art
> is defective.[18]

I cite this exchange at some length because it is fairly typical in revealing the
way in which the debate progresses. Palmer's attitudes are close to the Aristo-

telianism which Izevbaye enunciated in "Criticism and Literature in Africa" published in Heywood's *Perspectives on African Literature*. Izevbaye addresses himself to the same question as Dr. Irele—what kind of criticism will best serve African literature. He isolates three kinds of influences which criticism can have on an author's work (beyond the published state): criticism can be responsible for bringing the work to the public and affecting its reception either favorably or unfavorably; it may create taste for a particular kind of book and affect the production of books of a similar kind; it can elaborate the author's meaning in a work and may detect meaning beyond that intended by the author. The reference to the creation of taste (which also implies a capacity to make informed judgements) is an important part of Irele's "sociological criticism" but Izevbaye gives it less importance than his colleague and, ultimately, in the final judgements he makes, supersedes Irele's conclusions.

Izevbaye spends considerable time discussing the earliest and most effective form of criticism directed to African literature, criticism which was influenced by nonliterary interests—"the most important of which was nationalism or the desire to create an indigenous tradition that would be more or less independent of foreign models." This sort of emphasis was useful the author claims but currently the emphasis placed on the "referential nature of the literary work" causes two problems. The first of these has been the rejection of nonrealistic literature before it has been properly considered. (He cites as examples the early responses to Soyinka's *A Dance of the Forest*, Amadi's *The Concubine* and especially *The Palm-Wine Drinkard*.)

The second and more important problem is that often a writer is praised for the wrong reasons—he may not succeed in "persuading his public to accept him in his favorite role of seer and saviour of his society," yet his literary stature "has been enhanced by approving critics every time he writes on topical matters." The concluding paragraph of his essay, which states the kind of criticism Izevbaye would have, shows the degree to which he parts company with Irele and Ngugi.

> With this new emphasis in criticism, that is the suppression of the social reference of literature as a significant influence in criticism, it may be easier for critics to pay greater attention to the literary work itself. But the influence of the referential element in African criticism has not really been an intrusion. The social factor was important only because the literature itself was largely sociological. As the literature becomes less preoccupied with social or national problems and more concerned with the problems of men as individuals in an African society, the critical reference will be human beings rather than society, and the considerations which influence critical judgement will be human and literary rather than social ones.[19]

Thus we have three major expressions of the proper function or nature of criticism—that which is for total commitment and which, whilst not ignoring the art, places it in a position secondary to the effect the art has; secondly, a middle position which recognizes the imporance of Africanizing the literature, which attends to the social references of the works whilst being concerned with aesthetic factors; and thirdly, the objective kind of criticism which suppresses as much as can be the social reference of a work of literature until the art can be accounted for. This is not to say that anything in the way of an "art for art's sake" mentality has entered the picture. It is important to note this and to report Izevbaye's words on the subject. He says that "Many English-speaking African writers accept the notion that African art is functional, and that therefore the concept of art-for-art's-sake should not be allowed to take root in African thought"[20]—(but this is) "really a case of crying wolf when there is none, since pleasure itself is an artistic function . . ."[21]

We have said nothing of the role of the expatriate critic of African literature, though this is never far from the minds of anyone interested and involved in the subject. I noted that Achebe said recently in Kampala that Africans had allowed expatriates to get too big a hold on the criticism of African literature and pointed out some of the errors into which such critics can fall even with the best intentions. Achebe had said much the same things in 1964 in his "Where Angels Fear to Tread" article. And J. P. Clark was in agreement with Achebe in his various articles in *Présence Africaine, Nigeria Magazine* and other places. The nature of the complaint of these and others is not, it seems, with the right of the expatriate to engage in criticism, but with uninformed and possibly arrogant criticism, with errors oblivious to them arising out of the critic's lack of information about the culture from which the work springs. But the writing of non-African critics continues to appear in the journals of African editors. And these writers, critics and editors would likely accept the recommendations which Bishop offers at the close of his thesis where he says:

> The writer feels strongly that Western critics must accept the sovereignty of the African critic, and of the critical standards he chooses. On the other hand, it is felt equally strongly that the African critic must accept the sovereignty of the answers to the . . . question: "By what standards *do Westerners* judge African literature?" For the African cannot expect the Westerner to judge African literature by African critical standards, *even if he knows them.* The Westerner may be more or less well informed on the African context of the literature, . . . but he is only capable of *judging* the literature according to his own standards which, again, . . . derive from his own culture.[22]

It will be difficult to disarm the die-hard who feels that the non-African should not, indeed cannot make a useful comment on the works of writers from another culture. To follow this logic to its conclusion is to achieve an *ad absurdum.* In fact the argument will likely reach a *non-sequitur,* since literature is available to all who choose to read it, contemplate and write about it. So critical writing will continue to be done, chanced by those of other cultures, exposing themselves to the possibility of error and censure, but also the possibility of success. What must be guarded against, as Izevbaye has pointed out, "is the complacency of simple attitudes and the tyranny of uniformity."

Sunday Anozie's Genetic Structuralism is another example of the way in which formal academic training and exposure to the philosophical thinking of other people from another place and possibly another time can forge a link with one's own intellectual aspirations to produce a new way of looking at things and a new language to describe it.

Anozie articulates the system of Genetic Structuralism in *The Conch*, Volume III, No. 1 (March 1971). His subtitle for the article is "Notes towards a Sociological Theory of the African Novel." And he confines his examples here to "novels written and published originally in English or French by writers of African descent whose homes lie in any of the independent African states." He points out that other sociological approaches to the criticism of West African novels possess shortcomings which his new method will overcome. The first of these approaches is based on the chronology of the publication of novels which can lead to "anything from a mere statistical inventory of the novels or a barren compilation of facts and data relating to the author's lives to even such an undignified activity as writing a history of African literature." (Why this latter activity is undignified is not explained!) The second method of unsatisfactory criticism has been based on the nationality of the author and this, claims Anozie, "can lead from anything from a narrow perspective and simplistic view of the African novel to an atomistic categorisation into, say; the Igbo / Yoruba novel, the Nigerian fiction / Ghana fiction; African English novel / African French novel." The reasons for repudiating these approaches to judgement are less specific than what distinguishes them one from the other, but we can presume to have more on the subject from Anozie in due course. But Genetic Structuralism is defined here as

> an attempt to explain in terms of natural laws of growth and adaptation to milieu the causes of the dynamic changes, such as are taking place within the West African novel, considered as an organism. As envisaged however by its chief modern exponent, the French Professor Lucien Goldmann, himself also a disciple of Georges Lukacs, genetic structuralism is much more complex: it involves the problem of epistemology or the sociology of knowledge.[23]

Anozie describes the practice of Professor Goldmann at some length in order to clarify his own position, to elaborate the definition I have cited above. Anozie "fully subscribes" to Goldmann's views, and has written a full-length study, his monograph on Christopher Okigbo, according to the proscriptions of genetic structuralism. More than this, he is founder and editor of *The Conch*, a journal whose subtitle reads: "A Sociological Journal of African Cultures and Literatures" devoted to expounding, elaborating and testing the methodology of genetic structuralism.

Many people of different and possibly opposing critical persuasions will doubtless take issue with the method, or some of its tenets, as for example Anozie's claim that "A major achievement would be the suppression of all references to external systems, that is to say to other literatures or traditions, what most African critics do when they speak of influences." And some will be bothered by the claim made for a third advantage of the method which would afford "a set of objective criteria dynamically regulating the form and content of the literature [whereby] it would be fairly possible to forecast new developments, that is determine on the basis of known facts the laws of future evolution of the West African novel." Is this not perhaps establishing a pitfall to avoid a trap? It suggests a degree of mechanization which the writers themselves might not be too happy about; and they might be difficult to program.

Especially in light of that final quotation I think we might mention something which Anozie himself acknowledges as a possible limitation of his system: "One important disadvantage of genetic structuralism as a method of approach to the study of the African novel, however, needs to be mentioned. This consists in the little value it accords to aesthetic considerations within the art. This omission is not deliberate but results naturally from the method itself." One is moved to wonder how long an organism will live once its blood has been removed.

This brief survey of the growth and development of African literary criticism has hit only on the salients. The work of critics other than those mentioned here ought to be mentioned for the light they throw on the subject. One thinks of Bernth Lindfors and his articles arguing the abstractions of tradition and continuity, as well as those on individual writers. One thinks of G—C. M. Mutiso's recent *Socio-Political Thought in African Literature*. The book was published last year but deals with works of the imagination and of criticism up to 1968. Actually 1967 would be a more accurate date to suggest since none of the works cited in the bibliography and notes to the book is dated later than 1967. And it is not churlish to draw attention to this claim made in the Foreword: that "a very few critical books have come out since the completion of this work" is palpably not true.

The critical premises of the book are familiar and the book's great virtue is that it takes into account a lot of little-known writing from the 1940s and early 1950s and relates this body of writing to the familiar works in what is coming to be known as the first wave of African writing—that by Soyinka, Achebe, Clark, *et al*. Mutiso's analysis proceeds from the recognition that "all literature, to the extent that it deals with individuals in society, contains elements of social and political theory."

My choice of examples shows the wide spectrum of critical responses which African imaginative writing has provoked. And this variety of response and concern is typical of the criticism of other literatures in other places and times. We think of the various surveys of the history of the criticism of English literature, of the work of Wellek and Warren, of Plekhanov and the massive accounts of Lukacs. More relevant to the present needs of African criticism and its home in the academies might be those of the kind found in such handbooks as those prepared by James Thorpe[24]—those essays, written by William G. Moulton, Fredson Bowers, Robert E. Spiller and Northrop Frye in *The Aims and Methods of Scholarship in Modern Languages and Literatures,* and those in Thorpe's companion volume *Relations of Literary Study* with its essays by Rosalie Colie, Leon Edel, Frederick C. Crews, Leo Lowenthal, J. Hillis Miller, Bertrand H. Bronson, and again Northrop Frye who discuss such subjects as

Literature and History, Literature and Myth, Literature and Biography, Literature and Psychology, and Sociology, and Religion, and Music and Myth. Students of comparative literatures or modern literature in general should look
at these sorts of essays. And let me hasten to add should someone decide with
little charity to shoot the sitting duck, that I make no claim that there is an
exact relation with African writing, but merely to say what will be obvious to
the student of this literature that these various specialists in their essays attempt
to distinguish the essential relations between literature and another area of
intellectual concern. Then there is methodology which may well be appropriate
to the critical contemplation of literature. Methods which, as well, may remove
the writing of critical appreciations and reviews from the realm of the purely
personal and idiosyncratic. All of these various approaches seem to me to be
legitimate: the contemplation of literature is at the center of their concern and
the emphasis varies as critics seek to describe the relationship between the
literary and another element in the work under review. Those who read this
piece may well find fault with my identification of these two volumes of essays
edited by Professor Thorpe, thinking perhaps that I state personal preferences
and thus err in the same way as I claim Mrs. James has done. I no more mean
to suggest that these are the only books or essays on the subject than I mean
to imply that Mrs. James is unique in the way she treats Dr. Palmer. Both
represent convenient examples to illustrate the certain points I want to make.

So what I suggest is not mere slavish imitation of the comparative critical
attitudes or doctrines of a number of expatriate / Western critics who have
amassed impressive scholarly and academic credentials through the long and
systematic consideration of the various relationships which exist between literature and other intellectual pursuits, some of which like myth and religion are
as old as recorded systematic thought itself, others of which are relatively
recent—like psychology and sociology. What I suggest is that scholars and
advanced students in the universities, which have been the major centers of
creative and critical endeavor look into these findings, scrutinize them and test
their applicability to the African literary scene. Doubtless much of this sort of
activity is already going on—the example of Anozie's genetic structuralism
with his acknowledged debt to Levi-Strauss, Goldmann and Ruth Benedict,
members of the academies of France and America, being but one important
example. And it matters less at the stage whether Anozie is right or wrong: he
provokes intellectual enquiry, he elaborates meanings, he does the sort of
things which Izevbaye states as the possibilities of criticism.

One of the good things implied by the variety of critical attitudes which have
been and are espoused and defended is the recognition by students and prac-
tioners of literary criticism that their field of study, however exclusive it may
be made to seem in one sense, runs continuously into other academic studies
in all directions. At this level, the level of cultural studies, we see the development of the expression of cultural sensibility.

Notes

1   D. I. Izevbaye, "The State of Criticism in African Literature," *African Literature Today,* 7 (1975), 9.
2   Ibid.
3   Ngugi wa Thiongó, *Homecoming* (London, 1972), p. 11.
4   Ibid.
5   Grant Kamenju, "Black Aesthetics and Pan-African Emancipation," *Umma,* 2, 1 (1972), 58—59.
6   Ibid., p. 71.
7   T. R. M. Creighton, "An Attempt to Define African Literature," *African Literature and the Universities,* ed. Gerald Moore (Ibadan, 1965), pp. 84 ff.
8   D. I. Izevbaye, "African Literature Defined: the Record of a Controversy," *Ibadan Studies in English,* 1, 1 (1970).
9   Chinua Achebe, "In Defence of English? An Open Letter to Mr. Tai Solarin," *Morning Yet on Creation Day* (London, 1975), p. 87.
10 C. Jenewari, "A Case for the Development of Literature in the Native Language," *Oduma Magazine,* 2, 1 (August 1974), 52—53.
11 David Rand Bishop, Jr., *African Critics and African Literature: A Study of Critical Standards, 1947—1966,* (unpublished dissertation, Michigan State University, 1971), pp. 401—02.
12 Ibid.
13 Abiola Irele, Introduction to the *Contemporary African Literature Exhibition, University of Ife,* (Ile-Ife, 1972), p. xv.
14 Ngugi, op. cit.
15 Abiola Irele, "The Criticism of Modern African Literature," *Perspectives on African Literature,* ed. Christopher Heywood (Ile-Ife, 1971), p. 30.
16 Ibid., p. 20.
17 Ibid., p. 23.
18 Eustace Palmer, "Comment," *African Literature Today,* 7 (1975), 126—27.
19 D. I. Izevbaye, "Criticism and Literature in Africa," *Perspectives on African Literature,* op. cit., p. 30.
20 Ibid.
21 D. I. Izevbaye, "The State of Criticism in African Literature," *African Literature Today,* 7 (1975), 16.
22 Bishop, op. cit., p. 403.
23 Sunday O. Anozie, "Genetic Structuralism as a Critical Technique: Notes Toward a Sociological Theory of the African Novel," *The Conch,* 3, 1 (1971), 39.
24 James Thorpe, ed. *The Aims and Methods of Scholarship in Modern Languages and Literatures,* (New York, 1963); *Relations of Literary Study: Essays on Interdisciplinary Contributions,* (New York, 1967).

The Trinidad Awakening

Reinhard W. Sander

The emergence of West Indian fiction in the early 1930s is closely related to the appearance of two Trinidadian magazines: *Trinidad* and *The Beacon*. In the pages of these magazines, a group of intellectuals and writers (among them C. L. R. James, Alfred H. Mendes, Albert Gomes, and R. A. C. de Bois-siere) published essays, poetry and short fiction, and formulated basic postulates for an indigenous West Indian literature. Before we approach these magazines and analyze the group's development towards and conception of a theory of West Indian fiction, a brief discussion of the conditioning influences—social, political and literary—will help to present some general background.[1]

"Trinidad in 1930," writes Albert Gomes, the editor of *The Beacon*, in his autobiography,[2] "was a remote and forgotten back-water of the world. It lay deep and still in its sweaty sleep, tossing only occasionally when its comfortable dream touched furtively the nightmare into which it was to awaken abruptly in 1937." Trinidad, like almost every other British West Indian territory, was still a Crown Colony in 1930. "Discovered" by Columbus on his third voyage on July 31, 1498, Trinidad remained in Spanish possession and towards the end of the eighteenth century under French influence until it was captured by the British in 1797.[3] Since there was no gold in Trinidad, Spain had never been particularly interested in her colony. The consequence was that, apart from Guyana, Trinidad in 1930 comprised a population quite different from that of Jamaica, Barbados and the smaller British West Indian islands. The African slave population—very large in the islands with a developed sugar industry—amounted to a mere 10,000 in Trinidad in 1797.[4] The abolition of the Slave Trade in 1807 and Emancipation in 1833 prevented a substantial increase of African slaves under British rule. Indentured Asian labor, however, for more than ninety years filled the gap to ensure the growth of the Trinidadian sugar plantation. Thus, in 1930, the majority of Trinidad's population was of African *and* East Indian descent, with a small but powerful group of white Creoles (mostly of French and Portuguese origin) and of British expatriates. The sugar industry, although severely hit by one crisis after another, was still the dominant interest in the colony, joined by the oil industry after the discovery of oil in commercial quantities in 1910.[5]

Both the Crown Colony form of government and the sugar interest had disastrous effects on the intellectual and cultural development of the colony. James Stephen, a prominent British abolitionist, wrote in 1831 about West Indian planters: "Their lives are passed in a contracted circle amidst petty feuds and pecuniary embarrassments. There is no civilised society on earth so entirely destitute of learned leisure, of literary and scientific intercourse, and even of liberal recreation."[6] He could have repeated the same if he had had the opportunity of visiting the West Indies again a hundred years later. Kenneth Ramchand, the author of *The West Indian Novel and Its Background*, refers to the period before 1930 as that of "life without fiction." The plantocracy, if resident in the island, behaved in the way described by James Stephen, or after having established a fortune in the West Indies practiced "cultural absenteeism," residing in England, living off the profits from colonial exploitation and showing not the least interest in the colony. Towards the beginning of this century, the exceptional white Creole writer, such as Tom Redcam (pseud. for Thomas H. MacDermot) and Herbert de Lisser, appeared in the West Indies, but as a lone individual had no significant impact on the attitudes of the plantation society. Tom Redcam's attempt to create "The All Jamaica Library" which was to consist of "poetry, fiction, history and essays ... all dealing directly with Jamaica and Jamaicans, and written by Jamaicans" failed miserably.[7] There simply was no reading public in the West Indies.[8] The emerging middle class followed the example set by the plantocracy, and in addition showed "resistance ... to a native literature that was not the English literature they had been brought up to consider the only literature possible."[9] The masses of West Indians had not even developed sufficient reading skills since the introduction of elementary education after Emancipation in 1833. In fact, the demands of the Crown Colony system and the sugar industry discouraged education of any kind, as the following excerpt from a hearing before a Select Committee of the Trinidad Legislative Council in 1926 illustrates. A sugar planter, Mr. Robinson, is questioned by Committee member O'Reilly on the issue of child labor:

> Mr. O'Reilly: Do you think it is satisfactory to have a child of 10 working that number of hours (7 a.m to 5 p.m)?
> Mr. R.: This is an agricultural country. Unless you put the children on to working in the fields when they are young, you will never get them to do so later. If you want to turn all these people into a lot of clerks, caneweighers, and people of that sort, all you have to do is to prevent them working in the fields until they are 16 years old; then I guarantee you will have but very few labourers in the Colony, but if you train them to work in the fields, you will never have any difficulty.
> Mr. O'Reilley: You agree that the present system shuts them off from education?
> Mr. R.: They are well-fed!
> Mr. O'Reilley: I am talking of their education. If they are educated they don't want to be labourers?
> Mr. R.: No. Give them some education in the way of reading and writing, but no more. Even then I would say educate only the bright ones: not the mass. If you do educate the whole mass of the agricultural population, you will be deliberately ruining the country.[10]

The fate meted out to the colored population of the West Indies makes it clear why the first Afro-Caribbean novelist, Claude McKay, left for the United States in 1912. Although his novel *Banana Bottom,* published in 1933, deals with the kind of West Indian material later utilized by established West Indian writers, the quality of the majority of his works has earned him a place in Afro-American rather than West Indian literature.[11] Hardly anybody took notice of him once he had left Jamaica and had joined the creative forces of the "Harlem Renaissance."[12]

What distinguishes the writers and intellectuals who were involved in the publication of *Trinidad* and *The Beacon* from Tom Redcam, Herbert de Lisser, Claude McKay and a small number of other West Indian writers,[13] is primarily their appearance as a group, which fostered the exchange of views and theoretical discussions, and prevented creative loneliness and frustration. Each writer was assured of a small audience—the fellow-contributors to *Trinidad and The Beacon*; and as is evident from the sales of the magazines (*Trinidad:* about 1,000 copies; *The Beacon*: between 1,500 and 5,000 copies),[14] his writings were also read by a relatively large audience in Trinidad itself. It should be mentioned from the outset, however, that the reception of the magazines was not a friendly one. Alfred H. Mendes, the most prolific writer of the group and author of *Pitch Lake* (1934) and *Black Fauns* (1935), and Albert Gomes can still recall the furor the magazines created among the island's bourgeois public, "a libel action, frequent visits from the police, denunciation from the pulpit, pressure from both church and state, increasing opposition from the commercial community and chronic lack of funds."[15] It seems the Catholic establishment was the foremost enemy of *The Beacon* and "on one occasion ... organized a campaign to persuade advertisers to boycott the magazine, accusing it of immorality, atheism and communism."[16] However, adverse criticism only stimulated further productivity among the group, whose most important members were in their twenties and early thirties.

> *The Beacon* became much more than just a literary magazine and mouthpiece of a clique. Indeed, it became the focus of a movement of enlightenment spearheaded by Trinidad's angry young men of the Thirties. It was the torpor, the smugness and the hypocrisy of the Trinidad of the period that provoked the response which produced both the magazine and the defiant bohemianism of the movement that was built around it.[17]

Trinidad, edited by Alfred H. Mendes and C. L. R. James,[18] appeared only twice (Christimas, 1929, and Easter, 1930), but it is by far the more "literary" of the two magazines. The first issue contained eight pieces of short fiction, six poems, and an article on music. Alfred Mendes claims that it was "the first magazine of its kind that had appeared in Trinidad up until that point in the island's history"[19]; but to keep the record straight, we should at least mention a precursor and contemporary of *Trinidad*: a magazine called *The Quarterly Magazine*, edited and published by Austin M. Nolte, most copies of which seem to have completely vanished.[20] Anson Gonzalez, a young Trinidadian poet and critic, in his *Self-Discovery Through Literature: Creative Writing in Trinidad and Tobago* (1972)—a small volume of radio programs devoted to the tenth anniversary of Trinidad's Independence—remarks: "In creative writing, as in sport, in calypso, folk song and music, there seems to be a solid foundation, traditions, on which to build, legendary figures perhaps today debunked, who need being noticed for their contributions to the life of this beautiful, though troubled, land of ours."[21] Austin M. Nolte and his *Quarterly Magazine,* unfortunately, also remained lost and undiscussed during Anson Gonzalez's search into Trinidad's literary past. The critic laments that early works by Trinidadians "have in many cases almost totally disappeared from the scene."[22] Copies of *Trinidad* and *The Beacon* are, indeed, also very scarce,[23] and we hope that both magazines will be reprinted before it is too late.

Elsewhere in his booklet, Anson Gonzalez writes: "One of the giants, unacknowledged that is, of our literary world, who was making an effort to create a literary tradition not only for Trinidad and Tobago but for the entire West Indies as well, is Albert Gomes ... *The Beacon* was his baby and brainchild. With it he took Trinidad by storm for the better part of three years, and at this time he was merely twenty years old."[24] Albert Gomes, while studying and working in the United States between 1928 and 1930 had received a copy of *Trinidad,* and on his return to Trinidad in 1930 got introduced to the group around that magazine, whose members "met regularly and informally at Mendes' home where they listened to recorded music, argued way into the night, and read excerpts from each other's writings.[25] The group was disintegrating at that time, but became vigorously alive again once Gomes decided to publish *The Beacon. The Beacon,* which ran uninterruptedly from March 1931 through November 1933 (28 issues), differed vastly from *Trinidad.* Like *Trinidad* it featured indigenous short fiction and poetry (which unfortunately could not match the quality of the short fiction, remained imitative and suffered from neo-Romanticism, Victorianism and Exoticism),[26] but in its non-fictional sections it participated also actively in Trinidadian, West Indian and world affairs.[27] It is important to note that the group around *The Beacon,* although living in a remote colonial island, was well-informed about social and political activities not only in the British Empire, but also in the United States, Western Europe and the Soviet Union. C. L. R. James eagerly points out: "The origins of my work and my thoughts are to be found in Western European literature, Western European history and Western European thought."[28] He also draws attention to the extensive library and the amount of foreign magazines and newspapers which were at the disposal of the members of the group.[29] Through its contacts with the outside world it actually became part and parcel of the universal revolutionary spirit of the Thirties. For one thing, there were Nathan Schneider and Sheldon Christian, the American editors of *The Beacon,* who were involved in leftist movements in the United States. And Alfred H. Mendes remembers:

> We also had come to be known as the Communist group, and indeed in those
> years we were very sympathetic towards what was occurring in the Soviet
> Union.
> Most of us, you know, were on the border line—Imean we could easily have
> crossed the border, if we had had any influence directly brought to bear upon
> us to join the Communist Party.[30]

Like Mendes, almost all members of the groups remained fellow-travellers
during the early Thirties. The only one to cross the border was C. L. R. James,
who left Trinidad early in 1932 to become a renowned historian and political
theoretician. Only he could later say about himself, George Padmore and
Aimé Césaire: "We were educated not only in the literature and material life
of Western civilization, but we also became Marxists and were educated by
Marxism."[31] But for Albert Gomes, Alfred Mendes and most of the others,
the occupation with the Russian experiment became an important ideological
framework from which to criticize colonial society in Trinidad and to attack
the Crown Colony system. The opposition that Captain A. A. Cipriani, the
first of Trinidad's labor leaders, practiced as one of the elected members in
the Trinidad Legislative Council and as Mayor of Port-of-Spain in the immediate political realm was essentially supported in the editorials and political
articles of *The Beacon*. That *The Beacon* and Captain Cipriani were not on
friendly terms is one of those misfortunes one encounters so often among pro-
ponents of similar ideas. The Captain especially infuriated *The Beacon* group
during the crisis which developed around the Divorce Bill between 1930 and
1932 when as a Catholic he opposed that bill.[32] The emergence of Cipriani's
strong working-class movement after World War I had the same roots as the
upsurge of indigenous West Indian short fiction published in *Trinidad* and *The
Beacon*: the experience of World War I, the Soviet Revolution, the Great De-
pression, and the spirit of the Thirties. Captain Cipriani returned to Trinidad
a changed man after he had served in the British West India Regiment during
the war, and Mendes also testifies to that change for members of *The Beacon*
group in respect to writing:

> I think the motivating forces that drove us, willy-nilly, like a sort of one of
> the furies, into writing at all, stemmed from two world-shattering events at
> that early period of our lives.
> The first was of course, the first world war where a large number of us had
> been abroad, and indeed, even those of us who had not been abroad were
> influenced considerably by what was happening in the world, and the second
> event was the Russian Revolution. Those, I think, were the two events in our
> lives at that time which drove us into writing about our islands.[33]

The struggle for political Independence and the creation of a national literature went hand in hand from then on. With obvious enthusiasm *The Beacon* in
its pages also followed the events in another British crown colony, where
Gandhi began to make his name as a leader of the masses. For five issues *The
Beacon* even featured a special "India Section" which catered to the interests

of the East Indian population in Trinidad. "I feel," says Albert Gomes, "that the Indians had a distinctive culture whose features deserved to be reflected in a publication like *The Beacon*."[34] Articles about Africa catered to the Black population and attempted to create pride in the culture of the ancestral homeland. The race question was discussed at length and sparked off quite a controversy among contributors and readers of *The Beacon*. One of Albert Gomes's contributions entitled "Black Man," which in Kenneth Ramchand's words "is as fierce and relevant as any Black Power call today,"[35] brought the police to the house of the editor.[36] In the pages of *The Beacon* we also find the first interest in Caribbean history. Articles on local events like the Water Riots of 1903 and on Caribbean historical personalities foreshadowed the works of Eric Williams and C. L. R. James. *The Beacon* also served educational purposes in popularized accounts of various sciences, book, art and film reviews and the lengthy articles on music by H. McD. Carpenter. Although *The Beacon* died in November 1933, it was revived for one issue in November 1939. In 1937, Albert Gomes also finally realized a plan he had had in the early Thirties:[37] an anthology of Trinidadian writing entitled *From Trinidad: A Selection From the Fiction and Verse of the Island of Trinidad, British West Indies,* which featured a number of writers who had been associated with *The Beacon*.

It should be mentioned that the appearance of literary magazines in Trinidad was not an isolated phenomenon in the Thirties. The group around *Trinidad* and *The Beacon* established contacts with similar ventures in other islands. When it received *The Outlook,* edited by Clennell W. Wickham, and the first issue of *The Forum Quarterly*,[38] later edited by Gordon O. Bell—both magazines from Barbados—Albert Gomes wrote enthusiastically: "It proves conclusively that Barbados is not as English as we have been made to think."[39] And he added: "Recent publications in the West Indies suffice to explode the myth of isolation which travel writers are always so eager to apply to these islands. Good landscape, sugar and cocoa are not our only products."[40] The link with *The Forum Quarterly* was a lasting one and in its June 1932 issue that magazine featured a number of Trinidadian contributors.[41] A few Barbadians likewise appeared in the pages of *The Beacon,* and *The Beacon* was sold in Barbados where it received the usual hostile reception from the established press.[42] Towards the end *The Beacon* became, however, condescending towards *The Forum Quarterly,* but had to admit that it had "from time to time published good poetry."[43] In comparing theirs with other literary magazines, the Trinidadians were convinced that "outside of *The Beacon* and *The Royalian* there is no other magazine in the West Indies that publishes any fiction worthy of a second glance."[44]

It is indeed the short fiction for which *Trinidad* and *The Beacon* will be remembered. So far, unfortunately, hardly anybody has paid any significant attention to these cradles of West Indian literature. The same is also true of the Barbadian magazine *Bim,* published by Frank Collymore since 1942, and the Guyanese magazine *Kyk-over-al,* published by A. J. Seymour from 1945 to 1961.[45] Kenneth Ramchand is the only major critic who has paid tribute to the group around the Trinidadian magazines in his *The West Indian Novel and Its Background* and in an introduction to the 1971 republication of C. L. R. James's *Minty Alley* (1936).[46] Focussing on whom he considers the two leading figures in *The Beacon* group, Alfred Mendes and C. L. R. James, he discusses their novels and comes to the conclusion that "we can see the decisive establishment of social realism in the West Indian novel."[47] From the short fiction produced during the Thirties he selects C. L. R. James's "Triumph"[48] and evaluates it as "a good example of the realistic literature of the 'yard'."[49] In a future study we will follow Ramchand's example and discuss a selected amount of short fiction, but at present we want to show that the group around *Trinidad* and *The Beacon* had developed a theory of what fiction in the West Indies should deal with. In order to encourage literary expression in Trinidad, *The Beacon* had quite early in its existence organized a short story competition. When the contributions finally arrived, part of an editorial read:

We regret to write that few good stories have been received for this Competition. The majority of local fiction-writers obviously believe that gross exaggerations contribute to the artistic value of their stories. Several of the stories we have received read like advertisements for the enhancement of our tourist trade; others, like anecdotes from the Good Book and still more, like extracts from *True Story*. This however, might easily be attributed to that deep religious consciousness of which Trinidadians are so proud. We fail utterly to understand, however, why anyone should want to see Trinidad as a miniature *Paradiso,* where grave-diggers speak like English M.P.'s and *vice-versa.* The answer is obviously that the average Trinidad writer regards his fellow-countrymen as his inferiors, an uninteresting people who are not worth his while. He genuinely feels (and by this, of course, asserts his own feeling of inferiority) that with his people as characters his stories would be worth nothing. It is for this reason that he peoples them with creatures from other planets, American gangsters and English M.P.'s; and revives familiar plots and characters from *True Story* and other *nth* rate periodicals. It would be difficult to convince him that the exotic quality of his plot is immaterial and that it is difficult to write well of persons and things beyond one's ken. For those clerics and stern moralists who are always preaching and parading the moral cleanliness of "our fair isle" there are abundant surprises in the stories received for the competition. Sex is still "the dirty secret," but the aspiring local writer treats it with religious fervour; and we make bold to say that it is the axis on which his universe revolves. He prefers, however, to carry it around in his bosom rather than show it to his friends. We have never seen such bad love scenes before and not until the people of Trinidad begin to think more openly and less religiously of sex will local writers attain more artistic restraint and indifference in the treatment of sex in their stories. As it is, their treatment of the question is by far the ugliest, most unnatural and *civilized,* we have been up against. It is easy to understand and be sympathetic, however. They grow up among people who maintain an amazing silence in matters relating to sex and it is not unusual that the fascination of what is to them incomprehensible in sex should continue until late in life. We advise the local writer, however, to spend less time on florid descriptions of our hills, valleys, and the moonlight on the Queen's Park Savannah. Those things are only incidental to a good story. It is moreover, better to spend two days trying to analyse the sensations of your last tooth-ache than to continue to nibble away indefinitely at the distorted psyche of some New York gangster. Why is the local writer so eager to attach mystery to cut and dried Trinidad?[50]

On the occasion of a short story competition in the Barbadian *Forum Quarterly* the *Beacon* group simply wrote that "it is desirable that the stories should have a West Indian setting."[51] In these and similar comments we hear the first tentative voice of literary independence, which became stronger and stronger as the months went by. In the "Notes" for June, 1933, which defended C. L. R. James's story "Triumph" against an attack from *The Royalian*, we read for example: "It is important, moreover, that we break away as far as possible from the English tradition."[52] The Trinidadian writers were quite conscious of their pioneering contribution to the creation of an indigenous West Indian literature. They compared their efforts, though in an understatement, to those which created a national literature in the United States of America: "The day will come when we, like America, will produce our Walt Whitman; then and only then will the movement towards an art and language indigenous to our spirit and environment commence."[53] In fact, that movement had already commenced with the short fiction of writers such as C. L. R. James, Alfred H. Mendes, Ernest A. Carr, R. A. C. de Boissiere, Percival Maynard, and A. C. Thomasos. To return to the lengthy excerpt from the editorial quoted above, what *The Beacon* group advocated was writing which utilized West Indian setting, speech, characters, situations and conflicts. It warned against the imitation of foreign literature, especially against the imitation of foreign popular literature. Local color, however, was not regarded as a virtue by itself. A mere occupation with the enchanted landscape of the tropics (which is, however, very much present in *The Beacon's* poetry) did not fulfill the group's emphasis on realism and verisimilitude in writing. This emphasis on realism, it should be noted, is not a preculiarly West Indian phenomenon, but is evident in the renewed presence of realism in European and American literature during the Thirties—proletarian writing being the most thorough and radical manifestation of it. Realism combined with and supported by the Trinidadians' social and political ideology resulted in fiction that focussed on West Indian characters belonging to the lower classes. Daniel Guérin in his *The West Indies and Their Future* writes:

> A Caribbean culture only started to come into being when ... a minority split away from the middle classes and made contact with the people, turned its attention to their problems, studied their customs, their beliefs, what of African inheritance the people have kept alive, and voiced the people's aspirations and anger.[54]

Guérin is quite correct in stating elsewhere that "the Caribbean 'renaissance' located *itself first and most intensively in those islands which enjoy a relative political independence*: in Cuba, in Haiti,"[55] but we can notice the same process in the Trinidad "awakening." The group around *Trinidad* and *The Beacon* consisted essentially of middle-class people, with a slight racial preponderance of white Creoles and expatriates; but they as well as those middle-class members who were of African or Asian descent, or what is more likely in Trinidad a mixture of any of the major races,[56] "made contact" with Trinidad's lower classes in the pages of their magazines. The barrack-yard was of particular interest to the writers of short fiction. Alfred H. Mendes in an interview explained how the middle-class writer made his contact with the barrack-yarders:

> What I did in order to get the atmosphere, to get the sort of jargon that they spoke—the vernacular, the idiom—what I did was: I went into the barrack-yard that was then at the bottom of Park Street just before you came into Richmond Street, and I lived in it for about six months. I did not live completely there, but I ingratiated myself. They knew of what I was doing; they knew what I felt about their way of life—that I was sympathetic towards it. So I was *persona* very *grata*. I slept there frequently, and a lot of the incidents that appear in my second published novel, *Black Fauns*, were taken almost directly from my experience with the barrack-yarders.[57]

The lower classes in Trinidad consisted almost entirely of people of African and East Indian origin. Thus *The Beacon* group strongly attacked any West Indian publication in which the Black or East Indian majority did not receive its due place. The publishers of the *Jamboree Programme* were asked "how it is that in a booklet on Scouting published in and about an island where there are ten Negroes to every white person, there should be such a conspicuous absence of the portraits of Negroes."[58] *The Trinidadian*, another publication which began to appear during the early Thirties was condemned as being "no more Trinidadian than the Woolworth Building . . . an hallucitant for tourists." "Can we shut from their (the tourists') eyes the sordid spectacle of unclad, unwashed, unfed East Indians picking lice from each other's bodies in Marine Square?" queried the editor of *The Beacon*.[59]

If the bourgeois reading public in Trinidad was offended by *The Beacon's* interest in low-class life, it was infuriated by the magazine's nonchalant attitude towards sex. The editorial in connection with the short story competition quoted above indicates the group's demand for realism in matters concerning sex. Making serious contacts with the people obviously also forced the indigenous writer to emulate the people's notions about sex. Daniel Guérin who estimates that 50 to 60 percent of West Indian children are born out of wedlock writes: "The West Indian masses (unlike the West Indian middle classes) have remained close to nature: their superficial Christianity notwithstanding, they continue to view the sexual act as the most normal, the least reprehensible of things."[60] Among the writers of short fiction it was especially Alfred H. Mendes who focussed his interest on the complicated but natural sexual relationship in his barrack-yard pieces. His portraits of Trinidadian sweetmen and kept women elicited the angriest responses from the reading public in Trinidad. The first issue of *Trinidad* was violently attacked by a section of the press.[61] Alfred H. Mendes's reply in the second issue of *Trinidad* to the "hullabaloo" in Trinidad should be quoted at length because it is another vital document of the theory of fiction put forward by the group around the two Trinidadian magazines. The reply shows to what a large degree the Trinidadian writers participated in the universal revolutionary spirit of the Thirties and how in the Trinidadian case social realism was inseparable from sexual realism. Here is a brief excerpt:

> ... (T)he *Zeit Geist* is one of revolt against established customs and organic loyalties. Since the War, this revolt has been directed not so much against the Puritanism of the 16th century as against a degenerate form of it popularly known as Victorianism. This Victorianism, as exposed in the writings of most of the novelists of the period, insisted that maidens should be prim and proper, that the contours and lines of objects should be concealed by laces and embroideries, that philosophies should deny the reality of evil, that children should be spoon-fed with a thick soup of lies, and that the good life was conditioned by expurgated speech, going to church and in nine cases out of ten smiling when you should frown and frowning when you should smile ... But the creative artist is primarily concerned with the weaving of patterns: the material that he uses is so much grist to his mill, for he who is sincere about his literary work (or any other art-work for that matter) cannot stop to consider how much ugliness there is in the matter that comes his way. It would be silly to tell the architect not to build in stone because stone is rough and amorphous; to warn the sculptor to leave bronze alone because bronze is brown and blatant is like warning the priest and parson against heathens because they have no regard for *our* anthropomorphic god; even so it is futile and puerile to ask the writer of fiction to leave bodies and barrack-yards alone because they are obscene in the popular sense. It all depends on what literary treatment they receive, though it does not necessarily mean that, so treated, they shall be no longer obscenities; it simply means that they shall be obscenities presented for reasons other than raising the disgust or sexual desires of the reader.[62]

Along similar lines Elizabeth Peabody later wrote an article in *The Beacon* entitled "Defence of Modern Realism in Fiction."[63] It is also revealing that among the foreign writers whose works *The Beacon* group wanted to put across to their readers were Thomas Hardy, Ernest Hemingway, D. H. Lawrence, Turgenev, Dostoyevsky, Tolstoy and Arnold Bennett. The Russians were praised because of their realism and the theme of emancipation; Arnold Bennett was commended in a review by C. L. R. James because: "For the ordinary man he professed and obviously had a great admiration and respect."[64]

In theory and in practice, the West Indian writers of the Thirties are the direct ancestors of established writers such as Roger Mais, Vidia Naipaul, Samuel Selvon and George Lamming. When Anson Gonzalez in *Self-Discovery Through Literature* says about the early Trinidadian writers that "very few of them expressed any concern for middle and upper class themes,"[65] we notice in the works of the established West Indian writers that the preoccupation with the underprivileged West Indian, whether city-dweller or peasant, is a continuing feature of West Indian Literature.

Notes

1 Part of the present short study of Trinidadian magazines and short fiction in the Thirties is an excerpt from a Ph. D. dissertation in progress. The dissertation attempts to cover a number of literary magazines, especially *The Beacon, Bim,* and *Kyk-over-al,* in terms of their contributions to the cultural independence of the West Indies. The chapter on *The Beacon* will provide a thorough analysis not only of short fiction, but also of the poetry, editorials and articles published.

2 Albert Gomes's autobiography is entitled *Through a Maze of Colour.* We read the typed manuscript, which is kept in the Central Library of Trinidad and Tobago, in 1972. It is quite possible, though, that it has been published in book form in the meantime. Chapter II, "Rebel Journalist," pp. 22—42 of the typed manuscript, is an account of Gomes's editorship of *The Beacon.* Other personal accounts of or references to the publishing ventures of *Trinidad* and *The Beacon* are: C. L. R. James, "Discovering Literature in Trinidad: The Nineteen-Thirties," *Savacou,* 2 (September 1970), 54—60; C. L. R. James, *Beyond a Boundary* (London: Hutchinson, 1963, rpt. 1966, 1969), *passim;* "Interview with C. L. R. James," in *Kas-Kas: Interviews with Three Caribbean Writers in Texas,* ed. Ian Munro and Reinhard Sander (Austin: African and Afro-American Research Institute of the University of Texas, 1972), *passim;* "Talking about the Thirties (Interview with Alfred Mendes)," ed. Clifford Sealy, *Voices,* I, 5 (December 1965), 3—7; "The Turbulent Thirties in Trinidad: An Interview with Alfred H. Mendes," ed. Reinhard Sander, *World Literature Written in English,* 12, 1 (April 1973), 66—79.

3 Good introductions to Trinidadian and West Indian history are: Eric Williams, *History of the People of Trinidad and Tobago* (London: André Deutsch, 1964); Eric Williams, *From Columbus to Castro: The History of the Caribbean 1492—1969* (London: André Deutsch, 1970); Gordon K. Lewis, *The Growth of the Modern West Indies* (New York and London: Modern Reader Paperbacks, 1968); Daniel Guérin, *The West Indies and Their Future* (London: Dennis Dobson, 1961).

4 Williams, *History,* p. 47.

5 Ibid., p. 215.

6 Quoted in Williams, *History,* p. 90.

7 Cf. Kenneth Ramchand, *The West Indian Novel and Its Background* (London: Faber and Faber, 1970), pp. 54—55.

8 Albert Gomes recalls in *Through a Maze of Colour* (p. 8) that his father "considered reading books an unprofitable pastime, and so he regarded me with some suspicion when, at a very early age, I began to reveal a love for books and for the libraries where they were to be found."

9 Ramchand, *West Indian Novel,* p. 12.

10 Quoted in Williams, *History,* pp. 212—13.

11 An excellent discussion of Claude McKay as a "precursor" in the context of West Indian literature is Kenneth Ramchand's "The Road to *Banana Bottom,*" in his *The West Indian Novel and Its Background,* pp. 239—73.

12 It should be noted, though, that the group around *Trinidad* and *The Beacon* took notice of Claude McKay. We find a brief and rather negative review of *Banjo* in *Trinidad,* 1, 2 (Easter 1930), 135—36. In October 1933, however, a caption of the editorial in *The Beacon* (Vol. 3, No. 3, p. 51) reads: "A West Indian Novelist." Among other things, the editor points out that *Banana Bottom* "is a novel, we feel, that should be read

by everyone of our readers. For the first time the West Indian scene and character has been interpreted subjectively by a native West Indian." In the same issue (pp. 58—59), Albert Gomes writes a lengthy and quite favorable review of *Banana Bottom*. This review also contains an interesting criticism applicable to quite a number of African, Afro-American, and Caribbean novels dealing with a search for roots and rejection of Western civilization: "But in this novel there is something unconvincing about Bita's complete relinquishment of her foster-culture. McKay, I believe, underestimates the influence of a European training on the mind of the Negro. Its roots are far more secure; in itself it is less amenable to resilience."

13   For a "Year by Year Bibliography" of West Indian novels, see Ramchand, *West Indian Novel,* pp. 282—86 .

14   Information given by Alfred H. Mendes, cf. interview in *WLWE;* and by Albert Gomes in a personal communication, 4 November 1972.

15   Cf. Mendes, interview in *WLWE,* and Gomes, *Through a Maze of Colour.*

16   Gomes, personal communication, 4 November 1972.

17   Gomes, *Through a Maze of Colour,* p. 26—27.

18   C. L. R. James's name appears as co-editor only in the first issue of *Trinidad.* Cf. interview in *WLWE* for possible reason for James's withdrawing his name as co-editor in the second issue of Trinidad.

19   Mendes, interview in *WLWE,* p. 66.

20   We were only able to locate the Christmas 1930 issue of *The Quarterly Magazine,* which is the ninth issue of the magazine. This issue contains short fiction: "Bete Rouge" by Alfred H. Mendes, "Black Magic" by Edgar Jackson, "The Rise and Collapse of Samuel Prescott," by Wallace Donovan; poetry: "Cartagena de Indias (After Jose-Maria de Heredia)" by Louis E. Wharton, "The Whisper" by Joseph I. da Silva, "Your Rosary" by J. C. Superville, "The Look I Knew" by J. Chophee. Austin M. Nolte writes an editorial on "The War and Religion" and an article entitled "Insanity and Genius: A Study of the Traits of Famous Composers and Poets." La Loo Daniel writes "The Rubaiyat of Omar Khayyam" and E. D. Madoo analyzes Horace's poetry in a lengthy article entitled "Q. Horatii Flacci Carmini."

21   Anson Gonzalez, *Self-Discovery Through Literature: Creative Writing in Trinidad and Tobago* (Diego Martin, Trinidad: The Author, 1972), p. 1.

22   Ibid., p. 2.

23   Apart from the editor's complete set of *The Beacon,* there is *one* complete photocopied set in the library at U. W. I. St. Augustine. The Central Library of Trinidad and Tobago has a bound volume of *The Beacon,* which, however, misses a number of the 1933 issues and the 1939 issue. The latter library also possesses the two issues of *Trinidad.*

24   Gonzalez, *Self-Discovery,* p. 3.

25   Gomes, *Through a Maze of Colour,* p. 24.

26   The editor of *The Beacon* was aware of the poor quality of the poetry in the magazine. In "Notes of the Month" (3, 4, Nov. 1933), 74, he writes: "In this respect we make no claims for ourselves; we have always experienced and still experience great difficulty in choosing poetry for our columns. We receive a superabundance of bad verse which is, strictly speaking, fit only for the waste-basket. With fiction it is a different matter: Trinidad is in advance of the other islands."

27   The amount of poetry and short fiction even decreased some-what in the later issues of *The Beacon.* Already in April 1932 (Vol. 1, No. 12, p. 1),

the editor—aware of this trend—explained: "We want to encourage literary expression in the islands. That we have frequently deviated from our main purpose should surprise no one. Misery, Oppression and Want confront us at every turn. We could not make of art a mere luxury. It seemed a selfish thing to do."

28 James, "Discovering Literature," p. 54.

29 Cf. Ibid.

30 Mendes, interview in *WLWE*, p. 77.

31 James, "Discovering Literature," p. 55.

32 Cf. Alfred Mendes's response to the question, "What was the relationship of *The Beacon* to Captain Cipriani and his movement?" Interview in *WLWE*, pp. 75—76. Also cf. Gomes's *Through a Maze of Colour*.

33 Mendes, interview in *Voices*, p. 5.

34 Gomes, personal communication, 4 November 1972.

35 Ramchand, *West Indian Novel*, p. 64 (Footnote 1).

36 Cf. Gomes, *Through a Maze of Colour*, pp. 31—34.

37 Under the caption "A Proposed West Indian Publication," we find Gomes's plan outlined in the editorial of the December issue of *The Beacon* (Vol. 1, No. 9, p. 14): "The Editor of this paper thinks the time has arrived for an annual anthology of West Indian literature to be got together. The scheme is to publish at Christmas in each year, in book form, a collection of hitherto unpublished stories, plays, verses, essays and the like, with a view to drawing the people of the Caribbean closer together by that ageless bond of letters which among other peoples has never failed. The book will be advertised and it is hoped sold throughout the West Indies." Twelve years later, when Albert Gomes wrote a preface to *Best Poems of Trinidad*, ed. A. M. Clarke (Trinidad: Frasers Printerie, 1943), pp. 3—4, he recalled the success of *From Trinidad:* "When I was preparing *From Trinidad* for the printer, I asked a prominent Trinidad lawyer what he thought of the proposed publication. 'Well, you are a pioneer; you enjoy this sort of work ... but there's no support for that sort of thing in Trinidad.' That, in so many words, was his reply. The same reply, differently worded, but conveying the same meaning, came from many of my friends. *From Trinidad* was successful in a way that surprised my own fervent optimism. It sold well and was praised by persons whose discernment and sincerity I have never had any reason to doubt."

38 *The Forum Quarterly* was published by the Forum Club. A Barbadian correspondent later wrote in *The Beacon*, 3, 4 (November 1933), 90, about that club: "(It) is composed chiefly of the coloured and negro intelligentsia of the Colony. Members of this Body, apart from producing their own Quarterly, take an exceptionally keen interest in the historic background of the Negro, and presumably study current Negro Literature to a great extent."

39 *The Beacon*, 1,10 (Jan.—Feb. 1932), 24.

40 Ibid., p. 25.

41 These were Ralph Mentor ("Racial Relationship"—article), Olga Comma ("The Cigale"—poem), Olga Yaatoff ("Lime Trees"—poem), Later issues of the *The Forum Quarterly*, included material by Albert Gomes, Alfred H. Mendes, and C. L. R. James. *The Forum Quarterly*, a few copies of which are avaliable in the Barbados Public Library also had an interest in and links with Afro-America (cf. also footnote 38). We find an article on Langston Hughes, and articles by George Schuyler and W. E. E. DuBois.

42 The Barbados Advocate Weekly attacked The Beacon on its editorial page. Cf. The Beacon's rebuttal in 3, 2 (September 1933), 27—29.
43 The Beacon, 3, 4 (Nov. 1933), 74.
44 Ibid. (The Royalian, published by the Queen's Royal College Literary Society in Trinidad, seems to have completely disappeared.)
45 The lack of critical attention is particularly due to the unavailability of Trinidad, The Beacon, Bim, and Kyk-over-al. We are looking forward to the day when these magazines are reprinted. To my knowledge only three critics have written brief essays on the literary magazines: Edward Brathwaite, "Kyk-over-al and the Radicals," in New World: Guyana Independence Issue, ed. George Lamming and Martin Carter (Georgetown, Guyana: New World Group, 1966), pp. 55—57. "The Drift Towards the Audience," Chapter V in Kenneth Ramchand's The West Indian Novel and Its Background (London: Faber and Faber, 1970) pp. 63—74; Edward Baugh, "Frank Collymore and the Miracle of Bim," in New World: Barbados Independence Issue, ed. George Lamming and Edward Baugh (Kingston, Jamaica: New World Group, 1966—67), pp. 129—33; a revised and updated version of this last essay has been published as "Indroduction" to An Index to Bim, compiled by Reinhard Sander (St. Augustine, Trinidad and Tobago: University of the West Indies, Extra-Mural Studies Unit, 1973), pp. 7—17.
46 The introduction to C. L. R. James's Minty Alley (London and Port-of-Spain: New Beacon Books Ltd., 1971) is a slighty modified excerpt from Ramchand's Chapter V in The West Indian Novel and Its Background.
47 Ramchand, West Indian Novel, p. 65.
48 Trinidad, 1, 1 (Christmas 1929), 31—40.
49 Ramchand, West Indian Novel, p. 65.
50 The Beacon, 1, 10 (Jan.—Feb. 1932), 1—2.
51 The Beacon, 2, 1 (May 1932), 31.
52 The Beacon, 2, 12 (June 1933), 3.
53 Ibid.
54 Guérin, The West Indies, p. 80.
55 Ibid., p. 79.
56 For information on the racial identity of some of the members of The Beacon group, cf. Mendes, interview in WLWE, and Gomes, Through a Maze of Colour. In the context of the present paper this aspect seems to be irrelevant but has to be dealt with when discussing the controversy about the race question which occupied the pages of The Beacon for a number of issues.
57 Mendes, interview in WLWE, p. 71.
58 The Beacon, 2, 11 (May 1933), 2.
59 The Beacon, 3, 2 (September 1933), 29.
60 Guérin, The West Indies, p. 29.
61 Cf. "Editorial Notes," Trinidad, 1, 2 (Easter 1930), and "A Commentary" in the same issue.
62 Trinidad, 1, 2 (Easter 1930), 64 and 65.
63 The Beacon, 2, 6 (Oct.—Nov. 1932), 5—8.
64 The Beacon, 1, 4 (July 1931), 30.
65 Gonzalez, Self-Discovery Through Literature, p. 7.

A Checklist of Short Fiction in TRINIDAD (1929, 1930), THE BEACON (1931—1933, 1939), and FROM TRINIDAD (1937).
Abbreviations:

> T = *Trinidad*
> B = *The Beacon*
> FT = *From Trinidad*
> Roman numerals = volume numbers
> Arabic numerals = issue numbers

Note: Publication dates are omitted in the checklist. They are: T I/1 (Christmas 1929), T I/2 (Easter 1930), B I/1 (March 1931), B I/2 (May 1931), B I/3 (June 1931), B I/4 (July 1931), B I/5 (August 1931), B I/6 (September 1931), B I/7 (October 1931), B I/8 (November 1931), B I/9 (December 1931), B I/10 (Jan.-Febr. 1932), B I/11 (March 1932), B I/12 (April 1932), B II/1 (May 1932), B II/2 (June 1932), B II/3 (July 1932), B II/4 (August 1932), B II/5 (September 1932), B II/6 (Oct.-Nov. 1932), B II/7 (December 1932), B II/8 (February 1933), B II/9 (March 1933), B II/10 (April 1933), B II/11 (May 1933), B II/12 (June 1933), B III/1 (August 1933), B III/2 (September 1933), B III/3 (October 1933), B III/4 (November 1933), B IV/1 (November 1939), FT (1937).

The checklist is organized alphabetically by author and chronologically by entry.

Alexis, Henry C.: The Idiosyncracies of Samuel Worthing, B I/3, 18—21. Macuro, B I/6, 7—9.

Archibald, Charles H.: Rupert (A Sketch), B II/10, 13—14. No Reason for Laughter, FT, 34—41.

Archibald, John William: When the Old Man Died, FT, 13—15.

Archibald, Kathleen M.: The Answer, T I/2, 75—78. Beyond the Horizon, B I/3, 29—31. Clipped Wings, FT, 45—54.

Beattie, Margaret W.: Pastoral, B II/7, 18—19.

Benson, E. G.: Rene de Malmatre, T I/2, 101—108.

Burbank, Francis: Still Waters, B II/6, 18—19.

Carr, Ernest A.: Black Mother, B I/4, 8—13. The Box, B II/3, 11—16. The Crime, B II/7, 25—28.

Christian, Sheldon: Such Stuff as Dreams Are Made Of, B II/4, 24—26. Allegory of the Most Precious Treasure in All the World, B II/7, 23—24. The Grim Silence, B II/9, 17—19.

Collier, H. C.: The Mora Tree, B I/5, 15—16.

Collingwood, Norman: (Pseudonym for A. C. Thomasos) A Daughter of Jezebel, B II/9, 7—9. The Dougla, B II/10, 9—11.

Corlett, Dudley S.: The Drums of Delhi, B I/11, 26—28. Ju-Ju, B I/12, 21—22. Hermes and Aphrodite in Eden, B II/9, 20.

Da Silva, Joseph I.: The Thirteenth Spirit, T I/1, 11—13. The Pipe, T I/2, 109—118.

De Boissiere, R. A. C.: Miss Winter, T I/1, 3—9. Booze and the Goberdaw, T I/1, 45—50. A Trip to Town, T I/2, 82—100. The Woman on the Pavement, B I/8, 4—5. An Excursion, B I/9, 15—17. The Old Year Passes, FT, 19—29.

Deeble, Michael J.: Yacua: A West Indian Romance, B I/3, 9—14.

De Souza, Frank: Nocturne, B I/8, 18—19.

Evans, F. V. S.: Off Shore (A Sketch), T I/1, 27—28. On a Time, T I/2, 78—81. The Last Lot, T I/2, 127—131.

Farrell, Fred E.: The Other Side of the Picture, B II/2, 14—17.

Gomes, Albert: Day-Dreams, B II/7, 8—10.

Haweis, Stephen: On the Shelf, B I/8, 10—12.

James, C. L. R.: Triumph, T I/1, 31—40. Turner's Prosperity, T I/1, 51—53. Revolution, B I/2, 14—18. The Star that Would Not Shine, B I/3, 15—17.

Kelshall, T. M.: When Ignorance Was Bliss: An Extravaganza, B I/9, 11—12.

Maynard, Percival C.: The Hunt that Failed, B I/6, 1—6. Divorce and Mr.

The Early Work of George Lamming:
Poetry and Short Prose, 1946–1951

Ian H. Munro

From 1946 to 1951, George Lamming devoted himself to writing poetry, with only occasional excursions into prose. The *Caribbean Voices* series[1] broadcast a number of his poems,[2] and a smaller number appeared in various issues of *Bim*[3]; no collection of the poems has ever been made, however, so that except for the few which have been reprinted in anthologies,[4] his poetry is more or less inaccessible. Of the five short prose pieces he published, three have been anthologized.[5] A sixth prose work, entitled "Birthday Weather," which appeared in 1951, became in revised form the first chapter of *In the Castle of My Skin,* and appeared in the same issue of *Bim* as his last poem to be published, "Illumined Graves." Since the publication of *In the Castle of My Skin* (1953), Lamming has not returned to poetry.

Most of Lamming's published poetry and short prose is not of a very high quality. As one might expect of a young writer, it is experimental and often overly imitative, although considering the rather short span of time from his first published poem to his last, his abilities both as poet and prose writer developed remarkably. His best poems were written after he had arrived in England and was able to approach his experiences in the Caribbean with a measure of objectivity. Many of the earlier poems, written in the West Indies under the immediate pressure of circumstances there, suffer from a lack of objectivity, an intense but often confused emotional response which tends to wash out the sense of the poem. If quality were the sole criterion, a consideration of Lamming's work before *In the Castle of My Skin* could be limited to perhaps half a dozen poems and two or three of his prose pieces.

But if the early work is seen as a process of preparation for writing *In the Castle of My Skin,* then the whole body of work is relevant to a study of Lamming's development as a writer. *In the Castle of My Skin* is a novel of return to the familiar, biographical facts of the author's boyhood experience in Barbados and to an archetypal or static moment in which the past can be recovered and stabilized. Its peasant characters are firmly rooted in that moment, and isolated from historical events in the world outside, which reaches them only as rumor or as inexplicable violence. But their isolation is Lamming's version of what a West Indian critic, W. I. Carr, has called "a known and more or less comfortable world,"[6] in which the author's own sense of isolation from the West Indies he had left behind and the England he had encountered as an alien, could be overcome. An examination of his poetry and prose makes it clear that the novel is a culmination of a pattern of identification and alienation, beginning with Lamming's return to Barbados on vacation in 1947, after a year's absence in Trinidad.[7]

Prior to his return, Lamming had published only a few romantic, abstract poems, idealizing poetry and the poetic "persona," who is usually alone, secluded in a natural setting at a remove from the ordinary concerns of other men:

> Walking along the gravelled path pensively,
> Hearing the crisp notes of frogs whispering
> Or touched by two lovers' painful sighing,
> I do not feel alone.[8]

In this poem, entitled "Pitch Walk," the setting is not clear; its sole function is as a backdrop for the poet's sensibility. In a similar poem, "The Gardens," the setting is probably Port of Spain's Botanic Gardens, which are treated however as:

> ... a lovely background
> To weave these fibres,
> Intricate like the web of ancient spiders ...[9]

In several of these poems, there is a distinction made between the real—often equated with sexuality—and the ideal, the world of the imagination. One poem, which considers the proper function of poetry, reaches an extravagant conclusion:

> That poetry of tomorrow must be the beginning and the end.
> Passing from the dust of its first dreams
> Through the immaculate blackness of lower layers
> Taking baptism at the primal slime of the God-head
> Crucifying its early crust
> To bring salvation to its essential spirit
> E'er the rocks betray it
> Or the everlasting dead seek communion
> The poetry of tomorrow will be the poetry
> Of the infinite within the infinite.[10]

Lamming's visit to Barbados produced a series of poem with a more explicit social content, which were broadcast over *Caribbean Voices* early in 1948, under the collective title "The Islands." His first prose work to be published, "David's Walk," probably also developed from the return, although it appeared several weeks earlier than the "Islands" series. After a year in the more vital, materialistic society of Trinidad, Lamming was able to see some unique qualities in Barbadian life. His poem "For the People of Trinidad" suggests that he has left his insular countrymen behind; they had condemned Trinidad, "shaped you, Made you the monster," yet he had discovered a quite different island:

> Obtrusive, indulgent, unyielding
> In your desire to love all men.
> Oblivious to response, stumbling
> Insensibly against their hate.[11]

But the central theme of "David's Walk" and the "Islands" poems is the static, timeless character of Barbadian life, mixed with a nostalgic identification with the island as a personified entity, and a personal sense of loss and change. The essential stasis of Barbadian life as Lamming saw it is best represented by the character of the old man in "David's Walk," the prototype of Pa in *In the Castle of My Skin.*

"David's Walk" is less a story than a prose sketch with a number of scenes, loosely connected by the image of a walk which joins the rural village to the main road and symbolizes the continuity of peasant existence. In the opening scene, boys from the village pass along the walk on their way to school, ignorant of the pattern they are affirming. The author interjects an editorial comment:

> For five days of the week David's Walk offered this spectacle. It had become ritualistic. This desolate stretch of sand and stone had grown and spread out in the hearts of the people. The riotous laughing and general indiscretion of schoolboys who set the place ablaze during this year was no less glamorous, no less appealing than that which passed ten years ago. This was a continuation of the old; this was a carrying on from where their fathers had left off.[12]

The old man is a peasant figure who embodies this continuity in a conscious way. Like the peasant characters in *In the Castle of My Skin,* he values his relation to the landlord and the unchanging nature of rural Barbadian life. Again, tending to rely on direct statement rather than narration to make his point, Lamming editorializes:

> He learnt, among many things, the fear of God and the respect of his betters. He had grown up on an estate, cutting grass in the cruel heat of Tropical weather ... He felt that he was born into his position as a royal personage is born into the abundant splendour of royal things, and he believed fanatically that what he warranted by work and his guiding star could be appropriated by no force on earth. In his simple actions and in the drawling tones that communicated the secret thoughts that niggled at his mind, he embodied the hope and faith of all those who lived around him.[13]

The outlines of the character of Lamming's peasantry in *In the Castle of My Skin,* with their characteristic passivity and pride, are already apparent in the description.

In the second section of the piece, as a contrast to the life of the village, Lamming describes the activities in a sugar factory. There is no narrative relation between the two sections, so Lamming simply has the old man drop by the factory, which represents a different way of life from his own, characterized by noise, "the clash of iron and the shrill echo of whistles," and the camaraderie of the workers. The two ways of life are not in direct conflict in the story, but as in the earlier poetry they are certainly in contrast. The walk might be compared to Barbados in general, which in Lamming's poetry tends to be associated with quiet and an order which derives from the unthinking acceptance of stasis, while the factory parallels the noise and confusion of Trinidad and the modern world. This is indeed the dichotomy which Lamming sets up in the title poem of the "Islands" collection. The poem opens with a stanza suggesting that Barbados and Trinidad are alike in their relation to England:

> The island where all law, all knowledge,
> Aspiration, hope, even the challenge
> From the ostensible foe must expand
> To meet that other island, England, the Mother England.[14]

But in other respect they are quite different. Trinidad, with its "dark foreboding hills" and racially heterogenous population, is active and materialistic:

> This cosmopolitan producing the unpredictable mixture
> Of diverse races mingling their laughter with their tears,
> Expending all their toil for future years.

Barbados, with its coral beaches and relatively homogeneous population, is firmly tied to tradition:

> Living for nought, it seems, clinging to tradition
> With all the pride and tenacity of its mother,
> Caring for nought, striving to please no other.

The theme of "The Rock," another poem in the "Islands" group, is more obscure. Lamming has remarked that the poem was written in the village where he grew up, and that somehow "the experience of the Rock had got identified with all Barbados."[15] He equates the Rock with the solidity of the peasant experience and with the character of Papa Grandison who embodied that experience for him as a child. Clearly, "The Rock" is a poem which expresses his sense of change and loss of contact with the past. It begins:

> We looked on your countenance and found nothing
> That we could recognize, nothing to revive the memory...[16]

The symbol of loss is a rock which is submerged by the tide, its "mother," and loses its identity. The last stanza suggests that there is a historical dimension to the event:

> And so we wished that time and the age would change,
> Your mother would unclasp her arms, grant you your will,
> Perchance your lover should come back, take your hand
> And make you what you were before, a little island.

It is not simply the poet's absence in Trinidad which has made the island seem unfamiliar, then, but a discernible process of change.

The poetry and short prose written after the "Islands" group show a growing sense of confinement which parallels the development of Lamming's personal commitment to a writing career. The pattern of alienation, as the Guyanese poet Martin Carter has described it in the following passage, is a common phenomenon among West Indian writers:

> What we will discover upon considering the experience of our imaginary writer is that, like other members of the social stratum from which he comes, he suffers from a divided selfhood. On the one hand, here he is, living in a country, comparatively desperate in economic terms with no drawn lines separating social stratum from social stratum, and enduring daily assaults on his sensibility. On the other hand, here he is, speaking English as his mother tongue, assimilating the values instinct in the English language, and developing a world outlook which is, to the greatest extent, a little bit more than a mirror image of the recent past or contemporary movements in philosophy or aesthetics of advanced societies. In due course the imaginary person of whom I speak comes to the conclusion that if he remained and spent his life in the place of his birth there would be little chance of his ever attaining the goal to which his aspirations direct him. The atmosphere of the subsistence-oriented society chokes him; the philistinism of his peers numbs him . . .[17]

The social stratum Carter refers to is the middle-class, semi-professional group from which the writer is likely to come. The fact that Lamming was from a poor, semi-rural background does not alter significantly the validity of Carter's statement; the life of the ordinary folk of the islands in Lamming's poetry, insofar as he touches on it at all, is treated as an endless and hopeless struggle for existence, which the poet sees from a considerable distance. The fishermen in Lamming's poems of that name are the counterparts of the weary proletarians in Eliot's *Waste-Land*:

> Goodnight Peter, goodnight Arthur
> Goodnight, boys, goodnight.
> We may flick the shutters and curtain ourselves from the night
> Dispose of the empty bottles and cleave to our sheets
> But how shall we look upon the darkened weeds that festoon our
> shores
> Or whisper the final word to the broken vessels that house our
> souls?[18]

The only redeeming factor in their tedious life, the poet suggests, is their affection for the women who "guard the shore." The central idea of the poem is that their lives are divided between the "brute malice" of their perpetual struggle with the sea and human affection and emotion. In "The Seekers," one of the poems in the "Islands" series, Lamming deals with the West Indian peasantry in an even more remote manner. The poem is primarily an effort to arouse sympathy, through the most abstract generalizations:

> There are no bounds to their longing,
> There are no bounds to their striving
> And the heat of the day and the cold of the night
> Are like children in the eyes of desire,
> And the futurelessness of the years,
> And the hopelessness of their tears
> Sink quietly within the well of compassion.[19]

As in many of Lamming's poems written before 1950, there is an absence of genuine feeling or experience behind the moral statement. Lamming's distance from his experience is part of his alienation from the society and his difficulty in seeing it objectively.

The phenomenon which Carter defines is apparent in several of the poems Lamming published during 1948, and in his second prose work, "Birds of a Feather." The latter is an interesting piece with somewhat more structure than "David's Walk" and with experimentation in the symbolic use of description. The story begins with a vaguely Conradian scene which carries the main theme of the story symbolically, much as the opening chapter of *In the Castle of My Skin* is a blueprint for what follows:

> The silence was heavy and ominous as we waited for the strumming to continue. It came intermittently, a fine, wheezing sound like the blacksmith's pump in the distance, making us aware of our own existence. The dog gave a loud, insistent bark outside, and was on the verge of repeating the noise when the wind came in a powerful gust, flooding his lungs and muffling all sound. Through the iron bars which reinforced the dungeon it streamed like a torrent, powerful and uninterrupted, driving out the foulness and falling on us cold and refreshing. It revived our efforts at selfrecovery. When the strumming reached us again it seemed less hazy. It possessed rhythm and meaning this time.[20]

The dungeon is both the jail in which the narrator—a young West Indian—and two American companions are confined, and West Indian society as the narrator perceives it. Its isolation is emphasized by the sound of the stringed instrument, "flowing from the richness of civilized life" outside the walls, and by the wind, which acts as a renewing and revitalizing force, an image for the presence of Americans in the society.[21] Lamming does not sustain this symbolic style throughout the story, and there is a good deal of editorializing as well as several less satisfactory passages of symbolic description which seem to be indulged in for their own sake. In one such passage, the narrator and his friends pass a small village on the road, which becomes a symbol for the stability of peasant life in a technological world. "Withdrawn from the din and bustle of city life," he writes, "it seemed another world. The humility of its aspect and the dignity of its silence were like memories of the past."[22] After describing the church which looms over the village, Lamming focusses on a plane taking off from the base, a juxtaposition between two worlds like that employed in "David's Walk." The passage is an interesting example of the persistence of the image of village life in Lamming's imagination, but it has no actual relevance to the story.

The narrator and his American friends Dalton and Hendrickson are in jail as a result of a disturbance at a party given by the Flennings, who are what the narrator, with his inbred sense of social prestige, calls "symbols of a certain way of living; . . . they set the standards by which those in lower layers of society were judged."[23] The narrator is himself of the "lower layers," a "native of little worth in the judgement of those who formed the elite of my countrymen." His aspirations are checked by the judgement of this conservative group:

> Tradition! System! We lived under the awful shadow of those Gods. And then there was the war, and mingled with the gifts it brought to these parts was the treasure of the Americans. The Americans came and moved about our community like new brooms around a dust-laden room. And not a few were suffocated and choked and poisoned against them.[24]

At the party, the Americans offend the sensibilities of a West Indian and a fracas results. In the second section of the tsory, the narrator, Dalton and Hendrickson get together again and the narrator discovers that pressure has been brought to bear by Flenning to have them transferred back to the United States. After an evening of drinking, the three head back to the military base, the narrator reflecting at some length on the significance of the American presence and their eventual departure for himself and the society in general: if their departure will "strike the very foundations of my society" as had their arrival, he thinks, he is nevertheless "content to live the present to the fullest."

The climax of the story involves an inexplicable collision in the countryside with old Flenning, designed to show the real qualities of his class. He is drunk and curses Americans wildly for disrupting the established order, though the scene lacks the dramatic effect that Lamming no doubt wanted it to have. The story's most important feature, perhaps, is its characterization of the young narrator, who expresses some of Lamming's own feelings of confinement. "What I had to achieve," he says at one point, "was a way of escape."

Another symbolic treatment of the theme of confinement and frustration appears in the five poems published under the title "Variations on a Theme," which Lamming seems to have designed as a *Waste Land* in miniature. The first poem, "Prelude," opens on a note similar to the beginning of Eliot's poem:

> It is June now
> And it may have been December
> Or any other month of
> The long, cruel year.
> O Sun fagged to fickleness,
> Tentacles of fire recoiled,
> Cold and uncomforting the judas kiss.[25]

Lamming's attempts to create a symbolic structure for the poems revolve around his use of the sun, the "fire god," as a symbol for creativity, now "fagged to fickleness," and the moon, a symbol of motherhood and romantic illusions, "too proud To utter her weariness of the year's endeavour." But the symbolic texture is too dense and artificial for a clear meaning to emerge from any but the last poem. In the second poem, "Birth," a girl's virginity is lost as a result of illusions fostered by the romantic setting, but the moral conclusion —which seems to be that all romantic expectations are disappointed—is buried under a profusion of obscure symbols:

> Our dreams by cruel scythes are harvested;
> Virtue has placed a rose in nature's lap,
> The fires burn cold; infertile grows the seed
> And sin like wine is dancing in our cup.[26]

In the third poem, "Madonna," the betrayed virgin of the second poem has become a mother, "Cradling her heart's darling Moon petalled offering Of autumn revelry." In the first part of the poem she goes out "into the sunlight," and in the second part "retraced her steps from the sunlight," in despair. The third poem, "Retreat," opens with the question "Where shall we turn for a symbol of motherhood." The image of the mother is a recurrent one in Lamming's poetry. In "The Rock" she is identified with the identity-denying sea, and in "The Islands" with the all-embracing role of England. In a short story, "Of Thorns and Thistles," Mother Barton is an obsessed, hate-filled woman who dominates the life of her daughter.[27] In general, the mother in Lamming's early work is a tangible part of the forces which attempt to restrict freedom and identity. In the last poem of the "Variations" group, entitled "Epilogue" (the only poem with an identifiable theme), the mother begins the process of restricting the child's imagination:

> Yesterday the boy at the foot of the stairway
> Chalked castles of idiocy in relief,
> Hoisting his freedom like an ensign
> Turned tail to the importunate mother
> And made of the lunch hour an eternity of fun.[28]

The spirit of the child represents imaginative freedom which is synonymous in Lamming's poetry with an indifference to time. The image of the stairway is taken up again at the end of the four stanza poem. Time, says the poet, has become "measured out" in the course of the child's development:

> And the boy at the top of the stairway
> Poised for the ultimate plunge
> Into vast orgasm of achievement
> Knows only the academician's rod
> Unchallenged ritual of syllabus and calendar.

Thus the educational experience takes up where the mother leaves off. The poem reflects something of Lamming's negative attitude toward his own education, which receives harsher treatment in a later poem, "Satiric Lines" and in his description of the High School in *In the Castle of My Skin.*

The difficulty with the poems in "Variations on a Theme," with the exception of "Epilogue" perhaps, is that they fail to find a meaningful correlative for the poet's growing criticism of West Indian society. It is significant, then, that several of Lamming's last poems, including his best work, are in the form of a direct address to other West Indian writers or intellectuals, who have had similar experiences and with whom a basis of communication exists. The last poems, with a couple of exceptions, explore specific problems: the relation of the artist to West Indian society and to society in general, and the effect of exile, in the context of specific social experience.

In "West Indian Dutch Party," the context is the Dutch party, perhaps the most regular of social events in Trinidad.[29] The poem opens with the "persona" at a distance from the noise of the party. The music appears to be "straining and thinning itself" to reach him, and his mind dwells on serious moral questions which the determined superficiality of the party obscures:

> I watch the feeble footsteps of my mind
> Evade the glittering chatter
> To tread the fields of darkness:
> The battered skull of a soldier ...
> Famine and the starved ones ...
> The permanent disease of society ...[30]

In the second section of the poem, he focusses on the party itself, borrowing again from T. S. Eliot to suggest its mechanical regimentation:

> My friend in black regulates the pick-up
> And a familiar tune visits the senses
> Through the side door the ladies come
> Their faces smooth and polished
> The bottles and the glasses take their places ...

The poem concludes with images of water and ice, as the consciousness is submerged under the "Laughter and smiles" of what he calls, ironically, a "Characteristic evening, our evening." "West Indian Dutch Party" is, however, a rather superficial treatment of the central theme of Lamming's later poetry: the difficulty of functioning creatively amidst the constant demands made on the spirit by West Indian society. The artist, in Lamming's poetry, exists in a private world of humanistic, nonviolent values, surrounded by a materialistic and violent world. Inevitably, he is forced into rejecting his society in some way: its "glittering chatter" makes reflection difficult and its materialism and distorted values make his integrity and creativity irrelevant.

The social context of the artist's dilemma is clearer in "February 1949." The title refers to the granting of a new constitution to Trinidad early in 1949, after a period of political instability. The constitution allowed universal suffrage, and promised a greater measure of popular participation in the colonial regime.

The opening of Lamming's poem seems to treat this as the potential beginning of political maturity:

> The miracle of this moment is the confession of time:
> The cataclysmal growth, the sudden awakening from feathered
> dreams,
> Beware the infant gesture! Tread lightly this rubbled past
> Where obsolete and intimate are tolerable synonyms![31]

But the infant who steps from his cradle, "disclaiming allegiance to imbecility" with the promise of responsibility, is immediately menaced by the "garden," with its pervasive aura of decay:

> Each dewdrop is a bullet in disguise,
> Roses O sick to death of regal elegance
> Usurp the odour of subordinate manure,
> Inveigle (O crumbling unity of grass and soil!)
> The lunatic, the infant, the intruder.

As in "Variations on a Theme," the passage suggests that the landscape is partly to blame for the condition of the West Indies; its baroque richness conceals the reality of poverty and stagnation. In another poem, Lamming refers to islands "pebbled and coralled by the sea's deep kiss," whose "gardens subtly Conceal the midnight terror."[32] This image of beauty and tranquility concealing dark secrets had appeared in "David's Walk," where the old man recalls stories of villagers who have died or disappeared along the walk during its history, and it recurs at various points in *In the Castle of My Skin* as part of the allegorical level of the novel.

In the second stanza, Lamming addresses Willy Richardson, a fellow writer to whom the poem is dedicated:

> You who would scuttle the circle of these years,
> Mock freedom into cold submission of its unwashed linen . . .

Lamming argues that the urgency of the demand for political freedom has produced a social climate unfavorable to the writer. The repetitive pattern of West Indian history, "the circle of these years," has been replaced by a new, "original pattern":

> Arenas surrender their frontiers to the multitude
> Now met within sandstrewn arcs. Contestant and onlooker,
> The leading and the led fusing danger and delight
> In an original pattern, an automatic violence.

The final stanza puts the antipathy between the sensibilities of the intellectual and the political direction of the masses in the context of language:

> Here the conflagration of language is our modern choice,
> Enormous words that will not melt in the stale sun
> Of maternal promise.

"Trust not the gifts," warn the politicians, creating an atmosphere of distrust to which the poet's "subtle predictions" are irrelevant:

> . . . poets in peculiar attitudes in faraway places,
> Who strike their balance by the patient
> Selection of syllables and the dissolution of tears.

"February 1949" is the first of Lamming's published work which deals with an explicitly political theme, and its ambiguity toward the struggle for political change anticipates themes in his later fiction. In *In the Castle of My Skin,* the rioting strikers who invade the village presage major social changes in the whole archaic structure of colonial Barbados, but in the novel as in the poem the narrator's response to violence is divided, and he eventually finds himself outside of the process, unable to identify with what Lamming calls in one poem, "the multitude's monotonous cry For freedom and politics at the price of blood,"[33] in spite of his sympathy for the aims of the struggle.

The alternative is retreat into a private world, which is the subject of the last poem Lamming published before leaving the West Indies: "The Sculptor." The occasion for the poem is the completion by Karl Brodhagen, the Barbadian sculptor, of a bust of Lamming. The poet's contemplation of the bust leads him to contrast Brodhagen's enthusiastic creativity with his own silence, using Brodhagen as a model for the determination of the artist to escape the demands of the everyday world in his quest for imaginative freedom:

> Worshipping his world that requires no other dimension,
> This aproned butcher with all too primitive weapons
> Chopping the slabs of earth into recognisable forms,
> Must ponder yet another act of creation.
> What infant's cry from the neighbouring glade
> Or wife's prophetic mutterings of the season's curse
> Against his hallowed world could ever force
> Retreat to the simple demands of his tailoring trade?[34]

While the sculptor at his work is "in courtship with time's reservoir of pain," his neglected wife despairs at the passing of time; the stanza devoted to her complaints is dominated by images of decay and the destructive effects of time:

> I watch the seasons rust in their crime
> And days grow yellow with the odour
> Of my loss that tracks down time . . .

The sculptor's imaginative world, however, is akin to that of the child, whose "gambolling lunacies wreck time's ruse . . ." Artist and child exist in this timeless setting, while wife and family must suffer the consequences of the "indigent sculptor's" patient devotion to his craft. The final product is a "rusted beauty," rather than a timeless artifact, a portrait of the poet:

> That never showed so plain but by
> Your mirroring art and, your life's concomitant,
> Earth's blemish and its own grave bewilderment.

The artists retreat, then, is costly, but necessary if creativity is to be maintained. In *In the Castle of My Skin,* Brodhagen has his counterpart in the High School's first assistant, whose life is devided into different levels. For the writer, Lamming has remarked, "this private world is his one priceless possession, it is precisely from this point that everything else will proceed, and in these circumstances it cannot be sacrificed to the immediate neighborhood; because nothing can take its place."[35] Lamming's emigration to England in 1950, then, was a form of retreat or escape from a confining situation, from psychic pressures which—it is apparent in his poetry—had been accumulating for some time. England offered the advantages of a relative anonymity and a fertile climate of literary discussion in comparison to the rather artifical cultural milieu in Trinidad,[36] while his frequent appearances on the *Caribbean Voices* broadcasts held out the possibility of a literary career in England.

Relief at having escaped from the West Indies is expressed in a long, 135 line poem entitled "Satiric Lines." The main body of the poem is a sustained attack on the educational system as Lamming had experienced it, and particularly on the West Indian middle class. The poem is in the form of a monologue, addressing a fellow West Indian who had shared the same experiences and made the same journey. "It must not be the same again," the poem begins; their ability and creativity must no longer be wasted:

> Time was ours and we massacred the moment,
> Talent crying for mercy found no saint
> To atone its loss or possessor to repent
> The folly of years and their idle complaint.[37]

The poem goes on to recall their boyhood in the village, their mothers who "jockeyed in the traditional way" until they won scholarships to the High School, and their gradual separation from the village as they become educated:

> They made us prove we were now quite different
> From lads who played marbles on the village pavement . . .

They become, in effect, separated from their roots, as does G. in *In the Castle of My Skin,* but in the novel the division has profounder consequences. In "Satiric Lines," the experience is perhaps too close for objectivity or analysis, and the poem becomes a vituperative, rather tedious attack on the monotony and materialism of middle class life, which the poet has no desire to share.

"Our journey," he writes, "has been as cruel as any on a map Since we said farewell, farewell to all that," but the past lingers nevertheless, in their memory of the misguided devotion of their mothers,

> . . . the innocent mothers who
> Taught us after all what love might do.

"Birthday Poem (for Clifford Sealy)"[38] deals with the same subject, but much more effectively, in a series of sharp, occasionally brilliant scenes which tie together many of the ideas in the earlier work. The central figure is Clifford Sealy, a close friend of Lamming's during his years in Trinidad, who had remained behind. Both had come from poor families and been subject to the same dehumanizing experience:

> The freezing bastardy, the huddled tenantry
> Where children carry parents' pains like a uniform,
> The individual desire or despair mocking most faithfully
> Barometers that measure another's will
> Articulate only in their loyalty to life . . .

Sealy's reaction was to study Marxism in search of a political solution to the condition of the islands:

> Passion made politics a serious game
> And poverty your partner. How well I understood
> The intolerant gesture, the juvenile lust to murder
> An evil that had forged your life.

For Lamming, however, Sealy's Marxism is naive, since the problems are spiritual rather than economic. The islands are "cramped with disease no economy can cure," and the poet asks:

> What new fevers arise to reverse the crawl
> Our islands make toward their spiritual extinction?
> Do you still patrol the city's unsavoury sites
> Probing the prostitute's hearts, setting your intelligence
> An exercise in pity . . .

From the distance of exile, Lamming characterizes in a few ironic scenes the intellectual life of the West Indies:

> Young poets are decorated with foreign approval
> For precocious statements in a borrowed language . . .

and, in an intense but hopelessly illogical metaphor:

> Corruption is keen, time throbs
> With the ache of the proud and sensitive like you

> Who angrily wade through that vacuum
> Forever afloat on its oily seas ...

Yet in England, he has dicovered, the situations is not much different; the West Indian emigrés in London sustain illusions about their role:

> ... our people wear professions like a hat
> That cannot prove what the head contains,
> Success knows what grimace to assume,
> Mediocrity is informed with a bright sense of bluff ...

For the "proud and sensitive," then, there is no spiritual satisfaction in Sealy's "honest but innovent worship of the Russian regime," nor apparently in emigrating to England, where West Indian society is as superficial as at home. The solution the poem offers, predictably, is retreat and isolation. "We must suffer in patience," he tells Sealy: retreat to the "quiet shore" and reject "the multitude's monotonous cry For freedom and politics at the price of blood." Like the devoted Brodhagen, the artist must immerse himself in an aesthetic world of his own making:

> Live every moment in the soul's devouring flame
> Until we fold with the folding earth,
> Erect our final farewell in tree or cloud,
> Or (if possible) there is a new birth.

The movement from identification to retreat and isolation follows the pattern of Lamming's earlier poetry, and is taken up again in the two poems, "Dedication from Afar: A Song for Marian" and "Swans," which confront the experience of being an exile. For Lamming, as for the characters in his novel *The Emigrants,* emigration was a disturbing experience but also potentially liberating, since the exile is forced to confront the truth about himself as a colonial. A poem like "Birthday Poem," although it does recapitulate problems dealt with earlier, does so with a new clarity and objectivity. The perception, for example, that West Indian poets write in a "borrowed language" is sharpened after contact on their own ground with those who regard the English language as their own invention and possession. While the cultural stagnation and isolation of the islands becomes all the more evident after a residence in England, the West Indian can also discover his alienation from England as well, in whose values he had been nurtured. In this respect, exile can prove liberating, since it opens up wider perspectives on the identity.

In his poem "Swans," Lamming confronts the apparent serenity and order of the English scene, symbolized by swans on the Thames:

> Sailing the solitude of their customary waters
> Dark and dimpled in the windy morning,
> Instinct prompts a ritual of preening
> The rude arrangement of their feathers,

> And leaping with the leaping light of dawn
> They crown the river with a white perfection.[39]

"Ritual" and "custom" are here seen as natural and orderly, confirming the relation of the swans to their environment. In the third stanzas, day-trippers intrude, "the circus ... With its readymade apparatus of pleasures." Lamming describes them satirically, in much the same way as he characterizes the West Indian middle class, "swimming their lives through charted areas of water," but they are at least on familiar ground. The poet, on the other hand, is only an observer, whose sense of distance grows as time goes on:

> Sadly silently the late light falls,
> And the waving curl of water dies
> Where the winged white quietude at anchor lies.

"Swans" displays on the whole an unusual restraint in mood and language, so that the last stanza—though it states the conclusion towards which the whole poem moves—seems the less satisfactory. Like so many of Lamming's earlier poems, it attempts too much:

> Now blank desertion fills the senses,
> Over the howling city
> Louder than the cry of industry,
> The moon sheds a contagion of madness,
> And water fills the eyes of the visitor
> Entering the legend of this historic river.

In his short story "A Wedding in Spring," Lamming takes a comic view of the West Indian's distorted relation to England. Beresford, a West Indian, is to marry an English woman, to the disgust of his sister Flo, who insists "this Englan' turn his head an' make him lose his senses."[40] But for his other friends, West Indians from all the islands drawn together by their mutual isolation in London, the wedding is an opportunity for "teaching the English their own tune," as one character puts it. Beresford and his friend Knickerbocker outfit themselves elaborately in morning suits and top hats; one West Indian nick-named Lice-Preserver arrives in full evening dress with a sword. Predictably, their carefully-laid plans for impressing the English go awry. Flo sabotages the arrangements, the bridegroom arrives half an hour late, undignified and in disarray, on a bicycle, and a white poodle named Satire carries off his top hat. The story's central theme, taken up in depth in *The Emigrants,* is that the colonial in exile is a divided individual, who acts out of a sense that he is always subject to the scrutiny and judgement of the colonizer. The relation of the West Indians in the story to England remains, with the exception of Flo, one-dimensional. They continue to accept what Lamming, in *The Pleasures of Exile* calls the "myth" of England and of the colonial relation.

In his poem "Dedication from Afar: A Song for Marian," Lamming suggests that exile is a profound, existential condition which the West Indian shares with the Black American. The occasion for the poem is a concert given by the Black American singer Marian Anderson, in London. The first section of the poem is emotional and reintegrative in the sense that through her song, the poet is taken out of his immediate experience, represented by his self-conscious feeling he is "Parading my colour for an auditorium's gaze," and returned to the essential unity of his childhood experience. The second section of the poem, however, is meditative and disintegrative. The poet begins to reflect on the meaning of Anderson's songs; in his new role as exile they have a significance they could not have had in the West Indies where:

> ... sometimes we laughed at tall tales
> Burgeoning from the deep dark south
> Or bade our understanding stand neutral;
> For the bulletins were so unreal.
>
> Now I venturing from scattered islands
> To rediscover my roots
> Have found an impersonal city
> Where your tales are incredibly true,
>
> And I who had never sworn violence
> Nor charted courses for the heart's refusal
> To white, black, brown at home or afar
> Am urged to register with the outlaws.[41]

The "outlaws"—exiles and aliens like himself—observe one commandment: "Hate thy brother as thyself," and in the poem's conclusion he promises to "decorate my song in sackcloth For you and islands at anchor in the west," and contemplate their commandment, without committing himself to it.

In the penultimate stanza of "Song for Marian," having penetrated his alienation and discovered its depth, the poet asks a question which becomes essentially the theme of the work which follows:

> Where under the sun is our shelter?

It is not surprising, then, that in two of his last poems, and in "Birthday Weather," he should return to the West Indies of the "Islands" poems and "David's Walk," the static, timeless society in which a substantial and persistent part of his experience and imagination had remained rooted. In "The Boy and the Sea" he attempts—leaning all too heavily on Dylan Thomas's techniques, which strongly influenced his way of presenting the child's perspective both in the poetry and the novel—to evoke the untrammelled imaginative world of a boy of nine, the same age as G. at the beginning of *In the Castle of My Skin:*

> More punctual and deliberate than bird carol at dawn
> While water's wedding to the wilted weeds

In crystal accents screamed across the lawn,
I would awake with a child's wild, wandering will.[42]

The opening lines give a fairly good idea of the poem's theme, and its weaknesses. There is no controlling arrangement to the poem, as there is in almost all of Lamming's earlier work; instead, the poet seems to immerse himself in an imaginative world created by a profusion of metaphors and sense impressions. Like the children in *In the Castle of My Skin,* the boy, "Too early for lust or lullabies in love," is free to respond to what is around him. It is the child's secure, sensuous imagination which provides one part of the foundation on which the novel rests.

The other part is provided by the stable consciousness of the West Indian peasant, to whom Lamming returns in his last published poem, "The Illumined Graves". The poem deals with the annual observance of All Souls Day in the West Indies, and the emphasis is on the regularity with which the living return to the graves to re-establish their relation with the dead. The observance is "habitual" and "customary," but custom, the poet remarks, "carries its consoling fictions," which sustains the meager faith of the mourners. While the central comment of the poem is on the persistence of religious rituals in the lives of this "innocent tribe," it is significant that, at this point, Lamming should take up again the idea of continuity in West Indian life, the deeply habituated rituals which underlie the superficial "Englishness" of the West Indian.

"Birthday Weather," which combines the themes of the child's perception with the peasant's rooted outlook, appeared in 1951, and became the opening chapter of *In the Castle of My Skin* as well as a statement of the themes of the novel. But according to two writers who knew Lamming well when he lived in Trinidad, he had begun writing a novel even before leaving the West Indies, which he had discarded. The manuscript of the rejected novel has not reappeared, but the foregoing discussion of Lamming's development suggests that *In the Castle of My Skin* is the culmination of a certain period of development, and that his reaction to England was a necessary part of the shaping process. The return to Barbados in *In the Castle of My Skin* is an expression of Lamming's continued belief in a partly mythicized, partly allegorized, partly real world, in which the alienated West Indian experience had once had a whole, an integral and a valuable existence.

Notes

1   *Caribbean Voices* was broadcast weekly by the Carribbean and Colonial Service of the BBC from London; it provided for several years the main place where work from writers in all areas of the Caribbean appeared.

2   In all, forty-one poems and six prose works provide the material for this discussion. Of these, twenty-five first appeared in *Caribbean Voices* and five first appeared in *Bim*. Of the remainder, twelve poems apparently were not published, or at least were not found in the scripts of *Caribbean Voices* held by the library of the University of the West Indies at Mona,

Jamaica, although there are indications that these scripts are not complete. These unpublished poems were supplied in typescript by Mr. Cecil Herbert, a friend of Lamming's in Trinidad, with whom the poems were left. One story first appeared in an English periodical, *Lilliput.*

3   *Bim,* edited by Frank Collymore, is the most important of the group of literary periodicals which sprung up in the West Indies in the 1940s, and the only one still being published. At first confined to the work of Barbadian writers, it was expanded in the postwar period to include work by writers from throughout the Caribbean.

4   "Dedication from Afar: A Song for Marian" has been reprinted in *Caribbean Verse,* ed. O. R. Dathorne (London, 1967), and in *Caribbean Voices,* Volume I, ed. John Figueroa (London, 1966).
"Swans" has been reprinted in both the Dathorne and Figueroa anthologies.
"Birthday Poem (for Clifford Sealy)" has been reprinted in Volume II of the Figueroa anthology.
"Recollection" was also reprinted in Volume II of the Figueroa anthology.

5   "A Wedding in Spring" has been reprinted in *Four Hemispheres,* ed. W. H. New (Toronto, 1971), and in *West Indian Stories,* ed. Andrew Salkey (London, 1960).
"Birds of a Feather" has been reprinted in *Island Voices,* ed. Andrew Salkey (New York, 1970).
"Of Thorns and Thistles" appears in *West Indian Stories.*

6   W. I. Carr, "The West Indian Novelist: Prelude and Context," in *Consequences of Class and Color,* ed. David Lowenthal and Lambros Comitas (New York, 1973), p. 291.

7   Lamming left Barbados in 1946 to teach in Trinidad; he returned on vacation in mid-1947.

8   "Pitch Walk," an unpublished poem supplied in typescript by Mr. Cecil Herbert. Dated 1946.

9   "The Gardens," supplied in typescript by Mr. Cecil Herbert, is one of several early poems that was probably broadcast over *Caribbean Voices* but does not appear among the scripts in the University of the West Indies library at Mona, Jamaica. Dated 1946.

10 Untitled, undated and unpublished poem supplied in typescript by Mr. Cecil Herbert.

11 "For the People of Trinidad," *Caribbean Voices,* 4 January 1948. Reprinted in *Life and Letters,* ed. Robert Herring, LIX (1948), 122.

12 "David's Walk," *Caribbean Voices,* 17 August 1947. Reprinted in *Life and Letters,* LIX, pp. 116—21.

13 "David's Walk," *Caribbean Voices,* p. 5. In quoting from Lamming's work I have reproduced the text of the first published version if available, rather than later versions in anthologies. I have also ignored script changes made by the editors of *Caribbean Voices.*

14 "The Islands," *Caribbean Voices,* 4 January 1948.

15 *The Pleasures of Exile* (London, 1960), p. 226.

16 "The Rock," *Caribbean Voices,* 4 January 1948. Reprinted in *Life and Letters,* LIX, p. 123.

17 Martin Carter, *Man and Making—Victim and Vehicle.* The Edgar Mittelholzer Memorial Lectures, Fourth Series, October, 1971. (Georgetown, Guyana, 1971), p. 13.

18 "The Fishermen," *Caribbean Voices,* 18 July 1948. Reprinted in *Life and Letters,* LIX, p. 145.

19 "The Seekers," *Caribbean Voices,* 4 January 1948.

20 "Birds of a Feather," *Bim,* 9 (December 1948), p. 32. Appeared earlier in *Caribbean Voices,* 11 July 1948.

21 "Birds of a Feather" is not explicitly set in Trinidad, although the wartime impact of the American presence in the Caribbean was strongest there.

22 "Birds of a Feather," p. 38.

23 "Birds of a Feather," p. 33.

24 "Birds of a Feather," p. 34.

25 "Prelude," *Caribbean Voices,* 9 January 1949. Reprinted in *Tamarack Review,* 14 (Winter 1960).

26 "Birth," *Caribbean Voices,* 9 January 1949. Reprinted in *Tamarack Review,* 14 (Winter 1960).

27 "Of Thorns and Thistles," *Bim,* 10 (June 1949), 138—43.

28 "Epilogue," *Caribbean Voices,* 9 January 1949. Reprinted in *Tamarack Review,* 14 (Winter 1960).

29 Traditionally at a Dutch party, the guests bring the refreshments and the host provides a record player for dancing. Dutch parties can occur at any time during the week, but are a part of every social weekend in Trinidad.

30 "West Indian Dutch Party," *Caribbean Voices,* 22 August 1948.

31 "February 1949," *Bim,* 10 (June 1949), 111.

32 "The Sculptor," *Bim,* 11 (December 1949), 252—53.

33 "Birthday Poem (for Clifford Sealy)," *Caribbean Voices,* 24 September 1950.

34 "The Sculptor," *Bim,* 11 (December 1949), 252—53.

35 "The Negro Writer and His World," *Présence Africaine,* 8-9-10 (June—November 1956), 324.

36 For the last year or so of his stay in Trinidad, Lamming participated in meetings of the Readers and Writer's Guild, one of a number of literary groups in the islands. If anything, these societies served only to emphasize the gap between those with "literary interests" and the society at large. The Guild consisted of a few serious writers, of varying abilities, and a much larger number who regarded the meetings as a social occasion. Eventually, the Guild became entirely a social club. the result, perhaps, of an inability to take indigenous writers or their work seriously.

37 "Satiric Lines," *Caribbean Voices,* 3 September 1950.

38 "Birthday Poem (for Clifford Sealy)," *Caribbean Voices,* 24 September 1950.

39 "Swans," *Caribbean Voices,* 17 June 1951.

40 "A Wedding in Spring," reprinted in *West Indian Stories,* ed. Andrew Salkey (London, 1960). First appeared in *Lilliput.*

41 "A Dedication from Afar: Song for Marian," *Caribbean Voices,* 6 August 1950.

42 "The Boy and the Sea," *Caribbean Voices,* 1 April 1951.

43 "The Illumined Graves," *Bim,* 15 (December 1951), 165—66.

Journey into the Canje

Wilson Harris

Janheinz Jahn's remarkable achievement lies I am sure in his direct involvements in Africa, African literatures, African oral traditions, African history, sociology and so on. His involvement with African themes led him naturally to do research into African legend and transplated resources in the Americas and the Caribbean and to stress certain common rhythms. And it is here that it seems to me his methods of classification, though of interest, tend to turn away from specific re-creative and re-visionary perspectives that bear upon the reality of new community.

This is understandable because I would think that the enigma of African (indeed Asian, European and other cultural) values, in a New World heterogeneous context, raises issues—certainly for the imaginative writer—that have hardly been touched upon at all by historians and literary critics.

I want to look at some of these issues within certain strict limits and within the compass of the Canje river (an area in the Guianas) which I surveyed in the late 1940s and early 1950s. My last visit was around 1952.

The Canje is a deep but narrow tributary (scarcely more than one to two hundred yards wide) to the mile-to-two-mile wide Berbice and it discharges into the Berbice estuary, so close to the Atlantic Ocean that it seems almost an independent river in its own right.

It provides an invaluable irrigation resource for the Berbice/Corentyne sugarcane and rice-planting coastlands not only because of the tidal action upon it from the Atlantic which partially depletes but substantially conserves the river's resources; but also because the Canje catchment itself is affected by complexly eroding watersheds, with the Berbice on one hand and the Corentyne river on the other, that set up natural sluice gates of relief from pressure in time of great flood.

Equally the *indirect* drainage lines of the catchment, created by the unusual features of erosion and shifting accretion, are in league with the deep but restricted main Canje river itself, to hold back flow during the wet seasons in the headwaters of tributaries.

That holding asset is part of the irrigation potential that flows into the river, as the dry season commences, and builds the Canje which is tapped in turn by canals to the great sugarcane estates and rice farms on the Corentyne coastlands. (Sugar was a European capital investment in the 1940s and 1950s, rice an Eeast Indian peasant investment.)

This is an all too brief portrait of the drama of a particular catchment that feeds a region but it may help, I believe, to provide a sense of ironic pace to the elements that affects the small settlements of people who actually live in the Canje, on the banks of the river, and who are, in the main, of African descent.

They seem to mirror in their way of life a pressure of relatedness even as they eke out a living from woodcutting for the sugar estates and from occasional farming of vegetables and rice of a poor quality (since the soil of the Canje itself is not susceptible to rice growing). Legend has it that they are descended from rebels who escaped from the Berbice slave plantations in the eighteenth century. Thus an august tradition of conservative roots, in the teeth of a difficult environment, hedged around by a profound sense of oppression/persecution in and beyond place and time, persisted strongly in the small and diminishing groups I encountered in the late 1940s and early 1950s.

Indeed there was an enormous passivity grounded into the people I met then and a relation to the past as something or someone both dispossessed and godlike, both natural like a swamproot or a water creature and supernatural like a god—a god compounding the mystery of freedom with implacable hostility to a technology of change.

These are some of the aspects I attempted to weave into the novel *The Secret Ladder* which carries a confrontation between the "modern" engineer/surveyor (who comes to chart a comprehensive flood control project that would uproot entirely the inhabitants of the upper Canje) and the "ancient" Canje people themselves who invest in the landscape as if it were a fortress or a religious wall against barbarians.

There is an irony in that confrontation which is not immediately discernible and which perhaps I should now stress.

One cannot but note the location of "presentness" in "pastness" whether "presentness" has a technological engineering face or a ritual folk face.

Take the technological face first. The modern engineer is wrapped around by superior instruments and in the degree that he is nothing but an extension of those instruments becomes an involuntary creature of the past acting out a conformity to the technical rhythmic drum of the landscape.

To put it in another way: the landscape, in its very nature, consolidates a passive and conservative drum of supplies to which the engineer is geared and which he serves with all his intelligence like a tool that accommodates itself to a collective fate—it becomes a sophisticated gloss upon (even as it enhances) the furniture of the region. And that conformity—in the degree that it remains blind to the riddle of "presentness" set in "pastness"—is an invitation to terrorism or guerrilla activity by the folk, who become fearful of their own position turning into human flotsam and jetsam already in process of being submerged or borne away by a technical flood.

On the other hand it is a major task of the creative imagination to set up an activity of vision that is quite different to a conformable rhythm to the past. An activity, in fact, which *sees* in a new way the subtle and unspectacular play of indirections within history, so that it is possible not only to pick up the most sensitive ironic contours (whose erosive faculty one is inclined to dread) but also to begin to relate these to new windows upon what is vulnerable and essentially human in the way a culture reads or misreads given fortresses of place and time.

Now let us take the ritual folk face. The "ancient" rebel-slaves, like the modern engineer, in the degree that they are an extension of a static folk, are susceptible to a misconception of the freedom for which they stand. That freedom seems hemmed in once again by the fears of the past and a rhythm of terror is set in inevitable motion again. Thus the dialogue between art and science is susceptible to eclipse within the forces of the law which the modern engineer quite logically may be tempted to summon to combat the threat of disorder. And that summons could be the first step towards a reenactment in the mind of the folk of the bitter oppressions of the past (as they see it in the ritual static present).

I am suggesting that one needs a peculiar and original scale of activity in an imaginative fiction that bears upon the sort of problems I am discussing, to alert us to the enormous challenge involved in "subjective" fortresses, based upon the "slow motion" dance of a landscape and upon a state of such complex physical or environmental erosion that there builds accumulations of water (like gigantic natural moats)—in rapport with massive swamp vegetation—around hardwood trees on high, relatively substantial reefs of land.

An "activity of vision" that helps us to drift downwards and backwards through a passive world into the seeds of deepseated cultural reflections of asylum for rebel-slaves turning by degrees over the generations into "founding fathers" as the Canje folk conceived of themselves.

Take the vulnerable landscape (a landscape that conspired with them—became a medium of advantage for them in shaking off the enemy) into which their eighteenth century forebears came for the first time. Once they were ensconced in the body of the region they possessed not only a line of communication with the coast by way of the river (on which they could place their scouts) but a way of withdrawal into the green hell of the savannahs with its indirections and labyrinthine paths through which few pursuers would dare to follow.

All this converted itself into an art of brooding watchfulness and withdrawal in which the culture threaded dense secrets into apparently endless heavens and suns and stars like a shield or loom of fate/spaces/ corridors/unpredictable ladders/savannahs. (I do not wish to go into this in detail but the principle of many-levelled, many-faceted structure and the theme of contrasting horizons/spaces—"architectonics of self"—is latent, I believe, in a long immersion in the ironies of "the long-suffering geography of history" as I have described it elsewhere.)

No wonder over a couple of centuries the descendants of the rebel founding fathers did not see themselves (diminished and exhausted as their actual numbers were) as expendable settlement but as rooted in a timeless illusion which defied and resisted the Oppressor (with a Capital O).

It is essential, I think, to dwell on all this because resistance to oppression is a healthy principle of growth, except when it begins to take itself wholly for granted and a trauma of self-oppression takes over the present and the future and reenacts a perpetual state of historical oppression (as though the Historical Oppressor never vanishes and is alive in many extensions of ghost-sovereignty built into a technical age). The culture thus afflicted then becomes more and more susceptible to a misreading of both the inner and outer ground of change to which it relates intimately and concretely.

What is that "inner and outer ground of change"? This is a question one has to ask oneself in different imaginative ways again and again since it is grounded in many inimitable, so to speak, equations between place and people, between culture and culture, between past and present, between art and science that need to be appreciated in all their density even as they need to be unravelled as the naked heart of a quest for freedom.

There is a sense, I believe, in which "density" and "nakedness" occupy an interwoven scale that may illumine what most people sense (without necessarily articulating it) as implicit to freedom. And that "implicitness" left to itself—to function, as it were, in limbo fortresses—becomes fraught with self-deceptions.

For example let us take the uniform approaches of European and Caribbean Africanists who invest in the "drum" as the awakening of a people.

Clearly the accent on rhythm—on the African drum—is an enriching possibility but in its general application at the moment—as uniform instrument of value—it becomes an addiction and discloses the pathology of an age to dress itself up in dogmatic or animistic structure upon which society polarizes, technology polarizes, and so on. This state of affairs is true, I believe, of many other "uniform instruments of value" that rigidy/reify political and cultural institutions transplanted from Europe, Asia and elsewhere.

One is inclined to be trapped, I think, within the pathology of realism which tends more and more to look to dominant models and to evade the specific density of places and times until eruptive density becomes violent or catastrophic and evasion is no longer a practical pursuit within the body politic.

In a heterogeneous civilization one needs to define and redefine, again and again, what one means by "realism." Is realism an addiction to conquest, that breeds violence in turn, so that a virtue is made of homogeneity in order to mask all the more successfully the exploitation of "weak" cultures by "strong" cultures in the name of unity?

Is creativity, in the same token, an "esoteric" we despise in times of "good" realism—in times of order and domesticity—even as it becomes a forgotten scale upon which to grope and subsist, late in the day, when a necessity arises to heighten and deepen our perception of the susceptibilities of cultures to exploit each other or to be exploited by each other? It is here I believe—in the unravelling of such susceptibilities, in the dress/redress of resources, within the hardened state or habit of vision—that one approaches a kind of dialogue between eclipsed perspectives and dominant models of tradition.

Before I resume the issue of the African drum in the New World it may be helpful to look at new areas of density within the Christian icon in the Guianas to look at one such area anyway. I am thinking of the Arawak *zemi* which is rooted in "live metaphor," in a conception that sees "space" as a real resource, as real as wood or stone is, in the making of an object. Thus the Christian carpenter icon—in all its majesty—gains in rapport with the flexible spaces of the humble *zemi* and the theme of salvation relinquishes the motif of conquering mission and turns into a fruitful dialogue between heterogeneous "spaces."

Let me put it in another way. The dominant Christian dress or model with which one is familiar becomes curiously sensitive (in the complex I am discussing) to elements suppressed in a particular soil. That sensitivity unsettles the rigid proportions of pseudo-homogeneity—pseudo-unity—and a hint comes into play of a new living inwardness, a living body born of Arawak unsuspected elements within the habiliments of so-called superior and familiar institution.

It is in this sense that density is a revelation of interwoven features of attire and naked existence, of the living carpenter, the newborn curiously "nameless" maker of time. And this is implicit in the scale of the heterogeneous imagination as a medium of genuine community in an age when community itself needs to be born fresh if it is not to succumb to the doom of insoluble historical confrontations between reified world und helpless or consenting (no longer consenting) bodies.

I have listened to Edward Brathwaite read his poems to the accompaniment of the drum but I have also responded to the cautions that appear in those poems in lines such as

> After the *bambalula bambulai*
> he was a slave again.

The African drum, like every other transplanted instrument of value, becomes a uniform self-deception unless and until one sees the kinds of specific density, related to particular places and times, that may invade it. Indeed as an organ of universality the drum needs to pick up complex unravelling perspectives of self as profoundly re-creative if it is to bear upon, and remedy in part, not only the fears that haunt the black man in the Americas but a prospect that is already enveloping him of a hardened and insensible commerce of ritual.

Take the limbo dance—one of the most remarkable potential symbols in the theatre of the folk of the reassembly of disadvantaged cultures (I have commented upon this elsewhere in another essay).[1] This today is little more than a mere technique of dancers passing under a bar to entertain tourists and others at Caribbean and American nightclubs.

In the same token an addiction to rhythm as a uniform index of cultural ties between Africa and the Caribbean is the deadening of rhythm itself into a conformable drug of universality rather than a genesis of rhythm into poetic and dialectic self-discovery.

We need to define and re-define again and again not only what one means by "realism" but what one means by "universality." There is a universality, no doubt, of dominant frames and models but—as I have tried to show—this reifies and settles into an organ of conquest and fate in a heterogeneous context. So that without a rediscovery of that dominant and passive frame as a doorway through which one possesses a capacity to drift back into the ironies of the past, the imagination becomes inactive in the living present—it confirms the inertia of the living present—it sets a gloss upon the furniture of ritual—it is incapable of interwoven scale of new density and new spirit at the heart of one's time.

The black man in the Americas is haunted as much it would appear as anyone else by the loss of ancestral homelands or to put it differently by an "erosion of values." And the spectre of erosion heightens a sense of fear (particularly within apparently expendable cultures in the path of progress so-called).

In the Canje complex—if I may particularize again—a hint (more than a hint) exists that late twentieth century bastions of fear may now be rooted in an involuntary and complex erosion of systems of conquest: thus fear itself may grow ultimately into the last barrier to change. A new approach to universality is implicit in the kind of forgotten relation that exists between the fortress mentality of peoples and something born of the mystery of deity perhaps which is astronomically frail but infinitely beautiful in its human and vulnerable *indirect* presence. To put it another way: the fortress-cult of peoples which accumulates implacable models owes less to these in its paradoxical origins than to patterns of indirections it overlooks which are grounded in flexible resources of person, place and time.

This is not to underrate a necessity for symbols of collective security but to point out that "strength" lies in a vitality and energy that depletes itself to replenish itself. Such a scale of withdrawal/renewal puts a different face on "erosion of values."

The necessity exists today to begin to chart a conception of change at a time when cultures have no vision of change except as the new barbarism of technology.

Since the Renaissance, cultures have made a great deal of individual fortresses of freedom, so-called, but a time is already upon us when we need to transform this into the reality of the self—of private inviolate space—rooted nevertheless in the circulation of densities, dense proportions, dense populations. Indeed strategies of withdrawal and survival, of vitality and energy, may necessitate the breakdown of properties of implacable ritual if mankind is to survive at all as a human/humanizing spirit in dialogue with the natures of nature. And to conceive of "private space" is to endorse the marvellous "humanness" of the human person in all his and her frailty rather than to invest in proprietors of the globe.

Notes

1 "History, Fable and Myth in the Caribbean and the Guianas," in *Anagogic Qualities of Literature,* ed. Joseph P. Strelka. Yearbook of Comparative Criticism, vol. IV (University Park and London: The Pennsylvania State University Press, 1971), pp. 120—31.

Mainzer Afrika Studien

Herausgeber:
Gerhard Grohs, Ernst W. Müller, Leo Stappers
und Erika Sulzmann;
Institut für Ethnologie und Afrika-Studien,
Mainz

IN VORBEREITUNG:
Rambaek, Frank
**Die historische Entwicklung und gesellschaftliche Stellung
der Mischlinge Südafrikas. 1652 bis 1973**

Grohs, Elisabeth
Kisazi. Reiferiten der Zigua und Ngulu

Thies, Karl
Entwicklung der Beurteilung und Betrachtung der Naturvölker
Einleitung: Peter Heiligenthal
1976. Br., ca. 110 S., DM 24,—
Nachdr. d. Ausgabe Dresden 1899
Diese Untersuchung ist ein Beitrag zur Geschichte des ethnologischen Wissens, seiner
theoretischen und empirischen Entwicklung. In den Berichten der Reisenden, der
Missionare und ersten Ethnologen geht Thies den Spuren nach, die die europäische
Philosophie und Bewußtseinsstellung seit dem späten Mittelalter dort hinterlassen
haben; er zeigt, wie dann insbesondere die Philosophien Rousseaus, Herders und
Kants und der Wissenschaftsbegriff des 19. Jahrhunderts die ethnologische Begriffs-
und Theoriebildung fundamental geprägt haben. Thies' Schrift ist ein Vorläufer der
Forschungen, die Marcel Mauss unter dem Titel einer „Sozialgeschichte der Katego-
rien des menschlichen Geistes" forderte und eröffnete.

Pollak-Eltz, Angelina
Religiöse Kulte und Bewegungen der Afro-Amerikaner
1976. Br., ca. 260 S., DM 48,—
Die Religionen, Mythen und Riten der afrikanischen Kulturgruppen in Nord-, Mittel-
und Südamerika sowie im karibischen Raum sind das Thema dieser breit angelegten
Untersuchung. Neben bekannteren Kulten wie dem haitianischen Vodunkult und den
brasilianischen Xangokulten, Candomblé der Nago, Macumba in Rio und Umbanda
werden auch fast unbekannte wie der venezolanische Maria Lionza-Kult, die Kulte
der Buschneger Surinams, die Santeria auf Kuba und einige noch stark in afrikanischer Tradition stehende Negerkirchen Nordamerikas behandelt. Die Verfasserin
analysiert zunächst die traditionellen Religionen Westafrikas und geht dann den
Veränderungen und synkretistischen Verschmelzungen nach, denen sie im Zuge ihrer
zwangsweisen Verpflanzung in die Neue Welt unterworfen waren. Die „neuen"
Kulte werden sodann im Kontext der Traditionen und Zukunftsperspektiven der
Gesellschaften dargestellt, in denen sie sich herausgebildet haben. — Das Werk ist
die bislang vollständigste Untersuchung zu diesem Thema.

Studien und Materialien der anthropologischen Forschung (S.M.A.F.)

Müller, Hans-Peter
Die Geistertanzbewegung unter den nordamerikanischen Indianern als Entwicklungsproblem
Eine kulturanthropologisch-vergleichende Studie über Tradition und abweichendes Verhalten
1976. Br., ca. 250 S., DM 45,—
(S.M.A.F., Bd. I, Nr. 1)
Die Ghost-Dance-Bewegung wird nicht als Ausdruck der indianischen Kulturkrise, sondern als Übergangsphänomen von traditionellen Verhaltensformen zur partiellen Anpassung an die moderne Situation des Indianers analysiert. Die Studie ist ein Beitrag zu den Problemen des Kulturwandels und des Millenarismus und zur Entwicklungssoziologie.

Heiligenthal, Peter
Krise und Millennium
Versuch über ›Geschichte‹ in primitiven Gesellschaften und bibliographische Dokumentation eines wissenschaftlichen Themas
1977. Br., ca. 300 S., DM 58,—
(S.M.A.F., Bd. I, Nr. 2)
Im ersten Teil des Bandes wird das Problem der ›Geschichte‹ in primitiven Gesellschaften im Zusammenhang mit millenaristischen und messianischen Bewegungen untersucht. Den zweiten Teil nimmt eine Bibliographie ein, die die wissenschaftliche Literatur über die sozialreligiösen Bewegungen und Kulte in primitiven Gesellschaften und afro-amerikanischen Kulturgruppen für die Zeit von etwa 1875 bis 1975 erfaßt. Verzeichnet sind Monographien, vergleichende Untersuchungen, Aufsätze und Artikel in englischer, französischer, deutscher, italienischer, spanischer und portugiesischer Sprache.

Wischmann, Christine
Die mexikanische Fotonovela
Eine Untersuchung über Struktur, Ideologie und Rezeption von Massenliteratur in Mexiko und Lateinamerika
1976. Br., 284 S., 3 Abb., DM 38,— (S.M.A.F., Bd. I, Nr. 3)
Fotonovelas — Fotoromane — sind in Lateinamerika ein wesentliches Element der Volkskultur. Ihre Unterhaltungsfunktion beruht in erster Linie darauf, daß in ihnen die Wunschproduktion der „Kultur der Armut" angeregt, die Wunschprojektion jedoch gesteuert und in einer Scheinwelt aufgefangen und befriedigt wird. Mit diesem komplexen Problem setzt sich diese erste umfassende Untersuchung des Phänomens in deutscher Sprache auseinander. Der Begriff „Kultur der Armut" (O. Lewis) wird einer eingehenden Kritik unterzogen und durch ein Konzept ersetzt, das nicht auf affirmativen Voraussetzungen beruht.

Benzing, Brigitta
Studien über Ethno-Art
Essays zur ethnologischen Kunsttheorie und ihrer Kritik
1976. Br., ca. 120 S., DM 25,—
(S.M.A.F., Bd. I, Nr. 4)
Eine grundsätzliche kritische Analyse der ethnologischen Kunstforschung und ihrer theoretischen Konzeptionen aus materialistischer Sicht. Anstelle einer restriktiv-ästhetizistischen Betrachtungsweise ›primitiver Kunst‹ geht es in dieser Arbeit um einen Begriff von Kunst, der ihre Bedingtheit durch eine soziokulturelle Welt, ihre Funktion im Milieu ihrer Produzenten und ihren Warencharakter hervorhebt.

Korte, Werner
**Organisation und gesellschaftliche Funktion
unabhängiger Kirchen in Afrika**
Beispiele aus Liberia und Ansätze zu einer allgemeinen Theorie
1976. Br., ca. 400 S., DM 72,—
(S.M.A.F., Bd. II, Nr. 1)
Umfassende soziologische Analyse der unabhängigen Kirchen in Liberia. Der Verfasser hat das Material zu dieser Untersuchung während eines längeren Aufenthaltes im Lande gesammelt. Das komplexe Phänomen des kirchlichen Separatismus wird nach seinen ethnischen und sozialen Voraussetzungen, seinen Organisationsformen und seiner gesellschaftlichen Funktion untersucht; die Ergebnisse einer durchdachten und vorsichtigen Generalisierung runden die fundierte Studie ab.

Pollak-Eltz, Angelina
Indianische Relikte in der Volkskultur Venezuelas
1977. Br., ca. 200 S., DM 38,—
(S.M.A.F., Bd. II, Nr. 2)

Erdheim, Mario / Huonker, Thomas / Müller, Hans-Peter / Weiß, Florence
Krieg und Herrschaft in primitiven Gesellschaften
(Jivaro, Yanoama, Yatmül, Azteken)
1977. Br., ca. 300 S., DM 58,—
(S.M.A.F., Bd. II, Nr. 3/4)

Seiler, Signe
Wissenschaftstheorie in der Ethnologie
Zur Kritik und Weiterführung der Theorie von Thomas S. Kuhn anhand ethnographischen Materials
1977. Br., ca. 200 S., DM 38,—
(S.M.A.F., Bd. III, Nr. 1)

Zinser, Hartmut
Mythos und Arbeit
Studien über psychoanalytische Mytheninterpretation am Beispiel der Untersuchungen Géza Róheims
1976. Br., ca. 130 S., DM 26,—
(S.M.A.F., Bd. III, Nr. 2)
Die Diskussion um das keineswegs hinreichend geklärte Verhältnis von Ethnologie und Psychoanalyse wird durch Zinsers Studien beträchtlich gefördert. Das umfangreiche Werk des nun auch in Deutschland stärker beachteten Psychoanalytikers Géza Róheim bildet die Grundlage dieser subtilen Analysen vor allem der Róheimschen Interpretation australischer Mythen.

Enderwitz, Ulrich
Schamanismus und Psychoanalyse
Zum Problem mythologischer Rationalität in der strukturalen Anthropologie von Claude Lévi-Strauss
1976. Br., ca. 260 S., ca. DM 48,—
(S.M.A.F., Bd. III, Nr. 3/4)
Diese kritische Auseinandersetzung mit dem Werk von Lévi-Strauss hat u. a. den Vorzug, neben ihrem Gegenstand als durchaus eigenständige Position gelten zu können. Der Verfasser konfrontiert den Kategorienapparat der strukturalen Anthropologie mit dem der Psychoanalyse Sigmund Freuds und gewinnt daraus ein Instrumentarium, mit welchem er den Anspruch der strukturalen Anthropologie, die Ethnologie neu zu begründen, als falsche Unmittelbarkeit enthüllt. Ein ›metatheoretischer‹ Beitrag zur ethnologischen Selbstverständigung.